Truth may seem, but cannot be:
Beauty brag, but 'tis not she;
Truth and beauty buried be.

To this urn let those repair
That are either true or fair;
For these dead birds sigh a prayer.

Bacon

THE CITIES AND CEMETERIES

OF

ETRURIA.

ETRUSCAN MIRROR.

REPRESENTING "PHUPHLUNS," "SEMLA," AND "APULU;"

OR

BACCHUS, SEMELE, AND APOLLO.

THE
CITIES AND CEMETERIES
OF
ETRURIA.

Parva Tyrrhenum per æquor
Vela darem.
HORAT.

By ·GEORGE DENNIS.

THIRD EDITION.

IN TWO VOLUMES.—VOL. I.

WITH MAP, PLANS, AND ILLUSTRATIONS.

LONDON:
JOHN MURRAY, ALBEMARLE STREET.

TO

THE RIGHT HONOURABLE

SIR HENRY A. LAYARD, G.C.B.,

Her Majesty's Ambassador to the Sublime Porte,

ETC., ETC., ETC.;

THE MOST ILLUSTRIOUS AND MOST SUCCESSFUL EXCAVATOR OF THE AGE:

IN ADMIRATION OF

THE EMINENT POWERS AND MANIFOLD RESOURCES WHICH HAVE RENDERED

HIS CAREER ONE CONTINUAL TRIUMPH OVER DIFFICULTIES

SUCH AS FEW MEN HAVE HAD TO ENCOUNTER;

AND

IN GRATEFUL ACKNOWLEDGMENT OF ENCOURAGEMENT AND ASSISTANCE

RECEIVED FROM HIM DURING ANTIQUARIAN RESEARCHES IN

SICILY, LYDIA, AND THE CYRENAICA;

THESE VOLUMES

ARE RESPECTFULLY DEDICATED.

PREFACE TO THE FIRST EDITION.

THIS work is the fruit of several tours made in Etruria between the years 1842 and 1847. It has been written under the impression that the Antiquities of that land, which have excited intense interest in Italy and Germany during the last twenty or thirty years, deserve more attention than they have hitherto received from the British public; especially from those swarms of our countrymen who annually traverse that classic region in their migrations between Florence and Rome. A few Englishmen, eminent for rank or acquirements, have long been practically acquainted with the subject—but till the appearance of Mrs. Hamilton Gray's work on "The Sepulchres of Etruria" the public at large was in a state of profound ignorance or indifference. That lady is deserving of all praise for having first introduced Etruria to the notice of her countrymen, and for having, by the graces of her style and power of her imagination, rendered a subject so proverbially dry and uninviting as Antiquity, not only palatable but highly attractive. Her work, however, is far from satisfactory, as all who have used it as a Guide will confess; for there are many sites of high interest which she has not described, and on some of those of which she has treated many remarkable monuments have been subsequently discovered. It is to supply such deficiencies that I offer these volumes to the public. The interest and curiosity that lady has aroused in the mysterious race to which Italy is indebted for her early civilization, I hope to extend and further to gratify.

The primary object of this work is to serve as a Guide to those who would become personally acquainted with the extant remains of Etruscan civilization. The matter therefore is so arranged that the traveller may readily ascertain what monuments he will find on any particular site. I have deemed it advisable to add succinct notices of the history of each city, so far as it may be learnt from ancient writers, with a view to impart interest to the traveller's visit, as well as to give the book some value to those who would use it, not as a Hand-book, but as a work of classical and antiquarian reference. Yet as the former is its primary character, the traveller's wants and convenience have been particularly consulted—by statements of distances, by hints as to means of conveyance, as to the accommodation to be found on the road, and sundry such-like fragments of information, which, it is hoped, may prove the more acceptable to him, as they are intended for his exclusive use and benefit.

Some apology may be thought necessary for the copious annotations which give the work pretensions to something more than a mere Hand-book. As in the course of writing it I have had occasion to make frequent references to the classics and to modern works on archæology, it seemed to me, that by the insertion of my authorities I should avoid the charge of loose and unfounded statements; while at the same time, by collecting and arranging these authorities according to the several subjects on which they bore, and by pointing out the sources whence further information might be derived, I should be rendering service to the scholar and antiquary. Yet to avoid swelling the work to an undue extent, I have contented myself, for the most part, with simply indicating, instead of quoting. Though the exhibition of the process by which the work was constructed may be useless or even unpleasing to the general reader, to the student of these matters it will not prove unwelcome.

The obligations I have been under to Cluver, Müller, and other writers, living as well as dead, I must here acknowledge in general terms, as it would be impossible to state the source whence every reference or suggestion has been derived. Yet wherever I have availed myself of the labours of others, I have carefully verified their authorities, or, when that was impossible, have transferred the responsibility to the proper quarter.

I must also take this opportunity of paying my personal tribute of thanks to certain living antiquaries, whose names stand high in European estimation; particularly to Doctors Braun and Henzen, the secretaries of the Archaeological Institute at Rome, for their kindness in affording me facilities for the prosecution of my studies, especially by placing the copious library of the Institute at my command. To these I must add the names of Professor Migliarini of Florence, whose obliging courtesy has stood me in good stead when in that city; and of Mr. Birch, of the British Museum, who has favoured me with his notes of two sarcophagi at Musignano, described at page 489 of this volume. Nor must I forget to mention my friend and fellow-traveller Mr. Ainsley, to whom I am indebted for the free use of the notes of his Etruscan tours, as well as for several sketches used in illustrating this work.

The drawings of masonry, tombs, and other local remains have been mostly made by myself with the camera lucida. Those of portable monuments are generally copied from various works little known in England. Most of the plans of ancient sites are also borrowed, but two have been made by myself, and though laying no claim to scientific precision, will be found sufficiently accurate for the purposes of the tourist. The general Map of Etruria has been formed principally from Segato's Map of Tuscany, aided by Gell's and Westphal's Campagna di Roma, and by the official maps of the Pontifical State.

My chief aim throughout this work has been truth and accuracy. At least half of the manuscript has been written in Italy, and the greater part of it has been verified by subsequent visits to the scenes described. Notwithstanding, the book has, doubtless, its share of errors and imperfections. Those who take it up for mere amusement will think I have said too much, the scholar and antiquary that I have said too little, on the subjects treated,—on the one hand I may be accused of superficiality, on the other of prolixity and dulness. To all I make my apology in the words of Pliny—*Res ardua, vetustis novitatem dare, novis auctoritatem, obsoletis nitorem, obscuris lucem, fastiditis gratiam, dubiis fidem, omnibus vero naturam, et naturæ suæ omnia*—"It is no easy matter to give novelty to old subjects, authority to new, to impart lustre to rusty things, light to the obscure and mysterious, to throw a charm over what is distasteful, to command credence for doubtful matters, to give nature to everything, and to arrange everything according to its nature."

PREFACE TO THE SECOND EDITION.

Since the publication of the former edition of this work in 1848, many important and interesting discoveries have been made in Etruria. Long forgotten sites have been recognised as Etruscan; cemeteries of cities, known or suspected to have that origin, have been brought to light; and excavations have been carried on with more or less success in various parts of that land. Many painted tombs have been opened, and some have unfortunately been closed. The interest in such discoveries has so greatly increased, that museums have been established in not a few provincial towns, and private collections have become numerous. The subject of Etruscan antiquities, moreover, has received new light, and acquired fresh interest from similar researches in other parts of Italy, especially at Palestrina, and in the country north of the Apennines. In preparing then a new edition, it has been my task not only to visit the sites of these discoveries, and note them on the spot, with which object I have made four tours through Etruria during the last three years, but to collect the published records of all the researches made since 1848, and to incorporate notices of them with my original work. This I hope to have so far accomplished, that I believe very few discoveries of interest made since that date will be found to be unrecorded in these volumes. In short, it has been my aim to present to the public as complete an account of antiquarian researches in Etruria down to the present day, as the character of my work will permit. In one instance I have even ventured to overstep the limits originally assigned to it, and to introduce a description of the recent excavations at Bologna.

Not only has the work been considerably enlarged, but I have enriched it with numerous fresh illustrations, and with twelve additional plans of ancient cities; several of them rudely drawn by myself on the spot, yet true enough, I trust, to prove useful to those who may visit the sites.

I have little indebtedness to plead beyond what I have acknowledged in the course of the work. But I cannot omit to offer my thanks to my old friend Dr. Henzen, now Chief Secretary to the Archæological Institute of Rome, who kindly furnished me with introductions to those local antiquaries in Etruria, who could be of service to me; and to Padre Evola and Padre Di Marzo, Directors of the National and Communal Libraries of Palermo, for their indulgent courtesy in placing at my disposal whatever works it was in their power to supply. Nor must I fail to record my grateful sense of the kindness of another friend of my youth, E. W. Cooke, R.A., in most generously placing his Italian portfolio at my disposal, from which I have selected four sketches as illustrations.

I have no further acknowledgments to make, having revised the work under considerable disadvantages, during the intervals of official labour, without access to many books which were at my command in writing the original edition, and far from all friends who could render me personal assistance. My chief sources of information have been the admirable publications of the Archæological Institute of Rome.

I have had the gratification of learning that the former edition of this work, apart from literary and antiquarian considerations, has received the approval of not a few who have used it as a guide, on account of the conscientious accuracy of its descriptions. I trust that the present issue will maintain its reputation in this respect, for to ensure correctness has been my primary endeavour.

GEORGE DENNIS.

PALERMO, October, 1878.

CONTENTS OF VOLUME I.

INTRODUCTION.

CHAPTER I.

VEII.—The City.

CHAPTER II.

VEII.—The Cemetery.

CHAPTER III.

CASTEL GIUBILEO.—*FIDENÆ.*

CHAPTER IV.

MONTE MUSINO AND LAGO DI BRACCIANO.

CHAPTER V.

SUTRI.—*SUTRIUM.*

CHAPTER VI.

NEPI.—*NEPETE.*

CHAPTER VII.

CIVITA CASTELLANA.—*FALERII (VETERES).*

CHAPTER VIII.

FALLERI.—*FALERII (NOVI).*

CHAPTER IX.

FESCENNIUM.

CHAPTER X.

FERONIA AND CAPENA.

CHAPTER XI.

ORTE.—HORTA.

CHAPTER XII.

MONTE CIMINO.—MONS CIMINUS.

CHAPTER XIII.

VITERBO.—SURRINA.

CHAPTER XIV.

FERENTO.—FERENTINUM.

CHAPTER XV.

BOMARZO.

CHAPTER XVI.

CASTEL D' ASSO.—*CASTELLUM AXIA.*

CHAPTER XVII.

MUSARNA.

CHAPTER XVIII.

NORCHIA.—*ORCLE?*

CHAPTER XIX.

BIEDA.—*BLERA.*

CHAPTER XX.

PALO.—*ALSIUM*.

CHAPTER XXI.

CERVETRI.—*AGYLLA* OR *CÆRE*.

CHAPTER XXII.

SANTA SEVERA.—*PYRGI.*

CHAPTER XXIII.

SANTA MARINELLA.—*PUNICUM.*

CHAPTER XXIV.

CIVITA VECCHIA.—*CENTUM CELLÆ.*

CHAPTER XXV.

CORNETO.

TARQUINII.—THE CEMETERY.

CHAPTER XXVI.

CORNETO-TARQUINIA.—THE MUSEUMS.

CHAPTER XXVII.

TARQUINII.—THE CITY.

CHAPTER XXVIII.

GRAVISCÆ.

CHAPTER XXIX.

VULCI.

CHAPTER XXX.

CANINO AND MUSIGNANO.

CHAPTER XXXI.

TOSCANELLA.—TUSCANIA.

CHAPTER XXXII.

ISCHIA, FARNESE, AND CASTRO.

CHAPTER XXXIII.

PITIGLIANO AND SORANO.

LIST OF ILLUSTRATIONS IN VOLUME I.

LIST OF ILLUSTRATIONS.

xxiii

LIST OF PLANS IN VOLUME I.

THE ANUBIS-VASE—ETRUSCAN BLACK WARE.

INTRODUCTION.

ANTIQUARIAN research, partaking of the quickened energy of
the nineteenth century, has of late years thrown great light on
the early history of Italy. It has demonstrated, in confirmation
of extant records, that ages before the straw hut of Romulus
arose on the Palatine, there existed in that land a nation far
advanced in civilization and refinement—that Rome, before her
intercourse with Greece, was indebted to ETRURIA for whatever
tended to elevate and humanize her, for her chief lessons in art
and science, for many of her political, and most of her religious
and social institutions, for the conveniences and luxuries of peace,
and the weapons and appliances of war—for almost everything
that tended to exalt her as a nation, save her stern virtues, her
thirst of conquest, and her indomitable courage, which were

peculiarly her own : for verily her sons were mighty with little
else but the sword—

Stolidum genus—
Bellipotentes sunt magi' quam sapientipotentes.[1]

The external history of the Etruscans, as there are no native
chronicles extant, is to be gathered only from scattered notices in
Greek and Roman writers. Their internal history, till of late
years, was almost a blank, but by the continual accumulation of fresh
facts it is now daily acquiring form and substance, and promises,
ere long, to be as distinct and palpable as that of Egypt, Greece,
or Rome. For we already know the extent and peculiar nature
of their civilization—their social condition and modes of life—
their extended commerce and intercourse with far distant
countries—their religious creed, with its ceremonial observances
in this life, and the joys and torments it set forth in a future
state—their popular traditions—and a variety of customs, of all
which, History, commonly so called, is either utterly silent, or
makes but incidental mention, or gives notices imperfect and
obscure. We can now enter into the inner life of the Etruscans,
almost as fully as if they were living and moving before us,
instead of having been extinct as a nation for more than two
thousand years. We can follow them from the cradle to the
tomb,—we see them in their national costume, varied according
to age, sex, rank, and office,—we learn the varying fashions of
their dress, their personal adornments, and all the eccentricities
of their toilet,—we even become acquainted with their peculiar
physiognomy, their individual portraiture, their names and family
relationships,—we know what houses they inhabited, what furniture they used,—we behold them at their various avocations—the
princes in the council-chamber—the augur, or priest, at the altar
or in solemn procession—the warrior in the battle-field, or
returning home in triumph—the judge on the bench—the artisan
at his handicraft—the husbandman at the plough—the slave at
his daily toil,—we see them at their marriages, in the bosom of
their families, and at the festive board, reclining cup in hand
amid the strains of music, and the time-beating feet of
dancers,—we see them at their favourite games and sports,
encountering the wild boar, looking on or taking part in the
horse or chariot-race, the wrestling-match, or other palæstric

---

[1] Old Ennius (Ann. VI. 10) said this of
the Æacidæ, or race of Pyrrhus, not perceiving how much more applicable it was
to the Romans.

exercises,—we behold them stretched on the death-bed—the last rites performed by mourning relatives—the funeral procession— their bodies laid in the tomb—and solemn festivals held in their honour. Nor even here do we lose sight of them, but we follow their souls to the other world—perceive them in the hands of good or evil spirits—conducted to the judgment-seat, and in the enjoyment of bliss, or suffering the punishment of the damned.

We are indebted for most of this knowledge, not to musty records drawn from the oblivion of centuries, but to monumental remains—purer founts of historical truth—landmarks which, even when few and far between, are the surest guides across the expanse of distant ages—to the monuments which are still extant on the sites of the ancient Cities of Etruria, or have been drawn from their Cemeteries, and are stored in the museums of Italy and of Europe.

The internal history of Etruria is written on the mighty walls of her cities, and on other architectural monuments, on her roads, her sewers, her tunnels, but above all in her sepulchres; it is to be read on graven rocks, and on the painted walls of tombs; but its chief chronicles are inscribed on *stelæ* or tombstones, on sarcophagi and cinerary urns, on vases and goblets, on mirrors, and other articles in bronze, and a thousand *et cetera* of personal adornment and of domestic and warlike furniture—all found within the tombs of a people long passed away, and whose existence was till of late remembered by few but the traveller or the student of classical lore. It was the great reverence for the dead and the firm belief in a future life, which the Etruscans possessed in common with most other nations of antiquity, that prompted them to store their tombs with these rich and varied sepulchral treasures, which unveil to us of the nineteenth century the *arcana* of their inner life, almost as fully as though a second Pompeii had been disinterred in the heart of Etruria; going far to compensate us for the loss of the native annals of the country,[2] of the chronicles of Theophrastus,[3] and Verrius Flaccus,[4] and the twenty books of its history by the Emperor Claudius.[5]

> " Parlan le tombe ove la Storia è muta."

Etruria truly illustrates the remark, that "the history of an ancient people must be sought in its sepulchres."

---

[2] Varro, ap. Censorin. de Die Natali, XVII. 6.

[3] Schol. Pindar. Pyth. II. 3, cited by Müller, Etrusker. I. pp. 2, 197.

[4] Interp. Æn. X. 183, 198, ed. Mai.

[5] Suetonius, Claud. 42. Aristotle also

The object of this work is not to collect the *disjecta membra* of Etruscan history, and form them into a whole, though it were possible to breathe into it fresh spirit and life from the eloquent monuments that recent researches have brought to light; it is not to build up from these monuments any theory on the origin of this singular people, on the character of their language, or on the peculiar nature of their civilization,—it is simply to set before the reader a mass of facts relative to Etruscan remains, and particularly to afford the traveller who would visit the Cities and Cemeteries of Etruria such information as may prove of service, by indicating precisely what is now to be found on each site, whether local monuments, or those portable relics which exist in public museums, or in the hands of private collectors.

Before entering, however, on the consideration of the local antiquities of Etruria, it is advisable to take a general view of her geographical position and physical features, as well as to give a slight sketch of her civilization.

It is difficult to define with precision the limits of a state, which existed at so early a period as Etruria, ages before any extant chronicles were written—of which but scanty records have come down to us, and whose boundaries must have varied during her frequent struggles with her warlike neighbours.

We are told that in very early times the dominion of Etruria embraced the greater part of Italy,[6] extending over the plains of Lombardy to the Alps on the one hand,[7] and to Vesuvius and the Gulf of Salerno on the other;[8] stretching also across the peninsula from the Tyrrhene to the Adriatic Sea,[9] and comprising the large islands off her western shores.[1]

wrote on the laws of the Etruscans. Athen. Deipn. I. cap. 42.

[6] In Tuscorum jure pene omnis Italia fuerat.—Serv. ad Virg. Æn. XI. 567; X. 145; Liv. V. 33.

[7] Usque ad Alpes tenuére.—Liv. loc. cit.; Polyb. II. 17; Diodor. Sic. XIV. p. 321, ed. Rhod.; Scylax, Periplus, cited by Müller, Etrusk. einl. 3, 9; Justin. XX. 5. Catullus (XXXI. 13) calls the Benacus, now the Lago di Garda, a Lydian, i.e., an Etruscan, lake.

[8] The Etruscans at one time possessed the land of the Volsci, and all Campania, as far as the Silarus in the Gulf of Pæstum, or, as one account states, as far as the Sicilian sea. They took this land from the Greek colonists, who had driven out the

Osci, the original inhabitants; and then founded Capua and Nola. If Velleius Paterculus (I. 7) may be credited, this was 17 years before the foundation of Rome. Cato (ap. eund.) makes it as late as 471 B.C. Liv. IV. 37; Polyb. II. 17; Mela, II. 4; Strabo, V. pp. 242, 247; Plin. III. 9; Serv. ad Virg. Georg. II. 533.

[9] Liv. V. 33, 54; Plut. Camill. 16. The Adriatic received its name from the Etruscan town of Atria. Plin. III. 20; Strabo, V. p. 214.

[1] Elba, called Ilva by the Romans, and Æthalia or Æthale by the Greeks, belonged to Etruria, for Virgil (Æn. X. 173) classes it with the Etruscan states which sent assistance to Æneas. Diodorus, XI. p. 57; Pseudo-Aristotle, de Mirab. Auscult. c.

This wide territory was divided into three grand districts—that in the centre, which may be termed Etruria Proper; that to the north, or Etruria Circumpadana; and that to the south, or Etruria Campaniana. And each of these regions was divided into Twelve States, each represented by a city,[2] as in Greece,

95; Hecat. ap. Steph. sub voce. There was a close connection between it and the neighbouring maritime city of Populonia; and it is very probable that it was a possession of that city, unless both were under the sway of Volaterræ. See Vol. II. pp. 138, 215.

Corsica, the Cyrnus of the Greeks, was originally colonised by the Phocæans, who were driven out by the Etruscans, says Diodorus (V. p. 295, cf. XI. p. 67), by the Etruscans and Carthaginians combined, according to Herodotus (I. 166), and the island probably remained in the hands of the former to the last days of their independence, when it passed under the dominion of Carthage. Kallimachos, Delos, 19, cited by Müller, einl. 4, 6. It would seem, however, that Corsica was never fully occupied by the Etruscans, for it was a wild, forest-grown, little-populated land, and its inhabitants had the savage manners of a primitive state of society (Strabo, V. p. 224; Diodor. V. p. 295; Seneca, Consol. ad Helv. c. 6; Theophrast. Hist. Plant. V. 8); and it is very likely, as Müller conjectures, that it was a mere nest of pirates.

That Sardinia was a possession of the Etruscans is not so clear. The earliest settlers were Libyans, Greeks, Iberians, and Trojans, followed by the Carthaginians, about the middle of the third century of Rome. Strabo (V. p. 225) is the only ancient writer who mentions its being under Etruscan domination, and he says it was subject to the Tyrrheni, prior to the Carthaginian rule. · By these Tyrrhenes Müller (Etrusk. einl. 4, 7) thinks Strabo meant Etruscans, not Pelasgi, because he always made a distinction between these races; but Niebuhr (I. p. 127, Engl. trans.) maintains that they were unquestionably Pelasgians.

[2] The Twelve Cities of Etruria Proper will be presently mentioned.

In Etruria Circumpadana there were also Twelve cities, founded as colonies by the Twelve of Etruria Proper. Liv. V. 33;

Serv. ad Virg. Æn. X. 202. The capital is said by Virgil to have been Mantua (Æn. X. 203; Serv. ad loc.), though Pliny, with more probability, assigns that honour to Felsina, now Bologna. H. N. III. 20. A third city was Melpum, of which we know no more than that it stood north of the Po, was renowned for its wealth, and was destroyed by the Gauls on the same day that Camillus captured Veii. Corn. Nepos, ap. Plin. III. 21. Atria, or Adria, was a noble city and port of the Etruscans, and gave its name to the Adriatic Sea. Plin. III. 20; Liv. V. 33; Strabo, V. p. 214; Plut. Camill. 16; Varro, L. L. V. 161; Fest. v. Atrium. And Spina, at the southern mouth of the Po, though called an ancient Greek city by Strabo (loc. cit.) and Scylax (Geog. Min. I.), was certainly a Pelasgic settlement (Dion. Hal. I. c. 18, 28), and probably also Etruscan. Niebuhr, I. p. 36; Müller, Etrusk. einl. 3, 4. Müller thinks, from Strabo's mention of it, that Ravenna was an Etruscan town, and its name is certainly suggestive of such an origin. But Strabo (V. p. 213) says it was founded by Thessalians, i.e., Pelasgians, who, on being attacked by the Etruscans, allied themselves with the Umbri, who obtained possession of the city, while the Thessalians returned home. Cupra, in Picenum, was also probably Etruscan, for its temple was built by that people, and named after their goddess, Cupra, or Juno. Strabo, V. p. 241. And although Parma and Mutina (Modena) are not mentioned in history as Etruscan towns, we are justified in regarding them as of that antiquity, by the evidence of monuments found in their territory, which Livy tells us once belonged to the Etruscans. Liv. XXXIX. 55. We know the names of no other Etruscan cities north of the Apennines, though Plutarch (Camill. 16) asserts that there were eighteen cities of wealth and importance in that region.

There were Twelve chief cities also in Etruria Campaniana. Liv. V. 33; Strabo, V. p. 242. The metropolis was Capua,

where Athens, Sparta, Argos, Thebes—or in Italy of the middle
ages, where Venice, Genoa, Pisa, Florence—were representatives
of so many independent, sovereign states, possessed of extensive
territory.

Such seems to have been the extent of Etruria in the time of
Tarquinius Priscus, when she gave a dynasty to Rome, probably
as to a conquered city. But ere long the Gauls on the north and
east,[3] the Sabines, Samnites, and Greek colonists on the south,[4]
succeeded in compressing this wide-spread dominion into the
comparatively narrow limits of the central region. This may be
called Etruria Proper, because it was the peculiar seat of the
Etruscan power—the mother-country whence the adjoining
districts were conquered or colonised—the source where the
political and religious system of the nation took its rise—the
region where the power of Etruria continued to flourish long
after it had been extinguished in the rest of Italy, and where the
name, religion, language and customs of the people were preserved for ages after they had lost their political independence,
and had been absorbed in the world-wide dominion of Rome.

It is of Etruria Proper that I propose to treat in the following
pages.

It was still an extensive region of the Italian peninsula, comprehending almost the whole of modern Tuscany, the Duchy of
Lucca, and the Transtiberine portion of the Papal State; being
bounded on the north by the Apennines and the river Magra, on
the east by the Tiber, on the west and south by the Mediterranean. This region was intersected by several ranges of mountains, lateral branches or offsets of the great spine-bone of the

built by the Etruscans 800 years before
Christ, and called by them Vulturnum
(Strabo, loc. cit.; Liv. IV. 37; V. Paterc.
I. 7; Mela, II. 4), though Servius (ad
Æn. X. 145) derives its name from *Capys*,
which signified a "falcon" in Etruscan.
Nola also was of Etruscan foundation.
Vell. Pater. loc. cit. Dicæarchia, or Puteoli
(Pausan. VIII. 7; Steph. Byz. v. Ποτίολοι),
Pompeii, Herculaneum (Strabo, V. p. 247),
and Nuceria (Philistus, cited by Müller,
einl. 4, 2) were all once possessed by
the Etruscans; and Marcina in the
Gulf of Prestum, supposed to be Vietri,
was built by them. Strabo, V. p. 251.
Syrrentum, also, from the temple of the
Etruscan Minerva on its promontory, must
have belonged to that people (Stat. Sylv.

II. 2, 2; Steph. Byz. s. v. Συρέντιον); and
Müller would include Salernum. Posei-
donia, or Pæstum, also appears at one
time to have been possessed by the Etruscans, for Aristoxenus (ap. Athen. XIV.
31) says, that though of Greek origin, the
inhabitants had been completely barbarized
by the Etruscans or Romans, so as to have
changed their language and all their other
customs, retaining only one Greek festival,
in which they annually lamented their
degeneracy.

[3] Liv. V. 35; XXXVII. 57; Polyb. II.
17; Diodor. Sic. XIV. p. 321; Plin. III.
19; Plut. Camill.16; Isidor. Orig. XV. 1.

[4] Liv. IV. 37; Strabo, V. p. 247; Plin.
III. 9; Dionys. Hal. VII. p. 420, et seq.

peninsula—in the northern part in long chains, stretching in various directions—in the south, of inferior altitude, lying in detached masses, and separated, not by mere valleys, but by vast plains or table-lands. The geology of the two districts differs as widely as their superficial features. In the northern, the higher mountains, like the great chain of the Apennines, are chiefly composed of secondary limestone, and attain a considerable altitude ; the lower are formed of sandstone or marl. The southern district shows on every hand traces of volcanic action—in the abundance of hot springs and sulphureous waters —in wide plains of tufo and other igneous deposits, of even later date than the tertiary formations—and in the mountains which are chiefly of the same material, with beds of lava, basalt, or scoriæ, and which have been themselves volcanoes, their craters, extinct long before the days of history, being now the beds of beautiful lakes. Here and there, however, in this southern region, are heights of limestone ; now, like Soracte, rearing their craggy peaks from the wide bosom of the volcanic plain ; now, stretching in a continuous range along the coast. On these physical differences depend many of the characteristic features of northern and southern Etruria. The line of demarcation between these two great districts of Etruria is almost that which till lately was the frontier between the Tuscan and Roman States— i. e., from Cosa north-eastward to Acquapendente, and thence following the course of the Paglia till it mingles with the Tiber, near Orvieto.

Of the Twelve Cities or States of Etruria Proper, no complete list is given by the ancients, but it is not difficult in most instances to gather from their statements, which were the chief in the land. Foremost among them was TARQUINII, where the national polity, civil and religious, took its rise. This city was in the southern division of the land ; so also were VEII and FALERII, long the antagonists, with CÆRE, the ally, of Rome ; and VOLSINII, one of the last to be subdued. VULCI also was probably of the number. In the northern region were VETULONIA and perhaps RUSELLÆ near the coast,[5] CLUSIUM and ARRETIUM in the vale of the Clanis, and CORTONA and PERUSIA on the heights near the Thrasymene : while VOLATERRÆ stood

[5] Rusellæ is generally classed among the Twelve, but the question resolves itself into the comparative claims of that city and of Vulci, and I am inclined to give the preference to the latter, whose claims rest on monumental, not on historical evidence.

apart and ruled over a wide tract in the far north.[6] Beside these, there were many other towns, renowned in history, or remarkable for their massive fortifications still extant, for their singular tombs, or for the wonderful treasures of their sepulchral furniture, together with numerous castles and villages scattered over the country, many of which will be described in the course of this work.

Etruria was of old densely populated, not only in those parts which are still inhabited, but also, as is proved by remains of cities and cemeteries, in tracts now desolated by malaria, and relapsed into the desert; and what is now the fen or the jungle, the haunt of the wild-boar, the buffalo, the fox, and the noxious reptile, where man often dreads to stay his steps, and hurries away as from a plague-stricken land—

> Rus vacuum, quod non habitet, nisi nocte coactâ.
> Invitus—

of old yielded rich harvests of corn, wine, and oil,[7] and contained numerous cities, mighty, and opulent, into whose laps commerce poured the treasures of the East, and the more precious produce of Hellenic genius. Most of these ancient sites are now without a habitant, furrowed yearly by the plough, or forsaken as unprofitable wildernesses; and such as are still occupied, are, with few exceptions, mere phantoms of their pristine greatness—mean villages in the place of populous cities. On every hand are traces of bygone civilization, inferior in quality, no doubt, to that which at present exists, but much wider in extent, and exerting far greater influence on the neighbouring nations, and on the destinies of the world.

---

[6] The claims of these several cities will be discussed, when they are treated of respectively. The above is the classification which appears to me to be sanctioned by ancient writers; it agrees, save in the substitution of Vulci for Rusellæ, with that of Cluver (Ital. Ant. II. p. 453), and Cramer (Anc. Italy, I.). Micali (Ant. Pop. Ital. I. p. 140) adopts it with the exception of Falerii, for which he offers no substitute. Niebuhr (I. p. 118, et seq.) admits the claims of all, save Falerii and Cortona, and hesitates to supply the void with Fæsulæ, Cosa, or Capena. Müller (Etrusk. II. 1, 2; I, 3), to those given in the text, adds five—Pisæ, Fæsulæ, Saturnia or Cale-

tra, Vulci, and Salpinum—whose claims, he thinks, must be admitted, and suggests that they may have held that rank at different periods, or have been associated respectively with some one of the rest. Noël des Vergers ranks both Vulci and Rusellæ among the Twelve, and excludes Falerii. Étrurie et les Étrusques, I. p. 203.

[7] The fertility of Etruria was renowned of old. Diodorus (V. p. 316) says it was second to that of no other land. Liv. IX. 36; XXII. 3; Varro, Re Rust. I. 9, 44. The Romans, even in very early times, used to receive corn from Etruria, in times of famine. Liv. II. 34; IV. 12, 13, 25, 52.

The sites of the cities varied according to the nature of the ground. In the volcanic district, where they were most thickly set, they stood on the level of the plains, yet were not unprotected by nature, these plains or rather table-lands being everywhere intersected by ravines, the cleavings of the earth under volcanic action, which form natural fosses of great depth round the cliff-bound islands or promontories on which the towns were built. Such was the situation of Veii, Cære, Falerii, Sutrium, and other cities of historical renown. The favourite position was on a tongue of land at the junction of two of these ravines. In the northern district the cities stood in more commanding situations, on isolated hills; but never on the summits of scarcely accessible mountains, like many a Cyclopean town of Central Italy, which—

> "Like an eagle's nest, hangs on the crest
> Of purple Apennine."

Low ground, without any natural strength of site, was always avoided, though a few towns, as Luna, Pisæ, Graviscæ, Pyrgi, for maritime and commercial purposes, stood on the very level of the coast.

The position of the cities of Etruria is in some measure a key to her civilization and political condition.[8] Had they been on mountain-tops, we might have inferred a state of society little removed from barbarism, in which there was no security or confidence between the several communities. Had they stood on the unbroken level of the plains, we should have seen in them an index to an amount of internal security, such as nowhere existed in those early times. Yet is their medium position not inconsistent with a considerable degree of civilization, and a generally peaceable state of society. They are not such sites as were selected in later times, especially by the Romans; but it should be borne in mind, that the political constitution of early Italy, as of Greece, was entirely municipal—that cities were states, and citizens soldiers—and fortifications were as indispensable to the cities of old, as standing armies and fleets are deemed to be to the states of Modern Europe. The Etruscans especially appear to have trusted more to their ramparts than to the valour of their warriors.

Before we consider the institutions of Etruria, it may be well

---

[8] Strabo (XIII. p. 592) cites Plato as pointing out the position of cities as tests of civilization, illustrating this view by the successive cities of the Troad.

to say a word on the origin of the people, and the source of their civilization.

It must be remarked, that the people known to the Romans as Etruscans were not the original inhabitants of the land, but a mixed race, composed partly of the earlier occupants, partly of a people of foreign origin, who became dominant by right of conquest, and engrafted their peculiar civilization on that previously existing in the land. All history concurs in representing the earliest occupants to have been Siculi, or Umbri, two of the most ancient races of Italy, little removed, it is probable, from barbarism, though not nomade, but dwelling in towns.   Then a people of Greek race from Thessaly, the Pelasgi, entered Italy at the head of the Adriatic, and crossing the Apennines, and allying themselves with the Aborigines, or mountaineers, took possession of Etruria, driving out the earlier inhabitants, raised towns and fortified them with mighty walls, and long ruled supreme, till they were in turn conquered by a third race, called by the Greeks Tyrrheni, or Tyrseni, by the Romans Etrusci, Tusci, or Thusci,[9] and by themselves, Rasena,[1] who are supposed to have established their power in the land about 290 years before the foundation of Rome, or 1044 before Christ.[2]

The threads of the history, however, of these races are so entangled, as to defy every attempt at unravelment; and the confusion is increased by the indiscriminate application of the word Tyrrheni, which was used by the ancients as a synonym, sometimes of Pelasgi, sometimes of Etrusci.

Amid this confusion, two facts stand out with prominence. First—that the land was inhabited before the Etruscans, pro-

---

[9] Plin. III. 8, 19 ; Dion. Hal. l. c. 30, cf. Herod. I. 94. They were called Tyrseni, it is said, from the fortifications—τύρσεις— they were the first to raise in Italy (Dion. Hal. I. loc. cit.); and Tusci, or Thusci, from their frequent sacrifices—ἀπὸ τοῦ θύειν— Serv. ad Virg. Æn. II. 781 ; X. 164 ; Plin. III. 8 ; cf. Fest. v. Tuscos. Etruria is said to be derived from ἕτερος and ὅρος, because it lay beyond the Tiber. Serv. ad Æn. XI. 598. But the etymologies of the Romans are generally forced, and rarely to be depended on. Thuscia is a late word, not to be found in the earlier writers.

[1] Dion. Hal. I. c. 30. Some writers take Rasena to be but a form of Tyrseni, either a corruption from it, as Tyr—seni... Ra—seni ; or a contraction of it, as Ty—

raseni. Mannert. Geog. p. 308 ; Cramer, I. p. 161. The name " Rasna," or " Resna," is sometimes met with on the sepulchral urns of Etruria. A chain of mountains in Tuscany, not far from Arezzo, is said to have retained the name of Rasena to the present day. Ann. Inst. 1856, p. 77.

[2] This is the period which Müller (Etrusk. einl. 2, 2 ; IV. 7, 8) considers the commencement of the Etruscan era, referred to by Censorinus, de Die Natali, XVII. Helbig agrees with him. Ann. Inst. 1876, p. 227, et seq. Niebuhr (I. p. 138), however, would carry the first Etruscan sæculum as far back as 434 years before the foundation of Rome, or to 1188 B.C.

perly so called, took possession of it. And secondly—that the
Etruscans came from abroad. From what country, however, is
a problem as much disputed as any in the whole compass of
classical inquiry.

It is not compatible with the object of this work to enter fully
into this question, yet it cannot be passed by in silence. To
guide us, we have data of two kinds—the records of the ancients,
and the extant monuments of the Etruscans. The native annals,
which may be presumed to have spoken explicitly on this point,
have not come down to us, and we have only the testimony of
Greek and Roman writers. The concurrent voice of these—
historians and geographers, philosophers and poets—with one
solitary exception, marks the Etruscans as a tribe of Lydians,
who, leaving their native land on account of a protracted famine,
settled in this part of Italy.[3] The dissentient voice, however, is
of great importance—that of Dionysius of Halicarnassus—one of
the most accurate and diligent antiquaries of his times, and an
authority considered by many as sufficient to outweigh the vast
body of opposing evidence. His objections are two-fold. First
—that Xanthus, an early native historian of Lydia, well versed in
the ancient history of his land, makes no mention of any such
emigration, and never speaks of the Etruscans as a colony from
Lydia. Secondly—that neither in language, religion, laws, nor
customs, was there any similarity between the Lydians and
Etruscans—i.e. as they existed in his day. He consequently
maintained that the Etruscans were autochthons—a view not
held by any other ancient writer whose works have come down to

---

[3] "The father of history" is the first
that records this tradition. Herod. I. 94.
It is mentioned or alluded to also by Strabo,
Plutarch, and Lycophron among the Greeks,
and by a crowd of Roman writers—Cicero,
Pliny, Seneca, Valerius Maximus, Tacitus,
Paterculus, Appian, Virgil, Horace, Ovid,
Catullus, Silius Italicus, Statius, Tertullian, Festus, Servius, Justin, and Rutilius.
The tradition as related by Herodotus,
echoed by Servius, was this:— In the
reign of Atys there was a protracted
famine in Lydia; and in order to forget
their misery the people had recourse to
games and amusements, and invented dice,
and ball, the pipes and the trumpet;
abstaining from food on alternate days
when they gave themselves up to these new
diversions. For eighteen years they thus

continued to exist, but at length, their
condition being in no way improved, it was
agreed that half the nation should emigrate,
under the conduct of Tyrrhenus, the king's
son. After various wanderings, they
reached the coast of Umbria, and there
established themselves, exchanging the
name of Lydians for that of Tyrrhenians,
in honour of their leader. A more probable version of this emigration is given
by Anticleides, an Athenian historian (ap.
Strab. V. p. 221), who states that the
Pelasgi first colonized about Lemnos and
Imbros; and then some of them joined
Tyrrhenus the Lydian in his emigration to
Italy. This account is nearly in accordance
with that given by Plutarch (Romulus, 2),
that the Tyrrheni passed originally from
Thessaly to Lydia, and thence to Italy.

ns, yet suggested to him by the fact that they were unlike every other race in language, manners, and customs.[4] This view has been adopted by Micali, who may be suspected of national partialities, when he attempts to prove that the early civilization of Italy was indigenous.[5]

A different opinion was held by Niebuhr—that the Etruscans were a northern tribe who invaded Italy from the Rhætian Alps, and conquered the Tyrrhene-Pelasgi, the earlier possessors of the land,—that the true Etruscans were these Rhætian invaders, and that the term Tyrrheni was strictly applicable only to the Pelasgic, or subject part of the population. This theory is worthy of respect, as coming from such a source, but it is directly opposed to the statements of ancient writers.[6] Nor does the well-known fact that monuments like the Etruscan, and inscriptions in a character very similar, have been found among the Rhætian and Noric Alps, come to its aid. For though we are told by Livy and others, that the Etruscans occupied Rhætia, it was only when they had been driven by the Gauls from their settlements in the plains of the Po. All history concurs in marking the emigration to have been from the south northwards, instead of the contrary.[7] The subjoined specimen of Rhæto-Etruscan art confirms Livy's testimony as to the degeneracy and semi-barbarism of these Etruscan emigrants.[8]

---

[4] Dion. Hal. I. c. 28, 30.

[5] Micali, Ant. Pop. Ital. I. cap. VII.

[6] Niebuhr, I. p. 110, et seq. So great an authority naturally takes in its train a crowd of German writers, not unwilling to adopt an opinion so flattering to the *vaterland*. The view, however, of a Rhætian origin of the Etruscan race had been previously held by Freret, and by Heyne. It is founded on the resemblance of the name "Rasena," which the Etruscans gave themselves, to Rhæti—on the statement of the ancients that the Rhæti were of Etruscan origin—on the analogy certain dialects now spoken in these regions bear to the Etruscan—and on the fact that no earlier population than the Etruscan is recorded to have inhabited those mountains.

Niebuhr (II. p. 525) even supposes that at one time the Etruscan race extended north of the Alps into Alsace and the plains of Germany, and cites, in confirmation of his view, the walls on Mont Sainte Odilie, in the former country, which are very similar to those of Volterra, and unlike the works of the Gauls or Romans.

[7] Livy distinctly asserts the emigration to have been from the plains to the mountains, on the invasion of the Po-vale by the Gauls; and he, as a native of Padua, speaks with the more authority on this subject. Alpinis quoque ea gentibus haud dubie origo est, maxime Rhætis, quos loca ipsa effërarunt, ne quid ex antiquo præter sonum linguæ, nec eum incorruptum, retinerent. V. 33. He also states that the Twelve Etruscan cities of Northern Etruria were founded subsequently to those of Etruria Proper, being so many colonies of the original Twelve cities. Rhætos Thuscorum prolem arbitrantur, à Gallis pulsos, duce Rhæto. Plin. Nat. Hist. III. 24. Galli . . . sedibus Tuscos expulerunt. Tusci quoque duce Rhæto, avitis sodibus amissis, Alpes occupavêre : et ex nomine ducis gentes Rhætorum condiderunt. Justin. XX. 5.

[8] These figures form part of a procession

A modification of Niebuhr's view was held by Otfried Müller—that the later element in the Etruscan nation was from Lydia, yet composed not of natives, but of Tyrrhene-Pelasgi who had settled on the coasts of Asia Minor; and that the earlier lords of the land were the Rasena, from the mountains of Rhætia, who

FIGURES ON RHÆTO-ETRUSCAN BRONZES, FOUND IN THE TYROL.

in relief found, in 1845, at Matrai, a village on the northern slope of Mount Brenner, in the Tyrol. Besides this were found other singular reliefs, one of which has pugilists contending with the *cestus*, very like the scenes in the tombs at Chiusi and Tarquinii; pieces of amber and coral, *fibulæ* and rings of bronze. At Sonnenburg, 12 miles distant, many similar relics were in 1844 brought to light; together with cinerary urns of black ware, and knives of bronze. A few years previous, in a sepulchre at Zilli, in the ancient Noricum, were found two bronze casques, with inscriptions in a character very like the Etruscan. And in the valley of Cembra, 9 miles from Trent in the Tyrol, a bronze *situla*, or bucket, was discovered in 1828, bearing five inscriptions in a similar character; and it is remarkable that it was found near the torrent Lavis, and that that very word occurs in one of the inscriptions.

Giovanelli, Pensieri intorno ai Rezi, ed una inscrizione Rezio-Etrusca: Le antichità Rezio-Etrusche scoperte Presso Matrai; Micali, Monumenti Inediti, p. 331, *et seq.* tav. 53. At Vadena, in the Tyrol, Etruscan tombs have been found, one bearing an Etruscan inscription graven on its lid. Ann. Inst. 1856, pp. 76–78. Relics of very similar character, however, are discovered in districts never possessed by the Etruscans. Such are the Euganean inscriptions found in the Venetian territory, in that corner of Italy which Livy tells us never belonged to the Etruscans. Liv. V. 33. Such are the helmets with similar inscriptions, discovered in 1812 between Marburg and Radkersburg in Styria. Micali, Mon. Ined. loc. cit. And such is the gold torque, also with an Euganean inscription, found in 1835 in Wallachia. Micali, op. cit. p. 337; Bull. Inst. 1843 p. 95. But at Castel Vetro, near Modena

driving back the Umbrians, and uniting with the Tyrrheni on the Tarquinian coast, formed the Etruscan race.[9]

A more recent opinion is that of Lepsius, who utterly rejects the Rhætian theory of Niebuhr and Müller, pronouncing it most improbable that the arts and sciences, the literature and religious discipline, the refined civilization of Etruria, originated with a rude race of mountaineers from the Tyrol; although they may well have been introduced by the Tyrrhene-Pelasgi. He also rejects the Lydian tradition of Herodotus, chiefly on the ground of the silence of Xanthus, which he regards as conclusive evidence against it. His theory is that the Tyrrhene-Pelasgi, leaving Thessaly, entered Italy at the head of the Adriatic, made their first establishments at the mouths of the Po, eventually crossed the Apennines, and occupied Etruria, after conquering the Umbrians who then possessed it, from whom they took three hundred cities. He thinks there was no subsequent occupation of the land by any foreign people, but that the Umbrians continued to inhabit it as a subject race, like the Saxons in England after the Norman conquest, and that this mixture of Umbrians with Pelasgians, produced what is known as the Etruscan nation.[1]

Mommsen, the historian of Rome, rejects alike the Lydian origin of the Etruscans, and their identity with the Pelasgi, or the Tyrrhene pirates of the Ægæan seas, with whom they had

on the other hand, a bronze mirror has been found with figures precisely in the same style as those of Rhætia, and apparently by the same artist. Cavedoni, Ann. Inst. 1842, p. 67, et seq. tav. d'Agg. H.

In this northern district of Italy many relics have been found which substantiate its recorded possession by the Etruscans. Of the recent discoveries at Bologna, and at Marzabotto in its neighbourhood, a detailed account is given in Chapter LXIV. of this work. At Castel Vetro, and Savignano, near Modona, a number of tombs have been opened with similar furniture. Bull. Inst. 1841, pp. 75-79; 1868, p. 209; Ann. Inst. loc. cit. In the neighbourhood of Parma numerous objects have been found proving the existence of the same race in that region in very early times. Bull. Inst. 1875, pp. 140-149. At Arano and Rovio, in the district of Lugano, at Mendrisio, Ligurno, Sesto Calende, and in the Canton Ticino, many Etruscan antiquities have been discovered. Bull. Inst. 1875, pp. 200-203. At Trevisio in the Valtelline,

an Etruscan sepulchral inscription has been found. Bull. Inst. 1871, pp. 214-219. At Verona, at Ravenna, at Riusca, near Alessandria in Piedmont, and at Adria, genuine Etruscan inscriptions have been found (Lanzi. II. p. 649; Müller, I. pp. 140, 144, 164), and at the last-named place painted vases of great beauty, like those of Vulci and other cemeteries of Central Etruria, have been brought to light in abundance. Bull. Inst. 1834, pp. 135, 142; Micali, Mon. Ined. pp. 279-297, tav. 45, 46. In the hills above Rimini also, tombs very like the Etruscan have been discovered. Torini, I. p. 241.

[9] Müller, Etrusk. einl. 2, 4-12; 3, 10. This opinion is in part favoured by Plutarch (Romul. c. 2), who says the Tyrrheni passed from Thessaly to Lydia, and from Lydia to Italy. Cf. Strab. V. p. 221.

[1] Lepsius, Ueber die Tyrrhenischen-Pelasger in Etrurien. Nearly the same view was held by the late Mr. Millingen, Trans. Roy. Soc. Literat. II. 1834. Ann. Inst. 1834, p. 286.

nothing whatever in common. He ascribes the confusion between these people, made by the ancients as well as by the moderns, to the accidental resemblance between the names *Tursenni* (Etruscans), and the *Torrhebi*, or *Tyrrheni*, of Lydia, which resemblance seems to him the only foundation for the Lydian tradition of Herodotus. As the principal cities of Etruria were all in the interior (?), and as the movements of the Etruscans in historic times were always from north to south (?), he thinks the Etruscans must have reached the peninsula by land, and that their origin must be sought in the north or west of Italy, and probably in the Rhætian Alps, because the earliest inhabitants of that mountainous region spoke Etruscan even in historic times.[2]

It would take too long to record all the opinions and shades of opinion held on this intricate subject. Suffice it to say that the origin of the Etruscans has been assigned to the Greeks—to the Egyptians—the Phœnicians—the Canaanites—the Libyans—the Tartars—the Armenians—the Cantabrians or Basques—the Goths—the Celts, an old theory, revived in our own days by Sir William Betham, who fraternises them with the Irish—and to the Hyksos, or Shepherd-Kings of Egypt. I know not if they have been taken for the lost Ten Tribes of Israel, but, *certes*, a very pretty theory might be set up to that effect, and supported by arguments which would appear all-cogent to every one who swears by Coningsby.[3]

The reader, when he perceives how many-sided is this question, will surely thank me for not leading him deeply into it, yet may hardly like to be left among this chaos of opinions without a guiding hand. Amid the clash and conflict of such a host of combatants, who shall attempt to establish harmony?—and where there are "giants in the land," who shall hope to prevail against them?

No one, of course, in our days accepts in full the legend as

---

[2] Römische Geschichte, I. c. 9.

[3] Not to mention minor analogies, there is one of so striking a character, as satisfactorily to prove, not a descent from Abraham, but an intercourse more or less direct with the Hebrews, and at least an oriental origin. It is in the cosmogony of the Etruscans, who are said, on the authority of one of their own historians, to have believed that the Creator spent 12,000 years in his operations ; 6,000 of which were assigned to the work of creation, and as many to the duration of the world. In the first thousand he made heaven and earth. In the second, the apparent firmament, and called it heaven. In the third, the sea and all the waters which are in the earth. In the fourth, the great lights—sun, moon, and stars. In the fifth, every soul of birds, reptiles, and four-footed animals, in the air, earth, and waters. At the end of the sixth, man. Suidas, *sub voce* Τυῤῥηνία. To say that we recognise here a blending of Etruscan doctrines with the Mosaic account of the Creation, as Müller (III. 2. 7) observes, does not make the analogy less remarkable.

recorded by Herodotus, but it is received simply as bearing
testimony to the Lydian, or rather I should say Asiatic, origin of
the Etruscans. For my own part, I confess that I do not
perceive that the crowd of authorities who maintain that origin
have been put *hors de combat* by the dictum of Dionysius.
There seems to be life in them yet. They clearly represent the
popular traditions, not of the Romans only, but of the Etruscans
also, for what was current on such a matter among the former,
could hardly have been opposed to the traditions of the latter.
Besides, we have it on record that the Etruscans claimed for
themselves a Lydian origin. Tacitus tells us that in the time
of Tiberius, deputies from Sardis recited before the Roman
senate a decree of the Etruscans, declaring their consanguinity,
on the ground of the early colonization of Etruria by the
Lydians.[4] This popular tradition might not of itself be decisive
of the question, but when it is confirmed by a comparison of the
recorded customs and the extant monuments of the two peoples,
as will presently be shown, it comes with a force to my mind,
that will not admit of rejection.[5] I cannot yet consent to
consign it to " the limbo of unsubstantial fabrics " to which it
is contemptuously condemned by a recent writer on " the
Etruscans."[6]

[4] Tacit. Ann. IV. 55. This tradition
appears to have been at least as old as
Romulus. Plutarch (Rom. c. 25) relates
that that monarch, when he conquered
Veii, and granted her a truce for 100 years,
led the vanquished chief of the Veientines
in triumph through Rome. To commemorate this triumph the Romans, whenever
they offered a sacrifice for any victory,
were wont to lead an old man clad in a
toga prætexta and wearing a golden *bulla*
round his neck, from the Forum to the
Capitol, preceded by a herald who shouted,
" Sardians to sell ! "

[5] The argument of Dionysius rests on
the negative authority of Xanthus. Xanthus
was a Lydian, yet wrote in Greek, and was
somewhat earlier than Herodotus, who is
said to have taken some of his matter about
Lydia from him. Ephorus, ap. Athen.
XII. 11. Yet there is a doubt if Xanthus
were really the author of the history attributed to him, as Athenæus (loc. cit.) plainly
shows. Herodotus gives the tradition as
one current with the Lydians of his day.
The truthful historian of antiquity, whose

great merit is the simple trusting fidelity
with which he records what he heard or
saw, could not have invented it. He
doubtless heard it, and booked it just as
he heard it, not caring to strip it of its
incredible adjuncts. Xanthus probably
rejected it as unworthy of record, on
account of the mythical character of those
adjuncts.

[6] Contemporary Review, Oct. 1875, p.
719. Mr. Alexander Murray does not
advance a shadow of argument in support
of this condemnation. The drift of his
very interesting article on Etruscan art is
to suggest the probability, from a consideration of the close similarity of style between
the early silver coins of Thrace, and the
engraved scarabs of Etruria, that the
Etruscans and Greeks had common forefathers in the Pelasgi, and that this people
in Italy developed into the Etruscans—a
theory not very unlike that propounded by
Lepsius. But this is a very limited view
of a many-sided subject. Mr. Murray
omits to take into consideration the many
striking oriental analogies in the earliest

When a tribe like the Gypsies, without house or home, without literature or history, without fixed religious creed, but willing to adopt that of any country where their lot may be cast, with no moral peculiarity beyond their nomade life and roguish habits—when such a people assert that they come from Egypt or elsewhere, we believe them in proportion as we find their personal peculiarities, their language, habits, and customs, are in accordance with those of the people from whom they claim their origin. Their tradition is credible only when confirmed from other sources. But when a people, not a mere tribe, but spread over a large extent of territory, not a nomade, semibarbarous, unlettered race, but a nation settled for ages in one country, possessing a literature and national annals, a systematic form of government and ecclesiastical polity, and a degree of civilization second to that of no contemporary people, save Greece,—a nation having an extensive commerce, and frequent intercourse with the most polite and civilized of its fellows, and probably with the very race from which it claimed its descent,—when such a people lays claim traditionally to a definite origin, which nothing in its manners, customs, or creed appears to belie, but many things to confirm—how can we set the tradition at nought?—why hesitate to give it credence? It was not so much a doubtful fiction of poetry, assumed for a peculiar purpose, like the Trojan origin of Rome, as a record preserved in the religious books of the nation, like the Chronicles of the Jews.

If this tradition of the Lydian origin of the Etruscans be borne out by their recorded manners, and by monumental evidence, it must entirely outweigh the conflicting and unsupported testimony of Dionysius. Nay, granting him to have spoken advisedly in asserting that there was no resemblance between the two people in language, religion, or customs, it would be well explained by the lapse of more than a thousand years from the traditional emigration to his day,[7]—a period much more than sufficient to efface all superficial analogies between people so widely severed, and subjected to such different external influences, and a period during which the Lydians were

---

artistic works of the Etruscans, notably in the *bucchero* ware, and other such analogies in their system of government, their creed, religious discipline, habits, and customs, in which they differed widely from the Greeks, and which are not to be accounted

for by commercial relations, however intimate, with the East; and above all, he forgets the isolated character of their language, which bears not the remotest affinity to that of Greece.

[7] Velleius Paterculus (I. 1) states that

purposely degraded by Cyrus, till they had "lost all their pristine virtue,"[8] while the Etruscans, though also subjected to a foreign yoke, continued to advance in the arts of civilized life.[9]

No fact can be more clearly established than the oriental character of the civil and religious polity, the social and domestic manners, and the early arts of the Etruscans; and traces of this affinity are abundant in their monuments, especially in those of the most remote antiquity, which show none of the influence of Hellenic art.

Like the Assyrians, Babylonians, Egyptians, and Hindoos, the Etruscans were subject to an all-dominant hierarchy, which assumed to be a theocracy, and maintained its sway by arrogating to itself an intimate acquaintance with the will of Heaven and the decrees of fate. But here this ecclesiastical authority was further strengthened by the civil government, for the priests and augurs of Etruria were also her princes and military chiefs; so that with this triple sceptre of civil, religious, and military power, they ruled the people "as the soul governs the body." This state of things was purely oriental. It never existed among the Greeks or other European races; unless it find some analogy in the Druidical system. The divination and augury for which the Etruscans were renowned, and which gave them so peculiar a character among the nations of the west, were of oriental origin. Besides the abundant proofs given in Holy Writ of the early prevalence of soothsaying in the East, we have the authority of Homer and other pagan writers; and the origin of augury is particularly referred to Caria, an adjoining and cognate country to Lydia.[1] Cicero, indeed, classes the Etruscans with the Chaldees for their powers of divination, though they affected to read the will of Heaven, not in the stars, or in dreams, so much as in the entrails of victims, the flight of birds, and the effects of lightning.[2]

---

the Lydian emigration took place shortly after the Trojan War, at the time of the murder of Pyrrhus by Orestes at the temple of Delphi.

[8] Herod. I. 155, 156; Justin. I. 7. See Grote's "Greece," III. p. 283, et seq.

[9] In customs, however, as will be presently shown, there existed strong analogies between the Lydians and Etruscans. And Dionysius' statement as to the dissimilarity of language is of no account, if Strabo's assertion be true, that in his day not a vestige remained of the Lydian tongue,

even in Lydia itself. XIII. p. 631.

[1] Plin. VII. 57. Telmessus in Caria was particularly famed for its aruspices and soothsayers. Herod. I. 78, 84; Cicero, de Divin. I. 41, 42. Clemens of Alexandria (Strom. I. p. 306, ed. Sylb.) says the Carians were the first who divined from the stars, the Phrygians from the flight of birds, the Etruscans by aruspicy.

[2] Cicero, loc. cit. The same power, he tells us, was also possessed by other Asiatic people—the Phrygians, Cilicians, Pisidians, and Arabs. Cic. de Leg. II. 13. Divina-

The evidence of extant monuments seems to point to a close analogy between the religious creed of the Etruscans and those of oriental nations. Micali has written a work with the express purpose of establishing this analogy from the consideration of Etruscan monuments.[3] He contends that the antagonism of good and evil in the government of the universe, which entered so largely into the religious systems of the East, was held by the Etruscans also, and is set forth by the same external means of expression—either by the victories of deities over wild beasts or monsters, or by combats of animals of different natures. Such representations are seen in the colossal reliefs of Persepolis—on the monuments of Babylon and Nineveh—in the Osiris and Typhon of Egypt—and such abound on works of Etruscan art, particularly on those of most ancient character and date. But how far these representations on Etruscan monuments are symbolical, and how far they are parts of a conventional, decorative system derived from the East, it is not easy to pronounce. Such subjects are found also on works of primitive Hellenic art, and especially on those from the shores of Asia Minor. The same may be said of monsters of two-fold life—sphinxes, griffons, chimæras—and even of the four-winged demons of the Assyrian and Babylonian mythology, which abound also on Etruscan monuments, and are likewise found on early Greek vases. Yet the doctrine of good and evil spirits attendant on the soul—obviously held by the Etruscans[4]—favours the supposition that they held the dualistic principle of oriental creeds.

tion by lightning was the branch for which the Etruscans were especially distinguished, and in which they excelled all other people. Diod. Sic. V. p. 316; Dion. Hal. IX. p. 563; Seneca, Nat. Quæst. II. 32; Lucan. I. 587; cf. Cic. in Catil. III. 8; A. Gell. IV. 5; Claud. in Eutrop. I. 12. Cicero believed implicitly in their skill in soothsaying. De Divin. I. 18, 41, 42. Himself an augur, he must have studied deeply the books of the Etruscans on the subject.

Tum quis non, artis scripta ac monumenta volutans,
Voces tristificas chartis promebat Etruscis ?
De Divin. I. 12.

Joannes Lydus in his work De Ostentis, c. 27, gives, on the authority of Nigidius Figulus, a "Diarium Tonitruale, or Etrus-

can "thunder-calendar," for every day in the year, taken, he says, from the books of Tages. Servius also (ad Æn. I. 46) mentions Etruscan books on Lightning. Lucret. VI. 381; Cic. de Divin. I. 33; Amm. Marcell. XXIII. 5. The entire system of divination among the Romans, be it remembered, was derived from the Etruscans. It continued to be practised by them even to the close of the Empire, for we find the Etruscan aruspices consulted by Julian in the fourth (Amm. Marcell. XXV. 2, 7), and under Honorius in the fifth century of our era. Zosim. Hist. V. 41. See Müller, Etrusk. III.

[3] Monumenti Inediti, a illustrazione della Storia degli Antichi Popoli Italiani. Firenze, 1844.

[4] Vol. I. pp. 287, 342; II. p. 182.

The analogy of the Etruscan customs to those of the East
did not escape the notice of ancient writers. And here let me
remark that the Mysians, Lydians, Carians, Lycians, and
Phrygians being cognate races, inhabiting adjoining lands, what
is recorded of one is generally applicable to all.[5] "The
ascendancy of the Lydian dynasty in Asia Minor, with its
empire (real or fabulous) of the sea during its flourishing ages,
would naturally impart to any such tradition a Lydian form.
In any attempt, therefore, to illustrate the Etruscan origin or
manners from Asiatic sources, our appeals may safely be
extended to the neighbouring, whether kindred, or merely
connected, races."[6] The sports, games, and dances of the
Etruscans, adopted by the Romans, are traditionally of Lydian
origin.[7] The musical instruments on which they excelled were
introduced from Asia Minor,—the double-pipes from Phrygia,
the trumpet from Lydia.[8] Their luxurious habits were so
strictly oriental, that almost the same language is used in
describing them and those of the Lydians.[9] Even the common
national robe, the *toga*, was of Lydian origin.[1] Dionysius himself, after having stated that there was no resemblance whatever
between the customs of the Etruscans and Lydians, points out
that the purple robes worn in Etruria as *insignia* of authority,
were similar to those of the Lydian and Persian monarchs, differing only in form [2]—the oriental robe being square, the Etruscan

[5] Herodotus (I. 171) calls the Carians,
Mysians, and Lydians, κασίγνητοι. Strabo
(XIII. p. 628) says the boundaries between
Lydia, Phrygia, Caria, and Mysia, could
not be determined, and had given rise to
great confusion. Cf. XIV. p. 678 ; Plin.
V. 30.

[6] Quarterly Review, No. CLI. p. 56.

[7] Liv. VII. 2; Val. Max. II. 4, 3 :
Tertull. de Spect. I. 5 ; Appian, de Reb.
Punic. LXVI. Dice, which were a Lydian
invention (Herod. I. 94), were also much
used in Etruria, as we learn from history
(Liv. IV. 17), as well as from their being
frequently found in Etruscan tombs.

[8] Plin. VII. 57. Clem. Alex. Strom. I.
p. 306. The Lydian pipes were also famous,
Pind. Olymp. V. 44. One tradition ascribes
the invention of the trumpet to Tyrrhenus,
the Lydian colonist of Etruria. Pausan.
II. 21; cf. Serv. ad Virg. Æn. I. 71; Sil.
Ital. V. 12. Another refers it to Maleus,
the Etruscan prince of Regisvilla. Lactant.

ad Stat. Theb. IV. 224. The current belief
was that the trumpet was of Etruscan
origin. Strabo, V. p. 220 : Diod. V.
p. 316 ; Æschyl. Eumen. 567 ; Sophoc.
Ajax, 17 ; Athen. IV. c. 82 ; Virg. Æn.
VIII. 526 ; Serv. in loc. ; Clem. Alex.
Strom. I. p. 306 ; Pollux, IV. 11. Silius
Italicus (VIII. 490) specifies Vetulonia as
the site of its invention.

[9] Athen. XII. c. 11, 17 ; XV. c. 41 ;
Theopomp. ap. eund. XII. c. 14 ; Poseidon.
ap. eund. IV. c. 38 ; Diod. Sic. V. p. 316.
So Anacreon (ap. Athen. XV. c. 41) uses
Λυδοπαθής for ἡδυπαθής, and Æschylus
(Pers. 41) speaks of the ἀβροδίαιτοι Λυδοί.

[1] Tertull. de Pallio, I. ; cf. Serv. ad
Virg. Æn. II. 781. The Romans received
it from the Etruscans, who have therefore
a prior right to the title of *gens togata*.
Liv. I. 8 ; Flor. I. 5 ; Plin. VIII. 74 ;
IX. 63 ; Diodor. V. p. 316 ; Macrob. Sat.
I. 6 ; Festus v. Sardi.

[2] Dion. Hal. III. c. 61.

toga or τήβεννος, which answered to it, semicircular. The eagle, which Rome bore as her standard, and which she derived from Etruria, was also the military ensign of Persia.[3] The young women of Etruria are said, like those of Lydia, to have obtained their dowries by prostitution.[4] The singular custom of the Lycians, of tracing their descent by the maternal line, obtained also among the Etruscans, alone among the nations of antiquity.[5] And another custom which essentially distinguished the Etruscans from the Greeks, and assimilated them to the people of Asia Minor, was that they shared the festive couch with their wives.[6] Their language and the character in which it was written have very marked oriental analogies. But in their tombs and sepulchral usages the affinity of Etruria to Lydia and other countries of Asia is most strongly marked; and it is to be learned not only from extant monuments, but from historical records. These analogies will be pointed out in detail in the course of this work.

In one important particular there is also a striking analogy— in physiognomy. In many of the early monuments of Etruria the oriental type of countenance is strongly and unmistakably marked, a fact well illustrated by reference to the loving couple of life-size recumbent on the terra-cotta sarcophagus from Cervetri, now in the Louvre,[7] or better still, to the similar, but nude pair from the same site in the British Museum, who are portrayed in the woodcut at page 227 of this volume. There can be no mistake here. The type is purely oriental, nay Mongolian. Any one who has lived among Tartar tribes will at once recognize the characteristics of that race, especially in the obliquely placed eyes, which, as Mr. Isaac Taylor says, no Aryan ever possessed. In the Etruscan portraits of later times, these archaic peculiarities are in great measure lost. The mixture of races, it may be, on

---

[3] Cf. Dion. Hal. loc. cit. and Xenoph. Anab. I. 10.

[4] Cf. Herod. I. 93, and Plaut. Cistell. II. 3, 20.—

non enim hic, ubi ex Tusco modo
Tute tibi indigne dotem quæras corpore.

Chastity, if we may believe the accounts of the ancients, was little valued by either people; and this is a point in which they differed widely from the Greeks and early Romans. Strabo, XI. p. 532; Theopompus, ap. Athen. XII. c. 14; cf. Athen.

XII. 11. Horace complains of his Lyce as being much too obdurate for an Etruscan. Od. III. 10, 11. Strabo tells us that the ancient Armenians also prostituted their daughters before marriage.

[5] See Vol. I. p. 100.

[6] See Vol. I. p. 309. Herodotus (I. 172) mentions that the Caunians, a people of Asia Minor, were accustomed to hold *symposia*, or drinking-bouts, with their wives and families. Cf. I. 146.

[7] See Vol. I. p. 279.

the one hand, and the influence of Greek art on the other, tended to assimilate Etruscan portraiture to the European type.

The relation and connection of Etruria with the East is an established fact, admitted on all hands but variously accounted for.[8] To me it seems to be such as cannot be explained by commercial intercourse, however extensive, for it is apparent not merely on the surface of Etruscan life, but deep within it, influencing all its springs of action, and imparting a tone and character, that neither Greek example and preceptorship, nor Roman domination could ever entirely efface. So intimate a connection could only have been formed by conquest or colonization from the East. That such was possible all will admit,—that it was not improbable, the common practice of antiquity of colonizing distant lands is evidence enough ; sublime memorials of which we still behold on the shores of Italy and Sicily, in those shrines of a long-perished creed, now sacred to Hellenic genius. Had we been told that Mysia, Caria, Phrygia, or Lycia, was the mother-country of Etruria, we might have accepted the tradition, but as Lydia is specifically indicated, why refuse to credit it ? To what country of the East we may be inclined to ascribe this colonization, is of little moment. We must at least admit, with Seneca, that "Asia claims the Etruscans as her own."—*Tuscos Asia sibi vindicat.*[9]

LANGUAGE.

That which in an investigation of this kind would prove of most service is here unfortunately of no avail. The language of Etruria, even in an age which has unveiled the Egyptian hieroglyphics and the arrow-headed character of Babylon, still remains a mystery. This "geological literature," as it has been aptly termed, has baffled the learning and research of scholars of every nation for ages past ; and though fresh treasures are daily stored up, the key to unlock them is still wanting. We know the characters in which it is written, which much resemble the Pelasgic or early Greek,[1]—we can learn even somewhat of the

[8] Müller (Etrusk. einl. 2, 7) asserts "the unmistakable connection between the civilization of Etruria and Asia Minor." Even Micali, who maintains the indigenous origin of the Etruscans, sets forth their relation with the East in a prominent light, though explaining it as the result of

their commercial intercourse with the Egyptians, Phœnicians, Carthaginians, and other oriental people.

[9] Seneca, Consol. ad Helv. VI. ?.

[1] To the Pelasgi is referred the introduction of letters into Latium. Solin. Polyhist. VIII. Another tradition says

genius of the language and its inflections; but beyond this, and the proper names and the numerals on sepulchral monuments, and a few words recorded by the ancients,[2] the wisest must admit their ignorance, and confess that all they know of the Etruscan tongue, is that it is unique—like the Basque, an utter alien to every known family of languages. To the other early tongues of Italy, which made use of the same or nearly the same character, we find some key in the Latin, especially to the Oscan, which bears to it a parental relation. But the Etruscan has been tested again and again by Greek, Latin, Hebrew, and every other ancient language, and beyond occasional affinities which may be mere coincidences, such as occur in almost every case, no clue has yet been found to its interpretation,—and unless some monument like the Rosetta-stone should come to light, and some Young or Champollion should arise to decipher it, the Etruscan must ever remain a dead, as it has always emphatically been, a sepulchral, language.[3] Till then, to every fanciful theorist, who fondly hugs

they were brought to the Aborigines by Evander from Arcadia, and that the ancient Latin characters were the same as the earliest Greek. Tacit. Ann. XI. 14. The Etruscans are said by the same authority to have received their characters from Corinth through Demaratus. It is certain that all the ancient alphabets of Italy — the Umbrian, Oscan, Euganean, Messapian, as well as the Etruscan—bear an unmistakable affinity to the early Greek.

[2] All we know of the language from the ancients is confined to some thirty words, many of which are manifestly disguised by the foreign medium through which they have come down to us.

The names of certain Etruscan deities are also known, either from ancient writers or from monuments. Mr. Isaac Taylor (Etruscan Researches, p. 197 et seq.), from a careful comparison of mortuary inscriptions, has determined the precise meaning of certain words used in sepulchral formulæ :—

"Ril" = years.
"Avil" or "avils" = age, or aged.
"Leine" = lived.
"Lupu" = died.

If to this we add that the general, if not precise, meaning of two or three other sepulchral formulæ can be guessed at, and that "Clan" seems to mean son, "Sec,"

daughter, and "Hinthial," ghost, or spectre, we have the full extent of our knowledge of the Etruscan vocabulary.

[3] Lanzi states that in his day, besides the three classic languages, "the Ethiopic, the Egyptian, the Arabic, the Coptic, the Chinese, the Celtic, the Basque, the Anglo-Saxon, the Teutonic, the Runic, and what not," had been consulted in vain for the key to the Etruscan. Lanzi thought he had discovered it in the Greek, and to establish his theory put that noble language to sad torture, from which sounder criticism has released it. Dr. Arnold (History of Rome, pref. p. XIII.) expected the interpretation of the Etruscan to be discovered. And Müller (Etrusk. einl. 3, 10) entertained the hope that in some secluded valley of the Grisons or of the Tyrol, a remnant of the old Rhætian dialect might be discovered which would serve as a key to the Etruscan. He adds that Von Hormayr held the Surselvish dialect to be Etruscan. Within the last few years Müller's hope has been in some degree realised by the labours of a German scholar, who though he has found no key to the interpretation of the Etruscan, has at least shown that some remnants of a dialect very like it remain among the Alps of Rhætia. Steub, Ueber die Urbewohner Rätiens und ihren Zusammenhang mit den Etruskern. München, 1843. In travelling in 1842 among these Alps he was struck

himself into the belief that to him it has been reserved to unravel the mystery, or who possesses the Sabine faculty of dreaming what he wishes, we must reply in the words of the prophet. "It is an ancient nation, a nation whose language thou knowest not."

Were it not for this mystery of the language, the oriental analogies on the one hand, and the Greek features on the other, which are obvious in the recorded customs of Etruria and the monuments of her art, might be reconciled by the theory of a Pelasgic colony from Asia Minor. But the language in its utter loneliness compels us to look further for the origin of the Etruscan people.

For the benefit of travellers, who would spell their way through epitaphs, I subjoin the Etruscan alphabet, in the proper order of the characters, confronting them with the Greek.

A	ꓯꓯꓮ	N	ꟿꟿ
K (Γ ?)	><	Π	ꓵꓵ
E	ꓱꓱꓱ	Σ accented	MM
Digamma	ꓶꓶꓶꓶ	Q koppa	ρ
Z	‡‡ rarely	P	◁◁ρ◁
Aspirate	ᗺᗺH	Σ	₹₹₹
Θ	○⊙⊘◇◇	T	ꓕꓕꓬ
I	ǀ	Υ	VV rarely
K	ꓘꓘ	Φ	ΦΦ⊕⊘
Λ	ꓥꓶ	X	↓↓↓
M	ꟿꟿWW	Φ ?	88

with the strange-sounding names, on the high-roads as well as in the most secluded valleys. Mountains or villages bore the appellations of Tilisuna, Blisadona, Naturns, Velthurns, Schluderns, Schlanders, Villanders, Firmiaun, Similaun, Gufidaun, Altrans, Sistrans, Axams,—wherever he turned, these mysterious names resounded in his ears ; and he took them to be the relics of some long perished race. He tested them by the Celtic, and could find no analogy ; but with the Etruscan he had more success, and found the ancient traditions of a Rhæto-Etruria confirmed. Like many of his countrymen he rides his hobby too hard ; and seeks to establish analogies which none but a determined theorist could perceive. What resemblance is apparent to eye or ear between such words as the following, taken almost at random from his tables? — Carenna Tschirgant ; Caca = Tschätsch ; Velacarasa -. Vollgröss ; Caloruna = Goldrain ; Calusa Schleiss ; Calunoturusa .Schlanders ; Velavuna Plawen.

The Etruscan alphabet, it will be seen, wants the B, Γ, Δ, Ξ, Ψ, the H, and both the O and Ω.[4] In the custom of writing from right to left, and of frequently dropping the short vowels, the Etruscan bears a close oriental analogy. Indeed it is probable that like the Pelasgic, the Greek, and other kindred alphabets, this had its origin from Phœnicia.[6]

The numerals known to us by the name of Roman, are in reality Etruscan; and were originally not only read from right to left, but were inverted.

Professor Mommsen points out that there are two distinct phases in the Etruscan language, the earlier, as ascertained from the most ancient monuments, showing an abundance of vowels, and an avoidance of the juxta-position of two consonants; but by the gradual suppression of the vowels this sweet and sonorous tongue was transformed into one insufferably harsh and rough; forming such words as Tarchnas, Elchsentre, Achle, Klutmsta, Alksti, for Tarquinius, Alexandros, Achilleus, Clytæmnestra, Alcestis—in short, the character of the language was changed from an Italian to a German type. There are certain isolated analogies to other Italic tongues, the proper names in particular

[4] In the Etruscan alphabet of Bomarzo the second letter is a), and the *kappa* is wanting; while those of Chiusi, which are probably of earlier date, show the latter letter alone. In the alphabet of Rusellæ, however, which is apparently the most recent of all, there are not only both these characters, but the *koppa* in addition. It may be that the) had the sound of the *gamma*, though the existence of that letter in the Etruscan alphabet is not generally recognised. The 6fth letter in the Etruscan alphabet has the force of " ss " according to Lepsius, of " x " according to Müller; but it is now generally recognized as the equivalent of the Greek *zeta*. In the Bomarzo alphabet it has the peculiar form resembling an ε. For the Etruscan alphabet found at Bomarzo, see p. 172 of this volume; for that of Rusellæ, see Vol. II. p. 224; and for the three at Chiusi, Vol. II. p. 306. These last are supposed to be the most ancient. Gamurrini, Ann. Inst. 1871, pp. 156—166.

[6] Dr. Helbig very ingeniously demonstrates, from a consideration of the length of the Etruscan *secula*, as given by Varro (ap. Censorin. XVII. 5), that the alphabet must have been introduced into Etruria

between 750 and 644 B.C. Ann. Inst. 1876, p. 227 *et seq.* Whether the characters came directly from Phœnicia into Etruria, or were received through Greece, is a disputed point. Müller maintains the latter. Etrusk. IV. 6, 1. Mommsen is of the same opinion, and thinks they were imported by the Doric Chalcidians, who colonized the shores of Campania, and that the Umbrians received them from the Etruscans. Mr. Daniel Sharpe, speaking of the discoveries in Lycia, declares, that "it may be proved, from a comparison of the alphabets, that the Etruscans derived their characters from Asia Minor, and not from Greece." Fellows' Lycia, p. 442. The resemblance, indeed, of the Etruscan alphabet to the Lycian is striking—still more so that which it bears to the Phrygian, such as it is seen on the tombs of Dogan-lū. See Walpole's travels, and Steuart's Lydia and Phrygia. Dr. Klügmann marks three periods of Etruscan inscriptions, distinguishable by the form of the letters. The first, anterior to the Peloponnesian War, or to 431 B.C. The second, from that date to the First Punic War, or to 264 B.C. The third, from the Punic War to the Empire. Ann. Inst. 1873, p. 250.

being formed in accordance with the universal Italic system, but
with these exceptions the Etruscan language is as distinct from
all the Græco-Italic tongues, as are those of the Celts and Slavs
—a distinction recognized by the Romans themselves, who spoke
of the Etruscan and Gaulish as barbarous languages, of the
Oscan and Volscian as rustic dialects. The result of all our
investigations into the character of this mysterious language, is
that we seem to have sufficient authority for classing the Etruscans among the peoples of Indo-Germanic origin.[7]

While Professor Corssen, by a comparison of Etruscan inscriptions with other early languages of the Peninsula, arrives at the
conclusion that the Etruscan is an indigenous Italic tongue, the
Earl of Crawford and Balcarres has been led by confronting it
with the remains of the old German dialects, to believe he has
demonstrated its affinity to them, especially to those spoken by
the Thuringian tribes, the Visi-Goths and Ostro-Goths. I say
he believes he has proved this, for to say more were to hazard a
judgment, which in matters of such erudition I do not possess,
but as I do not hold to the Rhætian origin of the Etruscans, I
may consistently hope that the verdict of philologists on his lord-
ship's theory will be "not proven." The Rev. Robert Ellis also
maintains the Aryan character of the Etruscan language, believing
it to have close affinities to the Armenian, yet he admits the non-
Aryan character of its numerals, which he pronounces to be Ibero-
African. The Rev. Isaac Taylor stands alone in regarding the
Etruscan language as Turanian, and of the "Altaic, or Finno-
Turkic family of speech," but the method he adopts in his quest
of linguistic affinities, gathering them from different branches of
the Turanian stock in all parts of the world, is surely not philo-
sophical, and is hardly calculated to secure our confidence in his
deductions. "The key to the Etruscan language" Mr. Taylor
finds in a pair of ivory dice discovered at Vulci in 1847, and
incribed with the monosyllables MACH, HUTH, KI, SA, ZAL, THU.
Professors Max Müller and Corssen have questioned that these
words are the names of Etruscan numerals; but it may be fairly
presumed that the words were inserted in this instance instead of
the pips from 1 to 6 which are found on all other specimens of
Etruscan dice as yet brought to light. Granting them to be the
Etruscan names of the numerals, how are they to be arranged?
Here the interpreters differ widely, Ellis, Campanari, and Migliarini adopting one order, Taylor another, viz :—

[7] Röm. Gesch. I. c. 9.

1	2	3	4	5	6
Mr. Ellis— Mach	Thu	Zal	Huth	Ki	Sa.
Mr. Taylor—Mach	Ki	Zal	Sa	Thu	Huth.

Until their order is determined, the discovery of these numerals will add little to our knowledge of the Etruscan language.

GOVERNMENT.

The government of Etruria in external form bore some resemblance to a federal republic, each of its Twelve States or Cities having a distinct sovereignty, yet combining in a league of amity and mutual assistance—such a confederation, in fact, as existed in early times among the states of Greece. Yet the internal government of each state was an aristocracy, for the Etruscans hated a monarchy, and the kings we read of occasionally in Roman history were either the chief rulers of each state, or one chosen out of this body to preside over all, like the Doges of Venice or the Popes of Rome. The analogy in the latter case is strengthened by the double functions, political and ecclesiastical, of the Etruscan Lucumones. For these princes were all augurs, skilled in divination and the mysteries of "the Etruscan Discipline;" and when they met in solemn conclave at the shrine of the great goddess Voltumna, to deliberate on the affairs of the Confederation, one was chosen from among them as high priest or pontiff.[8] In Etruria, as in the Papal State, the same will decreed civil laws, and prescribed religious observances and ceremonies, all on the assumption of an unerring interpretation of the will of heaven.

Political freedom was a plant which flourished not in Etruria. The power was wholly in the hands of priestly nobles; the people had no voice in the government, not even the power of making themselves heard and respected, as at Rome. Whatever may have been the precise relation between the ruling class and their dependents, it is clear that it was akin to the feudal system, and that the mass of the community was enthralled. The state of society was not precisely that of the middle ages, for there was more union and community of interest and feeling than among

[8] Liv. V. 1 ; Serv. ad Virg. Æn. X. 202. Servius tells us that each of the Twelve Cities of Etruria was ruled by a *Lucumo*, or king, one of whom was supreme; ad Æn. II. 278 ; VIII. 65, 475; XI. 9. Porsena in his sovereign capacity brought down fire from heaven. Plin. II. 54. When Veii set up a real king, it gave great offence to the rest of the Confederation. Liv. V. I.

the feudal lords of Germany, France, or England. The commons must have been a conquered people, the descendants of the early inhabitants of the land, and must have stood in a somewhat similar relation to their rulers, to that which the Periœci of Laconia held to their Dorian lords, or the subjugated Saxons of England bore to their Norman conquerors. That they were serfs rather than slaves seems evident, from the fact that they formed the class of which the Etruscan armies were composed. The Etruscans possessed slaves, like the other nations of antiquity; [9] nay, their bondage was proverbially rigorous,[1]—but these were captives taken in war, or in their piratical expeditions. Niebuhr shows that "the want of a free and respectable commonalty—which the Etruscans, obstinately retaining and extending their old feudal system, never allowed to grow up—was the occasion of the singular weakness displayed by the great Etruscan cities in their wars with the Romans, where the victory was decided by the number and strength of the infantry." [2] It was also the cause of the inferiority of the Etruscan to the Greek civilization—of its comparatively stationary and conventional character. Yet had there been no slaves, and had the entire population been of one race, the lower classes could hardly have escaped enthralment, for it is difficult to conceive of a system of government more calculated to enslave both mind and body than that of the aristocratical augurs and aruspices of Etruria.

[9] Liv. V. I. 22. Dionysius (XI. p. 562) speaks of the Etruscan nobles leading the πενέσται, or serfs, out to battle against the Romans; and the "agrestium cohortes" mentioned by Livy (IX. 36), were probably of the same class. The rebellious slaves who usurped the supreme power at Volsinii are shown by Niebuhr to have been also serfs, not domestic slaves. Hist. Rom. I. p. 124; III. p. 546. See Vol. II. p. 22, of this work.

[1] This would appear from Martial, IX. 23. 4.—

Et sonet innumerâ compede Tuscus ager.

Cicero says the Etruscan pirates used to tie their living captives to the bodies of the dead (ap. Serv. ad Æn. VIII. 479); and Virgil relates the same of Mezentius, the tyrant of Agylla. Æn. VIII. 485.

[2] Niebuhr, I. p. 122. Engl. trans. The great historian, however, goes too far in asserting that the extant works of the Etruscans could not have been executed without taskmasters and bondmen (p. 129). Indeed the distinction between the public works of the Egyptians and Etruscans, admitted by Niebuhr himself—that all the works of the latter we are acquainted with have a great public object—is a sufficient refutation of this position. The works of the Etruscans are not ostentatious, useless piles, but such as might be produced in industrious, commercial, yet warlike communities, of no great extent, and under the influence of more popular freedom than was ever enjoyed in Etruria. The temples of Pæstum, Agrigentum, and Selinus, are examples of this

RELIGION.

The religion of Etruria in her earliest ages bore some resemblance to that of Egypt, but more to the other theological systems of the East. It had the same gloomy, unbending, imperious character, the same impenetrable shroud of mysticism and symbolism; widely unlike the lively, plastic, phantasy-full creed of the Greeks, whose joyous spirit found utterance in song. The one was the religion of a caste, imposed for its exclusive benefit on the masses, and therefore not an exponent of national character, though influencing it; the other was the creed of an entire people, voluntarily embraced from its adaptation to their wants—nay, called into being by them—and necessarily stamped with the peculiar impress of their thoughts and feelings. In consequence of increased intercourse with other lands in subsequent times, the mythology of Etruria assimilated in great measure to that of Greece; yet there was always this difference, that she held her creed, not as something apart from all political systems, not as a set of dogmas which deep-probing philosophy and shallow superstition could hold in common, and each invest with its peculiar meaning. No; it was with her an all-pervading principle—the very atmosphere of her existence—a leaven operating on the entire mass of society—a constant presence ever felt in one form or other—a power admitting no rival, all-ruling, all-regulating, all-requiring. Such was its sway, that it moulded the national character, and gave the Etruscans a pre-eminently religious reputation among the people of antiquity.[3] Like the Roman Catholic in after times, it was a religion of mysteries, of marvels, of ceremonial pomp and observances. It was, however, a religion of fear. The deities most dreaded received most adoration, and their wrath was deprecated even by the sacrifice of human life. Its dominance was not without one beneficial effect. It bound its votaries in fetters, if not of entire harmony, at least of peace. Those civil contests which were the disgrace of Greece, which retarded her civilization, and ultimately proved her destruction, seem to have been unknown in Etruria. Yet the power of her religion was but negative; it proved ineffectual as a national bond, as an incitement to make common cause against a common foe. The several States were often at variance, and pursued independent courses of action, and

---

[3] Liv. V. I—Geus ante omnes alias eo magis dedita religionibus, quod excelleret arte colendi eas. Arnob. VII.—Genetrix et mater superstitionis Etruria.

thus laid themselves open to be conquered in detail.[4] But so
far as we can learn from history, they were never arrayed in arms
against each other; and this must have been the effect of their
common religion. Yet it was her system of spiritual tyranny
that rendered Etruria inferior to Greece. She had the same
arts—an equal amount of scientific knowledge—a more extended
commerce. In every field had the Etruscan mind liberty to
expand, save in that wherein lies man's highest delight and glory.
Before the gate of that paradise where the intellect revels
unfettered among speculations on its own nature, on its origin,
existence, and final destiny, on its relation to the First Cause,
to other minds, and to society in general—stood the sacerdotal
Lucumo, brandishing in one hand the double-edged sword of
secular and ecclesiastical authority, and holding forth in the other
the books of Tages, exclaiming, to his awe-struck subjects,
"Believe and obey!" Liberty of thought and action was as
incompatible with the assumption of infallibility in the governing
power in the days of Tarchon or Porsena, as in those of Pius IX.

The mythological system of Etruria is learned partly from
ancient writers, partly from national monuments, particularly
figured mirrors. It was in some measure allied to that of
Greece, though rather to the early Pelasgic system than to that
of the Hellenes; but still more nearly to that of Rome, who in
fact derived certain of her divinities and their names from this
source.

The three great deities, who had temples in every Etruscan
city, were TINA or TINIA—THALNA or CUPRA—and MENRVA, or
MENERVA.[5]

TINIA was the supreme deity of the Etruscans, analogous to
the Zeus of the Greeks, and the Jupiter of the Romans—"the
centre of the Etruscan god-world, the power who speaks in the

[4] Five only of the Twelve assisted the
Latins against Tarquinius Priscus. Dion.
Hal. III. p. 189. Arretium, in 443, refused to join the rest in their attack on
Sutrium, then in the power of the Romans.
Liv. IX. 32. Veii, just before her capture,
estranged herself from the rest of the Confederation, which refused succour in her
need. Liv. V. 1, 17. When Sutrium and
Nepete are called the allies of Rome, and
are said to have besought assistance against
the Etruscans (Liv. VI. 3, 9, 10), this must
refer to the Roman, not the Etruscan population, for the latter, from the small size

of the towns, might easily be outnumbered
by a garrison. That the conquered portion
were ready to unite with their Etruscan
brethren when occasion offered, is proved
in the case of Nepete. Liv. VI. 10. Cære,
however, was in more independent alliance
with Rome, but even she at one time was
urged by the sympathy of blood to sever this
alliance; and it does not appear that she
was ever in arms against her fellow-cities of
the Etruscan Confederation. See Vol. I.
p. 233.

[5] Serv. ad Virg. Æn. 1. 426; II. 296.
To these three Tarquin added Mercury.

thunder and descends in the lightning." He alone had three separate bolts to hurl, and is therefore always represented on Etruscan monuments with a thunder-bolt with triple points in his hand.[6]

THALNA or CUPRA was the Etruscan Hera or Juno, and her principal shrines seem to have been at Veii, Falerii, and Perusia. Like her counterpart among the Greeks and Romans, she appears to have been worshipped under other forms, according to her various attributes—as Feronia, Uni, Eileithyia-Leucothea.[7]

MENRVA, as she is called on Etruscan monuments, answers to the Pallas-Athene of the Greeks. It is probable that the name by which the Romans knew her was of purely Etruscan origin.[8] She seems to have been allied to NORTIA, the Fortuna of the Etruscans.[9] Like her counterpart in the Greek and Roman mythology, she is represented armed, and with the ægis on her breast, but has sometimes wings in addition.[1]

There were Twelve Great Gods, six of each sex, called Dii Consentes or Complices. They composed the council of Tinia, and are called " the senators of the gods "—" the Penates of the Thunderer himself." They were fierce and pitiless deities, dwelling in the inmost recesses of heaven, whose names it was forbidden to utter. Yet they were not deemed eternal, but supposed to rise and fall together.[2]

[6] Plin. II. 53. Seneca (Nat. Quæst. II. 41) says that the first kind of bolt, which is monitory and not wrathful, Jove can hurl at his pleasure; the second he can hurl only with the consent of his Council of the Twelve Great Gods; and to hurl the third kind he is obliged to consult the Shrouded Gods. He is sometimes represented as a beardless youth. Gerhard, Etrus. Spieg. I. taf. 14. Some have sought an etymological relation between Tina and Zeus; others to Tonans, and others even to the Odin of the northern mythology, though this similarity is pronounced by Müller to be accidental. Etrusk. III. 3, 1. Gerhard, Gottheit. p. 27.

[7] We learn the name of Cupra from Strabo, V. p. 241, who states that the town of that name in Picenum took its name from the temple built there by the Etruscans, and dedicated to this goddess. The name Cupra has not been found on Etruscan monuments, where the goddess is generally called Thalna, though Gerhard (Gotth. d. Etrusk. p. 40) thinks this name is descrip-

tive of her as a goddess of birth and light. Feronia is said by Varro (V. 74) to be a Sabine goddess. Gerhard (Gotth. p. 8) takes her to be equivalent to Juno, Müller (III. 3, 8) to Tellus or Mania. See Vol. I. p. 129. For Uni, see Ann. Inst. 1851, tav. d'agg. G. H. For Eileithyia, see Vol. I. p. 292. The rites of the Etruscan Juno are described by Ovid, Amor. III. eleg. 13; cf. Dion. Hal. I. p. 17.

[8] So thinks Müller (Etrusk. III. 3, 2), notwithstanding that Varro asserts it to be Sabine. Ling. Lat. V. 74. Müller regards her as the only Etruscan divinity whose worship was transferred to Rome in all its purity.

[9] Gerhard (Gottheit. p. 10) thinks the relation between Minerva and Nortia is established by the fact of the annual nail being driven into the temple of the latter at Volsinii, and of the former on the Capitol. Gerhard takes Nortia for a Pelasgic divinity.

[1] As in a bronze figure from Orte, in the Museo Gregoriano, see Vol. II. p. 478.

[2] Arnob. adv. Nat. III. 40; Varro, de

Still more awful and potent were " the shrouded Gods,"—Dii Involuti—whose appellation is suggestive of their mysterious character; they ruled both gods and men, and to their decisions even Tinia himself was obedient. They were also called Dii Superiores.[3]

THE SHROUDED GODS?

The Etruscans believed in Nine Great Gods, who had the power of hurling thunderbolts; they were called Novensiles by the Romans.[4]   Of thunderbolts there were eleven sorts, of which Tinia, as the supreme thunder-god, wielded three.[5]   Cupra, or Juno, as one of the nine, also hurled her bolts.[6]   Menerva, the third, hurled hers at the time of the vernal equinox.[7]   Summanus hurled his bolts by night as Jupiter did by day, and received even

de Rust. I. 1 ; Martian Capella, de Nupt. I. 14.   Gerhard thinks they must include the eight thunder-wielding gods known to us, to which he would add Vertumnus, Janus or Apollo, Nortia or Fortuna, and Voltumna.   (Gotth. d. Etrusk. p. 23.

[3] Seneca, Nat. Quaest. II. 41 ; Festus, v. Manubiæ.   Gerhard (Gottheit. Etrusk. taf. 7) gives a singular plate of two veiled figures, sitting back to back, and with both hands to their mouths, which he thinks may represent " the shrouded gods."   They are taken from a drawing in the public archives of Viterbo, supposed to be a copy from some Etruscan monument, found in former

times ; perhaps a mirror, as Gerhard suggests, but more probably a bas-relief.   See the above wood-cut.

[4] Plin. II. 53 ; Manilius ap. Arnob. III. 38.   Varro (Ling. Lat. V. 74) says the name of Novensiles is derived from the Sabines.   Gerhard considers the Novensiles to belong, without doubt, to the Etruscan mythology.   Gotth. Etrusk. p. 3.

[5] Plin. loc. cit. : Servius (ad Æn. I. 46) states that in the Etruscan books on Things struck by Lightning, mention was made of twelve sorts of thunderbolts.

[6] Serv. loc. cit. ; VIII. 429.

[7] Serv. loc. cit. ; XI. 259.

more honour from the old Romans as a thunder-wielding god, than Jupiter himself.[8] VEJOVIS, or VEDIUS, though with a Latin name, was an Etruscan deity, whose bolts had the singular effect of making those they struck so deaf, " that they could not hear the thunder, or even louder noises."[9] Vulcan, or as the Etruscans called him SETHLANS, was another bolt-hurling god.[1] MARS was also one of these nine.[2] The last two are not mentioned, but it seems probable that one was SATURN, or it may be their great infernal deity MANTUS.[3] The ninth was probably Hercules —ERCLE, or HERCLE—a favourite god of the Etruscans.[4]

Besides these, were other great deities, as VERTUMNUS, or "the changeable," the god of wine and gardens, the Etruscan Bacchus;[5] though that god is sometimes also called PHUPHLUNS.[6] Allied to him, probably in more than name, was VOLTUMNA, the great goddess at whose shrine the confederate princes of Etruria held their councils.[7] With her also may be analogous, HORTA, whose name perhaps indicates a goddess of gardens, and from whom a town of Etruria derived its name.[8] APLU, or Apollo, often appears on Etruscan monuments, as god of the sun, being sometimes called USIL;[9] and so also TURMS, or Mercury;[1] and TURAN, or Venus;[2] and more rarely THESAN, the goddess of the

[8] Plin. loc. cit. ; Augustin. de Civ. Dei, IV. 23.

[9] Ammian. Marcell. XVII. 10, 2.

[1] Serv. ad Æn. I. 45. It is "Vulcanum" in some editions, and Müller (Etrusk. III. 3, 5) prefers it to "Junonem," which is Harmann's reading.

[2] Serv. ad Æn. VIII. 429 ; cf. Plin. II. 53. The name of the Etruscan Mars is not known, but that of the Sabine Mars, "Mamers," is inscribed in Etruscan letters on a fibula in the Gregorian Museum. Bull. Inst. 1846, p. 11.

[3] The Etruscans are said to have believed that thunderbolts came not always from heaven, but sometimes from the earth ; or, as some said, from the planet Saturn. Plin. II. 53. On this ground Müller (Etrusk. III. 3, 5) thinks Saturn was the eighth. So Gerhard, Gottheiten der Etrusker, p. 29. Servius (ad Æn. VIII. 430), indeed, says that some ascribed the power of hurling bolts to Auster.

[4] Müller (III. 3, 2) does not attempt to supply the ninth. Gerhard, however, from the evidence of monuments, takes it to have been Hercules, for on an Etruscan gem in his possession that god is repre-

sented armed with the thunderbolt as well as with his club. Gottheit. d. Etrusk. p. 23. Lanzi (II. p. 203) took the ninth to be Bacchus.

[5] See Vol. II. p. 33.

[6] As in the beautiful mirror represented in the frontispiece to this volume. The name seems connected with "Puphluns," the Etruscan form of Populonia. See Vol. II. p. 220.

[7] See Vol. II. p. 33.

[8] See Vol. I. p. 140. Gerhard, Gottheit. p. 35.

[9] As on a mirror in the Museo Gregoriano. See Vol. II. p. 432. This name, however, has been found attached to a female divinity on another mirror. Bull. Inst. 1847, p. 117.

[1] The name of this god on Etruscan mirrors is generally "Turms," or "Thurms ;" in one case he is called "Turms Aitas," or the infernal Mercury (Vol. II. p. 482), in another, "Mirqurios." Gerhard, Etrus. Spieg. II. taf. 182. He was associated by Tarquin with the three great gods. Serv. ad Æn. II. 296. Callimachus (ap. Macrob. III. 8) said that the Etruscans called this god Camillus.

[2] This name is so often attached to

dawn, Eos-Aurora;[3] and LOSNA, or LALA—the Etruscan Luna,
or Diana.[4] NETHUNS, or Neptune, also appears on monuments,[5]
though rarely, which is singular considering the maritime
character of the people; and Janus and Silvanus are also known
as Etruscan gods,[6] the double head of the former being a common
device on the coins of Volaterræ and Telamon.   Then there were
four gods called Penates—Ceres, Pales, Fortuna, and the Genius
Jovialis;[7] and the two Penates of Latium,—the Dioscuri,—
CASTUR and PULTUKE—were much worshipped in Etruria, as
we learn from monuments.[8] The worship of the mysterious
Cabeiri testified to the Pelasgic origin of a portion of the
Etruscan population.[9]

All these deities are more or less akin to those of other ancient
mythological systems, and what were of native origin and what of
foreign introduction, it is not always easy to determine. But
there were others more peculiarly Etruscan. At least if their
counterparts are to be found in the Greek and Roman mythology, they had a wider influence in Etruria, and occupied a
more prominent place in the Etruscan Pantheon. Such is the
goddess of Fate, who is generally represented with wings, sometimes with a hammer and nail, as if fixing unalterably her decrees

figures of Venus, that there can be no
question of the identity. Sometimes she
is represented with "Atunis" (Adonis),
or with "Elina" and "Menle" (Helen
and Menelaus), or with "Elina" and
"Elsntre" (Helen and Alexander). Gerhard, Et. Spieg. taf. 111, 115, 197, 198.
Tertullian (Spect. c. 8) says this goddess
was called Murtia.

[3] "Thesan" occurs on two mirrors in
the Gregorian Museum (Vol. II. p. 482).
Gerhard suggests a relation, and in one
case an identity, between Thesan and the
Themis of the Greeks. Gotth. p. 39;
Etrusk. Spieg. taf. 76.

[4] "Losna" is attached to the figure of
Diana on a mirror. Etrusk. Spieg. taf.
171; Lanzi, II. tav. VIII. 6. It is doubtless a form of Luna. "Lala" is found on
another mirror. Gerhard, Gottheit. taf.
II. 7.

[5] The name "Nethuns" occurs on a
mirror in the Gregorian Museum (Vol.
II. p. 482). Gerhard (Gottheit. pp. 2,
191) regards this as the Latin name, and
doubts if Neptune were an Etruscan deity,
though he is said to have been one of the
Penates (Arnob. adv. Nat. III. 40; Serv.

ad Æn. II. 325), but Müller (III. 3, 4)
says justly, if the name be not Etruscan,
that people must have had a god of the sea.

[6] A four-faced Janus was worshipped at
Falerii. Serv. ad Æn. VII., 607; Macrob.
Sat. I. 9. Silvanus was a Pelasgic god,
who had a celebrated shrine at Cære.
Virg. Æn. VIII. 600; cf. Liv. II. 7.

[7] Arnob. loc. cit.; Serv. ad Æn. II. 325.

[8] The Dioscuri are not recorded as Etruscan divinities by ancient writers, but they
are so frequently and distinctly represented
on the mirrors, that it is impossible not to
recognise them as Etruscan; indeed, they
are often mentioned by name. Gerhard,
Gottheit. pp. 2, 22, 46.

[9] The Cabeiri were the great gods of the
Pelasgic Samothrace, and certain passages
(Dion. Hal. I. c. 23; Macrob. Sat. III.
8) which ascribe their worship to the
Tyrrhenes, or Etruscans, may refer to the
Pelasgi. Müller, III. 3, 10. But Tarquin,
it is said, was initiated into the mysteries
of Samothrace. Serv. ad Æn. II. 296.
Gerhard sees in the three heads on the
Gate of Volterra, and in certain scenes on
mirrors, the three mysterious deities of
Lemnos. Gottheit. p. 13.

—an idea borrowed by the Romans; but more frequently with a bottle in one hand and a *stylus* in the other, with which to inscribe her decisions. She is found with various names attached; but the most common are LASA, and MEAN.[1] A kindred goddess is frequently introduced in the reliefs on the sepulchral urns, as present at the death of some individual, and is generally armed with a hammer, a sword, or torch, though sometimes brandishing snakes like a Fury.

What gives most peculiarity to the Etruscan mythology is the doctrine of Genii. The entire system of national divination, called "the Etruscan Discipline," was supposed to have been revealed by a Genius, called Tages—a wondrous boy with a hoary head and the wisdom of age, who sprung from the fresh-ploughed furrows of Tarquinii.[2] But the worship of the Lares and Penates, the household deities who watched over the personal and pecuniary interests of individuals and families, was the most prominent feature in the Etruscan mythology, whence it was borrowed by the Romans.[3] Thence it was also, in all probability, that the Romans obtained their doctrine of an attendant genius watching over every individual from his birth—

Genius natale comes qui temperat astrum,

who was of the same sex as the individual, and was called Genius when male, and Juno when female. Yet we find no positive proof of this doctrine among the Etruscans.[4]

Last, but brought most prominently before the eye in Etruscan sepulchral monuments, are the dread powers of the lower world. Here rule MANTUS and MANIA, the infernal deities of the Etruscan creed, whose names never occur on the native monuments, but are ascertained from Latin writers.[5] In fact, in two painted

---

[1] See Vol. I. p. 288.

[2] See Vol. I. p. 418.

[3] Müller, Etrusk. III. 4, 6, 7; Gerhard, Gottheit. d. Etrusk. p. 15.

[4] The Genii or demons who are introduced on Etruscan monuments to indicate a fatal event, are generally females—at least their sex in many instances does not correspond with that of the defunct. For the Genii and Junones see Vol. I. pp. 285-288.

[5] Mantus is the Etruscan Dispater. Serv. ad Æn. X. 199. From him the city Mantua received its name. Müller (III. 4, 10) thinks that the winged figure, armed with a mallet or sword, often introduced on Etruscan sepulchral urns in charge of the dead, is Mantus; though generally called Charun. Gerhard (Gottheit. taf. VI. 2, 3, gives two figures from urns in the Museum of Volterra, which, being crowned, most probably represent the King of Shades. Thus he was also depicted in the Campanari tomb at Vulci. See p. 466 of this volume. When two Charontic males are introduced into the same scene, as on the vase illustrated in the frontispiece to Vol. II. of this work, one may be intended for Mantus, or that which is not Charun may be a Thanatos, a personification of Death, or its messenger. Müller

tombs at Corneto and Orvieto, in which these divinities are depicted, they are designated by the corresponding Greek appellations of Hades and Persephone. In both those instances Mantus
is represented seated on a throne, with a wolf-skin on his head,
and a serpent in one hand, or twining round his sceptre. Mania
also, in the tomb at Corneto, has her head bristling with snakes.[6]
She was a fearful deity, who was propitiated by human sacrifices.[7]
Intimately connected with these divinities was CHARUN, the great
conductor of souls, the infernal Mercury of the Etruscans, the
chief minister of Mantus, whose dread image, hideous as the
imagination could conceive, is often introduced on sepulchral
monuments; and who, with his numerous attendant demons and
Furies, well illustrates the dark and gloomy character of the
Etruscan superstition.[8]

The government and religion of a country being ascertained,
much may be inferred of the character of its civilization. With
such shackles as were imposed on it, it was impossible for the
Etruscan mind, individually or collectively, to reach the highest
degree of culture to which society, even in those early ages,
attained. The intellect of Etruria, when removed from the
sciences and arts, and purely practical applications, was too much
absorbed in the mysteries of divination and the juggleries of
priestcraft. Even art was fettered by conventionalities, imposed,
it seems, by her religious system. Yet there is recorded evidence
that she possessed a national literature—histories,[9] tragedies,[1]

(III. 4, 9) suggests a relation to the
Mundus, the pit in the Comitium, which
was regarded as the mouth of Orcus, and
was opened three days in the year, for the
souls to step to the upper world. Varro,
ap. Macrob. I. 16; Fest. vv. Mundus,
Manalem Lapidem.

[6] See the woodcuts, Vol. I. p. 351; II.
p. 58.

[7] Mania is called the mother of the
Lares (Varro, L. L. IX. 61; Macrob. I. 7;
Arnob. adv. Nat. III. 41), or the mother
or grandmother of the Manes (Festus, sub
voce). Boys used annually to be offered to
her at the festival of the Compitalia, till,
on the expulsion of Tarquinius Superbus,
the heads of garlic and poppies were substituted. Macrob. Sat. I. 7. Müller
(Etrusk. III. 4, 12, 13) thinks she is
almost identical with Acca Larentia, the
foster-mother of Romulus, a divinity who

was transferred from the Etruscan into
the Roman mythology; and that she
answers also to the Lara or Larunda of the
Romans. Cf. Gerhard, Gottheit. p. 56.
For the various derivations of the name
suggested by Roman grammarians, see
Varro, L. L. IX. 61; Festus v. Maniae;
Servius ad Æn. I. 143; III. 63. But if
the name of this deity be Etruscan it is
useless to seek its origin in the Latin.

[8] See Vol. II. pp. 191-193.

[9] Varro, ap. Censorin. XVII. 6. Polybius (II. 17) speaks of histories of the
Etruscan dynasties. There was also an
historian of the name of Vegoja, a fragment of whose work is extant. See
Müller, IV. 5, 3: 7, 8.

[1] Varro (Ling. Lat. V. 55) mentions
Volnius, or Volumnius, a writer of Etruscan tragedies.

poems;[2] besides religious and ritual books;[3] and the Romans used to send their sons into the land of their hereditary foes to study its literature and language,[4] just as in later times the "old Christians" of Spain sent their youth to receive a knightly education at the Moslem courts of Cordoba and Granada.

History, moreover, attests the eminence of the Etruscans in navigation and commerce—for they were for ages "lords of the sea"[5]—in military tactics,[6] agriculture, medicine, and other prac-

[2] The Fescennines, or songs of raillery, were Etruscan. See Vol. I. p. 116. The Etruscan *histriones* or actors, danced and sang to the sound of the double-pipes. Liv. VII. 2. In their religious services also the Etruscans sang hymns to the honour of their gods or heroes. Dion. Hal. I. c. 21 ; Serv. ad Æn. VIII. 285. Lucretius (VI. 381) speaks of "Tyrrhena carmina" on divination by lightning. Müller, IV. 5, 1.

[3] The sacred or ritual books of the Etruscans are mentioned under many names by ancient writers — libri Etrusci — chartæ Etruscæ—scripta Etrusca—Tusci libelli—Etruscæ disciplinæ libri — libri fatales, rituales, haruspicini, fulgurales et tonitruales—libri Tagetici—sacra Tagetica—sacra Acherontica—libri Acherontici. The author of these sacred works on the "Etruscan Discipline," was supposed to be Tages. The names of Tarquitius, Cæcina, Aquila, Labeo, Begoë, Umbricius, are given as writers on these subjects, probably commentators on Tages.

[4] Liv. IX. 36 ; Cicero, de Divin. I. 41 ; Val. Max. I. 1, 1.

[5] Diod. Sic. V. pp. 295, 300, 316 ; Strabo, V. p. 222. They rivalled the Phœnicians in enterprise, founding colonies in the islands of the Tyrrhene Sea, and even on the coast of Spain, where Tarraco, now Tarragona (in whose name we recognise that of Tarchon), appears to have been one of their settlements (Auson. Epist. XXIV. 88)—a tradition confirmed by its ancient fortifications. Müller, Etrusk. I. 4, 6 ; Abeken, Mittelitalien, p. 129. Nay, the Etruscans would fain have colonised the far "island of the blest," in the Atlantic Ocean, probably Madeira or one of the Canaries, had not the Carthaginians opposed them. Diod. Sic. V. p. 300. It was this mutual spirit of maritime enterprise that led to a treaty between Carthage

and Etruria, which probably defined the limits of each people's commerce. Aristot. Polit. III. 9. The naval greatness of Etruria is symbolised on her coins, a common device on which is the prow of a ship, —copied on those of early Rome long before that city had a fleet or had achieved a naval triumph. Ovid (Fast. 1. 229) assigns a very different origin to the prow on Roman coins, but he relates the vulgar tradition.

Of the relations of Etruria with Egypt in very early times her sepulchres have yielded abundant proofs. But these relations were not always commercial, or of a friendly character. It is recorded in hieroglyphics on the great temple of Karnak, that as early as the fourteenth century B.C. the Etruscans (Tourshas) invaded Egypt, occupied a portion of it, and even threatened Memphis, but being defeated by Meneptah 1. of the Nineteenth Dynasty, 742 of them were slain, and 890 hands were cut off by the Egyptians. De Rougé, Revue Arch. 1867, pp. 35–45 ; 80–103. That Etruria had commercial relations with the far East, whether direct or indirect we cannot say, is proved by the discovery in a tomb at Vulci of a shell engraved with very archaic winged figures, which shell has been pronounced by conchologists to be of a species found only in the remote Indian seas, and chiefly in the waters of Japan. Bull. Inst. 1848, p. 59. It is evident that Etruria had also an extensive commerce by land, for bronzes which are recognized as Etruscan have been found in many countries north of the Alps. See p. lxxiii. n. 3.

[6] The military tactics of the Etruscans were celebrated. Diodor. V. p. 316. They fought in phalanx, and from them the Romans derived this their earliest military arrangement. Diod. Sic. XXIII. 1. Excerp. Mai ; Athen. VI. p. 273 ; cf. Liv. VIII. 8. Their large circular shields were also adopted by the Romans. Diod.

tical sciences; [7] above all in astronomy, which was brought by them to such perfection, that they seem to have arrived at a very close approximation to the true division of time, and to have fixed the tropical year at precisely 365 days, 5 hours, 40 minutes.[8]

If we measure Etruria by the standard of her own day, we must ascribe to her a high degree of civilization—second only to that of Greece. It differed indeed, as the civilization of a country under despotic rule will always differ from that of a free people. It resided in the mass rather than in the individual; it was the result of a set system, not of personal energy and excellence; its tendency was stationary rather than progressive; its object was to improve the material condition of the people, and to minister to luxury, rather than to advance and elevate the nobler faculties of human nature. In all this it assimilated to the civilization of the East, and of the Aztecs and Peruvians. It had not the earnest germ of development, the intense vitality which existed in Greece; it could never have produced a Plato, a Demosthenes, a Thucydides, or a Pericles. Yet while inferior to her illustrious contemporary in intellectual vigour and eminence, Etruria was in advance of her in her social condition and in certain respects in physical civilization, or that state in which the arts and sciences are made to minister to comfort and luxury. The health and cleanliness of her towns were insured by a system of sewerage, vestiges of which may be seen on many Etruscan sites; and the Cloaca Maxima will be a memorial to all time of the attention paid by the Etruscans to drainage. Yet this is said to have been

Sic. loc. cit. Another account, which Niebuhr (III. p. 99) calls in question, ascribes the origin of the Roman armour and weapons to the Samnites. Sallust, Catil. 51. The Romans probably borrowed the helmet from the Etruscans, as well as the word for it—*cassis*. Isid. Orig. XVIII. 14. An interesting specimen of an Etruscan helmet, with a Greek inscription, showing it to be of the spoils taken from the Etruscans by Hiero of Syracuse, is preserved in the British Museum.

[7] Virgil (Georg. II. 533) tells us that to agriculture Etruria owed her greatness—"sic fortis Etruria crevit."

The skill of the Etruscans as physicians is celebrated by Æschylus, ap. Theophrast. Hist. Plant. IX. 15; and Mart. Capella, de Geomet. VI. Their acquaintance with the vegetable world is recorded by Diodorus, V. p. 316. Cf. Plin. XXIV. 95. It must have been with the aid of science that they were enabled to bring down lightning from heaven; though the priests made the people believe it was by religious rites. Thus Porsena is said to have brought down thunderbolts by invocation. Plin. II. 54. And though Numa is said to have exercised the same power, which proved fatal to Tullus Hostilius, it was probably derived from Etruria. Plut. Numa; Ovid. Fast. III. 327; Plin. loc. cit.; XXVIII. 4.

[8] This is Niebuhr's opinion (I. p. 279). The ancient Aztecs of Mexico, and the Muyscas of South America, before their intercourse with Europe, had arrived at a still nearer approach to truth in their computation of time. Prescott's Mexico, I. p. 98, *et seq.*; Conquest of Peru, I. p. 117.

neglected by the Greeks.[9] In her internal communication Etruria also shows her advance in material civilization. Few extant remains of paved ways, it is true, can be pronounced Etruscan, but in the neighbourhood of most of her cities are traces of roads cut in the rocks, sometimes flanked with tombs, or even marked with inscriptions, determining their antiquity; and generally having water-channels or gutters to keep them dry and clean.[1] The Etruscans were also skilled in controlling the injurious processes of nature. They drained lakes by cutting tunnels through the heart of mountains, and they diverted the course of rivers, to reclaim low and marshy ground, just as the Val di Chiana has been rescued in our own times.[2] And these grand works are not only still extant, but some are even efficient as ever, after the lapse of so many centuries.

That the Etruscans were eminently skilled in tunnelling, excavating, and giving form and beauty to shapeless rocks, and for useful purposes, is a fact impressed on the mind of every one who visits the land. Their tombs were all subterranean, and, with few exceptions, hewn in the rock, after the manner of the Egyptians and other people of the East. In truth, in no

---

[9] Strabo, V. p. 235. Strabo says that the Greeks, in founding their cities, considered principally the strength and beauty of site, the advantages of ports, and the fertility of the soil ; whereas the Romans paid most attention to what 'the others neglected — paved roads, aqueducts, and common sewers. This distinction the Romans, in all probability, owe to the Etruscans. However, it is certain that vestiges of conduits and sewers are extant in many cities of Greece, though on a scale inferior, it is said, to those of Rome. Mure, Tour in Greece, II. p. 47. At Syracuse the ancient Greek aqueduct which transverses Epipolæ still supplies the modern town with water. There are remains of ancient Greek roads, both in Greece and her colonies in Italy, Sicily, Africa, and Asia Minor.

[1] The Romans are said to have been indebted to the Carthaginians for their paved roads. Isidor. Orig. XV. 16 ; cf. Serv. ad Æn. I. 426. But from the little intercourse the Romans maintained with that people in early times, it seems more probable that they derived this art from the Etruscans, who were their great preceptors in all works of public utility. There is no positive evidence of this ; but it is the opinion now

generally entertained. Micali (Ant. Pop. Ital. I. p. 150 ; II. p. 307) indeed maintains that there are remains of Etruscan paved roads still extant, such as that from Cære to Veii, and thence to Capena, constructed before the domination of the Romans.

[2] Such is the interpretation put by Niebuhr (I. p. 132) on Plin. III. 20—Omnia ea flumina, fossasque, primi a Sagi fecêre Thusci : egesto amnis impetu per transversum in Atrianorum paludes. Niebuhr declares the channels by which the Po still discharges itself, to be the work of the Etruscans. And in the territory of Perugia, and in Suburbicariau Tuscia, are traces of many lakes drained by the Etruscans, and now dried up ; "the tunnels are unknown and never cleared out, but still work." The Emissary of Albano, which there is every reason to regard as an Etruscan work, is a triumphant memorial of their skill in such operations. In such undertakings the Etruscans were rivalled by the Greeks of Bœotia, who in early, probably heroic times, constructed katabothra to drain the lake Copais, and convey the superabundant waters of the Cephissus into the Euripus.

point is the oriental character of the Etruscans more obviously marked than in their sepulchres; and modern researches are daily bringing to light fresh analogies to the tombs of Lycia, Phrygia, Lydia, or Egypt.

In physical comfort and luxury the Etruscans cannot have been surpassed by any contemporary nation. Whoever visits the Gregorian Museum of the Vatican, or that of Signor Augusto Castellani at Rome, will have abundant proofs of this. Much of it is doubtless owing to their extensive commerce, which was their pride for ages. In their social condition they were in advance of the Greeks, particularly in one point, which is an important test of civilization. In Athens, woman trod not by the side of man as his companion and helpmate, but followed as his slave; the treatment of the sex, even in the days of Pericles, was what would now be called oriental. But in Etruria, woman was honoured and respected; she took her place at the board by her husband's side, which she was never permitted to do at Athens;[3] she was educated and accomplished, and sometimes even instructed in the mysteries of divination;[4] her children assumed her name as well as their father's;[5] and her grave was honoured with even more splendour than that of her lord. It is not easy to say to what Etruria owed this superiority. But whatever its cause, it was a fact which tended greatly to humanize her, and, through her, to civilize Italy—a fact of which Rome reaped the benefit by imitating her example.

We have now to consider the arts of the Etruscans, from the remains of which we gather our chief knowledge of this people. That which is most peculiarly their own, and has partaken least of foreign influence, is their

ARCHITECTURE.

From history we learn very little of this art among them. We know that they were the chief architects of early Rome, that they built the great temple of Jupiter on the Capitol, and constructed the Cloaca Maxima,[6] and that Rome, whenever she

---

[3] See Vol. I. p. 309.

[4] Two illustrious examples of this are Tanaquil, the wife of Tarquinius Priscus, and the nymph Begoë. See Vol. I. p. 478; cf. II. pp. 163. Tanaquil is also said to have been deeply versed in mathematics and medicine (Schol. ad Juven. Sat. VI.

565; Fest. v. Prædia). Yet she was an industrious house-wife, a great spinner of wool (Plin. VIII. 74; Fest. v. Gaia Cæcilia), and an excellent helpmate to her husband. Suidas, v. Λεύκιος.

[5] See Vol. I. p. 100.

[6] Liv. I. 56.

would raise any public building, sent to Etruria for artificers. But of the peculiarities of Etruscan architecture we know from history little more than Vitruvius tells us of the plan and proportions of a temple in the Tuscan style.[6] We know too that Etruscan houses had frequently porticoes,[7] and a court, called *atrium* or *cavædium*, within them, so arranged that the water from the roof fell into a tank in the centre—a plan adopted by the Romans.[8] Unfortunately, not a vestige of an Etruscan temple, beyond some doubtful foundations, is now extant, to compare with Vitruvius' description;[9] yet numerous models of temples and houses are to be seen in Etruscan tombs, either hewn from the rock, or sculptured on sepulchral monuments; and there is no lack of materials whence to learn the proportions, style, and decorations of the former, and the arrangements, conveniences, and furniture of the latter. In truth Etruria presents abundant food to the inquiring architect; and he who would make the tour of her ancient cities and cemeteries, might add much to our knowledge of the early architecture of Italy. He would learn that the architecture of the Etruscans bore sometimes a close affinity to that of Egypt, sometimes to that of Greece or Rome, but had often remarkable native peculiarities. He would learn, also, beyond what Vitruvius tells him of the practice of the Etruscans to decorate the pediments of their temples with figures of clay or of bronze gilt,[1] that they must also have been adorned internally with paintings and reliefs, and that the whole, both within and without, must have glowed with colour, according to the polychrome system set forth in the tombs and sepulchral monuments.

[6] Vitruv. IV. 7. Müller (IV. 2, 3) thinks Vitruvius took his rules of an Etruscan temple from that of Ceres in the Circus Maximus, dedicated in the year of Rome 261. It is still disputed whether the so-called Tuscan order is an invention of the Etruscans, or a mere variety of the Doric. For notices of the Etruscan temple, see Müller, Etrusk. III. 6 ; IV. 2, 3—5 ; Inghirami, Mon. Etrus. IV. pp. 1—51 ; Abeken, Mittelitalien, pp. 202 — 233. Canina, Etruria Marittima, II., p. 153 —162.

[7] Diodor. Sic. V. p. 316.

[8] Vitruv. VI. 3 ; Varro, L. L. V. 161 ; Festus, v. Atrium ; Serv. ad Æn. I. 730.

[9] The reason why no Etruscan temples are standing, while so many of Egypt, Greece, and Rome are yet extant, seems to be that they were constructed principally of wood, which may be learnt from Vitruvius (IV. 7), who represents the *epistylia* as of wood, and the intercolumniations on that account much wider than in temples of the Greek orders. Something may also be learned from the analogy of the tombs, whose ceilings are generally cut into the form of beams and rafters, or into coffers —*lacunaria*—as in the Pantheon. Canina (Et. Mar. II. p. 152) accounts for this use of wood in Etruscan temples by the want of stone of sufficient strength to form *epistylia ;* but this objection is applicable only to the tufo in the southern part of the land, and in the neighbourhood of Chiusi.

[1] Vitruv. III. 3.

The remains of Etruscan architecture yet extant are found in the walls and gates of cities, in sewers, bridges, vaults, and tombs.

Nothing gives a more exalted idea of the power and grandeur of this ancient people than the walls of their cities.[2] These enormous piles of masonry, uncemented, yet so solid as to have withstood for three thousand years the destroying hand of man, the tempests, the earthquakes, the invisible yet more destructive power of atmospheric action, seem destined to endure to the end of time ; yet often show a beauty, a perfection of workmanship, that has never been surpassed. The style of masonry differs in the two great divisions of the land, and is determined in part by the nature of the local materials. In the northern district, where the rock is difficult to be hewn, being limestone, hard sandstone, or travertine, the walls are composed of huge blocks, rectangular in general, but of various sizes, and irregular arrangement, according as the masses of rock were hewn or split from the quarry ; and in some instances small pieces are inserted in the interstices of the larger blocks. There are also a few instances of the irregular, polygonal style, as in the so-called Cyclopean cities of Latium and Sabina. In the southern district the masonry is less massive and very regular, being *isodomon*, composed of parallelopiped blocks of tufo or other volcanic rock, which admits of being easily worked.[3]

In the earliest fortifications the gates were square-headed,

---

[2] There was a tradition, recorded by Dionysius (I. c. 30), that the Tyrrheni were the first who raised fortresses in Italy, and that thence they received their name. Cf. Tzetz. in Lycoph. 717.

[3] The masonry most common in this district is that to which I have applied the name *emplecton*, described Vol. I. pp. 65, 80. In measurement the blocks of this masonry generally correspond with the ancient Roman foot and modern Tuscan *braccio*. See Vol. I., p. 66 ; II. p. 339.

The peculiar ceremonies which the Romans observed in founding their cities, and which were observed in the case of Rome itself, they received from the Etruscans, with whom this was a very sacred rite. A day was chosen that was pronounced auspicious by the augurs. The founder, having yoked a bull and cow to a brazen plough, the bull outside, the cow within, ploughed a deep furrow round the intended city, while his followers turned all the clods inward to the city. The ridge thus raised marked the line of the future walls, and the furrow that of the fosse. Wherever the site of a gate was reached, the plough was lifted from the earth, and carried over the proposed roadway ; for the walls were deemed to be consecrated by the ceremony of ploughing, and had not the gateways been omitted, there could have been no entrances into the city. On either side of the walls a space called the *pomœrium* was also marked out, which was ever after sacred from the plough, and from habitation. Virgil (Æn. V. 755 ; Serv. in loc.) represents Æneas as founding a city according to the same rite. For authorities, see Vol. II. p. 228, n. 9 ; to which add, Dio Cass. Excerp. Mai, II. p. 527 ; Serv. ad Æn. V. 755 ; Isid. Orig. XV. 2.

spanned by lintels of stone or wood, and the arch, when found
in connection with such masonry, must be considered of subsequent construction. But in walls of later date the gates were
arched on the perfect cuneiform system, the massive voussoirs
holding together without cement. Indeed there is abundant
evidence in the architectural remains of Etruria that the perfect
arch was known and practised in that land at a very early period;
and that the Romans, who have long enjoyed the credit of its
invention, derived it from the Etruscans, is now set beyond a
doubt.

That the world is indebted to Etruria for the discovery of the
principle of the arch, would be difficult of proof. The existence
of arches among the tombs of Thebes and in the pyramids of
Nubia on the one hand,[4] and in a bridge in Laconia and a gateway in Acarnania on the other,[5] raises two rivals to contest the
honour of originality with Etruria; and a third may perhaps be
found in Assyria, if Mr. Layard's views of the date of the monuments at Nimroud be correct. But whichever of these leading
nations of antiquity may have discovered the principle, there can
be no doubt that it was the Etruscans who first practised it in
Italy; and, considering the inventive turn of this people and
their acknowledged skill in architecture, it is probable that the
principle of cuneiform sustentation was worked out by them,
whether prior or subsequently to its discovery in Egypt, Greece,

[4] Sir G. Wilkinson (Mod. Egypt. II.
pp. 189, 218) speaks of some tombs
vaulted with sun-dried bricks, which are
"proved" by the hieroglyphic inscriptions
they bear, to be as old as 1540 years B. C.
For two tombs with stone arches, one at
the foot of the Pyramids, the other at
Sakkara, he does not claim an antiquity
higher than 600 years before our era (op.
cit. I. pp. 357, 368), or a period about
cooeval with the Cloaca Maxima. This, I
believe, is also the antiquity claimed by
Mr. Layard for the Assyrian arches he has
discovered. Mr. Wathen, a professional
authority, who speaks from careful examination, while admitting that the tomb at
the foot of the Pyramids presents an instance of a perfect arch, declares that in
that of Sakkara, and in the earlier tombs
referred to by Wilkinson, the supposed
vaulting is a mere lining to the roof of the
tomb, hollowed in a friable rock, and does
not hold together on the wedge-principle.

Ancient Egypt, p. 234. His testimony is
confirmed by other architects who have
assured me, from personal inspection, that
these very ancient arches are apparent
merely, not real. There is as yet no evidence
to prove the arch much earlier than six centuries before Christ.

[5] The bridge referred to is that of
Xerokampo, in the neighbourhood of
Sparta, discovered by Dr. Ross of Athens.
It is on the true arch-principle, and surrounded by polygonal masonry (Ann. Inst.
1838, p. 140; Mon. Inst. II. tav. 57); but
it has been pronounced to be of late date
and Roman construction. The gateway is a
postern in the city of Œniadæ, whose walls
are also of polygonal masonry. Indeed,
this city is remarkable for exhibiting in its
several gates the progress from the flat
lintel to the perfect arch. See Vol. II. p.
250, n. 2. There are also some perfect
arches in the polygonal walls of Œnoanda,
in the Cibyratis, in Asia Minor.

or Assyria it is impossible to determine.[6]   As in those countries, there are here also extant instances of pseudo-vaults, prior to the invention of the arch, formed by the gradual convergence of blocks laid in horizontal courses.   These structures must be of very remote date, probably before the foundation of Rome.[7]

TOMBS.

Archæology has been called "the science of sepulchres." Those of Etruria are verily the fount whence we draw our chief knowledge of the civilization and arts of this wonderful people. So much will be said on this subject in the course of this work, that it is not necessary here to say much of the Sepulchres of the Etruscans.   But it may be well to point out a few of their characteristics.   A leading feature is, that they are always subterranean, being frequently hollowed in the living rock, either beneath the surface of the ground, or in the face of a cliff, or at the foot of a cliff, which was shaped by the chisel into a monument, and inscribed with an epitaph.[8]   Where the rock would not

[6] The earliest arched structure mentioned in history, and now extant, is the Cloaca Maxima constructed by Tarquinius Priscus (Liv. I. 38 ; Plin. XXXVI. 24)— unless the vault of the upper prison of the Mamertine be really that ascribed by Livy (I. 33) to Ancus Martius, which is very doubtful—and it dates from the middle of the second century of Rome, or about six hundred years before Christ.   How much earlier the principle of the arch may have been discovered, it is impossible to say ; but the perfection of the Cloaca Maxima might lead us to suppose a long previous acquaintance with this mode of construction. Canina (Cere Antica, p. 66) refers the first use of the true arch in Italy to the reign of Tarquinius Priscus (616—578, B.C.), to which conclusion he arrives from a comparison of the Cloaca with the Tullianum ; and he thinks that Tarquin must have brought the knowledge of it from Tarquinii, and that it was introduced there from Corinth by his father Demaratus; but for this there is no authority in ancient writers.

[7] The most remarkable instances of pseudo-vaults in Etruria are the Regulini-Galassi tomb at Cervetri, the Grotta Sergardi near Cortona, and the sepulchres lately opened by Signor Mancini beneath Orvieto.

A tomb of similar construction has been found at Cumæ.

[8] The only tomb of purely Roman times that I remember to resemble the Etruscan is that of the Nasones, on the Via Flaminia, a few miles from Rome.   Early tombs of Etruscan character, however, are found in Latium, Sabina, and other parts of Central Italy, and notably at Ardea of the Rutuli. Noël des Vergers, Étrurie, I. pp. 185-8. So occasionally also on Greek sites.   But of all the ancient sepulchres I have seen out of Italy, those of Cyrene bear the closest resemblance to the Etruscan, making allowance for the difference in the style of art. In that most remarkable and abounding Greek necropolis are streets of tombs carved in the cliffs, resembling temples or houses, with archaic Doric or Ionic façades, and bearing Greek inscriptions, or else built up in the form of small temples on the surface of the plain.   The city, for ages desolate, is surrounded by the homes of the dead, which have long survived the habitations of the living.   It has always struck me with surprise that at Cyrene, next door as it were to Egypt, there should be little or nothing of Egyptian art in the sculptured architecture of the tombs, while that style is a prominent

readily admit of such excavation, or where the soil was loose and friable, the tomb was sometimes a mere pit, or was constructed with masonry more or less rude, and heaped over with earth into the form of a tumulus.   There is nothing in all Etruria like some Greek and most Roman sepulchres, built up above the surface of the ground; unless, indeed, the tombs disinterred by Signor Mancini beneath Orvieto were originally left uncovered with earth.   The object of the Etruscans seems generally to have been to conceal their tombs rather than to display them, in which they differed from the Romans.[9]

Another characteristic of Etruscan tombs, which distinguishes them from the Roman, and allies them intimately with those of Egypt and Asia Minor, is that they frequently show an imitation, more or less obvious, of the abodes of the living. Some display this analogy in their exterior; others in their interior; a few in both. Some have more resemblance to temples, and may be the sepulchres of augurs or aruspices, or of families in which the sacerdotal office was hereditary. Yet it must be confessed that the analogy suggested by the external monument is often belied by the sepulchre it covers or contains, as is the case with the tumuli of Corneto and Cervetri, which, externally at least, resemble the huts of the ancient Phrygians,[1] yet

HUT-URN FROM ALBA LONGA.

characteristic of the rock-hewn monuments of Norchia, Castel d'Asso, and Sovana.

[9] Yet they often placed *stelæ* or *cippi* over their underground sepulchres, in the shape of columns, cubes, pine-cones, slabs, lions, or sphinxes. The strong resemblance the sepulchral slabs, with reliefs of men and animals, found at La Certosa, near Bologna, bear to those which marked the sites of the royal tombs at Mycenæ (see the woodcuts at pp. 52, 81, 86, 93, of Schliemann's Mycenæ), is worthy of notice.

Etruscan tombs, like the Greek and Roman, are occasionally found by the way-side, real monuments—*monimenta*—warnings and admonitions to the living. Varro, Ling. Lat. VI. 45.

[1] Vitruv. II. 1, 5. I have pointed out this analogy at p. 278 of this volume, yet I doubt if it be more than accidental, for the tumulus is a natural form of sepulchre, which would suggest itself to any people in any part of the world in an early stage of culture, from the facility of its construction. In a rude state of society, the body would be laid on the ground, or within it, and earth would be piled over it, both to protect it from wild beasts, and to mark the

cover tombs generally of quadrangular form. The idea of representing the abodes of the living in the receptacles for the dead, which is quite oriental, was not, however, confined to the Etruscans among the early people of Italy, as is proved by the singular cinerary urns found in the necropolis of Alba Longa, which are obvious imitations of rude huts formed of boughs and covered with skins,[2] as shown in the woodcut on the preceding page. There can be no doubt that the paintings on the walls of Etruscan tombs show the style, though perhaps not the exact subjects, of the internal decorations of their houses. The ceilings are often carved to imitate beams and rafters, or adorned with coffers, and the walls with panelling—couches and stools surround the chambers—weapons and other furniture are suspended from the walls—and easy arm-chairs, with foot-stools attached, all hewn from the living rock, are found in the subterranean houses of these Etruscan "cities of the dead." The analogy to houses in such instances has been truly said to hold in everything but the light of day. In this respect, Etruscan tombs have a peculiar interest and value, as illustrative of the plan, arrangements, and decorations, external and internal, of Etruscan houses: of which, as time has left us no trace, and history no definite description, we must gather what information we may from analogical sources. In the temples and houses of Etruria, be it remembered, we view those of early Rome, ere she had sat at the feet of her more accomplished preceptor, Greece.

PLASTIC ARTS.

Of the plastic and pictorial arts of the Etruscans it is not easy to treat, both on account of the vast extent of the subject, and because it demands an intimate acquaintance with ancient art in general, such as can be acquired only by years of study and experience, and by the careful comparison of numerous

---

site of its interment, and the more illustrious the dead, the loftier, safer, and more conspicuous would be the mound. I certainly cannot accept Mr. Taylor's theory ("Etruscan Researches," p. 42) that these sepulchral mounds are intentional imitations of tents, and that the masonry encircling their base was in itself useless, and therefore evidently a mere survival of the custom of surrounding tents with heavy stones to keep down the skins with which

they were covered. For no tumulus in Etruria has yet been found to contain a conical or bell-shaped chamber, corresponding with its external form; and the κρηπίς or podium of masonry, with which many, if not all, of these mounds were originally girt, was absolutely necessary to sustain the superincumbent earth, and to give the structure a permanent form.

[2] See Vol. II. p. 457.

works of various ages and countries. It has been laid down as an axiom, that "He who has seen one work of ancient art has seen none, he who has seen a thousand has seen but one."[3] I feel, therefore, reluctant to enter on a ground to which I cannot pretend to do justice, especially in the narrow limits to which I am confined. Yet it is incumbent on me to give the reader a general view of the subject, to enable him to understand the facts and observations he will meet with in the course of these volumes.

As the fine arts of a country always bear the reflex of its political and social condition, so the hierarchical government of Etruria here finds its most palpable expression. In the most ancient works of sculpture the influence of the national religion is most apparent; deities or religious symbols seem the only subjects represented, so that some have been led to the conclusion that both the practice and theory of design were originally in the hands of the priests alone.[4] These early Etruscan works have many points in common with those of the infancy of art in other lands, just as babes are very similar all the world over: yet, besides the usual shapelessness and want of expression, they have native peculiarities, such as disproportionate length of body and limbs, an unnatural elongation of hands and feet, drapery adhering to the body, and great rigidity, very like the Egyptian, yet with less parallelism. In truth, the earliest works of Etruria betray the great influence of Egypt;[5] and that of Assyria is also often manifest in early Etruscan, as in early Greek art, especially in the decorations. By degrees, however, probably from the natural progress common to all civilized countries, Etruscan art stepped out of the conventionalities which confined it, and assumed a more energetic character, more like the Greek than the Egyptian, yet still rigid, hard, and dry, rather akin to the Æginetic than the Athenian school, displaying more force than beauty, more vigour than grace, better intention than ability of execution, an exaggerated, rather than a truthful representation of nature. It was only when the triumph of Greek art was complete, and the world

[3] Gerhard, Ann. Inst. 1831, p. 111.

[4] Micali, Ant. Pop. Ital. II. p. 222.

[5] Strabo, who was personally acquainted with the antiquities of the respective lands, remarks the resemblance between the sculptured works of Egypt, Etruria, and early Greece. XVII. p. 806. It is by some maintained that this rigid and rectilinear Etruscan style was not necessarily imported from the Nile; for it is a style which nature in the infancy of art taught alike to the Egyptians, Greeks, and Etruscans, as it was not so much art, as the want of art.

acknowledged the transcendency of Hellenic genius, that Etruria became its humble disciple, and imitated, often with much success, the grand works of the Greek chisel and pencil. A distinctive national character is, however, generally preserved, for the tendency to realism, as opposed to Greek ideality, betrays itself even in the best works of Etruscan art.[6] The four styles into which Etruscan art may be divided are—1st, The Asiatic, which has Babylonian as well as Egyptian affinities; 2nd, The Etruscan, or Tyrrhene, as it is sometimes called; 3rd, The Hellenic, or Græco-Etruscan; 4th, That of the Decadence, which more resembles the Roman. The peculiarities of style, indeed, which distinguish Roman art from Greek, appear in great measure to have been borrowed from Etruria.

This classification pertains to all the imitative arts of the Etruscans. Though we may not agree with those who affirm that Etruscan art was but a variety of Greek, we may admit that in their infancy, while contemporaneous, they bore a considerable resemblance. Greek art, as well as Etruscan, was born on the shores of Asia Minor; both received strong impressions from Egypt and Assyria; but as they progressed they began to diverge, and this period of divergence is marked by the distinctive national style of Etruria. Subsequently they again approached, but it was no longer as equals. Etruria, confessing her inferiority, became the docile, earnest pupil of Greece, and was indebted to that influence for all that was most excellent and refined in her art-productions. She wanted, however, the genius, the inspiration of her master. She imitated his form, his manner, style, and general character, but failed to catch his spirit. The Etruscan artist carefully studied details, and strove to copy nature with fidelity, but failed to perceive that the distinguishing excellence of a Greek work of art lay in the harmony of all its parts, which rendered them all subservient to the expression of one leading idea; and that mere skill in working out details would not compensate for the absence of the spirit of unity and harmony pervading the whole.

[6] The specimens of Etruscan art that have come down to us confirm the assertion of Quintilian (XII. 10), that the statues of Etruria differed from those of Greece in *kind*, just as the eloquence of an Asiatic differed from that of an Athenian. Very similar in style to those of Etruria are the early plastic works of Latium and the few remains of Volscian art preserved to us, if indeed these be not Etruscan, either imported, or executed when the land of the Volsci was subject to Etruria. Witness the singular painted reliefs in terra-cotta, found at Velletri in 1784, and now in the Museum of Naples, illustrated by Inghirami, Mon. Etrus. VI. tav. T 4—X 4; cf. Micali, Ant. Pop. Ital. tav. LXI.

Like the craftsman described by Horace, the Etruscan could express with accuracy the nails, or imitate the flowing hair of his model, but he was an inferior artist after all—

> Infelix operis summâ, quia ponere totum
> Nesciet.

Of the imitative arts of Etruria the working in clay was the most ancient,[7] as modelling naturally precedes casting, chiselling, or painting. For their works in terra-cotta the Etruscans were renowned in ancient times,[8] and early Rome contained numerous specimens of them.[9] The Veientes in particular were famed for their works in clay.

Then followed the arts of casting and chiselling in bronze, for which the Etruscans were greatly renowned;[1] and their statues in metal not only filled their own cities, and the temples of Rome,[2] but were also exported to other lands.[3] In truth the Etruscans have the renown of being the inventors of this art in Italy.[4] Innumerable are the specimens of Etruscan toreutic statuary that have come down to us, and widely different are the degrees of excellence displayed, from the rudest, most uncouth attempts at

[7] Plin. XXXIV. 16; XXXV. 45.

[8] Præterea elaboratam hanc artem Italiæ, et maxime Etruriæ. Varro, ap. Plin. XXXV. 45. The most ancient specimens of Etruscan glyptic art yet disinterred are pronounced by Dr. Helbig to be three female figures in terra-cotta, draped in *chiton* and *peplos*, which were discovered, a few years since in a tomb at Cervetri, sitting on a chair hewn from the rock. Bull. Inst. 1866, p. 177.

[9] The most celebrated were the fictile statue of the god in the temple of Jupiter Capitolinus, executed by Turianus of Fregenæ, the *quadriga* on the *fastigium* of that temple, and the fictile statue of Hercules on the Capitol, all by the same artist (Plin. XXXV. 45; Vitruv. III. 3); though the *quadriga* is said to have been executed at Veii (see vol. I., p. 40). There was also a terra-cotta statue of Summanus on the *fastigium* of the same temple, which was struck down by lightning. Cic. de Divin. I. 10.

[1] Athenæus (XV. c. 60) speaking of the skill of the Etruscans in making lamps, calls them φιλοτέχνοι, and mentions their manifold art-productions — ποικίλαι ἐργασίαι. They obtained copper from their own mines

of Montieri—*Mons Æris*—near Massa; tin also from mines near Campiglia; and worked in bronze earlier than in iron, which as Lucretius (V. 1286) tells us, was a later discovery.

> Et prior æris erat, quam ferri, cognitus usus.

They had also an abundance of iron in the mines of Elba.

[2] Volsinii alone is said to have contained 2000 statues. Plin. XXXIV. 16. Tuscanica omnia in ædibus. Varro, ap. Plin. XXXV. 45. Tertullian (Apologet. 25) says they inundated the City. Etruscan bronze statues gilt also adorned the *fastigia* of the temples at Rome. Vitruv. III. 3, 5.

[3] Plin. XXXIV. 16. Antiquaries are now generally agreed that all the ancient bronzes found in various lands north of the Alps, from Switzerland to Denmark, and from Ireland to Hungary and Wallachia, are of Etruscan origin. Lindenschmit, Desor, Schuermans, Virchow, Worsaae, Genthe, cited by Gozzadini, Mors de Cheval Italiques, p. 40.

[4] Cassiodor. Var. VII. 15. Clem. Alex. Strom. I. p. 306.

representing the human form, to the glorification of its beauties, wrought with much of, if not all

> "The cunning they who dwell on high
> Have given unto the Greek."

In size they varied no less : from the minute figures of deities, or *lares*,[5] to statues of colossal dimensions, like that of the Apollo on the Palatine, which was fifty feet in height, and was as wonderful for its beauty as for its mass of metal.[6] One of the most interesting monuments of this art extant is the she-wolf of the Capitol, which has a historical renown.[7]

Not only in the representation of life, but in instruments for domestic and warlike purposes, did the Etruscan metal-workers excel.[8] Even in the time of Pericles, the Athenian poet Pherecrates sang of the Etruscan *candelabra* ;[9] "and what testimony," asks Müller, "can be more honourable for Etruscan art than the words of the cultivated Athenian, Kritias, the son of Kallæschros, a contemporary of Mys, who reckons as the best of their sort the Etruscan gold-wrought cups, and bronzes of every sort for the decoration and service of houses ;[1] by which we must understand *candelabra*, *krateres*, goblets, and even weapons ?"[2]   Even Pheidias himself gave to his celebrated

---

[5] These are the "Tyrrhena sigilla" of Horace, Ep. II. 2, 180; though Micali (Ant. Pop. Ital. II. p. 243) thinks the term refers to gems and scarabei. The "Tuscanica signa" of Pliny (XXXIV. 16), which were exported to many lands, were probably figures of larger size.

[6] Plin. XXXIV. 18.

[7] There is no doubt that it is either the figure mentioned by Dionysius (I. c. 79) as χάλκεον ποίημα παλαιᾶς ἐργασίας, and by Livy (X. 23) as existing in the year of Rome, 458, or that recorded by Cicero as having been struck by lightning. De Divin. II. 20 ; in Catil. III. 8. See Vol. II. p. 492.

Pliny (XXXV. 45) tells us, on the authority of Varro, that under the Kings, and for some years after, all the temples at Rome were decorated by Etruscan artists, but that two Greeks, Damophilus and Gargasus, painters as well as sculptors, were employed for the first time to embellish the temple of Ceres in the Circus Maximus, which was built about 493 B.C.

[8] The brass gates from the spoils of Veii, which Camillus was accused of appro-

priating to himself (Plutarch, Camil. 12), were probably adorned with reliefs. Müller, Etrusk. IV. 3, 4. Even as late as 205, B.C., under the Roman domination, Arretium, which seems to have been the Birmingham of Etruria, furnished the fleet which Scipio was fitting out for the invasion of Africa, with 30,000 shields, as many helmets, and 50,000 javelins, pikes, and spears, besides axes, falchions, and other implements sufficient for forty ships of war, and all in the space of forty-five days. Liv. XXVIII. 45.

[9] Ap. Atheu. XV. c. 60. For *candelabra* see Vol. II. pp. 190, 479.

[1] Τυρσηνὴ δὲ κρατεῖ χρυσότυπος φιάλη,
Καὶ πᾶς χαλκὸς ὅτις κοσμεῖ δόμον ἐν τινι
χρείᾳ.
Athen. I. c. 50.

[2] Müller, Etrusk. IV. 3, 4. Gerhard (Ann. Inst. 1837, 2, p. 143), however, is of opinion that these bronze works of the Etruscans had their origin in Greece. But the fact that Greek inscriptions have never been found on any of the Etruscan bronzes, seems opposed to this opinion. The inscriptions on the painted vases, on

statue of Minerva sandals of the Etruscan fashion.[3] From all this we learn, that if Etruria was indebted to Greece for the excellence she attained in the representation of the human form, the latter was ready to admit, and to avail herself of the native skill and taste of her pupil. And well may it have been so; for it were impossible that the Greeks should not admire such works as the bronze lamp in the Museum of Cortona, the casket from Vulci, and the exquisite specimens of gold filagree-work in the Museo Gregoriano, and in the collection of Signor Augusto Castellani.

ETRUSCAN CANDELABRUM.

The art of statuary was very ancient in Italy. It was either in wood or stone, the first being applied in very remote times to the images of the gods.[4] The Etruscans made use of this primitive material; for a very ancient Jupiter, carved from the trunk of a vine, was worshipped at Populonia.[5] Of their works in stone numerous specimens have come down to us, some on the façades or walls of their rock-hewn sepulchres, others in detached statues, but chiefly on sarcophagi and cinerary urns: for it was their custom to decorate these monuments with the effigies of the deceased, and with reliefs of various descriptions. The extant

the other hand, which confessedly have a Greek origin, are almost invariably in that language.

[3] Pollux, VII. 22; cf. Plin. XXXVI. 4, 4. The Etruscans paid particular attention to their feet—much more than the Greeks, who often went barefooted, whereas the former wore shoes or sandals, richly embossed and gilt, or fastened by gilt thongs (Pollux, loc. cit.; Plin., loc. cit.; Ovid. Amor. III. 13, 26), or high buskins (Ovid. loc. cit. I. 14). Thus Etruscan figures are

often represented naked in every other part but the feet. As in other articles of costume, the Etruscans here set the fashion to the Romans. It is probable that the sort of Etruscan calceus, which Servius (ad Æn. VIII. 458) says was worn by Roman senators, was the boot or buskin represented on the figures in the wall-paintings of Tarquinii. For further notices on this subject, see Müller, Etrusk. I. 3, 10–11.

[4] Plin. XXXIV. 16.

[5] Plin. XIV. 2.

sculpture of Etruria is indeed almost wholly sepulchral. It is not
in general so archaic or so peculiarly national in character as the
works in metal, and betrays rather the influence of Greek than of
Egyptian art. The most archaic productions of the Etruscan
chisel are the *cippi*, or so-called "altars," of fetid limestone, from
Chiusi and its neighbourhood, whose bas-reliefs show a purely
native style of art; together with a few large figures in relief, like
the warrior in the Palazzo Buonarroti at Florence, and the other
in the Museum of Volterra.[6] The latest are the cinerary urns of
Volterra and Perugia, which have often more of a Roman than
a Greek character, and were probably executed in the period of
Roman domination.[7] Yet it is from works of this description
that we learn most of the manners, customs, inner life, and religious creed, as well as of the costume and personal characteristics
of this singular people. There is often great boldness and expression in Etruscan sculpture, and generally much truth to nature;
but it rarely attains the beauty and grace which are found in the
pictorial and toreutic works of this people, and never the perfection of this art among the Greeks, to whom alone did heaven
reveal the full sentiment of human beauty.[8]

It may be well here to notice those works of the Etruscans
which have been distinguished as sculptural, or graven, such as
gems or *scarabei* in stone, and *specula* or mirrors in bronze.

SCARABEI.

Numerous as are Etruscan gems, none of them are cameos, or
with figures cut in relief; all are intaglios; and all are cut into
the form of the *scarabæus* or beetle. Nothing seems to indicate a
closer analogy between Etruria and Egypt than the multitude of
these curious gems found on certain sites in this part of Italy.
The use of them was, doubtless, derived from the banks of the
Nile; but they do not seem to stand in the same archaic relation

---

[6] For the *cippi* of Chiusi, see Vol. II.
p. 300. For the warriors in the Palazzo
Buonarroti of Florence and in the Museum
of Volterra, see Vol. II. pp. 106, 188.

[7] Micali (Ant. Pop. Ital. II. p. 246)
takes the Volterra urns to be, some of the
seventh or eighth century of Rome, others
as late as the Antonines, and others of still
later date. See Vol. II. p. 187.

[8] The inferiority of Etruscan sculpture
may perhaps in part be attributed to the
local stone, which except in the case of

alabaster and travertine, neither used in
very early times, was too coarse or too
friable to do justice to the skill of the
artist. The marble of Carrara, to which
Rome was so much indebted, does not
appear to have been known to the Etruscans at au early period, though that of the
Maremma and of the Circæan promontory
was used by them; yet comparatively few
works of the Etruscan chisel in marble have
come down to us. See Vol. II. p. 67.

to Etruscan art as the other works which betray an Egyptian analogy. They appear, however, to have served the same purpose as in Egypt—to have been worn as charms or amulets, generally in rings; yet it is probable that the Etruscans adopted this relic of foreign superstition without attaching to it the same religious meaning as the Egyptians did, who worshipped it as a god—as a symbol of the great Demiurgic principle.[9] The Etruscan *scarabæi* have a marked difference from the Egyptian, in material, form, and decoration;[1] and the frequent representations they bear from the Greek mythology seem to prove them of no very early date,[2] for such subjects rarely appear on works of archaic Etruscan art. From the heroic or palæstric subjects on these scarabs, it is thought that they were symbols of valour and manly energy, and were worn only by the male sex.[3]

Scarabæi have rarely been found on more than two sites in Etruria—Chiusi and Vulci. At the latter they are always in tombs, but at Chiusi they are found on the soil in a certain slope beneath the city, called, from the abundance of such discoveries, "The Jewellers' Field," where they are turned up by the plough, or washed to light by the rains.[4]

---

[9] Pliny (XXX. 30) tells us the beetle received this adoration because it rolled balls of dirt, alluding to its habit of pushing backwards with its hind feet small bits of dung or earth—verily the most grovelling idea of Deity that the human mind ever conceived. Pliny adds that Apion, the Egyptian, who sought to excuse the degraded rites of his countrymen, explained the worship of the beetle by some similarity in its operations to those of the sun—"a curious interpretation," as Pliny remarks.

[1] The genuine Egyptian scarabs are of smalt, porphyry, basalt, or some very hard stone; the Etruscan are of carnelian, sardonyx, and agate, rarely of chalcedony; a few have been found of smalt. The Egyptian are truthful representations of the insect; the Etruscan are exaggerated resemblances, especially in the back, which is set up to an extravagant height. The flat or under part of the stone, which is always the side engraved, in the Egyptian bears hieroglyphics, or representations of deities; in the Etruscan, though it sometimes shows imitations of Egyptian subjects, it generally bears figures or groups from the Greek mythology; the deeds of Hercules, and of the heroes of the Theban and Trojan wars,

being the favourite subjects. More rare are figures of the gods, and of the chimæras and other symbols of the Etruscan creed. And not a few have palæstric representations. These scarabs often bear designatory inscriptions in Etruscan characters.

[2] Great difference of opinion has been entertained as to the date of these gems. Gori (Mus. Etrus. II. p. 437) supposed them to be coeval with, or even anterior to, the Trojan War. Winckelman, though maintaining their high antiquity, took more moderate views. But it is now the general opinion, founded on a more intimate acquaintance and a wider range of comparison, that they cannot be referred to a very archaic period of Etruscan art. Mr. Alexander Murray, in an able article in the Contemporary Review for October, 1875, points out the striking analogy these scarabs of Etruria bear to the early silver coins of Thrace, to which he assigns the date of at least 500 B.C.

[3] One, however, which I have seen in the possession of the Canon Pasquini of Chiusi, was found set in an earring of gold. Bull. Inst. 1837, p. 46.

[4] See Vol. II. p. 297. *Scarabæi* are also found, though rarely, in other parts of

SPECULA,

or mirrors, are round or pear-shaped plates of bronze, often gilt or silvered, with the edge turned up, or slightly concave, having the outer side highly polished, and the inner adorned with figures engraved upon it. To the plate is attached a handle, often carved into some elegant form of life. The disk is seldom more than six or seven inches in diameter; it is generally encircled by a wreath of leaves, as shown in the specimen engraved for the frontispiece of this volume.[5]

For a long time these instruments went by the name of *pateræ*, and were supposed to have served as ladles for flour, or other light dry substances, used in sacrifices. Inghirami was among the first to reject this idea, and show them to be mirrors[6]—a fact now established beyond a doubt.[7] It is proved by representations of them, either on their own disks or on painted vases, in the hands of women, who are using them as mirrors—by the high polish they often retain, so bright indeed, as sometimes to fit them for their original purpose,—and by the discovery of them in caskets, with other articles of the female toilet.[8]

Italy, as at Palestrina in Latium (Abeken, Mittelitalien, p. 325). They have also been discovered in Greece. *e.g.* a celebrated one, bearing a Greek inscription, found among the ruins of Ægina (Bull. Inst. 1840, p. 140), and one from Attica, now in the Museum of Athens (Ann. Inst. 1837, 2, p. 144). In the British Museum are two found at Leucas in Acarnania. Gerhard is even of opinion that these gems may have had their origin in Greece. They have been found also in Asia Minor, at Tharros in Sardinia, and at Curium in Cyprus, where some have decided marks of a Phœnician origin. For the distinction between Egyptian and Phœnician scarabs, see an article by Mr. C. W. King in Cesnola's Cyprus, p. 353.

[5] A few mirrors have been found without handles, but these are liable to be confounded with the *capsulæ*, or cases for these instruments, which are formed of two round plates ornamented in a similar manner, or sometimes with reliefs, and hinged together like the valves of an oyster-shell. No instances have been found of Etruscan mirrors in the precious metals, or adorned with precious stones, or of so vast a size

as were used by the luxurious Romans. Seneca, Nat. Quæst. I. 17.

[6] Inghir. Mon. Etrus. II. pp. 1–77.

[7] Micali alone, to the last of his life, held to the old doctrine of *paterae*, a word now so completely superseded by *specula*, that he who would use it in reference to these instruments would scarcely be intelligible.

[8] Ann. Inst. 1840, p. 150; see also Gerhard's Etruskische Spiegel, pp. 82—4, for proofs of these instruments being mirrors. It has been supposed from certain scenes on painted vases, where women washing themselves at fountains are represented with these instruments in their hands, that they served a secondary purpose of casting water over the body, the concave side serving as a bowl to hold the liquid. Ann. Inst. 1840, p. 150—Braun. These mirrors are generally designated "mystic" by the Italians; and verily if mystic be synonymous with everything unreal, unnatural, and incomprehensible, the term is often not misapplied, for never were there more grotesque and ludicrous distortions of form and feature than are to be found on many of them.

Etruscan *specchj* may be divided into three classes.

First—those without any design on the inner surface. More than ordinary decoration is in these cases generally expended on the handles. Such mirrors are very rare.

Secondly—those with figures in relief. These are also met with but seldom.[9]

Thirdly—those with designs incised on the inner surface. These may be subdivided according to the subjects which they bear. First, and most numerous, are those which have scenes taken from the cycle of Greek mythology, or heroic fable, frequently illustrated by inscriptions, which are invariably in the Etruscan character, and often nationalised by the introduction of Etruscan demons. Next, those which bear representations or symbols of the divinities of the national creed, from the Nine Great Gods who wielded the thunder, through all the grades of their wild and multiform demonology, to the lowly Penates, the protectors of the individual hearth.[1] The last class portrays scenes of Etruscan life and manners; but of this a few instances only are known.

The art exhibited on these disks is not of primitive character, although a few have been found with archaic features, yet, though often extremely rude and feeble, it partakes less of the shortcomings of the period of infancy than of the carelessness of the Decadence; and it must be confessed that, except in comparatively few cases, such as that represented in the frontispiece to this volume, the elevation and perfection of the high style are not displayed.[2] These mirrors then cannot lay claim to a remote antiquity. Their date, indeed is pretty well determined by the fact that they are very rarely found in the same tomb with Greek painted vases, or if a vase by chance be found with them, it is in-

He who turns over Gerhard's illustrated volumes will find amusement, as well as instruction. That learned antiquary proves satisfactorily that these mirrors were instruments of personal rather than of sacred use, and served no other mysteries than those of the female bath and toilet (p. 76).

[9] A beautiful specimen of this class is in the Museo Gregoriano, representing Aurora carrying Memnon. See Vol. II. p. 481. Another, in the British Museum, represents Minerva overcoming Hercules. An exquisite example is in the possession of the Marchese Strozzi, of Florence. See Vol. II. p. 107.

[1] The most frequent representation is that of the winged goddess of Fate, some-times called "Lasa" (Vol. I. p. 288), or of the Dioscuri.

[2] The beautiful mirror in the frontispiece represents "Phuphluns," or Bacchus, embracing his mother "Semla," or Semele. It was found at Vulci, and is in the possession of Professor E. Gerhard of Berlin, who has illustrated it in his Etruskische Spiegel, taf. LXXXIII; cf. Mon. Ined. Inst. I. tav. LVI. A. The illustration here presented to the British public is drawn by Mr. George Scharf, from a cast of the original, reduced to half its size. It is one of the most beautiful specimens of Etruscan design on metal that have come down to us.

variably either of the Decadence, or of local origin.[3] And this fact proves that the importation or manufacture of Greek vases must have ceased, before these engraved mirrors came into use in Etruria. These monuments cannot be earlier than the fifth century of Rome,[4] and are probably later. Yet there is no branch of Etruscan antiquities more genuinely native—none more valuable to the inquirer, for the information it yields as to the mysterious language and creed of that ancient race; for the inscriptions being always in the native character, and designatory of the individual gods or heroes represented, these mirrors become a sure index to the Etruscan creed,—"a figurative dictionary," as Bunsen terms it, of Etruscan mythology; while at the same time they afford us the chief source and one of the most solid bases of our acquaintance with the native language.[5]

Akin to the mirrors are the *ciste*, or caskets, of bronze, with incised designs, which are occasionally found in Etruscan tombs, and chiefly at Vulci. They are more abundant at Palestrina, the ancient Praeneste, but whether of Etruscan or Latin origin is not easy to say, for the bronzes, and particularly the engraved works of the two lands, bear so close a resemblance that they often appear to be the productions of the same people, and even of the same master. The *ciste* of Palestrina, however, like the mirrors, sometimes bear inscriptions in early Latin. The art exhibited on these caskets is in some cases purely Greek, proving them to have been either imported, or the work of Greek artists resident in Italy. The most beautiful *cista* yet discovered is that known as the Ficoronian, from Palestrina, now in the Kircherian Museum at Rome,[6] and the best from Etruria is one from Vulci

[3] This is the experience of Signor Tommasi di Merigbi of Canino, after long continued excavations at Vulci. Bull. Inst. 1369, p. 174. It is the experience also of those who have dug at Chiusi and Corneto. Bull. Inst. 1870, p. 59 ; 1871, p. 93.—Helbig.

[4] From the association of these mirrors with the *ciste mistiche* in the tombs of Palestrina as well as of Vulci, it may be concluded that they came into use as sepulchral furniture, at least as early as the latter half of the third century B.C.

[5] Bull. Inst. 1836, p. 18. Hitherto these mirrors have been considered as peculiarly Etruscan, but of late years others like them have been found in the tombs of Athens, Ægina and Corinth. I have dis-

interred them also in Greek tombs in the Cyrenaica, but all without designs or inscriptions. Gerhard (Ann. Inst. 1837, 2, p. 143) supposes them to have had a Greek origin ; but it is remarkable that though they have often Greek myths, and Greek names, not one has ever been found in Etruria with a Greek inscription, though the inscriptions on the painted vases are almost invariably in that language. The same may be said of the other Etruscan works in bronze. Ann. Inst. 1834, p. 57 —Bunsen. Several mirrors, however, have been found with Latin epigraphs. These are generally from Palestrina. Gerhard, Etrusk. Spieg. taf. 147, 171, 182 ; Inghirami, Mon. Etrus. II. tav. 41.

[6] Vol. II. p. 497.

in the Gregorian Museum.[7] In date these caskets correspond with the mirrors, with which they are generally found, and to them the term "mystic" has also been applied with as little reason.

JEWELLERY.

In these volumes the jewellery of Etruria is frequently mentioned in terms of high admiration. It has been assumed that all the beautiful objects in gold and silver found in Etruscan tombs were the work of that ancient people. But Signor Augusto Castellani, the eminent jeweller of Rome, is of a different opinion, and as his authority on such matters is paramount, I make no apology for briefly stating his views, as communicated to me personally, and as published in his pamphlet entitled "Orificeria Italiana," Roma, 1872.

The most ancient jewellery of Italy has hitherto generally been ascribed to the Etruscans, but Signor Castellani distinguishes from the special style peculiar to that people two earlier styles proper to races who preceded them.

. First, the Pre-historic—a simple and semi-barbarous style, recognised in ornaments found in the earliest tombs of Veii, Cervetri, Corneto, Chiusi, Palestrina, and Bologna, of extremely rude workmanship and primitive forms, wrought with little gold, more silver, and an abundance of amber. To this style belong necklaces and bracelets of those three materials mixed, or of coloured glass, often with pendants in the shape of axes, vases, or other utensils; fibulæ of eccentric forms in gold, silver, or bronze, adorned with amber or variegated glass; thin plates of gold marked with straight or hatched lines; amulets of amber in the shape of monkeys, and other animals not found in Italy. It is a remarkable fact that articles of jewellery of similar character and style have been discovered also in Norway and Sweden, and even in Mexico. Signor Castellani does not attempt to determine to what particular race among the early inhabitants of Italy this primitive style should be ascribed, but is content to pronounce it Pre-historic.

After this comes a style of widely different character, not a development of the preceding, but so remarkable for the exquisite taste and elaborate workmanship it exhibits that there can be no doubt of its distinct origin. This style Signor Castellani attributes to the people who immediately preceded

[7] Vol. II. p. 489.

the Etruscans in Italy, *i.e.* the Pelasgians, whom he prefers to designate as "Tyrrhenes." He refuses to recognise this jewellery as Etruscan, because it is found not only in Etruria, but at Palestrina, Cumæ, Ruvo, and other sites in Italy, and also in Egypt, Assyria, Phœnicia, and the Crimea, showing that the people who produced it were widely scattered throughout the ancient world, and particularly on the coasts of the Mediterranean and Black Sea;[8] while the jewellery of the Etruscans has a distinct and peculiar character, not common to other people, and is found only on Etruscan sites.

The materials employed in this "Tyrrhene" style are gold, silver, bronze, amber, ivory, and variegated glass. The style is easily recognised by its elegant forms, the harmony of its parts, and the purity of its design, but chiefly by the marvellous fineness and elaboration of its workmanship. The patterns, which are always simple yet most elegant, and admirably harmonious, are wrought by soldering together globules or particles of gold, so minute as hardly to be perceptible to the naked eye, and by the interweaving of extremely delicate threads of gold; and are sometimes, but sparingly, interspersed with enamels.[9] Tiny figures of men, animals, or chimæras, exquisitely chased in relief or in the round, form another and favourite feature in the ornamentation. On a close inspection this jewellery astonishes and confounds by its wonderful elaboration; at a little distance it charms the eye by its exquisite taste, and

---

[8] Some of the gold ornaments found by Dr. Schliemann at Mycenæ have much of the character of this style, although the designs are effected not by granulated, or funiform, but by *repoussé* or intaglio work. See Mycenæ, illustrations, Nos. 281–292. But many of those discovered by General Cesnola at Curium in Cyprus, are unquestionably of the so-called "Tyrrhene" style, and are not to be distinguished from the best jewellery found in Etruscan tombs. See Cyprus, plate xxv. And this fact favours the view held by some that this early yet beautiful jewellery is to be ascribed to the Phœnicians, who at a very remote period were renowned as skilful workers in metal (πολυδαίδαλοι—Iliad. xxiii. 743; Odys. xv. 424; cf. 2 Chron. 2, 14; 1 Kings, 7, 14), and manufacturers of trinkets—ἀθύρματα—in which they traded to foreign lands (Odys. xv.

415; cf. Ezek. xxvii. 16, 22). That they excelled also in the art of jewellery, is evident from Homer's description of a Phœnician necklace of gold set with amber beads. Odys. xv. 459.

[9] It is undoubted that both the Greeks and Etruscans were acquainted with the art of enamelling, but they used it sparingly in their jewellery, being unwilling, thinks Signor Castellani, to cover too much of the beautiful hue of pure gold, then extremely rare, with coloured vitreous matter, which was comparatively common. Among the most remarkable works extant in enamelled gold of Greek and Etruscan origin, he specifies a crown in the Campana Museum, a necklace exhibited by himself in the Loan Collection at South Kensington in 1862, some earrings with swans found at Vulci, and others with peacocks and doves in the Campana collection.

the graceful character and harmony of its outlines. In fact it is the perfection of jewellery, far transcending all that the most expert artists of subsequent ages have been able to produce.

To this style belongs the most beautiful jewellery discovered in Etruria, and elsewhere in Italy, such as the gold ornaments from the Regulini-Galassi tomb, now in the Museo Gregoriano, and those, still more beautiful, recently found at Palestrina, and now exhibited at the Kircherian Museum at Rome.

Signor Castellani points out that the Hindoo jewellery, even of the present day, bears no slight resemblance to this ancient style. Though inferior in execution, and betraying a decline of taste, the method adopted of soldering minute grains or fine threads of gold, mixed with enamels, to the object, is precisely that employed by the Tyrrhenes of old.

The genuine Etruscan jewellery, says Signor Castellani, is very inferior both in taste and execution to that of the Tyrrhene style, of which it is a corruption. There is the same sort of relation between these styles that the works of the great painters of the *cinquecento* bear to those of the following centuries. The mode of workmanship is the same, yet the style has so degenerated that it may be pronounced *barocco*. No longer the minute granulations, the delicate thread-work, the charming simplicity in form and design which mark the earlier style. These are exchanged for forms of greater breadth and fulness; the purity of the lines gives place to the artificial and turgid, and the whole, though it makes a more striking appearance, has far less elegance, harmony, and elaboration.

Etruscan jewellery is of two descriptions, domestic and sepulchral: the former most substantial and durable, the latter very light and flimsy—witness the wreaths of gold leaves found encircling the helmets of illustrious warriors. The amber, coloured glass, enamel, and ivory used in the preceding style are rare in this, and give place to gems—chiefly garnet, onyx, and carnelian. Among the ornaments for personal use are earrings of various forms and dimensions, large *fibulæ* and brooches, massive gold rings, lentoid or vase-shaped *bullæ*, agate *scarabæi*; but in all these productions an inflated and artificial style, marking the decline of the art, is conspicuous.

The chief productions of this style come from the tombs of Corneto, Vulci, Chiusi, and Orvieto.

This ancient style of jewellery has come down traditionally to our own day. In a remote corner of the Umbrian Marches, at the little town of St. Angelo in Vado, hidden in the recesses of the Apennines, far from every centre of civilization, there still exists a special school of jewellery by which some of the processes employed by the Etruscans have been traditionally preserved. The beautiful peasant-girls of that district at their wedding feasts wear necklaces of gold filagree beads, and long earrings of the peculiar form designated *a navicella*, inferior in taste and elegance of design to the works of ancient art, yet wrought in a method which Signor Castellani does not hesitate to pronounce Etruscan.[1]

The art in which Etruscan genius and skill have achieved their greatest triumphs is PAINTING. This art is of very ancient date in Italy; for we hear of paintings at Cære in Etruria, which were commonly believed to be earlier than the foundation of Rome.[2]

The pictorial remains discovered in Etruria are of two kinds:— the scenes on the walls of sepulchres, and the paintings on pottery.

PAINTED TOMBS.

This is a most important class of monuments, for the variety and interest of the subjects represented, and the light they throw on the customs, domestic manners, and religious creed of the Etruscans, as well as on the progress and character of the pictorial art among them. We find these "chambers of imagery" chiefly in the cemeteries of Tarquinii and Clusium, though two have also been found at Cervetri, Vulci, and Orvieto, and a solitary one at Veii, Bomarzo, and Vetulonia respectively,—all of which will be described in the course of this work. They show us Etruscan art in various periods and stages of excellence, from its infancy to its perfection; some being coeval, it may be, with the foundation of Rome, others as late as the Empire; some almost Egyptian, others peculiarly native; some again decidedly Greek in character, if not in execution; others resembling the Graeco-Roman frescoes of Pompeii and Pæstum. There is the same

[1] The extraordinary earrings worn by the women of Forio in the Island of Ischia, may possibly have a similar traditional origin.

[2] Plin. XXXV. 6. These paintings were extant in Pliny's day; so also some in temples at Ardea and Lanuvium, of nearly equal antiquity. He remarks on the speedy perfection this art attained, as it seemed not to have been practised in Trajan times.

wide range as exists between the works of Giotto or Cimabue,
and those of Raffaele or the Caracci. In the Campana tomb
of Veii, which is the most ancient yet discovered, we have the
rudeness and conventionality of very early art—great exaggeration of anatomy and proportions—and no attempt to imitate the
colouring of nature, but only to arrest the eye by startling
contrasts.[3] Next in point of antiquity are the painted tiles which
lined the walls of certain tombs at Cervetri, where the human
figure is drawn with more truth to nature, though in bald outline,
and an attempt is even shown at the expression of sentiment, the
character of the whole remaining purely and specifically Etruscan.[4] In the earliest tombs of Tarquinii, though of later date,
the Egyptian character and physiognomy are strongly pronounced.
Of better style are other tomb-paintings on the same site and at
Orvieto,[5] which, though retaining a native character, with much
conventionality of form and colouring, show more correctness of
design, and a degree of elegance and refinement which betrays the
influence of Hellenic models. Earlier it may be, yet more free
and careless, are most of the wall-paintings at Chiusi, which
show us what Etruscan art with its strong tendency to realism
could effect, before it had felt the refining influence of Greece.[6]
Later, and far better, are some of the scenes at Tarquinii
which breathe the spirit and feeling of the Hellenic vases, where
there is a grace of outline, a dignity and simplicity of attitude,
and a force of expression, which prove the limner to have been a
master of his art, though this was not wholly freed from conventional trammels. Still later, with yet more freedom, mastery,
and intelligence, are some of the paintings on the same site,
and those found at Vulci, where rigidity and severity are laid
aside, where fore-shortening, grouping, composition, and even
chiaroscuro are introduced; which display, in a word, all the ease
and power of Græco-Roman frescoes of the close of the Republic
or commencement of the Empire.

There was little variety in the colours used in Etruscan wall-
paintings. In one early tomb at Chiusi, and in another of later
date at Bomarzo, the colouring is bichromatic—black and red
alone—"rubricà pictà et carbone." At Cervetri an early tomb
shows black, red, and white; the Campana tomb at Veii, black,
red, and yellow; the painted tiles of Cervetri, these four colours
burnt in with the tile. It was with these four colours alone that

---

[3] Vol. I. p. 34.   [5] Vol. II. pp. 55, 58.
[4] Vol. I. pp. 260-263.   [6] Vol. II. pp. 320, 332, 333.

the greatest painters of antiquity, Polygnotus, Zeuxis, Apelles and others, produced their immortal works.[7] Pliny dates the decline of the pictorial art from the introduction of purple and other hues, and laments that in his day there was not a picture worth looking at—"nunc nulla nobilis pictura est." In the tombs of Tarquinii, however, even in those which show the most archaic design, blue was used, and in one of the earliest, a decided green. The colours were invariably laid on in fresco.

The Etruscans painted not only the walls of their tombs, but often their coffins and cinerary urns. The latter, being generally of the Decadence, show crude and strongly contrasted hues on their reliefs, which are coloured in accordance with native conventionalities, and without any pretensions to pictorial skill. And although a better taste is occasionally displayed, there is too frequently a total disregard of harmony in the polychrome sculpture of Etruria. On the marble sarcophagi, however, in a few rare instances, we find some of the most exquisite productions of the Etruscan pencil, as regards both design and colouring, or it should more strictly be said, of the pictorial art in Etruria. Such paintings are executed on the flat surface of the marble. The most striking example of this monumental decoration hitherto brought to light, is the Amazon sarcophagus in the Etruscan Museum of Florence, which some critics claim as a purely Greek work, while others pronounce it to be the production of an Etruscan, deeply imbued with the spirit of Hellenic art. In this instance the colouring, though soft and harmonious, is less conspicuous for beauty, than the composition and design.[8]

PAINTED VASES.

The painted vases form the most comprehensive subject connected with art in Etruria. The vast multitude that have been brought to light, the great variety of form, of use, of story and myth, of degree of excellence in workmanship and design, the many questions connected with their origin and manufacture not yet satisfactorily answered, the diversity of opinions respecting them, render it impossible to treat fully of so extensive a subject in a narrow compass. My remarks, then, must necessarily be brief, and are offered for the sake of elucidating the frequent references to ancient pottery made in the course of this work:

[7] Plin. XXXV. 32 ; Cicero, Brutus, 18.   [8] See Vol. II. p. 96.

and rather with the hope of exciting interest in the subject than with the expectation of satisfying inquiry.

The most ancient vases found in Etruria are not painted, but rudely shaped by the hand, often not baked, but merely dried in the sun, without glaze, and either perfectly plain, or marked with bands of dots, zig-zags, hatched lines, meanders and other geometrical patterns, clumsily scratched on the clay when soft. Such is the pottery found in the "well-tombs" of Chiusi and Sarteano, and a few other sites in Etruria, and of the same character are the pots discovered in the necropolis of Alba Longa, buried beneath a stratum of *peperino*, or consolidated volcanic ash, and those found on the Esquiline, lying beneath the walls of Servius Tullius. Indeed, this very primitive pottery is by some regarded as pre-Etruscan, and is attributed to the Umbrians, Siculans, Oscans, or whatever early Italic race occupied the land prior to its conquest by the Etruscans.[9] The decorations on these vases were after a time drawn with more regularity and variety, and ultimately came to be stamped instead of incised, the geometrical designs giving place to imitations of animal life, birds, especially ducks, snakes, and rude attempts at representing the human form. Such was the earliest pottery of Veii and Caere; but on those sites we find a development of the art in large jars (*pithoi*), in stands, of brown or red ware, with heads or Egyptian-like figures in compartments or bands encircling the vase, and in flat relief, stamped on the clay when moist. Still later apparently was the *bucchero* ware of Chiusi and its neighbourhood, with figures in prominent and rounded

[9] As the geometrical style of decoration is the most ancient, and as it is found on the primitive pottery of Greece, the Greek islands, Italy, and also of Central and Northern Europe, Professor Conze broached the opinion that it must have been introduced into Italy as well as into Greece by the first Aryan invaders from beyond the Alps. This view is combated by Dr. Wolfgang Helbig (Ann. Inst. 1875, pp. 221–253), who shows that the earliest inhabitants of Italy, to judge from their remains—the people of the *terremare*, or fortified villages in the districts of Parma, Modena, and Reggio, had no such decorations on their pottery, or works in bone, horn, or bronze. Nor are such decorations found on the very earliest pottery of Sarteano, or of Poggio Renzo at Chiusi; nor on that of the northern necropolis of Alba Longa, where the singular hut-urns have been disinterred; nor on the fragments of vases discovered within the precincts of the temple of the Dea Dia, in the grove of the Arvales; nor on those found in the lowest vegetable stratum under the walls of Servius Tullius. It was only after Italy had been inhabited for some time that this system of decoration was developed or introduced; when we find it on the later pottery of Poggio Renzo, and of the Alban necropolis, and in the cinerary urns from the Benacci and Villanova diggings at Bologna. Helbig, finding the same style of decoration on pottery discovered at Nineveh, Jerusalem, Gaza, and Ascalon, assigns to it an Asiatic, and specifically a Semitic origin.

relief, representing deities, chimæras, and other symbols of the Etruscan creed, more rarely myths and scenes illustrative of native life and customs.[1] Though very archaic and Oriental in style, this pottery is not necessarily in every instance so early as it appears; for the peculiarities of a remote period and primitive stage of art may have been conventionally preserved, especially in sepulchral or sacred vessels, from one age to another.[2]

The earliest vases of genuinely Etruscan character, with painted decorations, which are extremely rare, bear archaic figures of men and animals rudely drawn in opaque white on the natural red of the clay, or in red on a creamy ground;[3] and in style they generally resemble the painted vases of the First or Doric style, with which they are probably contemporary. Such vases have been found chiefly at Cervetri.[4]

The painted vases found in multitudes in the cemeteries of Etruria, and commonly called Etruscan, are not for the most part of that origin, but Greek, though to some extent, it may be, of local manufacture. They do not, therefore, strictly come under our notice. Yet as they have been disinterred in even greater abundance in Etruscan cemeteries than in those of Greece and her colonies, as they were sometimes imitated by native artists, and as they exerted a powerful influence on Etruscan art, it is impossible to exclude them from our consideration.

They may be divided into three great classes.

First, the Egyptian, Phœnician, or Babylonian, as it is variously termed from the oriental character of its ornamentation, which has led some to ascribe its origin to those several peoples; but it is now more correctly regarded as primitive Greek, and particularly Doric.[5] Yet the term "ASIATIC" may not unaptly be applied to it as indicating the distinctive charac-

---

[1] A description of this ware is given in the chapters on Florence and Chiusi, Vol. II. pp. 76, 307. These vases are very rarely found in the same tomb with those that are painted, or if so accompanied, it is usually with those of the First or Corinthian style. Bull. Inst. 1875, p. 99. They are generally found with archaic bronzes, and invariably in tombs where the corpse has been interred, not burnt.

[2] This ware has in some very rare cases been found in the same tomb with painted vases with black figures, and with red in the early severe style, as in Mancini's ex-

cavations at Orvieto; but as such tombs always contain more than a single body, they may have served for interment at different periods; or the bucchero may have been interred as an antique relic.

[3] See Vol. II. pp. 47, 489, 490.

[4] Some of these vases from Cervetri have been found with polychrome decorations, in opaque colours, blue, white, and vermilion, laid on in fresco, as on the walls of the painted tombs. Micali, Mon. Ined. tav. 4, 5; Birch, p. 447.

[5] Gerhard, Ann. Inst. 1831, pp. 15, 201; Bunsen, Ann. Inst. 1834, pp. 63-70.

teristics of its style. This class of vases is of high antiquity,
by some supposed to date as far back as twelve centuries B.C.,
and it cannot be later than 540 B.C., the epoch of Theodoros
of Samos, whose improvements in metal-casting marked a new
era in ancient art.

The most primitive vases of this class rarely show representations of animal life, but are adorned with annular bands, zig-zags,
waves, meanders, concentric circles, hatched lines, *suastikas*, and
other geometrical patterns, often separated into compartments
by upright lines, like diglyphs or triglyphs; indeed the general
style of ornamentation closely resembles that on some of the
fragments of painted pottery found by Dr. Schliemann at Mycenæ.

KYLIX OF THE MOST PRIMITIVE STYLE.

An example of this primitive style is given in the *kylix* represented in the annexed woodcut, and another in the Appendix at
p. cxiii., which shows an Athenian *lebes* with three horses moulded
on the lid. These very archaic vases are believed to be primitive
Ionic Greek. "The absence of all human figures and of all inscriptions," says Dr. Birch, "and their analogies with Oriental
art, render it probable that some of them may be as old as the
heroic ages. None can be more recent than the seventh century,
B.C." [6]

Of rather later date are the vases of Doric character, which are
found in Etruria as well as in Greece, Sicily, Magna Græcia, and
the Greek islands, and may be looked for on any ancient site
which has an antiquity of not less than six centuries B.C. The
figures, which are painted on the pale yellow ground of the clay,
are generally arranged in several bands encircling the vase, and

[6] Ancient Pottery, p. 183. Dr. Birch
points out the resemblance some of the
earliest vases of this class bear in their
style of decoration to those found in the
sepulchres of the ancient Peruvians.

are brown rather than black, varied occasionally with purple, white, or crimson. They consist chiefly of wild beasts—lions, panthers, wolves, boars; of cattle—bulls, goats, rams, antelopes; of birds—swans, cocks, owls; or of sphinxes, griffons, and other compound mythical beings; arranged in pairs of opposite natures,

either facing each other, or engaged in combat; the oriental principle of antagonism being obviously set forth, as shown in the annexed woodcut of a Doric *aryballos*. Mixed with them are quaint representations of fruit and flowers, especially of the lotus.[7] On the later vases of the Doric style, human figures first appear, but often under the form of demons or genii, or of the four-winged divinities of oriental worship. Many vases of this class having been found at Corinth, and notably the celebrated Dodwell vase,[8] now at Munich, they have received the designation of "Corinthian." It is highly probable, indeed, that these vases were introduced into Etruria by Demaratus of Corinth,

ARYBALLOS, DORIC STYLE.

about 660 B.C. A few admirable examples, supposed to be importations from Corinth, have been discovered in the necropolis of Cervetri, and also some Etruscan imitations of this archaic style, a specimen of which is given at p. 283 of this volume. The design on these Corinthian vases corresponds in great part with that of the earliest painted tombs, such as the Grotta Campana at Veii, and also with the most archaic Etruscan bronzes. Were we to seek analogies to the art of other lands, it would be to the earliest works of the Greek chisel—to the reliefs from the Temple of Hercules at Selinus, or to the Agamemnon, Talthybios, and Epeios from Samothrace, now in the Louvre. These "Corinthian" vases mark the transition from the early Asiatic style to that of the Archaic Greek, or Attic, for without this intermediate class there appears to be so wide a difference between these styles, as to lead naturally to the conclusion that they are totally distinct in their origin.

---

[7] "The backgrounds with flowers appear, indeed, to have been copied from oriental or Assyrian art, which had ceased to exist in the sixth century B. C.; while the Asiatic style of the friezes, which resemble those of Solomon's temple and the Babylonian tapestries, likewise indicates an epoch of high antiquity." Birch, p. 158.

[8] Supposed to date from 574 B.C.

The annexed woodcut represents an archaic *lebes* from Athens, now in the British Museum. It is of the style which is supposed to have preceded the Corinthian. The figures are of a maroon colour, on a pale yellow ground.

ARCHAIC LEBES, FROM ATHENS.

The Second class of vases is commonly designated "Etruscan," or "Tyrrhene," from the abundance in which it is found in that part of Italy; in Campania it is called "Sicilian," for the same reason. The more correct appellation would be "Archaic Greek," for such is the character of the design, and the subjects and inscriptions are also purely Hellenic. This class is also appropriately designated "Attic," in distinction from the Doric character of the preceding class, and because the inscriptions are in that dialect. It continued to exist for about a century, from about 540 to 450 or 440 B.C., when it gave place to a still higher development of the ceramic art.[9]

The Second class is recognisable by its figures being painted

9 Dr. Brunn ascribes a large portion of the vases of this class found in Etruscan tombs to a much later period—to the third or even second century B.C., and regards them as local or imported imitations of original Greek vases of this class. He arrives at this conclusion from considerations both of palæography and style, which we have no room to specify, and must refer our readers to his work, "Probleme in der Geschichte der Vasenmalerei." That the Archaic Greek style was sometimes imitated in a subsequent age we have proofs in the Panathenaic vases of the Cyrenaica, which, though with black figures, bear dates of the fourth century B.C., one as late as 313 B.C. But that the generality of the vases of this class found in Etruria cannot be a century or two later than this, as Brunn opines, is clearly demonstrated by Helbig in his review of Brunn's pamphlet. Bull. Inst. 1871, pp. 85-96. While admitting that this archaic style may have been conventionally continued longer than is generally supposed, Helbig is not inclined to believe it was carried on later than the end of the fourth century B.C.

black on the ground of the clay, which is yellow, warming to red. The flesh of women, the hair of old men, the devices on shields, and a few other objects are painted white; the armour is sometimes tinted purple, and crimson is occasionally introduced on the drapery. The outlines, the muscles, and folds of drapery are marked by incised lines. Though the faces are invariably in profile, the eyes of the men are always round, of the women long and almond-shaped, of that very form usually represented in Egyptian paintings. In this class the human figure forms the principal subject of the design, which in the earlier works is hard, severe, and conventional; the attitudes rigid and constrained, often impossible; the forms angular, the muscular development exaggerated, the extremities of the limbs unnaturally attenuated, the hands and feet preposterously elongated. Yet with the progress of art these defects were in great measure remedied, and the design gradually became more natural and free, especially in the later works of this style, which sometimes show much truth and expression, and even spirit, with vigour of conception, and a conscientious carefulness and neatness of execution quite surprising. Yet none of this class are entirely free from the severity of archaic art. The figures bear the same relation to the sculptured reliefs of Ægina, that those on the Third class of vases do to the marbles of the Parthenon; indeed, these may be said to be of the Æginetic school, for they correspond not only in style, but in date. And though it may be questioned if all the extant pottery with black figures can claim so remote an antiquity, and if some of it be not rather a more recent imitation, the type of it belongs indisputably to the archaic period of Greek art. It will be understood that whenever vases with black figures are mentioned in the course of this work, a certain degree of archaicism of design is always implied. This style is found in connection with vases of more beauty and variety of form than the earlier class; the most common shapes being the *amphora*, or wine-jar; the *hydria*, or water-jar; the *kelebe*, or mixing-vase; the *oinochoë*, or wine-jug; the *kylix*, or drinking-bowl; and the *lekythos*, or oil-flask.

The subjects depicted on vases of this class are generally taken from the Heroic Cycle—the deeds of Hercules or Theseus, events of the Trojan War, or the wanderings of Ulysses, combats of the Greeks with the Amazons, of the Gods with the Giants, and similar fables from the Hellenic mythology. Very numerous also are scenes from the Dionysiac *thiasos*,—Sileni and Mænads dancing round the jolly god, who sits or stands in the midst, crowned with ivy, and holding a vine-branch or *thyrsos* in one hand, and a *kantharos* in the other. Another class of subjects, not so common, is the Panathenaic. On one side of the vase the great goddess of Attica stands brandishing her lance between two Doric columns, crowned with cocks; on the reverse are foot, horse, or chariot-races, or the wrestling, boxing, or hurling-matches, which took place at her annual festivals. Such vases, from the inscriptions they bear—"One of the prizes from Athens"—are proved to have been given to the victors on those occasions.[1] These subjects are peculiar to vases of the Second class. That the period to which this class of vases belonged overlapped that of the following class, and that for some time in the fifth century, B.C., the two styles were contemporary, is clear, not only from the advanced art of the later vases of the Second class, and from the hard, dry design of the earliest of the Third class, but also from certain instances where both styles are found on the same vase. Thus on a large *kylix*, found at Chiusi, but now in the Museum of Palermo, one half of the bowl is adorned with black figures on a red ground, the other with red upon black.

The Third class of Greek vases has justly been denominated "Perfect," as it partakes of the best art of that wonderful people. In these vases the ground is painted black, the figures being left of the natural reddish yellow of the clay, and the details are either marked with black lines, or with brownish red in the more delicate parts of the figures and drapery. These vases belong to the finest period of Greek art, but as some of the earliest with red figures retain the severe and archaic character of the preceding style, we may carry their age back to about 460 B.C. or even earlier.[3]

---

[1] The inscription is TONAϴENEϴEN-AϴΛON—τῶν Ἀθήνηθεν ἄθλων—sometimes with the prefix of EMI for εἰμί, as in the earliest known vase of this class, found by Mr. Burgon at Athens, and now in the British Museum. Pseudo-archaic vases of this class have also been found in the Cyrenaica, recognised as such by the affected archaicisms of style, and by the dates with which they are inscribed. The earliest dated vase yet known is one of six I discovered at Teucheira in that land, and it dates from the archonship of Polyzelos, or 367 B.C. Others, in the British Museum, the Louvre, and the Museum of Leyden, bear various dates, the latest being 313 B.C. Two of those in the British Museum dated in the archonship of Pythodemos, 336 B.C., were found at Cervetri. For notices of the Panathenaic vases see Böckh, Bull. Inst. 1832, pp. 91–98; Ambrosch, Ann. Inst. 1833, pp. 64–89; Secchi, Bull. Inst. 1843, p. 75.

[2] Birch states that recent discoveries show some of these vases to be as old as 480 B.C., and certainly prior to the age of Pheidias. p. 202. Bunsen assigns the vases of this style to a period between the 74th and 94th Olympiads (484–404, B.C.). Ann. Inst. 1834, p. 62.

They continued to be manufactured down to about 336 B.C., or to the accession of Alexander the Great, from which period dates the decline of the ceramic art. The best vases of this class are pre-eminent in elegance of form, in fineness of material, brilliancy of varnish, and in exquisite beauty of design, divested of that archaic severity and conventionality which distinguish the earlier classes. The sub-styles into which this class may be divided, are the Strong style, or the earliest, already mentioned, which belongs to the days of Pericles and Polygnotus; the Fine style, or that contemporary with Pheidias, Zeuxis, and Parrhasius; and the Florid or latest style, which marks the transition from the Perfect class to the Decadence, and was contemporary with Scopas, Praxiteles, and Lysippus.

The subjects illustrated are very similar to those on vases of the Second class, with the exception of the Panathenaic scenes; those of Bacchic character are also of less frequent occurrence, the predominating subjects being Greek myths, or representations of Greek manners. Little or nothing is to be learned from any of these painted vases of the customs, habits, traditions, or creed of the Etruscans. With very few exceptions all are purely Greek. The forms with which this style is associated are the *amphora*, the *krater*, or mixing-vase, the *kalpis*, an elegant variety of water-jar, the *œnochoë*, the *olpe*, the *kylix*, and the *lekythos*.

There is a class of vases belonging to this Third style, which have polychrome figures on a white ground, the colours being red, yellow, blue, purple, brown, and sometimes gold. These vases are generally of the *lekythos* form. They are rare everywhere, but particularly so in Etruria, though one of the very finest of this class was found at Vulci—the *krater* in the Gregorian Museum which represents Mercury handing the infant Bacchus to Silenus.[3] Beautiful specimens of this style have been found at Athens; a few also at Cameirus in Rhodes: and I have brought a few to light in my excavations in Sicily and the Cyrenaica.

No one can view the best works of this Third class without delight, and an intimate acquaintance with them begets in the man of taste an unbounded admiration. They are the source whence Flaxman drew his inspiration, and well would it be for the student of art to follow that master's example, and imbue his mind deeply with their excellences and beauties. The dignity of the conception and force of expression, at times rising

into the sublime, the chaste taste, the truth to nature, the purity
and simplicity of the design, and the force as well as the delicacy
of the execution, well entitle the best vases of this class to the
appellation of "Perfect." Never, perhaps, do they attain the
perfection of art displayed in the highest works of the Greek
chisel, yet there is a mastery, a spirit of beauty about them
which marks them as of the happiest and purest period of
Hellenic art. Though the Greek vase-painters were held of
small account in their own day, yet if the excellence of art
consist in conveying ideas by the fewest and most simple touches,
the merit of these artists is of a very high order.

The conquest of Asia by Alexander, by introducing metal vases
in the place of those of terra-cotta, was the cause of the decline of
Greek ceramic art. The period of Decadence dates then from
about 330 B.C., and was continued to about 150 B.C., when
metal had quite superseded earthenware. Vases of this class
continued to show red figures on a black ground, but white was
abundantly introduced, colour more sparingly, and gold also
occasionally in the ornaments and other accessories. They may
be recognised chiefly by the design, which, though often masterly
in the earlier vases of this style, is injured by affectation,
mannerism, and excess of ornament, and in the later vases is
coarse and careless in the extreme, with figures stumpy and inelegant. The most striking vases of this class are found in the
tombs of Puglia and Basilicata. They are often of enormous size
and exaggerated proportions, and of shapes unknown in the purer
days of ceramic art. The multitude of figures introduced, the
complexity of the composition, the general inferiority and
mannerism of the design, the flourish of the drapery, the lavish-
ment of decoration, in a word, the absence of that chasteness of
taste which gives the Perfect style its chief charm, indicate these
vases to belong to the period when Greek art was beginning to
trick herself out in meretricious embellishments, forgetful of her
sublime and god-like simplicity.

The vases of the Decadence found in Etruria are of more
modest dimensions, but display a sad decline from the beauty of
the earlier styles. They are almost always of local manufacture.
Those from Volterra are of pale clay, coarse forms, dull varnish,
most careless and rustic design ; large female heads *en silhouette*,
and scenes in which nude women are introduced, are the favourite
subjects. At Orvieto, where vases of somewhat similar character are found, there is also a peculiar pottery belonging to this

period, adorned, not with paintings, but with reliefs silvered, in imitation of vases of that metal.[4]

What use can this multitude of vases have served? Though now found only in tombs, it must not be supposed that they were all originally of sepulchral application. Those with Panathenaic subjects were given, probably full of oil, as prizes at the national games, as in Greece. Others may have been given as prizes at the palæstric fêtes, or as nuptial presents, or as pledges of love and friendship; and these are generally marked by some appropriate inscription. Many were doubtless articles of household furniture, for use or adornment;[5] and a few seem to have been expressly for sepulchral purposes, either as decorations of the tomb, or to contain the wine, honey, and milk, left as offerings to the *manes*,[6] or to make the customary libations, or more rarely to hold the ashes of the dead.[7] There can be little doubt, whatever purposes they may have originally served, that these vases were placed in the tomb by the ashes of the deceased, together with his armour and jewellery, as being among the articles which he most prized in life.

[4] Vol. II. p. 48. A choice collection of these peculiar vases is in the possession of Signor Augusto Castellani, at Rome. The fact of them all wanting a bottom shows them to have been made merely for decorative purposes. Bull. Inst. 1871, p. 18. Ann. Inst. 1871, pp. 5–27; Klügmann, tav. d'agg. A—C.

[5] Yet many of them are only varnished outside, and but partially—not at all within; so that they could hardly have served for liquids. Ann. Inst. 1831, p. 97. Many may have been used by the relatives at the *parentalia*, or funeral feasts, and left as sacred in the tomb.

[6] The notion of feeding the souls of the departed was very general among the ancients. In Egypt the tomb of Osiris, in the isle of Philæ in the Nile, contained 360 libatory vessels—χοαί—which were daily filled with milk by the priests. Diod. Sic. I. p. 19, ed. Rhod. In Greece the souls were supposed to be fed by the libations and feasts held at the sepulchre. Lucian, de Luctu, p. 509, ed. 1615. And so in Italy, where the *manes* were appeased by libations of wine, milk, and blood; and the wailing-women therefore beat their breasts to force out the milk, and tore their flesh to make the blood flow; all for

the satisfaction of the departed. Serv. ad Æn. V. 78. A similar custom, possibly of equal antiquity, prevails in China, of making an annual "feast for the hungry ghosts." It was the custom of the ancients to burn on the funeral pyre the vases containing oil, honey, or other offerings to the dead. Hom. Iliad, XXIII. 170; Virg. Æn. VI. 225; Serv. in loc. Vases are often found in the tombs of Etruria, as well as of Greece, and her colonies in Italy and Sicily, which retain manifest proofs of subjection to fire.

[7] This is sometimes the case with those of Sicily and Magna Græcia, especially of Apulia and Lucania, and frequently with the vases of La Certosa at Bologna; more rarely with those of Etruria Proper. A quaint but beautiful conceit on certain of these cinerary vases is uttered by Sir Thomas Browne, in his Hydriotaphia, chap. III. "Most imitate a circular figure, in a spherical and round composure; whether from any mystery, best duration, or capacity, were but a conjecture. But the common form with necks was a proper figure, making our last bed like our first; nor much unlike the urns of our nativity, while we lay in the nether part of the earth, and inward vault of our microcosm."

That these vases are found in such multitudes in Etruria is the more astonishing when we remember that almost all the tombs which contain them have been rifled in bygone times. It is extremely rare to find a virgin sepulchre. At Vulci, where the painted vases are most abundant, not one tomb in a hundred proves to be intact. It is obvious that those who in past ages violated these sepulchres were either ignorant of the value of the vases, or left them from superstitious motives—most probably the former, for they are often found broken to pieces, as though they had been dashed wantonly to the earth in the search for the precious metals. We know that the sepulchres of Corinth and of Capua were ransacked by the Romans in the time of Julius Cæsar, for the sake of these painted vases, which were called necro-Corinthian, and were then highly prized and of immense value; the art of making them having been lost;[1] but how it came to pass that the Romans never worked the vast mines of the same treasures in Etruria, some almost within sight of the Seven-hilled City, it is difficult to comprehend. They could hardly have been ignorant of the custom of the Etruscans to bury these vases in their sepulchres, and religious scruples could not have deterred them from spoliation in Etruria more than in Greece or the south of Italy. Such, however, is the fact, and the abundance of these vases in Etruscan tombs forbids us to believe that the extensive system of rifling, to which they have evidently been subjected, was by Roman hands. It was more probably carried forward at the close of the Empire, or by the barbarian hordes who overran Italy in the early centuries of our era.[2] Plunder

---

[1] Sueton., J. Cæs. 81. Strabo (VIII. p. 381) says the Romans did not leave a tomb untouched at Corinth in their search for the vases and bronzes. Robbers of tombs were not uncommon in ancient times, in Egypt and Greece as well as in Italy, and were execrated, as body-snatchers are at the present day. Pliny states that in his time fictile vases, by which he probably means those that were painted, fetched more money than the celebrated Murrhine vases, the cost of which he records (XXXV. 46; XXXVII. 7); and which are supposed to have been of porcelain. That these painted vases were very rare in his day is confirmed by the fact that not one has yet been discovered among the ruins of Pompeii or Herculaneum. Bull. Inst. 1871, p. 95.

[2] It is known that Theodoric, the Goth,

sanctioned the spoliation of ancient sepulchres, yet restricted it to the precious metals, commanding the ashes to be left—"quia nolumus lucra quæri, quæ per funesta scelera possunt reperiri;" and he justified his decree on the ground that that was not stolen which had no owner, and that that ought not to be left with the dead, which would serve to keep the living—"Non est enim cupiditas eripere quæ nullus se dominus ingemiscat amisisse." Cassiodor. Var. IV. 34. The same feeling was shown in the laws of the Twelve Tables, which forbade the burial of gold in sepulchres,—"Neve aurum addito,"—unless the teeth of the corpse happened to be fastened with it. "Quoi auro dentes vincti escunt, ast im cum illo sepelire urerevc, se fraude esto." Cicero, de Leg. II. 24.

was obviously the sole object, for the tombs of the poor, though opened, are left untouched; while those of the rich have been despoiled of the precious metals, the vases have been thrown down, the sarcophagi and urns overturned, and everything left in confusion, as though no corner had been unransacked. In the middle ages, traditions of subterranean treasures were rife in this land, and sorcerers were applied to for their discovery,[3] but it does not appear that any systematic researches were carried forward, as in earlier times, and again in our own day.

In the consideration of these vases the question naturally arises—if they are mostly of foreign character, either oriental or Greek, how came they in Etruscan tombs? This is a question which has puzzled many a learned man of our age. At the first view of the matter, when the purely Hellenic nature of the design and subjects, and especially the inscriptions in the Greek language and character, are regarded, the natural response is that they must have been imported; a view which receives confirmation from the recorded fact of an extensive commerce in pottery in ancient times.[4] Yet when, on the other hand, we bear in mind the enormous quantities of these vases that have been found in the Etruscan soil, that these spoils of the dead which within the last fifty years alone have been reaped by the excavator, may be reckoned, not by thousands, but by myriads, and that what have hitherto been found on a few sites only, can bear but a very small proportion to the multitudes still entombed —when the peculiarities of style attaching to particular localities are considered, the pottery of each site having its distinguishing characteristics, so that an experienced eye is seldom at a loss to pronounce in what part of the ancient world any given vase was found—it must be admitted that there are strong grounds for regarding many of them as of local manufacture.[5] Antiquaries,

---

[3] Micali, Mon. Ined. p. 362.

[4] Plin. XXXV. 46.—Hæc per maria terrasque ultro citroque portantur, insignibus rotæ officinis. The pottery of Athens was carried by the Phœnician traders to the far western coast of Africa, and bartered for leopard-skins and elephant-teeth. See Grote's Greece, III. p. 364.

[5] There are, moreover, facts which confirm this view. The inscriptions, though in Greek characters, are not unfrequently utterly unintelligible such collocations of letters as are foreign to every dialect of Greek. Half a dozen consonants, for instance, occur in juxtaposition. Ann. Inst. 1831, pp. 72, 122, 171, et seq. This unknown tongue, which is frequently found on vases of the Archaic style, may, in some cases be Etruscan in Greek letters. Ann. Inst. 1831, p. 171. In the place of characters a row of dots is sometimes found, as though the copyist would not venture to imitate what he did not comprehend. Yet from the extensive commercial intercourse of Etruria with Greece and her colonies, many of the Etruscans must have known Greek. Sometimes a genuine inscription appears to have been incorrectly

however, are much divided in opinion on this point, some maintaining all these vases to be importations from Greece or her
colonies; others, to be of Etruscan manufacture, in imitation
of Greek; and others, again, endeavouring to reconcile conflicting facts by imagining an extensive population of Greeks
settled for ages in Etruria, or at least bodies of Hellenic artists,
like the masonic corporations of the middle ages.

But after all what are the speculations of most antiquaries
worth, where there are no historic records for guidance, and
few other palpable data from which to arrive at the truth—where,
in a word, the question resolves itself into one of artistic feeling,
as much as of archæological erudition?[a] Not to every man is it
given to penetrate the mysteries of art—to distinguish the copy
from the original in painting or sculpture. Long experience,
extensive knowledge, and highly-cultivated taste, are requisite
for the discernment of those minute, indefinite, indescribable,
but not less real and convincing differences between the original
and the imitation. So it is with the ceramographic art. When
men, who to vast antiquarian attainments add the experience
of many years, whose natural taste has led them to make
ancient art in general, and Greek vases in particular, their express
study—who have visited every collection in Europe, and have
had thousands of specimens year after year submitted to their
inspection and judgment—when such men as Gerhard, Braun,
and Brunn, renowned throughout Europe for their profound
knowledge of the archæology of art, give their opinion that
there is something about many of the vases of Etruria, something in form, design, or feeling, which stamps them as imitations of those of Greece, distinguishable, by them at least, from
the genuine pottery of Attica—we may be content to accept
their opinion, though unable personally to verify it. This view
does not preclude the supposition that most of the vases found
in Etruria are of Greek manufacture, either imported from

---

copied, the blunders being such as could
hardly have been made by Greeks. Many
of the vases also have Etruscan monograms
beneath the foot, scratched in the clay
apparently before it was baked. On the
vases of Nola such monograms are also
found, but in Oscan characters. Gerhard,
Ann. Inst. 1831, pp. 74, 177.

[b] "Des jugemens qui émanent du sentiment," observes a shrewd and learned

Frenchman, "peuvent difficilement se
réduire en règle, et, sous ce rapport,
beaucoup d'amateurs presque ignorans
l'emporteraient sur les plus célèbres anti-
quaires, parceque, pour l'antiquité figurée,
les livres et les plus vastes études suppléent
moins au goût, que le goût et l'intelligence
ne peuvent suppléer à l'érudition." Duc
de Luynes, Ann. Inst. 1832, p. 146.

Greece or her colonies, or made by Greek residents in the former land. Gerhard, indeed, divides these vases into three classes.

I. Those purely Greek in character.

II. Those also Greek, but modified as if by Greek residents in Etruria.

III. Those of Etruscan manufacture, in imitation of Greek.

It is clear that though the art of painted pottery originated in Greece, it was more highly developed in Etruria and other parts of Italy. For there is a much greater variety of form and style in the vases of these countries than in those of Greece, and the descriptions common to both lands are carried to a much larger size in Italy.[7]

It is worthy of remark that most of the painted vases of Etruria—all those of the Second and Third styles—have an Athenian character. The deities represented are chiefly Attic —Athené, Poseidon, Phœbos, Artemis, Hermes, Dionysos, and Demeter. The myths also are generally Attic; so are the public games, and the scenes taken from ordinary life. Even the inscriptions, with a few exceptions, are in Attic Greek,[8] and belong, says Gerhard, to a period of short duration, and which can be determined with precision, being confirmed by the forms of the vases, by the design, and the subjects represented. It was not prior to the 74th Olympiad (484 B.C.), nor later than the 124th (284 B.C.)—or between the third and fifth centuries of Rome, when the Greek colonies of Italy were in the height of their power, and before Etruria had lost her independence.[9] The Attic character of these vases is the more remarkable, for from the only record we have of Greek artists emigrating to Etruria—namely, with Demaratus, the Corinthian—we might

---

[7] Gerhard, Bull. Inst. 1832, p. 75; Ann. Inst. 1837, 2, p. 134, et seq.

[8] The inscriptions are for the most part designatory; the several figures having their appellations attached. The names of the potter and painter are also not unfrequently recorded; the former being united with ΕΠΟΙΕΙ or ΕΠΟΙΕΣΕΝ; the latter with ΕΓΡΑΦΣΕ. Other inscriptions refer to the possessor of the vase, and either mention his name with the addition of ΚΑΛΟΣ, or have merely the latter word alone, or ΗΟ ΠΑΙΣ ΚΑΛΟΣ, showing the vase to have been a gift to some "beautiful youth." When this inscription is repeated

in the feminine, it probably marks a nuptial present. Other salutatory expressions are sometimes found, such as ΧΑΙΡΕ ΣΥ "hail to thee !" or ΗΟΣΟΝΔΕΠΟΤΕΕΥΦΡΟΝ "happy as possible !" On the vases for domestic use we often find ΧΑΙΡΕΚΑΙΠΙΕΙ —"hail, and drink !" or sometimes ΠΙΕΙΜΕ "drink me !" as though the goblet itself were speaking. The inscriptions on the Panathenaic vases have already been mentioned. The places where the vases were made are never indicated, as on the red pottery of Arretium.

[9] Ann. Inst. 1831, pp. 99, et seq. 201 ; Bull. Inst. 1831, pp. 154–7.

have expected that Doric vases and Doric inscriptions would have prevailed, whereas the fact is that such vases are of comparatively rare occurrence, and that such inscriptions are still more rare, found only on archaic pottery of the Corinthian class.

There are certain vases not mentioned above, because of such rare occurrence as hardly to form a class, which are undoubtedly of Etruscan manufacture; as they bear both Etruscan subjects and Etruscan inscriptions.[1] I am enabled to offer to the notice of the reader a specimen of these vases more remarkable than any yet discovered. It is a *krater* with volute handles, in the late style, with a Bacchic dance on one side,[2] and on the other a striking scene of the parting of Admetus and Alcestis, whose names are attached, between the figures of Charun armed with his mallet, and of another demon brandishing serpents. I have given it, as a very rare and curious specimen of undoubted Etruscan ceramography, in its natural colours, as a frontispiece to the second volume of this work.[3]

With the vases I close my notices of Etruscan art.

[1] Very few of this class are known. One, an *amphora* of ancient style, having birds with human heads, bears the inscription in Etruscan letters "Kape Mukathesa." Another, a *stamnos* in the Third style, shows a Victory writing the Etruscan word "Lasna" in an open book. Two other *amphoræ* of late style have inscriptions in a mixture of Greek and Etruscan, and one bears the name "Aruns" in Etruscan on the handle. Two others are *krateres*—one with Actæon ("Aitaiun" in Etruscan characters), defending himself against his dogs; *rev.* Ajax ("Aivas") falling on his sword; the other showing Ajax slaying a Trojan captive, and "Charun" standing by, ready to seize his victim; *rev.* Charun amid a group of three women, one called "Pentasila" (Penthesilea), another designated "Hinthial Turmucas." Ann. Inst. 1831, pp. 73, 175; 1834, pp. 54—56; pp. 264—294; Mon. Ined. Inst. II. tav. 8, 9.

[2] See the woodcut at p. 437 of this volume.

[3] This *krater* was found at Vulci, and was formerly in the possession of Dr. Emil Braun of Rome, through whose kindness I was enabled to offer this illustration, reduced from a tracing of the original. The scene represents Admetus—"ATMITE"—

at his last hour, when a Thanatos, or winged messenger of Death is come to claim him, and threatens him with serpents. As it had been decreed by the Fates that if one of his nearest relatives would become his substitute his life would be spared, his wife Alcestis—"ALKSTI," in Etruscan—comes forward to devote herself in his room, and takes a farewell embrace, while a second demon, apparently Charun himself, stands behind her with his mallet raised, about to strike the fatal blow.

The inscription between the last two figures would run thus in Roman letters—"Eca. Ersce. Nac. Achrum. Phlerthrce." It has been considered by Dr. Braun (Bull. Inst. 1847) pp. 81—86) to imply that Eca (a proper name) dedicated this vase to Acheron. But if I may suggest another version, in a matter which must be principally conjecture, I would say that "Eca" can hardly be a proper name, for it is found frequently in connection with Suthi, as a formula on sepulchral monuments, and is probably equivalent to *hæc*, or *ecce*. "Ersce," in which Dr. Braun finds an analogy to ἔργον, I would interpret by one of the few Etruscan words whose meaning has come down to us from the ancients—*arse*, which Festus says meant *averte*.

Such is the people to whose Cities and Cemeteries I propose to conduct the reader. From what has been already stated, he will expect to find traces of no mean degree of culture, and should he test my descriptions with his own eyes, he will not be disappointed. The Etruscans were undoubtedly one of the most remarkable nations of antiquity—the great civilizers of Italy—and their influence not only extended over the whole of the ancient world, but has affected every subsequent age, and has not been without effect, however faint, on the civilization of the nineteenth century, and of regions they never knew.

When we consider the important part they played among the nations of old, it is astonishing that the records of them are so vague and meagre. They did not, it is true, like the Greeks and Romans, trumpet their own fame to posterity, or at least, if it cannot be said

—nulli nota poetæ
Illa fuit tellus, jacuit sine carmine sacro,

none of the works of their poets and historians have come down to us.[4] And thus, had it not been for their tombs, we should have known them only through the representations of the Greeks and Romans, which give us a most unfavourable impression of them. For the Greeks describe them as pirates and robbers,[5] or as effeminate debauchees;[6] the Romans brand them

---

"Nac" is a particle, to which we have no clue, and whose meaning must be learned from the rest of the sentence. "Achrum" is apparently Acheron. Whether "Phlerthree" be one word or two, its meaning is pretty obvious, for "Phlere," or "Phleres," occurs frequently on votive bronzes, and in connection with "Turce," and is generally admitted to be a dedicatory formula. The meaning of the whole, then, I take to be this—"Lo! she saves him from Acheron, and makes an offering of herself." Dr. Birch takes it for the speech of Charun, and translates it, "I bear thee to Acheron." Ancient Pottery, p. 461. For another interpretation see Bull. Inst. 1847, pp. 86—88; for Lord Crawford's, see Etruscan Inscriptions, p. 37; for Mr. Taylor's, see Etruscan Researches, p. 308.

[4] "Troy herself," says Philostratus, "would not have been, had not Homer lived. He was verily the founder of Ilium" (cited by Lanzi, Sagg. II. p. 174).

[5] Many of the passages containing this charge refer doubtless to the Tyrrhene-Pelasgi rather than to the Etruscans, properly so called, but as the former race formed an ingredient in the population of Etruria, it is difficult always to draw the distinction. Yet there is still evidence enough to convict the Etruscans of this practice. Strabo, V. pp. 219, 220; VI. p. 207; Diod. Sic. V. p. 292; XI. p. 66. The Romans also laid this charge distinctly to the Etruscans. Cicero, de Repub. II. 4; Serv. ad Æn. VIII. 479; X. 184. See Niebuhr, I. p. 127, et seq. Piracy, however, in those days, be it remembered, was an honourable profession—a legitimate field for glory. Thucyd. I. 5; Justin. XLIII. 3.

[6] For the charges of inordinate luxury see the statements of Timæus, Poseidonius, and Theopompus ap. Athen. IV. c. 38; XII. c. 14, cf. 17; Diod. Sic. V. p. 316; Dion. Hal. II. p. 105; IX. p. 575. Niebuhr (I. p. 141) rejects the statements of Theopompus on this head, not only on

as sluggards, gluttons, and voluptuaries.[7] Yet the former acknowledged their power at sea, their commercial enterprise, and their artistic skill; and the latter were forced to confess that to Etruria they owed most of their institutions and arts : neither, however, have paid that tribute to her civilization which we now learn to be due, and the Romans have not admitted their full amount of indebtedness to it—a fact which is seen in the silence or merely incidental acknowledgment of their historians and poets, who would willingly have referred all the refinement of Rome to a Hellenic source.

Though the ancients were reluctant to admit the full worth of Etruria, it may be questioned if Niebuhr is correct in asserting that she has received from the moderns more than her due share of attention and praise. How far we Transalpines of the nineteenth century are indebted to her civilization is a problem hardly to be solved; but indelible traces of her influence are apparent in Italy. That portion of the Peninsula where civilization earliest flourished, whence infant Rome drew her first lessons, has in subsequent ages maintained its pre-eminence. It was on the Etruscan soil that the seeds of culture, dormant through the long winter of barbarism, broke forth anew when a genial spring smiled on the human intellect : it was in Etruria that immortality was first bestowed on the lyre, the canvas, the marble, the literature, the science of modern Europe. Here arose

> " the all Etruscan three —
> Dante and Petrarch, and scarce less than they,
> The Bard of Prose, creative spirit ! he
> Of the Hundred Tales of love."

It was Etruria which produced Giotto, Brunelleschi, Fra Angelico, Luca Signorelli, Fra Bartolemeo, Michel Angelo,[8] Hilde-

account of his being unworthy of credit, but because "there are no licentious representations on any Etruscan works of art." Though the accounts of Theopompus may be exaggerated, as Müller (Etrusk. I. 3, 12) supposes, yet Niebuhr is greatly mistaken as to the purity of the Etruscans. For to say nothing of the painted vases, which are illustrative rather of Greek than Etruscan manners, and on which the most abominable indecencies are sometimes represented, there is evidence enough on works of undoubtedly Etruscan art, such as sepulchral paintings and bronze mirrors, to convict the Etruscans of being little or

no better than their neighbours in purity of life.

[7] Virg. Æn. XI. 732 —Semper inertes Tyrrheni ! . . . . .
At non in Venerem segues nocturnaque bella ;
Aut, ubi curva choros indixit tibia Bacchi, Expectare dapes, et plenæ pocula mensæ. Hic amor, hoc studium.
Cf. Georg. II. 193 ; Catul. XXXIX. 11.

[8] Raffaele also, if he does not belong strictly to Etruria Proper, was born not far from the frontiers, and in a region once possessed by the Etruscans. Besides he was educated in the Perugian school. If

brand, Macchiavelli, "the starry Galileo," and such a noble band of painters, sculptors, and architects, as no other country of modern Europe can boast. Certainly no other region of Italy has produced such a galaxy of brilliant intellects. I leave it to philosophers to determine if there be anything in the climate or natural features of the land to render it thus intellectually prolific. Much may be owing to the natural superiority of the race, which, in spite of the revolutions of ages, remains essentially the same, and preserves a distinctive character ;[9] just as many traits of the ancient Greek, Gaul, German, and Spaniard may be recognised in their modern descendants. The roots of bygone moral, as well as physical, culture, are not easily eradicated. The wild vine and olive mark many a desert tract to have been once subject to cultivation. And thus ancient civilization will long maintain its traces even in a neglected soil, and will often germinate afresh on experiencing congenial influences,—

> " The wheat three thousand years interred
> Will still its harvest bear."

How else comes it that while the Roman of to-day retains much of the rudeness of former times—while the Neapolitan in his craft and wiliness betrays his Greek origin, and the Sicilian the lawlessness of his African forefathers—the Tuscan is still the most lively in intellect and imagination, the most highly endowed with a taste for art and literature ? May it not also be to the deep-seated influences of early culture that he owes that superior polish and blandness of manner, which entitle Tuscany pre-eminently to the distinction claimed for it of being " a rare land of courtesy ? "

we were to claim as the sons of Etruria the natives of those lands beyond the Apennines and the Tiber which once belonged to her, there would be very few illustrious Italian names, either of ancient or modern times, which would be excluded from the category.

[9] Micali (Ant. Pop. Ital. I. p. 101 ; III. p. 11), maintained the analogy in physical and craniological development, between the ancient Etruscans and the modern inhabitants of Tuscany.

No. 1. ETRUSCAN OINOCHOË, OF BUCCHERO.

APPENDIX TO THE INTRODUCTION.

ON THE FORMS AND USES OF GREEK AND ETRUSCAN VASES.

The Vases found in Etruscan tombs are of various forms, and served
different purposes; therefore to enable the reader to understand the frequent
mention made of them under their technical names in the course of this
work, I propose to arrange them under their respective classes.

It must be borne in mind that the greater part of the figured vases found
in Etruria are not Etruscan, although often so designated, but are Greek,
whether imported from Greece and her colonies, or of local manufacture by
Hellenic colonists, is a question not yet satisfactorily determined. But the
subjects on the painted vases, the inscriptions they bear, and the art they
display, are so unmistakably Greek as to determine their origin beyond a
doubt, and to distinguish them markedly from the ware proper to Etruria.
Etruscan imitations of Greek vases are occasionally brought to light, but the
genuine pottery of Etruria is quite Oriental in character, without a trace of
Hellenic influence. It is never painted, but is decorated with simple
geometrical patterns, scratched or stamped on the clay, or with figures in
relief, as shown in the woodcut No. 1, at the head of this Appendix. It is of
brown or black ware, made with the hand and not with the lathe, sun-dried

and unglazed, of rude workmanship, and often of clumsy form, and its adornments betray none of the elegance and refinement which breathe more or less from all the works of the Greeks. Yet in form these Etruscan vases do not differ so widely from the Greek, that they cannot be classified with them, and I shall therefore apply to them the nomenclature of the latter, so far as it can be ascertained. The generic name by which this early Etruscan ware is now known is "*búcchero*," and by this term it will be mentioned in the following pages. The term applied by the Greeks to black sepulchral pottery was *Libyes*, or "niggers."

The names of these ancient vases have been ascertained, in a few instances, from monumental sources, being attached to pots of certain forms introduced into scenes on painted vases; as the word "*hydria*" is written over a water-jar, on the celebrated François vase at Florence (Vol. II., p. 114); but more generally we have only the descriptions given of vases by certain ancient authors, especially Athenæus, which descriptions being in many instances vague, ambiguous, or contradictory, are far from throwing a satisfactory light on the subject. It must be confessed that, even after the critical researches of Panofka, Gerhard, Letronne, Ussing, and Thiersch, into this subject, the nomenclature of many of the shapes of ancient vases is in great measure arbitrary or conventional. As to the forms of numerous vases mentioned by Athenæus we are still utterly in the dark. We are, however, able to recognise the characters of the most common shapes and to classify the vases according to the purposes they were intended to serve.

Of the illustrations here given of the forms of ancient vases I would observe, that having been taken from various sources, and drawn at different periods, they are on no uniform scale, so that a large vase will often appear from the woodcut to be smaller than another to which it is really very superior in size, e.g. Nos. 6 and 7. The woodcuts indicate, therefore, the form and character of the several descriptions of vases, not their relative size.

Many of these woodcuts will probably be familiar to my readers from having appeared in the two editions of Dr. Birch's work on "Ancient Pottery," but availing myself of my right to claim my own thunder, I must mention that they originally illustrated the first edition of this work, ten years before they did duty for Dr. Birch.

The following classification will, I think, comprise all the most common forms of Greek vases.

Class I. Vases for holding or storing liquids, fruits, &c.,—*pithos, amphora, pelike, stamnos, lekane.*

II. Vases for carrying water,—*hydria, kalpis.*

III. Vases for mixing or cooling wine,—*krater, kelebe, oxybaphon, lebes, psykter.*

IV. Vases for drawing and pouring out wine, &c.,—*oinochoë, olpe, prochoos, kyathos, situla.*

V. Vases for drinking,—*kantharos, karchesion, skyphos, mastos, depas, kyathos, kylix, lepaste, pella, holkion, keras, rhyton, phiale, kothon.*

VI. Vases for ointments or perfumes,—*lekythos, aryballos, bombylios, askos, kotyliskos, alabastos, pyxis.*

Class I.—VASES FOR HOLDING OR PRESERVING LIQUIDS AND FOOD.

The largest vase of this class was the *pithos,* or wine-jar, a tall jar with a full body and wide mouth, with a lid, and generally without handles. It served also to hold oil, fruit, and other solids, and resembled in size and shape the large oil-jars of Southern Europe. The visitor to Pompeii may remember in the street of Mercury three oil-shops, full of these large *pithoi*, of coarse red ware, several of them mended of old with rivets of lead. The *pithos* was used also as an urn to contain burnt human ashes, and in the early days of Etruria, was often decorated with bands of small Egyptian-like figures in relief, and was also ribbed. An illustration of this jar as a cinerary urn is given in the woodcut annexed, No. 2. It was sometimes used also to hold the corpse, for two such jars being placed mouth to mouth, served as a rude coffin, and thus arranged they are not unfrequently found in the tombs of the Troad. It was this form of vase which served as the habitation of Diogenes, for his " tub " is thus represented on ancient monuments, —hence the Greek proverb " the life of a *pithos*," to express a mean and miserable existence. It was a brazen vase of this form, in which Eurystheus, in his terror at the bristly monster of Erymanthus, which Hercules was bringing him on his shoulders, endeavoured to hide himself—a subject often depicted, and with infinite humour, on the early Attic vases.

No. 2. PITHOS, FROM VEII.

The *amphora*, called by the Greeks *amphoreus*, is a two-handled vase of various forms, but generally tall and full-bellied. This is the most common of all ancient vases, and is found in connection with every period and style of art. The more ordinary description was of coarse unglazed but very hard ware, with a long cylindrical body and long neck, and with two angular handles, on the shoulders of which was generally stamped the name of the magistrate for the year, with sometimes the month in addition, and the device of the town where the vase was made. The foot always tapered to a point for penetrating the earth, as the pot could not stand without support. *Amphoræ* of this form are rarely found with decorations.

Amphoræ, even when decorated with paintings, are occasionally found with a pointed base, of which a beautiful example is preserved in the Museum of Perugia. See woodcut, No. 3.

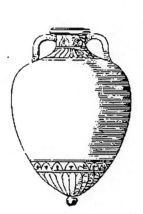

No. 3. AMPHORA WITH POINTED BASE.

No. 4. ETRUSCAN AMPHORA OF BUCCHERO.

In the early relieved ware of Chiusi, the *amphora* was of a quaint and peculiar form, of which the annexed woodcut (No. 4) is an illustration.

The *amphora* used in the earliest style of painted vases, is often, like the style itself, designated "Egyptian." It has plain handles, and the shoulders of the vase are rounded so as to meet the neck almost at right angles.

Amphoræ of the Second or Archaic Greek style, are commonly called "Tyrrhene." They have a fuller body and a thicker neck, and the greatest diameter of the vase is at about half its height. They are generally distinguished by squared handles, ornamented with floral decorations, and their shoulders, instead of meeting the neck abruptly, form with it a graceful curve. See woodcut No. 5. To this same period belongs the "Dionysiac" *amphora*, which differs generally from the former in having ribbed or reeded handles, and in having a taller and narrower neck; though it is chiefly distinguished by the Bacchic character of its subjects. Good examples of the Dionysiac *amphora* are given in the woodcut

No. 5. TYRRHENE AMPHORA. at p. 361 of this volume, which represents a scene in the "Tomb of the Painted Vases" at Corneto.

The "Panathenaic" *amphoræ*, or the vases given, filled with oil, as prizes at the palæstric games held at Athens in honour of the patron-goddess, are

No. 6. LATE PANATHENAIC AMPHORA.

No. 7. NOLAN AMPHORA.

also distinguished by their subjects rather than by their shape; the archaic vases, like the Burgon *amphora* in the British Museum, which is thought to be the earliest specimen of this class extant, being full-bellied, while those of later date are taller and more elegant, as in the woodcut No. 6, which is taken from one of six of these vases I found at Teucheira in the Cyrenaica, and which are now in the British Museum. All these vases have on one side a figure of Athene Promachos, with helmet, shield, and spear, in the attitude of attack, flanked by two Doric columns, generally surmounted by cocks, and usually bear the inscription—"Of the prizes from Athens." The reverse always shows one of the contests of the *pentathlon*, probably that for which the vase was awarded as a prize. Comparatively few of these vases have been discovered in Etruria. The Panathenaic vases have invariably black figures on a yellow ground, although the later ones, like that represented in the woodcut, being of the Macedonian period, are pseudo-archaic, or mere imitations of the earlier style.

The "Nolan" *amphora* is always of the Third style, with red figures, rarely more than one or two on each side, on the black ground of the vase. In shape it is slighter and more elegant than the forms already described; its handles are either reeded or twisted. Vases of this kind are found not only at Nola, but in Sicily, and also in Etruria, principally at Vulci. For elegance of form, surprising brilliancy of lustre, simplicity and purity of design, and beauty of execution, these Nolan *amphoræ* stand pre-eminent among the ceramic productions of antiquity. See woodcut No. 7.

To the same period and style belongs the *pelike*, a description of amphora shaped like a pear, with its greatest diameter near the base, and tapering upwards to the neck. It is of comparatively rare occurrence in Etruria, and almost always has red figures, though in Sicily it is sometimes found with black. See woodcut No. 8.

No. 8. PELIKE.

No. 9. STAMNOS.

Other varieties of the *amphora* are found, chiefly in Puglia and Basilicata, of much larger size, with taller and more slender forms, and handles elaborately moulded and decorated, in harmony with the more florid character of the paintings which adorn these vases. Numerous examples of them may be seen in the Museum at Naples, where they are designated according to the decorations of their handles, as *vaso a girelle, a rotelle, a mascheroni, a volute,* or, from some peculiarity of form, as *vaso a langella, a tromba.* This nomenclature, be it observed, is almost confined to Naples. It is not recognised in the higher parts of Italy, still less in the countries north of the Alps.

Connected with this same class, though by Gerhard referred to that of mixing-jars, is the *stamnos,* a very high-shouldered, short-necked, plethoric vase, with two small handles, not upright as in all the other varieties of the *amphora.* Vases of this form are generally found with red figures. They are still called by the same name in modern Greece. They were used to hold wine, oil, or fruit. See woodcut No. 9. The Apulian *stamnos* is a small and late variety of the same form, with tall upright handles and a lid, and is occasionally, though seldom, found in Etruria. It probably served to hold honey or sweetmeats. See woodcut No. 10.

The *lekane* was another vase for preserving food, and was somewhat of the form of a tureen or sugar-basin, having a full deep body, with a wide mouth, a lid, and two handles generally upright. The woodcut No. 11 shows an example. Vases of this form, when of large size, were used for washing the feet, as well as for other domestic but less cleanly purposes; and also for playing the Sicilian game of the *kottabos*.

No. 10. AMPULIAN STAMNOS.

Another form of the *lekane*, shown in the woodcut No. 12, is called by Panofka the *lopas*. It was probably this variety which was given full of sweets or savoury meats, as a nuptial present, and which the bride carried

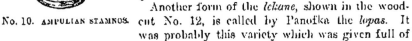

No. 11. LEKANE.   No. 12. LEKANE.

to the house of the bridegroom. The *lekanis* and *lekaniskos* were smaller varieties, and probably served for fruits or sweets at the table.

Class II.—VASES FOR CARRYING WATER.

The characteristic feature of water-jars is that they have three handles, two small horizontal ones at the shoulders, and one large vertical one at the neck. The generic term is *hydria*, but when used specifically, this name is applied to those of the earliest style which have a squareness about the shoulders, as shown in the woodcut No. 13, while a later and more elegant variety, with the shoulders rounded off, is generally called *kalpis*. See woodcut No. 14. But this distinction is conventional. The *hydria* is generally found in connection with the earlier styles, with black figures, the *kalpis* with red figures, though the latter is also occasionally found bearing archaic designs. Another point of difference is that the *hydria* has its principal subject on the body, and another with smaller figures on the shoulder; the designs on the *kalpis* are always confined to the body of the vase.

No. 13. HYDRIA.

The *hydria* is more commonly found in Etruria, the *kalpis* in the South of Italy. These water-jars were used by women alone, for whenever men are represented carrying water, it is invariably in an *amphora*. On certain early Attic vases, maidens are depicted on their way to and from the fountain. Each carries a *hydria* on her head, which when empty is lying on its side, just as the women of Central Italy carry their water-pots at the present day. But the *hydria*, when of bronze, was also used as a cinerary urn, and the *kalpis* was often given as a nuptial present to Athenian brides, filled with the water of the celebrated fountain of Callirrhoë. It was also used for perfumes, probably when too small to serve any other purpose, for vases of all forms are frequently found in miniature in Greek and Etruscan tombs, which can have been mere toys, or have served only for the toilet.

No. 14. KALPIS.

Class III.—MIXING-JARS.

These are characterised by their wide mouths, for the convenience of dipping the cups or ladles ; for the wine having been brought in the *amphora* to the banquet, was there poured into the *krater*, mixed with water, and handed round to the guests. *Krater* is the generic term, its name being expressive of its use ; but it is applied specifically to the elegant form shown in the woodcut No. 15, which is

No. 15. KRATER.

No. 16. LATE KRATER, ORVIETO.

confined to the third style of vase-painting. In Naples it is known as a "*vaso a campana.*" A late but elegant variety of the *krater* is shown in the woodcut No. 16. The more archaic style is generally connected in Etruria with the *kelebe*, which is known by its peculiar pillared handles, although the earlier vases of this form have often curved handles, as in the woodcut No. 17. Vases of this shape are more commonly found in Sicily and Southern Italy than in Etruria, and are there termed "*vasi a colonette*." They were frequently used as cinerary urns.

No. 17. KELEBE.

The vase represented in the woodcut No. 18, is sometimes called an *amphora* with volute handles, but considering the width of the mouth it should more properly be classed among the *krateres*. In this instance, it is an Etruscan imitation of a Greek vase. See Vol. I., p. 463. This form is not usual in Etruria, though common enough in Magna Graecia, where it

No. 18. ETRUSCAN KRATER.

No. 19. LATE KRATER, PERUGIA.

would be designated as "*vaso a volute.*" It is exemplified, however, in the François vase, the monarch of Attic vases, found at Chiusi, and now in the Museo Etrusco at Florence. See Vol. II., pp. 81, 113. A late but highly decorated variety of this form from Perugia is shown in the annexed woodcut, No. 19, which at Naples would be called a "*vaso a muscheroni.*"

The *oxybaphon* is another mixing-jar, of bell-shape (see woodcut No. 20), not of frequent occurrence in Etruria, though common in Magna Graecia and

No. 20. OXYBAPHON.

Sicily. By some the name has been supposed to mark it as a vinegar-cup —being derived from ὀξύς and βάπτω; but as its form and size establish an analogy to the *krater*, the "sharpness" in its etymology must refer rather to time than to taste, and its name must be significant of "dipping quickly." It is found only in connection with the later styles.

Another vase of this class was the *lebes*, a large vessel of caldron-shape, erroneously confounded with the *holmos*, or mortar. This form of vase is of very early date, and is frequently mentioned by Homer (*e.g.* Il. XXIII. 259) as awarded for a prize in the public games. It was often of metal, and stood on three feet; but it was also of earthenware, a very primitive specimen of which, from Athens, is given in the woodcut No. 21, with three horses on

No. 21. PRIMITIVE GREEK LEBES.   No. 22. ARCHAIC LEBES.

the lid, and the mysterious *suastika* among its adornments. A later, but still very archaic example from Athens, of large size, with a foot, and two handles, is in the British Museum, showing two large lions, facing each other, and each holding a paw over a flower; the ground of the vase being studded with rude geometrical patterns instead of flowers, among which the *suastika* is also prominent. An illustration of this singular vase is given at p. xci., of the Introduction. The bottom of the *lebes* is sometimes pointed or rounded to fit into a stand, like a huge cup and ball, as in the vase illustrated in the woodcut No. 22, which though of the archaic Doric period, is of later date than the preceding examples.

The *holmos*, or mortar, with which the *lebes* has often been confounded, was in the shape of a horn probably truncated, and about a cubit in height. Menesthenes, ap. Athen. XI. 86. It had straight sides, like many mortars at the present day.

In this class must be included the *psykter*, or wine-cooler, which was a large vase resembling a *krater* in form, but containing an inner pot for the wine, and a mouth or spout in its neck for the introduction of snow between the inner and outer walls of the vase, and an orifice in the foot to let

the water off. The purpose of this vase is obvious, and is indeed implied in
its name; although the description of it given by Athenæus (XI. 108) is
applicable rather to a large goblet, from which Plato, in his Symposium,
represents Socrates quaffing liberal potations all night long. It is a form of
very rare occurrence, and generally found with black figures. There is an
example in the British Museum of amphora-like form, having a Bacchic subject on one side, and Theseus slaying the Minotaur on the other. Another
psykter exists in the Etruscan Museum of Florence, where the form is that
of a *krater*, and the figures are yellow on a black ground. See Vol. II., p. 83.

Class IV.—Vases for drawing and pouring out Liquids.

The ewer or jug, of whatever form, in which the wine was transferred from
the *krater* to the goblets of the guests, was generically called *oinochoë*, but
this term is applied specifically, though conventionally, to a jug with a trefoil
spout, while that with a round even mouth without a spout is
called an *olpe*, or *olpis*, a term strictly applicable to the leathern
bottle or flask, containing the oil with which the athletes
anointed themselves in the *palæstra*. The ordinary form of
the *olpe* is shown in the woodcut No. 23. An earlier variety
from Chiusi, with a cock-crowned lid, illustrated in the woodcut No. 24, is of *bucchero*, the early black ware of Etruria. The
next cut shows another variety from Orvieto, with ribbed body,
ivy foliage painted on the neck, and handle decorated with a

No. 23. OLPE.

No. 25. OLPE, FROM
ORVIETO.

No. 24. ETRUSCAN OLPE.   No. 26. OINOCHOË.   No. 27. OINOCHOË, DORIC STYLE.

head in relief, No. 25. This vase is of late date, but the *olpe* form is generally associated with the most archaic styles of vase-painting, an example of
which is given in the woodcut, No. 80, at the end of this Appendix.

The ordinary form of *oinochoë* is seen in the woodcut. No. 26. Varieties in the early black relieved ware of Etruria are shown in woodcut No. 1, and at p. 318, Vol. II. Of the archaic Doric or Corinthian style an example is given in woodcut No. 27, which shows quaint animals and flowers in brown and purple on a pale yellow ground. A more elegant variety is exhibited in the Nolan jug, No. 28; a still later and beautiful variety in the ribbed vase, with ivy foliage and ribbons painted on its neck, No. 29; a charming though fantastic specimen at page 464 of this volume; and examples in bronze in woodcuts Nos. 30, 31.

No. 28. OINOCHOË, FROM NOLA.

No. 29. LATE OINOCHOË, SICILY.

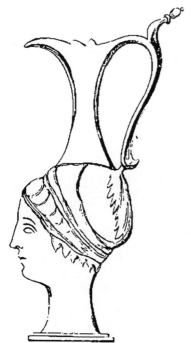

No. 30. BRONZE OINOCHOË.

No. 31. OINOCHOË OF BRONZE.

The *prochoos* is but a smaller variety of the *oinochoë*, being used for the same purpose, or as a jug from which water was poured on the hands of guests. It is generally supposed to have the form of the woodcut, No. 32. A variety of it, with a long spout, was termed *prochoos makrostomos*, of which an example is seen in the woodcut, No. 33, although Dr. Birch prefers to designate that form *epichysis*. These long beaked pots seem adapted to the pouring out of oil at the palæstric exercises.

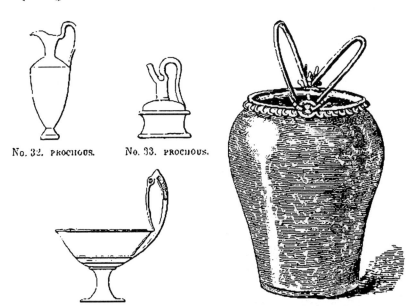

No. 32. PROCHOUS.   No. 33. PROCHOUS.

No. 34. KYATHOS.   No. 35. SITULA OF BRONZE.

The terms *oinochoë*, *olpe*, and *prochoos* are of generic application, and as we have but doubtful authority for attaching them to any specific shape of ewer, the above distinction may be regarded as conventional, and as adopted for the sake of convenience.

The *kyathos*, though generally classed among the goblets, was also used as a ladle for drawing the wine from the mixing-jar. See woodcut, No. 34.

The *situla*, or pail, for drawing water, was almost always of metal, and was so similar to the bucket of modern times, as hardly to require a description. An example of a bronze *situla* in the Etruscan Museum at Florence is given in woodcut No. 35. This form is sometimes rounded at the bottom, and, in archaic examples, is decorated externally with incised or relieved figures, as in two other *situlæ* in the said Museum (Vol. II. p. 104), and in another beautiful specimen in that of Bologna (Vol. II. p. 523).

Class V.—Cups and Goblets.

The drinking cups of the ancients were of various forms; indeed the Athenians alone are said to have had no less than 72 different descriptions of goblets. The most common forms, especially in Etruria, were the *kantharos* and the *skyphos*. The *kantharos* was a two-handled cup, sacred to Dionysus (Plin. XXXIII. 53; Macrob. Sat. V. 21) in whose hands it is generally represented on painted vases. The cup itself is rarely found decorated with paintings, at least in Etruria, where it is generally of plain black ware. This vase is supposed to take its name from some resemblance in form to that of the beetle—κάνθαρος—but it more probably took it from the boat or vessel of the same name (Athen. XI. 47, 48), though it is also said to have been called from the potter who invented it (Philetærus, ap. Athen. loc. cit.). The usual form is shown in the woodcut No. 36; a late variety with handles differently arranged, in the woodcut No. 37.

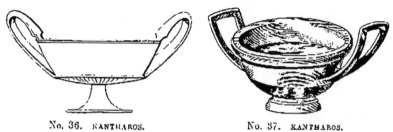

No. 36. KANTHAROS.　　　　No. 37. KANTHAROS.

The *Karchesion*, which was also a Bacchic cup, "cape Mæonii carchesia Bacchi" (Virg. Georg. IV. 380) appears to have resembled the *Kantharos*, but to have been larger, heavier, slightly compressed in the middle, and with long "ears" or handles reaching to the bottom. It is a form very rarely met with. Macrobius (V. 21) tells us it was extremely rare among the Greeks, and never found among the Latins. Athenæus says it is an extremely old form of vase. It was traditional that Jupiter gave a golden vase of this shape to Alcmena, as a love-token, which cup was supposed to have been preserved at Sparta (Athen. XI. 49). The form is found in the early black ware of Chiusi, and the finest specimen I have seen is in that

No. 38. KARCHESION, OF BUCCHERO.　　　No. 39. KARCHESION, OF BUCCHERO.

ware and in the possession of Signor Luigi Terrosi of Cetona. It is represented in the woodcut, No. 38. A still more quaint example with a lid, and relieved decorations, is given in the accompanying illustration of a vase from Chiusi, taken from the work of M. Noël Des Vergers: see woodcut No. 39.

A very common cup among the ancients was the *skyphos*, which seems to have been a generic name, but the term is applied, conventionally, to a full-bellied bowl with two horizontal handles. It was the cup of the peasantry, and was originally of wood and served for milk or whey, but afterwards was made of terra-cotta or silver. The name is derived from σκαφίς, a little boat (Anglicè, skiff, and ship). The *skyphos* was the cup of Hercules, as the *kantharos* was that of Dionysos (Macrob. V. 21). The usual form is shown in the woodcut No. 40, a shape which Panofka calls the *kotylos*, and Dr. Birch takes to be also that of the *kothon*, or cup of the Spartan soldiers. A later and more elegant example is given in a cup in my own possession, No. 41, with painted decorations; the incurved handles indicating an imita-

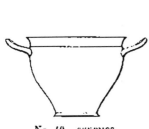

No. 40. SKYPHOS.   No. 41. SKYPHOS.

tion of metal. Vases of this description have sometimes a pointed bottom, so that to be laid down they must be emptied. A variety of this goblet, from its resemblance to a woman's breast, was called a *mastos*, a name given to it by the Paphians (Apollod. Cyren. ap. Athen. XI. 74). It was generally decorated with Bacchic figures, as in the woodcut No. 42; and was sometimes shaped like a head crowned with ivy, as in the cut No. 43. Both these examples are from Vulci.

No. 42. MASTOS.   No. 43. MASTOS.

The *kothon* was another form of cup carried by the Spartan soldiers on their expeditions, on account of its convenient form. For the brim being curved inwards the cup retained whatever sediment there might be in the water, while the pure fluid alone was imbibed. It is described as a circular, short-eared, and thick-mouthed cup, having a single handle, and being of striped colours (Athen. XI. 66, 67). Birch appears to confound it with the *skyphos*, and attaches the name of *kothon* to the form illustrated in woodcut No. 40. But there can be no doubt that the name applies to a flat, thick, and round-lipped bowl, with a single short handle, apparently for suspension, of which I possess several specimens, five and a half inches in diameter, and two inches high, all marked with black and red stripes on the hard yellow clay.

The *depas*, or *aleison*, was a cup with two ears or handles (Asclepiades ap. Athen. XI. 24, who quotes Homer, Od. XXII. 9). But the term *depas* appears to be generic, and to be often used, without any specific application, like the word *poterion*, yet as the name was applied to the cup of the Sun, in which Hercules crossed the sea to Erytheia (Athen. XI. 38, 39), it was probably proper to cups of a bowl-shape. I am inclined to believe, with Panofka, that when used specifically the term is applicable to the form given in the annexed woodcut, No. 44, which is copied from a vase in my possession.

No. 44. DEPAS.

The form of the Homeric δέπας ἀμφικύπελλον has given rise to much difference of opinion. Aristotle (Hist. Anim. IX. 40) uses the term to illustrate the forms of bees' cells, with a common base. There can be no doubt that he referred to certain cylindrical vases, like dice-boxes, with a bottom half-way up, so as to form a double cup, examples of which have been recently found in the cemeteries of Bologna, and which answer to the description of the *dactylotos* given by Philemon, ap. Athen. XI. 34. But the Homeric vase had two handles, and this has none. Dr. Schliemann thought he had found the δέπας of Homer in tall, straight-sided cups, "like champagne glasses with enormous handles," which he unearthed at Hissarlik (Troy, pp. 86, 158, 171); but that form is evidently the *holmos* described by Athenæus, XI. 86. The golden cup the Doctor found among "Priam's Treasure" (p. 326), of boat-shape, with a handle on either side, to enable it to be passed easily from hand to hand, has a far better claim to be the Homeric δέπας. So also the golden cups he disinterred at Mycenæ (see the illustrations at pages 231, 234, of his "Mycenæ"), are undoubted instances of this celebrated form. But we learn from Athenæus (XI. 24, 65) that opinions differed as widely as to the form of this vase among the ancient Greeks as among modern archæologists.

Another elegant form of vase, which is a *krater* in miniature, is the *krateriskos* or *krateridion*, which from its small size must be classed among the cups. The woodcut, No. 45, is from a vase in my collection.

No. 45. KRATERISKOS.

The *kyathos* was a cup with a single handle, and like the *kantharos*, is often represented in the hands of Dionysos on the painted vases. Unlike the *kantharos*, however, it is frequently found in painted pottery, an instance of which is given in the woodcut, No. 46. The *kyathos*, though used as a cup, also served as a ladle to draw wine from the *krater* (Plato, ap. Athen. X. 23), as already mentioned. The *kyathos* was also a measure, equal to $\frac{33}{40}$ of a pint. In the Etruscan black ware this form is not uncommon, and is shown in the cut, No. 47, which represents an early vase in the relieved ware of Chiusi.

No. 47.   KYATHOS, IN BUCCHERO.

No. 46.   KYATHOS.

No. 48.   EARLY KYLIX.

Very like the *kyathos* was the *kotylos* or *kotyle*, a small deep cup with one handle, said to be the most beautiful of all cups, and also the most convenient to drink from. Its precise shape has not been ascertained. It must have been in very common use, for there was an old Greek proverb, quoted by Athenæus (XI. 57), which said,—

> "There is many a slip
> Between cotylo and lip."

No. 49.   EARLY KYLIX.

The *kylix*, the most elegant of all ancient goblets, is a wide flat bowl on a slender stem. The most primitive form resembled a rude bowl of wood on a clumsy stand, and was decorated with meanders, and other geometrical patterns ; an example of it is given in the woodcut at page lxxxix of the Introduction. The earliest form with black figures on the yellow ground of the clay is shown in the woodcuts, Nos. 48 and 49. The later *kylix* sank to the form shown, woodcut No. 50; and still later, those with yellow figures assumed the more elegant shape given in the woodcuts Nos. 51, 52. These

No. 50.   KYLIX, FROM VULCI.

vases were generally painted inside as well as out; but in the earlier and more compact variety, shown in the woodcut, No. 48, the paintings are often

No. 51.   KYLIX.   No. 52.   KYLIX.

confined to the interior of the bowl. A late variety of the *kylix* is without a stem, and has only a moulded base. This form is supposed to be the *lepaste*, and to have borrowed its name from its resemblance to the limpet. —λεπάς—see the woodcut, No. 53. It is not of frequent occurrence in Etruria.

The *pella* or *pellis*, was another sort of cup, with a wide bottom, shaped somewhat like a pail, and originally used for milking cows and ewes (Athen. XI. 91). It is shown in the woodcut, No. 54.

No. 53.   LEPASTE.   No. 54.   PELLA.   No. 55.   HOLKION.

The term *holkion* is often applied to a cup-shaped vase on a tall stem, but without handles, as in the woodcut, No. 55. Birch assigns the name of *holmos* to a vase of this form, though elsewhere his description of the *holmos* accords with that of the *lebes* given at p. cxiii, No. 22. The *holkion* is a form very common in the Etruscan archaic black ware, and is often adorned with figures in relief, either in bands as in the woodcut, No. 56, or studding the edges, or stem of the vase, as in No. 57.

No. 56.   HOLKION, OF BUCCHERO.

No. 57.   HOLKION, OF BUCCHERO.

Another class of cups is that made in imitation of the head or body of some animal. The earliest form was the *keras*, which was originally the horn of an ox, adapted as a drinking-cup. The form is often represented on ancient vases, but rarely found in terra cotta. It was succeeded by the *rhyton*, a fantastic goblet, terminating sometimes in the human head, but more frequently in the head of some animal. It is particularly described at p. 91 of Vol. II. The *rhyton* is said by Athenaeus (XI. 97) to have been invented by Ptolemy Philadelphus scarcely three centuries before Christ, yet he also mentions that the word was used by Demosthenes. Theophrastus says the *rhyton* was given to heroes alone (cf. Athen. XI. 4). It was certainly of late date, for it is never found in connection with the earlier styles of vase-painting. Varieties of the *rhyton* are given in the

No. 58.   RHYTON.

No. 59.   RHYTON.

No. 60.   RHYTON.

woodcuts, Nos. 58, 59, 60. The last form was most common among the Etruscans; and even women are sometimes represented in effigy reclining at the banquet, with the horse-*rhyton* in their hand.

The cup, however, most frequently placed in the hands of the recumbent figures on Etruscan sarcophagi and cinerary urns is the *phiale*, or flat saucer-like bowl, without a stand; like the *patera* of the Romans. Instead of a handle, it has often a prominent boss in the centre, as in a shield, into whose cavity two fingers of the hand were introduced from beneath, to keep it steady. This form was designated *phiale omphalotos*, or *mesomphalos*, from the boss in the centre, and sometimes *akatos*, from its resemblance to a boat. The woodcut, No. 61, shows a bowl of this description with a hollow boss in the centre, surrounded by a race of four quadrigæ in relief. Such bowls are to be seen in the British Museum as well as in the Etruscan Museum at Florence.

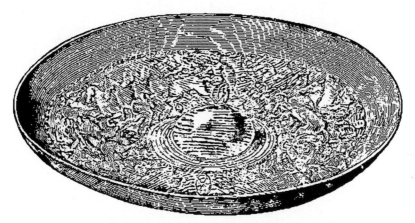

No. 61. PHIALE OMPHALOTOS, WITH RELIEVED DECORATIONS.

Class VI.—Ointment and Perfume Vases.

The principal vase of this class is the *lekythos*, or oil-flask, the form of which is well ascertained. In the earlier *lekythoi* with black figures, the body is full, largest at the shoulder, and tapering gradually to the base; the neck is short and joins the shoulder with a graceful curve. In the later style with yellow figures, the body is nearly cylindrical, the neck longer, and the shoulders flatter, the general form being much improved in elegance. See woodcut, No. 62.

The *lekythos* is much more abundant in the tombs of Greece, Magna Græcia, and Sicily, than in those of Etruria. In Greek tombs it was always laid by the side of the corpse, or on its breast, or placed in the corners of the sepulchre. In Sicily it is often found of large size. The largest *lekythos* in the British Museum is one I disinterred in the necropolis of the ancient Gela in that island. An illustration of it is given in the woodcut, No. 63. The figures in this instance are painted with various colours on a white ground; a

No. 62. LEKYTHOS.

No. 63. LEKYTHOS.

description of decoration very rare in Etruria, but common in Sicily as well as at Athens, which has yielded very beautiful *lekythoi* with polychromatic designs, generally of a later date than those of Sicily.

The *lekythos* of a later period was of smaller size, but of superior elegance, with an egg-shaped body on a broad base, with a still more slender neck, and a bell-shaped mouth. This form is shown in the woodcut, No. 64, and is sometimes called an *aryballos*. A more depressed form is given in the

No. 64. LEKYTHOS.   No. 65. LEKYTHOS.   No. 66. ARCHAIC LEKYTHOS.

woodcut, No. 65. Both these forms are more abundant in Magna Græcia than in Etruria. A very early variety, found only in connection with the

No. 67.   LATE LEKYTHOS.

most archaic designs on a pale yellow clay, is that like a truncated jug, No. 66. The latest variety, on the other hand, is also of white clay with polychrome designs of flowers, vases, and instruments, and is illustrated in the woodcut, No. 67, representing one from my excavations in the Cyrenaica, now in the British Museum.

The last four shapes are often denominated *aryballos*, a name given to such vases as resembled a purse, in being wide at the bottom and contracted at the top, like a purse drawn together, as Athenæus tells us, though he adds that some give the name to purses from their resemblance to vases of this form.

The earliest form of the *aryballos* was that in the cut, No. 68, but often without a base, as in No. 69, and as in the Doric vase of this form illus-

No. 68.   No. 69.   No. 70.   No. 71.
ARCHAIC ARYBALLOS.   ARYBALLOS.   EARLY ARYBALLOS.   ARYBALLOS.

trated at p. xc of the Introduction. Such forms are found only with the most archaic designs, of birds, beasts, or chimæras. A very early and quaint variety is shown in the woodcut, No. 70. A later form is given in the cut, No. 71. Like the *lekythos*, the *aryballos* was used for unguents, and was often carried on the person by a strap or string, for anointing the body after the bath.

Akin to these, and applied to the same purposes, was the *bombylios*, a narrow-necked pot, which received its name from the gurgling sound caused by the flow of the liquid from it. See the woodcut, No. 72. A quaint variety is shown in the cut, No. 73.

The *askos* is so called from its resemblance to the goat-skin, still so generally used in the South of Europe for the transport of wine and oil.

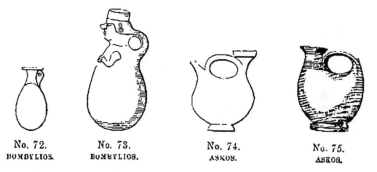

No. 72.
BOMBYLIOS.

No. 73.
BOMBYLIOS.

No. 74.
ASKOS.

No. 75.
ASKOS.

The annexed cuts show two varieties of this form, Nos. 74, 75. Pots of these forms, and of large size, are still common in Spain and Portugal, where they are used for water. By the ancients they seem to have been employed for the toilet alone.

The *kotyliskos* is a small pot with a single handle, in other respects like an *amphora* in miniature. See the woodcut, No. 76. It was used for unguents or perfumes.

The *alabastos*, or *alabastron*, is a name applied to those forms of ointment-vases, which have no feet; and to such as are in the shape of animals — hares, monkeys, ducks — or of heads and limbs of the human body. The most ordinary form of this pot is shown in the woodcut, No. 77. *Alabastoi* are often of oriental alabaster, but are also found of terra-cotta with a white or cream-coloured ground and black figures. The woodcut, No. 78, shows an *alabastos* of stone from Chiusi, carved into female faces above, and having a hole in the crown for pouring out the ointment or perfume. Another example of an *alabastron* in the shape of a figure of Isis is given in the cut, Vol. I., p. 458. Vases of this form were also used to hold ink or paint, for on Etruscan mirrors, a Lasa or Fate is not unfrequently represented with an *alabastos* in her left hand, and a *stylus* in her right.

Among the vases which served the purposes of the toilet, was the *pyxis* or casket, in which the ladies deposited their jewellery. It was originally, as its name implies, made of box-wood, but was sometimes of metal, or of ivory, and

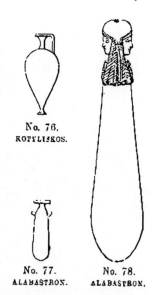

No. 76.
KOTYLISKOS.

No. 77.
ALABASTRON.

No. 78.
ALABASTRON.

also of terra-cotta, as in the woodcut, No. 79, and was then frequently decorated with beautiful paintings in the best style of ceramic art. Several exquisite specimens, one of them adorned with polychrome figures, from the tombs of Athens, are preserved in the British Museum.

No. 79. PYXIS.

In the nomenclature of these vases I have in most instances followed Gerhard, as his system is now generally adopted by antiquaries in Germany and Italy.

No. 80. GROUP OF ARCHAIC DORIC VASES.

LEKYTHOS—OLPE—ARYBALLOS—LEKANE—KYATHOS.

Appendix No. II.

ON AN ANCIENT CITY RECENTLY DISCOVERED IN THE TUSCAN MAREMMA.

I have just been informed by my friend, Mr. R. P. Pullan, of the existence of very extensive ruins on a height called Monte Leone, a few miles to the east of Monte Pescali, in the Maremma, north of Grosseto. He had heard of a great wall on this spot from Conte Bossi of Florence, who every winter visits this district for purposes of sport, and under the guidance of that gentleman he explored the site in May, 1877. He has already given some notice of his discovery in the "Academy" of 7th July last, but he has favoured me with further particulars to the following effect.

Monte Leone lies about two hours' ride to the east of the town of Monte Pescali, on the same range of heights which form the southern boundary to the valley of the Bruna, and at the distance of about six miles from Colonna di Buriano. For the first hour the way lies through the valley, then it turns to the right, and ascends an oak-covered hill which rises between Monte Pescali and Monte Leone. After an ascent of about an hour, lines of old wall come into view at intervals, peeping through the brushwood on the opposite side of the ravine to the east, and at a considerable height up the hill-side ; but to reach these remains it is necessary to make a *détour* by way of Batignano, and thence northward to Monte Leone. This height is covered with brushwood, thick and tangled, chiefly a sort of tall heather, through which it is difficult to force one's way. The wall is very extensive, inclosing all the upper part of the hill, and Mr. Pullan calculates that it may be at least ten miles in circuit. Owing to the density of the brushwood it is accessible only in parts. The first portion he reached disappointed him, as it was a mere heap of rough stones, piled together without any arrangement. In other parts, the construction appeared more systematic, but the masses of stone were still rough and unhewn, mere boulders, piled up to the height of seven or eight feet, without cement or jointing of any kind. The wall, which he found on measurement to be fully twenty feet in thickness, was composed of three parts,—an outer and inner facing, constructed of larger masses about three feet six inches long, and an intervening space filled with smaller stones or mere rubble. All the stones were alike undressed ; he looked in vain for any traces of tooling on them. At one end of the inclosure, on a northern spur of the height, he observed a semicircular work, about a quarter of a mile in diameter, with an outer wall of similar construction, some twenty or thirty feet in advance of it. He could perceive no traces of gateways, and no remains of buildings within the inclosure.

These facts, as well as the very rude style of construction, led him at first to take these walls for the *enceinte* of a camp, and he remembered that the Cisalpine Gauls, before their defeat by the Romans at Telamon, 225 B.C., were encamped somewhere in this neighbourhood. But the great extent of the inclosure, and the unusual thickness of its wall, seemed to preclude that idea. The former appeared even too spacious for an ancient city, and the construction of the latter was so unlike that of any Etruscan wall he had ever seen, being neither of the true Cyclopean style described by Pausanias—like certain ancient walls in Central Italy, those of Civitella, Olevano, and Monte Fortino, for instance—nor like any of the varieties of Etruscan masonry which approach more or less to regularity in the arrangement of the blocks, that he was naturally led to entertain doubts of its Etruscan antiquity. He was rather inclined to regard these as the ruins mentioned by Leandro Alberti, under the name of Vetulia or Vetulonia, which that old writer describes as those of a city surrounded by walls of large uncemented blocks, situated in a dense wood, and embracing a great extent of country ; and he was the more inclined to this view from the consideration that Alberti, having never seen those remains, but describing them at second-hand, may have been mistaken as to their exact position, which he places much further to the north, near Populonia. It is not easy, however, to believe that this ancient site discovered by Mr. Pullan is identical with that described by Leandro Alberti. A reference to his description, given at p. 206 of vol. ii., will show wide discrepancies, especially as regards situation. The ancient remains which Alberti took for those of Vetulonia, he places between the Torre di San Vincenzo and the headland of Populonia, three miles from the sea, five from the iron mines, and north of the Cornia—that is, in the near neighbourhood of Campiglia. But this newly found site is more than thirty miles distant from that town as the crow flies ; and there can be no doubt that the manuscript to which Alberti was indebted for his description, placed the supposed Vetulonia in the position indicated by him, for it was verified by Inghirami. The real question appears to be, whether the detailed description of Zacchio was, the mere creation of that writer's imagination, as Inghirami supposed, or whether the ruins, if they actually had an existence and were extant in Zacchio's day, have not, during the last four centuries, totally disappeared under the pilferings of the peasantry.

As attention has now been directed to this extensive inclosure discovered by Mr. Pullan, its character and antiquity cannot long remain a mystery.

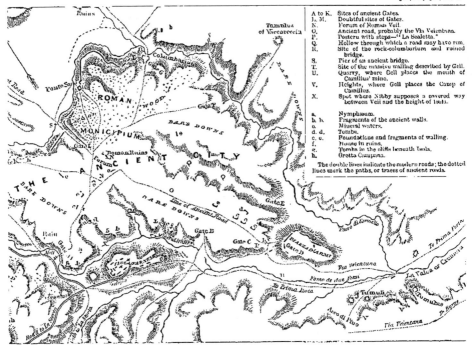

MAP OF VEII.

ADAPTED FROM GELL,

THE CITIES AND CEMETERIES

OF

ETRURIA.

CHAPTER I.

VEII.—THE CITY.

Hoc tunc Veii fuêre: quæ reliquiæ? quod vestigium?—FLORUS.

Sic magna fuit censuque virisque
Perque decem potuit tantum dare sanguinis annos ;
Nunc humilis veteres tantummodo Troja ruinas,
Et pro divitiis tumulos ostendit avorum. —OVID. Met.

OF all the cities of Etruria, none takes so prominent a place in history as Veii. One of the earliest, nearest, and unquestionably the most formidable of the foes of Rome—for nearly four centuries her rival in military power, her instructress in civilisation and the arts—the southern bulwark of Etruria—the richest city of that land—the Troy of Italy—Veii excites our interest as much by the length of the struggle she maintained, and by the romantic legends attending her overthrow, as by the intimate connection of her history with Rome's earliest and most spirit-stirring days. Such was her greatness—such her magnificence —that, even after her conquest, Veii disputed with the city of Romulus for metropolitan honours; and, but for the eloquence of Camillus, would have arisen as Roma Nova to be mistress of the world.[1] Yet, in the time of Augustus, we are told that the city was a desolation,[2] and a century later its very site is said to have been forgotten.[3] Though re-colonised under the Empire, it soon again fell into utter decay, and for ages Veii was blotted from the map of Italy. But when, on the revival of letters, attention was directed to the subject of Italian antiquities, its site became a point of dispute. Fiano, Ponzano, Martignano, and other places, found their respective advocates. Some, with

---

[1] Liv. V. 51—55. [2] Propert. IV. Eleg. x. 29. [3] Florus, I. 12.

Castiglioni, placed it at Civita Castellana; others, with Cluverius, at Scrofano, near Monte Musino; Zanchi at Monte Lupolo, above Baccano; while Holstenius, Nardini, and Fabretti assigned to it the site which more recent researches have determined beyond a doubt to belong to it. This is in the neighbourhood of Isola Farnese, a hamlet, about eleven miles from Rome, on the right of the Via Cassia, which agrees with the distance assigned to Veii by Dionysius and the Peutingerian Table.

The ancient road from Rome seems to have left the Via Cassia about the fifth milestone, not far from the sepulchre vulgarly, but erroneously, called that of Nero; and to have pursued a serpentine course to Veii. Instead of pursuing that ancient track, now distinguishable only by the sepulchres and tumuli at its side, travellers usually push on to La Storta, the first post-house from Rome, and beyond the ninth milestone on the Via Cassia. Hence it is a mile and a half to Isola by the carriage road; but the visitor, on horse or foot, may save half a mile by taking a pathway across the downs. When Isola Farnese comes into sight, let him halt awhile to admire the scene. A wide sweep of the Campagna lies before him, in this part broken into ravines or narrow glens, which, by varying the lines of the land-scape, redeem it from the monotony of a plain, and by patches of wood relieve it of its usual nakedness and sterility. On a steep cliff, about a mile distant, stands the hamlet of Isola—consisting of a large château, with a few small houses around it. Behind it rises the long, swelling ground, which once bore the walls, temples, and palaces of Veii, but is now a bare down, partly fringed with wood, and without a habitation on its surface. At a few miles' distance is the conical, tufted hill of Musino, the supposed scene of ancient rites, the Eleusis, or Delphi, it may be, of Etruria. The eye is next caught by a tree-crested mound in the plain beyond the site of the city; then it stretches away to the triple paps of the Monticelli, and to Tivoli, gleaming from the dark slopes behind; and then it rises and scans the majestic chain of Apennines, bounding the horizon with their dark grey masses, and rests with delight on La Leonessa and other well-known giants of the Sabine range, all capt with snow. Oh, the beauty of that range! From whatever part of the Campagna you view it, it presents those long, sweeping outlines, those grand, towering crests—not of Alpine abruptness, but consistently with the character of the land, preserving, even when soaring highest, the true Italian dignity and repose.

Isola is a wretched hamlet of ruinous houses, with not more than thirty inhabitants. Even the palace, which belongs to the Rospigliosi family, is falling into decay, and the next generation will probably find the place uninhabited. The caverns which yawn in the cliffs around whet the traveller's interest in the antiquities of Veii. In the little piazza are several relics of Roman domination, sculptural and inscriptive.

It is necessary to take Isola on the way to the ancient city, as the *cicerone* dwells there, and the key of the Painted Tomb is to be there obtained.

He who would make the tour of Veii must not expect to see numerous monuments of the past. Scarcely one Etruscan site has fewer remains, yet few possess greater interest. Veii lives in the page of history rather than in extant monuments; she has no Colosseum, no Parthenon, no Pyramids—few fragments even from which the antiquarian Cuvier may reconstruct her frame. The very skeleton of Veii has crumbled to dust—the city is its own sepulchre—*si monumentum requiris—circumspice!*

Yet is there no want of interest in a spot so hallowed by legend and history. The shadow of past glory falls as solemnly on the spirit as that of temple or tower. It is something to know and feel that "here was and is" not. The senses may desire more relics to link the present to the past; but the imagination need not here be "gravelled for lack of matter."

Since there are such scanty remains at Veii, few will care to make the entire circuit of the city, yet there are three or four spots of interest which all should visit—the Arx—the Columbarium—the Ponte Sodo—and the Painted Tomb. Beyond this there are but scattered fragments of walls—the sites of the gates, determined only by the nature of the ground—and the remains of several bridges.

I shall detail the track I took on my first visit, and the reader, with the aid of the Plan, will be enabled to trace the site of every object of interest within and around the walls of Veii.

My guide led the way into the glen which separates Isola from the ancient city, and in which stands a mill—most picturesquely situated, with the city-cliffs towering above it, and the stream sinking in a cascade into a deep gulley, over-shadowed by ilex. The road to the mill is cut through tufo, which presents some remarkable features, being composed of very thin strata of calcined vegetable matter, alternating with earthy layers, showing the regular and rapidly intermittent action of some neighbouring

volcano—the now extinct crater of Baccano or of Bracciano. The
bed formed by an igneous deposit had been covered with vegetation, which had been reduced to charcoal by a subsequent eruption,
and buried beneath another shower of earthy matter, which in its
turn served for a hotbed to a second crop of vegetation. That
these eruptions occurred at very short intervals is apparent from
the thinness of the charcoal layers. The whole mass is very
friable, and as this softness of the rock precluded the formation
of a water-trough on one side, so frequently seen in Etruscan
roads, to carry off the water from above, small pipes of earthenware were here thrust through the soft tufo in one of the cliffs,
and may be traced for some distance down the hill.[4] From the
mill a path leads up to the site of one of the ancient gates (A in
the Plan). Near this, which commands the view of Isola, given
in the woodcut, which is from a sketch by the author, are some
remains of the walls, composed of small rectangular blocks of
nenfro.[5]

Following the line of the high ground to the east, I passed
several other fragments of the ancient walls, all mere embankments, and then struck across bare downs or corn-fields into the
heart of the city. A field, overgrown with briers, was pointed
out by my guide as the site of excavations, where were found,
among other remains, the colossal statue of Tiberius, now in the
Vatican, and the twelve Ionic columns of marble, which sustain
the portico of the Post-office at Rome. This was probably the
Forum of the Roman "*Municipium Augustum Veiens*," which
rose on the ruins of Etruscan Veii. The *columbarium*, or Roman
sepulchre, hard by, must have been without the limits of the
municipium, which occupied but a small portion of the site of the
original city; when first opened, it contained stuccoes and
paintings in excellent preservation, but is now in a state of utter
ruin.

I next entered on a wide down, overrun with rank vegetation,
where tall thistles and briers played no small devilry with one's
lower limbs, and would deny all passage to the fair sex, save on
horseback. On I struggled, passing a Roman tomb, till I found
traces of an ancient road, slightly sunk between banks. This

---

[4] These pipes may be Roman, for *tubuli
fictiles* were often used by that people for
the conveyance of water.

[5] A volcanic stone, a species of tufo, distinguished from the ordinary red or yellow

tufo of the Campagna by its colour, a
dark grey, and by its superior hardness
and compactness—a difference thought to
be owing to its having cooled more slowly.

was the road from Rome to the *municipium*, and after crossing
the site of the ancient city in a direct line, it fell into the Via
Cassia.   I traced it a long distance southwards across the briery
down, and then into a deep hollow, choked with thickets, where
I came upon large polygonal blocks of basalt, such as usually
compose Roman pavement.   This was without the limits of the
Etruscan city in a narrow hollow, which separated the city from

ISOLA FARNESE, FROM THE WALLS OF VEII.

its Arx.   At this spot is a fragment of the ancient walls.   The
road ran down the hollow towards Rome, and was probably
known as the Via Veientana.   There are no remains of the gate.
    The Arx is a table-land of no great extent, rising precipitously
from the deep glens which bound it, save at the single point
where a narrow ridge unites it to the city.   Such a position would
mark it at once as the citadel, even had it not traditionally retained
its ancient designation in its modern name, Piazza d'Armi ; and
its juxta-position and connection with the city give it much
superior claims to be so considered, than those which can be
urged for the height of Isola Farnese, which is separated from
the city by a wide hollow.   There is also every reason to believe
that this was the site of the earliest town.   Here alone could the

founder of Veii have fixed his choice. The natural strength of
its position, and its size, adapted it admirably for an infant
settlement. In process of time, as its population increased, it
would have been compelled to extend its limits, until it gradually
embraced the whole of the adjoining table-land, which is far too
extensive to have been the original site; so that what was at first
the whole town became eventually merely the citadel. Such was
the case with Athens, Rome, Syracuse, and many other cities of
antiquity. There may possibly have been a second settlement at
Isola, which may have united with that on the Arx to occupy the
site of the celebrated city; just as at Rome, where the town of
Romulus, confined at first to the hill of the Palatine, united with
the earlier town on the Capitoline, to extend their limits as one
city over the neighbouring heights and intervening valleys.

I walked round the Piazza d'Armi, and from the verge of its
cliffs looked into the beautiful glen on either hand, through which,
far beneath me, wound the two streams which girded Veii, and
into the broader and still more beautiful hollow, through which,
after uniting their waters, they flowed, as the far-famed Cremera,
now known as La Valca, to mingle with the Tiber.[7] Peculiar
beauty was imparted to these glens by the rich autumnal tints of
the woods, which crowned the verge or clothed the base of their
red and grey cliffs—the dark russet foliage of the oaks, the
orange or brilliant red of the mantling vines, being heightened
by the contrast of the green meadows below. Scarcely a sign of
cultivation met the eye—one house alone on the opposite cliff—
no flocks or herds sprinkled the meadows beneath,—it was the
wild beauty of sylvan, secluded nature.

Far different was the scene that met the eye of Camillus, when
he gazed from this spot after his capture of Veii.[8] The flames
ascending from the burning city[9]—the battle and slaughter still
raging—the shouts of the victors and shrieks of the vanquished
—here, his victorious soldiers pressing up through the hollow
ways into the city, eager for spoil—there, the wretched inhabitants flying across the open country—yon height, studded with
the tents of the Roman army—the Cremera at his feet rolling
reddened down the valley towards the camp of the Fabii, whose
slaughter he had so signally avenged—all these sights and sounds

---

[7] The larger and more northerly stream
is the Fosso di Formello, the other the
Fosso de' due Fossi.

[8] Plut. Camillus. Dionys. Hal. Frag-

menta Mai, XII. 13.

[9] The city was not consumed, but Livy
(V. 21) states that the Roman soldiers set
it on fire.

melted the stern warrior to tears of mingled pity and exultation. Veii, so long the rival of Rome, had fallen, and her generous conqueror mourned her downfall. Like Troy, she had held out for ten long years against a beleaguering army: and like Troy she fell at last only by the clandestine introduction of an armed foe.

The story of the *cuniculus*, or mine of Camillus, is well known; how he carried it up into the temple of Juno within the citadel —how he himself led his troops to the assault—how they overheard the Etruscan *aruspex*, before the altar of the goddess, declare to the king of Veii that victory would rest with him who completed the sacrifice—how they burst through the flooring, seized the entrails and bore them to Camillus, who offered them to the goddess with his own hand—how his troops swarmed in through the mine, opened the gates to their fellows, and obtained possession of the city. Verily, as Livy sapiently remarks, "It were not worth while to prove or disprove these things, which are better fitted to be set forth on a stage which delighteth in marvels, than to be received with implicit faith. In matters of such antiquity, I hold it sufficient if what seemeth truth be received as such."

I wandered round the Arx seeking some traces of this temple of Juno, which was the largest in Veii. The sole remains of antiquity visible, are some foundations at the edge of the plateau, opposite the city, which may possibly be those of the celebrated temple, though more probably, as Gell suggests, the substructions of towers which defended the entrance to the citadel. Several sepulchral monuments have been here discovered; among them one of the Tarquitian family, which produced a celebrated writer on Etruscan divination,[1] and which seems from this and other inscriptions to have belonged to Veii. As none of these relics were Etruscan, they in no way militate against the view that this was the Arx, but merely show that it was without the bounds of the Roman *municipium*.

Of the *cuniculus* of Camillus no traces have been found. Not even is there a sewer, so common on most Etruscan sites, to be seen in the cliff beneath the Arx, though the dense wood which covers the eastern side of the hill may well conceal such openings; and one cannot but regard these sewers as suggestive of the *cuniculus*, if that were not a mere enlargement of one of them to admit an armed force. Researches after the *cuniculus* are not

---

[1] Plin. N. H. I. lib. 2. Macrob. Saturn. III. 7. cf. II. 16.

likely to be successful. Not that I agree with Niebuhr in doubt-
ing its existence; for though it were folly to give full credence
to the legend, which even Livy and Plutarch doubted, yet there
is nothing unnatural or improbable in the recorded mode of the
city's capture. When a siege of ten years had proved of no
avail, resort might well have been had to artifice; and the soft
volcanic rock of the site offered every facility for tunnelling.[e]
But if the *cuniculus* were commenced in the plain at the foot of
the height, it would not be easy to discover its mouth. The
entrance would probably be by a perpendicular shaft or well,
communicating with a subterranean passage leading towards the
Arx.

Returning into the hollow, through which runs the Via
Veientana, my eye was caught by a curious flight of steps, high
in the cliff on which the city stood. I climbed to them, and
found them to be of uncemented masonry, too rude for Roman
work, and similar in character to the walls of the Etruscan city;

Niebuhr (ii. p. 481, Eng. trans.) rejects the account, given by Livy, of the
capture of Veii : first, as bearing too close
a resemblance to the siege and taking of
Troy, to be authentic; and next, because
"in the whole history of ancient military
operations we shall scarcely find an authentic instance of a town taken in the same
manner." He thinks that the legend of
the *cuniculus* arose out of a tradition of a
mine of the ordinary character, by which a
portion of the walls was overthrown; because the besiegers would never have resorted to the arduous labour of forming a
cuniculus into the heart of the city, "when,
by merely firing the timbers, by which, at
all events, the walls must have been propt,
they might have made a breach." Now,
though there are many circumstances attending the capture, of too marvellous a
character to be admitted as authentic history, I must venture to differ from that
great man when he questions the formation
of the *cuniculus*. The fact is stated, not
only by Livy (V. 21), but by Plutarch
(Camil.), Diodorus (XIV., p. 307), Florus
(1. 12), and Zonaras (Ann. VII. 21).
The capture of Fidenæ by means of a
similar mine (Liv. IV. 22), Niebuhr thinks
not a whit better attested than that of
Veii; but Dionysius mentions a similar
capture of Fidenæ, as early as the reign

of Ancus Martius (III. p. 180); and Livy
records the taking of Nequinum or Narnia
in a similar manner, in long subsequent
times (X. 10). When Niebuhr states that
the walls of Veii might have been breached
by firing the timbers of the mine, it is
evident that he had not visited the site,
and wrote in perfect ignorance of its character. Such a remark would apply to a
town built in a plain, or on a slight elevation; but in a case where the citadel stood
on a cliff, nearly two hundred feet above
the valley (if Isola were the Arx, the height
was yet greater), it is obviously inapplic-
able; and this Niebuhr, in fact, admits,
when he says that "in Latium, where the
strength of the towns arose from the steep
rocks on which they were built, there was
no opportunity of mining." His argument,
then, against the *cuniculus* of Camillus
falls to the ground, because founded on a
misconception of the true situation of Veii.
His error is the more surprising as he had
the testimony of Dionysius (II.,p. 116),
that Veii "stood on a lofty and cliff-bound
rock."

Holstenius, who regarded Isola Farnese
as the Arx of Veii, speaks of the *cuniculus*
of Camillus being "manifestly apparent"
in his day (Adnot. ad Cluv., p. 54), but he
probably mistook for it some sewer which
opened low in the cliff.

therefore, I doubt not that this was a staircase leading to a postern gate of ancient Veii. The lower part having fallen with the cliff, these eight upper steps alone are left, and they will not remain long, for the shrubs which have interlaced their roots with the uncemented blocks, will soon precipitate them into the ravine.

ROCK-CUT TOMB AT VEII.

This curious staircase, La Scaletta, as it is called by the peasants, came to light in 1840, in consequence of the earth which concealed it having been washed away by unusually heavy rains. It is marked P in the Plan.

From the Arx the line of the walls ran northward, as indicated by the cliffs. I passed a few excavations in the rocks, and the sites of two gates,[3] and at length reached a wood, below

---

[3] The road from the second gate (F. in the Plan) ran past the Tumulus of Vaccareccia towards Pietra Pertusa, a remarkable cut through a rock near the Via Flaminia and four miles from Veii. The rock presents the appearance of an island rising out of a plain, which seems to have been originally a lake (Gell, Memor. Instit. I. p. 13).

which, on the banks of the stream, is a piece of broken ground,
which presents some curious traces of ancient times. It is a
most picturesque spot, sunk in the bosom of the woods, and strewn
with masses of grey rock, in wild confusion, full of sepulchral
excavations—literally honey-combed with niches; whence its
appellation of "Il Colombario." In one place the rock is hollowed into a chamber of unusually small size, with room for only
a single sarcophagus (see the woodcut on p. 9, which is from a
sketch by the author). The niches are of various forms, some not
unlike Etruscan, but all, it seemed to me, of Roman construction.
The most ancient Etruscan tombs of Veii are chambers excavated
in the rock, with rock-hewn couches for bodies or sarcophagi. As
the city was deserted soon after its capture in the year of Rome
358, all its Etruscan sepulchres must have been prior to that
date, and many of the niches within tombs are probably of high
antiquity, as in them have been found vases, mirrors, and other
objects of a purely Etruscan character. The smaller niches
served to hold lamps, perfume vases, cinerary urns, or votive
offerings, and those of elongated form contained the bodies of the
dead.[4] But the niches in the face of these cliffs have peculiarities, which mark them as of Roman origin, especially the
hole sunk within the niche for an *olla* or cinerary pot, as in the
Roman *columbaria*, instances of which are very rare in Etruscan
cemeteries.[5] Many of them are cut in the walls of rock, which
flank an ancient road sunk through a mass of tufo to the depth
of from twelve to twenty feet. Such roads are common in the
neighbourhood of Etruscan cities; several other instances occur
around Veii. In this case part of the polygonal pavement is
remaining with its kerb-stones, and the ruts worn by the ancient
cars are visible. On the top of the rock, on one side, are remains
of walls, which prove this to be the site of one of the city-gates.
(G. in the Plan.)

The road led directly from the Formello up to the gate, and
had evidently crossed the stream by a bridge. This is no longer
standing; but several large hewn blocks of tufo lie in the water;
and a little further up the stream, on the side opposite the city,
is a piece of walling, which has undoubtedly been the pier of the
bridge.[6]

---

[4] See the Appendix to this Chapter, Note I.

[5] Abeken (Mittelital. p. 258) regards these niches as Roman from the evidence

of the inscriptions found on the spot.

[6] Marked R. on the Plan. It is 20 feet wide, now only about 5 or 6 feet high, of small blocks of tufo cemented, in 6 courses,

I continued to follow the upward course of the Formello towards the Ponte Sodo. The banks of the stream, on the inner or city side, rose steep, rocky, and fringed with wood—the ash, beech, and ilex springing from the grey rocks, and hanging in varied hues over the torrent. Here and there, at the verge of the steep, portions of the ancient walls peeped through the foliage. Among them was a grand fragment of walling filling a natural gap in the cliff.[7] On the other hand were bare, swelling mounds, in which the mouths of caves were visible, the tombs of ancient Veii, now half choked with earth. One tomb alone, the Grotta Campana, which will be particularly described in the following chapter, now remains open. Here are also several vaults of Roman reticulated work.

It would be easy to pass the Ponte Sodo without observing it. It is called a bridge; but is a mere mass of rock bored for the passage of the stream. Whether wholly or but partly artificial may admit of dispute. It is, however, in all probability, an Etruscan excavation—a tunnel in the rock, two hundred and forty feet long, twelve or fifteen wide, and nearly twenty high. From above, it is not visible. You must view it from the banks of the stream. You at first take it to be of natural formation, yet there is a squareness and regularity about it which prove it artificial. The steep cliffs of tufo, yellow, grey, or white, overhung by ilex, ivy, and brushwood—the deep, dark-mouthed tunnel with a ray of sunshine, it may be, gleaming beyond—the masses of lichen-clad rock, which choke the stream—give it a charm apart from its antiquity.[8]

and much more neat and modern in appearance than the usual Etruscan masonry. Yet it is unlike late Roman work, and more resembles the remains of the *agger* of Servius Tullius, in the gardens of Sallust at Rome. Canina, who gives a drawing of this pier (Etruria Marittima, tav. 28), represents it as of a kind of masonry very common on early Etruscan sites, and which I take to be the *emplecton* of Vitruvius. See Chapter V., p. 79.

[7] Canina gives an illustration of this piece of wall (op. cit. I., p. 120, tav. 26), and represents it as of 18 courses in height, and of *emplecton*, at least in that style of masonry to which that name is applied throughout this work, although he does not so apply it. He takes it for part of the earliest fortifications of Veii, dating

some nine or ten centuries before Christ.

[8] Sodo, or solid, is a term commonly applied to natural bridges, or to such as in their massive character resemble them.

Gell (II., p. 323) thinks that the deep hollow through which the Formello here flows was not its original bed, but I could see no traces of a former channel, and am inclined to believe in the natural character of the hollow, by which the stream approaches the Ponte Sodo, and to think that there was a natural channel through the rock enlarged by art to obviate the disastrous consequences of winter floods. Canina (Etr. Marit. I. p. 121) believes the Ponte to be artificial.

Nibby (III., p. 432) calls the Ponte Sodo 70 feet long. He could not have measured it, as I have, by wading through

Upon this natural bridge is a shapeless mound in the midst of
an ancient roadway.   Gell sees in it the ruins of a square tower,
though it requires a brisk imagination to perceive such traces in
this overgrown mass; yet from its position, and from fragments
of walling hard by, it is evident that this was the site of a double
gateway.[9] (H in the Plan.) These fragments are traceable on
both sides of the gate.   To the left they rise high, and form the
facing to an *agger* or embankment which extends along the verge
of the slope for a considerable distance.   The blocks are smaller
than usual in Etruscan cities, being only sixteen inches deep,
and eighteen to twenty-four in length; yet there can be little
doubt that these were the once renowned fortifications—*egregii
muri*[1]—of Etruscan Veii.   A portion of the wall hereabouts has
been described and delineated by Gell, as being composed of
immense tufo blocks, ten or eleven feet long, based on courses
of thin bricks, a yard in length.   Again and again have I beat
the bush far and wide in quest of this singular fragment of
masonry, but have never been fortunate enough to stumble on it;
nor have I met with any one who has seen it.   Of late years the
wood has been greatly cleared on this side the city, but the
fragment is still sought in vain; and whether it has been torn
to pieces by the peasants, or lies hid in some of the thorny
brakes it is impossible to penetrate, I cannot say.

---

it. It is not cut with nicety, though it
is possible that the original surface of the
rock has been injured by the rush of
water through the tunnel, for the stream
at times swells to a torrent, filling the
entire channel, as is proved by trunks of
trees lodged in clefts of the rock close to
the roof, which remind one that this is
the *Cremera rapax* of Ovid (Fast. II.
205). There are two oblong shafts in the
ceiling, with niches cut in them as a
means of descent from above, precisely
such shafts as are seen in the tombs at
Civita Castellana, Fálleri, and other
Etruscan sites. Here they must have
been formed for the sake of carrying on
the work in several places at once. There
is a third at the upper entrance to the
tunnel, but not connected with it, as it
is sunk into a sewer which crosses the
mouth of the tunnel diagonally, showing
the latter to have been of subsequent formation to the system of drainage in the
city. Gell mistook the sewer for an aque-

duct, and the shafts for wells by which the
citizens drew water (II., p. 331). At this
end of the tunnel, the roof is cut into a
regular gable form, and is of much greater
elevation than the rest : it is continued
thus only for thirty or forty feet, as if the
original plan had been abandoned.

[9] Double gates such as this were common in Italy — the Porta Carmentalis of
Rome, the gates at Pompeii and Segni,
for instance — and not unknown to the
Greeks, being represented on monuments
and mentioned by their writers. It may
be doubted, however, whether the plural
number applied to gates, as to the celebrated Scæan gates of Troy (πύλαι Σκαιαί),
had reference to a gate like this, or to
one with a double portal connected by a
passage, as the Porta all' Arco of Volterra.
Canina (Arch. Ant. V. p. 96) thinks the
latter. The plural term would also apply
to a single gate with folding doors—*portæ
bipatentes*—Virg. Æn. II. 330.

[1] Liv. V. 2.

A little above the Ponte Sodo, where the ground sinks to the edge of the stream, and where many troughs in the rocky banks indicate the spots whence blocks have been quarried for the construction of the city, I observed, on the left bank, a fragment of walling with the same peculiarities as that described by Gell, and more massive than any other I had seen at Veii. From its position with regard to the gate, which may here be traced on the city side of the stream, it had evidently formed the pier of a bridge. Its width was ten feet. The largest block was only three feet nine inches by two feet four, but this was massive in comparison with those of the city walls. The absence of cement proved its antiquity. The whole rested on three layers of long sun-burnt bricks, or tiles.[2] Yet their position was no proof of the antiquity of their collocation, for they might have been inserted in aftertimes to repair the foundations, just as the massive walls of Volterra are here and there underbuilt with modern masonry. There is nothing, however, in the material which militates against the antiquity of the structure. Bricks were used in the remotest ages, and in most parts of the ancient world.[3] The Etruscans, so skilled in pottery, must have been acquainted with their use; Arretium, one of the cities of the League, is said to have been walled with brick; and we know that the Veientes in particular were famed for their manufactures of baked earth.[4] If the bricks in this masonry really formed part of the original structure, they lead one to suspect that the walls of other Etruscan cities may have been formed in part of the same materials, which, when the cities fell into decay, would have formed a quarry for the construction of villages. The destruction of Etruscan fortifications, however, in the volcanic district of the land, may be accounted for without this supposition—the small size, lightness, and facility of cleavage of the tufo blocks composing the extant fragments, must in all ages have proved a temptation to apply them to other purposes.

About three quarters of a mile above the Ponte Sodo is another

---

[2] This site is marked S. in the plan. On a subsequent visit, I was grieved to see that this pier had been almost destroyed. Canina gives a drawing of this pier. Etr. Marit. tav. 29.

[3] According to Sanchoniatho, bricks were invented before mankind had learned to construct villages, or to tend flocks. The Tower of Babel was built of bricks. We have the testimony of Moses also as to their early use in Egypt, corroborated by extant monuments; and Herodotus informs us that the walls of Babylon were built of brick. For their use in Greece, see Pausanias (I. 42, II. 27, V. 5, X. 35); and in other countries, see Vitruvius (II. viii. 9) and Pliny (N. H. XXXV. 49).

[4] Plut. Publicola. Serv. ad Æn. VII. 188. Festus roce Ratumena.

bridge, called Ponte Formello, whose piers are of *nenfro*, undoubtedly ancient, possibly of Etruscan construction, though not of the earliest period; but the existing arch is of mediæval brickwork. The road which crosses the Formello by this bridge runs to the village of Formello and to Monte Musino, six miles distant.

Crossing this bridge, and following the line of the ancient walls as indicated by the nature of the ground, I presently came to a cross-road, cut through tufo banks, and leading into the city. (Gate K.) It is clearly an ancient way; fifty years ago its pavement was entire,[4] but, owing to the pilferings of the peasantry, scarcely a block is now left.

The road that crosses the Formello runs direct, for half-a-mile, to the Ponte dell' Isola, a bridge over the Fosso de' due Fossi, the stream which washed the southern walls of Veii. The city walls followed the line of bank on the left, which turns off towards the mill, while the road leads directly to the Ponte d' Isola. This is a picturesque bridge of a single arch, twenty-two feet in span.[5] Antiquaries have pronounced it to be of very ancient date—connected with the original plan of the city. But to my eye the very small size of the blocks, and the cement used in its construction, are opposed to so high an antiquity.

A doubt may arise as to the antiquity of these bridges at Veii, as well as of any others which claim an Etruscan origin, seeing that no stone bridge was erected at Rome before the year 575, the date of the Pons Æmilius,[7] long after the entire subjugation of Etruria, and more than two centuries after the capture of Veii. Is it possible that the Romans, if they found such structures existing in the conquered land, could have refrained from introducing such additions to the beauty and convenience of the City? —how could they have remained satisfied for centuries with a single bridge, and that of wood? But it must be remembered that the Tiber was one of the ramparts of Rome; that the Pons Sublicius was equivalent to a draw-bridge, being so constructed as to be readily taken to pieces on an emergency; that it was maintained, in its wooden state, as a religious duty, and committed to the especial care of the priests, who hence derived their

---

[4] Nibby, III. p. 433.

[5] The piers are 14½ feet wide; the lower courses are of *nenfro*; the rest of tufo; all alike cemented. The masonry is not unlike that of the Ponte Formello, and of the pier of the ruined bridge near the Columbarium gate.

[7] Plut. Numa.

name of *pontifices;* and it was not till after the conquest of
Etruria, the downfall of Hannibal, and when all fear of a foe at
the gates of the City was removed, that a permanent bridge was
constructed.   The Romans of that day had no need to go beyond
their own walls for the model of a stone arch; they had had it
for ages in the Cloaca Maxima.

From the Ponte d'Isola, a pathway leads to the mill.   Here I
had completed the circuit of Veii.   Gell calls it more than four
miles in circumference, but his own map makes it of much
greater area.   Nibby seems nearer the truth, in calling it seven
miles round, which more nearly agrees with the statement of
Dionysius that Veii was equal in size to Athens,[8] said to have
been sixty stadia in circumference, *i.e.* seven miles and a half,[9]
or at the lower estimate of ten stadia to the mile, the common
itinerary stadia of Greece, six miles in circuit.   The Rome of
Servius Tullius, which Dionysius also compares to Athens, was
about the same extent.[1]

Such then is Veii—once the most powerful,[2] the most wealthy
city of Etruria,[3] renowned for its beauty,[4] its arts and refinement,
which in size equalled Athens and Rome, in military force was
not inferior to the latter,[5] and which for its site, strong by nature
and almost impregnable by art,[6] and for the magnificence of its
buildings and the superior extent and fertility of its territory,
was preferred by the Romans to the Eternal City itself, even
before the destruction of the latter by the Gauls,[7]—now void
and desolate, without one house or habitant, its temples and
palaces level with the dust, and nothing beyond a few fragments
of walls, and some empty sepulchres, remaining to tell the traveller that here Veii was.   The plough passes over its bosom,
and the shepherd pastures his flock on the waste within it.   Such

---

[8] Dionys. II. p. 116.

[9] So says the Scholiast on Thucydides,
II. 13; but the great historian himself
merely states that the extent of that part
of the city which was guarded was 43
stadia; and the Scholiast adds that the
unguarded part, or the space between the
Long Walls, which united the city with the
Piræus, and the Phaleric Wall, was 17
stadia in breadth.

[1] Dionys. IV. p. 219; and IX. p. 624.

[2] Dionys. II. p. 116; Liv. IV. 58.

[3] Liv. II. 50; V. 20, 21, 22.   Florus
(I. 12) and Plutarch (Camil.) attest its
wealth by the spoil that fell into the hands

of the conquerors.   Eutrop. J. 18.

[4] Liv. V. 24.

[5] Plut. Camillus.

[6] Urbe validâ muris ac situ ipso mu-
nitâ, Liv. I. 15, V. 2.   Dionys. loc. cit.,
and IX. p. 593; Plut. Romul. and Camil.

[7] Liv. V. 24.   Arnold (I. p. 212) questions
the authority of Livy on this head, and
also the sincerity of the Romans, if they
said it; without good grounds, it seems
to me.   Dionysius (Frag. Mai, XII. 14)
in some measure confirms Livy by saying
Veii was in no way inferior to Rome as a
residence.

must it have been in the earlier years of Augustus, for Propertius
pictures a similar scene of decay.

> Et Veii veteres, et vos tum regna fuistis ;
>   Et vestro posita est aurea sella foro ;
> Nunc intra muros pastoris buccina lenti
>   Cantat, et in vestris ossibus arva metunt.

> Veii, thou hadst a royal crown of old,
>   And in thy forum stood a throne of gold !—
> Thy walls now echo but the shepherd's horn,
>   And o'er thine ashes waves the summer corn.

Lucan also speaks of its desolation :—

> Gabios, Veiosque, Coramque
> Pulvere vix tectæ poterunt monstrare ruinæ.

How are we to account for this neglect ? The city was certainly
not destroyed by Camillus, for the superior magnificence of its
public and private buildings was a temptation to the Romans to
desert the Seven Hills. But after the destruction of Rome by
the Gauls, Veii was abandoned, in consequence of the decree of
the Senate threatening with the severest punishment the Roman
citizens who should remain within its walls; and Niebuhr's
conjecture may be correct, that it was demolished to supply
materials for the rebuilding of Rome, though the distance would
almost preclude the transport of more than the architectural
ornaments. Its desolation must have been owing either to the
policy of Rome which proscribed its inhabitation, or to *malaria ;*[8]
otherwise, a city which presented so many advantages as almost
to have tempted the Romans to desert their hearths and the
sepulchres of their fathers, would scarcely have been suffered to
fall into utter decay, and remain so for nearly four centuries.
The Romans most probably ceased to maintain the high cultivation of its territory, and it became unhealthy, as at the present
day. This was the case with the Campagna in general, which
in very early times was studded with towns, but under Roman
domination became, what it has ever since remained—a desert,
whose wide surface is rarely relieved by habitation.

After the lapse of ages the site was colonised afresh by
Augustus; but the glory of Veii had departed—the new colony

---

[8] Dionysius, however (Excerpta Mai,
XII. 14), tells us the air of Veii was very
healthy, which is more than can be said of
it now-a-days ; some of the inhabitants of
Isola being constant sufferers from the
malaria fever.

occupied scarcely a third of the area of the ancient city, and struggled for a century for existence, till in the days of Adrian it again sunk into decay. Yet it is difficult to credit the assertion of Florus, that its very site was forgotten. "This, then, was Veii!—who now remembers its existence? What ruins?—what traces of it are left? Hardly can we credit our annals, which tell us Veii has been."[9] For the inscriptions found on the spot prove that the colony continued to exist to the fourth century of our era.

I have now described my first walk round Veii; but many a day, and in all seasons, have I spent in wandering over the site and around the walls of this once renowned city. I was wont to take up my quarters at La Storta, and step over at daybreak; and, with a luncheon in my pocket and a draught from the Cremera, I cared not to return till the landscape was veiled in the purple shadows of evening.

Every time I visit Veii I am struck with the rapid progress of destruction. Nibby and Gell mention many remains which are no longer visible. The site has less to show on every succeeding year. Even masonry, such as the pier of the bridge over the Fosso di Formello, that from its massiveness might seem to defy the pilferings of the peasantry, is torn to pieces, and the blocks removed to form walls or houses elsewhere, so that, ere long, it may be said of Veii, "Her very ruins have perished "— *etiam perire ruinæ*.

Occasionally, in my wanderings on this site, I have entered, either from curiosity or for shelter, one of the *capanne* scattered over the downs. These are tall, conical, thatched huts, which the shepherds make their winter abode. For in Italy, the low lands being generally unhealthy in summer, the flocks are driven to the mountains about May, and as soon as the great heats are past, are brought back to the richer pastures of the plains. It is a curious sight—the interior of a *capanna*. A little boldness is requisite to pass through the pack of dogs, white as new-dropt lambs, but large and fierce as wolves, which, were the shepherd not at hand, would tear in pieces whoever might venture to approach the hut; but, with one of the *pecoraj* for a Teucer,

<hr>

[9] Flor. I. 12. The Roman colony—the *Municipium Augustum Veiens* of the inscriptions—could never have been of much importance, though the inscriptions mention several temples, a theatre, and baths; for Strabo, who wrote in the reign of Tiberius, speaks of it as an insignificant place in his time—as one of the πολίχναι συχναί of Etruria (V. p. 226).

nothing is to be feared. The *capanne* are of various sizes. One I entered not far from Veii was thirty or forty feet in diameter, and nearly as high, propped in the centre by two rough masts, between which a hole was left in the roof for the escape of smoke. Within the door lay a large pile of lambs—there might be a hundred—killed that morning and already flayed, and a number of shepherds were busied in operating on the carcasses of others; all of which were to be despatched forthwith to the Roman market. Though a fierce May sun blazed without, a huge fire roared in the middle of the hut; but this was for the sake of the *ricotta*, which was being made in another part of the *capanna*. Here stood a huge caldron, full of boiling ewes'-milk. In a warm state this curd is a delicious jelly, and has often tempted me to enter a *capanna* in quest of it, to the amazement of the *pecoraj*, to whom it is "vilior algâ." Lord of the caldron, stood a man dispensing ladlefuls of the rich simmering mess to his fellows, as they brought their bowls for their morning's allowance; and he varied his occupation by pouring the same into certain small baskets, in which it is conveyed to market; the serous parts running off through the wicker, and the residue caking as it cooled. On the same board stood the cheeses, previously made from the cream. In this hut lived twenty-five men, their nether limbs clad in goat-skins, with the hair outwards, suggestive of the satyrs of ancient fable; but they had no nymphs to tease, nor shepherdesses to woo, and never

> —————————"sat all day
> Playing on pipes of corn, and versing love
> To amorous Phillida."

They were a band of celibats, without the vows. In such huts they dwell all the year round, flaying lambs, or shearing sheep, living on bread, *ricotta*, and water, very rarely tasting meat or wine, and sleeping on shelves ranged round the hut, like berths in a ship's cabin. Thus are the dreams of Arcadia dispelled by realities!

To revert to the early history of Veii.[1] That she was one of the most ancient cities of Etruria may be inferred from the pitch

---

[1] It has been suggested by Orioli (Ann. Inst. 1833, p. 22) that Veii may be derived from Vedius, or Vejovis, one of the Etruscan deities, just as Mantua was derived from another, Mantus (Serv. ad Æn. X. 198). According to Festus (ap. Paul. Diac.) Veia is an Oscan word, signifying *plaustrum*, a waggon; hence probably *veho*.

of power she had attained in the time of Romulus.[2] That she was one of the Twelve of the great Etruscan Confederation cannot be doubted. Her vast size, superior to that of every other Etruscan city whose limits can be ascertained—the great extent of her territory, and the numerous towns dependent on her[3]—her power, opulence, and magnificence—would make it sufficiently evident, without the express testimony of Livy and Dionysius to the fact.[4]

Of the history of Veii we know no more than her contests with Rome. She is one of those numerous cities of antiquity, whose records are mere tissues of wars—bloody trails across the field of history. While regretting that our knowledge of them is confined to such events, we should remember that, had not such wars been chronicled, the very names of these cities would most probably never have come down to us. Whatever mention of Veii we find in ancient writers is as the antagonist of Rome. No less than fourteen wars with that power are on record. The Veientes indeed are called by Florus "the unceasing and annual enemies of Rome"—assidui vero et anniversarii hostes.

The first six wars were with the Kings of Rome, and as in all this history the man, and not the lion, drew the picture, we are told that the Roman monarchs were always triumphant, whether against Veii alone, or the united forces of Etruria.[5]

---

[2] Dion. Hal. II. p. 116. She is called "antiquissima et ditissima civitas" by Eutropius (I. 18). Veii is not mentioned by Virgil among the cities of Etruria in the time of Æneas, but nothing can be fairly deduced from this against her antiquity, seeing that the poet is equally silent of Arretium, Perusia, Volsinii, Rusellæ, and Volaterra, some of which most assuredly existed at that period, as Perusia, traditionally very ancient (Serv. loc. cit.) and Volaterra, of whose colony (Populonia) Virgil makes mention (Æn. X. 172).

[3] Plut. Romul. Dion. Hal. III. p. 181; also Frag. Mai, XII. 14. The territory of Veii, before it was curtailed by the Romans, extended on the south and east to the Tiber (Plin. III. 9), and on the south-west to the sea, embracing the Salinæ, or salt-works, at the mouth of the river (Dion. Hal. II. p. 118; Plut. Romul.). On the west, it adjoined the territory of Cære, though the frontier line is not defined. Müller (Etrusk. II. 2, 1) is of

opinion that Sabate, on the Lake of Bracciano, was in the Veientine territory; and that even Sutrium and Nepeto were also included. On the north, it met the *Ager Faliscus*. On the east, it must have embraced all the district south of Soracte and eastward to the Tiber, or, in other words, the *Ager Capenatis*, because Capena was a colony of Veii (Cato ap. Serv. ad Æn. VII. 697. Niebuhr, I. p. 120; Müller, Einl. 2, 14; and II. 1, 2); and Feronia, under Soracte, was also in the *Ager Capenatis*, Fidenæ was another colony of Veii. Of the *Ager Veiens*, we further know that it produced a red wine of inferior quality, too bad to be drunk on festive occasions: Horat. II. Sat. 3, 143; Pers. Sat. V. 147; Mart. I. epig. 104, 9; II. 53, 4; III. 49.

Pliny (XXXVII. 69) and Solinus (I. p. 16) speak of a precious stone found at Veii,—Veientana gemma—which was black bordered with white; perhaps onyx.

[4] See the Appendix, Note II.

[5] Tarquinius Priscus, indeed, is said

Seventh War.—In the year 245, Veii joined Tarquinii in the
attempt to replace Tarquinius Superbus on his throne. They
encountered the forces of the young Republic near the Arsian
Wood; Aruns, the son of Tarquin, and Brutus, the first Consul,
fell by each other's hands, and the victory remained undecided.
In the following night an unearthly voice, thought to be that of
the god Silvanus, was heard proceeding from the wood—" The
Etruscans have lost one more man in the fight; the Romans
are therefore the victors."[6] This war terminated with the celebrated march of Porsenna on Rome. Too well known are the
romantic events of that campaign to need recording.

> " How well Horatius kept the bridge
> In the brave days of old,"—

how Scœvola braved the fire, and Clœlia the water—and how the
Clusian chieftain strove to emulate these deeds of heroism by his
chivalrous magnanimity—all these events are familiar to us as
household words.

In the year 272 broke out the ninth war with Rome, during
which occurred the most interesting incident in the annals of
Veii. In the year 275, the war still continuing, the Veientes at
one time even threatening the City itself, which was pressed upon
at the same time by the Æqui and Volsci, an instance of patriotic
devotion was called forth, such as few ages have produced. Cæso
Fabius, the consul, and chief of the noblest and most powerful of
Roman *gentes*, rose in the Senate, and said—" Well know ye,
Conscript Fathers, that to keep the Veientes in check there is
need of a fixed garrison, rather than of a powerful army. Look
ye to our other foes; leave it to the Fabii to deal with Veii. We
will engage to uphold the majesty of the Roman name. The
Republic hath need of men and money elsewhere; be this war at
our own cost." The next day the whole *gens* of the Fabii, three

to have conquered the whole of Etruria,
which in token of submission sent him
the Etruscan *insignia* of authority, thence-
forth adopted by the Romans. Dionys.
Hal. III. pp. 193, 195; Flor. I. 5. Nei-
buhr (I. p. 379) justly questions the truth
of this tradition of the entire conquest of
Etruria by Tarquin, which is not noticed
by Livy or Cicero; yet thinks the union
of Rome with Etruria may be seen in it.
It seems probable that this conquest was
an invention of the old annalists, to
account for the introduction of the Etruscan symbols of royalty—the twelve lictors
with their fasces, the golden crown, the
ivory chair, the purple robe, the eagled
sceptre—which were traditionally adopted
about this time. But it were more reasonable to account for their introduction by
the accession of an Etruscan prince to the
throne of Rome.

[6] Liv. II. 6, 7; Dion. Hal. V. p. 288—
290; Plut. Publicola.

hundred and six in number, all of patrician blood, marched forth
from Rome, the consul himself at their head, amid the admiration,
the prayers, and joyful shouts of the citizens.　One single family
to meet an entire people, the most powerful of Etruria!　"Never,"
says Livy, "never did an army so small in number, or so great in
deeds, and in the admiration of their countrymen, march through
the streets of Rome."[7]　When they reached the Cremera, they
pitched their camp on a precipice-girt hill, and further protected

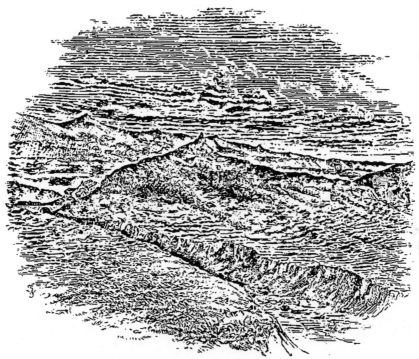

CASTLE OF THE FABII.

it by a double fosse and numerous towers.　There they maintained themselves for a year against all the efforts of their
enemies to dislodge them, ravaging the lands of Veii far and
wide, and routing the forces sent against them—till in the year
276 the Consul Æmilius Mamercus defeated the Veientes, and
forced them to sue for peace.[8]

[7] Liv. II. 48, 49; Dion. Hal. IX. p. 571
—573.　Dionysius says there were fully
4000 in the band, most of them πελάτοι τε
καὶ ἑταῖροι, and 306 only of the Fabian
gens.　Festus also says (voce Scelerata
Porta) that there were some thousands of

clientes.　Both these statements Niebuhr
(II. p. 195) thinks greatly exaggerated. A.
Gellius (XVII. 21), says there were 306
"with their families."
[8] Liv. II. 49; Dion. Hal. IX. p. 573—
576.

Tenth War.—In the following year, 277, the Veientes again declared war against Rome, and commenced by attacking the Fabii, who had not withdrawn from their camp. Knowing that open force was of little avail against these heroes, they had recourse to stratagem. They sent out flocks and herds, as if to pasture; and the Fabii beholding these from the height of their castle, sallied forth, eager for the spoil. As they were returning with it the Etruscans rushed from their ambush, and overwhelming them by numbers, after a long and desperate resistance, cut them to pieces, not one escaping save a boy, who lived to preserve the race and be the progenitor of Fabius Maximus.[9] The slaughter of the Fabii was but the prelude to a signal victory of the Veientes; and, had they followed up their advantage, Rome itself might have fallen into their hands. As it was, they took possession of the Janiculan, where they maintained themselves for many months, till they were routed by the Roman Consuls, from whom they obtained a truce for forty years.[1]

Twelfth War.—In the year 316 the Fidenates threw off the yoke of Rome, and declared for Veii. The Veientes espoused their cause, and put to death the ambassadors sent by Rome to demand an explanation. The Etruscan army encountered their foes on the banks of the Tiber, below Fidenæ, the scene of so many former defeats, and were again routed by the Dictator Mam. Æmilius; their king, Lars Tolumnius, being slain by the sword of A. Cornelius Cossus;[2] yet two years after, the allied army of Veii and Fidenæ marched up to the very gates of Rome, but were routed by the Dictator A. Servilius, who captured Fidenæ.[3]

So again in the thirteenth war which broke out in 326, the Veientes and the Fidenates crossed the Tiber, and struck terror into the City of Romulus. Their course, however, was soon

[9] Liv. II. 50 ; Dion. Hal. IX. p. 577—580. Florus, I. 12. Dionysius gives another version of this slaughter, which, however, he discredits as improbable. It is that the whole body of the Fabii left their camp to offer up a sacrifice at their family shrine in Rome; and, journeying along, heedless of danger, they were suddenly attacked by the Veientes, who rushed from their ambush, and cut them to pieces. Dionysius' reasons (IX. p. 578) for regarding this version as apocryphal are not deemed valid by Niebuhr (II. p. 202), nor by Arnold (I. p. 217), who prefers it to the other tradition. Ovid (Fast. II. 195—242) recounts the story as given in the text. See also Diodor. Sic. XI. p. 40, ed. Rhod. A. Gellius, XVII. 21. Dion. Cass. Excerpta Mai, XXI.

[1] Liv. II. 51, 53, 54. Dion. Hal. IX. pp. 582—5, 592-4.

[2] Liv. IV. 17—19. Propert. IV. Eleg. 10 Dion. Hal. Excerpta Mai, XII. 2.

[3] Liv. IV. 21, 22.

checked; for they were again utterly routed by Mam. Æmilius and Cornelius Cossus, on the very field of their former triumph. Fidenæ was taken and destroyed, and Veii obtained a truce for twenty years.[4]

Fourteenth War.—In 347, the truce having expired, war broke out afresh; and in 349 the Romans laid seige to Veii,[5] a fate which would earlier have befallen her, had it not been for the great strength of her position and fortifications, which rendered her conquest almost hopeless; but Rome being at peace elsewhere, was now enabled to pour out all her strength against her ancient foe.[6] In 352 Veii obtained the assistance of the Falisci and Capenates, who saw that she was the bulwark of Etruria against Rome, and should she fall, the whole land would be open to invasion, and they, as the nearest, would be the next to suffer. The diversion thus created, together with dissension in the Roman camp, operated greatly in favour of the Veientes, so that at one time they had possession of the Roman lines; but they were ultimately driven out, and their allies put to the rout.[7] In 356, when the siege had already endured eight years, a remarkable phenomenon occurred, which was considered a portent of some fearful event. In the height of summer, when elsewhere the streams were running dry, the waters of the Alban Lake, without any evident cause, suddenly rose to an extraordinary height, overflowing their barrier—the crater-lip of an extinct volcano—and threatened to burst it and devastate the Campagna. Sacrifices were offered up, but the gods were not appeased.[8] Messengers were despatched from Rome to consult the oracle at Delphi as to the meaning of this prodigy. In the mean time, at one of the outposts of the camp before Veii, the soldiers, as often happens in such situations, fell to gossiping with the townsfolk instead of fighting; and one of them, a Roman centurion, who had made acquaintance with an old citizen, renowned as a soothsayer, began one day to lament the fate of his friend, seeing that when the city was taken, he would be involved in the common destruction. But the Veientine laughed thereat, saying, "Ye maintain an unprofitable war in the vain hope of taking this city of Veii, knowing not that it is revealed by the Etruscan Discipline, that when the Alban Lake shall swell, the gods will not abandon Veii, unless its waters be

---

[4] Liv. IV. 30—35.

[5] Liv. IV. 58, 61. Diod. Sic. XIV. p. 247.

[6] Liv. IV. 61; V. 1.

[7] Liv. V. 8, 12, 13.

[8] Dionys. Frag. Mai, XII. 8.

drained off, so as not to mingle with the sea." The centurion pondered these words in his mind, and the next day met the old soothsayer again, and under pretext of consulting him on certain signs and portents, led him far from the walls of Veii; then suddenly seizing him in his arms, bore him off to the Roman camp. Thence he was taken before the Senate, to whom he repeated his prophecy, saying that the gods would not have it concealed, for thus it was written in the books of Fate. The Senate at first distrusted this prophecy; but, on the return of the messengers from Delphi, it was confirmed by the oracle of the god—"Romans, beware of letting the water remain in the Alban Lake: take heed that it flow not to the sea in a natural channel. Draw it off, and diffuse it through your fields. Then shall ye stand victors on the walls of Veii." In obedience to the oracle a tunnel was bored through the rocky hill, which still, as the Emissary of Albano, calls forth the admiration of the traveller; and verily it is a marvellous work for that early age —the more so, if completed, as Livy asserts, within the short space of one year.[9] In 357 the Veientes received further suc-cour from Tarquinii, by which their prospects of deliverance were raised; more especially when their allies obtained a victory, which struck terror into the citizens of Rome, who hourly ex-pected to see a triumphant foe beneath their walls.[1] But the tables were soon turned; for Camillus, now appointed dictator, first routed the forces of the allies, and then, taking a hint, it may be, from the Alban Emissary, which was by this time com-pleted, began to work his celebrated *cuniculus*, "a very great and most laborious undertaking," into the citadel of Veii. Then were the oracle and the prophecy of the soothsayer accomplished, and Veii fell, proving her power even in her final overthrow—

Vincere cum Veios posse laboris erat—[1]

"for, though beleaguered," as Livy states, "for ten long years, with more injury to her foe than to herself, she was at last over-come by stratagem, not by open force."[3]

It is instructive to observe how similar are the fruits of super-stition in all ages, and under various religious creeds. The scene

---

[9] For an account of the Alban prodigy, see Dionys. Frag. Mai, XII. cap. 8—11; Liv. V. 15, 16, 17, 19; Cic. de Divin. I. 44, and II. 32; Val. Max. I. 6, 3; Plut. Camil.; Zonaras, Annal. VII. c. 20.

[1] Liv. V. 16, 18.
[2] Propert., Lib. IV. Eleg. X. 24.
[3] Liv. V. 19, 21, 22; Flor. I. 12; Plut. Camil.

between Camillus and the statue of Juno, the patron goddess of
Veii, which he wanted to remove to Rome, is precisely such as
has been reported to occur in similar circumstances in more
recent times. Said Camillus to the goddess, " Wilt thou go to
Rome, Juno?" The image signified assent by bowing her head;
and some of the bystanders asserted that they heard a soft voice
whispering assent.[4] Ancient writers frequently report such
miracles—that statues broke into a sweat, groaned, rolled their
eyes, and turned their heads—precisely such miracles as are
related by modern enthusiasts or impostors.

The relation which the height of Isola Farnese bore to the
ancient city has been the subject of much difference of opinion.
Some have regarded it as the Arx of Veii, which Camillus
entered through his *cuniculus*. That it may have been inhabited
and fortified at an early period is not improbable; but there
are strong reasons for believing that it was not so in the time
of Camillus. Others, with still less probability, have considered
it the site of the Castle of the Fabii.[5] To me it seems evident
that at the time of the conquest it was nothing more than part
of the necropolis of Veii. The rock is hollowed in every direction
into sepulchral caves and niches, most of them apparently Etruscan; not only in the face of its cliffs, but also on the table-land
above. Now it is clear that such must have been its character in
the days of Camillus, for the Etruscans never inhabited nor
walled in a site that had been appropriated to burial; and
though it may originally have been fortified, yet once made
sacred to the dead, it must ever have remained so. The principal
necropolis of Veii lay on the opposite side of the city, but the
Etruscans did not confine their cemeteries to any particular side
of their cities, but availed themselves of any ground that was
convenient for the purpose of burial.

To see the Ponte Sodo, the Columbario, and the Painted
Tomb, which are within a short distance of each other, will not
occupy more than two hours; the Arx, lying in another direction,
will require another hour; and the entire circuit of the city, in-
cluding the above lions, can be accomplished in four or five.
The *cicerone* will provide asses, if required,—possibly saddles.
Visitors should bring their own provender with them, or, the
guide will provide refreshment, which may be eaten without

---

[4] Liv. V. 22. Plut. Camil. Dionysius
(Excerp. Mai, XII. 17) says the goddess
repeated her assent in an audible voice.

According to Livy, it was not Camillus
who put the question.

[5] See Appendix, Note III.

alarm, in spite of the suspicion expressed by a lady writer that Isola is a sort of Cannibal *Island*.[6] All fear of bandits, suggested in the same quarter, may be dispensed with, and "mounted *contadini*, covered with togas and armed with long iron-shod poles," may be encountered without trepidation as honest drovers in quest of cattle.

Veii is of such easy access that no visitor to Rome should fail to make an excursion thither. It is not more than a couple of hours' drive from the gates, and though there be little of attraction on the road beyond views of the all-glorious Campagna, and though the site of the ancient city be well-nigh denuded of its ruins, yet the intense interest of a spot, so renowned in history,—

> " And where the antique fame of stout Camill
> Doth ever live—"

and the tomb now open with its marvellous paintings and strange furniture, which carry the mind back with realising force to the earliest days of Rome, render a trip to the site of Veii one of the most delightful excursions in the neighbourhood of the Eternal City.

APPENDIX TO CHAPTER I.

NOTE I.—SEPULCHRAL NICHES, AND MODES OF SEPULTURE. See p. 10.

Sepulchral niches are found in the rocks in the neighbourhood of other ancient cities in the southern district of Etruria, but nowhere in such abundance and variety as at Veii. Hollowed rocks like these, with their faces full of small sepulchral niches, are almost unique in Etruria, though abundant at Syracuse, and other Greek sites of Sicily. Tombs full of niches are not unfrequent in Etruria, but as they are almost always found in exposed situations, rifled of all their furniture, it is difficult to pronounce on their antiquity. Their similarity to the *columbaria* of the Romans, is suggestive of such an origin, while the want of the *olla* hole, already mentioned, and the fact of being hollowed in the rock, instead of being constructed with masonry, distinguish them from the Roman *columbaria*. It is not improbable that these pigeon-holed tombs of Etruria are of native origin, and that the Romans thence derived their idea of the *columbaria*, most likely from those of Veii, the nearest city of Etruria. Canina (Etr. Marit. 1. p. 123) is of this opinion, and takes these niches at Veii to be all prior to the Roman conquest. By some the pigeon-holed tombs in Etruscan cemeteries are regarded as of late date, indicating a period when burning had superseded burial. Micali

---

[6] Sepulchres of Etruria, p. 109.

(Mon. Ined., pp. 163, 370), who is of this opinion, thinks all such tombs on this site posterior to the fall of Veii. But cremation was of far higher antiquity. The Greeks, in the earliest times, certainly buried their dead ; such was the custom in the time of Cecrops, and of fable (Cic. de Leg. II. capp. 22, 25), yet in Homeric times burning was practised, as in the case of Patroclus and of Hector. The expense of the pyre, however, as we find it described by Homer (Il. XXIII. 164, et seq.; XXIV. 784, et seq.), and by Virgil (Æn. XI. 72, et seq.), must have put it out of the reach of the community. My own excavations in various Greek cemeteries convince me that, with that people, burial was the rule, burning the exception. De Jorio, a practised excavator, maintains that burial among the Greeks of Magna Græcia was to burning as ten to one—among the Romans as one to ten (Metodo per frugare i Sepolcri, p. 28; cf. Serradifalco, Ant. di Sic. IV. p. 197). Philosophic notions of purification or of resolving the frame into its original elements, may have had to do with the practice of burning. My own experience as an excavator in Greek cemeteries convinces me that both methods were practised coevally. Cinerary urns were generally deposited in a hole at no great depth and covered with a slab or tile. So at least I have invariably found them in Greek necropoles, mixed with tombs hollowed in the rock, or constructed of masonry.

The practice of the Romans also in the earliest times was to bury, not burn their dead (Plin. Nat. His. VII. 55), the latter mode having been adopted only when it was found that in protracted wars the dead were disinterred. Yet burning also seems to have been in vogue in the time of Numa, who, as he wished to be interred, was obliged to forbid his body to be burned (Plut. Numa). Perhaps the latter custom had reference only to great men. Ovid represents the body of Remus as burnt (Fast. IV. 853-6). In the early times of the Republic, interment was the general mode ; cremation, however, seems to have gradually come into use—the Twelve Tables speak of both (Cic. de Leg. II. 23)—yet certain families long adhered to the more ancient custom, the Cornelian gens for instance, the first member of which, who was burnt, was Sylla the Dictator, who, having dishonoured the corpse of Marius, feared retaliation on his own remains (Plin. loc. cit. Cic. de Leg. II. 22). Burning, at first confined to heroes, or the wealthy, became general under the Empire, but at length fell out of fashion, and was principally applied to the corpses of freedmen and slaves, and in the fourth century after Christ was wholly superseded by burial. Macrob. Sat. VII. 7.

With the Etruscans it is difficult to pronounce whether inhumation or cremation was the earlier, as instances of both together are found in tombs of very remote antiquity. With them, as with the Greeks and Romans, both methods seem, in later periods of their history, to have been practised contemporaneously. In certain sites, however, one or the other mode was the more prevalent. At Volterra, Chiusi, Perugia, and the northern cities generally, cremation was the fashion ; at Tarquinii, Cære, and the other cities of the great southern plain, it was rare, and interment was almost universal. The antiquity of cremation is confirmed by the cinerary hut-urns of Albano, which analogy, as well as the position in which they were found, indicates to be of very ancient date—by the well-tombs of Poggio Renzo, the earliest sepulchres of Chiusi—and by the very archaic character of some of the "ash-chests" and cinerary pots found in Etruscan cemeteries.

Note II.—Veii one of the Twelve. See p. 19.

That Veii was one of the Twelve principal cities of Etruria is implied by Livy (II. 6), and by Dionysius (V., p. 288), when they state that it united with Tarquinii, the metropolis of Etruria, in assisting Tarquinius Superbus to recover his throne, and again, where the example of Veii, in throwing off the yoke of Servius Tullius, was followed by Cære and Tarquinii (Dion. Hal. IV., p. 231), undoubtedly cities of the Confederation. It is stated explicitly, where Tullius grants peace to the Twelve Cities, but mulcts the aforesaid three, which commenced the revolt, and instigated the rest to war against the Romans. It is clearly shown by Dionysius (Frag. Mai. XII. 13), when he calls it "a great and flourishing city, not the least part of Etruria;" and also (VI., p. 398), when he calls Veii and Tarquinii "the two most illustrious cities of Etruria;" and again (IX., p. 577), when he says that the Veientes, having made peace with Rome, "the eleven Etruscan people who were not parties to this peace having convened a council of the nation, accused the Veientes, because they had made peace without consulting the rest." It is also clearly shown by Livy (V. 1), in that the king of the Veientes was disappointed because another had been chosen by the suffrages of the Twelve Cities to be high-priest of the nation, in preference to himself. Livy elsewhere (IV. 23) states, that Veii and Falerii sent ambassadors to the Twelve people to demand a council of the nation, at the Voltumnæ Fanum. This might, at first sight, be interpreted as indicating these two cities as not of the Twelve; but on further consideration it will be seen that the term "Twelve Cities" was a common, or as Müller (II. 1, 2, n. 20) calls it, "a standing expression," and is not opposed to the idea of the two cities being included. They sought for a convention of the Twelve, of which they formed a part. Had it not been so they could scarcely have acted an independent part; the cities to which they were subject would have made the demand. When, at a later date, Capena joined Falerii in a similar request (Liv. V. 17), it should be remembered that Veii was then closely beleaguered, and Capena being her colony, might aptly act as her representative. Where Livy mentions the Twelve Cities, after the fall of Veii (VII. 21), it can only mean that the number being a fixed one in each of the three divisions of Etruria, like the Thirty Cities of Latium, and the Twelve of the Achæan League, the place of the city that was separated was immediately supplied by another (Niebuhr. I., p. 119). But were all these historical proofs wanting to show Veii to have been one of the Twelve, her large size, as determined by existing remains—an extent second to that of no other Etruscan city—would be evidence enough.

Note III.—Isola Farnese, and the Castle of the Fabii. See p. 25.

Though at first view it would seem that a site so strongly fortified by nature as the rock of Isola, would naturally have been chosen for a citadel, yet there is good ground for rejecting the supposition. Its isolation—separated as it is from the city by a broad glen of considerable depth, is strongly opposed to the idea. Nibby, indeed, who regards Isola as the Arx, takes a hint from Holstenius (Adnot. ad Cluv., p. 54), and thinks it may have been connected with the city by means of a covered way between parallel walls, as Athens was with the Piræus; but no traces of such a structure are visible, and it probably never existed save in the worthy Professor's imagination. Livy (V. 21) makes it clear that the Arx adjoined the city, for, on the former being captured by Camillus, the latter immediately fell into his hands, which could not have been the case had Isola been the Arx, for its possession by an enemy, in those days of non-artillery, would have proved an annoyance, but could have little affected the safety of the city. There is every reason to believe, as already shown, that Isola was only a portion of the necropolis. If nothing more than Roman *columbaria*, and Roman funeral inscriptions, had been found on the spot, there would be room for doubt, seeing that sepulchral remains of that nation have also been found on the Piazza d'Armi, the true Arx, as well as within the walls of Etruscan Veii; which fact, however, only proves the small size of the Roman *municipium*. But the numerous Etruscan tombs on the height of Isola, and the absence of every trace of such sepulture on the Piazza d'Armi, seem alone, independently of their position with regard to the city, to afford a strong argument in favour of the opinion that the latter, and not Isola, was the Arx of Veii.

It is surprising that Isola should ever have been mistaken for the Castle of the Fabii. The objection raised by Gell, that it is not on the Cremera, scarcely seems valid, for who is to pronounce with certainty which of the two confluents bore the ancient name? It seems incredible, however, that the band of the Fabii should have been allowed to take up a position at so short a distance from Veii, overlooking its very walls, and that they should have succeeded in raising a fortress here, and strengthening it with a double fosse and numerous towers (Dion. Hal. IX., p. 573). Dionysius says they fixed their camp on an abrupt and precipice-girt height on the banks of the Cremera, which is not far distant from the city of Veii; a description which will apply to any such site between Veii and the Tiber, though scarcely to the hill of Isola, hardly two bow-shots from the walls. Ovid (Fast. II. 205), as well as Dionysius, seems to imply that their camp was between Veii and Rome, and Livy (II. 49) indicates a similar position, when he says, that they were on the frontier between the Etruscan and Roman territories, protecting the one from foes, and devastating the other ; and again more decidedly, when he asserts that the Veientes, on attacking the castle of the Fabii, were driven back by the Roman legions to Saxa Rubra, where they had a camp. Now, Saxa Rubra was on the Via Flaminia,[1] some miles distant, and it is evident that had Isola been the Castellum Fabiorum, the nearest place of refuge for the Veientes would have been their own city, and it is not to be believed that they could not have reached some one of its many gates even though attacked in flank by the Roman horse, as Livy states. The site claimed for the Fabian Camp by Nibby and Gell, but first indicated by Nardini (Veio Antico, p. 180), is on the right bank of the Cremera, near its junction with the Tiber, on the steep heights above the Osteria della Valchetta, and overhanging the Flaminian Way, about half-way between Veii and Rome, on which height are still remains of ancient buildings, though not of a style

[1] Cluverius (Ital. Antiq. II. p. 527) places Saxa Rubra at Borghetto, ten miles from Rome; Holstenius, Cramer, and Gell, somewhat nearer the City, at Prima Porta, five miles from Veii. That it was on or near the Flaminian Way is evident, not only from a passage in Tacitus, "Antonius per Flaminiam ad Saxa Rubra venit" (Hist. III. 79), but from the Peutingerian Table and Jerusalem Itinerary, which agree in placing it on this Via, nine miles from Rome. That it was not far from the City is clear from Cicero (Phil. II. 31). Martial (IV., ep. 64. 15) shows that it could be seen from the Janiculan, and that it was a place of small importance—*breves Rubras.*

which can be referred to so early a period. The Fabii could not have chosen a more favourable spot than this for holding the Veientes in check, because it dominated the whole valley of the Cremera, then the boundary, as Livy implies, between the Roman and Etruscan territories, protected the former from incursions, and also held in check the Fidenates, should they have rebelled and attempted to form a junction with their kinsmen of Veii. See the woodcut at p. 21, made from a sketch by the author.

The ruins on the summit of this height are of late Roman and of mediæval times—there is not a fragment that can be referred to the Republican era; only in the face of the cliff is a sewer cut in the rock, like those on Etruscan sites, showing the spot to have been inhabited at an earlier period than the extant remains would testify. On the height on the opposite side of the glen, are some Roman ruins of *opus incertum*, of prior antiquity.

Neither of these eminences has more than *situation* to advance as a claim to be considered the site of the "Præsidium Cremeræ." If we look for an objection, we might suggest that the distance, six miles, from Veii, seems too great, but, till a stronger claim is urged for some other site, we may be content to regard this as the Thermopylæ of the Fabii.

GROTTA CAMPANA, AS IT WAS DISCOVERED.

CHAPTER II.

VEII.—THE CEMETERY.

Non è il mondan romore altro ch' un fiato
Di vento, ch' or vien quinci, ed or vien quindi,
E muta nome, perchè muta lato.—DANTE.

                    The noise
Of worldly fame is but a blast of wind
That blows from diverse points, and shifts its name
Shifting the point it blows from.—CARY.

It is to be regretted that so little is to be seen of the long-forgotten dead of Veii. It was the largest, and, in Romulus' time,
the most mighty of Etruscan cities, and yet in scarcely another
cemetery are there so few tombs to be seen. The hills around
the city without doubt abound in sepulchres, all hewn out of the
rock according to the universal Etruscan custom, but with the
exception of those around the hamlet of Isola, which from the
exposure of ages have lost almost all form and character, one
alone remains open to give the traveller an idea of the burying-
places of the Veientes. Yet excavations are frequently, almost
yearly, carried forward, mostly by dealers in antiquities at Rome;
but as lucre is their sole object they are content to rifle the
tombs of everything convertible into cash, and cover them in
immediately with earth. Many tombs, it is true, have no peculiar
features—nothing to redeem them from the common herd of

sepulchres, of which, *ex uno disce omnia;* but some discrimina-
tion should be exercised as to this, and the filling up should not
be left to caprice or convenience.   Surely, among the multitude
that have been opened, some containing treasures in gold,
jewellery, and highly ornamented bronzes, not a few must have
been found remarkable enough for their form or decorations to
have demanded preservation.

Of tumuli there is no lack, though they are not so abundant as
at Cervetri and Corneto : some· of them have been proved to be
Roman. That on the east of the city, called La Vaccareccia,
with its crest of trees so prominent an object in the Campagna,
has been excavated, but without success. Like the rest, it was
probably raised over some Lucumo or distinguished man among the
Veientes, but whether it be the tomb of Propertius, king of Veii,
or of Morrius, the Veientine king who instituted the Salian rites
and dances, as Gell suggests, or of some other prince unknown to
fame, is mere matter of conjecture.

This tumulus is worthy of a visit for the magnificent view
which it commands of the Campagna. There are several other
tumuli or barrows in the valley of the Cremera below the Arx,
and also on the heights on the right bank, which may have been
raised over the slain in some of the bloody combats between the
citizens and Romans during the ten years' siege, or they may be
individual or family sepulchres. On these heights Gell thinks
Camillus must have pitched his camp in the last siege of Veii.
At their base is a singular archway in the rock, whether natural
or artificial is not easy to say, called L'Arco di Pino, which, with
its masses of yellow and grey tufo, overhung with ilices, forms a
most picturesque object in form and colouring, and claims a place
in the visitor's sketch-book. Several other large tumuli lie on
the west and north of the city, and may be observed on the right
of the modern road to Baccano.

The solitary tomb remaining open in the necropolis of Veii was
discovered in the winter of 1842–43 by the late Marchese Campana, so well known for his unrivalled collection of Etruscan
vases and jewellery.   It is of very remarkable character, and
has fortunately been preserved for the gratification of the traveller,
with its furniture untouched, almost in the exact condition in
which it was discovered.

When I first knew Veii, its necropolis possessed no interest;
though a thousand sepulchres had been excavated, not one remained open, and it was the discovery of this tomb that led me

to turn my steps once more to the site. As I crossed the ancient city, I perceived that the wood which had covered the northern side had been cut down, so as no longer to impede the view. The eye wandered across the valley of the Formello, and the bare undulations of the necropolis opposite, away to the green mass of Monte Aguzzo northwards, with the conical and tufted Monte Musino behind it, and the village of Formello on a wooded slope below—a wild and desolate scene, such as meets the eye from many a spot in the Campagna, and to which the baying of the sheep-dogs in the valley beneath me, and the sharp shriek of the falcon wheeling above my head, formed a harmonious accompaniment—and yet, whether from the associations connected with this region, or the elevating effect of the back-ground of glorious Apennines, it is a wildness that charms—a desolation that, to me at least, yields a delight such as few scenes of cultivated beauty can impart. From this point I descried the site of the tomb, in a hill on the other side of the valley of the Formello, where deep furrows on the slopes marked recent excavations.

The tomb, in compliment to its discoverer, has been termed

La Grotta Campana.

Half way up the slope of a mound, the Poggio Michele, is a long passage, about six feet wide, cut through the rock towards the centre of the hill. At the entrance on each side crouches a stone lion, of that quaint, singular style of sculpture, that ludicrously clumsy form, which the antiquary recognises as the conventional mode among Etruscan sculptors of representing the king of beasts. At the further end of the passage crouch two similar lions, one on each side of the door of the tomb—all intended as figurative guardians of the sepulchre.[8] The passage

---

[8] Inghirami (Mon. Etrus. I., p. 216) rejects this notion, on the ground that they could not frighten violators, who, if they had overcome their dread of the avenging Manes, so as to attempt to plunder a sepulchre, would not be deterred by mere figures in stone. But he argues from a modern point of view, and does not allow for the effect of such palpable symbols of vengeful wrath, upon the superstitious minds of the ancients. Figures of lions, as images of power, and to inspire dread, are of very ancient use, and quite oriental.

Thus, Solomon set lions around his throne (1 Kings X., 19, 20), and the Egyptians and Hindoos placed them at the entrance of their temples. That they were at a very early period used by the Greeks as figurative guardians, is proved by the celebrated gate of Mycenæ. The monuments of Lycia, now in the British Museum, and the tombs of Phrygia, delineated by Steuart (Ancient Monuments of Lydia and Phrygia), show this animal in a similar relation to sepulchres; and moreover establish a strong point of analogy between Etruria and the East.

is of ancient formation, and has merely been cleared out by the spade of the excavator.

The door, of which the *custode* keeps the key, is a modern addition—the ancient one, which was a slab of stone, having been broken to pieces by former excavators; for it is rare to find an Etruscan tomb which has escaped the spoilers of every previous age, though the earliest riflers, after carrying off the precious

metals and jewellery, often left every other article, even the most beautiful vases, untouched. It is a moment of excitement, this—the first peep within an Etruscan painted tomb; and if this be the first the visitor has beheld, he will find food enough for wonderment. He enters a low, dark chamber, hewn out of the rock, whose dull greyish hue adds to the gloom. He catches an imperfect glance of several jars of great size, and smaller pieces of crockery and bronze, lying on benches or standing on the floor, but he heeds them not, for his eye is at once riveted on the extraordinary paintings on the inner wall of the tomb, facing the entrance. Were there ever more strangely devised, more grotesquely designed figures?—was there ever such a harlequin scene as this. Here is a horse with legs of most undesirable length and tenuity, chest and quarters far from meagre, but barrel pinched in like a lady's waist. His colour is not to be told in a word—as Lord Tolumnius' chestnut colt, or Mr. C. Vibenna's bay gelding.   His neck and fore-hand are red, with yellow spots—his head black—mane and tail yellow—hind-quarters and near leg black—near fore-leg corresponding with his body, but off-legs yellow, spotted with red.   His groom is naked, and his skin is of a deep-red hue.   A boy of similar complexion bestrides the horse; and another man precedes him, bearing a hammer, or, it may be, a *bipennis*, or double-headed axe, upon his shoulder; while on the

croup crouches a tailless cat or dog, parti-coloured like the steed, with one paw familiarly resting on the boy's shoulder.   Another beast, similar in character, but with the head of a dog, stands beneath the horse.   This is but one scene, and occupies a band about three feet deep, or the upper half of the wall.

In the band below is a sphinx, standing, not crouching, as is usual on ancient Egyptian monuments, with a red face and bosom, spotted with white—straight black hair, depending behind —wings short, with curling tips, and striped black, red, and yellow —body, near hind-leg and tail of the latter colour, near fore-leg black, and off-legs like the bosom.   A panther, or large animal of the feline species, sits behind, rampant, with one paw on the haunch, the other on the tail of the sphinx; and beneath the latter is an ass, or it may be a deer, of smaller size than the panther.   Both are painted in the same curious parti-colours as those already described.

On the opposite side of the doorway (for there is a door in
this wall, opening into an inner chamber), in the upper band, is a
horse, with a boy on his back, and a "spotted pard" behind
him sitting on the ground.   In the lower band is another similar
beast of great size, with his tongue lolling out and a couple of
dogs beneath him.   All these quadrupeds are of the same curious
patchwork of red, yellow, and black.[9]

To explain the signification of these figures I pretend not.
In quaintness and peculiarity of form they strongly resemble the

animals represented on the vases of the most archaic style, and
like them had probably some mystic or symbolic import; but who
shall now interpret them? who shall now read aright the hand-
writing on these walls?   Panthers are frequently introduced into
the painted tombs of Etruria, as figurative guardians of the dead,
being probably sacred to Mantus, the Hades of the Etruscans.
The boys on horseback I take to be emblematical of the passage
of the soul into another state of existence, as is clearly the case
in many cinerary urns of later date; and the figure with the
hammer is probably intended for the Charon of the Etruscans.
There is nothing of an Egyptian character in the faces of the
men, as in some of the oldest monuments of Etruria, where the
figures have more or less of the Egyptian physiognomy, according

---

[9] These harlequin figures are not unique.
They have been found also in a painted
tomb at Cervetri, and to a lesser extent
are to be seen in the tombs of Tarquinii,
where, however, they cannot pretend to so
high an antiquity.

to their degree of antiquity. The features here on the contrary are very rudely drawn, and quite devoid of any national peculiarity, seeming rather like untutored efforts to portray the human face divine.[1] Indeed, in this particular, as well as in the uncouth representations of flowers interspersed with the figures, and of the same parti-coloured hues, there is a great resemblance to the paintings on early Doric vases—nor would it be difficult to find points of analogy with Assyrian reliefs on the one hand, and with Mexican paintings on the other. The sphinx, though with an Egyptian *coiffure*, has none of that character in other respects, for the Egyptians never represented this chimæra with wings, nor of so attenuated a form. The land of the Nile however may be seen in the ornamental border of lotus-flowers, emblematical of immortality, which surmounts the figures.

On either side of this tomb, and projecting from the walls, is a bench of rock about two feet and a half high, on each of which, when the tomb was opened, lay a skeleton ; but exposure to the air caused them very soon to crumble to dust. One of these had been a warrior, and on the right-hand bench you still see portions of the breast-plate, and the helmet entire, which once encased his remains. Observe the helmet—it is a plain bronze casque of the simplest form. On one side of it is a hole, which seems by the indentation of the metal to have been caused by a hard blow. Turn the casque about and you will observe on the opposite side a gash, evidently formed by the point of a sword or lance from within ; proving this to have been the fatal wound which deprived the wearer of life.

> " Through teeth and skull and helmet
>   So fierce a thrust was sped,
> The good sword stood a hand-breadth out
>   Behind the Tuscan's head."

On the same bench you see the iron head, much corroded, and the bronze rest of a spear—it may be the very weapon which inflicted the death-wound. And how long since may that be ? If it were not subsequent to the decorations of the tomb—and the fact of this warrior being laid out on one of the rock-hewn benches, goes far to prove him one of its earliest occupants—it must have been in very remote antiquity. The most untutored eye can perceive at a glance that the paintings belong to a very early age of the world. After having carefully studied every

---

[1] The woodcut on p. 34 fails to give the strange rudeness of the features.

other painted tomb now open in Etruria, I have not a moment's
hesitation in asserting, that this is in point of antiquity pre-
eminent; and, I believe, that few other tombs in Italy, though
unpainted, have any claim to be considered anterior to it. Its
great antiquity is confirmed by its contents, all of which are of
the most archaic character. Campana was of opinion that if it
did not precede the foundation of Rome it was at least coeval
with that event. I am not inclined to assign to it an inferior
antiquity.[2] The wall within the doorway is built up with masonry
of very rude character, uncemented, belonging to an age prior to
the invention of the arch; for the door is formed of blocks gradually converging towards the top, as in the oldest European
architecture extant—in the style of the Cyclopean gateways of
Greece and Italy—those mysteries of unknown antiquity. On
one side of the door indeed there is some approximation to the
arch—cuneiform blocks like *roussoirs*, and one also in the place
of a key-stone; but if this be not mere accident, as might be
supposed from the blocks not holding together as in a true arch,
it shows merely a transition period, when, though somewhat of

---

[2] It is now universally admitted that
the decorations of this tomb are the earliest
works yet known of Etruscan wall-paint-
ing. It is more easy, however, to determine their relative antiquity, than to fix
their precise date. Though there are
features unquestionably oriental, there is
here no imitation of the Egyptian, all is
genuinely national, and characteristic of
the primitive Etruscan school.

Dr. Helbig, of the Archæological Institute
of Rome, says of these paintings, "The
design is rude, and shows a want of decision almost childish. The bodies of the
beasts are all out of proportion. The
artist could not express the finer parts of
the human form, such as the fingers, and
the eye, which is represented without a
pupil, and in two of the figures is out of
its proper place; nor in the countenances
is there any variety of form and expression.
The influence of archaic Greek art is clearly
distinguishable. The bodies of the men
are delineated according to the same laws
of style which we find in the Corinthian
and Attic vases." Ann. Inst. 1863,
pp. 337—341. Dr. H. Brunn, of Munich,
cannot admit that these paintings show
the true archaic Greek style, and is of
opinion that the rudeness and defects of

the design, which he would ascribe rather
to the unskilfulness of the individual artist,
than to the imperfect development of the
art, give them an appearance of higher
antiquity than really belongs to them. He
does not, however, dispute that they are
the earliest works of pictorial art yet
discovered in Etruria. Ann. Inst. 1866,
p. 418.

Few painted tombs have been discovered
in Greece. One in the island of Ægina has
only four figures sketched in charcoal on the
walls of rock, representing a Bacchic
dance. The style is free and masterly.
Several painted tombs also have been found
at Pæstum, a few at Cyrene in Libya, and
some also in Lycia. Pausanias (VII. c. 22)
describes one near the city of Tritæa,
painted by Nicias, the Athenian. "On
an ivory chair sits a young woman of great
beauty; before her stands a maid-servant,
holding an umbrella, and a youth quite
beardless is standing by, clad in a tunic
and a purple *chlamys* over it, and by him
stands a slave with some javelins in his
hand, leading dogs such as are used by
hunters. We were not able to divine their
names; but we all alike conjectured that
here a husband and wife were interred in
the same sepulchre."

the principle of the arch was comprehended, it was not brought to perfection. Now as there is every reason to believe that the arch was known to, and practised by, the Etruscans at a very early period, prior to the reign of the Tarquins, when the Cloacæ of Rome were constructed, it is obvious that the masonry in this tomb indicates a very high antiquity.

The skeleton on the other bench was probably that of the wife of this warrior, as no weapons or armour were found on the couch. But these were not the sole occupants of the tomb. The large jars on the floor were found to contain human ashes, probably of the dependents of the family; if so, they would indicate that, among the Etruscans of that age, to bury was more honourable than to burn—or at least they prove that both modes of sepulture were practised at a very early period. There are four of these jars (see the annexed woodcut), about three feet high, of dark brown earthenware, and ornamented with patterns in relief or colours; also several smaller jars of quaint, squat form, with archaic figures painted in the earliest style of Greek art, representing in one instance a dance of Bacchanals.[3]   A

CINERARY JAR, GROTTA CAMPANA.

bronze *præfericulum* or ewer, and a light *candelabrum* of very simple form, stand on the bench, by the warrior's helmet. Several bronze *specchj*, or mirrors, and small figures of men

[3] This is some of the earliest painted pottery of Veii, and is very similar to that found at Cære. That of purely Etruscan manufacture, peculiar to Veii, consists of vases and jars of similar description, of plain black or brown ware, but with figures *scratched* upon the clay when wet, or else moulded in very low relief. Such plain ware is the most abundant on this site; painted vases are comparatively rare. Those in the archaic style with animals and chimæras are sometimes of extraordinary size, larger than any Panathenaic vases. There are also some with black figures in the archaic style, and even with red figures on a black ground, sometimes of a noble simplicity; yet, in spite of the beauty of conception and design, the rigidity and severity of the early school are never wholly lost. We may hence infer that vase-painting had not reached its perfection when Veii was captured. This is a fact worthy of attention as tending to fix the era of the art. For as Veii was taken in the year of Rome 358, and remained uninhabited and desolate till the commencement of the Empire, we have sure grounds for ascribing all the pottery found in its tombs to a period prior to 396 B.C.

For a description of the vases of Veii, see "Descrizione de' Vasi dell' Isola Farnese, &c., di Secondiano Campanari, Roma, 1839," with a review of the same in Bull. Inst. 1840, pp. 12—16. Also Micali, Mon. Ined., p. 156, et seq. tav. XXVII.; and p. 242, tav. XLI.

or gods in terra-cotta, and of animals in amber, were also found in the tomb.

Of similar description is the furniture of the inner and smaller chamber. The ceiling has two beams carved in relief; showing that even at a very early period Etruscan tombs were imitations of the abodes of the living. A low ledge of rock runs round three sides of the chamber, and on it stand as many square cinerary urns or chests of earthenware, about eighteen inches long and a foot high, each with an overhanging lid, and a man's head projecting from it, as if for a handle; probably intended for a portrait of him whose ashes are stored in the urn[4] (see the annexed woodcut). On the same ledge are

eight tall jars, some plain, others painted— banded red and yellow. Two stand in pans of terra-cotta, with a rim of animals of archaic form, beautifully executed in relief. There are other smaller jars or vases, all probably of cinerary character. In the centre of the apartment stands a low brazier of bronze, nearly two feet in diameter; which must have served for burning perfumes to destroy the effluvium of the sepulchre.

CINERARY URN, GROTTA CAMPANA.

The walls of this inner chamber are unpainted, save opposite the doorway, where six disks or "crowns," as Campana calls them, are represented as suspended. They

---

[4] Such urns as this are almost the only specimens yet found of the fictile statuary for which Veii was of old renowned, though a few *antefixæ* and decorated tiles have been brought to light. The fictile *quadriga* made at Veii by order of Tarquinius Superbus was, like the Palladium, one of the seven sacred things, on the preservation of which the power and safety of Rome were believed to depend—the others being, Cybele's needle, the ashes of Orestes, Priam's sceptre, Ilione's veil, and the Salian bucklers. Serv. ad Æn. VII. 188. The legend of the *quadriga* is worth recording. Tarquin had bespoken one or more such cars of earthenware to adorn the pediment of his new temple on the Capitoline, according to the Etruscan fashion in architecture; but the clay, instead of shrinking as usual, swelled so as to burst the mould, and not to be extracted from the furnace; and the Etruscan soothsayers interpreting this as betokening increase of dominion to the possessor, the chariot was retained at Veii. Shortly after, however, a chariot-race was held at this city, and the victor having received his crown was leaving the arena, when his horses suddenly took fright, and dashed off at full speed towards Rome; nor did they stop till they arrived at the foot of the Capitol, where they threw out and killed their driver at the gate, afterwards called from his name, Ratumena. Whereon the Veientes, terrified at this second portent, gave up the earthen *quadriga* to the Romans. Plut. Publicola. Festus v. Ratumena. Plin. H. N. VIII. 65. XXVIII. 4. XXXV. 45.

are fifteen inches in diameter, and are painted with a mosaic-work of various colours, black, blue, red, yellow, and grey, in such small fragments, and with such an arrangement, as if they were copies of some kaleidoscopic effect. They are too small for shields; and the whole disk being filled with colour, precludes the idea of crowns or chaplets. They were probably intended for *paterœ* or drinking-bowls, and the colour may indicate some style of ornamentation of which no examples have come down to us.[5] Above them are many stumps of iron nails, formerly supporting vases, the originals, it may be, of these painted disks; and around the door between the two chambers are many similar traces of nails. It was a common custom to suspend vessels, and jugs of terra-cotta or bronze in this manner in Etruscan tombs; but, as no fragments of such were found at the foot of the wall, it is probable that something of a more perishable nature, or so valuable as to have been removed by previous spoilers, was here suspended.

At the entrance of this double-chambered tomb, and opening on the same passage, is another small tomb, evidently an appendage to the family-vault, and apparently of more recent formation. It is the porter's lodge to this mansion of the dead—and not metaphorically so, for Etruscan tombs being generally imitations of houses, the analogy may be concluded to hold throughout; and these small chambers, of which there are often two, one on each side of the *ostium*, or doorway, answer to the *cellulœ janitoris,* or *ostiarii*—not here within the entrance, as usual in Roman houses, but just outside—*janitor ante fores*—and it is highly probable that the lions here found were in place of the dog in domestic houses—*custos liminis—Cave canem!* Here were probably interred the slaves of the family, who were frequently buried at the doors of their masters' sepulchres. This little chamber has a bench of rock on one side, on which are rudely carved the legs of a couch, with a *hypopodium* or long low stool beneath it; representing respectively the banqueting-couch and accompanying stool, so often pictured on the walls of Etruscan tombs. The body was probably extended on its rocky bier without coffin or sarcophagus. No vestiges of it, or of its habiliments, now remain—nothing beyond sundry small articles of pottery, perfume-vases, drinking-cups, plates,

---

[5] The analogy of a *phiala* with similar decorations, depicted in the hands of a banqueter in the Grotta della Pulcella, at Corneto, leaves no doubt that these disks were intended to represent drinking-cups.

bowls, and bronze mirrors—the usual furniture of Etruscan sepulchres.

The rock out of which these tombs are hewn is not tufo, but an arenaceous clay, of greyish-brown hue, indurating by exposure to the air. This is a fair specimen of the Etruscan tombs found at Veii, though in general they have not more than a single chamber. Sometimes they are formed with a rounded, sometimes with a gabled ceiling, always alike hewn out of the rock.

One peculiarity of this sepulchre remains to be noticed. In most Etruscan tombs there is some inscription, either on sarcophagus, or urn, on *cippus*, or tile, or it may be on the inner walls, or external façade; but to whom this belonged, no epitaph, no inscription whatever, remains to inform us. Here was interred some bold but unfortunate chieftain, some Veientine Lucumo, not less brave, not less worthy, it may be, of having his name preserved, than Achilles, Ulysses, Æneas, or half the heroes of antiquity; but he had no bard of fame to immortalise his deeds.

> " Vain was the chief's, the hero's pride !
> He had no poet—and he died ;
> In vain he fought, in vain he bled !—
> He had no poet—and is dead."

More than this we know not of him. His deeds may have been sung by some native Homer—some compatriot may have chronicled his valour with the elegance and poetic fire of a Livy, or the dignified pen of a Tacitus, but they and their works have alike perished with him. It might be that his renown was so great that it was deemed a vain thing to raise a monumental stone—his deeds spoke for him—they were such as his friends and admiring countrymen fondly imagined could never die; so they laid him out on his rocky bier, fresh, it would seem, from the battle-field, with his battered panoply for a shroud, and there

> "They left him alone with his glory."

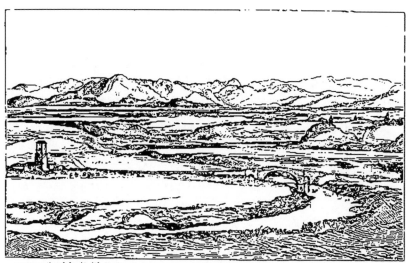

THE ANIO AND PONTE SALARO.

CHAPTER III.

CASTEL GIUBILEO.—*FIDENÆ.*

. . . . tot vacuas urbes !—LUCAN.

Revolving, as we rest on the green turf,
The changes from that hour when He from Troy
Went up the Tiber. ROGERS.

IF from Veii the traveller follow the course of the Cremera for five or six miles it will lead him to the Tiber, of which it is a tributary. In the cliffs of the lonely but beautiful ravine through which it flows he will observe in several places sepulchral caves, particularly at the end nearer Veii; and on reaching the mouth of the glen, he will have, on the right, the ruin-capt heights which are supposed by Nibby and Gell to have been the site of the Castle of the Fabii.

Exactly opposite the mouth of this glen, and on the other bank of the Tiber, rises the hill which was once crowned by the city of Fidenæ. This, though beyond the bounds of Etruria Proper, being on the left bank of the Tiber, was an Etruscan city,[1] and in all probability a colony of Veii; for Livy speaks of the consanguinity of the inhabitants of the two cities, though

---

[1] Liv. I. 15. Strab. V., p. 226. Plutarch (Romul.) says Fidenæ was claimed by Veii.

some writers assign to it a Latin origin.[2] It seems at least to have been dependent on Veii, and was frequently associated with her in opposition to Rome. Its history, indeed, save that on several occasions it fell into the hands of the Romans, is almost identical with that of Veii.

The traveller who would visit the site of Fidenæ had better do so from Rome ; for unless, like Cassius, he be prepared to

> "leap into the angry flood
> And swim to yonder point,"

he will find no means of crossing " the troubled Tyber ; " and rapid and turbulent is the current at this point, as it was in ancient times.[3] It is but a short excursion—only five miles—from Rome, and the road lies across a very interesting part of the Campagna. There are indeed two roads to it. One, the carriage road, runs direct from the Porta Salara, and follows the line of the ancient Via Salaria. But the traveller on foot or horseback should quit the Eternal City by the Porta del Popolo, and leaving the Florence road on the left, take the path to the Acqua Acetosa. Here a green hill—one of those bare, square table-lands, so common in the Campagna—rises on the right. Ascend it where a broad furrow in the slope seems to mark the line of an ancient road. You are on a plateau, almost quadrangular in form, rising steeply to the height of nearly two hundred feet above the Tiber, and isolated, save at one angle where it is united to other high ground by a narrow isthmus. Not a tree—not a shrub on its turf-grown surface—not a house—not a ruin—not one stone upon another, to tell you that the site had been inhabited. Yet here once stood Antemnæ, the city of many towers—turrigeræ Antemnæ,[4]—one of the most ancient of Italy.—

> ——Antemnaque prisco
> Crustumio prior.[5]

[2] Dionysius (II., p. 116) says that Fidenæ was originally a colony of Alba, formed at the same time as Nomentum and Crustumeria. Virgil, Æn. VI. 773. Steph. Byz. *sub voce.* Solinus (Polyhistor, II., p. 13) says it was settled by Ascanius himself. According to Plutarch (Romul.), Fidenæ, in the time of Romulus, was possessed by the Sabines. Niebuhr (II., p. 455, trans.) thinks the Fidenates were originally Tyrrheni, and that when Livy calls them Etruscans, it is through the ordinary confusion between the Tuscans and Tyrrhenes. Müller (Etrus. Einl. 2. 14) thinks there must have been in the population of Fidenæ the same three elements as in that of Rome—Etruscans, Latins, and Sabines. Livy (I. 27) makes it clear that the native language of the Fidenates was not Latin.

[3] Dionysius (III. p. 165) notices this fact.

[4] Virg. Æn. VII. 631.

[5] Sil. Ital. VIII. 37. cf. Dion. Hal. II., p. 103.

Not a trace remains above ground. Even the broken pottery, that infallible indicator of bygone civilisation, which marks the site and determines the limits of habitation on many a now desolate spot of classic ground, is here so overgrown with herbage that the eye of an antiquary would alone detect it. It is a site strong by nature, and well adapted for a city, as cities then were ; for it is scarcely larger than the Palatine Hill, which, though at first it embraced the whole of Rome was afterwards too small for a single palace. It has a peculiar interest as the site of one of the three cities of Sabina, whose daughters, ravished by the followers of Romulus, became the mothers of the Roman race.[6] Antemnæ was the nearest city to Rome—only three miles distant —and therefore must have suffered most from the inhospitable violence of the Romans.

It was a bright spring morning when I first visited the spot. All Rome was issuing from its gates to witness the meeting of the huntsmen at the tomb of Cæcilia Metella. Shades of Flaccus and Juvenal! can ye rest amid the clangour of these modern Circenses ? Doth not the earth weigh heavy on your ashes, when "savage Britons," whom ye were wont to see "led in chains down the Sacred Way," flaunt haughtily among your hearths and altars ?—when, spurning the sober pleasures of the august and solemn city, in the pride of their wealth and power, they startle all Rome from its propriety by races and fox-hunts, awakening unwonted echoes among the old sepulchres of the Appian Way, and the ruined aqueducts of the Campagna ?

Here, beyond the echo of the tally-ho, I lay down on the green sward and gave myself up to enjoyment. Much was there to afford delight—the brightness and beauty of the scene —the clear blue sky—the genial warmth of the sun, by no means oppressive, but just giving a foretaste of his summer's might—there was the interest of this and other sites around—and there was Livy in my hand. No one can thoroughly enjoy Italy without him for a companion. There are a thousand sites and scenes which might be passed by without interest, but which, once touched by the wand of this magician, rise immediately into life and beauty. Be he more of a romancer than historian—I care not ; but prize him as among the first of Roman *poets*. To read him thus, reclining on the sunny sward, with all the influ-

[6] Liv. I. 9, 10; Dionys. II., p. 101; Plut. Romul. The other two were Cænina and Crustamium.

ences of nature congenial, and amid the scenes he has described,
was perfect luxury.

Here no sound—

> Confusæ sonus urbis et illætabile murmur—

told of the proximity of the city. Rome seldom, save on great
festive occasions, raises her voice audibly. Never does she roar
tempestuously like London, nor buzz and rustle like Paris or
Naples—at the most she utters what Carlyle would call, " an
inarticulate slumberous mumblement."

> " The City's voice itself is soft, like Solitude's."

She is verily more " blessed " in the want than in the possession
of the " noise and smoke " of Horace's time.—

> Omitto mirari beatæ
> Fumum et opes strepitumque Romæ.

Far beneath me, at the foot of the steep cliff which bounds
Antemnæ to the north, flowed the Anio, not here the "head-
long" stream it shows itself at Tivoli, and higher up its course,[7]
but gliding soberly along to lose itself in the Tiber.[8] Beyond
it, stretched a long level tract of meadow-land, dotted with
cattle ; and, bounding this, a couple of miles or more distant,
rose another eminence crested by some building and jutting out
from the adjoining heights till it almost overhung the Tiber.
This was Castel Giubileo, the site of the ancient Fidenæ. On
the low hills to the right, Romulus, when at war with that city,
laid his successful ambush.[9] But in the intervening plain was
fought the desperate conflict between the Romans and the allied
forces of the Veientes and Fidenates, in the reign of Tullus
Hostilius. With Livy's vivid page before me, it required little
imagination to people the scene anew, and to picture the Romans
encamped at the confluence of the streams at my feet, and the
army of Veii crossing the Tiber, and joining the troops of Fidenæ
in yonder plain. Tullus Hostilius marches his forces along the
Tiber to the encounter. Mettus Fuffetius, his ally, the leader

---

7 " Præceps Anio." Hor. I. Od. 7,
13. Statius, Silv. I., 5, 25.

8 Varro (de Ling. Lat. V. 28) says the
name of the city was derived from its
position. "Antemnæ, quòd ante amnem

qui Anio influit in Tiberim." cf. Servius
(ad Æn. VII. 631) and Festus (v. Am-
nenses).

9 Liv. I. 14. Dion. Hal. II., p. 117.
Plut. Romul. Frontin. Strat. II. 5. 1.

of the Albans, meditating treachery, and willing to throw his weight into the heavier scale, is creeping up the hills on the right, where with his army he remains a spectator of the combat, till fortune befriends the Romans. Here I see the Fidenates flying back to defend their city; and there the Veientes are driven into the Tiber, or cut down in numbers on its banks. And I shudder to behold in imagination the terrible vengeance inflicted by the victorious Roman upon his treacherous ally.[1]

On the same field was fought many a bloody fight between the Romans and Etruscans. Here, in the year of Rome 317, the Fidenates, with their allies of Veii and Falerii, were again defeated, and Lars Tolumnius, chief of the Veientes, was slain.[2] And a few years later, Mamilius Æmilius and Cornelius Cossus, the heroes of the former fight, routed the same foes in the same plain, and captured the city of Fidenæ.[3] Here too, Annibal pitched his camp when he marched from Capua to surprise the City.[4]

I turned to the right, and there, at the foot of the hill, the Ponte Salaro, a venerable relic of antiquity, spanned the Anio. It may be the identical structure which, in the year of Rome 393, was the scene of many a fierce encounter between the Romans and Gauls encamped on opposite banks of the stream, and on which Manlius Torquatus did combat with the gigantic Celt who had defied the Roman host, and like another David, smote his Goliath to the dust.[5]

I turned to the left, and the ruins on the further bank of the Tiber marked the supposed site of the Castle of the Fabii; nearer still several crumbling towers indicated the course of the Flaminian Way; and yon cave at the base of a cliff was the celebrated tomb of the Nasones. Further down the Tiber was the Ponte Molle, the scene of Constantine's battle with Maxentius, and of the miracle of the flaming cross. On every hand was some object attracting the eye by its picturesque beauty, or exciting the mind to the contemplation of the past.

The Ponte Salaro is on the line of the ancient Via Salaria, the high road to Fidenæ. It is a very fine bridge, of three arches; the central one, eighty feet in span, and about thirty above the

[1] Liv. I. 27, 28. cf. Dion. Hal III., p. 161—172. Flor. I. 3. Val. Max. VII. 4. 1. Ennius, Ann. II. 30, et seq. A. Vict., Vir. Ill., IV.
[2] Liv. IV. 17, 18, 19.
[3] Liv. IV. 32, 33, 34.
[4] Liv. XXVI. 10.
[5] Liv. VII. 9, 10. Serv. ad Æn. VI. 825. Aul. Gell. IX. 13. cf. Dio Cassius, Excerp. Mai, tom. II. p. 530.

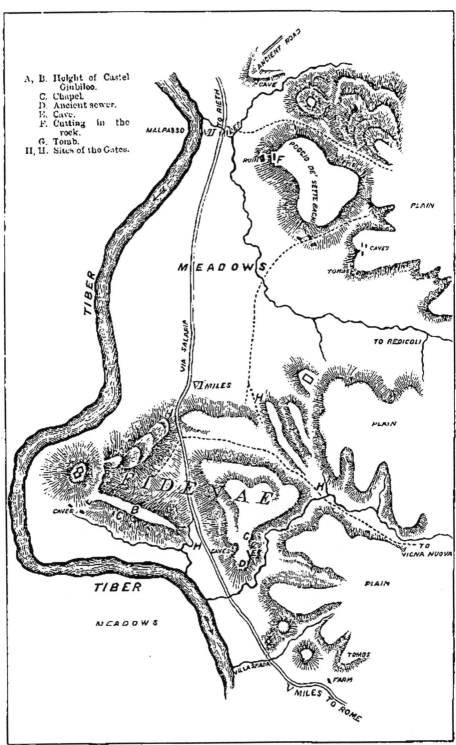

A, B. Height of Castel
Gìubiloo.
C. Chapel
D. Ancient sewer.
E. Cave.
F. Cutting in the
rock.
G. Tomb.
H, H. Sites of the Gates.

ANCIENT ROAD

CAVE

TO RIETH

MALPASSO

II MILES

RUINS

F

POGGIO DE' SETTE BAGNI

PLAIN

MEADOWS

CAVES

TOMBS

TO REDICOLI

VIA SALARIA

VI MILES

H

D

PLAIN

FIDENAE

H

CAVES

B

C

TO
VIGNA NUOVA

CAVES

H

CAVES

G

D

PLAIN

TIBER

TIBER

MEADOWS

TOMBS

VILLA SPADA

FARM

V MILES TO ROME

PLAN OF FIDENÆ.

stream ; the side ones stilted, and not more than twelve feet in span. The structure is faced with travertine ; but this indicates the repairs made by Narses in the sixth century after Christ ; the original masonry, which is uncovered in parts, is of tufo, in the Etruscan style, and may possibly be of Etruscan construction ; as it may be presumed were many of the public edifices of Rome and her territory for the first few centuries of her existence. Its masonry is rusticated, and in the arrangement and dimensions of the blocks precisely similar to that of the ancient walls at Sutri, Nepi, Civita Castellana, Bieda and other Etruscan sites in the southern district of the land.[6]

Just beyond the bridge is an *osteria*, in what was once a Roman sepulchre, where he who foots it to Fidenæ may refresh himself with decent wine. The road runs through the meadows for a couple of miles to Castel Giubileo. In the low hills to the right are caves, which have been tombs. Just before Fidenæ, at a bend in the road, stands the Villa Spada, the height above which is supposed to be the site of the Villa of Phaon, the scene of Nero's suicide.

The first indications of the ancient city are in the cliffs on the right of the road, in which are remains of tombs with niches, and a sewer, all excavated in the rock beneath the city-walls —walls, I say, but none exist, and the outline of the city is to be traced only by the character of the ground and the extent of the fragments of pottery. The height above the tombs bears these unequivocal traces of bygone habitation ; and at certain parts on the edge of the cliffs are remains of *opus incertum*, probably of some Roman villa. The hill of Castel Giubileo, on the other hand, has also formed part of the city, and its steep, lofty, and isolated character leaves little room to doubt that here was the Arx of Fidenæ. A farm-house now crests its summit, raised to that elevation for protection, not from man's attack, but from a more insidious foe, the malaria of the Campagna. The ancient Via Salaria, whose course the modern road follows, passed between these two eminences, as does the railroad, that is, through the very heart of Fidenæ. In the cliff beneath the farm-house is another tomb. The whole face of the steep, when I first visited it, was frosted over with the bloom of wild pear-trees, and tinted with the flowers of the Judas-tree—

[6] This bridge was blown up in 1867, when Garibaldi was threatening Rome, and has been rebuilt, the piers being the only portion now remaining of the ancient structure.

> " One white empurpled shower
> Of mingled blossoms."

Had the whole of the city been comprehended on this height, it would be easy to understand Livy's description; "the city, lofty and well-fortified, could not be taken by assault;"[7] but as it also covered the opposite eminence, the walls which united them must have descended in two places, almost to the level of the plain. These were the vulnerable points of Fidenæ, and to them was perhaps owing its frequent capture. It seems probable, from the nature of the position, that the earliest town was confined to the height of Castel Giubileo. Yet, in this case, Fidenæ would scarcely answer the description of Dionysius, who says, "it was a great and populous city" in the time of Romulus.[8] This was doubtless meant in a comparative sense, in reference to the neighbouring towns. Fidenæ, however, could never have been of great size or importance. It was little more than two miles in circuit. Its vicinity to and frequent contests with Rome gave it a prominence in history, to which, from its inferior size and power, it was hardly entitled.

Making the circuit of Castel Giubileo, you are led round till you meet the road, where it issues from the hollow at the northern angle of the city.[9] Besides the tombs which are found on both sides of the southern promontory of the city, there is a cave, running far into the rock, and branching off into several chambers and passages. Fidenæ, like Veii, is said to have been taken by a mine;[1] and this cave might be supposed to indicate the spot, had not Livy stated that the *cuniculus* was on the opposite side of Fidenæ, where the cliffs were loftiest, and that it was carried into the Arx.

The chief necropolis of Fidenæ was probably on the heights to the north-east, called Poggio de' Sette Bagni, where are a number of caves; and here, also, are traces of quarries, perhaps those of the soft rock for which Fidenæ was famed in ancient times.[2]

The ruin of Fidenæ is as complete as that of Antemnæ. The hills on which it stood are now bare and desolate; the shepherd tends his flocks on its slopes, or the plough furrows its bosom. Its walls have utterly disappeared; not one stone remains on

---

[7] Liv. IV. 22.

[8] Dion. Hal II., p. 116.

[9] This is the steepest and most impregnable side of Fidenæ, and as such is referred to by Dionysius (V., p. 310), and

more expressly by Livy (IV. 22).

[1] Liv. loc. cit. Dionysius (III., p. 180) mentions a prior capture of Fidenæ by Ancus Martius by means of a *cuniculus*.

[2] Vitruv. II. 7. Plin. XXXVI. 48.

another, and the broken pottery and the tombs around are the sole evidences of its existence. Yet, as Nibby observes, "few ancient cities, of which few or no vestiges remain, have had the good fortune to have their sites so well determined as Fidenæ." Its distance of forty stadia, or five miles from Rome, mentioned by Dionysius,[3] and its position relative to Veii, to the Tiber, and to the confluence of the Anio with that stream, as set forth by Livy,[4] leave not a doubt of its true site.

The history of Fidenæ is a series of struggles with Rome, of captures and rebellions, if the efforts of a people to free themselves from a foreign and unwelcome yoke may be thus designated. We have no less than eight distinct captures of it recorded.[5] Livy sneeringly remarks, "it was almost more often captured than attacked."[6] It was first taken by Romulus, and by him made a Roman colony; and such it continued, save at intervals when it threw off the yoke, till its final capture and destruction in the year of Rome 328.[7] Its destruction was an act of policy on the part of Rome. She had experienced so much annoyance from the towns in her immediate neighbourhood, especially from Fidenæ, which she had subdued again and again, and re-colonised with Romans, but which, from the hostility of the Etruscan inhabitants, was ever a thorn in her side, that to rid herself of these foes at her very gates, she destroyed or suffered to fall into decay Fidenæ, Antemnæ, Veii, and other towns of the Campagna. The destruction of Fidenæ was complete, and in after ages its desolation became a bye-word.

> Gabiis desertior atque
> Fidenis vicus.[8]

Yet its site seems to have been inhabited in the time of Cicero,[9] and still later it was a village, or more probably only the site of some private villa.[1] Under the Empire it seems to have risen in

---

[3] Dion. Hal. II., p. 116; III., p. 167; and X., p. 648. Strabo V., p. 230.

[4] Liv. I. 14, 27; IV., 17, 21, 31, 32, 33, 34; see also Dionysius III. pp. 165, 181, 191, 193.

[5] See the Appendix to this Chapter.

[6] Liv. IV. 32,—prope sæpius captas quam oppugnatas.

[7] Florus (I. 12) speaks of it as having been burnt by its inhabitants. Yet not many years after, shortly after the Gauls had evacuated Rome, we hear of the Fidenates, in conjunction with some of the

neighbouring people, suddenly rising, and striking such terror into the Romans, that they commemorated the event ever after by a public festival on the Nones of July, called "Populifugia" or "Poplifugia." Varro de L. L. VI. 18. Macrob. Saturn. III. 2. Dionysius, however (II., p. 118), gives a different version of the origin of this festival.

[8] Hor. I. Epist. XI. 7.

[9] Cic. de Leg. Agrar. II. 35.

[1] Strabo V., pp. 226, 230.

importance, for an amphitheatre of wood was erected there, in the
reign of Tiberius, which gave way during the performance, and
twenty, or as some accounts say, fifty thousand persons were
mutilated or crushed to death by its ruins. It must not, however, be supposed that such was the population of Fidenæ in
those times, for Tacitus states that a great concourse had flocked
thither from Rome, the more abundant from the propinquity of
the place.[2]

Though there are few local antiquities—little more than associations of the olden time—remaining at Fidenæ, the scenery
should alone be sufficient to attract the visitor to the spot. From
these heights you look down on "the yellow Tiber" winding
through the green valley—rafts floating down its stream, and
buffaloes on its sandy banks, slaking their thirst, or revelling in
its waters. That opening in the cliffs on its opposite bank is the
glen of the Cremera, whose waters, oft dyeing the Tiber with
crimson, told the Fidenates of the struggles between their kinsmen of Veii and the common foe. Those ruins on the cliff above
the glen are supposed to mark the site of the Castle of the Fabii,
that band of heroes, who, like Leonidas and his Spartans, devoted
themselves to their country, and fell in her cause. Further, in
the same direction, yon distant tree-capt mound points out the
site of Veii; it is the tumulus of Vaccareccia. On the high
ground to the left may be recognised the palace at Isola Farnese,
and the inn of La Storta; and the solitary towers at intervals
between this and Rome, mark the line of the Via Cassia. There
you see the undulating heights around the lake of Bracciano; and
the grey head of the Ciminian beyond; the tufted cone of Monte
Musino; and that pyramid of Nature's raising, Soracte, rarely
now snow-capt as in days of yore, but towering in dark and lonely
grandeur from the plain. Do you seek for snow?—turn to the
range of Apennines, whose frozen masses are glittering like ice-
bergs in the sun, piled above nearer and darker heights, among
which Monte Gennaro, the "Lucretilis amœnus" of Horace, stands
prominent; and at its feet Tivoli, ever dear to the poet—

"Sit meæ sedes utinam senectæ !"—

sparkles out from the dense olive-groves. There, where the
purple range sinks to the plain, "cool Præneste" climbs the
steep with her Cyclopean walls. Here, as your eye sweeps over

[2] Tacit. Ann. iv. 62, 63 ; cf. Sueton. Tiber. 40.

the bare Campagna, it passes the site of many a city, renowned
in the early history of Italy, but now, like Fidenæ and Antemnæ,
in utter desolation, and lost to the common eye.[3]   And there, on
the slope of the Alban, that most graceful of mountains, with its
soft flowing outlines and long drawn swells, still brightened by
towns—once stood Alba, the fostermother, and rival of Rome ;
Tusculum with its noble villas and its Academy, where the
greatest of Romans lived, wrote, debated, taught, and where

" Still the eloquent air breathes, burns, with Cicero ; "—

and from its highest peak shone the Temple of Jove, the common
shrine of the Latin cities, a worthy altar to the King of Heaven.
Then, after again sweeping the surface of the wide Campagna,
strewn in this quarter with league-long lines of ruined aqueducts,
with crumbling tombs, and many a monument of Roman grandeur, your eye reaches at length the Imperial City herself.   She
is in great part concealed by the intervening Pincian, but you
catch sight of her most prominent buildings — the pinnacled
statues of St. John Lateran, the tower and cupolas of Sta. Maria
Maggiore, and the vast dome of St. Peter's ; and you look in
imagination on the rest from the brow of Monte Mario, which rises
on the right, crested with dark cypresses and snow-white villas.

APPENDIX TO CHAPTER III.

Note.

FIDENÆ was taken, 1st, by Romulus, who pursued the routed citizens
within the gates. Liv. I., 14 ; Dion. Hal. II., p. 116 ; Plut. Romul.
  The 2nd time by Tullus Hostilius, who reduced it by famine. Dion.
Hal. III., p. 172.
  The 3rd by Ancus Martius, by means of a *cuniculus.* Dion. Hal. III., p. 180.
  The 4th by Tarquinius Priscus, by storm.   Dion. Hal. III., p. 194.
  The 5th in the year of Rome 250, by the Consuls Valerius Poplicola, and
Lucretius Tricipitinus, also by storm, Dion. Hal. V. p. 310.
  The 6th in the year 256, by the Consul Largius Flavus, by famine. Dion.
Hal. V., p. 325.
  The 7th in the year 319, by the Dictator A. Servilius Priscus, by means of
a *cuniculus.* Liv. IV., 22.
  The 8th, and last time, in the year 328, by the Dictator Mam. Æmilius
Mamercinus, in the same manner as it was first taken by Romulus (Liv. IV.,
34), though Florus (I., 12) says it was set on fire by its own citizens.

[3] Pliny (III. 9) enumerates fifty-three
towns of ancient Latium, which in his day
had utterly perished, without a trace remaining—*interiere sine vestigiis ;* among
them were Antemnæ and Fidenæ.

CHAPTER IV.

MONTE MUSINO AND LAGO DI BRACCIANO.

Nor rough nor barren are the winding ways
Of hoar antiquity, but strowed with flowers.—T. WARTON.

On Lough Neagh's banks as the fisherman strays,
  When the clear cold eve's declining,
He sees the round towers of other days
  In the wave beneath him shining.—MOORE.

THE next Etruscan town of any note in history northward from
Veii was Sutrium, but there is an intervening district, containing
several sites of that antiquity, which merit the traveller's attention. Moreover, this district possesses much geological interest,
for it contains no less than four extinct craters, three of them
now lakes, and one, the Lago Bracciano, the largest sheet of
water in Etruria after the Thrasymene and the "great Volsinian
mere."

The high-road northwards from Storta pursues the line of the
ancient Via Cassia, of which I was unpleasantly reminded by the
large blocks of basalt which had formed the ancient pavement,
and were now laid at intervals by the side of the road—*proh
pudor !*—to be Macadamised for the convenience of modern
travellers. This is, alas, too often the case in Italy, where the
spirit of utilitarianism is fully rife. If a relic of antiquity be
convertible into cash, whether by sale or by exhibition, it meets
with due attention ; but when this is not the case, nobody cares
to preserve it—the very terms in which it is mentioned are those
of contempt—it is *il pontaccio*—or, *le muraccia*—and "worth
nothing ;" or, if it can be turned to any account, however base,
the most hoary antiquity will avail it nought. Stones are torn
from the spots they have occupied twenty, or five-and-twenty
centuries, where they served as corroborations of history, as
elucidations of national customs, as evidences of long extinct
civilisation, and as landmarks to the antiquary—they are torn

thence to be turned to some vile purpose of domestic or general convenience. This is not an evil of to-day. It existed under the old governments of the Peninsula as fully as under that of Victor Emmanuel. Let us hope that a government which professes to reverence and prize memorials of the past, will put a stop to such barbarous spoliations and perversions; or the ancient monuments of Italian greatness will ere long exist in history alone.

Just after leaving La Storta, a road branches to the left towards Bracciano and its Lake. It follows nearly the line of the ancient Via Clodia, which ran through Sabate, Blera, and Tuscania, to Cosa. The first station on that Way beyond Veii was Careiæ, fifteen miles from Rome, represented by the ruined and utterly deserted, but highly picturesque, village of Galera, which stands on a cliff-bound rock, washed by the Arrone, about a mile off the modern road. The only mention of Careiæ is made by Frontinus and the Itineraries, and there is no record of an Etruscan population here, yet there are said to be remains of ancient walls on the west of the town, and Etruscan tombs in the cliffs around.[1] The modern town dates from the eleventh century, and was a possession of the Orsini family, whose abandoned castle with the tall *campanile* form the most prominent features in this scene of picturesque desolation.

Two miles beyond La Storta bring you to the Osteria del Fosso, a lonely way-side inn. The stream here crossed is that of I due Fossi, which washes the western walls of Veii. In the wood-hung cliffs around are traces of Etruscan tombs, part of the necropolis of that city.

Seven miles more over the bare undulating Campagna to Baccano, the ancient Ad Baccanas, a place like many others in Italy, known to us only through the Itineraries, once a Roman *Mutatio*, and now a modern post-house, situated in a deep hollow, originally the crater of a volcano, and afterwards a lake, but drained in ancient times, by emissaries cut through the encircling hills. At the eighteenth milestone is one, cut through the rocky soil to the depth of about twenty feet, which Gell seems to think may have been formed in ancient times, but I believe it to be modern, and the work of the Chigi family, the territorial lords of Baccano.[2]

---

[1] Front. de Aquæd. II., p. 48. Gell, II. c. Galeria. Nibby II., p. 92.

[2] I followed it for some distance, and found that after receiving one or two streamlets, it loses altogether its artificial character, and so continues till it finds

Nothing like the Alban Emissary now exists in the hollow. On the height however towards Rome there are several *cuniculi*, which drain the water from an upper basin of the crater. They are carried through Monte Lupolo, a lofty part of the crater rim. Here are also a number of holes in the upper part of the hill, said to be of great depth, and called by the peasants "*pozzi*," or wells; probably nothing more than shafts to the emissaries. It was these passages that were mistaken by Zanchi for the *cuniculus* of Camillus, and which led him to regard this as the site of ancient Veii.

The lake is now represented by a stagnant pond in the marshy bottom of the crater, which makes Baccano one of the most fertile spots in all Italy—in malaria. Fortunately for the landlord of La Posta, summer is not the travelling season, or his inn would boast its fair reputation in vain. This neighbourhood in the olden time was notorious for robbers, so that the "Diversorium Bacchanæ" passed into a proverb.[3] Let the traveller still be wary; though he be in no peril of assault, he may yet fall a victim to some *perfidus caupo*, who thirsting for foreign spoil "expects his evening prey." In the ridge of the surrounding hills are several gaps, marking the spots by which ancient roads entered the crater. On Monte Razzano, the hill above Baccano, are some ruins called, on dubious authority, Fanum Bacchi—though it is probable that the Roman *mutatio* derived its name from some such shrine. There is a large cave on the said Mount, which is vulgarly believed to contain hidden treasures. From the hills of Baccano, travellers coming from Florence are supposed to get their first view of Rome. But the dome of St. Peter's may be distinctly seen in the Campagna horizon, from the Monte Cimino, a distance of forty miles, or twice as far as Baccano.

Two miles to the north of Baccano, and to the right of the road to Florence, lies Campagnano; the first view of which, with Soracte in the back-ground, is highly picturesque. It is a place of some size and importance, compared to other villages of the Campagna, and its position, and some caves in the neighbourhood, seem to mark it as of Etruscan origin. A few Roman remains are to be seen in the streets.

a natural vent from the crater at Madonna del Sorbo, three miles to the south-east of Baccano, where it forms one of the sources of the Cremera. I observed other deep clefts opening upon it, and running towards the mountains in the same quarter; but, as they all sink towards the lake, they cannot be emissaries: they are either natural clefts, or they have been sunk for roads.

[8] Dempster, de Etrur. Reg. II., p. 161.

From Campagnano a path runs eastward, first through vine-yards, and then across a wide valley of corn, to Scrofano, five miles distant. This is a small secluded village, also of Etruscan origin, for the cliffs around it, especially to the west, are full of tombs ; among them are several *columbaria*. It lies at the foot of Monte Musino, that curious tufted hill which is seen from every part of the Campagna, and is thought to have been the site of ancient religious rites. The name Musino is generally supposed to be a corruption of the Ara *Mutiæ*, which was in the territory of Veii,[4] though some place the Ara at Belmonte, nearer the Flaminian Way.[5] The hill is conical, of volcanic formation, the lower slopes being composed of ashes and scoriæ, strewed with blocks of lava. It is ascended by broad terraces leading spirally to the summit, on which are the remains of a large circular structure, which, Gell suggests, may have been the Altar. There is also a large cavern near the summit, reported, like that of Monte Razzano, to contain great treasures ; access to which is said to be debarred by an iron grating—so far within the mountain, however, that no one can pretend to have seen it. The clump of oaks and chestnuts which tufts the hill-top, is sacred from the axe, though the wood on the slopes is cut from time to time ; and the only explanation of this which I could obtain, was, that the said clump preserves Scrofano from the sea-wind, which is deemed unhealthy, and that, were it cut, the wind, instead of pursuing its course at a great elevation, would descend upon the devoted village.[6] This seems so unsatisfactory, that I cannot but regard it as a modern explanation of an ancient custom, the meaning of which has been lost in the lapse of ages and the change of religious faith. The immunity of the clump is in all probability a relic of the ancient reverence for a sacred grove. Gell justly remarks of the artificial terraces round this hill and the building on the summit, that this extraordinary labour can only be accounted for by concluding the place was sacred. The analogy, indeed, of the winding road still extant, which led to the temple of Jupiter

---

[4] Plin. II. 98. Dempster (Etr. Reg. II. p. 140) thinks it should have been spelt "Murciæ," Murcia or Murtia being another name for the Etruscan Venus. Tertullian, de Spect. cap. VIII. Pliny (XV. 36) derives the name of Murcia from the myrtle, which was sacred to that Goddess—ara vetus fuit Veneri Myrteæ, quam nunc Murciam vocant. According to the same writer (II. 98) the soil at the Ara Mutiæ was so peculiarly tenacious, that whatever was thrust in could not be extracted. Nardini (Veio Antico, p. 260) asserts that the same phenomenon is to be observed on the slopes of Monte Musino.

[5] Westphal, Röm. Kamp., p. 135.

[6] Gell (I., p. 166) gives another version of this belief.

Latialis on the summit of the Alban Mount, is sufficient authority for such a conclusion. The terraces here, however, are too broad for simple roads; the lower being sixty, the upper forty feet in breadth. Gell imagines them to have been formed for the Salii, or for the augurs of Veii—the rites of the former consisting in dancing or running round the altar. The local tradition is, that the Monte was the citadel of Veii,[7] though that city is confessed to be at least six miles distant, and it has hence received its vulgar appellation of La Fortezza; and the cave is believed to be the mouth of Camillus' *cuniculus*. The said *cuniculus* is also to be seen—so say the village oracles—at a spot two miles distant, on the way to Isola Farnese, called Monte Sorriglio (or Soviglio), in a subterranean passage, wide enough for two waggons to pass, which runs eight miles under ground to Prima Porta, on the Flaminian Way, where Camillus is pronounced to have commenced his mine. These things are only worthy of mention as indicative of the state of local antiquarian knowledge, which the traveller should ever mistrust.

In summer it is no easy matter to reach the summit of Monte Musino, on account of the dense thickets which cover its slopes. The view it commands, however, will repay any trouble in the ascent, which is easiest from Scrofano, whence the summit may be a mile distant. The most direct road to Scrofano from Rome is by the Via Flaminia, which must be left to the right about a mile or more beyond Borghettaccio, where a path pursues the banks of a stream up to the village. It may also be reached through Formello, either directly from the site of Veii, whence it is six miles distant, or by a path which leaves the modern Via Cassia at the Osteria di Merluzzo, near the sixteenth milestone. From this spot it is about six miles to Scrofano.

The ancient name of Scrofano is quite unknown. Its present appellation has no more dignified an origin than a sow (*scrofa*— possibly from an ancient family of that name),[8] as appears from the arms of the town over one of the gateways, which display that unclean animal under a figure of San Biagio, the "Protector"

---

[7] This tradition is probably owing to the recorded opinion of Cluverius (Ital. Ant., II., p. 530), that Scrofano was the site of ancient Veii. Such traditions generally originate with the priests, who often dabble in antiquarian matters, though rarely to the advancement of science, being too much swayed by local prejudices,—and

their *dictum* is naturally accepted by their flocks. Who, indeed, should gainsay it? "In a nation of blind men, the one-eyed man is king," says the Spanish proverb.

[8] Nibby (III. p. 77) records a derivation, which, as he says, "is not to be despised;" —certainly not, if Monte Musino were hallowed ground—Scrofano, *a sacro fano*.

of the place. Almost the only relic of early times is a Roman *cippus* of marble under the Palazzo Serraggi.

From Baccano, two tracks, cut in ancient times in the lip of the crater-lake, and retaining vestiges of Roman pavement, run westward to the lonesome little lakes of Stracciacappa, and Martignano (Lacus Alsietinus), and thence continue to the spacious one of Bracciano (Lacus Sabatinus); branching to the right to Trevignano and Oriolo, and to the left to Anguillara and Bracciano.[9]

The lake of Bracciano (Lacus Sabatinus), like every other in this district of Italy, is the crater of an extinct volcano. It is nearly twenty miles in circuit, and though without islands, or other very striking features, is not deficient in beauty.

Sabate, which gives its name to the lake, is not mentioned as an Etruscan town, though it was probably of that antiquity.[1] It must have stood on or near the lake, though its precise site has been matter of dispute. By some it has been thought to have occupied the site of Bracciano, but at that town there are no vestiges or even traditions of antiquity, the earliest mention of it in history being of the fourteenth century. Some have supposed it to have stood on the eastern shore, while others take it to be the city mentioned by Sotion as engulfed of old beneath the waters of the lake.[2] It has been reserved for M. Ernest Desjardins, a learned and enterprising Frenchman, who has taken great pains to trace out the stations on the Viæ Clodia and Cassia, to determine its true site. This is at Trevignano, a little village on the northern shore of the lake, lying at the foot of a rock of basalt, now crested by a mediæval tower.[3]

M. Desjardins has arrived at this conclusion, both by carefully working out the position of Sabate from the Itineraries, and by finding early Etruscan remains on the spot. He noticed, on issu-

---

[9] The "Sabatia stagna" of Silius Italicus (VIII., 492) probably included the neighbouring lakelets of Martignano and Stracciacappa.

[1] The earliest mention of it is in the year 367, after the fall of Veii and Falerii, when the conquered territory was given to the Etruscans who had favoured Rome in the contest, and four new tribes, one called Sabatina, were formed. Liv. VI. 4, 5. Fest. v. Sabatina. The town, in fact, is not named except in the Peutingerian Table; but there can be no doubt of its existence.

[2] Cluver II. p. 524. Nibby I. p. 325.

Holstenius (ad Cluver. p. 44) and Westphal (p. 156) point out some ruins at a spot more than a mile beyond Bracciano, near S. Marciano or S. Liberato, as those of Sabate, but Nibby declares them to be the remains of a Roman villa of the early Empire.

Sotion (de Mir. Font.) says a town was swallowed up by this lake, and that many foundations and temples and statues might be seen in its clear depths.

[3] The discovery is recorded in the Ann. Inst. 1859, pp. 84—60.

ing from the gate of the village facing the west, the only gate now remaining, a large fragment of walling of squared blocks of rather regular masonry, which he declares to be in perfect conformity with the Etruscan fortifications of Cortona and Perugia.[4] This masonry, which is probably of basalt or other hard volcanic stone, proves the existence of an Etruscan town on this spot, and as there are no other such remains on the shores of the lake, there can be no doubt that here stood Sabate.

At the Bagni di Vicarello, three miles beyond, there are abundant remains of Imperial times, villas and baths, which mark the site of the Aquæ Apollinares.[5] Here in 1852, in clearing out the reservoir of the ancient baths, a most interesting discovery was made of a large collection of copper coins from the earliest *æs rude* and *æs signatum* of Etruria down to the money of the Empire; as well as of sundry silver vases—all votive offerings, now preserved in the Kircherian Museum at Rome.

The Forum Clodii is generally supposed to have stood at Oriuolo, but M. Desjardins places it on the hill above S. Liberato, on the west of the lake, where are some extensive Roman remains. On the ancient road, between this and Bieda stands the ruined town or castle of Ischia, supposed, but on no authority, to be one of the Novem Pagi of antiquity.[6]

I retain pleasurable reminiscences of a midsummer ramble on the shores of this lake. My path ran first over flats of corn, then falling beneath the sickle—next it led through avenues of mulberries, whitening the ground with their showered fruit, while

---

[4] Nibby (III. p. 287) had previously suspected this to be an Etruscan site from this fragment of ancient masonry, which he described as composed "of irregularly squared blocks, joined together as in the walls of Collatia, Ardea, and other very ancient cities." M. Desjardins (op. cit. p. 48) finds fault with this description, and declares there is not the least resemblance between this fragment and the walls of the Latin towns on the south of the Tiber. I cannot add my testimony in this instance, the walling having escaped my observation when I passed that way; but I can reconcile these conflicting descriptions by the authority of another French antiquary, who describes the walls of Ardea as composed "of enormous blocks cut in regular parallelograms, and put together without

cement, like those in the walls of Volterra, Populonia, Cosa, or Rusellæ. I measured some of these blocks, which are as much as 3 mètres in length." Noël des Vergers, Etrurie, I., p. 182.

[5] Desjardins, Ann. Inst. 1859, pp. 34—60. The fact is determined beyond a doubt by a number of dedicatory inscriptions in honour of Apollo found on the spot.

[6] Westphal (p. 157) thinks the Novem Pagi are represented by the neighbouring sites of Viano, Ischia, Agliola, Barbarano, &c. But this is mere conjecture. The only mention of them is by Pliny (N. H. III. 8), who places them in his list of Etruscan towns between Nepet and Præfectura Claudia Foroclodii, but as his list is alphabetical, it gives us no clue to their position.

the whole strip of shore was covered with the richest tessellation of wheat, hemp, maize, flax, melons, artichokes, overshadowed by vines, olives, figs, and other fruit trees, intermingling with that "gracious prodigality of Nature," which almost dispenses with labour in these sunny climes—and then it passed the hamlet of Trevignano and the wrecks of Roman luxury at Bagni di Vicarello, and climbed the heights above, where cultivation ceases, and those forest aristocrats, the oak, the beech, and the chestnut, hold undisputed sway. From this height the eye revels over the broad blue lake, the mirror of Italian heavens,—

> " It was the azure time of June,
>   When the skies are deep in the stainless noon—"

reflecting, on one shore, the cliff-perched towns of Anguillara and Bracciano—the latter dominated by the turretted mass of its feudal castle—and on the other, the crumbling tower of Trevignano, backed by the green mountain-pyramid of Rocca Romana. But the glassy surface of the lake does not merely mirror remains of the olden time, for in its clear depths, it is said, may still be seen the ruins of former days, on certain parts of its shores. There is no doubt that the waters are now higher than in ancient times—proof of which may be seen in a mass of Roman reticulated work off the shore near Vicarello ; and in the fact recorded by Nibby and Desjardins, that the ancient road between that place and Trevignano is now submerged for a considerable distance.

APPENDIX TO CHAPTER IV.

NOTE.

The stations and distances on the Via Clodia are thus given by the Itineraries.

ANTONINE ITINERARY.			PEUTINGERIAN TABLE.		
Roma			Roma		
Careias	. . . . M.P. XV.		Ad Sextum . . . . M.P. VI.		
Aquas Apollinaris	. . .XVIII.		Careias . . . . . VIIII.		
Tarquinios .	. . . XVII.		Ad Nonas . . . . . VIIII.		
Cosam	. . . . XV.		Sabate . . . . . —		
			Foro Clodo . . . . —		
			Blera . . . . . XVI.		
			Tuscana . . . . . VIIII.		
			Materno . . . . . XII.		
			Saturnia . . . . XVIII.		
			Succosa . . . . . VIII.		
			Cosa . . . . . —		

THE AMPHITHEATRE OF SUTRI, FROM THE ENTRANCE.

CHAPTER V.

SUTRI.—*SUTRIUM.*

Graminoum campum, quem collibus undique curvis
Ciugebant silvæ; mediâque in valle theatri
Circus erat.   Virg.

Imaginare amphitheatrum . . . . quale sola rerum natura possit effingere.
                                 Plin. Epist.

It was a bright but cool morning in October, when I left the
comfortless inn of Baccano, and set out for Sutri. The wind
blew keenly in my teeth; and the rich tints of the trees wherever
they appeared on the undulating plain, and the snow on the
loftiest peaks of the Apennines, proved that autumn was fast
giving place to winter.

About four miles from Baccano on the Via Cassia is Le Sette
Vene, a lonely inn in the midst of an open country. It is one of
the largest and most comfortable hotels between Florence and
Rome, on the Siena road. Close to it is an ancient Roman
bridge of a single arch, in excellent preservation.

The next place on the Via Cassia three miles beyond Sette
Vene, is Monterosi, which does not appear to have been an Etruscan site. It is commanded by a conical height, called Monte di

Tucchetti, crested with some ruins of the middle ages. The view from it well repays the small difficulty of the ascent; for it commands the wide sea-like Campagna—Soracte, a rocky islet in the midst, lorded over by the snow-capt Apennines—the sharp wooded peak of Rocca Romana on the one hand, and the long sweeping mass of the Ciminian on the other.

Monterosi has two inns, both wretched. L'Angelo is said to be the better. Of La Posta I have had unpleasant experience,— *animus meminisse horret!* Hence there is a carriageable road following the line of the old Via Cassia to Sutri, the ancient Sutrium, seven or eight miles distant;[1] but as very inferior accommodation is to be had there, the traveller who would take more than a passing glance at that site had better drive on to Ronciglione, and visit it thence.

Soon after descending from Monterosi, and after passing a small dreary lake and crossing a stream of lava, the road divides; the right branch leading northward to Nepi, Narni and Perugia; the other, which is the Siena road, running in a direct line to Ronciglione, which, as it lies on the lower slope of the Ciminian, is visible at a considerable distance. In truth, it bears quite an imposing appearance, with its buildings stretching up the slope, and its white domes gleaming out from the wooded hill. The celebrated castle-palace of Capraruola, the *chef-d'œuvre* of Vignola, also adorns the slope of the Ciminian a few miles to the right.

But the beauties of Ronciglione are not to be seen from a distance. The town is romantically situated on the brink of a deep ravine, with precipitous cliffs, in which many caverns, originally sepulchres, mark the site of an Etruscan town.[2] Its memory and name, however, have utterly perished. Ronciglione has very tolerable accommodation; even a choice of hotels—the Aquila Nera and the Posta—and the traveller will do well to

---

[1] The distance of Sutrium from Rome was thirty-three miles.

VIA CASSIA.

ITINERARY OF ANTONINUS.		PEUTINGERIAN TABLE.	
Roma		Roma	
Baccanas M.P.	XXI.	Ad Sextum M.P.	VI.
Sutrio	XII.	Veios	VI.
Forum Cassi	XI.	Vacanas	VIIII.
		Sutrio	XII.
		Vico Matrini	(VII.)
		Foro Cassii	IIII.

Its present distance is thirty-two miles, but the measurement is taken from the modern gate, a mile from the Forum, whence the distances were anciently calculated.

[2] "Not far from Capraruola," says Bonarroti (Michael Angelo's nephew), "I saw an Etruscan inscription in letters almost three feet high, carved in the rock, through which the road to Sutri (as I understood) is cut, but on account of the loftiness of the site distrusting my copy, I do not venture to give it," p. 98, ap. Dempst. II.

make it his head-quarters for excursions to Sutri, which lies about three miles to the south. It must be confessed, however, that the road to it is wretched enough, and if it resemble the ancient approaches to the town, it would incline us to believe that the proverb *ire Sutrium* (to be prompt) was applied ironically.

Like most of the ancient towns in Southern Etruria, Sutrium stood on a plateau of rock, at the point of junction of two of the deep ravines which furrow the plain in all directions,[3] being united to the main-land of the plain only by a narrow neck. The extent of the town, therefore, was circumscribed; the low but steep cliffs which formed its natural fortifications forbade its extension into the ravines. Veii, whose citadel occupied a similar position, crossed the isthmus, and swelled out over the adjoining table-land, just as Rome soon ceased to be confined to the narrow plateau of the Palatine. But the same principle of growth seems not to have existed in Sutrium, and the town appears never to have extended beyond the limits prescribed by nature. It was thus precluded from attaining the dignity of a first-rate city, yet on account of its situation and strong natural position it was a place of much importance, especially after the fall of Veii, when it was celebrated as one of "the keys and gates of Etruria;" (claustra portæque Etruriæ); Nepete, a town similarly situated, being the other.[4] As a fortress, indeed, Sutrium seems to have been maintained to a late period, long after the neighbouring Etruscan cities had been destroyed.

The modern town occupies the site of the ancient, and is probably composed of the same materials. Not that any of the ancient *Sutria tecta* are extant, but the blocks of tufo of which the houses are constructed, may well have been hewn by Etruscan hands. Every one who knows the Italians, is aware that they never cut fresh materials, when they have a quarry of ready-hewn stones to their hands. The columns and fragments of sculpture here and there imbedded in the walls of houses, prove that the remains of Roman Sutrium at least were thus applied. There are some fine fragments of the ancient walls on the south side of the town, and not a few sewers opening in the cliffs beneath them.

---

[3] The ground in the neighbourhood of Sutri is much broken, and some parts answer to the description given by Livy (IX. 35)—aspreta strata saxis.

[4] Liv. VI. 9; IX. 32. Strabo (V. 9), however, classes it among the cities of Etruria with Arretium, Perusia, and Volsinii, and Plutarch (Camil.) calls it "a flourishing and wealthy town," εὐδαίμονα καὶ πλούσιαν πόλιν. i

As the walls of Sutri are similar to those of most of the
Etruscan cities in the southern or volcanic district of the land,
I shall describe the peculiarity of their masonry. The blocks
are arranged so as to present their ends and sides to view in
alternate courses, in the style which is called by builders "old

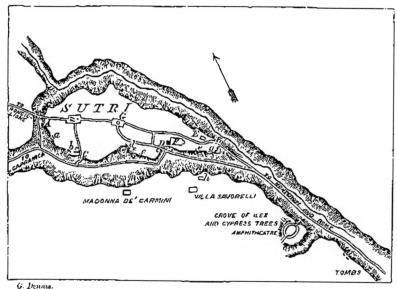

G. Dennis.

ROUGH PLAN OF SUTRI.

A. Porta Menona.	*a.* Etruscan wall, nine courses.	
B. ,, Romana.	*b.* ,, ,, seven ,,	
C. ,, di Mezza.	*c.* ,, ,, four ,,	
D. ,, Vecchia.	*d.* ,, ,, seven ,,	
E. ,, Furia.	*e.* ,, Sewers, cut in rock.	
F. Cathedral.	*f.* Mediæval bastion.	
G. H. Piazze.	*g.* Columbarium.	
	h. Madonna del Parto.	

English bond," or more vulgarly, "headers and stretchers;" but
as this masonry is of classic origin, I will designate it by the
more appropriate term of *emplecton*, which was applied by the
Greeks to a similar sort of masonry in use among them[5]—a term
significant of the interweaving process by which the blocks were
wrought into a solid wall. The dimensions of the blocks being
the same, or very nearly so, in almost every specimen of this
masonry extant in Etruria,[6] I will give them as a guide in future

---

[5] Vitruv. II., VIII. 7. For further
remarks on *emplecton* masonry, see
Appendix.

[6] The only exceptions I remember are at
Cervetri, where the dimensions are smaller.

descriptions, in order that when the term *emplecton* is used, it
may not be necessary to re-specify the dimensions. This
masonry is *isodomon*, i. e. the courses are of equal height—about
one foot eleven inches. The blocks which present their ends to
the eye are generally square, though sometimes a little more or
a little less in width; and the others vary slightly in length, but
in general this is double the height, or three feet ten inches. It
is singular that these measurements accord with the length of the
modern Tuscan *braccio* of twenty-three inches. The same description of masonry was used extensively by the Romans, under
the kings and during the Republic, in Rome itself, as well as
in Latium and Sabina, and was brought to perfection in the
magnificent wall of the Forum of Augustus; but that it was also
used by the Etruscans in very early times is attested by their
walls and tombs; so that while it is often impossible to pronounce any particular portion to be of Etruscan or Roman origin,
it may safely be asserted that the style was Etruscan, imitated
and adopted by the Romans.[7]

Sutri has four gates; one at the end of the town towards
Ronciglione, another at the opposite extremity, and two on the
southern side. A fifth in the northern wall is now blocked up;
and it is said that this and the two on the opposite side are the
original entrances, and that the two at the extremities have been
formed within the last century. If so, Sutrium had the precise

---

[7] The earliest walls of Rome—those of
the Roma Quadrata, on the Palatine—are
of this masonry, and of the precise dimensions mentioned above. So are also
those of the second period, on the Aventine. Roman masonry, however, of this
description, especially on the south side
of the Tiber, is often of inferior dimensions, as in the Porta Romana of Segni,
where the courses are only eighteen inches
deep, and the Porta Cassamaro of Ferentino,
where they are still less—from fourteen to
seventeen inches. The specimens in Etruria are much more uniform. Mr. Bunbury,
in his new edition of Sir William Gell's
Rome (p. 328), questions whether these
walls of Sutri, or in fact any masonry of
this description found on Etruscan sites, be
of Etruscan construction, and asserts that
" it is certain that it is not found in any
Etruscan cities of undoubted antiquity;"
referring it always to the Romans. True
it is that the walls of Falleri, which he

cites, were built by a Roman colony in this
style (see the woodcuts at pages 97 and 101);
but what can be said to the masonry of
precisely the same character and dimensions, which may be traced in fragments
around the heights of Civita Castellana,
marking out the periphery of a city which
is now universally admitted to be no
other than the Etruscan Falerii, — destroyed, be it remembered, on its conquest? How is it that in no case in
Etruria is this masonry found based on a
different description, as though it were
Roman repairs of earlier fortifications, but
is always found at the very foundations,
and often in positions where the walls
must have been completely secure from
the contingencies of warfare? And what
can be said to the numerous instances of
its existence in connection with undoubted
Etruscan tombs at Cervetri and Corneto,
if it were not employed by the Etruscans
as well as by the Romans?

number of gates prescribed by the Etruscan ritual.[8]   Over that at
the western end the claims of the town to distinction are thus set
forth—"SUTRIUM ETRURIÆ CLAUSTRA, URBS SOCIA ROMANIS COLONIA
CONJUNCTA JULIA;" and over the Porta Romana, the other modern
gate, are painted the arms of the town—a man on horseback,
holding three ears of corn—with the inscription "A PELASGIIS
SUTRIUM CONDITUR." Now, though the village fathers should
maintain that the latter epigraph is a quotation from Livy,
believe them not, traveller, but rather credit my assertion that
there is no historic evidence of such an origin for Sutri—for on
no substantial authority doth this derivation rest.[9]

Though Sutrium was undoubtedly an ancient Etruscan city,[1]
we know nothing of its history during its independence.   The
first mention made of it is its capture by the Romans.   It is
singular that, in all the notices we have of it, we find it engaged in war, not like Veii and Fidenæ with the Romans, but
with the Etruscans.   It was taken from the latter at an early
period, probably in the year U.C. 360 ;[2] and in 371, or seven years
after the Gallic conquest of the City, it was made a Roman
colony.[3]   From the date of its capture, so soon after the fall of
Veii, it seems probable it was one of the towns dependent on
that city, like Fidenæ; yet it is nowhere mentioned in such a
connection.[4]   It was celebrated for the fidelity to its victors
displayed in several sieges it sustained from the confederate
Etruscans.   The first and most remarkable was in the year 365,
when it was besieged, as Livy tells us, by almost the whole force
of Etruria, and compelled to surrender; and the miserable inhabitants were driven out, with nothing but the clothes on their
backs.   As the sad train was pursuing its melancholy way on

---

[8] Servius (ad Æn. I. 426) says no Etruscan city was deemed perfect that had less
than three gates.

[9] The only shadow of authority for such
an origin is derived from the "Catonis
Origines" of Annio of Viterbo, that
"most impudent trifler and nefarious
impostor," as Cluverius styles him, but
whose forgeries long passed as genuine.
Here we find, "Sutrium à Pelasgia condi-
tum, ab insigni grano dictum." Sutrium
is probably the Latinized form of the
Etruscan appellation. We find "Sutrinas"
and "Suthrina" in Etruscan inscriptions,
which Vermiglioli (Iscriz. Perug. I. pp.
174, 256) thinks have reference to this

town, though evidently proper names.

[1] Steph. Byzant. voce Σούτριον.

[2] Diodorus (XIV. p. 311, ed. Rhod.)
states that the Romans attacked it in this
year.

[3] Vell. Paterc. I. 14. It must have
been one of the colonies of the Triumvirate, for it is called in an inscription in
the church Colonia Julia Sutrina
(Grüter, 302, 1). Festus (voce Municipium) speaks of it as a municipium.
Frontin. de Col.

[4] Müller's Etrusker, II. 2, 1. The
passage in Livy (XXVI. 34), "in Veiente,
aut Sutrino, Nepesinove agro," can only
refer to the contiguity of the lands.

foot towards Rome, it chanced to fall in with the army of Camillus, then on his road to relieve their city, which he imagined still held out. The dictator, moved by the prayers of the princes of Sutrium, by the lamentations of the women and children, bade them dry their tears, for he would soon transfer their weepings and wailings to their foes; and well did he keep his word. That self-same day he reached the town, which he found an easy prey, for the gates were unguarded, the walls unmanned, and the victorious Etruscans intent only on gathering the spoil. In a very short time he was master of the place; the Etruscans submitted almost without resistance, and ere night he restored the inhabitants to their homes, and reinstated them in their possessions. Thus Sutrium was taken twice in one day.[5] From the rapidity of this exploit the proverb "ire Sutrium" took its rise.[6] The gateway, now blocked up, on the northern side of the town, is pointed out as that by which Camillus entered, and hence it has received the name of Porta Furia, from the gentile name of the dictator. But such an antiquity is apocryphal; for the gate as it now exists is of the middle ages, and has an arch slightly, yet decidedly, pointed.[7] It is now blocked up, and does not seem to have been used for centuries.

In U.C. 368, Sutrium was again taken by the Etruscans, and rescued by Camillus;[8] and in 443, it was long besieged by the same foes, but saved by Fabius and Roman valour.[9] Near Sutrium, too, after Fabius had returned from his expedition across the Ciminian Mount, he signally surprised the Etruscans, and slew or captured sixty thousand.[1] Sutrium is subsequently mentioned by several ancient writers,[2] and the last intimation of its existence in classic times is given by an inscription of the time of Adrian.[3] It seems never to have shared the fate of Veii and Fidenæ—to have lain uninhabited and desolate for centuries; for its existence can be traced through the middle ages down to our own times.

[5] Liv. VI. 3; Plut. Camil.; Diod. Sic. XIV. p. 325.

[6] Plautus, Cas. Act. III., sc. I. 10. Festus voce Sutrium.

[7] Yet Canina (Etruria Marittima I. pp. 72, 76) maintains it to be an ancient Etruscan gate, and refers it to the time of Tarquinius Priscus.

[8] Liv. VI. 9.

[9] Liv. IX. 32, 33, 35. Diodor. XX. pp. 772–3.

[1] Liv. IX. 37.

[2] Strabo, V. p. 226; Liv. X. 14; XXVI. 34; XXVII. 9; XXIX. 15. Sil. Ital. VIII. 493. Appian. B.C., V. 31. Festus voce Municipium. Plin. III. 8. Ptol. Geog. p. 72, ed. Bert. Front. de Colon. Tertullian (Apolog. 24) mentions a goddess Hostia, or, as some editions have it, Nortia, worshipped at Sutrium. Müller (Etrusk. III. 3, 7) would read it, Horta.

[3] Nibby voce Sutrium.

On descending from the Porta Romana, I entered a glen, bounded by steep cliffs of red and grey tufo, hollowed into caves. To the right rose a most picturesque height, crowned with a thick grove of ilex. Over a doorway in the cliff was this inscription :—"Here stay thy step ; the place is sacred to God, to the Virgin, to the repose of the departed. Pray or pass on." I did neither, but entered, and found myself, first in an Etruscan sepulchre, and then in a Christian church—a little church in the heart of the rock, with three aisles, separated by square pillars left in the tufo in which the temple is excavated, and lighted by windows, also cut in the rock which forms one of the walls. It is believed by the Sutrini to have been formed by the early Christians, at a time when their worship was proscribed within the town. That it is of early date cannot be doubted ; the walls of the vestibule and the ceiling of the church retain traces of frescoes of the thirteenth or fourteenth century. The altar-piece was an old fresco of the Madonna and Child, which was under repair by a young artist of Sutri. This gentleman took me into an adjoining cave, which served as a sacristy, and showed me a door, which, he said, led to catacombs, supposed to communicate with those of Rome, Nepi, and Ostia. There are many wild legends connected with these mysterious subterranean passages ; the truth is that, though their extent has been greatly exaggerated, they are very intricate, and it is not difficult to lose oneself therein. On this account the Sutrini have blocked up the door leading to their subterranean wonders. Finding I had not yet seen the lions of Sutri, the young artist threw down his brush and palette, and insisted politely on doing the honours of his native town. He pointed out a cavern adjoining the vestibule of the church, now a charnel-house, full of human bones. The vestibule itself had originally been an Etruscan tomb, and the church, in all probability, another, enlarged to its present dimensions. It is called La Madonna del Parto.

On the top of the cliff, in which the church is excavated, stands the villa of the Marchese Savorelli, in a beautiful grove of ilex and cypress, which had attracted my eye on leaving the gate of Sutri. I walked through the grove to the further edge of the cliff, and lo ! the amphitheatre of Sutri lay beneath me—a structure which, from its unique character, and picturesque beauty, merits a detailed description.

THE AMPHITHEATRE.

Imagine a miniature of the Colosseum, or of any other amphitheatre you please, with corridors, seats, and vomitories; the seats in many parts perfect, and the flights of steps particularly sharp and fresh. Imagine such an amphitheatre, smaller than such structures in general, not built up with masonry, but in its every part hewn from the solid rock, and most richly coloured—green and grey weather-tints harmonising with the natural warm red hue of the tufo; the upper edge of the whole not merely fringed with shrubs, but bristling all round with forest trees, which on one side overshadow it in a dense wood, the classical ilex mingling with the solemn cypress;—and you have the amphitheatre of Sutri. The imagination of a Claude or a Poussin could not have conceived a sylvan theatre of more picturesque character.

Apart from its natural charms, this amphitheatre has peculiar interest, as being probably the type of all those celebrated structures raised by Imperial Rome, even of the Colosseum itself. We have historical evidence that Rome derived her theatrical exhibitions from Etruria. Livy tells us that the *ludi scenici*, "a new thing for a warlike people, who had hitherto known only the games of the circus," were introduced into Rome in the year 390, in order to appease the wrath of the gods for a pestilence then desolating the city—the same, by the way, which carried off Furius Camillus; and that *ludiones* were sent for from Etruria who acted to the sound of the pipe, in the Tuscan fashion. He adds, that they were also called "*histriones*"—*hister*, in the Etruscan tongue, being equivalent to *ludio* in the Latin.[4] All this is corroborated by Valerius Maximus; and Tertullian and Appian make it appear that the very name of these sports was indicative of their Etruscan origin,[5] *ludio a Lydiá*—the traditional mother-country of the Etruscans. The Roman theatres of that day must have been temporary structures of wood, the first permanent theatre being that erected by Pompey A. U. C. 699, which still exists in Rome. We also learn from Livy that the Circus Maximus was built by Tarquinius Priscus, the first of the Etruscan dynasty of Rome, who sent for race-horses and pugilists to Etruria,[6] where such and kindred games must have been

---

[4] Liv. VII. 2.

[5] Val. Max. II. 4. 3; Tertul. de Spectac. V.; Appian de Reb. Punic.

LXVI.

[6] Liv. I. 35; cf. Dionys. Hal. III. p. 200. Herodotus (I. 167) mentions the

common, as they are represented on the walls of many painted tombs, and on sarcophagi, cinerary urns, and *cippi*. We have historical evidence also, that the gladiatorial combats of the Romans had an Etruscan origin.[7] Therefore, though we find no express mention of circi, theatres and amphitheatres in use among the Etruscans, we may fairly infer their existence. There is strong ground for the presumption that the edifices they used were copied by the Romans, as well as the performances;[8] and if a building of this description be discovered in Etruria, it may well, *primâ facie*, urge a claim to be considered as of Etruscan construction.[9] It is true that some authorities of weight regard this amphitheatre of Sutri as Roman and of Imperial times, founding their opinion on its architectural details,[1] although an argument drawn from that source is far from conclusive, as we shall afterwards have occasion to show; but on the other hand

---

institution of such games at Agylla. Valerius Maximus (loc. cit.), on the other hand, states that the Circensian games were first celebrated by Romulus, under the name of Consualia. Dionys. II. p. 100; Virg. Æn. VIII. 636. It seems probable that the *Ludi Circenses*, introduced by Tarquin, were a new form of the original Consualia of Romulus. Boxing to the sound of the flute is said by Eratosthenes (ap. Athen. IV. c. 39) to have been an Etruscan custom.

[7] Nicolaus Damasconus, ap. Athen. loc. cit. In confirmation of which statement, we may mention that the name *Lanista*, which was given to the superintendent or trainer of the Roman gladiators, was an Etruscan word (Isid. Orig. X., 247). Müller (Etrusk. IV. 1, 10) is of opinion that the origin of the custom of gladiatorial combats at funerals should be referred to the Etruscans; "at least such a sanguinary mode of appeasing the dead must have appeared a very suitable oblation to the Manes among a people who so long retained human sacrifices."

[8] The existence of theatres is strongly implied by the passage of Nicolaus Damascenus above cited, who says, "The Romans held their gladiatorial spectacles not only at public festivals and in theatres, receiving the custom from the Etruscans, but also at their banquets."

[9] As we know there was no amphitheatre erected in Rome before the time of

Cæsar, when C. Curio constructed one of wood, in separate halves, which could be brought together into an amphitheatre, or swung round at pleasure into two distinct theatres (Plin. Nat. Hist., XXXVI. 24, 8); and as we know that the first stone building of this description was erected by Statilius Taurus in the reign of Augustus (Dio Cass. LI. 23; Sueton. Aug. 29), and that the Colosseum, and all the other amphitheatres extant, were constructed during the Empire;—the question naturally arises, How, if such edifices previously existed in Etruscan cities, there were none erected at Rome, or in her territories, before the time of Cæsar? for we know that until the amphitheatre was introduced, the Romans were content to hold their wild-beast fights and *naumachiæ* in the Circus, and their gladiatorial combats in the forum, at the banquet, or at the funeral pyre. It may be that in the construction of amphitheatres, Etruria did not long precede Rome, and that this of Sutri, if it be really of Etruscan origin, is not to be referred to the remote days of the national independence, but rather to a period before all native peculiarities in art and customs had been completely obliterated.

[1] Nibby (*voce* Sutrium) considers it of the time of Augustus; Canina (Etr. Marit. I. p. 56) thinks it an imitation of Roman structures of this description, while Micali (Ant. Pop. It. I. p. 145) regards it a Etruscan.

the structure has certain characteristics of a native origin, which may be observed in the cornice of the *podium* which surrounds the arena—in the doors in the same, narrower above than below, and above all in its mode of construction which is decidedly un-Roman, and peculiarly Etruscan; while the irregularity of the structure—the seats and passages being accommodated to the natural surface of the rock—and its singular, nay rustic, simplicity, distinguish it widely from the known amphitheatres of the Romans.[2]   In one sense it is undoubtedly Roman, for it cannot claim an antiquity prior to the conquest of Sutri.

This curious relic of antiquity is an ellipse—the arena being, according to my measurement, one hundred and sixty-four feet in length, by one hundred and thirty-two in its greatest breadth. The doors in the podium open into a vaulted corridor which surrounds the arena.   This corridor, with its doors, is of very rare occurrence; found elsewhere, I believe, only at Capua and Syracuse.[3]   Above the podium rise the benches; at the interval of every four or five is a *præcinctio* or encircling passage, for the convenience of spectators in reaching their seats.   There are several of these *præcinctiones*, and also a broad corridor above the whole, running round the upper edge of the structure; but such is the irregularity and want of uniformity throughout, that their number and disposition in few parts correspond.   Above the upper corridor, on that side of the amphitheatre which is overhung by the garden Savorelli, rises a wall of rock, with slender half-columns carved in relief on its face, and a cornice above, but both so ruined or concealed by the bushes which clothe the rock, as to make it difficult to perceive their distinctive character.   In the same wall or cliff are several niches or recesses, some upright, high enough for a man to stand in; others evidently sepulchral, of the usual form and size of those in which bodies were interred. The upright ones, being elevated above the level of the *præcinctio*, were probably intended to hold the statues of the gods, in whose honour the games were held.[4]   Such a thing was unknown,

---

[2] The only other amphitheatres I know, which are in parts rock-hewn, are those of Syracuse, Ptolomais in the Cyrenaica, and Dorchester.

[3] The *podium*, or parapet, now rises only three or four feet above the ground, but the arena has not been cleared out to its original level.   The corridor that surrounds it is between five and six feet high, and the same in width.   Similar doors in the *podium* I have observed in the stadium at Ephesus.

[4] Nibby conjectures these to have been for the *designatores*, or persons whose office it was to assign posts to the spectators; in other words, masters of the ceremonies.   But Plautus (Pœn. prol. 19) intimates, as indeed it is more natural to suppose, that the *designatores* walked about, and handed people to their seats,

I believe, in Roman amphitheatres; but I remember something like it in Spanish bull-rings—a chapel of the Virgin in a similar position, in the very roof of the gallery, before which the *matador* kneels on entering the arena, to beg her protection in his encounter with the bull. The horizontal recesses, on the other hand, have clearly no connexion with the amphitheatre, but are of subsequent formation, for in almost every instance they have broken through the half-columns, and destroyed the decorations of the amphitheatre, proving this to have fallen into decay before these sepulchral niches were formed, which are probably the work of the early Christians.

Another peculiarity in this amphitheatre is a number of recesses, about half-way up the slope of seats. There are twelve in all, at regular intervals, but three are vomitories, and the rest are alcoves slightly arched over, and containing each a seat of rock, wide enough for two or three persons. They seem to have some reference to the municipal economy of Sutrium, and were probably intended for the magnates of the town.[5] At the southern end is a vomitory on either side of the principal entrance; at the northern, on one side only of the gateway. The latter vomitory is now a great gap in the rock, having lost the flight of steps within it, which must have been supplied with wood or masonry. The other vomitories are perfect.[6] They have grooves or channels along their walls to carry off the water that might percolate through the porous tufo; and similar channels are to be seen in other parts of the amphitheatre, and furnish an argu-

---

instead of shouting to them from a fixed station on the top of the building. If it were a theatre instead of an amphitheatre, we might suspect them to be for the ἠχεῖα or brazen pots which were used for throwing out the voice, though Vitruvius tells us (V. 5) that these were placed among the seats of the theatre; but there could have been no need of this in an amphitheatre, where all appealed to the eye, nothing to the ear.

[5] The number twelve may not be without a meaning, as there were twelve cities in each of the three divisions of Etruria. The only parallel instance is in the theatre of Catania, in Sicily, which had four similar recesses. (Serrad. Antich. Sicil. v. p. 13.) "Till the year 558 of Rome, the senators had always mingled indiscriminately with the people at public spectacles. But Atilius Serranus and L. Scribonius, ædiles, followed

the suggestion of the elder Africanus, and set aside this custom by appointing separate places to the senators and the people, which estranged the minds of the populace, and greatly injured Scipio in their esteem" (Val. Max. II. 4. 2; Liv. XXXIV. 54). Augustus assigned to every rank and each sex a distinct place at the public shows (Suet. Aug. 44).

[6] They are seven or eight feet high at the mouth, and the same in width, with a well-formed arch; but within the passage the arch is depressed, almost like that of the later Gothic. They contain flights of steps relieved by landing-places. The entrance-passage is hewn into the form of a regular vault, sixteen or seventeen feet high, and about the same in width. Its length is sixty-eight feet, which is here the thickness of the rock out of which the structure is hewn.

ment for its Etruscan origin; as this is a feature very frequently observed in the rock-hewn sepulchres and roads of Etruria. The sharpness of the steps in some parts is surprising, but this is explained by the fact that this amphitheatre, only within the last thirty-five years, has been cleared of the rubbish which had choked and the trees which had covered it for centuries, so that its existence was unknown to Dempster, Gori, Buonarroti, and the early writers on Etruscan antiquities.[7] We are indebted for its excavation to the antiquarian zeal of the Marquis Savorelli, its present proprietor. Its worst foe seems to have been Nature, the tufo being in parts split by the roots of trees, remains of its forest covering, now reduced to mere stumps, which are too deeply imbedded to be eradicated.

The exterior of this structure exhibits no "arches upon arches," no corridors upon corridors—it is in keeping with the simplicity and picturesque character of the interior. Cliffs of red tufo in all the ruggedness of nature, coloured with white and grey lichens, hung with a drapery of ivy or shrubs, and crowned with a circling diadem of trees, with the never-to-be-forgotten group of ilices and cypresses on the table-land above—Sutri itself, at a little distance on another rocky height, the road running up to its open gate, and its church-spire shooting high above the mass of buildings—the deep dark glens around, with their yawning sepulchral caverns, dashing the scene with a shade of mystery and gloom.

A little down the road, beyond the amphitheatre, in a range of tufo cliffs, are many sepulchral caverns; some remarkable for their sculptured fronts. Not one of these façades remains in a perfect state; but there are traces of pediments, pilasters, and half-columns, with arches in relief, and fragments of mouldings of a simple character. In their interiors, some are small and shallow, others deep and spacious; some have flat ceilings, others are vaulted over, now with a perfect, now with a depressed arch; and some have simple cornices in relief surrounding the chamber. In some there are benches of rock for the support of sarcophagi; in others these benches are hollowed out to receive the body— and in many are semi-circular cavities recessed in the walls for a similar purpose. All these features are Etruscan characteristics, but most of these sepulchres bear traces of an after appropriation to Roman burial, in small upright niches, similar to those in

7 It is simply mentioned by Müller (Etrusk. II. p. 241, n. 49).

SUTRI AND ITS AMPHITHEATRE, FROM THE ROAD TO ROME.

Drawn by G. Dennis.

Roman *columbaria*, which have the same variety of form as in those in the rocks at Veii, and like them, contain sunken holes for the *ollæ*, of which there are from two to six in each niche. In one instance the niches are separated by small Doric-like pilasters, hewn out of the tufo. A feature that distinguishes them from the niches of a genuine Etruscan character is that they want the usual groove running round the back of the recess and opening in two holes in front, to carry off the moisture that might percolate the rock. The façades of many tombs on this site have similar grooves, which sometimes form a sort of graven pediment over the doorway.

Not one of these open sepulchres remains in a perfect state. The Spaniards have a proverb, "An open door tempts the devil to enter." Such has been the fate of these sepulchres—in all ages they have been misapplied. The Romans, both Pagan and Christian, introduced their own dead. In the dark and turbulent ages succeeding the fall of the Empire, they were probably inhabited by a semi-barbarous peasantry, or served as the lurking-places of banditti; and now they are commonly used as wine-cellars, hog-sties, or cattle-stalls, and their sarcophagi converted into bins, mangers, or water-troughs.

Beyond the sculptured tombs, in a field by the road-side, I found a sepulchre differing from any I had yet entered. It was divided into several chambers, all with recesses excavated in their walls to contain bodies, with or without sarcophagi—in tiers of shelves one above the other, like berths in a steamer's cabin. Such an arrangement is often observed in the catacombs of Italy and Sicily, and would lead one to suspect these tombs to have had a Christian origin, were it not also found in connection with Etruscan inscriptions at Civita Castellana, and Cervetri.

Some distance beyond is a cave called the Grotta d' Orlando, a personage, who, like his Satanic Majesty, has his name attached to many a marvel of nature and of art in the southern countries of Europe. He it was who cleft the Pyrenees with one stroke of his sword, Durandal, with the same ease with which he had been wont to cleave the Saracens from crown to seat. This Grotta may have been an Etruscan tomb, of two chambers, the outer and larger supported by a square pillar. But what has it to do with Orlando? Tradition represents that hero, while on his way to Rome in the army of Charlemagne, as having lured away some maid or matron of Sutri, and concealed her in this

cave, which would scarcely tempt an Æneas and Dido at present.[8]
On the same cliff with the Villa Savorelli is a ruin, pointed out
as the house in which Charlemagne took up his abode, when on
his way to Rome, to succour Adrian I., but it is evidently of
much later date.   Nor is Orlando the only hero of former times
of whom Sutri has to boast.   She lays claim to the nativity of
that much execrated character, Pontius Pilate, and a house is
still shown as the identical one in which he was born; though
the building is obviously of the middle ages.

There are other curious traditions hanging about this old
town of Sutri.   At the angle of a house in the main street is
an ass's or sheep's head of stone, minus the ears, which, like
the Moorish statues in the vaults of the Alhambra, is believed to
have been placed there as the guardian of hidden treasure.   Not
that any stores of wealth have yet been brought to light, for no
one has been able to determine on what spot the eyes of this
mysterious ass are fixed; but its existence is not the less
implicitly believed, and not by the vulgar only.   The artist who
accompanied me round Sutri, and his father, who is one of the
principal inhabitants, had jointly made researches for the said
treasure.   Thinking they had discovered the direction of the
asinine regards, they hired an opposite house, commenced delving
into its foundations, and doubted not to have found the object of
their search, had they not been stopped by the authorities, who,
wishing to keep the spoils to themselves, had forbidden all
private enterprise in this line.   He had made however more
profitable excavations.   He had opened tombs in the ground
above the sculptured cliffs, and had brought to light vases,
bronzes, and other valuable relics of Etruscan date.   Sutri has
been so little explored, that it is probable many treasures of
antiquity are yet to be found in its neighbourhood.   The tombs
hollowed in the cliffs have been rifled ages since, but those below
the surface, with no external indications, have in some cases
escaped the researches of former plunderers.   It is among these
alone that art-treasures are to be expected.

The traveller will find no inn at Sutri; and even for refreshment he must be dependent on the good-will of some private
townsman, who will dress him a meal for a consideration.

In the glen to the west of the town, on the road to Capranica,

[8] It is not improbable that this legend
originated in those stanzas of Ariosto (XII.
83–91), in which he represents his hero as

meeting the fair Isabella in a cave:—

" Era bella sì, che facea il loco
  Salvatico, parere un paradiso."

there is a cavern of large dimensions, but of natural formation, at the mouth of which is a church called, La Madonna della Grotta. The cave is extremely picturesque, its roof stalactited with pendent ferns.

The Via Cassia runs beyond Sutri through this wooded ravine to Capranica, another Etruscan site with a few tombs and sewers, but nothing of extraordinary interest. It is now a place of more importance than Sutri, having 3000 inhabitants—excellent fruit and wine—mineral waters beneficial in disorders of the kidneys, bladder, and spleen, (ask for the Fonte Carbonari, for so the spring is dubbed by the peasantry, instead of Carbonato)— and, what is of more importance to the traveller, possessing a *hospitium* formerly kept by a butcher, Pietro Ferri, where, if he will not find comfort, he may be sure of its best substitute, unbounded civility and readiness to oblige. The women here wear the skirt of their gowns over their heads for a veil, like Teresa Panza and other Manchegas, and being very brightly arrayed, are always picturesque. I could perceive no Roman remains at Capranica, the ancient name of which has not come down to us. It is three miles distant from Sutri, eight or more from Vetralla also on the Via Cassia, three from Bassano, four from Ronciglione, and nine from Oriuolo. On this latter road I found in several spots remains of Roman pavement, and about halfway from Oriuolo, or near Agliola, I observed a long portion of the road entire, running directly between the two towns, and probably a cross road connecting the Claudian and Cassian Ways. The church of San Vincenzo, on a height above Bassano, is a conspicuous object in this district, and is the great shrine of the neighbourhood, where, on the first fortnight in November, a general "*perdono*" is dispensed, and the country folks flock in thousands to obtain remission.

Beyond Capranica, some three or four miles, and a little off the road to the left, are the ruins of Vicus Matrini, a station on the Via Cassia, still retaining its ancient name, but having little to show beyond a few crumbling towers and sepulchres, all of Roman date; and a mile or so beyond it, is a way-side *osteria*, called Le Capannaccie, which has sundry relics from the said ancient station embedded in its walls. This is the highest point of the road, which here crosses the shoulder of the Ciminian, but its rise is so gradual as to be scarcely perceptible. The first part of the road from Capranica passes through shady lanes, orchards, and vineyards; then it traverses wide tracts of corn-land—the most wearisome scenery to the summer traveller, when the sun's glare is reflected with sickening intensity from the ever-restless, ever-dazzling surface. He who has crossed the torrid plains of the Castilles, La Mancha, or Estremadura, under a dog-day sun, will readily acknowledge that *segetes* are *lætæ* only in poetry or to the eye of the proprietor. A gradual descent of four miles, mostly through orchards, leads to Vetralla, on the verge of the great central plain of Etruria, which here bursts upon the view. The road from Rome to this place, a distance of forty-three miles, follows as near as may be the line of the ancient Via Cassia. It is still carriageable throughout; indeed, a " diligence " runs to Vetralla once or twice a week, professedly in nine hours, which are increased indefinitely at the convenience of the driver.

APPENDIX TO CHAPTER V.

Note.—Emplecton Masonry, vide p. 65.

I am aware that this interpretation of *emplecton* differs from that generally adopted, especially by Italian writers on ancient architecture, who take it to be descriptive of masonry formed of two fronts of squared blocks, with the intervening space filled with rubbish and mortar; thus forming "three crusts," as Vitruvius says, " two of facings, and a middle one of stuffing." This, however, was the mode employed by the Romans, as an expeditious substitute for the more solid construction of the Greeks, as Vitruvius (II., 8) expressly asserts; but the application of the term *emplecton* to it, was evidently an abuse. The Italians err in taking the word to be significant of *filling in, stuffing*, as though it were derived from ἐμπίπλημι or ἐμπλήθω, to *fill up*, instead of ἐμπλέκω, to *weave in*—a word expressive of the peculiar arrangement of the blocks. Marini, in his edition of Vitruvius (Rome, 1836, I., p. 97) commits the error of rendering ἐμπλέκω by *impleo*. Orsini, in his Dictionary of Vitruvius, makes *emplecton* to mean "something full or to be filled." Baldus, in his Lexicon, makes the same blunder, which De Laetus, in his, quarrels with, but does not correct, though he quotes Salmasius (Exercit. Plin., p. 1231), who comes nearer the mark, and acknowledges its derivation from πλέκω; but only perceives an analogy with the dressing of women's hair, where the outside is made smooth, while the inside remains rough, as this masonry is described. Canina also (Arch. Ant. V., p. 130) explains *emplecton* as signifying the stuffed masonry above mentioned, but thinks it applicable to constructions of small stones like bricks (VIII., p. 104). This stuffed masonry was used extensively by the Romans, especially in small work, and it was even employed by the Greeks on a larger scale, as the remains of their cities testify. It may be seen also in part of the Cyclopean walls of Arpinum, and even in the Etruscan ones of Volterra. Pliny (Nat. Hist., XXXVI. 51) says it was called *diamicton, i.e.*, mixt-work.

The Greeks, however, sometimes, as at Pæstum, Syracuse, and elsewhere in Sicily, bound the facings of their walls together by solid masonry. So Pliny remarks, in his description of *emplecton*, though he says, where it was not possible, they built as with bricks, which evidently means, as bricks were used in facings merely, the rest being filled in with rubbish. The point aimed at, according to the same writer, was to lay the blocks so that their centres should fall immediately over the joinings of those below them.

Vitruvius, however, is the best authority for the application of *emplecton* to solid masonry, for, after mentioning it as descriptive of a style used by the Greeks, and after distinguishing the Roman variety, he says, "Græci vero non ita ; sed plana (coria) collocantes et longitudines chororum alternis coagmentis in crassitudinem instruentes, *non media farciunt*, sed e suis frontatis perpetuum et in unam crassitudinem parietem consolidant. Præterea interponunt singulos perpetuâ crassitudine utrâque parte frontatos, quos διατόνους appellant, qui maxime religando confirmant parietum soliditatem." This is a just description of the walls of Falleri, which, not being mere embankments, display the blocks in some parts "stretching through" from side to side. I would not maintain that the term *emplecton* should be confined to this sort of masonry. It is also applicable to that where the *diatoni* or cross blocks, instead of occurring in alternate courses, and continuously, are found only from time to time ; it is applicable, in short, to any masonry where the principle of *interweaving* is preserved. I use it throughout this work to designate that species of *opus quadratum*, which is so common in ancient structures in the southern district of Etruria, as well as in Rome and its neighbourhood.

There are difficulties, I own, in this passage of Vitruvius, describing Greek masonry ; in fact, the text is generally admitted to be corrupt, as the variety of readings prove ; but it is still clear that the term *emplecton*, however misapplied by the Romans, or their descendants, was properly confined by the Greeks to masonry, of which an interweaving of the blocks was the principle. The analogy to brick-work, indicated by Vitruvius (cf. II. 3), is confirmatory of this. Abeken (Mittelitalien, p. 151) is the only writer besides myself, so far as I am aware, who takes this view of *emplecton*.

An excellent example of Greek *emplecton* masonry is presented by the Castle of Euryalus in Epipolæ at Syracuse, where the four towers above the fosse, and the piers for the drawbridge within the fosse, are of this masonry rusticated, but it is on a rather smaller scale than is usual in Etruria.

CHAPTER VI.

NEPI.—*NEPETE.*

Where Time hath leant
His hand, but broke his scythe, there is a power
And magic in the ruined battlement,
For which the palace of the present hour
Must yield its pomp, and wait till ages are its dower. —BYRON.

IF on reaching the Guglia, or sign-post, beyond Monterosi,
instead of taking the road to Ronciglione and " Firenze," the
traveller follow the more holy track of " Loreto," three short
miles will carry him to Nepi. Let him remark the scenery
on the road. He has left the open wastes of the Campagna
and entered a wooded district. It is one of the few portions
of central Italy that will remind him, if an Englishman, of
home. Those sweeps of bright green sward—those stately wide-
armed oaks scattered over it, singly, or in clumps—those neat
hedge-rows, made up of maples, hawthorns, and brambles, with
fern below, and clematis, dog-roses, and honeysuckles above ;
they are the very brothers of those in Merry England. The
whole forms a lively imitation of—what is most rare on the
Continent—English park-scenery ; and it requires no stretch of
fancy to conceive oneself journeying through Surrey or Devon-
shire.

The first view of Nepi dispels the illusion. It is a quaint-
looking town. A line of crumbling wall, laden with machicolated battlements, and a massive castle within rising high
above it, would give it the appearance of a fortress, were it not
for the square red tower of the cathedral with its white pyramid
of a spire, shooting high and bright into the deep blue sky.
Behind it soars Soracte, its serrated mass blued by distance ;
and far away in the horizon is the range of snow-capt Apennines.

On entering the gate the eye is caught by a fine piece of
ancient walling, in nineteen courses, or about thirty-six feet and
a half in height, and of considerable length. Its crumbling

weather-worn condition proclaims its antiquity, and the size and arrangement of the blocks mark its Etruscan character. Just within the inner gate is another fragment of less extent, only ten courses high, and still more decayed. These are probably the very walls which Camillus and his soldiers scaled when they stormed the town, 386 years before Christ.[1]

But instead of entering the town, cross the court-yard to the right, and pass through another gate in the fortifications.[2] Here you are on the brink of the ravine which bounds Nepi on the south. The view of the cliff-bound city—of the profound, lonely ravine—of the lofty venerable walls of the keep, with their machicolated battlements towering above you—of the lowly mill at their feet, vying with them in picturesque effect, as it shoots out a jet of foam which sinks in a cascade into the glen—would alone claim admiration. But there is yet more for the attention of the antiquary. At the verge of the cliff, to which, indeed, it forms a facing or embankment, and only a few steps from the gate of the town, is another bit of the ancient walling of Nepete, and the most perfect specimen remaining. It is of four courses only, in an excellent state of preservation. Like the two other portions mentioned, it is of *emplecton*, precisely similar to the walls of Sutri.

The wall, of which this is a fragment, seems to have extended along the face of the precipice. Much seems to remain imbedded in a mass of Roman *opus incertum*, which apparently once faced the whole structure, showing the priority of the *emplecton*.[3] If this formed part of the walls of Nepete, the ancient must have been somewhat larger than the modern town.

This is all I could perceive of the ancient walls of Nepete. These portions, be it observed, are on the weakest side of the town, where it receives no protection from nature. On every other

[1] Liv. VI. 10.

[2] The road from this gate is a by-path to Sette Vene, shorter by several miles, but said to be a wretched track, utterly impracticable for vehicles.

[3] Nibby (II. p. 400) thinks these relics of the ancient walls of Nepi are of Roman construction, and of the time of the colony formed here A. U. C. 381, because their masonry is analogous with that of the walls of the new Falerium (Falleri) raised not long after that date. Canina (Etruria Marittima I., p. 72) takes the same view. But it is also precisely similar to the masonry of the ancient walls at Civita Castellana, which they admit to be Etruscan. There is no reason to suppose that these walls at Nepi are of less ancient construction. The discovery since their day of the walls of Roma Quadrata proves that this style of masonry was used in the earliest days of Rome, and as we find it also in very primitive cities and tombs in Etruria, there can be no doubt that it was originally employed by the Etruscans, and imitated by the Romans.

side, as it is situated on a long cliff-bound tongue of land between
two ravines that meet at its tip, there was little need of walls.
But at the root of the tongue, where the ground on which the
city stands meets the unbroken level of the Campagna, it was
most strongly fortified in ancient times; and this necessity continuing throughout the troubled period of the middle ages, the
walls were preserved as much as might be, or replaced, where
dilapidated, by the strong line of fortifications and flanking
bastions, which still unite the ravines. From the analogy of
other Etruscan cities, it is probable that the inhabitants were
not satisfied with the natural protection of their precipices, but
surrounded the city with walls, which, in after times, were
demolished, probably for the sake of materials to build or repair
the edifices of the town.

My aim being simply to point out objects of antiquarian
interest, I shall say little of the modern representative of Nepete.
It is a small town, not larger than Sutri; and its position is
very similar, though the plateau it occupies rises much higher
from the ravines, and the cliffs are in most parts more precipitous. As regards its natural strength it has certainly no less
claim than Sutri to the title of " key and portal of Etruria."[4]

In strolling around the place, I was surprised at the small
number of tombs. The opposite cliff of the ravine to the south,
has not a single cave; and on the other side of the town there
are far fewer than usual in the immediate vicinity of Etruscan
sites, which present facilities for excavation. The Nepesini seem
to have preferred burying their dead beneath the surface of the
ground, to hollowing out tombs or niches in the cliffs; and the
table-lands around the town are probably burrowed thickly with
sepulchres. In the rock on which the modern walls are based,
close to the gate that opens to Civita Castellana, are traces of
sepulchral niches; and here also a sewer, like those at Sutri,
opens in the cliff. The ravine is spanned by a bridge,[5] and
also by an aqueduct with a double tier of arches, the work of the
sixteenth century.

No one should cross this bridge without a pause. The dark
ravine, deepening as it recedes, leading the eye to the many-
peaked mass of Soracte in the distance, by the towers and battle-

[4] Liv. VI. 9.

[5] The stream below is said by Nibby to
retain the classic name of Falisco, though
all my inquiries called forth no more elevated appellation than " La Buttata della
Mola," or the Mill-force. The stream in the
opposite ravine is called " Cava-terra "—
i. e., Earth-digger.

ments of the town on one hand, and by a stately stone-pine raising its spreading crest into the blue sky on the other, is set off like a picture in its frame. It is one of those scenes in which you could scarcely suggest an improvement—in which Nature rivals the perfection of Art.

There is little to detain the antiquarian traveller in Nepi. In the Piazza, beside a fine fountain of large size, are several Roman altars and statues found in the neighbourhood, one of them having reference to the goddess Feronia; and a mutilated bas-relief of a winged lion.

Of the old inn, "La Fontana," no one speaks well; and I retain a most uncomfortable remembrance of it. A new *locanda*, "Hôtel de la Paix," has since been opened, in which the traveller will fare well enough—but let him look to his bill—*suspice finem!*

Nepete never took a prominent part in history; at least, we find little more than incidental mention of this town. It early fell under Roman dominion, for in the year 368, a few years after the capture of the City by the Gauls, we find it mentioned with Sutrium, as an ally of Rome; both towns seeking assistance against the Etruscans, by whom they were attacked. Nepete surrendered to the Etruscans, because a portion of the inhabitants were better affected towards their countrymen than towards their recent allies; but it was retaken at the first assault by Camillus; and the rebellious citizens met their punishment from the axes of the lictors.[6] It was made a Roman colony ten years later than Sutrium, or seventeen years after the Gallic capture of the City.[7] Both these towns enjoyed municipal honours of the highest class, that is, while retaining their own internal administration, they were admitted to the full rights and privileges of Roman citizenship.[8]

There seems to have been some particular bond of union between Nepete and Sutrium; for they are frequently coupled together by ancient writers.[9] Similar bonds seem to have existed among other Etruscan cities, even those of the Confederation; for instance, Arretium, Cortona, and Perugia appear to have had a minor league among themselves[1]—a *vinculum in vinculo*—a bond arising, as in this case, from proximity and community of interest.

---

[6] Liv. VI. 9, 10.

[7] Vell. Pat. I. 14. Livy (VI. 21) makes it to be the same year as Sutrium, or A. U. 371.

[8] Festus, *voce* Municipium.

[9] Liv. VI. 9; X. 14; XXVI. 34; XXVII. 9; XXIX. 15. Festus (loc. cit.).

[1] Liv. IX. 37; Diod. XX. p. 773.

Nepete, like Sutrium, has retained its name,[2] and maintained an existence from ancient times. Under the Empire, it seems to have been of inferior consequence;[3] but in the middle ages it rose greatly in importance, and at one period exercised no little influence over Rome herself.[4] It is now an insignificant town, with about 1500 inhabitants.

Nepi is five miles distant from Monterosi, eight from Civita Castellana, five from Falleri by a path through the woods, the line of the ancient Via Amerina; seven from Sutri by a short cut, and nine by the carriage-road.

---

[2] It is called Nepete by Livy, and by inscriptions, but Nepita by Strabo (V. p. 226), Nepo by Paterculus and the Peutingerian table, Nepet by Pliny (III. 8), Nepeta by Ptolemy (Geog. p. 72), Nepis by Frontinus (de Col.), Nepetus by Dionysius (XIII. ap. Steph. Byz.).

[3] Strabo (V. p. 226) classes Sutrium with Arretium, Perusia, and Volsinii, as cities πόλεις) of Etruria; while Nepete is mentioned among the smaller towns (πολίχναι).

[4] This was in the eighth century, when Totone, Duke of Nepi, created his brother Pope, under the title of Constantine II., and maintained him in the seat of St. Peter for thirteen months. "Nepi seems at that epoch to have risen like a meteor, and rapidly to have sunk to her former condition."—Nibby, voce Nepi.

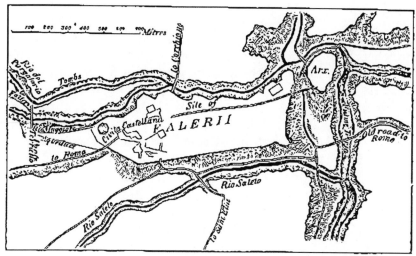

PLAN OF FALERII.   *From Canina.*

CHAPTER VII.

CIVITA CASTELLANA.—*FALERII (VETERES).*

Faliscis,
Mœnia contigimus victa, Camille, tibi.—OVID. Amor.

Poi giunsi in una valle incolta e fiera,
Di ripe cinta e spaventose tane ;
Che nel mezzo sù un sasso havea un castello,
Forte, e ben posto, e a maraviglia bello.—ARIOSTO.

FROM Nepi, which is thirty miles from Rome, the high road
runs direct to Civita Castellana, a distance of nearly eight miles ;
but to the traveller on horse or foot I would recommend a route,
by which he will save two miles. On passing the bridge of Nepi,
let him turn immediately to the right ; a mile of lane-scenery
with fine views of Nepi will carry him to Castel di Santa Elia, a
small village, which looks much like an Etruscan site, and was
perhaps a *castellum* dependent on Nepete. The road to it and
beyond it seems in parts to have been ancient, cut through the
tufo ; there are few tombs by its side, but here and there portions
of masonry, serving as fences to the road, may be observed,
which are of ancient blocks, often found in such situations. He
then enters on a bare green down, rich in the peculiar beauties
of the Campagna. A ravine yawns on either hand. That on the
right, dark with wood, is more than usually deep, gloomy, and
grand. Beyond the other runs the high road to Civita ; and in

that direction the plain—in winter an uniform sheet of dark rich brown from the oak-woods which cover it, studded here and there with some tower or spire shooting up from the foliage—stretches to the foot of the Ciminian Mount. Ronciglione and Capraruola gleam in sunshine on its slopes, each beneath one of its dark wooded peaks. The towers of Civita Castellana rise before him. Towns shine out from the distant mountains of Umbria and Sabina. The plain on the right is variegated in hue, and broken in surface. Soracte towers in lonely majesty in the midst; and the chain of Apennines in grey or snow-capped masses billows along the horizon. A goatherd, shaggy with skins, stands leaning on his staff, watching the passing traveller; and with his flock and huge baying dogs, occupies the foreground of the picture. Just so has Dante beautifully drawn it—

> " Le capre
> Tacite all' ombra mentre che 'l sol ferve,
> Guardate dal pastor che 'n su la verga
> Poggiato s' è, e lor poggiato serve."—*Purg.* XXVII. 76.

> All in the shade
> The goats lie silent, 'neath the fervid noon,
> Watched by the goatherd, who upon his staff
> Stands leaning; and thus resting, tendeth them.

A stone-piled cross by the way-side, recording that here

> "Some shrieking victim hath
> Poured forth his blood beneath the assassin's knife,"

seems strangely at variance with the beauty and calm of the scenery.

To reach Civita Castellana by this road, you must cross the wide and deep ravine which forms its southern boundary. The high-road, however, continues along the ridge, approaching the town by level-ground, and enters it beneath the walls of the octagonal fortress—the masterpiece of Sangallo, and the political Bastille of Rome, when the Pope retained his temporal sovereignty.

What traveller who has visited Rome, before the days of railroads, has not passed through Civita Castellana? There is scarcely any object in Italy better known than its bridge—none assuredly is more certain to find a place in every tourist's sketchbook; and well does it merit it. Though little more than a century old, this bridge or viaduct is worthy of the magnificence

of Imperial Rome; and combines with the ravine, the town on its
verge, the distant Campagna, Soracte, and the Apennines, to
form one of the choicest unions of nature and art to be found
in that land where, above all others, their beauties seem most
closely wedded. Yet beyond this, little or nothing is known of
Civita Castellana. Not one in five hundred who passes through
it, and halts awhile to admire the superb view from the bridge, or
even descends from his carriage to transfer it to his sketch-book,
ever visits the tombs by the Ponte Terrano. Still fewer descend
to the Ponte di Treia; and not one in a thousand makes the tour
of the ravines, or thinks of this as a site abounding in Etruscan
antiquities. My aim is to direct attention to the objects of
antiquarian interest with which Civita Castellana is surrounded.

Very near the bridge, and on the verge of the cliff on which
the town is built, is a portion of the ancient walls, of tufo, in
emplecton, seventeen courses in height, and precisely similar in
the size and arrangement of its blocks, to the walls of Sutri and
Nepi, already described. It forms an angle at the verge of the
precipice, and is nothing more than a *revêtement* to the ground
within.[1]

If you here enter the town, and continue down the long street
on the left, you will arrive at the nunnery of St. Agata, at the
north-east angle of the plateau, on which Civita is built. By its
side is a road cut in the rock, which a very little experience will
tell you is Etruscan. It has on one side a water-course or gutter
sunk in the tufo, which, after running high above the road for
some distance, discharges its waters over the precipice. There
are tombs also—genuine Etruscan tombs—on either hand, though
the forms of some are almost obliterated, and others are sadly
injured by the purposes they are now made to serve—shepherds'
huts, cattle-stalls, and hog-sties. They are mostly in the cliff,
which, as the road descends rapidly to the valley, rises high
above your head. Here, too, opening in the cliff, are the mouths
of several sewers, similar to those at Sutri and the Etruscan sites
described.[2]

---

[1] Canina gives illustrations of three
pieces of the walls on this north side of
the ancient city, and represents them all
as showing the ends only of the blocks.
Etruria Marit. tav. 6. All the fragments
which I saw were certainly of that masonry
which I have designated as *emplecton*, and
which shows the ends and sides of the

blocks in alternate courses.

[2] These sewers are about 6 ft. in height,
2 ft. 6 in. wide at the bottom, tapering to
1 ft. 6 in. at the top. One runs into the
rocks some little distance, and then rises
in an upright square chimney, into which
another passage opens horizontally above.

It was probably these subterranean passages being ignorantly mistaken for the *caniculus* of Camillus that gave rise to the notion of this being the site of Veii; but such sewers are to be found beneath the walls of every Etruscan city in the tufo district of the land, where the rock would admit of easy excavation, and are found also on all the ancient sites of the Campagna, even in the Capitoline, Palatine, and Aventine hills of Rome. Here you are at the extreme angle of the plateau of Civita Castellana; the ravine spanned by the celebrated bridge opens on one hand, while another and wider glen lies on the other, bounding the plateau to the east.[3] The road passes two ruined gateways of the middle ages, and winds down into this valley, through which flows the Treia, spanned by a neat bridge of three arches. Here stands a large building in ruins; the table-land of Civita rises above your head in a range of steep, lofty cliffs of red tufo, based on a stratum of white sandy breccia. At the brow of the cliff, just above the bridge, is a long line of wall of the middle ages, in one place based on more ancient masonry of larger blocks, evidently part of the Etruscan walls, the very " mœnia alta " sung by Ovid.[4] A sewer in the cliff beneath them rivals them in antiquity.

This line of cliff runs due north and south for some distance— it then suddenly turns at right angles, where a glen opens to the west, and the streamlet of the Saleto, or, as it is also called, the Ricano, issues from it to unite its waters with those of the Treia. It is a lonely and wild, but attractive spot. No sign of man save in the stepping-stones over the stream, or in the narrow track through the meadows or brushwood. Not a sound to remind you of the neighbourhood of the town over your head. The lofty cliffs on either hand bare their broad faces with a contrasted expression—smiling or scowling as they catch or lose the sun.

Here it is advisable to cross the stream to get a better view of the cliffs of the city. Soon after entering this glen you may perceive a portion of ancient wall sunk in a hollow of the cliff, and

---

[3] Gell points out this angle of the cliff pierced by tombs and sewers as the site of the ancient city (which he supposes to have been Fescennium), intimating his opinion that the city occupied this corner of the plateau only (I. p. 292). Had he made the tour of the height of Civita Castellana, he would have observed unequivocal traces of the ancient city in several places widely distant, proving that it was not confined to a mere corner of the plateau, but extended over the whole area, whose limits are defined by natural boundaries, and was thus one of the largest cities in the south of Etruria. This peninsular platform, which he mistook for the site of the entire city, was probably that of the Arx.

[4] Ovid. Amor. III., Eleg. XIII. 34.

filling a natural gap. You may count as many as twelve courses. A little beyond you meet with another piece in a similar situation, and of five or six courses. You cannot inspect the masonry as you could wish, on account of the height of the cliff, which rises more than two hundred feet above your head, and, as the wall is at the very brink of the precipice, it is obviously not to be viewed from above. A practised eye, however, has no difficulty in determining its character—the difference between it and the mediæval masonry, a long line of which presently follows, is most decided. Below this wall, and half-way up the cliff, are many tombs, with traces also of sewers.

At the Ponte Saleto, where you meet the short cut from Civita to Nepi, you cross the stream, and take the road to the city, passing many tombs hollowed in the rock, resembling those near the Ponte Terrano, which will presently be described. The cliff here turns to the north-west, and a path runs along its brow, outside the modern walls. On this side there is rather a natural fosse than a ravine, for the cliff rises nearly one hundred feet above the lower part of the isthmus which unites the plateau of Civita with the plain of the Campagna. It is probable that wherever the cliffs were not sufficiently steep they were scarped by art, to increase the natural strength of the position—no difficult task, as tufo has a tendency to split vertically. Remains of the ancient walls may be observed in the foundations of the modern, from which they are easily distinguished by the superior massiveness of the blocks, by their different arrangement, and by the absence of cement. It will be remarked that all these fragments of ancient walling either exist in situations at the verge of the precipice, most difficult of access, or serve as foundations to more modern walls; whence it may be inferred that the rest of the ancient fortifications have been applied to other purposes; and a glance at the houses in the town suffices to show that, like Sutri, Civita is in great measure built of ancient materials.

Passing round the castle of Sangallo, you re-enter the town by an adjoining gate, where are traces of an ancient road cut in the rock at the verge of the precipice, which bounds the city on the north; its character marked by the tombs at its side. The wall of the city must here have been on the top of the rock in which the tombs are hollowed and the road sunk; and it seems most probable that here was the site of a gate, and that the modern fortress stands without the walls of the ancient city. It is curious to observe how close to their cities the Etruscans buried their dead—even up to the very gates; though very rarely within the walls, as was the custom in some of the cities of Greece, and occasionally permitted at Rome.[5] These tombs are large conical niches or pits, eight or nine feet high, by six in diameter. They are very common in the tufo district of Etruria, and are also met with in the neighbourhood of the ancient cities of Latium, in the Campagna south of the Tiber, and at Syracuse and other ancient sites in Sicily. Some have supposed them depositories for grain,[6] and were they found only as close to ancient cities as in this case, this would be probable enough; but around Civita there are others in very different situations; and having seen them on other Etruscan sites, far outside the ancient walls, and in the midst of undoubted tombs, I have not the smallest doubt of their sepulchral character. Besides, they have, almost invariably, above the cone a small niche of the usual sepulchral form, as if for a *cippus*, or for a votive offering. I think it not unlikely that they contained figures of stone or terra-cotta, probably the effigies of the deceased, which were at the same time cinerary urns, holding their ashes,—such figures as have been found in several cemeteries of Etruria.

Instead of entering the town, follow the brink of the precipice to the Ponte Terrano—a bridge which spans the ravine, where it contracts and becomes a mere bed to the Rio Maggiore. It has a single arch in span, but a double one in height, the one which carries the road across being raised above another of more ancient date. Over all runs an aqueduct of modern construction, which spares the Civitonici the trouble of fetching water from the bottom of the ravines.

The cliffs above and below the bridge are perforated in every direction with holes—doorways innumerable, leading into spacious tombs—sepulchral niches of various forms and sizes—here, rows of squares, side by side, like the port-holes of a ship of war—there, long and shallow recesses, one over the other, like an open cupboard, or a book-case, where the dead were literally laid upon

[5] For this custom in Greece, see Becker, Charicles. Excurs. sc. IX. At Rome it was forbidden by the Twelve Tables to bury or burn the dead within the walls, but the privilege was occasionally granted to a few, illustrious for their deeds or virtues. Cic. de Leg. II. 23. Plut. Publicola.

[6] The corn-pits for which these tombs have been taken were called σειροί or σιροί

by the Greeks of Cappadocia and Thrace. Varro, de Re Rust. I. cap. 57. But these Pollux (Onomast. IX. cap. 5. s. 49) mentions among the parts of a city, with cellars, wells, bridges, gates, vaults; whence we may conclude they were within the walls. Such pits are still known in Sicily by the name of *Sili*.

the shelf,—now again, upright like pigeon-holes,—or still taller and narrower, like loop-holes in a fortification. This seems to have been the principal necropolis of the Etruscan city. If you enter any of the tombs in the faces of the low cliffs into which the ground breaks, you will find one general plan prevailing, characteristic of the site. Unlike those of Sutri, where the door opens at once into the tomb, it here leads into a small ante-chamber, seldom as much as five feet square, which has an oblong hole in the ceiling, running up like a chimney to the level of the ground above. The tomb itself is generally spacious— from twelve to twenty feet square, or of an oblong form—never circular—mostly with a massive square pillar in the centre, hewn out of the rock, or, in many cases, with a thick partition-wall of rock instead, dividing the tomb into two equal parts. The front face of this, whether it be pillar or projecting wall, is generally hollowed out, sometimes in recesses, long and shallow, and one over the other, to contain bodies, sometimes in upright niches, for cinerary urns or votive offerings. Around the walls are long recesses for bodies, in double or triple tiers, just as in the catacombs and tombs of the early Christians. The door-posts are frequently grooved to hold the stone slabs with which the tombs were closed. The chimney in the ceiling of the ante-chamber probably served several purposes—as a *spiramen*, or vent-hole, to let off the effluvium of the decaying bodies or burnt ashes—as a means of pouring in libations to the Manes of the dead—and as a mode of entrance on emergency after the doors were closed. That they were used for the latter purpose is evident, for in the sides of these chimneys may be seen small niches, about a foot or eighteen inches one above the other, manifestly cut for the hands and feet. These chimneys were probably left open for some time, till the effluvium had passed off, and then were covered in, generally with large hewn blocks. Similar trap-doorways to tombs are found occasionally at Corneto, Ferento, Cervetri, and elsewhere in Etruria, but nowhere in such numbers as at Civita Castellana and Fálleri, where they form a leading characteristic of the sepulchres.[7]

A few of these tombs have a vestibule or open chamber in front, sometimes with a cornice in relief, benches of rock against

---

[7] I have opened tombs with such entrances at Teuchira in the Cyrenaica; and the tombs of Phrygia, described by Stewart (Ancient Monuments of Lydia and Phrygia, pl. vii.), had similar trap-doors, b they had no other mode of entrance, the façade having merely a false doorway, as in the tombs of Castel d'Asso and Norchia.

the walls for the support of sarcophagi, and niches recessed above, probably for votive offerings. In one instance there is a row of these niches, five on each side the doorway, high and narrow, like loopholes for musketry, save that they do not perforate the rock. Sometimes a large sarcophagus is hollowed out of a mass of rock. It is not uncommon to find graves of the same form sunk in the rock in front of the tomb, probably for the bodies of the slaves of the family, who, in death as in life, seem to have lain at their masters' doors.

In the front wall of the tomb next to that with the row of niches, is an inscription in Etruscan letters,—" Tucthnu "— which I do not recognise as an Etruscan name. It is probable that this is but part of the original inscription, the rest being obliterated. The letters retain traces of the red paint with which, as on the sarcophagi and urns generally, they were filled, to render them more legible. No other tomb could I find on this site with an Etruscan inscription on its exterior; it does not seem to have been the custom in this part of Etruria, as in some necropoles north of the Ciminian, to engrave epitaphs on the rock-hewn façades of the sepulchres.

On the inner wall of a large tomb, close to the Ponte Terrano, is an Etruscan inscription of two lines rudely graven on the rock, and in unusually large letters, about a foot in height.[8] It is over one of the long body-niches, which are hollowed in the walls of this tomb in three tiers, and is of importance as it proves these niches to be of Etruscan formation, and not always early Christian, as many have imagined. Further proof of this is given by the tombs of Cervetri—that of the Tarquins, for example.[9]

From the tombs on this site we learn that it was the custom here to bury rather than to burn the dead—the latter rite seems to have been more prevalent at Sutrium. These differences are worthy of notice, as every Etruscan city had its peculiar mode of sepulture; though there is in general much affinity among those in the same district, and in similar situations.

The Ponte Terrano is a modern structure on an ancient basement. The northern pier, to the height of ten courses and to the width of twenty-three feet, is of *emplecton* masonry—

---

[8] It is given by Buonarroti (ap. Dempst. II., tav. 82, p. 26), who visited it in 1691, and by Gori and Lanzi. Mr. Ainsley gives a different reading. Bull. Inst. 1845, p. 189.

[9] Padre Garrucci (Ann. Inst. 1860, p. 269, tav. G.) gives several other inscriptions from tombs on this spot, which he pronounces to be in the ancient Faliscan character and language.

Etruscan in style and in the size and arrangement of the blocks. Above it is small irregular masonry of modern times. The opposite pier is of rock, overhung with ivy and ilex. The lower arch is of the middle ages, so that the bridge unites in itself the work of three distinct epochs. Its antiquity has scarcely been noticed by former writers.[1]

Whoever would see the chief beauties of Civita Castellana, should descend into the deep ravine on this side of the town. The most convenient path is near the great bridge or viaduct. It is a zigzag track, cut through the tufo, and of ancient formation, as is proved by the water-troughs at its side, and by the tombs in the rocks.

From the bottom of the descent the bridge is seen to great advantage, spanning the ravine with its stupendous double tier of arches, with a grandeur that few viaducts, save the Pont du Gard, can surpass. A mimic cataract rushes down the cliff to join the stream—a rustic mill or two nestling beneath the bridge, are the only other buildings visible, and contrast their humility with its majesty, as if to show at one glance the loftiest and meanest efforts of man's constructive power. Whoever has seen the magnificent Tajo of Ronda, in the south of Spain, will recognise immediately some resemblance here; but this ravine is by no means so profound—the bridge is of a different character, wider, lighter, less solid, and massive—and here are no cascades, and lines of ivy-grown mills, as on the Rio Verde. Nevertheless, there is much in the general features of the ravine to recall to the memory the glorious Tajo de Ronda.

The cliffs, both above and below the bridge, are excavated into tombs and niches of various forms, but few have retained their original shape. It must be confessed that the Etruscans often displayed great taste in selecting the sites of their sepulchres. Where could be found a more impressive, a more appropriate cemetery, than a ravine like this—a vast grave in itself, sunk two hundred and fifty feet below the surface—full of grandeur and gloom?

The ravine, moreover, is fertile in the picturesque. Ascend the course of the stream, and just above a rustic bridge you obtain a fine view of the Ponte Terrano spanning the glen in the distance, the Castle cresting the precipice on the left, and a ruined tower frowning down upon you from the opposite height. The

---

[1] Gell and even Nibby seem to have overlooked it. Westphal alone (Römische Kampagne, p. 139) mentions it as ancient.

cliffs rise on either hand, of yellow and red tufo, dashed with grey, white, or brown, with occasional ledges of green; the whole crested with ilex, and draped here and there with ivy, clematis, and wild vine. Below the great bridge you have still more of the picturesque. The walls of warm yellow cliff, variegated with foliage, here approach so close as to make this a mere chasm—the fragment of Etruscan walling crowns the precipice on the right—huge masses of cliff fallen from above, lie about in wild confusion, almost choking the hollow—tall trees shoot up from among them, by the banks of the stream, but are dwarfed into shrubs by the vast height of the all-shadowing cliffs.

There is no lack of accommodation at Civita Castellana. The principal inn, La Posta, has received a bad name on account of the alleged extortion and insolence of the landlord. At La Croce Bianca, however, the traveller will find comfortable accommodation, civility and attention. Sausages are not now famous here, as in ancient times.[2] Civita Castellana contains scarcely more than two thousand souls, and extends over but a small part of the area occupied by the Etruscan city; which is now for the most part covered with gardens and vineyards. This city, from its size, must have been of considerable importance among those of Southern Etruria. It was formerly supposed to be Veii, and there is an inscription in the cathedral, calling the church " Veiorum Basilica;" but this opinion has not the slightest foundation—its distance from Rome being three times greater than that of Veii, as mentioned by Dionysius.[3] Gell supposes it to have been Fescennium, but gives no reason for his opinion, in which he follows Müller and Nardini.[4] There is much more probability that it is the ancient Falerium, or Falerii, so prominent in the early history of the Roman Republic. My reasons for holding this opinion will be given in the next chapter, when I treat of the ruined town, a few miles distant, now called Fálleri.

[2] Varro (L. L. V. 111) says they were called *Falisci ventres.* So also Martial. IV. epig., 46. 8.; cf. Stat. Silv. IV. 9,

35.

[3] Dion. Hal. II. p. 116, ed. Sylb.

[4] Gell), I. p. 290.

PORTA DI GIOVE, FALLERI.

CHAPTER VIII.

FÁLLERI.—*FALERII (NOVI)*.

Ebbi improvviso un gran sepolcro scorto, . . .
E in brevi note altrui vi si sponea
Il nome e la virtù del guerrier morto.
Io non sapea da tal vista levarmi,
Mirando ora le lettre, od ora i marmi.—TASSO.

Gaudent Italiæ sublimibus oppida muris.—CLAUDIAN.

THE road from Ponte Terrano leads to Santa Maria di Fálleri,
or Fálari, a ruined convent on another ancient site, about four
miles from Civita Castellana. After two or three miles over the
heath, you reach the Fosso de' Tre Camini, and where you cross
the stream are traces of an ancient bridge. Just before coming
in sight of Fálleri, you reach a tomb, which, as you come suddenly
upon it, cannot fail to strike you with admiration. A wide recess
in the cliff is occupied by a spacious portico of three large arches,
hewn out of the rock, and with a bold cornice of masonry above,

of massive tufo blocks, now somewhat dislocated, and concealed
by the overhanging foliage. A door in the inner wall of the
portico, of the usual Etruscan form, slightly narrowing upwards,
opens into the sepulchre. Sepulchre! to an unpractised eye the
structure looks far more like a habitation; and in truth it is an
imitation of an ancient abode. The portico is surrounded by

PORTICOED TOMB WITH CORNICE OF MASONRY, FALLERI.

an elegant cornice, carved in the rock; the door, to which you
ascend by steps, is ornamented with mouldings in relief. Within
it, is a small antechamber, with the usual chimney or funnel in
its ceiling; and then you enter a spacious, gloomy sepulchre. Its
flat ceiling is supported in the midst by a massive square pillar,
in the face of which are three long, shallow niches, one over the
other; and in the walls of the tomb are smaller niches for urns
or votive offerings. Under the portico the rock is cut into
benches for sarcophagi, and long holes are sunk in the ground
for the reception of bodies, which, with the exception of being
covered over with tiles, must have been exposed to the passers-
by, as the arches of the portico could hardly have been closed.

The cornice around the portico and the mouldings of the door are almost Roman in character; yet in form and arrangement the tomb is too nearly allied to the Etruscan tombs of this district to be of Roman construction. It is probable that the Romans appropriated it to their own dead; and possible that they added these decorations; but, though an architectural adornment be proved to have been used by that people, it by no means follows that they originated it. Had not history informed us that the Corinthian capital was of Greek origin, the frequency of it in the ancient buildings of Rome and Italy, and its rarity in Greece, might have led us to a different conclusion. Now, we know almost nothing of Etruscan architecture from written records; and therefore when we find, in a position which favours an Etruscan origin, architectural decorations analogous to those used by the Romans, it were illogical to pronounce them necessarily to be the work of the latter. On the contrary, it were quite as reasonable to regard them as Etruscan, knowing that, before the time of the Empire at least, the Romans were mere imitators of the Etruscans and Greeks in the arts, servile enough in that respect—*imitatores, servum pecus!*—however they may have taken the lead of the world in arms. Nevertheless, whether Etruscan or Roman, the tomb is probably of a late period.

This is the only instance known of an Etruscan tomb with a cornice of masonry, and it was thought to be unique also as regards its portico; but I was fortunate enough to discover a group of tombs of similar charcter, very near this, which were before unknown.[1]

Among them is one which seems also to have had a portico, but the cliff out of which it was hewn is broken away. What now forms its front, has been the inner wall, if not of a portico, of an antechamber or outer tomb, and on it, to my astonishment, I found a Latin inscription, in very neatly formed letters, about four or five inches high, graven deep in the tufo.

L. VECILIO. VI. F. E
PO . . AE. ABELES.
LECTV. I. DATV
. . VECILIO. L. F. ET. PLENESTE
. ECTV. I. AMPLIVS. NIHIL
INVITEIS. L. C. LEVIEIS. L. F.
ET. QVEI. EOS. PARENTARET
NE. ANTEPONAT

---

[1] One has two arches in its portico; another has only one standing, though it seems to have had two more; and a third is a mere portico of two arches, without

The last line was buried in the earth, and having no instrument at hand, I could not uncover it; but I communicated the
discovery to the Archæological Institute[2] of Rome; and my
friend, Dr. Henzen, one of the secretaries, proceeded immediately to Falleri to inspect the inscription. To him is due the
discovery of the last line, which explains the whole. To him
also am I indebted for the correction and explanation of the
inscription.

"To Lucius Vecilius, son of Vibius and of Polla (or Pollia)
Abeles, one bed (sepulchral couch) is given—to ... Vecilius,
son of Lucius and of Plenesta, one bed.—Let no one place
anything before (i.e., another body in) these beds, save with the
permission of Lucius and Caius Levius, sons of Lucius, and (with
the permission) of whoever may perform their obsequies (i.e.
their heirs)."

The beds are the long niches in the walls of the tomb, of
which there are eleven. The inscription is curious for its ancient
Latinity alone; but most interesting as an evidence of the fact
that the Romans made use of the tombs of the Etruscans, or else
constructed sepulchres precisely similar. No one can doubt the
Etruscan character of this particular tomb, and yet it belonged to
the Roman family of the Levii, who gave it or let it out to the
Vecilii, as we know to have been frequently the case with the *ollæ*
of Roman *columbaria*. The mention of the mother's name after
the father's is a genuine Etruscanism.[3] It is general in Etruscan
epitaphs, and was retained even under Roman domination, for
some sarcophagi bear similar epitaphs in Latin, with "*natus*"
affixed to the mother's name in the genitive or ablative. But
those sarcophagi were found in Etruscan tombs, in the midst of
others with Etruscan inscriptions, and are only the coffins of the
latest members of the same families, belonging to a period when
the native language was being superseded by that of the conquerors. This may be the case here also—the Levii may have
been an Etruscan family; as indeed seems highly probable. If
not, we have here a Roman usurpation of an Etruscan sepulchre,
or it may be an imitation of the Etruscan mode of burial, and

an inner chamber, the portico itself being
the tomb, as is shown by the rock-benches
within it.

[2] See Bull. Iustit. 1844, p. 92.

[3] This custom the Etruscans must
have derived from the East, as it was not
practised by the Greeks or Romans; but

the Lycians always traced their descent
through the maternal line, to the exclu-
sion of the paternal—a fact recorded by
Herodotus (I. 173), and verified by
modern researches. Fellows' Lycia, p.
276. The Etruscans being less purely
Oriental, made use of both methods.

also an instance of the adoption of the customs of that people by the Romans.[4]

Just beyond these tombs the city of Falleri comes into view. And an imposing sight it is—not from its position, for it is on the very level of the plain by which you approach it—but from

THE WALLS OF FALLERI, FROM THE EAST.

its lofty walls and numerous towers, stretching away on either hand to a great distance in an almost unbroken line, and only just dilapidated enough to acquire a picturesque effect, which is heightened by overhanging foliage. You approach it from the east, at an angle of the wall where there is an arched gateway on either hand—one still open[5], the other almost buried in the earth.

[4] Dr. Henzen, who is *facile princeps* in the archæology of inscriptions, refers this to a remote period, undoubtedly to the time of the Republic, and before the establishment of the Colonia Junonia by the Triumvirate, and considers the tomb as one of the most ancient on this site. Bull. Inst. 1844, pp. 129, 161–8. In the neighbourhood of this tomb Signor Guidi, in 1851, opened five others which contained a number of inscriptions in a character and language neither Etruscan nor Latin, and therefore pronounced to be Faliscan. They were painted on sepulchral tiles. Eight were written like the Etruscan, from right to left, and two in Roman letters, from left to right. The characters

of the ten differed from the Etruscan in the forms of the A, E, P, R, and in the use of the O, assimilating more to the Greek. But the language was much more akin to the Latin. Copies of these inscriptions are given in Ann. Inst. 1860, tav. d'Agg. G. H., and they are explained by Padre Garrucci (op. cit., pp. 272–9), who refers them to the sixth century of Rome.

[5] This gate, as will be seen in the woodcut, has a tower immediately to the left of him who approaches it, which is contrary to the precepts of Vitruvius (I. 5), who recommends that the approach to a city-gate be such, that the right side of the foe, which is unprotected by his shield, may be open to attack

The walls here are about seven feet thick, and in thirteen courses, or about twenty-five feet high; they are of red tufo blocks, of the size usual in the *emplecton* masonry of Etruria, fitted together without cement and with great nicety. In parts the tufo has lost its surface, but in others the masonry looks as sharp and fresh as though it had been just constructed, without a sign of age beyond its weather-stained coating of grey. Both walls and towers are perpendicular or nearly so; the latter, which are at unequal distances, but generally about one hundred feet apart, are square—about seventeen feet wide, and projecting ten feet. They are external only; the inner surface of the wall, which rises high above the level of the ground within, is unbroken by projections; it is similar in appearance to the outer surface, though not so neatly smoothed and finished.

Following the northern wall of the city, after passing ten towers, you reach a small arched gate or postern. Outside it are remains of Roman tombs of *opus incertum*, on mounds by the side of the road which issued from this gate; blocks of basalt, now upturned by the plough, indicate its course. It was the Via Amerina, which ran northward to Horta and Ameria. Passing a breach which Gell takes for a gateway, you next cross a long wall or embankment stretching away at right angles from the city; it is of ancient blocks, probably taken from the city walls. A little beyond is what seems a window, high in the wall and partly blocked up, but it is a mere hole cut in later times.

On turning the corner of the wall you reach the Porta di Giove, a fine gate in excellent preservation, flanked by towers. The arch-stones and encircling moulding are of peperino; and in the centre over the key-stone, is a head in bold relief. Why called Giove I do not understand; it has none of the attributes of Jupiter, but in its beardless youth and gentleness of expression, seems rather to represent Bacchus or Apollo.[6] See the woodcut

---

from the ramparts. The angular form of this city, and of the towers in its walls, is also at variance with the rules laid down by the same author, who denounces angles, as protecting the foe rather than the citizen.

[6] Canina takes the head to be that of Juno, rather than of Jupiter, as she was the great goddess of the Falisci. Etruria Marit. I. p. 70. The gate is nearly eighteen feet in height, and ten feet eight inches in span. The depth of its door-posts is more than seven feet, which is also the thickness of the city wall. The imposts are also of peperino—above them the arch is blocked up with brickwork.

Canina is inclined to regard this gate as Etruscan. He says (Archit. Ant. VI. p. 54), from a comparison of it with those of Pæstum and Volterra, that it cannot be otherwise than of early date, and not wholly Roman, as some have supposed; and again (Ann. Inst. 1835, p. 192) he cites the head on the keystone as a proof

at the head of this chapter. Within the gate is a double line of
ancient wall, flanking a hollow way or road, which now leads to the
ruined convent of Santa Maria di Fálleri, the only building standing within the walls.[7]

The wall soon turns again and follows the course of the valley
through which flows the Miccino. Here it is based on low tufo
cliffs, in which are the mouths of several sewers. On this side it is
for the most part greatly dilapidated: sometimes you lose sight of it
altogether for a considerable distance, then again trace it by

TOMBS IN THE CLIFFS AT FALLERI.

detached portions or by towers only, which jet boldly into the
valley on projecting masses of cliff. The rock beneath the walls
is in many places hollowed into niches or caves, once evidently
tombs; and on the other side of the stream are tall cliffs, full
of long sepulchral niches one above the other, where the Falerians
of old stored up their dead—shown in the above woodcut On

of this sort of decoration being Etruscan.
It was also extensively used by both Greeks
and Romans.

[7] Just within the gate, to the right as
you enter, is a sewer-like hole, now blocked

up, which seems to have been a window.
It is not visible from without, because the
ancient wall just in that part is faced
with mediæval masonry; but its form is
distinguishable.

that side also are the remains of several Roman tombs—massive piles of *opus incertum*, towering high above the light wood that covers that bank of the stream. This necropolis has been little explored, and I regret that I have not been able to give it due examination. Dr. Henzen found one tomb here with a Christian inscription.[8]

One of the city-towers stands on a projection of the cliff where the wall makes a semicircular bend inwards. Beneath this tower is a tomb of unusual size, square and lofty. It would seem at first sight to have been formed as a cellar to the tower, but further observation shows that it was of prior formation, for its original doorway is blocked up by the masonry of the tower itself. Whence it may be inferred that the city was of subsequent construction, and that the tomb had been profaned by the founders. Near this is another instance of the city-wall blocking up an ancient tomb. Facts of importance, as bearing on the question by whom and in what age the city was built.

A little beyond this you reach another deep recess in the line of cliff, with a magnificent mass of walling rising to the height of twenty-eight courses, or fifty-four feet, and stretching completely across the hollow. In the centre is a gate, the Porta del Bove, fine in itself, but appearing quite insignificant—a mere drain-hole in the vast expanse of wall.[9] Towers, bannered with oak-saplings, and battlemented with ivy, crest boldly the projecting cliffs at the angles of the recess. "Desert caves, with wild thyme and the gadding vine o'ergrown," yawn around. Soracte soars bluely in the distance above the wooded glen. The whole scene is one of picturesque grandeur, rendered more impressive by the silence, loneliness, and desolation.[1]

---

[8] Bull. Inst. 1844, p. 168.

[9] This is perhaps the loftiest relic of ancient city-walls extant in Italy, save the Bastion in the polygonal walls of Norba in Latium, which is about the same height. The wall of the Forum of Augustus at Rome, in the same style of masonry, is, however, considerably higher.

[1] The gate derives its present appellation from something carved in relief on its key-stone, which may once have been a bull's skull, a favourite ornament of gateways among the Romans. Another appellation, Porta della Puttana, is yet more difficult of explanation. Within are traces of a vaulted passage, much wider than the gate itself, leading up to the higher ground of the city. It must have been a very steep ascent, as the gate opens at the bottom of a deep gulley, and the ground within is almost on a level with the top of the wall. A large tree, now reduced to charcoal, lies prostrate on the ramparts, which, when it flourished high above the wall, must have greatly increased the picturesque effect from below. The gate is 8 feet in span, and the depth of the arch, or the thickness of the wall in this part, is 9 feet. There are 13 voussoirs in the arch, 3 feet 9 inches deep, fitted together with great neatness—all are of tufo, and are rusticated in the return facing of the arch.

Opposite the Porta del Bove are the remains of a bridge over the Miccino, the piers on both banks being still extant.

The southern wall of the city extends but a short way beyond the Porta del Bove. It then turns to the north; and after passing nine towers in excellent preservation, you come to the site of another gate, now destroyed. Outside it, a Roman tomb rises to a considerable height. From this spot, a short distance

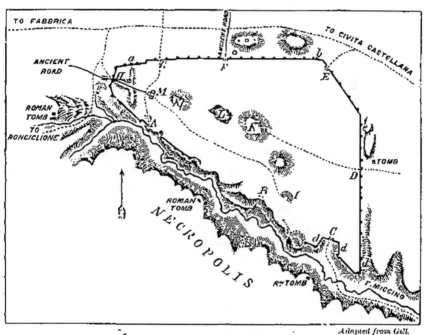

PLAN OF FALLERI.

Adapted from Gell.

A to H.	Gates in the city-walls.	L.	Supposed site of Forum.
C.	Porta del Bove.	M.	Church of Sta. Maria di Fálleri.
F.	Gate represented in woodcut, p. 101.	a.	Window in the wall.
		b.	Small gate, almost buried.
H.	Porta di Giove. See woodcut, p. 97.	c.	Pyramid, and other Roman tombs.
I.	Theatre.	d d.	Loftiest portions of the walls.
K.	Ruins.	e e.	Sewers cut in the rock.

carries you to the gate at the north-eastern angle, where you complete the tour of the city. According to Gell, the circuit of the walls is 2305 yards, or more than one English mile and a third.[2] The form of the city is a right-angled triangle, with the angles truncated. About fifty towers are standing, and eight or nine gates may be traced. "Perhaps," as Gell remarks, "no place presents a more perfect specimen of ancient military architecture."

[2] Gell, I. p. 421.

Within the walls there are but few remains. On the spot
where the theatre was found nothing can now be traced of the
seats or arches. A high bank, encircling a hollow, marks the
outline. Here, as on the other spots where excavations have been
made, are fragments of cornices and columns of travertine and
marble, and other traces of the Romans. Several fine statues
have been found on this spot.[3]

The only building now standing within the walls is the convent
of Sta. Maria di Fálleri, but even this shares in the ruin of the
spot, and, instead of chaunt and orison, resounds with the bleat-
ing of sheep and lowing of oxen. It is of the Lombard style, so
common in the ecclesiastical architecture of Italy, but of a
more simple character than usual. It is constructed of the materials of the ancient city, and apparently is of the twelfth century.

We have now to consider the origin and ancient name of this
city. That an Etruscan population occupied this or a neighbouring site is evident from the multitude of tombs and niches
excavated in the cliffs, undoubtedly of that character, and too
remote to belong to the city which occupied the site of Civita
Castellana. The walls are certainly in the Etruscan style as
regards the masonry; but this is not decisive of their origin, for
precisely the same sort of masonry was employed in the earliest
walls of Rome, and is to be seen in other places south and east
of the Tiber; in almost every case, however, prior to the Empire.
Nibby[4] is of opinion from the method of fortification, from the
arching of the gateways, and from the sculpture and mouldings,
as well as from the fact that the theatre and other ancient relics
within the walls are unequivocally Roman, that the remains now
extant belong to a Roman city. Canina, on the other hand, a
superior authority on architectural matters, sees much Etruscan
character in the gateways.[5] As before her intercourse with
Greece, Rome was indebted to Etruria for all her arts, as well as
for most of her institutions, religious, political, and social; it may
well be that this city was built under the Roman domination, but
that Etruscan artists and artisans were employed in its construction. The name of the original town, moreover, seems preserved
in its modern appellation, which it possessed through the middle

[3] The theatre is said to have been cut
in the rock, like the amphitheatre of Sutri
(Bull. Inst. 1829, p. 57). It was excavated in 1829 and 1830. It seems to
have been of the time of Augustus, from a
statue of Livia as Concord, and some muti-

lated statues of C. and L. Cæsar, which
were found among its ruins. A fine
statue of Juno has also been excavated
within the walls of Falleri.

[4] II. p. 27.

[5] See note 6, p. 102.

ages, and which indicates it as the Falerii of the Etruscans. Let us consider what is said of that town by ancient writers.

At an early period, says tradition, shortly after the Trojan war, a body of Greeks from Argos, led by Halesus, or Haliscus, son of Agamemnon, settled in this part of Italy,[6] drove out the Siculi, who then possessed it, and occupied their towns of Falerium and Fescennium.[7] Whether they were subsequently conquered by the Tyrrheni or Etruscans, or entered into alliance with them, does not appear, but it is certain that they were incorporated with that people, and under the name of Falisci[8] continued to possess this part of Etruria till its conquest by Rome. Yet they were always in some respects a distinct people; their language was said to differ from the Etruscan;[9] and even as late as the time of Augustus, they retained traces of their Argive origin, in their armour and weapons, and in various customs, especially in what regarded their temples and religious rites. The temple of Juno at Falerii is said to have been the counterpart of that dedicated to the same goddess at Argos, i.e. the Heræum, and her worship to have been similar.[1] There seems to have been a third city, Faliscum, similar in origin to the other two, and deriving its name from the chief of the original colonists.[2]

We see then that there were three cities, probably not far removed from each other, inhabited by a race, which, though

[6] Dion. Hal. I. p. 17. Ovid. Fast. IV. 73, and Amor. III. Eleg. 13, 31. Cato ap. Plin. III. 8. Serv. ad Æn. VII. 695. Steph. Byzant. v. Φαλίσκος. Solinus II. p. 13. All agree as to the Argive origin of the Falisci, save Justin (XX. 1), who derives them from the Chalcidenses —an origin which Niebuhr (III. p. 179) rejects.

[7] Dionys. Hal. I. pp. 16, 17. Neither Dionysius, Cato, nor Stephanus makes mention of Halesus as the founder. Servius (ad Æn. VII. 695) points out the change of the initial Ll. into F., the adoption by the Romans of the Æolic digamma to express the Greek aspirate, —sicut Formiæ, quæ Hormiæ fuerunt— ἀπὸ τῆς ὁρμῆς.

[8] Dionysius (loc. cit.) calls this Argive colony Pelasgi, and the similarity, almost amounting to identity, of this word to Falisci is remarkable; in fact it is not improbable that the appellation Falisci was one simply indicative of their Argive i. e. Pelasgic) descent.

[9] Strabo, V. p. 226.

[1] Dion. Hal. loc. cit. Ovid. Amor. III. Eleg. 13, 27, et seq. : see also Fasti, VI. 49. This Juno had the epithet of Curitis or Quiritis, as we learn from Tertullian (Apolog. 24) —and from inscriptions found on the spot (Holsten. ad Cluv. p. 57. Gruter, p. 308, 1). In the Sabine tongue Quiris signifies "lance," she was therefore the "lance-Juno," and is represented holding that weapon. Plut. Romul. Minerva also was worshipped at Falerii. Ovid. Fast. III. 843. Mars seems to have been another god of the Falisci, as they called the fifth month in their calendar after his name. Ovid. Fast. III. 89. A four-faced Janus was also worshipped here, whose statue was carried to Rome, where the temple of Janus Quadrifrons was erected to receive it. Serv. ad Æn. VII. 607. Festus (v. Strop-pus) speaks of a festival kept by the Falisci under the name of Strupearia, but in honour of what deity he does not mention.

[2] See Note I. in the Appendix to this Chapter.

of Greek origin, was, at the period it is mentioned in Roman
history, to all intents and purposes, Etruscan; amalgamated,
like the inhabitants of Agylla, Cortona, and other Pelasgic cities
of Etruria, with the mixed race of the Tyrrhenes, and bearing,
from the general testimony of ancient writers, the generic name
of Falisci.

Of these three cities, Falerii, or Falerium, as it is indifferently
called, was evidently the most important. There is every reason
to believe it one of the Twelve cities of the Confederation.[3]
Plutarch says it was so strong by nature and so admirably
prepared to sustain an attack, that the citizens made light of
being besieged by the Romans,[4] even though led by Camillus;
and according to Livy the siege bid fair to be as tedious as that
of Veii;[5] which could not have been the case had not the city
occupied a site strong by nature as well as by art. Ovid speaks
of the steepness of the ascent to the celebrated temple of Juno
within the city.[6] Zonaras also mentions the natural strength
of its position on a lofty height.[7] All descriptive of a site
widely different from that of Fálleri, and perfectly agreeing
with that of Civita Castellana, which, in accordance with Cluverius, Holstenius, Cramer, and Nibby, I am fully persuaded is
the representative of the Etruscan Falerium.

There it is we must place the scene of the well-known story of
the treacherous schoolmaster.

The Falerians, trusting in the strength of their town, regarded
with indifference the Roman army encamped about it, and pursued their ordinary avocations. It was the custom of the Falisci,
derived probably from their Greek ancestors, to have a public
school for the tuition of the male children of the citizens. The
schoolmaster during the siege took his boys out of the city for
exercise, as usual in time of peace, and led them daily further
from the walls, till at length he carried them to the Roman
camp, and delivered them up to their foes. As among them
were the children of the principal citizens, he thought by this
act to transfer to the Romans the destinies of the city itself, and
thus purchase for himself the favour of Camillus. But the
Roman general, with that noble generosity and inflexible virtue
which characterised many of his countrymen of early times,

---

[3] See Note II. in the Appendix to this Chapter.

[4] Plut. Camil.; see also Val. Max. VI. 5. 1.—mœnia expuguari non poterant.

[5] Liv. V. 26.

[6] Amor. III., Eleg. 13, 6.

[7] Zonar. Ann. VII. 22; and VIII. 18.

scorned to profit by such baseness, and sternly replied,—"Not to such wretches as thyself art thou come with thy base offers. With the Falisci we have no common bond of human making; but such as nature hath formed, that will we ever respect. War hath its laws as well as peace; and its duties we have learnt to execute, whether they demand our justice or our valour. We are arrayed, not against that tender age which is sacred even in the moment of successful assault, but against those who, though neither injured nor annoyed by us, took up arms and attacked our camp at Veii. Them hast thou surpassed in iniquity; and them will I overcome, as I have the Veientes, by Roman skill, determination, and valour." Then commanding the wretch to be stript, and his hands to be bound behind his back, he delivered him to the boys, who with rods and scourges drove him back to the city. The anxiety and terror of the inhabitants at the loss of their children was turned to joy on their return, and they conceived such admiration of the Roman general that they forthwith surrendered the city into his hands.[8]

This was in the year of Rome 360; but the Falisci, as a people, are mentioned in Roman history as early as the year 317;[9] from which time, to the capture of the city, they several times warred against Rome, in alliance with either the Veientes, Fidenates, or Capenates. The Falisci remained subject to Rome till the year 397, when they revolted, and joined the Tarquinienses, but were subdued by the dictator, Marcius Rutilus.[1] In 461 they joined the other Etruscan cities in the final struggle for independence.[2] In 513, after the first Punic war, they again revolted; but were soon reduced.[3] Zonaras, who has given us an account of this final capture, says that "the ancient city situated on a steep and lofty height was destroyed, and another built in a place of easy access."[4] The description of the latter, which will not apply at all to the site of Civita Castellana, agrees precisely with that of Fálleri, which, as already shown, stands on two sides on the actual level of the plain, and on the third, on cliffs but slightly raised from the valley—such a situation, as, by analogy, we know would never have been chosen by the Etruscans, but is not at all inconsistent

[8] Livy, V. 27. Plut. Camil. Dion. Hal. Excerp. Mai, XII. c. 16. Val. Max. VI. 5, 1. Florus. I. 12. Frontin. Strat. IV. 4. Zonaras, VII. 22.

[9] Liv. IV. 17.

[1] Liv. VII. 16, 17. Diod. Sic. XVI. p. 432.

[2] Liv. X. 45, 46.

[3] Polyb. I. 65. Val. Max. VI. 5. Eutrop. II. 28. Zonaras, Ann. VIII. 18. Orosius, IV. 11.

[4] Zonar. loc. cit.

with a Roman origin.' Regarding Fálleri, then, to be the city rebuilt at this period, all difficulty with regard to its name is removed. It is not necessary to suppose it the Etruscan Falerii; for the name of the original city was transferred with the inhabitants to this site, which has retained it, while the ancient site lay desolate, it is probable, for many ages,[6] till long after the fall of the Empire, in the eighth or ninth century of our era, the strength of its position attracted a fresh settlement, and it was fortified under the name of Civitas Castellana.

That Civita was the site of the original, and Fálleri of the second city of Falerii, is corroborated by the much superior size of the former, and by the fact that no Roman remains have been discovered there, while they abound at the latter place.[7]

This is the opinion regarding Falerii held by most antiquaries of note, and it seems clear and consistent.[8] Some few, as Nardini, Müller, Gell, and Mannert, led astray by the resemblance of the name, view Fálleri as the original Falerii, and without just grounds regard Civita Castellana as the site of Fescennium.

Regarding, then, the remains of Fálleri as belonging to Roman times, the resemblance of its walls and gates to Etruscan masonry and architecture is explained by the date of their construction, as they belong to a period when the Romans were imitators of the Etruscans in all their arts; besides, the inhabitants were still of the latter nation, though they had received a Roman colony. This may also, to some extent, explain its tombs, which, with a few exceptions, are purely Etruscan. Nevertheless, as already shown, there is ground for believing that such tombs existed here long prior to the erection of the walls of Fálleri, and therefore that a genuine Etruscan town occupied a neighbouring site—but where that town may have stood, or

---

[5] See Note III. in the Appendix to this Chapter.

[6] The "apple-bearing Falisci" mentioned by Ovid (Amor. III., Eleg. 13), as the birthplace of his wife may have been Fálleri; but the temple of Juno continued in his day to occupy the original site, as is proved by his mention of the walls conquered by Camillus, and the steep ascent to the town,—difficilis clivis via—there being nothing like a steep to Fálleri. The dense and venerable grove, too, around the temple, may perhaps mark the desolation of the site, though a grove generally sur-

rounded every temple. It is probable, however, that there was still some small population on this spot, as usual in the immediate neighbourhood of celebrated shrines, and to that Ovid may have referred under the name of Falisci. The Colonia Junonia, referred to by Frontinus (de colon.)—quæ appellatur Faliscos, quæ a III viris est assignata—and in an inscription found at Fálleri, must apply to the second city.

[7] Nibby, II. v. Falerii.

[8] See Note IV. in the Appendix to this Chapter.

what its name may have been, I pretend not to determine. It was probably some small town dependent on Falerii, the name of which has not come down to us.

Fálleri was on the Via Amerina which branched from the Via Cassia at Le Sette Vene, and ran northward through Nepi to Todi and Perugia. It is five miles from Nepi, as set down in the Table, and three from Corchiano on the same line of ancient road. In this direction, or northwards from Fálleri, the road may be traced by fragments more or less perfect almost as far as Orte, on the Tiber.[9]

For my guide to Fálleri I took a man from Civita Castellana, named Domenico Mancini, a most civil fellow, simple but intelligent, and, what is more than can be said for Italian guides in general, satisfied with a just remuneration. Having tended cattle or sheep all his life-time in the neighbourhood, he knows the site of every *grotta* or tomb, and in fact, pointed out to me those with the porticoes and Latin inscription, which were previously unknown to the world. The antiquity-hunter in Italy can have no better guide than an intelligent shepherd; for these men, passing their days in the open air, and following their flocks over the wilds far from beaten tracks, become familiar with every cave, every fragment of ruined wall, and block of hewn stone ; and, though they do not comprehend the antiquity of such relics, yet, if the traveller makes them aware of what he is seeking, they will rarely fail to lead him to the sites of such remains. The visitor to Fálleri who would engage the services of the said Domenico, must ask for " Domenico, detto Figlio del Re," or the King's Son ; which is no reflection on any crowned head in Europe, but is a *sobriquet* belonging to him in right of his father, who was generally called " The King," whether from his dignified bearing, or from out-topping his fellows, like Saul, I know not. These *cognomina* are general among the lower orders in Italy—a relic, doubtless, of ancient times—and no one seems ashamed of them ; nay, a man is best known by his nickname. At Sutri I was guided by a Sorcio,—or " Mouse"— (remember the three great Republican heroes of the same name,

---

[9] The distances on the Via Amerina are thus marked in the Peutingerian Table :

Roma		
Ad Sextum	M.P. VI.	
Veios	VI.	
Vacanas	VIIII.	
Nepe	VIIII.	
Faleros	V.	
Castello Amerino	XII.	
Ameria	VIIII.	
Tuder	—	
	VI.	
Vetona	XX.	
Pirusio	XIII.	

P. Decius Mus!); at Narni, I was driven by Mosto, or "New Wine;" at Chianciano by the "Holy Father" himself; and at Pitigliano I lodged in the house of Il Bimbo, or "the Baby." I should mention that this son of the shepherd-king of Civita Castellana, will provide the traveller with horses at three francs each per diem.

APPENDIX TO CHAPTER VIII.

NOTE I.—THE THREE TOWNS OF THE FALISCI.—See page 107.

NIBBY doubts the existence of a third town, and thinks that Faliscum is merely another name for Falerium, seeing that Falisci was the name of the people, and Falerii of their city; just as the inhabitants of Rome were called Quirites, and of Ardea, Rutuli. Cluver (II., p. 544) is much of the same opinion. Now, though "Falisci" was undoubtedly the name of the race, as shown by most writers, particularly by Livy, and though sometimes employed, in this sense, indifferently with Falerii, and though Faliscum, Falisca, or Falisci, is often confounded with Falerii the town, as by Ovid, Pliny, Diodorus, (XIV., p. 310), and perhaps by Servius; yet Faliscum is mentioned by Strabo (V., p. 226), by Stephanus (v. Φαλίσκος), and Solinus (II., p. 13), in addition to Falerium. The last-named author speaks of the three cities in the same passage,—ab Haleso Argivo Phaliscam; a Phalerio Argivo Phalerios; Fescennium quoque ab Argivis. See Müller's opinion on this passage (Etrusk. IV., 4, 3, n. 31). Strabo also mentions "Falerium and Faliscum" in the same breath; and as by the former he must mean the second, or Roman Falerii, seeing that the original Etruscan city had ceased to exist long before his time, it is clear that the latter must refer to some other place—probably the Æquum Faliscum which he indicates as lying on the Flaminian Way between Ocriculum and Rome. See Note III.

NOTE II.—FALERII ONE OF THE TWELVE.—See page 108.

That Falerii was one of the Twelve Cities of the Etruscan Confederation, there is every reason to believe. Its position, in a portion of Etruria which could scarcely belong to Veii, or to Volsinii, the nearest cities of the League —its size, much superior to any of the known dependent towns, and second only to Caere and Veii, among the cities south of the Ciminian—and the importance ascribed to it by ancient writers—make it highly probable that it was one of the principal cities of Etruria. Cluver (II., p. 545) thinks the fact may be deduced from the passage of Livy (IV. 23) already commented on, in connection with Veii (ut supra, p. 28). Müller thinks Falerii has equal claims to this honour with Veii and Caere; and that it was much too powerful, and acted too independently, to be the colony of another city. Etrusk. II. 1, 2. Eutropius (I. 18) says it was not inferior to Veii. Dempster (de Etruriâ Regali, II. p. 52) places Falerii among the Twelve. Niebuhr is not of this opinion; perhaps because he regarded the Falisci as Æqui, rather than as Etruscans. Hist. Rom. I. pp. 72, 119, Eng. trans.

Note III.—Æquum Faliscum.—See page 110.

Niebuhr (Hist. Rom. I. p. 72, Eng. trans.) is of opinion that the epithet of Æqui, attached by Virgil (Æn. VII. 695) and Silius Italicus (VIII. 491, cf. V. 176) to the Falisci, was applied to them because they were Æqui or Volsci, and remarks that the names Falisci and Volsci are clearly identical. Müller (einl. II. 14), however, shows that the Etruscan element was predominant at Falerii; that the city was never found in political connection with the Sabines, Umbrians, or Æquians, but solely with the Etruscans, and thinks that the epithet refers to the position of the second city of Falerium in the plain, as stated by Zonaras. Servius, however, in his comment on this passage of Virgil, interprets Æqui as, "Just, because the Roman people, having got rid of the Decemvirs, received from the Falisci the Fecial laws, and some supplements of the XII. Tables which they had had from the Athenians." Cluver (Ital. Ant. II. p. 538) and Müller (Etrusk. II. 3, 6) refute this statement; and the latter will not allow that they were called Æqui Falisci, either from their uprightness, or their origin from the race of the Æqui, as Niebuhr supposes; but solely from the situation of their second city. I pretend not to reconcile the variances of such authorities; but merely point out the glaring anachronism of which the Mantuan bard is guilty, provided the opinion of Müller be correct. The same epithet, however, in another case—Æquimælium—we are expressly told, was significant of the level nature of the ground (Dion. Hal. Excerp. Mai, XII. 1). It seems to me more probable, from a comparison with Strabo (V. p. 226), that Æquum Faliscum was a synonym not of Roman Falerii, but of Faliscum, the third city of the Falisci. See Note I. and note *, on page 123.

Note IV.—Falleri not the Etruscan Falerii.—See page 110.

The name of most weight in the opposite scale is that of Müller; but though his opinion was "the result of careful consideration," it is, in this case, of no weight, seeing that it is founded on a mistaken view of the local characteristics of Fálleri, which, it is evident, he had never visited. He has been misled by false statements, and his arguments, on such premises, are of course powerless. He says (Etrusker, einl. II., 14), "the walls of the ancient city of Falerii, built of polygonal blocks of white stone, uncemented, are situated on the heights about three miles to the west of Civita Castellana; and the site is still called Falari." He takes his information, as to the position of the ruins, from Nardini (Veio Antico, p. 153), and from Sickler's Plan of the Campagna, a map full of inaccuracies, both in names and sites: though he owns that Cluver, Holstenius, and Mazzocchi state that Fálleri is in the plain. But it is on this false notion that he founds his main argument, which is the correspondence of the position of Falari with that ascribed to Falerii, by ancient writers. Again, he says, "it is quite incredible that such massive walls as these are the work of the conquered Falisci, or of a Roman colony. Falari must therefore be regarded as the ancient Falerii." Now, there are no polygonal walls in existence in Southern Etruria, save at Pyrgi on the coast; and the blocks of which those of Falerii are composed are of the comparatively small size, usually employed in Etruscan cities in this part of the land, and precisely accord in dimensions and arrangement with those of Roma Quadrata, of the Tabularium, and many other remains in and around Rome. The second town of Falerii—

Æquum Faliscum, as he calls it—he places, with Nardini, on some undetermined site in the Plain of Borghetto, near the Tiber, because Strabo says it was near the Via Flaminia. Civita Castellana, he follows Nardini and the early Italian antiquaries, in supposing to be the ancient Fescennium, and contents himself with saying that it cannot be Falerii.

It should be stated that Festus offers a singular derivation for the name of this city—Faleri oppidum à sale dictum—which Cluver (II. p. 542) explains as the consequence of a blunder in transcribing from the Greek authors—ἀπὸ τοῦ ἅλος instead of ἀπὸ τοῦ 'Αλήσου. Its obscurity is in some measure relieved by Servius (ad Æn. VIII. 285), who calls Alesus the son of Neptune, and by Silius Italicus (VIII. 476), where he refers to Halesus as the founder of Alsium, on the sea-coast. Some readings, however, of Festus give " Faleri à fale"—fala meaning something lofty, being derived, say Festus, from the Etruscan word falando, which signifies heaven.

CORCHIANO, AN ETRUSCAN SITE.

CHAPTER IX.

FESCENNIUM.

Festa dicax fundat convicia Fescenninus.—SENECA.

Hem! nos homunculi indignamur, si quis nostrûm interiit aut occisus est quorum vita brevior esse debet, cum uno loco tot oppidûm cadavera projecta jaceant?
SERV. SULPIT., Epist. ad M. Tull. Cicer.

THE second town of the Falisci, Fescennium, or Fescennia, or Fasceninm, as Dionysius calls it, was founded, like Falerii, by the Siculi, who were driven out by the Pelasgi; traces of which latter race were still extant in Dionysius' day, in the warlike tactics, the Argolic shields and spears, the religious rites and ceremonies, and in the construction and furniture of the temples of the Falisci.[1] This Argive or Pelasgic origin of Fescennium, as well as of Falerii, is confirmed by Solinus.[2] Virgil mentions

---

[1] Dion. Hal. I. pp. 16, 17.
[2] Solin. II. p. 13. Servius, however, ascribes to Fescennium an Athenian origin, and calls it a town of Campania (ad Æn. VII. 695).

Fescennium as sending her hosts to the assistance of Turnus;[3] but no notice of it, which can be regarded as historical, has come down to us; and it is probable that, as a Faliscan town, it followed the fortunes and fate of Falerii. It was a Roman colony in the time of Pliny.[4] We know only this in addition, that here are said to have originated the songs, which from an early period were in use among the Romans at their nuptials;[5] and which were sung also by the peasantry in alternate *extempore* verses, full of banter and raillery.[6]

To the precise site of Fescennium we have no clue, though, from its connection with Falerii, and the mention made of it by Virgil, we may safely conclude it was in the district between Soracte and the Ciminian mount, *i. e.* in the *ager Faliscus*. Müller's opinion, that it occupied the site of Civita Castellana, has been shown to be incorrect. The assumption of Cluver, that it is represented by Gallese, a village about nine miles to the north of Civita Castellana, seems wholly gratuitous; he is followed, however, in this by subsequent writers—*magni nominis umbra.*[7] The truth is, that there are numerous Etruscan sites in this district, none of which, save Gallese, have been recognised as such, so that, in the absence of definite description by the ancients, and of all monumentary evidence on the several localities, it is im-

---

[3] Virg. Æn. loc. cit.

[4] Plin. III. 8.

[5] Servius, loc. cit. Festus *voce* Fescennini versus. Plin. XV. 24. Catul. LXI. 126. Seneca, Medea, 113. Claudian gives a specimen of Fescennina, on the nuptials of Honorius and Maria. Festus offers a derivation—quia *fascinum* putabantur arcere—which Müller (Etrusk. IV. 5. 2. n. 8.) thinks is not satisfactory. Dr. Schmitz, in Smith's Dictionary of Antiquities, objects to the Fescennian origin of these songs, on the ground that "this kind of amusement has at all times been, and is still, so popular in Italy, that it can scarcely be considered as peculiar to any particular place." He further maintains that these songs cannot be of Etruscan origin, because Fescennium was not an Etruscan, but a Faliscan town. But whatever may have been the origin of the Palisci, ages before we find mention of the Fescennine verses, they had been incorporated with the Etruscan Confederation, and were as much Etruscans as the citizens

of Cortona, Cære, Alsium, Pyrgi, all which cities had a Pelasgic origin.

[6] Livy (VII. 2) calls them — versum incompositum temere ac rudem. Catullos (loc. cit.)—procax Fescennina locutio. So also Seneca (loc. cit.). Fescennine seems to have been a proverbial synonym for "playing the fool." Macrob. Saturn. II. 10. In their original character these Fescennines, though coarse and bold, were not malicious; but in time, says Horace, the freedom of amiable sport grew to malignant rage, and gave rise to dissensions and feuds; whereon the law stept in, and put an end to them altogether. Epist. II. I. 145. Augustus himself wrote Fescennines on Pollio, who would not respond, save with a witty excuse—non est facile in eum scribere, qui potest proscribere.— Macrob. Satur. II. 4.

[7] Cluv. Ital. Antiq. II. p. 551. Nibby, II. p. 28. Cramer, I. p. 226. Abeken's Mittelital. p. 36. Westphal, Map of the Campagna.

possible to pronounce with certainty which is the site of
Fescennium.

This district lying between the Ciminian on the west, Soracte
on the east, the Tiber on the north, and the modern Via Cassia
on the south, with the exception of the road which passes
through Nepi and Civita Castellana to Ponte Felice, is to
travellers in general, and to antiquaries in particular, a *terra
incognita*. This tract of country, though level, is of exceeding
beauty—not the stern, barren grandeur of the Campagna around
Rome—but beauty, soft, rich, and luxuriant. Plains covered
with oaks and chestnuts—grand gnarled giants, who have lorded
it here for centuries over the lowly hawthorn, nut, or fern—such
sunny glades, carpeted with green sward!—such bright stretches
of corn, waving away even under the trees!—such " quaint
mazes in the wanton groves! "—and such delicious shady dells,
and avenues, and knolls, where Nature, in her springtide frolics,
mocks Art or Titania, and girds every tree, every bush, with a
fairy belt of crocuses, anemones, purple and white cistuses,
delicate cyclamens, convolvuluses of different hues, and more
varieties of laughing flowers than I would care to enumerate.
A merrier greenwood you cannot see in all merry England; it
may want the buck to make it perfect to the stalker's taste;
but its beauty, its joyousness, must fill every other eye with
delight—

> " It is, I ween, a lovely spot of ground,
>   And in a season atween June and May
>   Half prankt with spring, with summer half embrowned . .
>   Is nought around but images of rest,
>   Sleep-soothing groves, and quiet lawns between,
>   And flowery beds that slumb'rous influence kest
>   From poppies breathed, and beds of pleasant green."

Ever and anon the vine and the olive come in to enrich, and a
flock of goats or of long-horned cattle[8] to animate the landscape,
which is hedged in by the dark, forest-clad Ciminian, the naked,
craggy, sparkling Soracte, and the ever-fresh and glorious range
of Apennines, gemmed with many a town, and chequered with
shifting shadows.

All this is seen on the plain; but go northwards towards the

---

[8] The waters or the pastures of this
district, the "ager Faliscus," were supposed by the ancients to have the property
of turning cattle white (Plin. Nat. His. II.
106. Ovid. Amor. III. Eleg. 13, v. 13),
but the local breed is now of the grey hue
common in the Campagna. This district
was anciently fertile in flax (Sil. Ital. IV.
223). There is little enough, either of
produce or manufacture, at present.

Tiber, and you find that you are far from being on low ground; the river flows five hundred feet beneath you, through a valley which in fertile beauty has few rivals, even in Italy. Or attempt to approach some one of the towns whose spires you see peering above the woods of the plain; and many a ravine, darkly profound, unseen, unthought of till you stand on its brink, yawns at your feet, and must be traversed to its uttermost recesses ere you attain your object. In these lower regions you are amid scenes widely different from those on the upper level. Your horizon is bounded by walls of rock, but what it wants in distance it gains in intrinsic beauty. The cliffs, broken into fantastic forms, and hollowed into caves of mysterious interest, display the richest hues of brown, red, orange, and grey; wood hangs from their every ledge, and even crests their brows—a wood as varied in mass as in tint—ilex, ash, alder, oak, chestnut—matted together with ivy, vines, clematis, and honeysuckle; a stream winds brawling through the hollow, here spanned by a rustic bridge, there sinking in a mimic cascade; now struggling among the fallen, moss-grown crags, now running riot through some lowly mill, half hid by foliage. A white shrine or hermitage looks down from the verge of the cliff, or a bolder-featured town, picturesque with the ruin of ages, towers above you on an insulated mass at the forking of the glen; so lofty, so inaccessible is the site, you cannot believe it the very same town you had seen for miles before you, lying in the bosom of the plain. Such are the general outlines of the scenery; but every site has its peculiar features, which I shall only notice in so far as they have antiquarian interest.

About six miles northwards from Civita Castellana lies Corchiano, now a wretched village of five or six hundred souls, ruined by the French at the beginning of the century, and never rebuilt. There is nothing of antiquity within the walls, but the site is clearly Etruscan. No walls of that origin are extant, but the ravines around contain numerous sepulchres, now defaced by appropriation to other purposes. Traces of Etruscan roads, too, are abundant. On the way to Gallese, to Ponte Felice, and to Civita Castellana, you pass through deep clefts, sunk in the rock in ancient times; and in the more immediate neighbourhood of the village are roads cut in the rock, and flanked by sepulchres, or built up on either hand with large blocks of tufo, which have every appearance of remote antiquity. The tombs have no remarkable features—being mostly square chambers, with benches

of rock around, and sometimes with a pillar or partition-wall in
the centre.   There are some *columbaria* as at Fálleri, and not a
few of those singular conical tombs, sunk in the ground, and
having an opening above, which abound at Civita Castellana.
But the most remarkable monument on this site is about half a
mile from Corchiano, on the road to Fálleri.   After crossing the
river—the Rio Fratte—you ascend to the level of the plain by a
road sunk in the tufo, on the wall of which is carved an Etruscan
inscription, in letters fifteen inches in height, with an intaglio of
at least three inches—

ꟼƧƎIꟼꟼⱯ · ꟼƎꟻ · ꟼⱯⱭⱭⱯⱢ

or LARTH. VEL. ARNIES.   On the rock just beyond there has been
another inscription, but one letter only is now traceable.   There
is no appearance of a tomb, and the rock does not seem to have
been hewn into a monumental form, yet the inscription of a
proper name, in such a situation (and complete in itself, as the
smooth surface testifies), can hardly have been other than sepulchral.   Here, at least, is proof positive of the Etruscan antiquity
of the road, and a valuable guide by which to judge of other roads.
There has been a water-course down one side, and, a little above
the inscription, a sewer, just like those beneath the walls of
Etruscan cities, opens on the road, bringing the water from the
ground above into the course; and again, some distance below the
inscribed rock, another similar sewer opens in the tufo, and
carries the water through the cliff, clear of the road, down to the
river.   Both sewers have evidently been formed for no other
purpose; and have every appearance of being coeval with the
road.   This, which ran here in Etruscan times, must be the same
as that afterwards called by the Romans Via Amerina; it led
northward from Nepi, through Fálleri, to the Tiber near Orte.
Corchiano, the ancient name of which is utterly lost,[9] was also on
the road, perhaps a *mutatio*.

[9] Among the sepulchral incriptions of
Chiusi, we find the proper name of
"Carcu" "Carca" "Carcna," and
"Carcuni," which in Latin would be
Carconia.   Mus. Chius. II. p. 218.
Lanzi, II. pp. 348, 409, 432, 455.   The
name of "Curcli," which bears a strong
affinity to Corchiano, occurs in an inscription said by Buonarroti to be cut on some
rocks in the mountains near Florence (p.
95, ap. Dempst. II.).   The name Carconia
in Faliscan letters occurs in one of the
sepulchral inscriptions found in 1851 near
Sta. Maria di Fálleri.   Ann. Inst. 1860,
tav. G.

There is considerable interest around Corchiano, and the antiquary or artist, who would explore the neighbourhood, would do well to make it his head-quarters, as it is centrally convenient, and accommodation might formerly be had in the house of the butcher of the place, Giuseppe Lionidi. The persons who entertain strangers at these out-of-the-way places are often butchers, and generally well to do in the world, that is, as well-doing is esteemed in Italy. At such places the traveller cannot look for comfort, but he will generally meet with great attention from the whole household.

About two miles from Corchiano on the road to Bassanello, at a spot called Puntone del Ponte, is a singular tomb, with a sort of court in front sunk in the rock,[1] and with the remains of a portico, of which but one square pillar is now standing. On the inner wall of the portico, high under the cornice, is an Etruscan inscription, which is imperfect, but seems to state the age of the defunct. In its general style this sepulchre resembles the triple-arched tomb at Fálleri. It now serves as a pig-sty; therefore beware of fleas—swarming as in Egyptian plagues—beclouding light nether garments!

Seven miles north of Corchiano, on the road to Orte, is Bassanello, perhaps an Etruscan site. There is nothing of interest here; but half-way between it and Corchiano, is a deserted town called Alcano or Liano, alias Sta. Bruna, from a ruined church on the site. The walls and other ruins, so far as I could see, are mediæval, and highly picturesque; but there are tombs of more ancient date in the cliffs beneath the walls, and in the neighbourhood. In many parts of this road you trace the Via Amerina, by the line of basaltic blocks, running almost due N. and S., and in one part, near the Puntone del Ponte, you tread the ancient pavement for some distance.

Three miles from Corchiano and nine from Civita Castellana, lies Gallese, the town which has been supposed to occupy the site of Fescennium. It stands, as usual, on a mass of rock at the junction of two ravines. It has evidently been an Etruscan site, and though no walls of that construction are extant, there are several sewers in the cliffs beneath the town, and plenty of tombs in the rocks around. Within the town are a few Roman remains, fragments of columns, inscriptions, and bas-reliefs, but nothing

---

[1] This court in front of the portico must represent the vestibule described by Cœcilius Gallus (ap. A. Gell. XVI. 5; Macrob. Sat. VI. 8) as a vacant space before the door of the house, through which lay the approach to it.

which throws light on the ancient name of the place. This, however, has been determined by a worthy *canonico* of Gallese, now deceased, to be the Æquum Faliscum, mentioned by Strabo, Virgil, and Italicus, and he wrote a work thereon, still in manuscript, entitled, "La Antica Falisca, o sia notizie istoriche della città di Gallese, dal Canonico Teologo Amanzio Nardoni." His is not a new idea, for on the front of the Palazzo Comunale or Town-hall is inscribed—

SÆCULA DUM VIVENT DURABIT VITA PHALISCIS.

The derivation of Gallese from Halesus, or Haliscus, the son of Agamemnon, and reputed founder of the Faliscan race, is plausible enough; but another less venerable origin has been sought for the name by the townspeople, who have assumed for the arms of the town a cock—Gallese *a gallo*. Æquum Faliscum seems, from Strabo, to have been on the Flaminian Way, but Gallese lies about midway between that and the Via Amerina, two or three miles from each. The town is circumscribed by nature, and can never have been of importance—scarcely large enough to be the ancient Fescennium. Gallese is very accessible by railway from Rome, from which it is 74 chilomètres distant, and three miles from the station bearing its own name.

Six miles north-west of Corchiano lies Vignanello, also an Etruscan site, but with no remains of interest. It is a mean and dirty town with a villanous *osteria*, yet of such importance that a vehicle, miscalled *diligence*, runs thither from Rome twice a week. Four miles beyond is Soriano, another ancient site, possibly the Surrina Vetus whose existence may be inferred from the "Surrina Nova" which occupied the site of Viterbo. It is boldly situated on the lower slope of the dark Ciminian, lorded over by its venerable castle; and retains many a picturesque trace of the earthquake which shattered it in the last century.

I had the fortune to discover the site of an ancient city in this district, which seems to me to be more probably that of Fescennium than any one of those yet mentioned. It lies about a mile and a half west of Ponte Felice, on the way thence to Corchiano, and the site is indicated by a long line of walling, an embankment to the cliffs on one side of a ravine. From the character of the ground the city must have been of great size, for it is not the usual narrow ridge between two ravines, but a wide area, some miles in circuit, surrounded by ravines of great depth; more like the site of the ancient Falerii, on the heights of Civita Castel-

Juna, than of any other town in this neighbourhood. The area of the city is covered with dense wood, which greatly impedes research; on it stands the ruined church of San Silvestro, which gives its name to the spot. The wall is the facing to a sort of natural bastion in the cliff, considerably below the level of the city. It is so conspicuous that I am surprised to find no mention of it in any work on the Campagna, not even in Westphal or Nibby.

Forcing a way through pathless thickets, I climbed to the wall and found it to extend in an unbroken mass for 150 or 200 feet.[2] In the size and arrangement of its blocks it is more like the fragments at Tarquinii and Cære, than any other remains I can recollect in Etruria. The whole is much ruined in surface, and bears the appearance of very high antiquity. It has evidently been the wall of a city, for no mere castle would have had a bastion such as this, nor would it have occupied such a site, on a ledge of the cliff, completely commanded by higher ground; and though in the style of its masonry it differs somewhat from the general type, yet in its position, as a *revêtement* to the cliff, it exactly corresponds with the usual walling of Etruscan cities. That such is its character is corroborated by the existence of numerous tombs, not in the cliffs of the ravines, but, as at Nepi, on the level of the high ground opposite, together with fragments of walling, and sewers which were probably intended to drain this level and keep the tombs dry.

The size of this city, so much superior to that of the neighbouring Etruscan towns, and its vicinity to the Via Flaminia which ran just below it to the East on its way to the Tiber and Otricoli, greatly favour the view that here stood Fescennium. Not that that city is known to have been on the Flaminian, but the ancients generally made their roads to accommodate any place of importance that lay in the same direction;[3] and that

---

[2] About eight or ten courses are standing, formed of tufo blocks, from 18 to 22 inches in height, and square, or nearly so (not alternating with long blocks as in the usual *emplecton*), and laid often one directly over the other, as in the Tullianum prison, and other very early structures.

[3] The ancient road departed from the line of the modern Via Flaminia about Aqua Viva, leaving Civita Castellana two or three miles to the left, and continued to Borghetto, crossing the Tiber by the bridge now in ruins, called Le Pile d' Augusto; but its precise course through this district has not been determined. Westphal, Röuis. Kamp. p. 136. It did not run to the original Falerii, because that city had been destroyed before its formation, and the second Falerii was accommodated by the Via Amerina. But Fescennium continued to exist under the Empire, and therefore was most probably connected with the City by a road.

Fescennium was of more importance than the many nameless Etruscan towns in this district, it is fair to conclude from the mention of it by Dionysius and Virgil, and from its being coupled with Falerii, one of the cities of the Confederation.   If it were certain that Æquum Faliscum was not merely another name for Falerii, it might well have occupied this site, for Strabo seems to indicate it as being on the Flaminian Way, between Otricoli and Rome, which must mean somewhat on the Roman side of the former place.[4]   In one of the three Itineraries, indeed, which give the stations on the Flaminian, a town of that name is placed in this neighbourhood; but on the wrong bank of the Tiber. Neither Fescennium nor Æquum Faliscum is mentioned by Ptolemy.   If this be the site of Fescennium, as the latest mention of that town is made by Pliny, it is probable that at an early period of the Empire it fell into decay, and was deserted, like so many other Etruscan towns, and "the rejoicing city became a desolation, a place for beasts to lie down in."   Its only inhabitants are now the feathered tribes, and the only nuptial songs which meet the ear are those of countless nightingales, which in spring-time not only "smooth the rugged brow of Night," but even at noonday fill the groves and ravines with tuneful echoes,

"Stirring the air with such a harmony"

as to infuse a spirit of joy and gladness into this lonely and desolate spot.

---

[4] Strabo, it must be observed, does not speak from his own knowledge, but records it as a report—οἱ δὲ Αἰκουμφαλίσκον λέγου- σιν, &c. (V. p. 226).   This is according to the version of Cluver (II. p. 538), who reads it *Æquum Faliscum*, an emendation of the evidently corrupt text also approved of by Müller (Etrusk. einl. II. 14, n. 101). Both these authorities, however, take this for a synonym of the second Falerii, which was built in the plain, not of the third city (Faliscum) of the Falisci.

CAPENA, WITH SORACTE IN THE DISTANCE.

CHAPTER X.

FERONIA AND CAPENA.

Hæc duo præterea disjectis oppida muris.—VIRG.

Itur in agros
Dives ubi anto omnes colitur Feronia luco
Et sacer humectat fluvialia rura Capenas.—SIL. ITAL.

ANOTHER Etruscan city which played a prominent part in the early history of Rome, was Capena.[1] It is first mentioned by Livy in his account of the last Veientine war, when it united with Falerii in assisting Veii, then beleaguered by the Romans. The latter city, from her power and proximity to Rome, was the bulwark of Etruria; and it was foreseen by the neighbouring people, that should she fall, the whole land would be open to invasion.[2] Falerii and Capena, fearing they would be next attacked, made strenuous attempts to raise the siege, but finding their efforts vain, they besought the aid of the great Confederation of Etruria.[3] Now, it had so happened that the Veientes had greatly offended the Confederation, first, by acting contrary to

---

[1] Capena is evidently a name of Etruscan origin. A tomb of the family of "Capeni," or "Capenia," was discovered at Perugia in 1843 (Vermigl. Scavi Perugini, p. 9). Among Etruscan family names, we meet with "Capnas" (Verm. Isc. Perug. 1. p. 226) and "Capevani," (Lanzi II. p. 371) probably a derivation from Capena with the insertion of the digamma. In the tomb of the Cilnii, the name "Canpna" occurs.

Signor Giulietti of Chiusi has an urn inscribed "Thania Capuei." Stephanus calls this town *Capinna*.

[2] Liv. V. 8.

[3] Liv. V. 17. Cato (ap. Serv. ad Æn. VII. 697) states that Capena was a colony of Veii, which would be an additional reason for her eagerness to assist the latter in her extremity.

the established custom of the land, in taking to themselves a
king; and in the next place, their king had made himself
personally obnoxious by interrupting the solemn games—an act
amounting to sacrilege.   So the Confederation had decreed that
no succour should be afforded to Veii so long as she retained her
king.[4]   To the representations of the Falisci and Capenates, the
magnates of Etruria in conclave assembled, replied, that hitherto
they had refused Veii assistance on the ground that as she had
not sought counsel of them, neither must she seek succour, and
that they must still withhold it, being themselves in peril from
the sudden invasion of the Gauls.[5]   The two allies nevertheless
persisted in their efforts to raise the siege, but in vain : their
lands were several times ravaged, and their armies overthrown ;[6]
and on the fall of Veii, the fate they had anticipated befell them.
Their territories were again invaded, and though the natural
strength of their cities preserved them from assault, their lands
were laid waste, and the produce of their fields and orchards
utterly destroyed.[7]   The territory of Capena was particularly
fertile,[8] and such a blow as this was more efficacious than the
sword, for it compelled the citizens to sue for peace, though at
the expense of their independence.   A few years later (A.U. 365)
the Roman citizenship was granted to such of the inhabitants of
Veii, Falerii, and Capena, as had sided with Rome in the recent
struggle ; and the conquered territory was divided among them.[9]
Such means did Rome employ to facilitate her conquests, and
secure them more firmly to herself.

That Capena continued to exist as late as the time of
Aurelian, is proved by scattered notices in ancient writers and
by inscriptions.   From that time we lose sight of her.   Her
site probably became desolate ; and her name was consequently
forgotten.   When interest was again awakened in the antiquities
of Italy, she was sought for, but long in vain.   Cluver[1] placed
Capena at Civitella San Paolo, not far from the Tiber ;
Holstenius,[2] at Morlupo ; while Galetti, from the evidence of
inscriptions discovered on the spot,[3] has determined it to

---

[4] Liv. V. 1.
[5] Liv. V. 17.
[6] Liv. V. 12—14. 19.
[7] Liv. V. 24.
[8] Cicero pro Flac. XXIX.
[9] Liv. VI. 4.   Those of Capena were
formed into a new tribe, called *Stellatina.*
Festus, s. voce. cf. Liv. VI. 5.

[1] Cluv. II p. 549.
[2] Adnot. ad Cluv. p. 62.
[3] Galetti, Sopra il Sito di Capena, p.
4—23.   One of these inscriptions is now
at Morlupo, another in the church of S.
Oreste, and a third in that of S. Silvestro,
on the summit of Soracte. cf. Gruter, p.
189. 5. and 466. 6.   Fabretti, p. 109.

have been at Civitucola, an uninhabited hill, half-way between the two.[4]

This hill lies far from any high road or frequented path, and still further from any town where the traveller may find accommodation—in a part of the Campagna which is never visited by strangers, save by some adventurous antiquary, or some sportsman, led by his eagerness far away from his accustomed haunts. It was more accessible when the Via Flaminia was in use as the high-way from Rome to Civita Castellana, for it lies only five or six miles off that road. The nearest point on the railroad from which it may be visited is Monte Rotondo, from which station it is about five miles distant; but when I visited it, the nearest point was Civita Castellana, sixteen or eighteen miles distant, and it was a long day's journey there and back, on account of the nature of the country to be traversed, which is practicable only on foot or on horseback. In truth it was necessary to leave Civita at break of day, to avoid the risk of being benighted—no agreeable accident in a country so lonely, and whose inhabitants are not well reputed for honesty.

Domenico, my guide to Fálleri, could not attend me to Capena, and sent his brother in his stead—Antonio, commonly called "Il Re"—the King—a *nom de guerre* which, as the eldest son, he had inherited from his father. Domenico, I learned, was having his pigs blessed. A mad dog had attacked them, and the hogs had defended themselves stoutly, rushing upon and goring him with their tusks till they trampled his dead body under their feet. They paid dearly for it, however; ten of them were bitten in the conflict, and to save them from hydrophobia Domenico had sent to the *sacerdote* to bless them and put the iron of San Domenico on their foreheads.

I requested an explanation.

Saint Domenick, it seems, was once on a time on his travels, when his horse dropped a shoe. He stopped at the first farrier's he came to, and had it replaced. The farrier asked for payment.

---

[4] Cramer, I. p. 231; Nibby, *voce* Capena; Gell, I. p. 263. Dempster (Et. Reg. II. p. 179) made the blunder of placing it in Latium, on the Appian Way, because the Porta Capena of Rome opened on that road, as Servius (ad Æn. VII. 697) had said:— Porta Capena juxta Capenos est. There can be little doubt that the Gate derived its name, not from Capena, which lay in the opposite direction, but from Capua, and that the termination is but the early Latin adjectival form, as we know it to have been the Etruscan. Frontinus indeed (de Aquæd., p. 27) says the Via Appia led —a portâ Capenâ usque ad Capuam; and Dionysius (VIII. p. 483) calls the gate πύλη Καπυίνη.

The saint-errant was as astonished as the knight of La Mancha could have been at such a demand; but with less courtesy he said to his horse, "Give him back the shoe." Whereupon the obedient animal flung out his heels, and with a blow on the forehead laid the farrier dead. Domenico in his simplicity could not perceive that the farrier was at least as worthy of his hire as the priest, to whom he had paid three pauls for saying a benediction over his hogs, and branding their foreheads with the mark of a horse-shoe.

For the first five miles the road was the modern Via Flaminia, which after crossing the Treia, ascends to the level of the Campagna, and continues through a country partially wooded and cultivated, yet not without beauty, to the foot of Soracte. The mountain itself is sufficient to obviate all tedium on the ride. At first it presents the form of a dark wedge or cone, the end towards you being densely clothed with wood; but as you approach it lengthens out gradually, peak after peak disclosing itself, till it presents a totally different aspect—a long serrated ridge, rising at first in bright green slopes from the plain, then darkening above with a belt of olive-groves, and terminating in a bald crest of grey rock, jagged and craggy, its peaks capt with white convents, which sparkle in the sun like jewels on a diadem. The whole mass reminds one of Gibraltar; it is about the same length—more than three miles—it rises to about the same height above the plain [5]—it has the same pyramidal form when foreshortened, a similar line of jagged peaks. But there is less abruptness, and more fertility. There is not the stern savage grandeur of the Spanish Rock; but the true Italian grace and ease of outline—still the beautiful though verging on the wild.

At the Romitorio, a hamlet of a few ruined houses, I left the Via Flaminia, and striking across some fields and through a wood, ascended, by wretched tracks saturated with rain, to the olive-groves which belt the mountain. The view on the ascent is magnificent—the vast expanse of the wild, almost uninhabited, Campagna at my feet—here dark with wood, from which the towers of a few towns arose at wide intervals—there sweeping away in league after league of bare down or heath—the double-headed mass of the Ciminian on the right—the more distant

---

[5] Gibraltar is about 1500 feet above the sea. Soracte, according to Nibby, is 2150 French feet; according to Gell, 2270 French feet in height. Westphal calls it 2200 feet. But the plain from which Soracte is viewed, being considerably elevated above the sea, the heights of the two mountains *appear* nearly equal.

Alban on the other hand—the sharp wooded peak of Rocca Romana between them—the varied effects of light and shade, of cloud and sunshine, as storms arose from time to time and crossed the scene, darkening and shrouding a portion of the landscape, which presently came forth laughing in brilliant sunshine; while the lowering cloud moved on, blotting out one object after another on which the eye but a moment before had been resting with delight.

On emerging from the wood, Sant Oreste was seen before us, situated on a bare elevated shoulder of the mountain. From the rocky ridge leading to the village a new scene comes into view. A richly wooded valley lies beneath, with the Tiber winding through it; and the Apennines rise beyond, peak above peak in steps of sublimity, and stretch away far to the south till they sink all faint and grey into the Latin valley, at the steep of Palestrina.

The rock of which the mountain is composed here starts up in bold crags on every side; it is a sort of limestone, called from its colour "*palombino;*" it is not however of dove-colour alone, but it is to be found of various shades of grey, and sometimes almost white. Among these crags a path winds up to the summit of the mountain. Here the traveller will find a colony of recluses, and the several churches of Sta. Lucia, La Madonna delle Grazie, Sant Antonio, and San Silvestro. The latter stands on the central and highest peak of the mountain, and is generally supposed to occupy the site of the ancient temple of Apollo, to which deity Soracte was sacred.[6] It can boast of no small antiquity itself, having been founded in A.D. 746, by Carloman, son of Charles Martel, and uncle of the celebrated Charlemagne, in honour of the saint whose name it bears.

Sant Oreste is a wretched village, with steep, foul streets, and mean houses—without any accommodation for the stranger. I was at once impressed with the conviction that it must have been an Etruscan site. Its situation is too strong by nature to have been neglected, and is just such as would have been chosen for a city in the northern part of Etruria; the plateau rising just as high above the plain as those of Cosa, Rusellæ, and Saturnia. At the foot of the steep and rocky hill on which the village stands I found confirmation of my opinion in a number of tombs

[6] Virg. Æn. XI. 785. Sil. Ital. V. 170.—VII. 662.—VIII. 494; Plin. VII. 2; Solinus, Polyhist. II. p. 15. Nibby fancied the name of the Mount was Pelasgic, and suggested Σωρός—ἀκτή as its derivation.

in the tufo cliffs. I did not observe any remains of ancient walls on the height, but if they were of tufo—as is most probable, since that sort of rock is hewn with so much facility, that notwithstanding the transport of the blocks up the hill, there would have been less labour than in preparing the hard limestone close at hand [7]—they may have been destroyed for the sake of materials to construct the houses of the village. What may have been the name of the Etruscan town which occupied this site is not easy to determine; but I am inclined to agree with Nibby in regarding it as Feronia, which Strabo says was situated under Soracte, and its name seems to be preserved in that of Felonica, a fountain at the foot of this hill, on the road to Civitella di San Paolo.[8]

At or near Feronia was a celebrated temple to the goddess of that name, which, like many ancient shrines, stood in a thick grove—Lucus Feroniæ.[9] She seems to have been identical with Proserpine,[1] and was worshipped by the Sabines, and Latins, as well as by the Etruscans.[2] Hither, on yearly festivals, pilgrims resorted in great numbers from the surrounding country, many to perform vows and offer sacrifice—and those who were possessed with the spirit of the goddess, walked with naked feet over heaps of burning coal and ashes, without receiving injury [3]—and

---

[7] This was done at Tivoli, whose walls are volcanic (Gell, II. p. 272), though the rocks are travertine and limestone; so also at Palestrina, and again at Segni, where a gate and a portion of the walls are of tufo, though the rest are formed of the natural limestone of the hill on which the city stands. The *palombino* of Soracte was quarried by the Romans, and is classed by Vitruvius (II. 7) with travertine, as a stone of moderate hardness, a mean between tufo and *silex* or lava.

[8] Nibby, II. p. 103; Strab. V. p. 226. Gell thinks, quite unnecessarily it seems to me, that this Felonica is "the site of the temple, grove, and fountain of Feronia." Holstenius (Adnot. ad Cluver. p. 60) also placed Feronia in the plain about a mile from S. Oreste, where he said there were extensive remains of a town. The site he referred to is probably that indicated by Westphal (Römis. Kamp. p. 136), as occupied by an unimportant ruin, and vulgarly called Feronia. It lies between the Flaminian Way and the mountain.

[9] Liv. I. 30, XXVI. 11, XXVII. 4; Sil. Ital. XIII. 83; Plin. III. 8. Strabo (loc.

cit.) calls Feronia a city, and says the Grove was on the same spot. This must not be confounded with the other Lucus Feroniæ in the north of Etruria near Luca, which Ptolemy (Geog. p. 72, ed. Bert.) places among the "inland colonies" of that land,—still less with the Temple of Feronia mentioned by Virgil (Æn. VII. 800) as situated in a green grove—viridi gaudens Feronia luco— which was near Terracina and the Circæan promontory. It is to this latter shrine and the fountain attached to it that Horace refers on his journey to Brundusium (Sat. I. 5, 24).

[1] Dion. Hal. III. p. 173. According to Servius (ad Æn. VII. 799) Juno, as a virgin, was also called Feronia. Servius elsewhere (VIII. 564) calls Feronia the goddess of freed men, who, in her temple at Terracina, placed a *pileus*, or felt scull-cap, on their shaven crowns. Here also was a stone bench, inscribed with these words: "Bene-meriti servi sedeant, surgent liberi."

[2] Dion. Hal. loc. cit.; Liv. XXVI. 11; Varro, de Ling. Lat. V. 74.

[3] Strab. V. p. 226. The same is related of the shrine of Apollo on this mountain.

many merchants, artisans, and husbandmen, taking advantage of the concourse, brought their goods hither for sale, so that the market or fair held here was more splendid than any other in Italy.[4] From the numerous first-fruits and other gifts offered to the goddess, her shrine became renowned for its riches, and was decorated with an abundance of gold and silver. But it was despoiled by Hannibal on his march through Italy.[5] It was however maintained till the fall of paganism in the fourth century. That the temple itself stood on a height seems probable from the fact, mentioned by Livy, of its being struck by lightning.[6]

In a geological point of view, Soracte is interesting. It is a mass of limestone rising out of the volcanic plain, not resting, as Gell supposed, on a basis of tufo. One of those convulsions of the earth, which ejected from the neighbouring craters the matter which constitutes the surface of the Campagna, upheaved this huge mass of limestone, and either drove it through the superincumbent beds of tufo; or, what is more probable, upraised it previous to the volcanic disturbances of this district, when the Campagna lay beneath the waters of the ocean.

Sant Oreste is about eight miles from Civita Castellana, or about half way from that town to the site of Capena. On journeying this latter half of the road, I learned two things, by which future travellers would do well to profit—first, not to attempt to cross an uncultivated country without a competent guide, especially on fête-days, when there are no labourers or shepherds in the fields; secondly, to look well to the horses one hires and to ascertain before starting that they have been fed, and, if need be, to carry provender for them. The animals hired in these country-towns are mere beasts of burden, overworked and underfed, accustomed to carry wood, charcoal, or flour, and with

Plin. N. H. VII. 2; Solinus, II. p. 15; Virgil, Æn. XI. 785, et seq.; Sil. Ital. V. 177, et seq.

[4] Dion. Hal. III. p. 173; cf. Liv. I. 30.

[5] Liv. XXVI. 11; Sil. Ital. XIII. 84, et seq. Cramer (I. p. 232, 309) opines that the temple Hannibal rifled was one to the same goddess at Eretum in Sabina, and quotes Fabretti (Insc. Ant. p. 452), who states that inscriptions have been found near Eretum which mention a temple to Feronia at that place. Livy, however, records a tradition that Hannibal spoiled this said shrine in the *ager Capenatis*, on his

road from Reate to Rome, "turning out of his way from Eretum," which he must certainly have done, if Monte Rotondo be the site of Eretum, as Cluver (II. p. 667) supposes. The battle of Eretum, in which the Sabines were defeated by Tullus Hostilius, was the consequence of that people having laid violent hands on some Romans at the fair of Fanum Feroniæ. Dion. Hal. loc. cit. cf. Liv. I. 30.

[6] Liv. XXXIII. 26. It has been suggested that the Temple of Feronia stood on the site of the Church of S. Abondio, near Rignano. Ann. Inst., 1864, p. 130.

difficulty to be urged out of their usual deliberate pace. Their mouths are as tough and insensible as their hides ; the whip is of little avail, and spurs are indispensable. As these are not always to be had, it is advisable for whoever would explore the by-roads of Italy, to add a pair to his luggage.

Antonio, my guide, had never been beyond Sant Oreste, but the road I wished to take was pointed out to us so clearly by some people of that town, that it seemed impossible to miss it. But among the lanes and hollows at the foot of Soracte we were soon at fault—took a wrong path—wandered about for an hour over newly-ploughed land, swampy from recent rains—at length found the right path—lost it again immediately on a trackless down— and then, like Dante, found ourselves at the middle of our journey in a dark and savage wood. No poet,—" od ombra od uomo certo "—nor any other being, came to our assistance, for not a sign of humanity was in sight ; and, to crown our difficulties, one of the horses sunk from exhaustion, owing to want of food. Remembering the proverb, " sacco vuoto non regge in piede,"—" an empty sack will not stand upright,"—we transferred what refreshments we had brought for our own use to our horses' stomachs, and quietly awaited their time. Patience—no easy virtue when the rain was coming down in deluging showers —at length overcame all difficulties, and we found ourselves in the right track, on the banks of the Grammiccia, which led us to the site of Capena.[7]

The city crowned a hill of some elevation, rising steeply from the valley, and whose highest point is now crested with some ruins, called the church of San Martino ; by which name the spot is known among the peasantry, and not by that of Civitucola, as I had been led by former writers to suppose ; the latter appellation being assigned to the spot by some documents of the middle ages. The whole declivity was frosted over with the blossom of the wild pear-trees which cover its face. Through these I had to climb by sheep-tracks, slippery with the rain. The ruins just mentioned are the only remains on the height on which the city stood. They are of opus incertum, and probably formed part of a villa of Imperial times, which may subsequently have been converted into a Christian chapel. That a city originally stood here, however, there are unequivocal proofs in the broken pottery which thickly strews the hill. It occupied

[7] The stream itself seems to have been anciently called Capenas. Sil. Ital. XIII. 85. It is now sometimes called Fosso di San Martino.

an elevated ridge on one side of a deep hollow, which Gell supposes to be an extinct crater, and which is now called Il Lago.

No remains of walls could I find, save at the western angle, overhanging the Lago, where a few blocks mark the foundations; but on the slopes beneath, to the south and east, many blocks lie scattered about.[8] The form of the city, however, is easily traced by the pottery, and character of the ground: it was long and narrow, especially narrow in the centre of its length, near the ruins of San Martino. Its circumference can hardly have been a mile and a half, and this marks it as a town of inferior importance. The highest part was to the west, and there, in all probability, was the Arx. I observed the sites of three gates, —one at the eastern, one at the western extremity, and one to the south, where the land narrows opposite the ruin. By this gate alone vehicles could have reached the city, so steep are the cliffs and slopes around it. After making the tour of Capena, it is easy to comprehend how the Roman armies several times entered the territory, and laid it waste, but never attacked the town. It was as elevated as Falerii, and could on no side be approached on level ground.

I could perceive no tombs in the cliffs around or beneath the city, and one only in the low ground, to the north.[9]

The view from the height of Capena is wildly beautiful. The

[8] Gell states that the walls may be traced by their foundations round the summit of the hill; but either he was deceived by the natural breaks of the tufo rock, which at a little distance may be easily mistaken for masonry, or the blocks since his time have been carried off by the peasantry.

[9] That this is the true site of Capena has been called in question. Excavations made here of late years tend to prove that the cemetery, rather than the city, of Capena occupied this hill of S. Martino. For these researches have brought to light many sepulchres, some described as of peculiar form, being sunk like shallow wells beneath the surface, with niches hollowed in the sides, one to contain the corpse, and the others the objects of art buried with it. These articles were, as usual, of terra cotta, bronze, and glass, but of different periods. Some of the vases were of very primitive forms, with figures of animals painted or scratched on them in bands, and of very

archaic art. In some of the later tombs pots were found bearing inscriptions, either in early Latin, or in a character neither Etruscan nor Faliscan, and which therefore suggested the existence of a dialect peculiar to Capena. Dr. Henzen refers these inscriptions to the sixth century of Rome. Bull. Inst., 1861, pp. 143–150.

With the meagre notices we possess of these excavations, it would be premature to pronounce that this hill was not the site of Capena. The slopes beneath many Etruscan cities are full of tombs, and the discovery of Roman sepulchres, even on the plateau above, would not be opposed to the existence of habitation in earlier times. Until we can ascertain the exact position of the tombs which have yielded the archaic articles, or until further excavations decide the question, we may keep our judgment in abeyance as to the site of Capena.

deep hollow on the south, with its green carpet: the steep hills
overhanging it, dark with wood—the groves of Capena, be it
remembered, were sung by Virgil[1]—the bare swelling ground to
the north, with Soracte towering above: the snow-capt Apennines
in the eastern horizon: the deep silence, the seclusion: the
absence of human habitations (not even a shepherd's hut) within
the sphere of vision, save the distant town of Sant Oreste,
scarcely distinguishable from the grey rock on which it stands;—
compose a scene of more singular desolation than belongs to the
site of any other Etruscan city in this district of the land.

A visit to this site will scarcely repay the antiquary for the
difficulty of reaching it. But the scenery on the way is delightful, especially between San Martino and Rignano, about seven
miles distant, which road I took on my return. It is a mere
mule-track, and passes over very rough ground. Now it descends
into ravines picturesque with cliff and wood, and with an overshot
mill, it may be, in the hollow—now pursues the level of the
plain, commanding glorious views of Soracte, with a changing,
but ever beautiful foreground of glen, heath, wood, or corn-land.
On the approach to Rignano, the view is particularly fine; for
beneath the town opens a wide ravine which seems to stretch up
to the very base of Soracte, its cliffs overhung with wood, and a
pretty convent nestling in its bosom. Around Rignano the land
presents a singular stratification of white and grey rock—the
white, called "cappellaccio," is a sort of friable tufo; the grey,
with which it alternates, is a sandstone, in very thin layers.

Rignano is a miserable town; tolerably flourishing, it is said,
when the Via Flaminia, on which it stands, was the high road to
Rome, but now falling into decay. It is evidently a Roman site,
for altars, cippi, fragments of statues and cornices, and other
traces of that people, abound in the streets. There is also a
curious relic of the middle ages, a primitive cannon, made like
a barrel, with staves of iron hooped at intervals, and with rings
attached to serve as handles. It is the counterpart of one I have
seen, I think, in the armoury of Madrid. Rignano lays claim to
be the birthplace of the infamous Cæsar Borgia.

Around the church of S. Abondio, which stands on a wooded
height near Rignano, are many ancient remains, which, from the

---

[1] Lucosque Capenos.—Æn. VII. 697.
But the groves here referred to may with
equal probability be those around the shrine
of Feronia, which was in the Ager Capenatis. Liv. XXVI. 11, XXVII. 4, XXXIII.
26. Cato also mentions—lucus Capenatis
(ap. Priscian. IV. p. 36, ed. Ald.).

description given, appear to be all of Roman times. From the marble columns and capitals, the numerous fragments of architecture, and the sarcophagi and inscribed *cippi* which encumber the spot, it is concluded that a temple, of such magnificence as not to belie the description we have of the Fanum Feroniæ, formerly stood here; and it is inferred that this must be the site of that celebrated shrine. As we are not told, however, of the existence of Etruscan antiquities on the spot, we may hesitate to accept the inference, until we have more precise information as to the locality.[2]

No one who values comfort will care to enter the *osteria* of Rignano. Woe betide the man who is compelled to pass a night within its walls. To avoid the companionship of squalid monks and disgusting cripples, I resolved to push on for Civita, though it was almost dark, and there were still nine miles before our jaded beasts. By the time we reached the Romitorio, Soracte loomed an indistinct mass against the sky. Near this my guide pointed out a tree by the road-side, in which when a boy he had taken refuge from the wolves. He was returning from Rignano one winter's night, when the ground was covered with snow. On reaching this spot he heard their howlings in the wood by the road-side. They seemed to scent him, for he had barely time to climb the tree when it was surrounded by a dozen yelling demons, whose eyes, he said, shone with "the fire of hell." The tree was then but a sapling, and bent fearfully with his weight; so that he was in dread lest it should break and precipitate him among them. After a time of terrible suspense he was left alone, and at break of day ventured to descend, and with the protection of the Virgin reached Civita in safety. At that time the wood was very thick on Soracte, and afforded shelter to multitudes of wolves and bears which were wont to ravage the Campagna for miles round. Some years later the wood was cut, and the wild beasts disappeared with it, and retired to the Apennines.

The wolves of Soracte were celebrated in ancient times. Servius relates that sacrifices were once being offered on this mount to Pluto, when some wolves rushed in, seized the smoking

[2] Signor Fabio Gori points out these ruins in Ann. Inst. 1864, p. 130. He states that the site lies immediately under Soracte, and in the *ager Capenatis*, as may be learned from the discovery on the spot of inscriptions referring to that town. An ancient road branched from the Via Flaminia, and ran directly up to the hill of S. Abondio.

entrails from the altar, and bore them away to a cave, which emitted pestiferous vapours.[3]   The shepherds pursued them thither, but were arrested by these fumes. A pestilence was the consequence. They consulted the oracle, and received for answer that the plague would be staid when they imitated wolves, i.e., led a life of rapine. So they became robbers by divine authority. Hence they were called Hirpini Sorani, or Pluto's Wolves, from *hirpus*, which signified a wolf in the Sabine tongue, and *Soranus*, another name for Dis Pater.[4]   It was the descendants of these Hirpini, or Hirpi, who made the annual sacrifice to the god of the mountain, and performed the marvellous feat of walking bare-footed over live coals.[5]   This exploit seems to have continued in fashion to a late period; at least to the third century of our era, for Solinus speaks of it as existing in his day. Varro suspected jugglery, and would allow nothing supernatural in it, for he says they rubbed their soles with a certain medicament.

Wolves are not the only beasts for which Soracte was renowned. There was a race of wild goats—*capræ feræ*—perhaps roebucks, on the mountain, which could leap more than sixty feet at a bound! Well done, old Cato![6]

At Sommavilla, a village on the Sabine side of the Tiber, opposite Soracte, tombs have been found containing vases and other furniture, extremely like those of Etruria.[7]

---

[3] On the eastern side of the mountain, near the church of Santa Romana, is a cave, with deep fissures near it, called Le Voragini, which emit foul vapours. Hence the fable related by Servius must have taken its rise. Pliny (II. 95) seems to refer to these fissures, yet says the vapours were fatal to birds alone. But elsewhere (XXXI. 19) he cites Varro as saying that fatal effects were produced by a fountain on all birds which tasted it. To this spring Vitruvius (VIII. 3, 17) seems also to allude; though he places it—agro Falisco viâ Campanâ in campo Corneto. This fountain, Nibby (III. p. 112) thinks is represented by the Acqua Forte, in the plain between Soracte and the Tiber, about two miles from Ponzano.

[4] Serv. ad Æn. XI. 785 ; cf. VII. 696. Festus (*voce Irpini*) and Strabo (V. p. 250) say the Irpini were a colony of Samnites,

and were so called from Irpus, their leader, which word signified a wolf in the Samnite tongue. The Samnites, be it remembered, were of the Sabine race. Varro de L. L. VII. 29. Servius says the mountain was sacred to the Manes, but other ancient writers concur in stating that it was sacred to Apollo.

[5] Plin. Nat. Hist. VII. 2; Varro ap. Serv. ad Æn. XI. 787. Solinus, Polyb. II. p. 15. See p. 129, note 3.

[6] Cato ap. Varron. Re Rust. II. cap. 3.,

[7] For an account of these discoveries, see Bull. Inst. 1836, p. 172, Braun ; 1837, p. 95; p. 70—73, Braun ; p. 209—213, Fossati; Bull. 1838, p. 71. At Sestino, in the Umbrian Apennines, a bronze mirror, with dancing figures and Etruscan inscriptions incised, has recently been discovered, Bull. Inst. 1875, p. 88.

ORTE, FROM THE ROAD TO THE VADIMONIAN LAKE.

CHAPTER XI.

ORTE.—*HORTA*.

Et terram Hesperiam venies, ubi Lydius, arva
Inter opima virûm, leni fluit agmine Thybris.—VIRGIL.

By the rushy-fringed bank,
Where grows the willow and the osier dank,
My chariot stays.—MILTON.

ONE of the most delightful excursions I ever made in Italy
was up the Tiber, from Rome to Orte. It was as far back as 1846,
long before the railway whistle had been heard in the Papal
States, and when the great "Etruscan river" was almost a sealed
book to travellers; for in those days the roads through the valley
of the Tiber were mere country tracks, in few parts carriageable.
Inns there were none fit for any one above the condition of a
day-labourer. I therefore considered myself highly fortunate in
having an opportunity of doing the river in a steamboat! This
was a small tug of some fifteen or twenty tons, which had recently
come from England to fetch charcoal from Porte Felice, when
the state of the river would permit it. The craft had no accommodation whatever. My artist friend and I were happy to find
space enough on the grimy deck to stretch our limbs at night,
instead of seeking shelter in some filthy and well populated
locanda on shore, knowing from experience that a by-road bed
in Italy is not likely to prove

"a perfect Halcyon nest,
All calm, and balm, and quiet and rest."

It was a voyage of two or three days, for the current was strong against us, and the boat came to an anchor at dusk, when the "mali culices ranæque. palustres" feelingly reminded us of Horace's discomforts on his road to Brundusium. Like him again in the morning, we lost much time in starting, for the sun was well up before we got under weigh. But these were annoyances of little moment. To balance them we had a plethoric basket of provisions, some flasks of excellent wine to cheer us, with "allaying Tyber" *ad libitum ;* we had youth, health, good appetites, enthusiasm, and no end of enjoyment, for the scenery was not only beautiful but novel, and every turn in the river brought new and picturesque objects into view, or produced fresh combinations of those already familiar.

Times are indeed changed, when you can now run to Orte by rail in a couple of hours—too scanty a time to enjoy the all-glorious landscapes on the road ; but as the line keeps the Sabine bank for the greater part of the way, you have more comprehensive views of Soracte and the Etruscan shore, than you can obtain from the river itself. You pass the caverned heights of Antemnæ, you shoot like an arrow through the heart of Fidenæ, and as you rush on, you catch exciting glimpses of the Alban Mount, of the Latin valley, with Palestrina at its mouth, of Tivoli on the slope of Monte Gennaro, of the nearer triple-papped Monticelli, and of the snow-capped, "olive-sandalled Apennines" in the horizon. Your first halt is beneath Monte Rotondo, near which Garibaldi was discomfited in 1867 ; the little brook you here cross is no other than the Allia— "infaustum nomen ! "—the scene of the disastrous defeat of the Romans by the Gauls in the year 390 (364 B.C.) which was followed by the capture and destruction of the City by Brennus. This is the nearest station to the site of Capena, which lies on the right bank, about half-way between this and the next station of Passo di Correse ; but if you are bound thither, get out at Monte Rotondo, where you can obtain beasts and a guide.[1] In the plain, opposite the Passo, lie the "Flavinia arva" of Virgil, if the village of Fiano represent, as is generally supposed, the Etruscan town of Flavina.[2] Beyond Fiano on the same side, on the crest of the wooded hills which here embank the river, stands Nazzano, which has been proved by recent excavations to be an Etruscan site. Its necropolis occupies the plateau of Caraffa, about half a mile to the north of the town, and it has yielded

[1] See the last chapter, p. 126. [2] Virg. Æn. VII. 696 ; Sil. Ital. VIII. 492.

vases with both black and red figures, besides various articles in bronze.[3] There can be little doubt that others of the many towns within view, if subjected to similar research, would be found to occupy Etruscan sites; not excluding those on the Sabine bank, for the territory of Etruria, which at one time extended from the Alps as far south as Pæstum, could not have been rigidly bounded by this narrow stream, and must at that period have embraced all the region between the Tiber and the Apennines; and the Umbrians and cognate Sabines must have continued to feel the civilizing influences of Etruria, even when no longer under her dominion.[4]

At Montorso, the next station, the valley narrows almost to a gorge, and becomes more than ever picturesque, for the river here forms sharp bends, which give great variety to the land-scape. The yellow banks are overhung with trees, festooned with honeysuckle and wild vine, or sink into stretches of pebbly beach, the haunt of thirsty wallowing buffaloes; above them on either hand, rise wooded heights, studded with towers and towns, castles and convents, the whole dominated by the rocky crests of Soracte, sparkling with many shrines. It is an exquisite bit of what is most rare in Italy—river-scenery. After all, the most striking and interesting feature of the Tiber valley is Soracte, which you seem in your progress upward completely to circum-ambulate. On the way to Monte Rotondo its southern slopes, familiar to Romans, meet the eye. From Passo di Correse the mountain looks like a sharp cone or wedge of rock, soaring above the wooded hills at its base. As you advance it gradually opens out again, till from Stimigliano it presents its northern flank fully to the eye, the intervening hills which have hitherto concealed all but its crest, here sinking to the plain, and displaying the mountain mass from base to summit. Another valley presently opens to the left, through which winds the Treja, which after washing the castled crags of Civita Castellana, here falls into the Tiber. On a low red cliff at the point of junction, a tall ruined tower, through whose walls the blue light of heaven is visible, forms a picturesque object in the scene. It is known as the Torre Giuliana, and is of mediæval times, though tombs and sewers in the cliffs mark the site as originally Etruscan. The tower is shown in the woodcut on the next page.

Here you cross the Tiber into Etruria, and continue in that

[3] Bull. Inst. 1873, pp. 113–123, Helbig.
[4] For the discovery of Etruscan objects

in Sabina, see p. 135, note 7; also Ann. Inst. 1858, p. 240; Bull. Inst. 1866, p. 213.

land as far as Orte, passing beneath the mediæval ruins of
Borghetto, another picturesque village on an Etruscan site,
below which is the Ponte Felice, by which the old post-road
from Rome crossed the Tiber on its way to Narni, Terni, and
Foligno.

The station of Gallese is three miles from the town of that
name, which, as already stated, occupies an Etruscan site, by

TORRE GIULIANA, PASSO DI CIVITA, ON THE TIBER.

some supposed to be that of Fescennium.[5] From this point
Soracte is again seen foreshortened, reassuming the form of a
wedge or cone.

, ORTE is 83 kilomêtres, or 52 miles from Rome by railroad.
Here the two lines from Florence to Rome, one by Chiusi, the
other by Perugia, form a junction.

Orte lies on the right bank of the Tiber, about twelve miles
above Ponte Felice, and crowns the summit of a long narrow
isolated ridge of tufo rock. Beneath the walls of the town this
ridge breaks into naked cliffs, and then sinks gradually in slopes
clad with olives and vines to meet the Tiber and the plain.
Viewed from the north or south its situation appears very similar
to that of Orvieto, though far from being so elevated and imposing, but from the east or west it has a less commanding
though more picturesque appearance. At its western end the
ridge is particularly narrow, terminating in a mere wall of cliff,
called La Rocca, which communicates with the town by a viaduct.

[5] See Chapter IX. p. 120.

Thus the plan of the whole takes the form of a battledore, of which the handle is the Rocca and the body the town. Orte is still a place of some importance; and though its air in summertime be in no good repute, it retains its population throughout the year. The only place of entertainment for the traveller is the "Antica Trattoria e Locanda" of the Bell, but "it is not enough to have a clean tablecloth," as the proverb says; for if you make a tolerable meal by day, you furnish forth a dainty feast by night to thousands of hungry banqueters, whose nimbleness gets them off scot-free, though credit is not the order of the house, as is pompously set forth in the *cucina*—

> " *Credenza è morta—*
> *Il creditor l' ha ucciso—*
> *Amico, abbi pazienza,*
> *Piacer ti farò, ma non credenza.*"

Of the ancient history of Horta, we have no record, unless the notice by Virgil, the application of which to this town has been doubted, be received as historical.[1] We know, however, from better authority than that of the Mantuan bard, namely, from its extant monuments, that Horta was an Etruscan city, and the archaic character of those remains even leads us to regard it as among the most ancient in the land. The only other mention of it is by Pliny, who cites it among the "inland colonies" of Etruria;[2] but we learn from inscriptions that it was one of the military colonies of Augustus.

Orte preserves no vestiges of its ancient walls, nor is there a sign of high antiquity in either of its three gates. Nothing of classic times, in fact, is to be seen within the town save a few Roman relics. The Ortani show a house on the walls as Etruscan, but—*credat Judæus!* Let no one, however, express such a doubt within the walls of Orte, for he will have to combat not merely the prejudices of her 3000 inhabitants, but a formidable array of piety and learning in her clergy.

---

[1] Qui Tiberim Fabarimque bibunt, quos
      frigida misit
   Nursia, et Hortinæ classes, populique
      Latini.—Æn. VII. 715.

[2] Plin. III. 8. Padre Secchi, the learned Jesuit of Rome, follows Müller (Etrusk. III. 3, 7,) in thinking the place derives its name from Horta, an Etruscan goddess equivalent to the Roman "Salus," and distinct from Nortia or Fortuna, the great deity of Volsinii. This goddess Horta is mentioned by Plutarch (Quæst. Rom. XLVI), who says her temple was always kept open. A distinction between her and the Etruscan Fortuna is indicated by Tacitus (Ann. XV. 53). Secchi, Il Musaico Antoniniano, p. 47, n. 5.

"Odi, vedo, e tace,
Se vuoi viver in pace."

These gentlemen, whose want of experience in such matters may well excuse this blunder, deserve all credit for the interest they take in the antiquities of their town. To the learned canon Don Giovanni Vitali I am especially indebted for his courtesy in furnishing me with information about the excavations which have been made at Orte, and in giving me copies of inscriptions there brought to light which his antiquarian zeal has preserved from oblivion. What little I have to say of the Etruscan antiquities of Orte, as scarcely anything is now to be seen, I derive from his lips, and from those of Signor Brugiotti, a gentleman who took part in these excavations.

To the south of the town, at the distance of a mile or more, rise lofty, cliff-bound heights, apparently ranges of hills, but in fact the termination of the high table-land of the Campagna. Here, near the Convent of Bernardines, a few tombs are seen in the cliffs, and in the rocks on the plain above are others, said to resemble those of Castel d'Asso, hereafter to be described, having a false moulded doorway in the façade, an open chamber beneath it, and the sepulchre itself below all, underground. Excavations were made in this plain in 1837, with no great profit. They were carried forward, however, more successfully by an association of the townsmen, under the direction of Signor Arduini, on a still loftier height to the south-west of Orte, near the Capuchin Convent, where the tombs had no external indications, but lay beneath the surface of the ground. The articles found were similar in character to those from the neighbouring site of Bomarzo—no figured pottery, but common and rude ware of various forms, articles of glass, and bronzes in abundance. Among the latter were candelabra of great elegance and beauty, now in the Gregorian Museum at Rome, tripods, mirrors, vases with figured handles, and small statues of deities. A winged Minerva, with an owl on her hand, is, perhaps, unique in metal, though the goddess is so represented on painted vases. A leaden spade, which must have been a votive offering, is curious as the type of those still in use in this part of the country. *Alabasti* of glass, figured blue and white. Egg-shells in an entire state, often found in Etruscan tombs. A singular jar of earthenware, hermetically sealed, and half-full of liquid, which was heard when the jar was shaken, and when it was inverted would exude from a porous part in drops of limpid water. If testimony be here trustworthy, this must be the most ancient bottled liquid extant.

Numerous cinerary urns of terra cotta or *nenfro* were brought to light, generally quite plain, with inscriptions; sometimes with a head projecting from the lid, as at Veii; as many as sixty have been found in one tomb. Only one large sarcophagus, with a reclining figure on its lid, was discovered; whence it is evident that the Hortani burnt rather than buried their dead. Coins and other relics of Roman times were occasionally found in the sepulchres along with articles of undoubted Etruscan antiquity. One instance was found of a painted tomb, in which a bear was represented chained to a column; but I could not ascertain if this were of Etruscan or Roman art. It was almost immediately destroyed by the peasantry.[3]

In the cliffs beneath the town are a few tombs, now greatly defaced, some of them *columbaria*; and near the gate of S. Agostino is a sewer of the usual size and form. On the banks of the Tiber, below the town, are the remains of a Roman bridge which carried the Via Amerina across the river on its way to Tuder and Perusia. The bridge was repaired during the middle ages, and the masonry of its piers, now standing on the banks, and of the masses prostrate in the water, is of that period. Castellum Amerinum, the last stage on the Via Amerina within the Etruscan territory, which was distant twelve miles from Falerii and nine from Ameria, must have been in the near neighbourhood of Orte, probably on the heights to the south of the town, near the spot where the modern road from Corchiano begins to descend into the valley of the Tiber.

If you follow the Tiber for about four miles above Orte, you will reach, on the right bank, the "Laghetto" or "Lagherello," or "Lago di Bassano," so called from a village in the neighbourhood. In it you behold the Vadimonian Lake of antiquity, renowned for the defeat of the Etruscans on two several occasions—first, by the Dictator, Papirius Cursor, in the year 445, when after a hard-contested battle the might of Etruria was irrecoverably broken;[4] and again, in the year 471, when Cornelius Dolabella utterly routed the allied forces of the Etruscans and Gauls on its shores.[5] In after times it was renowned for its floating

---

[3] For other notices of the results of these excavations, see Bull. Inst. 1837, p. 129.

[4] Liv. IX. 39.

[5] Flor. I. 13. Polyb. II. 20. Eutrop. II. 10. Florus relates this as occurring before Fabius crossed the Ciminian, while in fact it was nearly 30 years after; unless indeed he is here anticipating the event,

islands,[6] a minute description of which is given by the younger Pliny:—

"They pointed out to me a lake lying below the hill, the Vadimon by name, and told me certain marvellous stories concerning it. I went thither. The lake is in the form of a wheel lying on its side, even all round, without sinuosity or irregularity, but perfectly uniform in shape, as though it had been hollowed out and cut round by the hand of man. The water is whitish rather than blue, inclined to green, and turbid, of sulphureous smell, medicinal taste, and glutinous quality. The lake is but moderate in size, yet it is affected by the winds and swells into waves. No vessel is on its waters, for it is a sacred lake, but grassy islets, covered with reeds and rushes, float on its bosom, and on its margin flourish the plants of the rankest marshes. Each of these islets has a distinct form and size, and all have their edges smoothed off, from constantly rubbing against the shore and against one another. All are equal in height and in buoyancy, for they sink into a sort of boat with a deep keel, which is seen from every side; and there is just as much of the island above as below water. At one time these islands are all joined close together, like a part of the mainland; at another they are driven asunder and scattered by the winds; sometimes thus detached, the wind falling dead, they float apart, motionless on the water. It often happens that the smaller ones stick to the greater, like skiffs to ships of burden; and often both large and small seem to strive together in a race. Again, all driven together into one spot, add to the land on that side, and now here, now there, increase or diminish the surface of the lake; and only cease to contract it, when they float in the middle. It is a well-known fact that cattle attracted by the herbage, are wont to walk on the islets, mistaking them for the shore of the lake; nor do they become aware that they are not on firm ground, till borne away from the shore, they behold with terror the waters stretching around them. Presently, when the wind has carried them again to the bank, they go forth, no more aware of disembarking than they were of their embarkation. The water of this said lake flows out in a stream which, after showing itself for a little space, is lost in a cave, and runs deep underground; and if anything be thrown into it before it thus dives, it is brought to

and mentions it out of its chronological order. But there is probably some confusion between the two routs at the Vadi-

monian. No author mentions both.

[6] Plin. Nat. Hist. II. 96. Senec. Nat. Quæst. III. 25. Sotion, de Mir. Font.

light again where it emerges. I have written of these things to
thee, thinking they would be as novel and pleasing to thee as to
myself, for we both delight in nothing so much as the works of
Nature." [7]

The lake lies beneath the heights, in the plain by the banks of
the Tiber; but he who would expect Pliny's description to be
verified, might search for ever in vain. It is, indeed, no easy
matter to find the lake ; for it has so shrunk in dimensions, that
what must have been a spacious tract of water in the olden time,
is now but a small stagnant pond, almost lost in the tall reeds
and bulrushes that wave over it. These we may conclude represent the islets, which either never had an existence, or have now
clubbed together to stop up the lake.[8] The water has still a
sulphureous appearance, though not too highly flavoured for the
frogs, whose croakings mingling with the shrill chirrup of the
cicala, rise eternally from the pool. I fancied I saw the stream
of which Pliny speaks, in a small ditch which carries the super-
fluous water towards the Tiber ; but I did not perceive it to take
a subterranean course.

Whoever visits the Vadimon, will comprehend how it was that
decisive battles were fought upon its shores. The valley here
forms the natural pass into the inner or central plain of Etruria.
It is a spot, indeed, very like the field of Thrasymene—a low,
level tract, about a mile wide, hemmed in between the heights
and the Tiber, which here takes the place of that lake ; but the
heights rise more steeply and loftily than those by the Thrasymene,
and are even now densely covered with wood, as no doubt they
were in ancient times, the celebrated Ciminian forest extending
thus far. Though the Consul Fabius had once passed that fearful
wood, it was against the express command of the Senate ; so
when the Etruscans were next to be attacked, the Roman general,

---

[7] Plin. Epist. VIII. 20.

[8] This process is still going forward in
certain lakes in Italy—in the Lago d' Isole
Natanti, or Lake of Floating Islands, near
the road from Rome to Tivoli, and well
known from the description of Sir Hum-
phry Davy in his "Last Days of a Philosopher" (see also Westphal's Römische
Kampagne, p. 108), and also in the Lacus
Cutiliæ in Sabina, renowned by the
ancients for its floating islands, and now
called the Pozzo Ratignano. "Its banks
appear to be approaching each other by in-
crustation ; there is no shelving shore, the

rock being suspended over the lake, like
broken ice over a deep abyss." The waters
are sulphureous, yet there are fish in the
lake. "The phenomenon of floating islands
may still be observed ; they are nothing
more than reeds or long coarse grass, the
roots of which bound together by the petri-
fying nature of the water, are sometimes
detached from the shore." Gell's Rome,
II. p. 370. Floating islands are common
enough in the great rivers of South America.
I have seen them even far at sea, carried
out by the tide.

instead of again crossing the mountain, turned its extremity, and there encountered the Etruscan army drawn up in this natural pass into their land, leagued together by a solemn bond to defend their country to the utmost—a determination which caused them to offer so desperate and extraordinary a resistance.[9]

The vale of the Tiber is here rich and beautiful—the low ground highly cultivated with corn, wine, and oil; the slopes on the Etruscan side clothed with dense oak-woods, on the Umbrian with olive-groves and vineyards; the towns of Giove and Penna crown the latter heights; Bassano overhangs the lake from the former. Looking up the stream, Mugnano is seen on its hill, backed by the loftier ground of Bomarzo; looking down, the horizon is bounded by the distant range of the Apennines, with their "silent pinnacles of aged snow."

Bassano has been supposed by Cluver,[1] Cramer,[2] and others, to be the Castellum Amerinum on the Via Amerina, mentioned by the Peutingerian Table, because it overhangs the Vadimon, as Pliny describes the Amerine estate—*Amerina prædia*—of his wife's grandfather to have done.[3] But the Castellum must have been near Orte, as already stated, because the road took a direct course from Nepi to Ameria, and the distance, twenty-six miles, between these places is correctly stated by the Table, but would have been considerably increased had the road made a *détour* to Bassano. Besides, I have myself traced the road by its fragments from Nepi to within a mile or two of Orte, and its course is due north and south, without deviation; and there can be no doubt that it crossed the Tiber by the bridge at Orte, now in ruins. The ground about Bassano may nevertheless have been called Amerine, though the Castellum itself was three or four miles distant.

Bassano is a miserable place, without accommodation for the traveller; and with no signs of antiquity, or anything to interest, beyond its picturesque scenery. It lies on the railway from Rome to Florence, ninety-one kilomètres, or fifty-seven miles from the former city. It is nearly two miles from the Vadimonian Lake, five from Orte, by the direct road, four or five from Bomarzo, seven or eight from Soriano, and the same from Vignanello.

---

[9] Livy says,—non cum Etruscia toties victis, sed cum aliquâ novâ gente, videretur dimicatio esse,—(IX. 39). Müller (II. 1. 4) and Mannert (p. 422) seem to me to be in error in supposing that the Etruscans made their stand on this spot on account of the sacredness of the lake. The nature of the ground, with which those writers seem to have been unacquainted, sufficiently accounts for the fact.

[1] Ital. Ant. II. p. 551.

[2] Ancient Italy, I. p. 224.

[3] Plin. Epist. loc. cit.

CHAPTER XII.

MONTE CIMINO.—*MONS CIMINUS.*

Cimini cum monte lacum.—VIRGIL.

How soon the tale of ages may be told !
A page, a verse, records the fall of fame.
The wreck of centuries—we gaze on you
O cities, once the glorious and the free !—
The lofty tales that charmed our youth renew,
And wondering ask if these their scenes can be.
                                        HEMANS.

WHO that has seen has not hailed with delight the exquisite
little lake of Vico, which lies in the lap of the Ciminian Mount,
just above Ronciglione ? I saw it for the first time one evening
when I strolled up from that town, and came upon it unex-
pectedly, not aware of its close proximity. The sun was sinking
behind the hills, which reared their broad, purple masses into
the clear sky, and shaded half the bosom of the calm lake with
their hues—while the other half reflected the orange and golden
glories of an Italian sunset. Not a sound broke the stillness,
save the chirping of the *cicala* from the trees, whose song served
but to make the silence heard—and not a sign of human life was
there beyond a column of smoke wreathing up whitely in front of
the dark mountains. When I next visited the lake, it was under
the glare of a noonday sun—its calm surface, deepening the
azure of the sky into a vivid sapphire, was dashed at the edge
with reflections of the overhanging woods, in the richest hues of
autumn ; and with Siren smiles it treacherously masked the
destruction it had wrought.[1]

---

[1] The waters of this lake, the ancient
Lacus Ciminus, are said to cover a town
called Succinium, or Saccumum, engulfed
by an earthquake (Ammian. Marcell. XVII.
7, 13 ; Sotion. de Mir. Font.). The latter
writer states the same of the Lacus Sabatinus, or Lago Bracciano. The lake is
evidently the crater of an extinct volcano.
Fable, however, gives it another origin.
When Hercules was on this mount, he was
begged by the inhabitants to give them
some proof of his marvellous strength ;
whereon he drove an iron bar deep into the
earth. When they had tried in vain to stir

Who has not hailed with yet higher delight the view from the summit of the long steep ascent which rises from the shores of the lake to the shoulder of the mountain—more especially if he be for the first time approaching the Eternal City?—for from this height, if the day be clear, he will obtain his first view of Rome.   There lies the vast, variegated expanse of the Campagna at his feet, with its framework of sea and mountain.   There stands Soracte in the midst, which

> "from out the plain
> Heaves like a long-swept wave about to break,
> And on the curl hangs pausing."

The white convent of San Silvestro gleams on its dark craggy crest, as though it were an altar to the god of poetry and light on this his favourite mountain.   There sweeps the long range of Apennines, in grey or purple masses, or rearing some giant, hoary peak, into the blue heaven.   There flows the Tiber at their feet, from time to time sparkling in the sun as it winds through the undulating plain.   Far in the southern horizon swells the Alban Mount with its soft flowing outlines; and apparently at its foot, lies Rome herself, distinguishable more by the cupola of St. Peter's than by the white line of her buildings. Well, traveller, mayest thou gaze, for even in her present fallen state

> Possis nihil urbe Româ
> Visere majus.[2]

Nor must the dense- and many-tinted woods, which clothe the slopes of the mountain around and beneath, be passed without notice.   It is the Ciminian forest, in olden times the terror of the Roman,[3] and still with its majestic oaks and chestnuts vindicating its ancient reputation—*silvæ sunt consule dignæ !*

On descending from the crest of the pass on the road to Viterbo, a new scene broke on my view.   The slopes around and

---

it, they besought the hero to draw it forth, which he did; but an immense flood of water welled up from the hole, and formed the Ciminian Lake. Serv. ad Æn. VII. 697. The height on the northern shore is called Monte Venere—a name it is said to owe to a temple of Venus, that once occupied the summit. But so far as I can learn, the existence of a temple here rests on tradition alone.

[2] Horat. Carm. Sæc. 11.
[3] It was so dreaded by the ancient Romans, that the Senate, even after the great rout of the Etruscans at Sutrium, in the year 444, dispatched legates to the consul Fabius, charging him not to enter the wood (Liv. IX. 36 ; Florus, I. 17); and when it was known that he had done so, all Rome was terror-struck (Liv. IX. 38).

beneath were still densely clothed with wood—a wide plain again lay at my feet—mountains also rose beyond—the sea glittered in a golden line on the horizon—a lake shone out from the plain—even Soracte had its counterpart: the general features of the scene were the same as on the other side of the mountain, but there was more tameness, more monotony in their character, and the same stirring interest did not attach to every spot as the site of some historic event or romantic legend; nor was there one grand focus of attraction to which every other object was subordinate. Yet was it a scene of high interest. It was the great Etruscan plain, the fruitful mother of cities renowned before Rome was—where arose, flourished, and fell that nation which from this plain as from a centre extended its dominion over the greater part of Italy, giving laws, arts, and institutions to the surrounding tribes, and to Rome itself—the twin-sister of Greece in the work of civilising Europe. I could not, as the consul Fabius once did from this same height, admire "the rich fields of Etruria,"[4] for the plain is in most parts uncultivated, with here and there a few patches of wood to relieve its monotonous bareness.

With what pride must an Etruscan have regarded this scene twenty-five centuries since. The numerous cities in the plain were so many trophies of the power and civilisation of his nation. There stood Volsinii, renowned for her wealth and arts, on the shores of her crater-lake—Tuscania reared her towers in the west—Vulci shone out from the plain, and Cosa from the mountain—and Tarquinii, chief of all, asserted her metropolitan

---

[4] Liv. IX. 36—opulenta Etruriæ arva. If it were not expressly stated by Livy that —juga Ciminii montis tenebat, it would be more reasonable to suppose that Fabius crossed from Sutrium by the line of the subsequent Via Cassia, than that he should have scaled this much loftier, more difficult, and dangerous pass. Possibly he chose it as being wholly undefended. He was the first Roman, it is said, who dared to penetrate the dread Ciminian forest, which before his time had never been trod even by the peaceful traveller. It is impossible to believe this statement, and that the forest was utterly pathless (Liv. loc. cit. Flor. loc. cit.), for as the Mount originally stood in the heart of Etruria, there must have been sundry passes across it for communication between the several states.

Besides, as Arnold (Hist. Rome, II. p. 249) observes, the range could not have formed "an impassable barrier." The highest peak rises 3000 feet above the sea, but there are very deep depressions between its crests ; and the shoulder to the south, crossed by the Via Cassia, is of so slight an elevation, that the rise is scarcely perceptible. The difficulty must have lain rather in the density of the forest than in the height of the mountain. Niebuhr (III. p. 279) also disputes Livy's statement, but suggests that the mountain may have been left in a savage state by mutual agreement to serve as a natural frontier between Latium and Etruria. He was evidently, however, quite ignorant of the pass by the Vadimonian Lake, between the foot of the Mount and the Tiber.

supremacy from her far-off cliff-bound heights.   Nearer still, his eye must have rested on city after city, some in the plain, and others on the slope beneath him; while the mountains in the horizon would have carried his thoughts to the glories of Clusium, Perusia, Cortona, Vetulonia, Volaterræ, and other cities of the great Etruscan Confederation. How changed is now the scene! Save Tuscania, which is still inhabited, all within view are now desolate.   Tarquinii has left scarce a vestige of her greatness on the grass-grown heights she once occupied; the very site of Volsinii is disputed; silence has long reigned in the crumbling theatre of Ferentum; the plough yearly furrows the bosom of Vulci; the fox, the owl, and the bat, are the sole tenants of the vaults within the ruined walls of Cosa : and of the rest, the greater part have neither building, habitant, nor name —nothing but the sepulchres around them to prove they ever had an existence.

Did he turn to the southern side of the mountain ?—his eye wandered from city to city of no less renown, studding the plain beneath him—Veii, Fidenæ, Falerii, Fescennium, Capena, Nepete, Sutrium—all then powerful, wealthy, and independent.   Little did he foresee that yon small town on the banks of the Tiber, would prove the destruction of them all, and even of his nation and language, of his religion and civilisation.

CHAPTER XIII.

VITERBO.—*SURRINA.*

Cernimus exemplis oppida posse mori.—Rutilius.

Multa retro rerum jacet, atque ambagibus ævi
Obtegitur densâ caligine mersa vetustas.—Sil. Italicus.

Almost every town in Italy and Spain has its chronicle, written generally by some priest or monk, who has made it a labour of love to record the history, real or imaginary, of his native place from the creation down to his own time. In these monographs, as they may be termed, the great object appears to have been to exalt the antiquity and magnify the pristine importance of each respective town, often at the expense of every other. It is this feeling which has ascribed to many of the cities of Spain a foundation by Japhet or Tubal-Cain; and to this foolish partiality we owe many a bulky volume replete with dogmatical assertions, distortions of history, unwarranted readings or interpretations of ancient writers; and even, it may be, blackened with forgery.

Among those who have been guilty of this foulest of literary crimes, stands foremost in impudence, unrivalled in voluminous perseverance, Fra Giovanni Nanni, commonly called Annio di Viterbo, a Dominican monk of this town, who lived in the fifteenth century. He was a wholesale and crafty forger; he did not write the history of his native place, but pretended to have discovered fragments of various ancient writers, most of which are made, more or less directly, to bear testimony to its antiquity and pristine importance. Besides these fragments of Berosus, Manetho, Archilochus, Xenophon, Fabius Pictor, Cato, Antoninus, and others, he forged, with the same object, a marble tablet, with an edict purporting to be of King Desiderio, the last of the Lombard dynasty, in which it is decreed that " within one wall shall be included the three towns, Longula, Vetulonia, and Tirrena, called Volturna, and the whole city thus formed shall be called Etruria or Viterbum," which city Annio further attempted to prove one of the Twelve, and the metropolis of ancient Etruria. His forgeries for some time imposed on the world; but they have been long exposed, and he is now universally branded as an impostor.[1]

One of his statements, however, that Viterbo was the site of the Fanum Voltumnæ, the shrine at which the princes of Etruria were wont to assemble in solemn conclave to deliberate on the affairs of the Confederation—has been assented to by many who denounce him, and is an opinion that has found supporters among antiquaries of note.[2] That the Fanum was somewhere in this district is probable enough; but as Livy, who alone mentions it, has given no clue to its locality,[3] and as no inscriptions have thrown light on the subject, it can be but pure conjecture to assign it to this or that particular site. Viterbo, inasmuch as it contains a church named Santa Maria in Volturna, may be allowed to put in some claim to that honour, certainly stronger than can be urged for Castel d' Asso. Yet such is far from amounting to positive evidence, for, to say nothing of the corruption of words in the course of two thousand years, Voltumna or Volturna was a deity of the Etruscans, and probably had temples in various parts of the land.

That the long lost Vetulonia occupied this or a neighbouring site, is an opinion held not only by Annio, and the early antiquaries of Italy, but even in our own times has found its advocates, who cite in support of their views the oriental magnificence of the sepulchres of Norchia and Castel d' Asso.[4] A much more probable site will be indicated for Vetulonia in a subsequent chapter.

Though Viterbo has been a bone of contention to archæologists, ever since the days of Annio, its name contains a clear indication of its antiquity, being evidently compounded of *Vetus urbs.*[5] There are, moreover, indisputable proofs of the existence of an Etruscan town on this spot, in the numerous sepulchral caves in

---

[1] The authenticity of the Desiderio decree has been much disputed. Even Holstenius (Adnot. ad Clurer. p. 68) contended for its authenticity; and as late as 1777 Faure maintained it to be genuine.

[2] Cluverius, II. p. 565. Cellarius, Geog. Ant. I. p. 581. Ambrosch, Mem. Inst. IV. p. 149.

[3] Liv. IV. 23, 25, 61; V. 17; VI. 2.

[4] Inghir. Mem. Inst. IV. p. 98 et seq. This has been ably controverted by Dr.

Ambrosch, in his reply to the letters of Inghirami on the subject.

[5] Yet old Fazio degli Uberti could find another derivation—

　"Che nel principio Veghionza fu detta,
　Sino al tempo che a Roma fu nemica,
Ma vinta poi agli Roman dilecta,
　Tanto per le buone acque e dolcie sito
　Che'n vita Erbo del suo nome tragecta."
　　　　　DITTAMUNDI, III. cap. 10.

the cliffs around, and in the tombs which from time to time have been excavated, yielding genuine Etruscan objects. No remains of the ancient town itself are extant, beyond the foundations of a bridge near the cathedral, composed of large rectangular blocks of *emplecton* masonry, rusticated and uncemented, and sundry sewers cut in the neighbouring cliffs. The blocks are of the same hard *peperino* that forms the pavement of the town. In dimensions and arrangement they are like Etruscan; but the general style of the masonry, and the peculiarity of the material, so different from the red tufo rock on which these piers rest, induce me to pronounce them of Roman construction; if they be not, as Canina suggests, a re-construction, in still later times, of the ancient materials.[6] The name of the ancient town seems from Latin inscriptions to have been Surrina or Sorrina,[7] and it appears to have occupied the cliff-bound plateau on which the Cathedral stands.

In the Palazzo Comunale, in an upper room, is shown the marble tablet with the decree of the king Desiderio, already mentioned, the authenticity of which has given rise to so much discussion,[8]—and the Tabula Cibellaria, another of Annio's forgeries, by which he sought to make it appear that his town was as ancient as Corythus, or prior to the foundation of Troy. When I first knew Viterbo, there was a respectable collection of Etruscan relics up-stairs, comprising sepulchral urns, conical *cippi* with inscriptions, small idols of bronze, and other objects of the same metal, pottery of *bucchero*, black or uncoloured, showing antiquity, not richness or elegance—with few of the beautiful figured vases, so abundant on the more luxurious sites of Vulci,

[6] Canina (Etruria Marit. Vol. II. p. 70, tav. 100) gives an illustration of this piece of walling.

[7] The existence of a "Surrina or Sorrina Nova" is made known by sundry inscriptions, most of which have been found in the neighbourhood. Muratori, 201, 6, and 1083, 8; Mariani, de Etrur. Metrop. p. 125. The names of Surina, and Civitas Surinæ, were attached to the place in the middle ages; Suriannm, also, is said often to occur in old documents. Orioli (Nouvel. Ann. Inst. 1836, p. 41) says, the town of Surrina Nova stood half a mile from Viterbo, just where Annio placed it, between the Grotta di Riello, the stream of the Arcione, and the modern baths, where are numerous ruins and manifest traces of a

town. Marini (Frat. Arval. II. p. 424), referred Surrina Nova to Soriano on the eastern slope of the Ciminian; but Orioli would rather consider that town to be the Surrina Vetus, from which this, distinguished as Nova, may have been originally peopled. To me, however, it appears more probable, that the old town of this name was that on the very site of Viterbo, on the heights of the Cathedral, as already stated, and that when the Roman settlement was made on the lower ground, indicated by Orioli, it received the epithet of "Nova," while that on the original site was distinguished only as "the old town,—*vetus urbs*—of which Viterbo is obviously a derivative.

[8] It may be found in Gruter, p. 220.

Tarquinii, or Clusium. But all these objects have been carried away by the Jesuits, and nothing is now left but a few monuments from Musarna, stored in a room on the ground floor. Here are sixteen sarcophagi of *nenfro*, some with bas-reliefs on the sides, and all with the effigy of the deceased of life-size reclining on the lid.   They are all from the newly discovered Etruscan town of Musarna, and from one tomb, which we learn from the inscriptions to have been that of the family "Alethnas," a name suggestive of a Greek origin. A singular feature in these inscriptions is that they are not confined to the sarcophagi and lids as usual ; but some are carved on the recumbent effigies themselves, in one case on the bosom, in three on the thigh—as if the figures were of bronze instead of stone. Another peculiarity is that the flesh of some of the males is coloured yellow instead of red. In the relief, on one sarcophagus, a soul is represented in a *biga*, led by a demon, and followed by Charun. The art displayed in these monuments is very rude, but it is the rudeness of the Decadence, not of primitive art.

The only other collection of Etruscan antiquities at Viterbo is in the possession of Signor Giosafat Bazzichelli, the proprietor of Castel d'Asso, the discoverer of Musarna, and the explorer of many other cemeteries in the great Etruscan plain, and is the accumulated fruit of his researches. He is also the Government Inspector of excavations for this district. Of his courtesy and readiness to impart the results of his experience, I retain a grateful recollection. He possesses some beautiful Greek vases in the Second style, from Corneto, of which the following are the most noteworthy :—

Amphora.—Four naked, phallic Fauns in procession, each carrying a draped Mænad on his shoulder, one of whom is playing the lyre, and two the double-pipes.

Amphora.—A *quadriga* drawn by horses of surprising life and spirit.

Amphora.—Hercules overcoming Nereus.

Amphora.—Hercules contending with the Amazons.

Some other vases of the same form and style, with a brilliant lustre, and in wonderful preservation—all from Corneto.

You see here—what is not seen elsewhere—the produce of excavations at Castel d'Asso. The vases, which are numerous, are in a very early style, but for the most part pseudo-archaic, mere Etruscan imitations of the so-called Phœnician style. When confronted with genuine vases of that style, the imitation is palpable. Yet they are not of late date, but contemporaneous, for they are always found in the same tombs with vases of *bucchero,* the earliest native pottery of Etruria. There are other painted vases in the late style of Magna Graecia, and these also are local imitations. So that Castel d'Asso produces pottery of a very early and a very late period—of 600 B.C. and of 250 B.C.—while the art of the intervening centuries is not represented. The tombs with architectural façades probably belonged to this interval; for, though ransacked long ages since, the fragments of pottery found in them are not of the archaic *bucchero,* but of ordinary plain ware of a later date. Signor Bazzichelli possesses a beautiful bronze *specchio,* from this site, representing Venus (TURAN) and Adonis (ATUNS) embracing; another, of Hercules overcoming Hippolyta, Queen of the Amazons; with other mirrors of inferior art, and numerous strigils, among them one of iron, retaining fragments of the cloth in which it was wrapt.[9]

In the wall of the church in front of this palace, is a Roman sarcophagus of marble, bearing a bas-relief of a lion contending with a boar. An inscription shows it to have been raised in honour of a Viterbian damsel of the twelfth century, who had such extraordinary beauty, that, like Helen, she became the cause of a war—"causa teterrima belli." On her account the city was besieged by the Romans; and after unsuccessful assaults they agreed to raise the siege, on condition that the fair Galiana displayed her charms from the ramparts—an instance of "the might, the majesty of loveliness" never surpassed in any age.

It may partly be owing to this Italian Helen that the daughters of Viterbo still enjoy a proverbial reputation for beauty. But these are delicate matters, not to be handled by an antiquary. What more shall I say of Viterbo? It was the second city in the Papal State within the limits of ancient Etruria, and can still boast of thirteen or fourteen thousand inhabitants, and in former times was often the residence of the Popes. I will say nothing of the remains of Santa Rosa, the holy patroness of the city—of the pulpit of San Bernardino of Siena—of the celebrated "Deposition" of Sebastian del Piombo, from the design of Michael Angelo—of the palace where Olimpia Pamfili held her revels—of the Gothic Cathedral, stained with the royal blood of England[1]—of the quaint Episcopal palace adjoining, whose vast hall has witnessed

[9] Bull. Inst. 1874, p. 257.

[1] The cathedral is dedicated to S. Lorenzo, and occupies the site of a temple to Hercules, mentioned in early Christian documents.

the election of some half-dozen popes—are they not all recorded by Murray?   Yet I must testify to the neatness and cleanliness of Viterbo—to the Tuscan character of its architecture—to its well-paved, ever dry streets—to its noble fountains, proverbial for their beauty—and I must not omit the abundant civility experienced in the hotel of the "Angelo," which the traveller should make his head-quarters while exploring the antiquities of the neighbourhood.

THE THEATRE OF FERENTO—THE CENTRAL GATE.

CHAPTER XIV.

FERENTO. *FERENTINUM.*

Si te grata quies, et primam somnus in horam
Delectat ; si te pulvis strepitusque rotarum,
Si lædit caupona ; Ferentinum ire jubebo.—Horat.

The neighbourhood of Viterbo is rich in antiquities. It was not usual with the southern Etruscans to build on the summits of lofty mountains, or even on the higher slopes— therefore no remains are found on the Ciminian itself—but all along its base stood city after city, now for the most part in utter desolation, yet whose pristine magnificence can be traced in the sepulchres around them. The vast plain, also, north of the Ciminian, now in great part uncultivated, and throughout most thinly inhabited, teems with vestiges of long extinct civilisation.

Five miles north of Viterbo, on the left of the road to Monte Fiascone, and near the Ponte Fontanile, is a remarkable assemblage of ruins, called Le Casacce del Bacucco. One is an edifice of two stories, by some thought a temple of Serapis, most probably because they fancied they could trace a corruption of this

word in its name, Bagni delle Serpi.[1] It is more vulgarly called
La Lettighetta, or the Warming-pan. Then there are several
quadrilateral buildings, evidently baths; one retaining traces of
some magnificence, being surmounted by an octagon which
originally supported a cupola. From the character of these
ruins, and the abundance of thermal springs in this district, it
has been with great probability supposed that this is the site of
the Aquæ Passeris of antiquity.[2] All these ruins are clearly of
Roman times; but there is one monument on this site apparently
of Etruscan construction. It is a mound of tufo shaped like a
cone, hollowed into a tomb, and girt with rectangular travertine
masonry, like the tumuli of Tarquinii. Its interior is very
plain.[3]

Considerably to the east of Bacucco, and about five miles north
of Viterbo stand the ruins of an Etruscan city, now called Férento
or Férenti. It is the ancient Ferentinum of Etruria,[4] the birthplace of the emperor Otho; and must not be confounded with the
town of the same name in the land of the Hernici. That, the
"Ferentinum of the rock," stands on the summit of a lofty hill,

---

[1] Excavations were made here in 1830,
and statues and mosaic pavements were
brought to light. Bull. Inst. 1831, p. 84;
Ann. Inst. 1835, 1—7. Camilli.

[2] Cluver (II. p. 561). The Peutingerian
Table places Aquæ Passeris between Forum
Cassii and Volsinii, eleven miles from the
former, and nine from the latter. If Vetralla be the site of Forum Cassii, the
distance to Bacucco is about correct, but
thence to Volsinii is fourteen miles; and
this distance Cluverius thinks was originally
stated by the Table, but that XIIII. was
corrupted by the transcriber into VIIII.
which might very easily occur.

Professor Orioli also, who has published
a long Latin inscription, found near Viterbo,
referring to the springs and course of these
"Aquæ Passerianæ," is of opinion that the
baths occupied the site of Bacucco. (Ann.
Instit. 1829, p. 174—179.) But Canina
takes the Bullicame to be the Aquæ Passeris,
because there are no other hot springs in the
neighbourhood to which Martial's description can apply—fervidi fluctus Passeris (VI.
Epig. 42). The name of Le Serpi, vulgarly
given to the building at Bacucco, may be a
corruption of "Scirpinnum," an estate
mentioned by the said inscription as traversed by the Via Ferentiensis. Etr.

Marit. II., p. 133.

[3] Bull. Inst. 1831, p. 85. It is considered by Lenoir (Annali dell' Inst. 1832,
p. 277), from the character of its mouldings,
to be of Roman construction, in imitation
of tombs genuinely Etruscan; but I have
already shown, in treating of the tombs of
Falleri, that a resemblance to Roman architecture is not necessarily an evidence against
an Etruscan origin; and it is clear that the
Romans could as well imitate the Etruscans
in the mouldings as in the general character
of the tomb. For an illustration of this tomb,
see Mon. Ined. Inst. I. tav. XLI. 16.

[4] By Strabo (V. p. 226), Tacitus (Hist.
II. 50), Pliny (III. 8), and Suetonius (Otho
1.), it is called Ferentinum; by Ptolemy
(Geog. p. 72, ed. Bertii) Pherentia; by
Vitruvius (II. 7) Ferentum. It may also
be referred to as Ferentum by Suctonius
(Vespas. 3). It seems to have given name
to an Etruscan family, mentioned on a
sepulchral urn of Perugia—"Aruth Phrenti-
nate Pisico." It is strange that Vermiglioli,
who gives this inscription (Iscriz. Perug.
I. 319), should have thought of an analogy
with the Frentani of Samnium, or with the
Ferentinates of Latium, rather than with
this town of Etruria.

and to the traveller from Rome to Naples by the upper road, is
an object of interest on account of its massive Cyclopean walls;
this is on the level of the great Etruscan plain, girt about, however, by profound ravines. Nor must it be confounded with
Ferentum in Apulia, a town also situated in a plain,

———————arvum
Pingue tenent humilis Ferenti.[5]

We have no record of this town in Etruscan times, though the
sepulchres around it give sure evidence of such an antiquity. It
must have been a dependency of Volsinii. The earliest mention
of it is in the time of Augustus, when it was a Roman colony of
small importance,[6] and, if the passage of Horace which heads
this chapter refer to this town,[7] it was then a quiet, secluded,
country village. Then we hear of it as the birthplace of the
Emperor Otho;[8] and as the site of a temple of Fortune,[9] probably the Etruscan goddess, Nurtia, who had a celebrated shrine
at Volsinii, not many miles distant. It continued in existence
after the fall of the Empire, and rose into the importance of an
episcopal see,[1] but was utterly destroyed in the eleventh century,
by the Viterbesi, in their zeal to exterminate a heresy with which
its inhabitants were tainted, that heresy being that they represented Christ on the cross with his eyes open, instead of being
orthodoxly closed!

The area of the town is covered with ruins of the three epochs
into which its history may be divided. The greater part are
foundations of houses and other structures of the middle ages.
There are considerable remains of Roman pavement of polygonal
blocks of basalt; and several Roman structures in ruin, among
which a tower with a vaulted roof is prominent. Some of the
ruins of later date are raised on foundations of Roman antiquity.
The walls of the town are in great part overthrown, but fragments
of them remain, and many of the rectangular blocks which com-

[5] Hor. III. Od. 4, 15.

[6] Strabo, V. p. 226; Frontinus (de
Colon.) also calls it a colony; Vitruvius (loc.
cit.) and Tacitus (Hist. II. 50) a municipium.

[7] Cluver (II. p. 563) is decidedly of this
opinion; and shows that it could not have
applied to the other Ferentinum, which
was precisely amid the dust and the noise

of that great thoroughfare, the Latin Way.
Cramer (I. p. 225) follows his opinion.

[8] Sueton. Otho I.; Tacit. Hist. II. 50;
Aur. Vict. Imp. Otho.

[9] Tacit. Annal. XV. 53.

[1] Cluver. II. p. 562. Camilli, Mon. di
Viterbo, pp. 62, 84. An inscription recorded by Orelli calls it "splendidissima
civitas."

posed them, lie scattered on the slopes around.[2] The sites of several gates are distinctly traceable.

But the grand monument at Férento is the theatre. In its perfect state it must have been a truly imposing edifice; even now, though all the winds of heaven play through its open arches, it is a most majestic ruin, with every advantage of situation to increase its effect on the senses. For it stands on the brink of a precipice, overhanging a wooded and picturesque ravine, amid solitude, ruin, and desolation, where for centuries man has left his dwelling to the falcon, the owl, the bat, the viper, and the lizard, and where his foot or voice now rarely calls forth echoes— with the wide plain on every hand, the dark gloomy mass of the Ciminian in front, the swelling Mount of Fiascone behind, and the snowy ranges of the Umbrian Apennines in the horizon.

The stage-front of the theatre is one hundred and thirty-six feet in length, of massive masonry, composed of large rectangular volcanic blocks uncemented; not, as in the Etruscan walls already described, laid lengthways and endways in alternate courses, but like those in the northern division of the land, arranged rather with regard to the size and form of the blocks themselves than to any predetermined order or style of masonry. From its peculiar character, and its evidently superior antiquity to the rest of the structure, I am inclined to regard this façade as Etruscan. The construction of its gates might be cited as an objection. There are seven of these, the largest in the centre,— all with flat architraves composed of cunciform blocks holding together on the principle of the arch, though without cement; as is proved in one gateway, where, the masonry being dislocated, the keystone has slipt down several inches, yet is still supported by the contiguous blocks.[3] This mode of construction, like the arch itself, has generally been supposed a Roman invention; but

---

[2] The extant portions of the walls are generally of small masonry, either Roman or of "the low times;" but there are fragments on the northern side, of more ancient date and more massive character. They are indeed very peculiar, the blocks being nearly square, without any regularity in size or arrangement, and being often let into one another,—more like the masonry of that singular quadrangle on the Via Appia, which Gell called the "Campus Sacer Horatiorum," but which Canina, with much more probability, regards as an *ustrina*, than any other ancient walling in Etruria; though there is also some resemblance to the pier of a ruined bridge at Veii, mentioned at page 10 of this work.

[3] This has fallen since the above was written, and the architrave is destroyed. Its place is seen to the left in the woodcut at page 156.

The central gate, which is represented in the woodcut, is more than 12 ft. in height, and is 10 ft. 2 in. wide; the next on either hand, 8 ft. 1 in.; the next two, 7 ft. 6 in.; and the outer gates, 7 ft. 3 in. in width.

there is now little doubt that the arch in Italy had an Etruscan origin; therefore, seeing the perfection to which the arched vault had been brought at a very early age in the Cloaca Maxima, there is nothing in the peculiar style or construction of this flat arch which militates against its being of Etruscan formation; for the principle of cuneiform sustentation once discovered, the progress from one application of it to another must have been short and easy.

This massive masonry rises to the height of ten courses. On it rests a mass of Roman brickwork, of Imperial times, with several arched openings, intended to admit light into the passage within. This passage, or *postscenium*, which runs the whole length of the façade, is about four feet wide, and its inner wall, or the *scena*, is also of red Roman brick. One vast mass of this wall has been loosened from its foundation, probably by the same convulsion of nature which dislocated the gateway, and reclines against the outer wall, adding much to the picturesque effect of the ruins. The passage must have been a means of communication for the actors behind the scenes, and in two parts it widens into a chamber—the *parascenion* of the Greek theatre—for their convenience in changing costumes. Within the theatre all is ruin—a chaos of fallen masonry, shapeless masses of rock and red brick-work, overgrown with weeds and moss—the *orchestra* filled up to the level of the stage—not a seat of the *cavea* remaining, that part of the theatre being only distinguishable by the semicircle of arches which inclosed it. These are of regular and massive masonry, of a hard grey tufo whitened by lichen—a whiteness quite dazzling in the sunshine. The semicircle which they originally formed is not complete. Commencing with the first arch at the south-western angle of the arc, there are eleven in an unbroken series; then occurs a gap, where one has been destroyed; then follow nine more in succession; and six or seven are wanting to complete the semicircle. Attached to the first is another, at an angle with it, indicating the line of the chord of the arc, the division between the *cavea* and the *proscenium*; and its distance from the walls of the *scena* shows the depth of the stage. These arches are beautifully formed, the blocks shaped with uniformity, and fitted with great nicety, though without cement.[4] Canina, the Roman architect, regards them as an in-

---

[4] These arches vary from 7½ ft. to 9 ft. in span. They are based on pillars about 3 ft. square, each a single block of stone, supporting a simple lip-impost, also a single block; as is likewise the mass raised on it, from which springs the arch on either side.

terior structure only, and thinks there was an outer range of arches for the external adornment of the theatre, as in those of Pompeii, and of Marcellus at Rome. He says that, from its excellent state of preservation, the scena in this ruin gives us a more complete idea of that part in ancient theatres than can be derived from any other remain of the same description extant, particularly in the distinction between the "royal gate" in the centre, and the "stranger-gates" on either hand.[5] Canina pronounced this theatre a Roman structure, as late as the time of Otho ;[6] yet the lower part of the façade has an air of much superior antiquity, and from its resemblance to the masonry of other Etruscan sites, has strong claims to be considered Etruscan.[7]

Ferentum, though small, and probably at no time of political importance, was celebrated for the beauty of its public monuments. Vitruvius cites them as exhibiting "the infinite virtues" of a stone hewn from certain quarries, called "Anitianæ," in the territory of Tarquinii, and especially in the neighbourhood of the Volsinian Lake. This stone, says he, was similar to that of the Alban Mount in colour, i.e., it was grey like peperino ; it was proof alike against frost and fire, and of extreme hardness and durability, as might be seen from the monuments of Ferentum, which were made of it. "For there are noble statues of wondrous workmanship, and likewise figures of smaller size, together with foliage and acanthi, delicately carved, which albeit they be ancient, appear as fresh as if they were but just now finished." The brass-founders, he adds, find this stone most useful for moulds. "Were these quarries near the City, it would be well to

---

The length of the chord of the arc, or the greatest width of the theatre, according to my measurement, is exactly 200 English feet. The depth of the stage is 33 feet.

[5] Vitruv. V. 6. The seven gates in the outer wall are a very unusual number ; but in the scena there is only the legitimate number of three ; the rest opening into the postscenium alone. There are no traces of a portico at the back of the theatre, as was common in Greek edifices of this description. Vitruv. V. 9.

This is certainly the best preserved scena in Italy ; but that of Taormina in Sicily is more perfect, having a second story ; and that of Aspendus in Pamphylia is entire, with three stories inside, and four outside, as I learn from the drawings of my friend, Mr. Edward Falkener.

[6] Etr. Marit. II., pp. 132, 141. The plan of this theatre, and its measurements in Tuscan braccia, are given in the Annals of the Institute 1839. Tav. d' Agg. F.

[7] The semicircle of arches, though of the same material as this façade, and very massive, seems, from the regularity of its masonry, to be of later date. I regard it as Roman. That the brickwork is but a repair of a more ancient structure is most clear, from the irregularity of the upper line of the masonry below it, and from the brickwork filling up its deficiencies. See the woodcut at page 156. It appears to me probable that the original Etruscan theatre having fallen into decay, Otho, or one of the early Emperors, put it into repair.

construct everything of this stone."[8]　Pliny speaks of this stone
in the same laudatory terms, but calls it a white *silex*.[9]　Canina
takes this stone to be *nenfro*;[1] but *nenfro* was found at Gabii,
and was well known and much used at Rome.　Moreover, *nenfro*
has not the properties assigned to this stone by Vitruvius.
When last at Férento, I sought particularly to obtain light on
this subject.　Among the numerous blocks with which the site is
strewed, I remarked very few fragments of architectural decoration; nothing that would at all bear out the praises of Vitruvius.[2]
The cliffs beneath the town are a sort of travertine; yet the
masonry of the theatre is of a yellowish tufo, not unlike *nenfro*;
and the town walls are composed of the same or of limestone.
This latter, which is also found in abundance among the scattered masses, seems too hard for the chisel.　I could perceive
nothing which answered to the description of Vitruvius.

In the neighbourhood of Férento are sepulchres, some of
Roman, but most of Etruscan construction.　A few of these are
tumuli, not of the large size seen at Veii, rather like those so
abundant at Tarquinii; but the majority are caves hollowed in the
rocks.　Orioli mentions some remarkable tombs in a plain near
the town, called Piano de' Pozzi, because these tombs are entered
by oblong wells or shafts sunk to a great depth in the earth, with
niches cut in the sides for the feet and hands, as in the tombs of
Civita Castellana and Falleri.　One of the shafts into which he
descended was eighty feet deep, another, one hundred and
twenty; and at the bottom were horizontal passages, opening at
intervals into sepulchral chambers.[3]

The visitor may vary his route on his return to Viterbo, by
way of Vitorchiano, a small town three or four miles from Férento.
A competent guide, however, is requisite, for there is merely a
foot-path.　Vitorchiano seems to have been an Etruscan site, from

---

[8] Vitruv. II. 7.

[9] Plin. Nat. Hist. XXXVI. 49.

[1] Canina, Arch. Ant. VIII. p. 86.
But he subsequently altered his opinion,
and in his last work (Etruria Marit. II.,
p. 40) he asserts that the quarries in question have been recently found near Bag-
narèa, and that the stone is now used at
Rome for pavements.　He maintains that
the lower part of the *scena* and the arches
of the *cavea* of the theatre at Ferento are
all constructed of the stone from these
quarries (II. p. 142).

[2] There is a stone, quarried at Manziana,
near the Lake of Bracciano, which has
some of the properties ascribed to that mentioned by Vitruvius and Pliny, and is
much used in Rome, at the present day, for
moulds for metal-casting.

[3] Orioli ap. Inghir. Monumenti Etruschi
IV. p. 189.　In Magna Græcia also such
tombs have been found, the shafts to which
are sunk sometimes perpendicularly, like
wells, sometimes obliquely, as in the
Egyptian pyramids. — De Jorio. Sepol.
Ant. p. 10.

the slight excavations which have been made in its neighbourhood. Its ancient name is unknown, but in 1435 it was colonised
by the inhabitants of Norchia, who deserted their native town on
account of its insalubrity, and migrated hither. Hence its modern
name Vitorchiano (Vicus Orclanus).[4] It possesses the exclusive
right of providing servants for the Senator of Rome—that solitary
representative of the mighty body which once ruled the world.
This privilege is derived, tradition asserts, from classic times, and
was accorded in perpetuity to Vitorchiano by a certain emperor,
because one of its townsmen extracted a thorn from his foot. In
virtue thereof, every forty years, the principal families in the place
assemble and draw lots for their order of annual service ; each
family sending one of its members to Rome in its turn, or selling
the privilege, which custom has fixed at a certain price. The
truth of this may be tested by any one who chooses to inquire on
the Capitol of the Senator's servants, distinguished by their red
and yellow, beef-eating costume. The validity of the privilege
was contested, some years since, and the Vitorchianesi came off
with flying colours.

[4] Ann. Inst. 1833, p. 21.

CHAPTER XV.

BOMARZO.

Miremur periisse homines ?—monumenta fatiscunt,
Mors etiam saxis nominibusque venit.—Ausonius.

Ecce libet pisces Tyrrhenaque monstra
Dicere.   Ovid.

About twelve miles east of Viterbo, on the same slope of the
Ciminian, is the village of Bomarzo, in the immediate neighbourhood of an Etruscan town where extensive excavations have been
made. The direct road to it runs along the base of the mountain,
but the excursion may be made more interesting by a détour to
Férento, which must be done in the saddle, the road being quite
impracticable for vehicles.

From Férento the path leads across a deep ravine, past the
village of Le Grotte di Santo Stefano, whose name marks the
existence of caves in its neighbourhood,[1] and over the open heath
towards Bomarzo. But before reaching that place, a wooded
ravine, Fosso della Vezza, which forms a natural fosse to the
Ciminian, has to be crossed, and here the proverb—*Chi va piano
va sano*—must be borne in mind. A more steep, slippery, and
dangerous tract I do not remember to have traversed in Italy.
Stiff miry clay, in which the steeds will anchor fast; rocks
shelving and smooth-faced, like inclined planes of ice, are the
alternatives. Let the traveller take warning, and not pursue this
track after heavy rains. It would be advisable, especially if ladies
are of the party, to return from Férento to Viterbo, and to take
the direct road thence to Bomarzo. A diligence runs daily
between Viterbo and the railway station at Orte, passing not far
from Bomarzo.

[1] I could not learn that excavations had
been made here, though at Monte Calvello,
about 1½ mile beyond, Ruggieri of Viterbo
excavated in 1845 for Prince Doria, but
with no great success. He found, however,
another well-tomb, similar to those of
Féreuto, the shaft to which was 127 palms
deep.

This is a village of considerable size situated on a wooded cliff-bound platform, with an old castle of the Borghese family at the verge of the precipice. It commands a glorious view of the vale of the Tiber, and the long chain of Umbrian and Sabine Apennines to the east; of the vast Etruscan plain to the north, with Monte Fiascone like a watch-tower in the midst, and the giant masses of Monte Cetona and Monte Amiata in the far horizon. Like most villages in the old Papal State, Bomarzo is squalid in the extreme; so that as we rode down its main street, not a house could we see whose exterior promised decent accommodation. We pulled up at one of the best, the Casa Fosci, to which we had been directed as a place where travellers were entertained.

One great point of contrast between France and Italy—I may say, between northern and southern Europe—is that in every French village or hamlet, be it ever so small, there is some one house, often several, where Pierre or Jean so-and-so "donne à boire et à manger," or "loge à pied et à cheval;" but in Central and Southern Italy such signs are as rare as notices of spiritual refreshment and halting-places for the devotee are abundant. Here and there a withered bush at a doorway shows that wine may be had within; but as to an inn, except on the great high-ways—you might as well look for a club-house. Some one or more of the most respectable inhabitants of these country-towns and villages is always, however—thank Mercury!—ready to entertain the traveller, for a consideration—for what will not an Italian do for gain?—especially the Romans, who, however unlike in some points, resemble their ancestors in thirst for foreign spoil. "Omnia Romæ cum pretio"—holds good now as in Juvenal's day. This occasional Boniface is generally a man of decayed fortunes, and, as in this instance, shows his gentle blood by his courtesy and attention, and by doing everything that the slender resources of a country village will allow, to contribute to the traveller's comfort. The ruder sex may be content with their modicum of this, and thank God it is not less, but should ladies desire to explore the antiquities of Bomarzo I can scarcely recommend them to make more than a flying visit.

The site of the Etruscan town, which Bomarzo represents, lies on a platform nearly two miles to the north of the village, separated from it by the deep ravine of La Vezza. From the brow of the further height the valley of the Tiber opened beneath us, the royal river winding through it, washing the base of many a town-capt height, of which that of Mugnano was the nearest and most prominent, and that of Orte the most distant, while midway lay the Vadimonian lake, on whose shores the Roman eagle twice soared in triumph, and the fate of Etruria was doubly sealed as a dependent nation.[2]

The first ruin which met our eye was some Roman baths, in three parallel vaults of *opus incertum*, very massive in character. They are clearly of Roman construction; for cement, though not unknown to the Etruscans, was rarely, if ever, used in their architecture—never to such an extent as to form the principal portion of the masonry. This ruin is without the ancient town, and the platform on which it stands, called Pian della Colonna, is united to that of the town by a narrow neck of land. Here Ruggieri of Viterbo made excavations for Prince Borghese, and found no less than twenty *specchj* in one tomb.[3]

On passing this strait, fragments of pottery, bricks, and wrought stone strewn over the ground, showed us we were on the site of former habitation; but no more definite remains could I perceive than some fragments of red tessellated pavement—probably marking the site of an *impluvium*, or tank in the court of a private house. The town must have been of very small importance, for its size is limited by the natural boundaries of cliffs, save at the narrow neck already mentioned; and the space thus circumscribed forms a single field of no great dimensions. Of the ancient walls not one stone remains on another; but beneath the brow of the hill on the east lie a few of the blocks, of red tufo, and of the dimensions usual in Etruscan walls in the volcanic district. In the cliff, on the same side, are two sewers opening in the rock, similar to those on other Etruscan sites.

The name of this town in Etruscan times we have no means of determining. It has been supposed to be Mæonia, or Pneonia, but there is no authority for this in ancient writers. By others it has been thought to be Polimartium; but as this is a name mentioned only in works of the middle ages,[4] it may have had no connection with the Etruscan town, but may have been simply the original of the village of Bomarzo.

The existence of an Etruscan town on this site had for ages been forgotten, when some years since it was proved by the dis-

---

[2] See Chapter XI. Mugnano claims to be the birthplace of Biagio Sinibaldi, a famous traveller of the olden time, who visited Ceylon, Japan, the Eastern Archipelago, China, and Tartary, at a date when Europe imported little from the East but fables and the plague. May not his own existence be called into question?—may he not be an European embodiment of the oriental myth of Sinbad the Sailor?

[3] Bull. Inst. 1845, p. 21.

[4] Dempster de Etrur. Reg. II. p. 110.

covery of tombs containing articles of value and interest. Excavations were commenced in 1830, and have since been carried on with various success.

The platforms to the south and west of the town seem to have been the chief depositories of its dead. A few tombs are seen in the cliffs beneath the walls, but the greater part are sunk deep below the surface of the ground as at Tarquinii and Vulci, and were entered by long narrow passages, descending obliquely. Though very many have been excavated, few now remain open; the greater part, as at Veii and Vulci, have been reclosed, in order to save for tillage the few yards of earth occupied by the entrance-passages. Many tombs do not merit preservation, but on the other hand it is well known that some of the most interesting opened in former years in this and other cemeteries are not now to be entered, and their very sites are forgotten.

The principal group of tombs that still remain open, is on the edge of the hill facing Bomarzo. Two of them merit a few words of description. One is called

Grotta della Colonna

from a massive pillar of Doric-like simplicity, which supports the ceiling. The chamber is about thirteen feet square, and seven in height, with a roof slightly vaulted, in the form of a camber-arch. The door is of the usual Etruscan form, smaller above than below, like Egyptian and Doric doorways; and the wall on each side of it, within the tomb, is lined with masonry— a rare feature in Etruscan tombs, especially in those of subterraneous excavation. The blocks are very massive and neatly rusticated, a clear proof that this style of masonry was used by the Etruscans; a fact also attested by other remains on Etruscan sites. It is worthy of remark that this style, which probably originated in Etruria, is still prevalent in this part of Italy; and the grand palaces of Florence and Siena, so far as masonry is concerned, may be purely traditional imitations of those of Etruscan Lucumones, raised five-and-twenty centuries ago.

The character of this tomb is most solemn and imposing. The rock-hewn pillar in the midst, more simple and severe than any Doric column[5]—the bare, damp walls of rock—the massive

---

[5] Canina cites this as the most striking example of a Doric-like column among the very few to be found in Etruscan tombs, and points out its similarity to the rock-hewn columns in the tombs of Beni-Hassan. Etruria Marit. II., p. 166. This column is singularly formed, the side facing the door being rounded, the back squared. The

blocks of masonry—the yawning sarcophagus with its lid over-thrown, and the dust of the long-forgotten dead exposed to view—the deep gloom never broken but by the torch of the curious traveller—all strike the soul with a chill feeling of awe.

GROTTA DIPINTA.

Let us leave this tomb and enter another hard by. We are in a chamber whose walls, gaily painted, are alive with sea-horses snorting and plunging—water-snakes uprearing their crests and gliding along in slimy folds—dolphins sporting as in their native element—and,—can we believe our eyes?—grim and hideous caricatures of the human face divine. One is the head of an old man, with eye starting from its socket, and mouth wide open as though smitten with terror. Another is a face elongated into a coffin form, or like the head of an ox, with one eye blotted from his visage, and the other regarding you with a fixed stare, no nostrils visible, the mouth gaping above a shapeless chin, and the hair standing out stiffly from the head, as though electrified. I could not readily bring myself to believe that this caricature was of ancient execution; but, after minute examination, I was convinced that it was of the same date, and by the same hand, as the other paintings in this tomb, which are indubitably Etruscan. All are drawn in the same broad and sketchy style, with red and black crayons—" rubricâ picta aut carbone."

In the centre of one wall is a third head, no caricature, and probably the portrait of the Etruscan for whom the tomb was constructed, and whose ashes were found in his sarcophagus. The other two heads may represent respectively Charun and Typhon, i.e. the angel or minister of Death, and the principle of Destruction, both of whom are usually depicted as hideous as the imagination of the artist could conceive.[6]

Hippocampi and water-snakes are symbols frequently found in Etruscan tombs, either depicted on the walls, or sculptured on sarcophagi and urns. They are generally regarded as emblematic of the passage of the soul from one state of existence to another, an opinion confirmed by the frequent representation of boys

shaft is 5 ft. high, and 18 inches in dia-meter, with a plain base. The capital is 2 ft. square, with its lower edge bevelled down to the shaft. The whole is crowned by an abacus, 4 ft. square, and, like the capital, about 1 ft. deep.

[6] Typhon is here, as elsewhere in this work, used conventionally, to express a di-vinity of Etruscan mythology, whose name has not yet been ascertained, but who bears some analogy to the Typhon of Egyptian and Greek mythology. See Chapter XXV.

riding on their backs. This view is, moreover, borne out by their amphibious character—horse and fish, snake and fish—evidently referring to a two-fold state of existence. The dolphins, which form a border round the apartment, painted alternately black and red, are a common sepulchral ornament, and are supposed to have a similar symbolical reference ;[7] though they have also been considered as emblematic of the maritime power of the Etruscans, the "sea-kings" of antiquity.[8] The rolling border beneath them represents the waves, in which they are supposed to be sporting—

> circum clari delphines in orbem
> Æquora verrebant caudis, æstumque secabant.

Next to the Typhon-head is a large jar, sketched on the wall, out of which two serpents with forked tongues are rising. The demons or genii of Etruscan mythology are commonly represented brandishing these reptiles in their hands, or with them bound round their brows or waists, and sometimes, as in this case, having them by their side. That snakes were also made use of by the Etruscan priests and soothsayers, as by the Egyptian, to establish their credit for superior powers in the minds of the people, as evincing control over the most deadly and untractable creatures in existence, may be learned both from history and from sepulchral monuments,[9] and it is possible that those used in the service of the temples were kept in such jars as this.[1]

---

[7] Gori Mus. Etr. II. p. 236.- Inghirami Mon. Etrus. I. p. 160. Some have imagined that the dolphins so frequently introduced on Etruscan sepulchral monuments have reference to the story of Dionysos, told in the Homeric Hymn to that god, who, when seized by some Tyrrhene pirates, assumed the form of a lion (v. 44), or, as Apollodorus has it, turned the mast and oars into serpents, and filled the ship with ivy and the music of pipes, which so terrified the crew that they leaped into the sea, and were transformed to dolphins. Apollod. III. 5, 3. cf. Ovid. Met. III. 575, et seq. Serv. ad Æn. I. 67. Hyginus, 134. Nonnus, Dionys. XLV. p. 1164, ed. Hanov. 1605. Eurip. Cycl. 112. But it is clear that these pirates were Tyrrhene Pelasgi, of the Lydian coast, not Etruscans. See Niebuhr, I. p. 42. Müller, Etrus. einl. 2, 4, and I. 4, 4. The dolphin was

called from this fable—Tyrrhenus piscis—Seneca, Agam. 451. cf. Stat. Achil. I. 56. The dolphin is also an emblem of Apollo, who once assumed its form, and drove a ship from Crete to Crissa. Hom. Hym. Apol. 401, et seq.

[8] Τυρρηνοὶ βαλλαττοκρατοῦντες. Diod. Sic. V. p. 295, 316. Strabo V. p. 222.

[9] Livy (VII. 17) records that the Etruscan priests made use of these animals to strike terror into their foes. See also Florus. I. 12, and Front. Strat. II. 4, 17.

[1] The serpent was an object of divination among the Latins (Ælian. Nat. An. XL cap. 16), and probably also among the Etruscans, as it continues to be among certain people of Asia and Africa. Serpents were worshipped by the Egyptians, and cherished in their temples (Ælian. X. cap. 31, XI. 17, XVII. 5), and the Greeks kept representations of them in the temples of

In this tomb was found the curious sarcophagus, now in the British Museum, of temple-shape, with a pair of serpents, in knotted coils on the roof; and it appears highly probable, from this and the other adornments of the sarcophagus, as well as from the serpent-jar painted on the wall, that this was the sepulchre of some *augur* or *aruspex*, skilled in the mysteries of "the Etruscan Discipline," and in interpreting the will of Heaven.   His name, we learn from his sarcophagus, was "Vel Urinates," a family name met with in other parts of Etruria;[2] and his portrait is probably seen on the right-hand wall.[3]

From the freedom of the sketches on the walls, from the Greek character of the ornaments, and the peculiar style of the

---

Bacchus (Schol. ad Aristoph. Plut. III. sc. 2, 690), probably because this reptile was a symbol of regeneration and renovation. The serpent is also a well-known emblem of Apollo, of his son Æsculapius, and of Minerva in her character of Hygieia.

The Romans also connected the serpent with the worship of the Lares; this reptile being always found on the Lararia of the houses at Pompeii.   The serpent indeed seems to have been used by the Romans as a mark of sacredness.   They were wont to paint it on walls for the same purpose that the modern Italians paint crosses or souls in purgatory.

Pinge duos angues: pueri, locus
            est sacer: extra, &c.,

says Persius (Sat. I. 113).   Whether it be a traditional custom, or a mere coincidence, I know not, but the modern Italians, especially the Romans, are very fond of chalking huge serpents on walls, generally chained to a post.

Serpents were regarded by the ancients as genii of the place where they were found; or as ministers to the dead; as when Æneas sees one issue from the tomb of his father he was

            Incertus geniumne loci, famulumne
                        parentis
            Esse putet.-- Æn. V. 95.

So also Val. Flacc. Argon. III. 458.—Umbrarum famuli.   So says Isidore (Orig. XII. 4)—Angues apud gentiles, pro geniis locorum erant habiti semper.   Seneca (de Irâ II. 31) speaks of them at banquets, gliding among the goblets on the table; so also Virgil describes the serpent mentioned above, taking part in the funeral feast

(Æn. V. 90).

            —agmine longo
            Tandem inter pateras et levia pocula
                serpens,
            Libavitque dapes. . . . . .

cf. Val. Flacc. loc. cit.   It is probable that the serpent was delineated on the walls of tombs, not so much to mark the sacredness of the spot, as to keep it inviolate by exciting the superstitious terror of intruders.

[2] The name Urinates is inscribed on a rock-tomb at Castel d' Asso.   It occurs also among the Etruscan family names of Perugia, Volterra, and Chiusi.

[3] This sarcophagus is unique.   It seems from the sloping roof, joint-tiles, and antefixæ, to have represented a house or temple, yet nothing like a door is visible.   The lid has a winged sphinx at each end of the ridge, and in the middle are a pair of serpents curiously knotted together like ropes. The antefixæ are female heads, probably Larvæ, as on the black pottery of Chiusi and Sarteano.   At each end of the monument are griffons, or beasts of prey, devouring antelopes, and on the sides at each angle is a figure, also in relief, one representing Charun with his hammer and a crested snake in his hand; another, a winged female genius, with a drawn sword; a third, a similar figure, with an open scroll; and the fourth, a warrior, with sword and shield.   The whole was originally covered with stucco and coloured, and traces of red, black, and blue, may still be detected.   The name—Vel Urinates—is inscribed on one side just beneath the lid.

A plate of it is given, Mon. Ined. Instit. I. tav. XLII., and Etruria Marit. tav. CXX.

sarcophagus, this tomb cannot be of early date. It must be some centuries later than the Grotta Campagna at Veii, coeval with the latest painted tombs of Corneto, probably subsequent to the conquest of Etruria, though betraying no foreign influence, save in its style of art, and the character of its adornments.[4]

This is the only painted tomb yet found in this necropolis. The generality of sepulchres on this site are quadrilateral, of moderate size, with a broad ledge or bench of rock round three sides, on which lay the bodies, sometimes in sarcophagi, sometimes uncoffined, with a lamp of terra-cotta or bronze at the head of each; and weapons, vases, and other sepulchral furniture around. These benches were occasionally hollowed into sarcophagi, which were covered by large sun-burnt tiles, three feet or more in length. Body-niches, so common at Sutri, Civita Castellana, and Falleri, are seldom found on this site; and even small niches for lamps or vases are rare. I observed one tomb under the town-walls, which seems to have been circular, with a pillar in the centre—the usual form of the sepulchres of Volterra. In some instances, sarcophagi have been found not in tombs, but sunk like our modern coffins, a few feet below the surface of the ground, covered with large tiles, or stone slabs. These were for the bodies of the poor. At this site they did not always bury their dead; for vases are often found containing calcined remains.

As every necropolis in Etruria has its peculiar style of tomb, so there is a peculiarity also in the character of the sepulchral furniture. On this site the beautiful painted vases of Vulci and Tarquinii are not common; those, however, with yellow figures, are not so rare as the more archaic, with black on a yellow ground; but they are seldom in a good style of art. Articles of bronze, often of great richness and beauty, are abundant; consisting of helmets, often gilt, shields, greaves, and other portions of armour; vases of different forms; *specchj*, or mirrors, figured with mythological scenes; tripods and *candelabra*; and long thin plates of this metal gilt, covered with designs in relief. Besides these have been found swords and bows of steel. But perhaps the most remarkable article in bronze here found is an *aspis*, or circular shield, about three feet in diameter, with a lance-thrust

---

[4] The tomb is 18 ft. long by 15 wide, and nearly 7 high in the middle; the ceiling is cut as usual into the form of the roof of a house, with a beam along the centre, and rafters sloping from it downwards on either side. The floor is said to have been covered with cement. The walls are coated with a fine white stucco to receive the colour, not here, as at Veii and Chiusi, laid on the rock itself.

in it, and its lining of wood, and braces of leather still remaining, after the lapse of more than 2000 years.   Go to the Gregorian Museum, and behold it suspended on the walls; for the Pope purchased it of Signor Ruggieri, the fortunate excavator, for the sum of 600 *scudi*.   It was found suspended from the wall, near the sarcophagus of its owner, and the rest of his armour hung there with it—his embossed helmet, his greaves of bronze, and his wooden-hilted sword of steel.   In one tomb on this site a skeleton was discovered still retaining fragments of its shroud; and in another a purple mantle was found covering two vases and a garland of box![5]   In a third was a little cup of ordinary ware, but bearing on its foot an inscription, which proved to be no other than the Etruscan alphabet.   What was the meaning of it in such a situation is hard to say—to us it is suggestive only of a present to a child.   Though originally of little worth, it is now a rare treasure, being, until very recently, the sole instance known of an alphabet in the Etruscan character.[6]   Here is a fac-simile of it—

All these articles are now in the possession of the Prince Borghese.   The fullest description of the excavations at Bomarzo will be found in the work of Don Luigi Vittori, arch-priest of the village.[7]

[5] Vittori, Mem. Polim. p. 38.

[6] A little pot was discovered at Cervetri some few years since, inscribed with an alphabet and primer; and a tomb at Colle, near Volterra, opened two or three centuries ago, had a somewhat similar epigraph on its walls.   But in both those cases the letters were Pelasgic, not Etruscan.   Here, however, is an alphabet which is admitted to be in the latter character.   The order adopted is singular.   In Roman letters it runs thus:—A, C, E, V, Z, H, TH, I, L, M, N, P, S, R, S, T, U, TH, CH, PH.   The fifth, or the *zeta*, is of a very rare form.   The usual form of the Etruscan *zeta* is ‡.   It will be observed that there are two *thetas*; the ante-penultimate letter in the alphabet may also be a *phi*.   The difference between the two *sigmas* is supposed by Lepsius to consist in the first being accented, and the other not; but they are often used indifferently in the same word.

Another Etruscan alphabet has lately been found scratched on a black bowl, now in the Museum at Grosseto, but the place of its discovery I could not ascertain.   It closely resembles this of Bomarzo in the order, and generally in the form of the letters, but contains twenty-two instead of twenty.   See Chapter XLVII.   In the Museum at Chiusi are three Etruscan alphabets, all fragmentary, carved on slabs of tufo.   They are of earlier date than the two mentioned, and the letters, which do not observe the same arrangement, run from left to right.   See Chapter LIII.

[7] For other particulars regarding the excavations on this site, see Annali dell' Inst. 1831, p. 116 (Gerhard); 1832, p. 284; 1832, p. 269 (Lenoir); Bullettini dell' Inst. 1830, p. 233; 1831, p. 6; p. 85; p. 90; 1832, p. 195; 1834, p. 50.

We returned to Viterbo by the direct road along the foot of the Ciminian Mount. It presents many picturesque combinations of rock and wood, with striking views of the Etruscan plain, and the distant snow-capt mountains of Cetona and Amiata. This district is said to be rich in remains of Etruscan roads, sepulchres, and buildings.[8] I observed in one spot a singular line of rocks, which, at a short distance, seemed to be Cyclopean walls, but proved to be a natural arrangement; and I remarked some traces of an ancient road; but beyond this, I saw nothing—no tombs or other remains of Etruscan antiquity.[9] About two miles from Viterbo is the village of Bagnaja, with the celebrated Villa Lante of Vignola, and thence the curious in natural phenomena may ascend to the Menicatore, or rocking-stone, near the summit of the mountain—an enormous block of *peperino*, about twenty-two feet long, twenty wide, and nine high, calculated to weigh more than two hundred and twenty tons, and yet easily moved with a slight lever.

[8] Ann. Instit. 1832, p. 282 (Knapp).

[9] At Corviano, about three miles from Bomarzo, on this road, there is said to be a singular tomb, composed of a very long corridor lined with masonry, ending in a narrow passage which terminates in a well. On the corridor open four chambers. Orioli, who describes it, could not pronounce whether it was Etruscan, Roman, or of the Low Empire. (ap. Ingh. IV. p. 189, tav. XXXXI. 2.) The passage and shaft are quite Etruscan features.

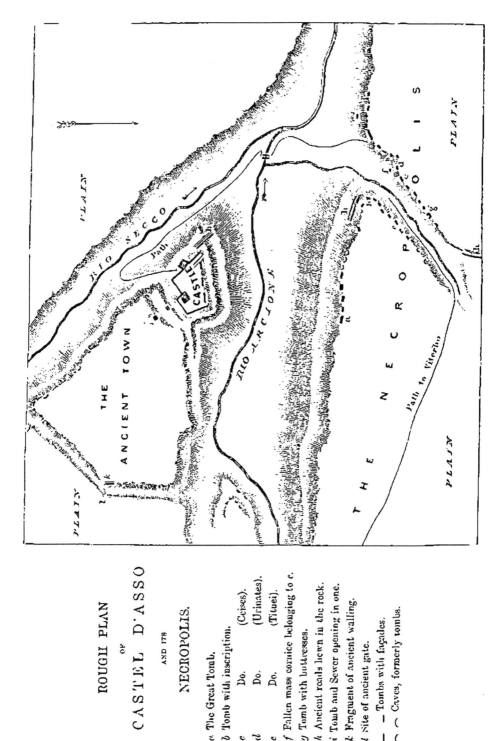

ROUGH PLAN
OF
CASTEL D'ASSO
AND ITS
NECROPOLIS.

a The Great Tomb.
b Tomb with inscription.
c Do. (Ceises).
d Do. (Urinates).
e Do. (Tituei).
f Fallen mass cornice belonging to *c*.
g Tomb with buttresses.
h Ancient reads hewn in the rock.
i Tomb and Sewer opening in one.
k Fragment of ancient walling.
l Site of ancient gate.
— — Tombs with façades.
⌒ ⌒ Caves, formerly tombs.

CHAPTER XVI.

CASTEL D'ASSO.—*CASTELLUM AXIA.*

Sovr' a' sepolti le tombe terragne
Portan segnato quel ch' elli eran pria.—DANTE.

Here man's departed steps are traced
But by his dust amid the solitude.—HEMANS.

THE best guide to the Etruscan antiquities of Viterbo and its neighbourhood used to be Ruggieri, a *caffettiere* of that city who, though a master-excavator himself, would condescend, for a consideration, to act the cicerone. His mantle has now fallen on a certain Fanali, who also acts as guide to Castel d' Asso, an Etruscan necropolis, which was first made known to the English public by the lively description of Mrs. Hamilton Gray. It lies about five miles to the west of Viterbo, and can be reached by the light vehicles of the country, though more easily on horse-back.[1]

From the gate of Viterbo, the road descends between low cliffs, here and there hollowed into sepulchres. At the extremity of this cleft is a large cave, called Grotta di Riello, once a sepulchre, and a spot long approached with superstitious awe, as the depository of hidden treasure guarded by demons. But a small Virgin having been erected at the corner of the road hard by, the worthy Viterbesi can now pass on their daily or nightly avocations without let or hindrance from spiritual foe. The same evil report is given of another sepulchral cavern, not far off, called Grotta del Cataletto.

[1] It is first found under this name in the works of Annio of Viterbo. Orioli (Ann. dell' Inst. 1833, p. 23) asserts that its true name is Castellaccio, as it has always been, and is still, called by the lower orders of Viterbo; but the Baron Bunsen, on the other hand, maintains that, though there is a ruined tower some miles distant called Castellaccio, this site is always mentioned by the shepherds and peasantry as Castel d' Asso. Bullett. dell' Inst. 1833, p. 97. My own experience agrees with that of Orioli, and I have found peasants who did not understand the name of Castel d' Asso, but instantly comprehended what site I meant by Castellaccio.

About a mile and a half from Viterbo we entered on the open
heath, and here columns of steam, issuing from the ground by
the roadside, marked the Bulicame, a hot sulphureous spring,
which has the honour of having been sung by Dante.[2] It is
apparently in a boiling state, but is not of intolerable heat.[3] It
is inclosed by a circular wall, and being carried off in small
channels, flows steaming across the plain. This is almost the
only active intimation of those latent fires which, in past ages,
have deposited the strata of this district. It lies midway between
the Lake of Bolsena and that of Vico, both craters of extinct
volcanoes. The high temperature and medicinal qualities of
these waters have given rise to baths in their neighbourhood, and
from the many ruins around, there seem to have been similar
edifices in former ages, at least as far back as Roman times.[4]

We were now on the great Etruscan plain, which was here
and there darkened by wood, but unenlivened by towns or
villages; no habitations visible on its vast expanse save the
distant towers of Toscanella, and a lonely farm-house or crumbling ruin studding its surface at wide intervals. Our guide,
being then new in his trade, mistook one of these ruins for
another, and, after wandering a long time over the moor, fairly
confessed he was at fault. So we took the road into our own
hands, and with much difficulty, in consequence of the numerous
ravines with which the plain is intersected, reached the brink of
the wide glen of Castel d'Asso. Just opposite the ruined castle
which gives its name to the site, we found a smaller glen, opening at an angle into the large one, and here we descended, and
presently came upon the object of our search. Tomb after tomb,
hewn out of the cliffs, on either hand—a street of sepulchres; all
with a house-like character! They were unlike any Etruscan
tombs I had yet seen; not simply opening in the cliffs as at
Sutri and Civita Castellana, nor fronted with arched porticoes as
at Falleri, but hewn into square architectural façades, with bold
cornices and mouldings in high relief, and many with inscriptions
graven on their fronts, in the striking characters and mysterious
language of Etruria.

Such a scene is well calculated to produce an impression on a

---

[2] Inferno, XII. 117, and XIV. 79.

[3] Fazio degli Uberti, in his Dittamundi,
lib. III. cap. 10, says it is so hot that in
less time than a man can walk a quarter of
a mile you may boil all the flesh off a sheep,
so as to leave it a mere skeleton.

The heat is said to be not greater than
60° Reaumur. Ann. Inst. 1835, p. 5.

[4] Canina takes the Bulicame to be the
Aquæ Passeris of Martial, VI. Epig. 42,
ut supra, p. 157, note 2.

CASTEL . D'ASSO, FROM THE NECROPOLIS.

Drawn by Geo. Dennis

sensitive mind, especially on one to whom an Etruscan necropolis is a novel spectacle. The solemnity of the site—the burial-place of long-past generations, of a people of mysterious origin and undetermined antiquity—their empty sepulchres yawning at our feet, yet their monuments still standing, in eternal memorial of their extinct civilization, and their epitaphs mocking their dust that has long ago been trampled under foot or scattered to the winds—all this cannot fail to excite reflection. Then the loneliness, seclusion, and utter stillness of the scene—the absence of all habitation—nothing but the ruined and picturesque castle on the opposite precipice, and the grand dark mass of the Ciminian, looking down on the glen—tend to make this more imposing than other Etruscan cemeteries which are in the immediate neighbourhood of modern habitations.

As I advanced down the glen I found that the tombs continued round the face of the cliffs, on either hand, into the great valley, in a line opposite the ruined castle. There might be thirty or forty of them—not all, however, preserving their monumental façades — occupying an extent of cliff about half a mile in length.[5]

The façades are formed by the face of the cliffs being hewn to a smooth surface, save where the decorations are left in relief; the height of the cliff being that of the monuments, which vary, in this respect, from twelve to thirty feet. The imposing effect of these tombs is perhaps increased by their form, which is like that of Egyptian edifices and Doric doorways, narrower above than below, the front also retreating from the perpendicular—a form ordinarily associated in our minds with the remotest antiquity. Still more of Egyptian character is seen in the massive horizontal cornices, which, however, depart from that type in receding, instead of projecting from the plane of the façade.[6] These cornices, in many instances, are carried round the sides of the monument, and even where this is not the case, each tomb is quite isolated from its neighbours; a broad upright groove, or a flight of steps cut in the rock, and leading to the plain above, marking the separation. In the centre of each façade is a rod-moulding, describing the outline of a door; in some instances

---

[5] Orioli (ap. Inghir. Mon. Etrus. IV. p. 175) makes it to be a mile and a half in length, but the learned Professor has here decidedly stretched a point.

[6] The mouldings of the cornice are the torus, the fascia, the ogee, and the *becco di civetta*, or lip-moulding, generally arranged in the same relative order, but varying considerably in proportions and boldness. See the Appendix, Note L.

having panels recessed one within the other, as in the annexed woodcut. This is not the entrance, but merely the frontispiece

MOULDED DOOR.

to the tomb, and the title is generally engraved on the lowest and most prominent *fascia*, or, in some cases, on the flat surface of the façade just over the moulded door.[7] The letters are seldom six inches in height, though, from the depth of their intaglio, they can be read in the sunshine from a considerable distance. Not half the tombs have inscriptions, and not all of these are legible; yet, in proportion to the number of monuments, there are more inscribed façades at Castel d'Asso than in any other Etruscan necropolis, save that of Sovana. Most of these inscriptions seem to indicate the name of the individual or family buried below, but there are others, the precise meaning of which can be only conjectured.[8]

So much for the title-page of these sepulchres. The preface comes next, in the form of a chamber hollowed in the rock, receding, in most instances, a little from the face of the monument above it, and vaulted half over, by the rock being left to project at the base of the façade. The front seems to have been always open.[9] On the inner wall, and directly beneath the moulded door of the façade, is a similar false door, sometimes with a niche in its centre.[1] Here the funeral feast may have been held; or the corpse may have been laid out in this chamber, before its transfer to its last resting-place in the sepulchre beneath; or here the surviving relatives may have assembled to perform their annual festivities in honour of the dead; and the niche may have held a lamp, a *cippus*, or a vase of perfume to destroy the effluvium, or in it may have been left an offering to the infernal deities, or to the *manes* of the deceased.

Directly beneath this second moulded door, is the real

<hr />

[7] This system of false doors in the façades of tombs, obtains in the ancient rock-hewn sepulchres of Phrygia, which, indeed, have many other points of analogy with those of Etruria (see Steuart's Ancient Monuments of Lydia and Phrygia, Lond. 1842), and also in those of Lycia, which have often recessed panellings. See Sir C. Fellows' works, and the monuments from Xanthus now in the British Museum. Moulded doorways often occur also in Egyptian monuments, and sometimes with recessed panellings, as in

the above woodcut; as on a granite sarcophagus in the Museum of Leyden.

[8] All the inscriptions that remain legible are given in the Appendix, Note II.

[9] Some of the smaller tombs are without this open chamber, and have the entrance-passage immediately below the façade. This intermediate chamber is a feature almost peculiar to the tombs of Castel d'Asso, and Norchia.

[1] As in the woodcut in Chap. XIX. page 216.

entrance to the sepulchre, generally twenty, sometimes thirty or forty feet below the uppermost moulding. It is approached by a narrow and shelving passage, cut through the rock in front of the monument, running down at an angle of about forty degrees, and originally cut into steps. The door, like the false ones above it, tapers upwards, but is often arched. Forcing my way down these passages, mostly choked with rocks and bushes, and squeezing my body through the doorways, now often nearly reclosed with earth, by the aid of a taper, without which nothing would have been visible, I explored most of the sepulchres. They are now half filled with earth, and I had to crawl on all-fours, over upturned sarcophagi, fragments of pottery, and the bones and dust of the ancient dead.

The tombs are of various sizes, some very spacious, others extremely small—all rudely hollowed in the rock, and most of a quadrilateral form. The ceilings are generally flat, though sometimes slightly vaulted ; and I do not recollect an instance of beams and rafters in relief, so common in other cemeteries. The resemblance to houses is here external only. Some have the usual benches of rock against the walls for the support of sarcophagi : in others are double rows of coffins, sunk in the rock, side by side, like beds in a hospital or workhouse, and with a narrow passage down the middle. In one tomb these sunken sarcophagi radiate from the centre. The bodies, when laid in these hollows were probably covered with tiles.

I was greatly surprised at the studied economy of space displayed in these sepulchres—a fact which entirely sets aside the notion that none but the most illustrious of the nation were here interred. The truth is, that the tombs with the largest and grandest façades have generally the meanest interiors. The last tomb in the great glen, in the direction of Viterbo, is externally the largest of all, and a truly magnificent monument, its façade rising nearly thirty feet above the upper chamber ;[2] and it is natural to conclude that it was appropriated to some great chieftain, hero, or priest ; yet, like all its neighbours, it was not a mausoleum for a single individual, but a family-vault, for it contains eight or ten sarcophagi of *nenfro*. Unlike the figure-lidded sarcophagi and urns, so common in many Etruscan cemeteries, these correspond with the tombs themselves in their simple, massive, and archaic character, having no bas-reliefs

---

[2] It is seen in the woodcut at p. 177, which shows the range of cliff-hewn tombs in the glen opposite the Castle.

or other sculptured ornaments, and, in their general form, resembling the sarcophagi of Lydia and Phrygia. I did not
observe a single instance of a niche within the tomb itself, but
in the wall of the passage, just outside the door, there is often
one, which was probably for the *cippus*, inscribed with the name
of the family to whom the sepulchre belonged.

From their exposed position, there is every reason to conclude
that these tombs, like those of Sutri, Civita Castellana, and
Falleri, were rifled at an early period. As soon as the sacredness attaching to them as the resting-place of the dead had worn
off, they must have fallen a prey to plunderers. Their site being
always indicated by their superincumbent monuments, whatever
of their contents the earlier spoilers might have spared must
inevitably have been carried off or destroyed in subsequent ages.
It is absurd to expect that anything of value should be found in
our own days in these open tombs. But in others excavated of
late years in the plain above, have been found various articles of
bronze, *specchj* with figures and inscriptions, tripods, vases, large
studs representing lions' heads, besides articles of gold and
jewellery, scarabei, &c., with painted vases, some of great beauty
and archaic design, though in general mere native imitations of
the Greek.[3] A collection of antiquities from this site may be
seen at Viterbo, in the possession of Signor Bazzichelli, the
present proprietor of Castel d'Asso.[4]

Only one tomb did I perceive which, in any striking particular,
differed from those already described. It is in the narrow glen.
On each side of the false door of the façade is a squared buttress
projecting at right angles, and cut out of the rock which formed
the roof of the upper and open chamber. These buttresses are
surmounted by cornices, and have a small door-moulding on their
inner sides, like that on the façade. The sepulchre itself, in this
instance, is of an unusual form—elliptical. Orioli has described
a singular sepulchre at Castel d'Asso, which differs wholly from
those already mentioned, being a cavity for a body, sunk in the
surface of the plain and surrounded by an ornamental pattern,
cut in the tufo.[5] I looked in vain for this; but nearly opposite

---

[3] Orioli, Ann. Inst. 1833, p. 33, and ap.
Inghir. Mon. Etrus. IV. p. 188. Urlichs,
Bull. Inst. 1839, p. 75. Abeken (Mittelitalien, p. 256) is mistaken in supposing
these articles were found in the façaded
tombs.

[4] *Ut supra*, p. 153. See also Bull. Inst.

1874, p. 257.
[5] Orioli, ap. Inghir. Mon. Etr. IV. p.
189, tav. XXXIX, 3. The same writer
(p. 209) speaks of a tomb on this site with
two *phalli* scratched on its walls. I did
not perceive such symbols in any of these
tombs

the castle, I remarked a deep well or shaft sunk in the plain, which doubtless was the entrance to a tomb, such as exist at Férento. There can be no doubt, from the analogy of other sites, and from the excavations already made, that sepulchres abound beneath the surface of the plain.

In a country like our own, where intelligence is so widely diffused, and news travels with telegraphic rapidity, it were scarcely possible that monuments of former ages, of the most striking character, should exist in the open air, be seen daily by the peasantry, and remain unknown to the rest of the world for many ages. Yet so it is in Italy. Here is a site abounding in most imposing remains of the olden time, bearing at every step indisputable traces of by-gone civilisation, scarcely six miles from the great thoroughfare of Italy, and from Viterbo, the largest city in all this district ; and yet it remained unknown to the world at large till the year 1808, when Professor Orioli, of Bologna, and the Padre Pio Semería, of Viterbo, had their attention directed to the wonders of this glen.[6]   I am persuaded that Italy is not yet half explored—that very much remains to be brought to light ; a persuasion founded on such discoveries as this, which are still, from time to time, being made, of which I may cite the Etruscan necropolis of Sovana, discovered by my fellow-traveller, Mr. Ainsley—even more remarkable than this of Castel d'Asso—and sundry monuments of the same antiquity, which it has been my lot to make known to the world.   In fact, ruins and remains of ancient art are of such common occurrence in Italy as to excite no particular attention.   To whatever age they may belong— mediæval, Imperial, Republican, or pre-historical—the peasant knows them only as "*muraccia*," and he shelters his flock amid their walls, ploughs the land around them, daily slumbers beneath their shade, or even dwells within their precincts from year to year ; and the world at large knows no more of their existence than if they were situated in the heart of the Great Desert.

The general style of these monuments—their simplicity and

<hr />

[6] The gentleman who has the honour of having indicated the site to Orioli, is Signor Luigi Anselmi, of Viterbo, who is well stored with local antiquarian knowledge. He has also made excavations in the necropolis of Castel d'Asso. The place had been long known as the site of a ruined castle, and was even mentioned under its present name by Annio of Viterbo, in the fifteenth century ; indeed, the name is painted on the ceiling of the principal hall of the Palazzo Comunale, at Viterbo, which must be more than 200 years old (Orioli, Ann. Inst. 1833, p. 24), but it was not recognised as an Etruscan site till the year 1808.

massive grandeur, and strong Egyptian features—testify to their high antiquity; and this is confirmed by the remarkable plainness of the sarcophagi, and by the archaic character of the rest of their furniture, so far as it is possible to judge of it. They may safely be referred to the days of Etruscan independence.

This ancient cemetery clearly implies the existence of an Etruscan town in its neighbourhood; and the eye of the antiquary needs not the extant remains to point out the site on the opposite cliff, just at that spot where a tongue of land is formed in the plateau, by the intersection of a deep glen opening obliquely into the great valley. Here, accordingly, besides numerous remains of the middle ages, to which the castle wholly belongs, may be traced the outline of a town, almost utterly destroyed, indeed, but, on one side, towards the east, retaining a fragment of its walls in several courses of rectangular tufo blocks, uncemented, which have every appearance of an Etruscan origin. The site is worthy of a visit for the fine view it commands of the tomb-hewn cliffs opposite. The extent of the town, which is clearly marked by the nature of the ground, was very small, about half a mile in circuit. What may have been its ancient name is a question to determine. By Mrs. Hamilton Gray it has been conjectured to be the Fanum Voltumnæ, the shrine of the great goddess of the Etruscans, where the princes of Etruria were wont to meet in a grand national council; but for this there is no authority; Viterbo, as already shown, has stronger claims to that honour, and still stronger will hereafter be urged for another site. It has been suggested, and with high probability, that it may be the site of the Castellum Axia, mentioned by Cicero as near the farm of Cæsennia, the wife of A. Cæcina, his client.[7] Its very small size shows it could never

[7] Cicero pro Cæcinâ; cf. cap. VI. and VII. Cluver (II. p. 521) could not determine the site of Castellum Axia; but Mariani (de Etrur. Metrop. p. 45) as early as 1728, declared it to be Castel d'Asso. The objection urged by Orioli (Ann. Instit. 1833, p. 24) that Castel d'Asso is too distant from Tarquinii to be included within its territory, as the Castellum Axia seems to have been, is not valid, for Tarquinii, as the metropolis of the land, most probably had a more extended *ager* than usual; besides, the lake of Belsena, which is more remote from that city, is called by Pliny (Nat. His. II. 95,—lacus Tarquiniensis—

and by Vitruvius (II. 7) is said to be—in finibus Tarquiniensium. If the strong resemblance of the name, the agreement in the distance from Rome, said by Cicero (loc. cit. cap. X.) to be less than 53 miles (i.e. by the Via Cassia), as well as in the position on a height (cap. VII.), be taken into account, there can be little doubt that this is really the site of the Castellum Axia. Cacina, however, objects to place the Fundus Cæsenniæ here, because it is only fifty miles from Rome, and would rather place it at Castel Cardinale, three miles further to the north. Etr. Marit. II., p. 51.

have been more than a mere fortress. This could have been only its Roman name; as to its Etruscan appellation, we are still at a loss. It is not improbable, however, that it bore a somewhat similar name in Etruscan times. Acsi, we know, from a tomb at Perugia, to have been a family name among that people; and it was not uncommon for them, as well as for the Romans and other nations, to derive their family names from those of countries, cities, towns, or rivers.

ROCK-HEWN TOMB, NEAR CASTEL D'ASSO.

At the mouth of the wide glen of Castel d'Asso is a mass of rock, hewn into a sort of cone, and hollowed into a tomb, with a flight of steps cut out of the rock at the side, leading to the flat summit of the cone, which, it is conjectured, was surmounted by a statue.[8] About a mile from Castel d'Asso is a very spacious tomb, with decorated front, called Grotta Colonna,[9] which is near enough to have formed part of this same necropolis.

[8] Lenoir, Annali dell' Inst. 1832, p. 276.
[9] The Grotta Colonna is nearly 70 feet long by 16 wide. It contains a double row of coffins sunk in the rock, with a passage down the middle. Orioli, ap. Ingh. Mon. Etr. IV. p. 197, 218. See also tav. 38. 3.

APPENDIX TO CHAPTER XVI.

NOTE I.—MOULDINGS OF TOMBS AT CASTEL D'ASSO. See p. 179.

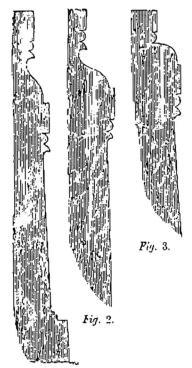

Fig. 3.

Fig. 2.

Fig. 1.

FIG. 1 shows the moulding of the façade of the great tomb, mentioned at page 181. This arrangement is that generally followed at Castel d'Asso, but with varieties in the proportions of the parts, and in the boldness of the general character—as seen in fig. 2. A few of the monuments are moulded as in fig. 3; but this arrangement is more common at Norchia, where, however, the former system also obtains. These three mouldings are not on an uniform scale. All the façades on this site fall slightly back, as in the annexed cuts.

The specimens of mouldings from this necropolis, published by Gell, and copied by Mrs. Hamilton Gray, are very incorrect; though Sir William flattered himself that they were "the only specimens of real Etruscan mouldings that have ever been seen in our country." Canina (Etruria Marit. tav. 97) gives illustrations of some of these mouldings, which ought to be accurate. In his restorations, he represents the tombs as being each surmounted by a pyramid of masonry, but I could perceive no traces of such superstructures.

NOTE II.—INSCRIPTIONS. See p. 180.

The inscriptions at Castel d'Asso are the following, which I give in Roman letters :—On a tomb on the left of the small glen, " ARNTHAL CEISES."

On one at the mouth of this glen on the same side is " ECASUTH . . . " which is but the commencement of the inscription.

On a tomb on the opposite side of the glen, " . . . . . RINATE . . . LVIES " . Orioli (Ann. Inst. 1833, pp. 31-2) reads it " URINATES . . . LVIES " . . The initial of the first word was very probably U, as the name Urinate occurs in other inscriptions—the sarcophagus from Bomarzo, for instance, now in the British Museum (see page 170), and on cinerary urns from Perugia, Volterra and Chiusi. On the last named site a sepulchre of this family was discovered in 1859. Conestabile, Bull. Soc. Colomb. iii., pp. 7–12.

Near this is a tomb, part of whose cornice has fallen. On the fragment yet standing, you read " Ecasu ; " and on the prostrate mass is the rest of the inscription, " INESL. TITNIE," so that the inscription, when entire, read thus :

ƎIⴹⵏⵔ·ⵏⵎƎⵏ⵪ ◇∨ⵏ⵪◇Ǝ

On a tomb in the great valley is " INESL," which is but a fragment.

On a fallen mass Orioli read " . . . . UTHIK . SL . . . "

Orioli (ap. Ingh. iv. p. 218 ; Ann. Instit. 1833, pp. 34, 52) read on two tombs these numerals, IIAXX and IIIIIIIAXX, which doubtless recorded the ages of the dead therein interred.

The recurrence of ECASUTHINESL shows it to be a formula. It is found also on other sites, and has given rise to much conjecture. SUTHINA is frequently found on bronze figures, which appear to have been votive offerings. Lanzi (II. pp. 481, 494) derived SCTHI from σωτηρία, in which he is followed by Vermiglioli (Iscriz. Perug. I. p. 133) and Campanari (Urna d' Arunte), who deduced the formula from ἡκα and σωτήρ. One antiquary (Bibliot. Ital. Magg. 1817) sought its interpretation in the Latin—*hic subtus inest.* Professor Migliarini of Florence, also sought a Latin analogy—*ecce situs*, or *hic situs est* (Bull. Inst. 1847, p. 86). The " Ulster king-at-arms," (Etruria Celtica, I. p. 38) finds it to be choice Erse, and to signify " eternal houses of death ! " Whatever it mean, it can hardly be a proper name. Beyond this, we must own with Orioli (loc. cit.), that " we know nothing about it, and our wisest plan is to confess our ignorance."

CHAPTER XVII.

MUSARNA.

Though nought at all but ruines now I bee,
And lye in mine own asbes, as you see ;
Verlame I was ; what bootes it that I was,
Sith now I am but weedes and wastefull grass ?—SPENSER.

MOST of the ancient cities of Etruria which have been discovered of late years, have been found fortuitously by travellers,
native or foreign, who, with more or less knowledge of the
subject, chancing to traverse ground far from the beaten tracks,
have been attracted by the local monuments yet extant, and
have recognised them as of Etruscan antiquity. But in 1850
the existence of an Etruscan town was made known to the world
in a novel manner—as "the fruit of diligent and persistent researches," made by Signor Giosafat Bazzichelli of Viterbo, acting
on information furnished by Professor Orioli. In searching the
archives of that city, the learned Professor found mention, in a
chronicle of the thirteenth century, of two old towns, one called
"Sorena," near the Bulicame, the other named "Civita Muserna,"
(in other documents Musana, or Musarna,) which towns, like the
Theban brothers of old, were recorded to have fought so long,
and so fiercely, that at length they utterly destroyed each other.

The site of Sorena or Surrina, the Etruscan representative of
Viterbo, had long been known ; it remained only to discover that
of Musarna, whose existence was confirmed by other mediæval
documents. As Orioli was personally unable to undertake the
task of exploring the wide and desolate Etruscan plain, he
delegated it to Signor Bazzichelli, who under his auspices succeeded eventually in rescuing from obscurity the long-forgotten
town, and in proving it to be of Etruscan antiquity.

On visiting the Macchia del Conte, a vast estate belonging
to the Counts of Gentili, about 7 miles west of Viterbo, on the

road to Toscanella, Signor Bazzichelli was fortunate enough to discover the site in question. Leaving the high road at the bridge of the Leja, turning to the left, and following the course of that stream for about a mile, he reached a ruined castle on a lofty cliff, bearing the name of Cordigliano. Leaving this old fortress by its eastern gate, and skirting the line of precipices which turn to the south, at the distance of little more than a mile he came to another height, overhanging the vale of the Leja, and called Civita. It was crested with the remains of an ancient town, which he recognised at once as Etruscan. The platform on which it stood is elliptical, the longer axis running from north-east to south-west. On the north it sinks in a fearful precipice to the valley of the Leja; on the west it is bounded by the same deep ravine; and on the south it is separated from the adjacent plain by an enormous fosse, of the length of the town, sunk with immense labour in the rock, and bounded at each extremity by the ruins of a tower. On the east of the town is a hollow, partly natural, partly artificial, which sinks to the vale of the Leja. The area of the town is very limited, so that it is difficult to regard it as more than a castle, or at most a fortified village.[1] All round the height stretch the Etruscan walls, in parts rising some height above the surface and in admirable preservation, in others, level with the plain, though the foundations may be distinctly traced throughout. The walls are of regular masonry, composed of large blocks of tufo, joined with wonderful nicety, though without cement, and arranged in alternate courses of long and short blocks, in the style usual in the southern cities of Etruria, and which in this work is described as *emplecton.* Beneath the walls, the cliffs on every side of the town are perforated with sewers.[2]

The town had four gates, two on the south side, one in the west, and one in the north wall. The principal entrance was from the south-east by a bridge hewn from the rock, spanning the fosse, of which mention has been made, and thus uniting the platform of the city with the adjacent plain. There is a similar

[1] Canina (Etr. Marit. II. p. 135) takes both Musarna and Cordigliano, from their very small size, to have been mere estates, the habitations of the proprietor and his retainers, inclosed by walls. He regards Castel Cardinale to be the Fundus Cæcunniæ of Cicero (pro Cæcina), as its distance, fifty-three miles, from Rome exactly corres- ponds with that of the farm of Cicero's client.

[2] The fragments of these walls delineated by Canina (Etr. Marit. tav. 119) show that early description of masonry, in which the blocks present their ends only to the eye, as in the walls of Tarquinii and Cære.

bridge at the other extremity of the fosse, each being protected by a large tower, as already stated, whose foundations alone are extant. Within the walls are many remains of ancient buildings, with a few traces also of still later occupation.

The town lies between two castles, which form, as it were, its suburbs. The nearest is Castel Cardinale, hardly a gunshot distant, on the further side of the valley of the Leja. It retains many remains of mediæval times. The other, or that already mentioned as Cordigliano, is at a somewhat greater distance, situated on a platform very similar as regards position, but much more circumscribed than that occupied by the town. The isthmus of rock which united it to the plain was in this instance also crossed by a deep fosse, which barred the approach to the castle. The height was anciently enclosed by walls of massive, un-cemented masonry, fragments of whose foundations are extant, and have been recognised as Etruscan. Numerous similar blocks strew the steep slopes beneath, overturned probably by some convulsion of nature, unless we are rather to believe the tradition which attributes it to the hostility of the Sorenesi. Beneath this castle, in the valley of the Leja, is the pier of an ancient bridge which once spanned the stream. The existence of these castles in close vicinity to the town, suggests a considerable population in ancient times, but this part of the plain is now utterly desolate and uncultivated.

This ancient town of course had its necropolis, and, as usual in southern Etruria, there were visible traces of it in tombs hewn in the neighbouring cliffs, some with façades like those at Castel d'Asso and Norchia, though in a simpler and severer style.[3] Other sepulchres were covered by tumuli, which rose above the plain; but most were sunk deep below the surface, and were reached by long passages with flights of steps hewn from the living rock.[4]

Soon after the discovery of this town, a party of gentlemen, with Bazzichelli at their head, repaired to the site to explore the necropolis. They opened the tumuli, dug into the hill slopes, and dived beneath the plain, but they found that almost all the sepulchres had been rifled in former times. In a hill to the west of the town they opened tombs in great numbers, both in the upper stratum of calcareous rock, and in the red tufo beneath it;

[3] One of these tombs is of remarkable character, having square holes, like windows, in its façade.

[4] Illustrations of some of the sepulchres at Castel Cardinale will be found in Canina's Etruria Marittima, tav. 99.

and they found the tombs to extend for a long distance in this
hill, lying in tier above tier from the foot of the slope to the very
summit. They were of small size, rudely hewn from the rock,
generally square in plan, and sometimes divided into two by a
wall left in the rock, and fronting the entrance. In some the
ceilings were carved in imitation of beams and rafters; others
were surrounded by benches of rock, on which were still stretched
skeletons. The sepulchres sunk beneath the plain, were sometimes mere pits rudely lined with tiles; these were the resting-
places of the poorer inhabitants. Here were also found spacious
chambers, in one instance supported by massive piers of rock.
In this tomb they found more than forty large sarcophagi of
nenfro, lying in tiers around the walls, nearly all with lids
bearing the effigies of the deceased as large as life, and with
Etruscan inscriptions on the lids or coffins, though sometimes
incised on the figures themselves, either on their bodies or on
their legs—a feature quite peculiar to this site. The inscriptions
proved the tomb to belong to the family "Alethnas." Rude and
coarse as was the art displayed in these figures, there was much
character and life-like expression in the countenances, which
were evidently portraits. The men reclined with a drinking-bowl
in their right hand, their flesh coloured red as usual. The
women were represented with rich dresses and ornaments, and
holding fans. The eyes of many were coloured blue. Sixteen
of the sarcophagi from this tomb are now to be seen in the
Museum of Viterbo.

In other tombs the sarcophagi were simple chests of stone
without ornament of any kind. One was of archaic character,
like the early monuments of Chiusi, with flat reliefs representing
a funeral procession. Of similar style was a square *cippus*, displaying a winged Charun, armed with a mallet. Many articles
of bronze were brought to light, generally of an early style of art
—mirrors, with figures incised; strigils, one with an inscription;
coins, sometimes in the mouths of the skeletons; spear-heads,
one retaining in its socket fragments of its wooden shaft; a
Satyr's head in relief, of exquisite workmanship; a candelabrum
on a tripod of human legs. Little or no figured pottery was
disinterred on this site, but there were three beautiful masks
of terra-cotta, painted red and blue, with strange head-dresses of
ribbons. In one tomb were found a pair of skulls, male and
female, the former with the indentation of the leaden acorn from
his foeman's sling, which had struck him in the forehead; and

with a fracture of the parietal bone from some other weapon, which was probably his *coup de grâce*. Orioli says the profiles of these skulls were of the true Italian cast, the face elongated, the chin sharp and prominent, "almost of the type of our Dante." [5]

It does not appear to me that Orioli has established the identity of this Etruscan town with the Muserna or Musana of the chronicles he cites. He takes it for granted rather than proves it. The only clue to its position given by the chronicles is, that it lies "towards the Veia." The only mention indeed of Civita Musarna is found in the apocryphal records of Annio of Viterbo, who represents it as a ruined town, built by Hercules, near "Coriti Lyanum," and places it five miles from Viterbo, not far from the Vadimonian lake, a position which would tally better with that of Bomarzo, than of the town in question. But Orioli assumes the "Veia" to be identical with the Leja, and the "Coriti Lyanum" of Annio to be Cordigliano, and prefers the name Musarna to Muserna or Musana, because Mastarna and a few other words in Etruscan have the same termination.

Whether Musarna be the correct appellation of this ancient town or not is of little moment. Until a more likely one is found for it, we may be content to accept this nomenclature for want of a better.

---

[5] For further particulars regarding this Etruscan town, and especially for the inscriptions in the Alethnas tomb, see Bull. Inst. 1850, pp. 22--30; pp. 35—44; pp. 89—96.

THE TEMPLE-TOMBS, NORCHIA.

CHAPTER XVIII.

NORCHIA.—ORCLE?

Quid sibi saxa cavata—
Quid pulchra volunt monumenta?—PRUDENTIUS.

There is a temple in ruin stands,
Fashioned by long-forgotten hands.—BYRON.

AT the same time, and by the same parties that Castel d'Asso was made known, there was brought to light another Etruscan necropolis, of even greater extent and higher interest. It lies more to the west, about fourteen miles from Viterbo, among the wooded glens which here intersect the great Etruscan plain, and in the neighbourhood of a ruined and desolate town, known by its mediæval name of Norchia. Besides numerous rock-sepulchres, similar to those of Castel d'Asso, this necropolis contains two of a more remarkable character—imitations of temples, with porticoed façades and sculptured pediments, thought to be unique in Etruria, until the discoveries of Mr. Ainsley, at Sovana. It is a spot which should not fail to be visited by every one who feels interest in the antiquities of early Italy.

Norchia is reached with most ease from Vetralla, from which it is six or seven miles distant. The road from Viterbo to Vetralla skirts the base of the Ciminian, but has little of the picturesque beauty of that from Viterbo to Bomarzo. The village of San

Martino is passed on the left, high on the slope of the mountain.
At S. Ippolito, half-way between Viterbo and Vetralla, a line of
low aqueduct and other remains of Roman buildings are passed,
which mark the site of ancient baths, and probably also of a
station on the Via Cassia, which, after crossing the shoulder of
the Ciminian, in its way from Sutrium, and passing through
Forum Cassii, hard by Vetralla, turned northward across the
great plain to Volsinii. The road, for the rest of the way to
Vetralla, follows the line of the ancient Cassian, fragments of
whose pavement were visible when first I travelled this road.

Vetralla stands at the western base of the Ciminian, and its
position on a cliff-bound ridge between two ravines, the ancient
rock-cut road by which you approach it, and numerous grottoes
in the cliffs around, are so many proofs that it occupies the site
of an Etruscan town. The antiquity of the place seems implied
in its name, which has been supposed to be a corruption of *Vetus
Aula*,—the derivation of the former part of the word at least can
hardly be gainsaid. Forum Cassii, as already stated, was a
station on the Cassian Way, eleven miles from Sutri, and twelve
from Aquæ Passeris, lying about a mile to the E.N.E. of Vetralla,
and its position is marked by the church of Santa Maria in
Forcassi, corrupted by the peasantry into "Filicassi." There is
nothing to be seen on this spot beyond two Roman vaults, and a
mass of *opus incertum*.[1]

Vetralla is a place of some importance, having 6000 inhabitants.
Viterbo is celebrated for its beautiful women, but verily good
looks are more abundant at Vetralla—

> " Uno ha la voce.
> L'altro maugia la noce."

This town is forty-three miles from Rome, eleven or twelve from
Sutri, nine from Viterbo, twelve from Monte Romano, twenty-
one from Corneto, thirty from Civita Vecchia, and eighteen from
Toscanella. All these roads, save the last, are carriageable.

The sole interest of Vetralla, to the antiquary, consists in its
being the best point whence to lionise the two Etruscan sites of
Norchia and Bieda, which are each about six miles distant. Not
that the *osteria*, for it is nothing more, of Vetralla, has very
inviting quarters; it lacks many things—comfort more than all;

---

[1] Canina places Forum Cassii at Vetralla, though recognizing this as an Etruscan
site. Etruria Marit. II., p. 54.

but it is the best accommodation the neighbourhood for miles round can afford. Yet I may not do the place justice, for on three several occasions I have spent some days there in the month of November, when the weather was either extremely wet or lowering; and after a long day's work, often in rain, always in mud, cold, and gloom, the want of comfort at night may have been more severely felt. I have visited it also in the height of summer, but being caught in a thunder-storm, my reminiscences of the Vetralla hostelry were not brightened. A guide to Norchia or Bieda may be obtained at the *osteria* of Vetralla.

Norchia lies W.N.W. from Vetralla. For the first three miles you follow the high road to Corneto. Here, in a glen to the right of the road, may be observed many traces of sepulture, indicating the existence of some Etruscan town, whose name and memory have perished, unless these tombs belong to the necropolis of Norchia, three miles distant, to which the path here turns to the right. It is more likely, however, that they mark the necropolis of some town near at hand. Canina takes that town to be Cortuosa, which, with Contenebra, was captured by the Romans in the year 367 (B.C. 387), ten years after the fall of Veii. Contenebra he supposes to be no other than Norchia.[2] For the latter half of the way, the road dwindles to a mere path, or vanishes altogether as you cross the wide desert heath, or dive into the deep glens with which it is in every direction intersected. Nothing can be more dreary than this scenery, on a dull November day. The bare, treeless, trackless moor has scarcely a habitation on its broad melancholy expanse, which seems unbroken till one of its numerous ravines opens suddenly

[2] Etruria Marittima, II., p. 50. He founds this opinion on the statement of Livy (VI. 4) from which he infers that these were the first towns that were attacked by the Romans on entering the territory of Tarquinii. Cortuosa, as the nearest, was the first assailed, and offered no resistance, which he attributes to the inferior strength of its position, the cliffs in this neighbourhood having no great elevation. Contenebra made more resistance, and kept the Romans at bay for several days, being protected, he asserts, by strong fortifications, and was of more importance, being mentioned by Livy as a "city," while Cortuosa was a mere "town." This opinion of Canina, however, will not bear examination. He forgets that to reach this spot the Romans must have already passed Vetralla, an undoubted Etruscan site, which, as nearer Rome, has a better claim to be regarded as Cortuosa. Livy, moreover, ascribes the easy conquest of that town to its being attacked by surprise; and he represents Contenebra as being compelled to surrender on account of the paucity of its inhabitants, they being unable to resist the continuous attacks of the Romans, who, dividing their forces into six bodies, kept up the assault with fresh troops, night and day, till they wearied the citizens into a surrender. Of the fortifications on which Canina bases his opinion that Norchia was the site of Contenebra, I shall have occasion to speak presently.

at your feet. The mountains around, which, in brighter weather, give beauty and grandeur to the scene, are lost in cloud and mist; even Monte Fiascone has shrouded his unaspiring crest. In the ravines is always more or less of the picturesque; yet their silence and lonesomeness, their woods almost stript of foliage, and dripping with moisture, have a chilling effect on the traveller's spirits, little to be cheered by the sight of a flock of sheep pent in a muddy fold, or of the smoke of the shepherd's fire issuing from a neighbouring cave, suggestive of savage comfort.

Little heeded we, however, the dulness of the weather. Hastily we threaded these glens, eager to reach the famed necropolis. The few tombs we did see here and there in the cliffs, served but to whet our appetite. At length we turned a corner in the glen, and lo! a grand range of monuments burst upon us. There they were—a line of sepulchres, high in the face of the cliff which forms the right-hand barrier of the glen, some two hundred feet above the stream—an amphitheatre of tombs! for the glen here swells into something not unlike that form. This singular glen is perhaps the most imposing spot in the whole compass of Etruscan cemeteries.[3]

The eye, as it ranges along the line of corniced sepulchres, singles out one of the most remote—one, whose prominent and decorated pediment gives it, even at a distance, an unique character. In our way towards it, we passed huge masses of rock-cornice, split from the cliffs above, and lying low in the valley. We found that what looked like one tomb at a distance, was in fact a double tomb, or rather a tomb and a half, seeing that the half of one of the pediments has fallen. Its peculiarity consists in this—that while all the sepulchres around are of the severely simple style of Castel d'Asso, approximating to the Egyptian, these two are highly ornate, and with much of the Greek character. Instead of the bold horizontal cornices which surmount the other tombs, here are pediments and Doric friezes, supported on columns; and, what is to be seen on the exterior of very few other Etruscan monuments, the *tympana* are occupied with figures in high relief. The inner wall of the portico is also adorned with reliefs, at least under the remaining half of the mutilated façade.

---

[3] It is said by Lenoir (Annali dell' Instit. 1832, p. 291) that the slope from the base of the tombs down to the banks of the stream was cut into steps, about two feet and a half high. I could perceive no traces of them; but if they existed they must have greatly increased the resemblance of the glen to an amphitheatre.

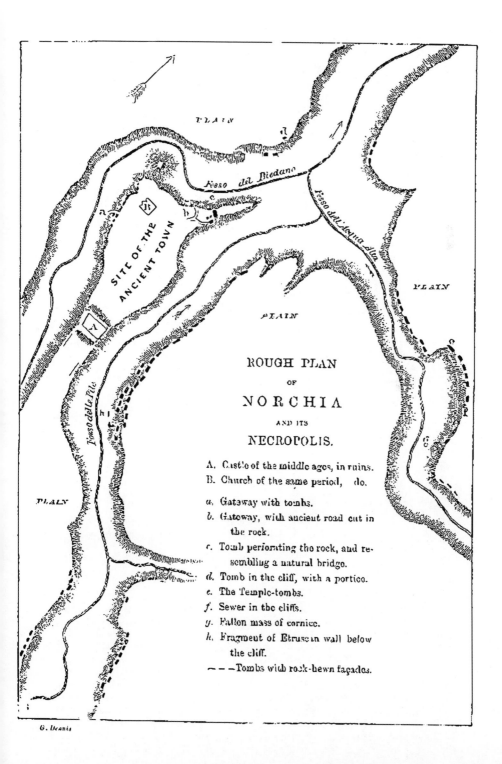

PLAIN

Fosso del Biedano

SITE OF THE ANCIENT TOWN

PLAIN

Fosso dell'Acqua alta

PLAIN

Fosso delle Pile

PLAIN

ROUGH PLAN

OF

NORCHIA

AND ITS

NECROPOLIS.

A. Castle of the middle ages, in ruins.
B. Church of the same period,   do.

a. Gateway with tombs.
b. Gateway, with ancient road cut in the rock.
c. Tomb perforating the rock, and resembling a natural bridge.
d. Tomb in the cliff, with a portico.
e. The Temple-tombs.
f. Sewer in the cliffs.
g. Fallen mass of cornice.
h. Fragment of Etruscan wall below the cliff.
– – – Tombs with rock-hewn façades.

G. Dennis.

Our first impression was the modern date of this double tomb, compared with those of archaic character around; and then we were naturally led to speculate on its origin. Who had made this his last resting-place? Was it some merchant-prince of Etruria, who had grown wealthy by commerce—or, it might be, by piracy—and who, not content with the simple sepulchres of his forefathers, obtruded among them one on the model of some temple he had seen and admired in his wanderings through Greece or Asia Minor? Was it a hero, renowned in Etruscan annals—some conqueror of Umbrians and Pelasgians—some successful opposer of that restless, quarrelsome city, that upstart bully of the Seven Hills? There, in each pediment, were figures engaged in combat—some overthrown and prostrate—others sinking to their knees, and covering their heads with their shields—one rushing forward to the assault, sword in hand—another raising a wounded warrior. All this, however, may have been the ornament of the temple from which this double-tomb was copied; or it may have had a symbolical meaning. Yet that he had been a warrior seemed certain, for in the relief within the portico were shield, mace, and sword suspended against the wall, as if to intimate that he had fought his last fight;[4] and beneath was a long funeral procession. Could he have been a Greek, who, flying from his native land, like Demaratus of Corinth, became great and powerful in this the home of his adoption, yet with fond yearnings after his native soil, raised himself a sepulchre after the fashion of his kindred, that, though separated from them in life, he might in some sort be united with them in death? No—he must have been an Etruscan in blood and creed; for this same procession shows certain peculiarities of the Etruscan mythology—the winged genius of Death, with three other figures in long robes, bearing twisted rods—those mysterious symbols of

---

[4] It was the custom of the Greeks and Romans, on retiring from active life, to dedicate to the gods the instruments of their craft or profession. Thus Horace (Od. III. 26) proposed to suspend his arms and lyre on the wall of the temple of Venus. The temple-form of this tomb is suggestive of such an explanation; though, on the other hand, it was not uncommon to indicate on the sepulchre itself the profession of the deceased by the representation of his implements or tools, or by scenes descriptive of his mode of life. A well-known but curious instance of this is seen in the baker's tomb at the Porta Maggiore of Rome, and another in the cutler's monument in the Galleria Lapidaria of the Vatican. Another, more analogous to this Norchian sepulchre, is seen on a vase, described by Millingen (Peintures de Vases Grecs, pl. XIX.), where within an *ædicula* or shrine stands the figure of the deceased, with his shield and greaves suspended above his head. The custom is still retained in the East. I have observed frequent instances of it in Armenian burial-grounds.

the Etruscan Hades—conducting the souls of two warriors with funeral pomp, just as in the Typhon-tomb at Corneto.

I have spoken of columns. None are now standing,[5] but it is evident that the heavy projecting entablatures have been so supported—that of the entire tomb by four, traces of whose capitals and bases are very distinct—that of the broken one, whether by four or six it is difficult to say; more probably by the latter. In neither case do they seem to have been more than plain square *antæ*, the inner ones similar to those at the angles of the portico. They were all left in the rock out of which the façades are hewn, and the softness and friability of the tufo accounts for their destruction.

The entablatures at a distance seem Doric, but a nearer approach discloses peculiar features. The pediments terminate on each side in a volute,[6] within which is a grim, grinning face with prominent teeth, a Gorgon's head, a common sepulchral decoration among the Etruscans. Over two of the three remaining volutes is something, which from below seems a shapeless mass of rock, but on closer examination proves to be a lioness or leopard,—specimens of the *acroteria*, with which the ancients were wont to decorate their temples.[7] Other peculiarities may be observed in the *guttæ*, the triglyphs, the dentilled cornice above them, and the ornamented *fascia* of the pediment—all so many Etruscan corruptions of the pure Greek.[8]

The tomb whose façade is entire, is more ancient than its fellow, as is proved by the bas-relief in the portico of the latter encroaching considerably on the wall of the former. Yet with some trifling exceptions they correspond.[9] Indeed the sculptures

---

[5] The pillar at the right-hand angle of the entire tomb was standing when Orioli first visited these monuments. Ann. Inst. 1833, p. 36.

[6] The pediments to these tombs prove them to be imitations of temples, or of very distinguished houses—if we may judge from the analogy of the Romans, among whom pediments were such marks of dignity, that Cicero says (de Orat. III. 46) if you could build in heaven, where you have no showers to fear, yet you would never seem to have attained dignity without a pediment. Julius Cæsar, as a great mark of distinction, was allowed a pediment to his house. Flor. IV. 2. cf. Cic. Phil. II. 43.

[7] Lions were symbolic guardians of sepulchres; and as such were often placed at the entrances of tombs, or painted within them over the doorway—and are sometimes found in a similar position as *acroteria* to porticoes, as in a temple-like sarcophagus at Chiusi, which bears a relief of a death-bed scene. Micali. Mon. Ined. tav. XXII. They are also often found carved on the lids of sarcophagi, one at each angle, as if to guard the effigy of the deceased. Panthers or leopards are also sepulchral emblems, and are frequently represented in the pediments of painted tombs.

[8] The *guttæ* are inverted, having the points downwards, and they are only three in number. The triglyphs are without the half-channels on their outer edges, and are therefore more properly diglyphs.

[9] The pediment is rather higher in the

in the two pediments are by some considered as relating to the same subject; though what that may be, it is not easy from the dilapidated state of the figures to decide. One has conjectured it to represent the contest for the body of Patroclus; another the destruction of Niobe's children; one has seen in it an interment, or games of chance, and the gladiatorial combats which the Etruscans held at their funerals; while a fourth regards it as the representation of some dispute about peace or war at the Fanum Voltumnæ. The attitudes of the figures alone—and in some cases not even these—are distinguishable. All the details which would give character and meaning are effaced. The broken half of the pediment does not serve to clear up the mystery, though it was discovered, half buried in the earth, with the figures in excellent preservation, and was removed to Viterbo, where it is still to be seen in the possession of Signor Giosafat Bazzichelli.[1] Whatever be the subject of these sculptures, they have not the archaic Etruscan character displayed in the bas-relief beneath the portico.

The surface of this rocky wall is so much injured, that doubt must ever hang over certain parts of this relief. Thus much is clear and unequivocal—that there is first a large, circular, convex shield,[2] like the *aspis* of the Greeks, and then a mace, both suspended against the wall. Next is a figure, now almost effaced, which from its large open wings must be that of a genius.[3] Over this is a plumed helmet, either worn by a figure behind the genius, not now distinguishable, or more probably suspended.

---

older tomb. This has no *guttæ* like the other. The portico is loftier in the imperfect monument.

[1] A plate of it, with the rest of the relief, is given in the Mon. Ined. Inst. I. tav. XLVIII.

[2] Orioli (Ann. Inst. 1833, p. 38) thinks here was originally a boss of metal in the centre of the shield, but there are now no traces of such an ornament. In the rock-hewn temple-tombs of Phrygia, the shields found on the architraves or pediments are bossed. Those represented in Etruscan monuments have very seldom a boss, and are always circular, like the Argolic shields and the ἀσπίδες εὐκύκλοι of the Homeric heroes; Diodorus (Eclog. lib. XXIII. 3) says the Romans at first used a square shield, but afterwards exchanged it for the *aspis* of the Etruscans. Similar shields are found sculptured on tombs in Pam-

phylia, as well as on city-walls. See Fellows' Asia Minor, pp. 175, 192, where Ezek. xxvii. 11, is cited in illustration. They were also suspended by the Greeks in their sepulchres; as in the pyramid between Argos and Epidaurus, described by Pausanias (II. 25, 7). From the frequency of them painted or sculptured in the tombs of Cervetri and Corneto, they seem to have had a votive meaning among the Etruscans, as well as among the Greeks and Romans. The latter people used to emblazon them with the portraits of their ancestors or with their heroic deeds. Pliny (XXXV. 3).

[3] One wing is most distinct. There is a corresponding arched ridge where the other ought to be. Orioli (Ann. dell' Inst. 1833, p. 53) thinks this figure represents Venus Libitina, the goddess who presided over funerals. It is certainly a female, for the prominence of the bosom is manifest

Another figure seems to have followed, and above it hangs by a cord a short curved sword[4]; a second helmet succeeds, which seems to be worn by a figure ; then a straight sword suspended ; and three draped figures, about the size of life, probably representing souls, each bearing one of the mysterious twisted rods, close the procession.[5] This may have been continued in the former half of the relief, now utterly destroyed.   It is clear that the ground of the whole has been originally painted red, and traces of the same colour, and of yellow, may be observed here and there about the figures ; and from the same on the fallen half of the pediment, it is certain that the reliefs of both *tympana* and of the portico—and probable that the architectural portions of the tombs also—were thus decorated.   This is one among numerous proofs in tombs, sarcophagi, and urns, that the Etruscans, like the Egyptians, Greeks, and Romans, had a polychrome system of decorating their architecture and sculpture.

Various are the opinions of archæologists as to the date of these monuments.   All are agreed on one point, that both the architecture and sculpture are decided imitations of the Greek.   They have been considered as early as Demaratus, the father of Tarquinius Priscus, to whose time belongs the first historical mention of the influence of Greek over Etruscan art ; but the spirit and freedom of the sculptures in the pediments, do not indicate so early an age ; while the somewhat archaic stiffness and quaintness of the three figures which close the procession in the portico, seem to show, that art had not entirely thrown aside the conventional trammels of its infancy.   I think then we shall not be far from the truth in referring them to the close of the fourth century of Rome.[6]

---

[4] Similar curved swords are represented on several Etruscan monuments. A curved steel sword, with the sharp edge on the inner side, as in a scythe, found in an Etruscan tomb, was formerly in the Campana collection at Roma.

[5] Such rods as these have been found represented on only two other Etruscan monuments, the Typhon-tomb of Tarquinii, where they are borne in a procession very similar to this, and the Tomb of the Reliefs at Cervetri. Their precise meaning is unknown. Orioli (Ann. Inst. 1834, p. 161) suggests that they may be either *funalia*, links used at funerals, made of papyrus or rope twisted and covered with wax or pitch (Virg. Æn. I. 781. Serv. in

loco), or that they may have an affinity to the sacred and golden bough—*fatalis virga* —torn from the grove of Proserpine, and borne by Æneas into hell as a gift to that goddess. Virg. Æn. VI. 136, 406, 636. Ovid. Met. XIV. 114. Urlichs (Bull. Inst. 1839, p. 45) suggests that they may be magisterial rods. It is possible they are emblems of supplication ; as Orestes sat at the altar with a topmost branch of olive wound round with much wool. Æschyl. Eumen. 43.

[6] Gerhard sees no rigidity in the reliefs of the pediments such as might be expected in monuments in the midst of others of so very ancient a character ; and thinks the design shows rather the decadence than

There are no moulded doors in the façades of these tombs, as in those adjoining, and at Castel d'Asso; but the resemblance to temples is sufficiently obvious. The analogy is strengthened by a depression in the stylobate of the unbroken tomb, which seems to indicate the steps leading up to the portico. In the porticoes being aræostyle, or having very wide intercolumniations, and in some minor particulars, these monuments may illustrate the temple of the Tuscan order, described by Vitruvius;[7] but in most points the façades have more of a Greek character.[8] Of the proportions and adornments of the columns nothing can now be said.

The external magnificence of these temple-tombs raises anticipations of a corresponding degree of adornment within. But these are soon destroyed. The tombs, which are entered as usual by narrow, steeply-descending passages, are like the plainest at Castel d'Asso—large chambers rudely hollowed in the rock, utterly devoid of ornament, and containing a double row of sarcophagi sunk in the tufo, with an economisation of space which quite dispels the notion of their being the burial-places, each of an illustrious hero or Lucumo. They are, in fact, like most of those around them, family sepulchres.

Let not the traveller suppose that in these tombs he has seen all the wonders of Norchia. The glen which contains the temple-tombs opens to the west on a wide area where four glens meet. Immediately opposite, as you emerge on this space, are a few fine detached tombs, almost at the foot of the cliffs. To the left, on a tongue of land which projects into the hollow between two other ravines, stands the ruined and picturesque church of Norchia,

---

infancy of art; yet considers them prior to the Roman conquest of Etruria (Bull. dell' Inst. 1831, pp. 84, 89). Urlichs views them as of a subsequent period (Bull. dell' Inst. 1839, p. 45). Their similarity to the reliefs of the sarcophagi and urns is noticed by several writers.

[7] Vitruv. IV. cap. 7, cf. III. 3. Lenoir (Ann. Inst. 1832, p. 290) points out the correspondence of these façades with the aræostyle temples of the Etruscans—*baryeæ, barycephalæ, humiles, latæ*. When I speak, in the text, of the resemblance to temples, I refer to the apparent character of these tombs, for it is possible that they are imitations, not of temples, but of mere houses; seeing that the Etruscans are known to have had porticoes to their abodes, which

they so constructed to free themselves from the confusion and annoyance of crowds of attendants. Diod. Sic. V. p. 316.

[8] The Cavaliere del Rosso is said to have proved that the dimensions of these tombs are on the scale of the Greek cubit. Ann. Inst. 1833, p. 56. Their general dimensions may be learned from the woodcut at p. 193, by the figures under the portico, which are nearly the size of life; but to be more explicit, the length of the broken façade is 15 ft. 6 in.; of the entire one, 25 ft. 6 in. The portico is about 9 ft. high, and projects 4 ft. The height of the entablature is 8 ft. 6 in., and of the entire façade, 17 ft. 6 in., exclusive of the stylobate, which averages about 5 ft. in height.

marking the site of the Etruscan town.   The glen to the west of this contains very few tombs, but that on the opposite side abounds in them, especially in the cliffs facing the town, where they rise in terraces or stand in picturesque groups, half hidden by wild luxuriant foliage.   A few may also be seen on the opposite side of the stream in the cliffs which are terminated by the ancient town.   Altogether the monuments in this glen are very numerous—twice as many as are to be found at Castel d'Asso, and more interesting from their variety; for though in general character they resemble the tombs of that necropolis, in their details they are often dissimilar, and differ also more widely from each other.   It may suffice to state that the variations are observable rather in the façades and mouldings than in the open chambers

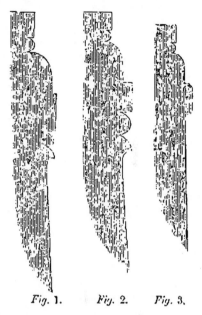

Fig. 1.   *Fig.* 2.   *Fig.* 3.

MOULDINGS OF TOMBS AT NORCHIA.[2]

or the tombs beneath.   No other example is there of a temple-tomb at Norchia; yet high above the detached monuments in the open area just mentioned, is a portico recessed in the cliff.   It is scarcely intelligible from below, and is rather difficult of access. It is composed of three recesses, separated by prominent pilasters rounded in front like half-columns, and having curious fluted capitals.   Each recess is stuccoed, and seems to have been coloured.   It is obvious that this elevated portico was not a mere tomb-stone, like the monuments around, but a sepulchre itself, each recess serving as a niche for the deposit of a sarcophagus. It bears a strong analogy to some Greek tombs in the island of Thera, recessed in the cliffs in a similar manner.[1]

The tombs at Norchia are more numerous than at Castel d'Asso.   There must be at least fifty or sixty with distinct sculptured façades, besides many others in ruin.   I sought in vain

[2] The mouldings of *Fig.* 1 are most common at this site.   Those of *Figs.* 2 and 3 are varieties.   Those also most common at Castel d'Asso see *Figs.* 1 and 2 in the woodcut at page 186) are to be found at Norchia, but less frequently.

[1] Mon. Ined. Inst. III. tav. 25, 3.   Ann. Inst. 1841, p. 17.

for one described by Orioli[2] as having a trapezium cut in the rock
above its façade, in all probability to represent the roof to that
sort of *cavædium* which Vitruvius terms *displuviatum*. Nor could
I find another, said by the same antiquary to have a sphinx in
prominent relief on each of the side-walls of the façade.[3] It
is singular that not a single Etruscan inscription has been found
in this necropolis. Excavations have been made on this site by
Signor Desiderio of Rome, but nothing of value was brought to
light.

The Etruscan town of which these tombs formed the necropolis,
occupied the site of the ruined church of Norchia. Its position
on a sharp point of land at the junction of two glens, and in relation to the tombs around, would alone tend to indicate this as the
site of ancient habitation. But there are also remains of ancient
gateways cut through the cliffs; though no vestiges of Etruscan
walls are visible—all the ruins on the height belonging to the
middle ages. The size of the ancient town was very small,
scarcely larger than that at Castel d'Asso, though the number
and magnificence of its sepulchres indicate a place of some
importance. Its name is involved in obscurity. We know that
in the ninth century it was called Orcle;[4] but that such was its
original appellation it is impossible to determine, as no mention
is made of it by ancient writers.[5] Canina takes it to be Contenebra, and so marks it on his map, but has no authority for this

[2] Ap. Ingbir. Mon. Etrus. IV. p. 199,
tav. XLII. 2. Ann. Inst. 1833, p. 30.

[3] Annali dell' Inst. 1833, p. 29. So also
Lenoir (Ann. Inst. 1832, p. 295), who
speaks of but one, a colossal sphinx, cut in
the rock among the tombs.

[4] In an epistle of Leo. IV., "to the
good man the Bishop of Toscanella," given
by Orioli (Annali dell' Instit. 1833, p.
20), which, singularly enough, mentions
the "*petra ficta*" without the city—most
probably referring to the temple-tombs. In
the same letter are also mentioned "*cava
scamerata*" and "*cava caprilis*"—i.e. a
cave with chambers, and one where goats
were kept.

[5] Orioli (op. cit. p. 22) suggests that it
may be identical with Nyrtia, mentioned by
the ancient scholiast on Juvenal (X. 74) as
a town, the birthplace of Sejanus, giving
its name to or deriving it from the goddess
Nurtia or Fortuna, spoken of by the Satirist
in the text, or that it derives its name from

Orcus, as Mantua was so called from Mantus. But seeing that it was called Orcle as
early as the ninth century, it is quite as
probable that it derives its name from
Hercules, who was worshipped by the
Etruscans as Ercle—just as Minerva gave
her name to Athens, and Neptune his to
Posidonia or Pæstum.

Orcle was partly deserted in early times
on account of the unhealthiness of the site,
and the emigrants removed to Vitorchiano
(Vicus Orclanus), whither in 1435, under
the pontificate of Eugeno IV., the rest of
the inhabitants removed, and the town was
destroyed. Orioli, Ann. Instit. 1833, p. 21.
Though Orioli lays claim to the discovery
of this site, it was indicated as Etruscan a
century before his time by Mariani (De
Etrur. Metrop. p. 46, compare his map),
who speaks of "Horchia. Sic appellabatur
dea Etruscorum ibi culta. Norchiam nunc
dicunt, ut Nannium pro Annio, Nannum pro
Annæ."

nomenclature, which is mere conjecture.[6] In its present state of utter desolation, it has charms as much for the artist as for the antiquary. Who that has visited this spot can forget the ruined church of Lombard architecture, wasting its simple beauty on the stupid gaze of the shepherd, the only frequenter of these wilds ? Who that has an eye for the picturesque, can forget the tall cliffs on which it stands—here, perforated so as to form a bridge,[7] there, dislocated, and cleft to their base,—the rich red and grey tufo half-mantled with the evergreen foliage of cork, ilex, and ivy ? Who can forget the deep glens around, ever wrapt in gloom, where the stillness is broken only by the murmurs of the stream, or by the shriek of the falcon—solitudes teeming with solemn memorials of a past, mysterious race—with pompous monuments mocking their very purpose ; for, raised to perpetuate the memory of the dead, they still stand, while their inmates have for long ages been forgotten ? He who has visited it must admit, that though name-less and unchronicled, there are few sites in Etruria more in-teresting than this—none which more imperatively demand the attention of the antiquary.

[6] In his map he places the ancient town on the broad platform between the Fosso delle Pile and the Fosso dell' Acqua Alta, and thus represents it as a place of first-rate size, which we know Contenebra was not, for it had but a scanty population (Liv. VI. 4). Canina founds his opinion on a piece of ancient walling on the spot marked *h* in my plan, which he takes to be a portion of the walls of the Etruscan town, and he thereon pronounces it to have been "strongly fortified in most ancient times," so as to have been able to resist the Romans for several days (Etr. Marit. II., p. 51). But this bit of wall is not on the brow of the cliff as the fortifications would be, but in the valley at their feet; and if it protected anything, it was the tombs in the cliffs above it. (See Canina's illustration, tav. XCII.) It can have formed no part of the city-walls. I see no reason to alter my opinion that the Etrus-can town stood on the height, now occupied by the Lombard church.

[7] Orioli (Ann. Inst. 1833, p. 20) says there is an ancient Roman bridge of regular masonry over the Biedano, below the town ; but I did not perceive it. He also mentions a road cut in the rock, and called the "Cava Buja," on whose wall is carved a Latin in-scription. The only instance of a rock-hewn road that I could perceive is near the natural bridge, and it is now choked with fallen masses of rock.

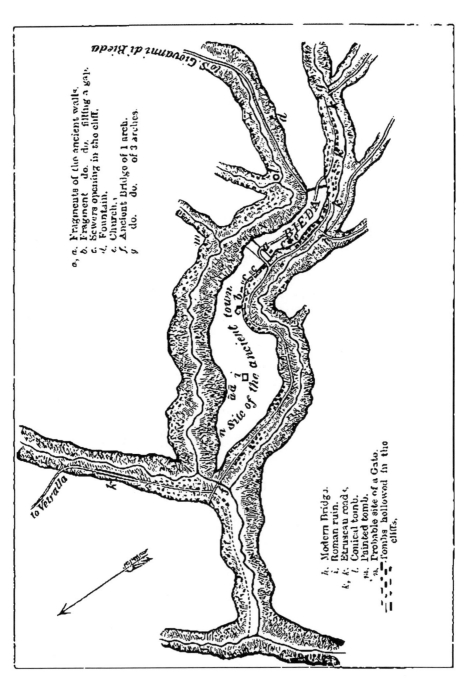

a, a. Fragments of the ancient walls.
b. Fragment do. do. filling a gap.
c. Sewers opening in the cliff.
d. Fountain.
e. Church.
f. Ancient Bridge of 1 arch.
g. do. do. of 3 arches.

h. Modern Bridge.
i. Roman ruin.
k, k. Etruscan roads.
l. Conical tomb.
m. Painted tomb.
n. Probable site of a Gate.
n. Tombs hollowed in the cliffs.

Giovanni di Bieda

BIEDA

a a a a Site of the ancient town.

to Vetralla

ROUGH PLAN OF BIEDA AND ITS NECROPOLIS.

G. Dennis.

CHAPTER XIX.

BIEDA.—*BLERA.*

Data sunt ipsis quoque fata sepuleris.—JUVENAL.

Some things in it you may meet with, which are out of the common road; a Duke there
is, and the scene lies in Italy.—BEAUMONT AND FLETCHER.

ANOTHER Etruscan site of great interest, but very little known,
is Bieda, a village five or six miles south-west of Vetralla. It is
the representative of the ancient town of Blera, of which its
name is a corruption.[1] Blera could not have been a place of
importance, under either Etruscans or Romans. Not once is it
mentioned by ancient historians, and its name only occurs in the
catalogues of geographers.[2] We know that it was a small town
at the commencement of the Empire;[3] that it was on the Via
Clodia, between the Forum Clodii and Tuscania; and there ends
our knowledge of it from ancient sources. That it had an existence in Etruscan times, we learn, not from the pages of history,
but from the surer records of its extant monuments.

Bieda is best visited from Vetralla. The road for the first two
miles is the highway to Corneto and Civita Vecchia. We then
turned off to the left, crossed some downs by a mere bridle-path,
forded a stream in a wild, deep hollow, and reached the brow
of a hill, whence the village of Bieda came into view, crowning
an opposite height. The scenery here was very romantic. The
height of Bieda was lofty and precipitous, and as usual was a
tongue of rock at the junction of two glens, which separated it
from corresponding heights of equal abruptness. These glens,

---

[1] When *l* in Latin words follows a con-
sonant, the Italians are wont to change it
into *i*; as from *clarus, planus, flamma,*
they make *chiaro, piano, fiamma;* and *r*
is sometimes changed into *d*, as *rarus* into
rado, porphyrites into *porfido.* Blera must
have been called Phlera, or Phlere, by the
Etruscans, since they had no *b* in their

language. "Phleres" is a word which
often occurs in Etruscan votive inscriptions.

[2] Strabo V. p. 226. Ptolem. Geog. p. 72,
ed. Bertii. Plin. Nat. His. III. 8.

[3] Strabo classes it among the πολίχναι
συχναί of Etruria.

or ravines, were well clothed with wood, now rich with the tints
of autumn. Wood also climbed the steep cliffs, struggled for a
footing among the wild masses of tufo split from their brow, and
crowned in triumph the surface of the platforms above.

On descending the rocky slope, we found ourselves in the
Etruscan necropolis. The slope was broken into many ledges,
and the cliffs thus formed were full of caverns—sepulchre after
sepulchre above, beneath, around us—some simply hollowed in
the rock and entered by Egyptian doorways, some mere niches,
and others adorned with architectural façades; from the banks of
the stream to the brow of the height the whole face of the hill
was thus burrowed.

I had been struck at Castel d'Asso with the street-like arrangement of the tombs, and at Norchia with their house-like character;
but I had been unwilling to consider those features as other than
accidental, and had ascribed them to the natural peculiarities of
the ground. But here, I felt convinced that they were intentional, and that this assemblage of sepulchres was literally a
necropolis—a city of the dead.

Here were rows of tombs, side by side, hollowed in the cliff,
each with its gaping doorway; here they were in terraces, one
above the other, united by flights of steps carved out of the rock;
here were masses split from the precipice above, and hewn into
tombs, standing out like isolated abodes—shaped, too, into the
very forms of houses, with sloping roofs culminating to an apex,
overhanging eaves at the gable, and a massive central beam to
support the rafters. The angle of the roof, I observed, was that
still usual in Italian buildings—that angle, which being just
sufficient to carry off the rain, is naturally suggested in a climate
where snow rarely lies a day. I have spoken only of the exterior
of the tombs. On entering any one of them, the resemblance
was no less striking. The broad beam carved in relief along the
ceiling—the rafters, also in relief, resting on it and sinking
gently on either side—the inner chamber in many, lighted by a
window on each side of the door in the partition-wall, all three
of the same Egyptian form—the triclinial arrangement of the
rock-hewn benches, as though the dead, as represented on their
sarcophagi, were wont to recline at a banquet—these things were
enough to convince me that in their sepulchres the Etruscans, in
many respects, imitated their habitations, and sought to make
their cemeteries as far as possible the counterparts of their cities.

The cliff-bound height of Bieda at its termination is sharp as

a wedge. On it stood the ancient town as well as the modern
village, but they did not occupy precisely the same site ; the
former from the fragments of ancient wall at the verge of the
precipice on both sides the height, seems to have extended to the
very tip of the tongue of land ; while the latter is removed almost
a mile further back.

At the point of junction of the two ravines, where the streams
from each also meet, is an ancient bridge, of one wide arch, based
on the rocky banks of the stream, and approached by a gradually
ascending causeway of masonry, which, as well as the bridge, is
of tufo cut from the cliffs around.[4] The parapets have been
overturned, probably by the large shrubs which flank it, in-
sinuating their roots among the uncemented masonry, and
threatening ultimately to destroy the whole structure. The only
means of approach to Bieda from this side is by this ancient
bridge, which was probably on the Via Clodia.

From this point there seem to have been anciently two roads
to the town—one leading directly up to the summit of the wedge-
shaped table-land, the other still in use, running beneath the
precipice to the right, and sunk deep in the tufo rock. The cliffs
between which it passes are hollowed out for the reception of the
dead, not, as at Veii, in square or upright niches, which could
hold only an urn or vase, but in low-arched recesses, as at
Falleri, of sufficient length to contain a body, with a deep hollow
for it to lie in, and a groove around it for a lid of stone or terra-
cotta, apparently serving also to carry off the water which might
trickle from the ground above. Nor are there wanting sepulchral
chambers hollowed in these cliffs, nor the water-channel formed
in the rock on one side of the road to keep it dry and clean, and
free from deposits from above.

The road to Bieda creeps beneath the cliffs of the ancient town,
which are honey-combed with sepulchral caverns, broken and
blackened with smoke. Here and there among them tall upright
openings in the cliff show the mouths of ancient sewers, and at
intervals are fragments of the Etruscan wall along the verge of
the cliff; in one spot filling a natural gap, as at Civita Castellana.
The masonry is of rectangular blocks of tufo, of the size and

---

[4] In order to accommodate the masonry
to the ascent of the road, a course of wedge-
like form was introduced, which gives a
slight rising towards the arch. Similar
edge courses I have observed in the walls
of several Etruscan and Umbrian cities—
Populonia, Fiesole, Perugia, Todi—and this
feature is also to be seen in the substructions of the Appian Way, near Aricia.

arrangement which I have described under the name of *emplecton*. The ancient town certainly occupied part, perhaps the whole, of the modern village. It must have been very long and narrow, since the height on which it stood forms but a ridge—a mere spine-bone—between the parallel glens.

Bieda, like every town and village off the main roads throughout the Roman State, is a wretched place, " in linked *squalor* long drawn out," with no *osteria* where the traveller, who values comfort, could venture to pass the night. There is but one respectable house, and here we were stopped by the Count of S. Giorgio, who stood at the door waiting to receive us. He apologised for delaying us; but said that the presence of strangers was of such rare occurrence in this secluded village, that he could not allow us to pass without inquiring if he could be of service to us. We learned that he was from Turin, but having bought some estates in this part of Italy, he had acquired therewith the title of Duke of Bieda, the honour of magistracy, and almost feudal dominion over the inhabitants of this village and its territory. The purchase could only be effected on these terms, and on the condition of his residing six months in the year on this spot, which he regarded as a veritable exile from civilisation. He pointed out a ruin opposite, as once the palace of the Counts of Anguillara, the old feudal lords of Bieda, who, among other barbarous privileges, claimed that of forestalling every bridegroom in their domain—by insisting on which the last of these fine old Roman gentlemen, three centuries since, fell a victim to popular fury, and his mansion was destroyed. Yet much of the power of its feudal chiefs has descended to the present lord of Bieda, who told us he was almost absolute; that his will was law; that he had power over the lives and properties of his tenants, being supreme judge of both civil and criminal causes— in a country, be it remembered, where trial by jury was then unknown. His rule, however, seemed based on love, rather than on fear—more akin to that of the chief of a clan than to feudal seigniory, on the one hand, or to the authority of an English landowner over his tenantry, on the other.

The Count courteously proposed to act as our *cicerone* to the antiquities of the neighbourhood, and mounted his steed to accompany us.

Our first object was an ancient bridge of three arches, which lay in the ravine to the south-east of the town. The Count led the way down the descent, through a narrow cleft, sunk some

ANCIENT BRIDGE OF THREE ARCHES, BELOW BIEDA.

Drawn by Geo. Measom.

twenty feet in the tufo, with a channel or furrow in the middle, so deep and narrow that the horses could scarcely put one foot before the other, and we were obliged to adhere to the Horatian maxim, *in media tutissimus*, lest our legs should be crushed against the walls of rock.

On emerging from this cleft, the triple-arched bridge stood before us. The central arch was a true semicircle, thirty feet in span; the side arches were only ten feet wide, and stilted. All were formed of rusticated blocks, with edges so sharp and fresh that it was difficult to believe it the work of two hundred years since, much less of two thousand; but the first step I set on the bridge convinced me of its high antiquity. The central arch has been split throughout its entire length, probably by an earthquake; the blocks, being uncemented, have been much dislocated, but few have fallen. It is clear that this split occurred at an early period; for in crossing the bridge, passengers have been obliged to step clear of the gaps, which in some parts yawn from one to two feet wide, and, by treading in each other's footsteps, have worn holes far deeper than pious knees have done in the steps at A'Becket's shrine, or in the Santa Scala at Rome. They have worn a hollow pathway almost through the thick masses of rock; in some spots entirely through—a perpendicular depth of more than three feet.[5]

From the superior neatness of its masonry, I have no hesitation in assigning to this bridge a later date than to that on the other side of Bieda. That being of similar masonry to the town-walls, may well be of Etruscan construction. This may be as late as the Roman domination in Etruria, yet is in the Etruscan style, and the work probably of Etruscan architects, like other public works in Rome and her territories, raised in the earlier ages of the City, in consequence of the system she adopted of supplying her own deficiencies in the useful and ornamental arts by the superior skill of her neighbours. It must be remembered that this part of Etruria was not conquered before the fourth

[5] The bridge is of tufo, usually soft, flaky or friable, but here of a peculiarly close, hard character, as is shown by the remarkable sharpness of the rustications. And it must be observed that for ages the bridge must have been impassable to beasts, for the same earthquake that split the arch caused the outer part of it on one side to fall; this, however, having been repaired during the middle ages, as the masonry attests, all further necessity of following the foot-worn track was obviated, yet the bridge was still scarcely practicable for beasts. It is evident that the hollow pathway has been worn wholly by human feet, and prior to the repairs of the bridge in the middle ages.

century of Rome; yet the Etruscans must previously have had
bridges over these streams; and that they could raise perfect
arches in much earlier times the Cloaca Maxima remains to
attest. These bridges have an air of greater antiquity than the
two at Veii, which have been accounted Etruscan. It is probable
that they were both on the line of the Via Clodia, which passed
through Blera on its way to Tuscania.

The Count declared that the bridge was an enigma, as none
could perceive by what road it had anciently communicated with
the town—the cleft by which we had descended not being deemed
of sufficient antiquity. But to me it was plain as the cliffs that
rose around me, that this very cleft had formed the ancient
approach to Bieda from this side; for I had observed, almost
throughout its length, traces of the water-channels recessed at
the foot of its rocky walls, just above the original level of the road;
and it was no less clear that the deep and narrow furrow along
which we had steered with so much difficulty, had been worn by
the feet of beasts through many ages, as from the narrowness of
the road they had been constrained always to keep in the middle.

The scenery in the hollow is very fine. Just beyond the bridge
the glen again forks and the cliffs rise to a vast height. I do not
recollect a site in the volcanic district of Etruria, save Sorano in
Tuscany, where the chasms are more profound, and the scenery
more picturesque, than around Bieda.

Close to the bridge is a large cave, the cliff above which was
pitted with bullet marks, which were thus explained by the
Count:—"Every tenant of mine on returning home from the
wild-boar chase, if successful, discharges his piece against this
rock, and I, or my steward, answer the summons by appearing on
the top of the cliff and claiming the boar's thigh as my right."

Between these ancient bridges, and just below the town, is a
modern bridge, overhung by a ruined tower of the middle ages,
and in the opposite steep is another artificial cleft in the rock—
another Etruscan roadway. From this height the whole face of
the slope below Bieda is seen honeycombed with caves, originally
sepulchres, extending in terraces and scattered groups down to
the banks of the stream. It is a very warren of tombs, used by
the Biedani as hog-sties, cattle-stalls, or wine-cellars. The
application to the former purposes is a profanation, but of the
latter change who shall complain ?—

> " Better to hold the sparkling grape
> Than nurse the earthworm's slimy brood."

At the top of the ascent we were in an undulating plain, apparently an unbroken level, with the village of Bieda in the midst. The Count pointed out the extent of his domain, which was far too large for the limited number of his tenantry. At the close of every year he assembles his vassals, as they may be called, and having determined what part of his estate is to be cultivated, and having partitioned it into lots, he makes them draw for the several portions. He takes a share of the produce in lieu of rent.

On our return to the village we visited the church, in front of which stood a Roman sarcophagus with a good bas-relief, found in the neighbourhood. We were not a little surprised to see in this secluded place a genuine altar-piece of Annibale Caracci—the Scourging of Christ. At the Count's mansion we found a sumptuous repast spread for us, and refusing his pressing invitation to stay the night, we groped our way in the dark to Vetralla—thus closing our first day at Bieda, and one of the most agreeable of our Etruscan travel.

Bieda is a site which deserves much more attention than it has yet received from antiquaries. In no Etruscan necropolis are the tombs hollowed in the face of cliffs more numerous. The glens on every side of the town abound in them, and they face every point of the compass, though here, as elsewhere, few have a northern or eastern aspect. On this account, the cliffs on the western side of the town, even under the very walls, are honey-combed with tombs, while scarcely one is to be seen on the opposite side of the glen, or in the cliffs beneath the town on the east. For variety of character the tombs of Bieda are particularly interesting. At Castel d'Asso there is much monotony; even at Norchia, with a few striking exceptions, one prevailing fashion is maintained throughout. But Bieda, without any marked peculiarities of its own, seems to unite those of many other *necropoles*. Here we find tombs with architectural façades, like those of Castel d'Asso and Norchia, but in general differently moulded, and in a simpler and severer style. Here are many, as at Civita Castellana and Sutri, having a mere doorway, without any inscription or external decoration. Here are the body-niches of the same two cemeteries—the columbarium-tombs of Toscanella and Bolsena, and even something like the curious cliff-columbarium of Veii—the house-like tombs of Sovana; and certain rock-hewn isolated monuments, square or conical, of a character rarely seen elsewhere. In one instance is a bench cut

out of the rock in front of a tomb—a practical "*Siste Viator!*"
which I have observed also on other sites.

In cornices there is a great variety at Bieda. One struck

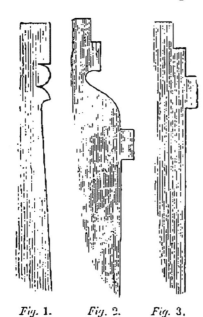

me as very peculiar; it had no
rounded mouldings, but three
distinct *fasciæ*, retreating one
above the other, and though not
ornamental, its simplicity and
massiveness made it very imposing. See the woodcut, fig. 3.
The moulded door, which frequently occurs on the façades, is
in no instance like those of Castel
d'Asso and Norchia, but invariably as in the woodcut below.
In most instances this is a
mere moulding, or pseudo-door;
in others, a real one; in others
again it forms a framework to a
small niche, which must have
contained an urn or vase, pro-

Fig. 1.　　*Fig.* 2.　　*Fig.* 3.

MOULDINGS OF TOMBS AT BIEDA.

bably with the ashes of the
deceased.

These door-mouldings are very common in Etruria. On some
sites, Cervetri, Toscanella, Vulci, and Chiusi, for instance, they

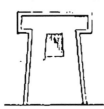

are found, not on the face of cliffs as here, but
at the entrances to sepulchres, many feet below
the surface; and sometimes within the tombs
themselves. They are also often found on
cinerary urns, of house or temple shape. The
form is truly Doric, particularly as it is seen at

MOULDED DOOR AT
BIEDA.

Bieda; it is found also in archaic monuments
of the Doric colonies in Italy and Sicily.[c]

Whether it be the representation of the ordinary door, or a mere
sepulchral ornament, with or without a symbolical meaning, has

---

[c] At Cefalù, the ancient Cephalœdium,
in Sicily, where it is found in connection
with Cyclopean masonry,—and at Canosa,
the ancient Canusium, in Apulia, in a
tomb of four chambers in every respect
extremely like the Etruscan, discovered in
1825. The architrave, however, is by no
means so heavy in this as in the Etruscan
tombs, but more like the Doric. This tomb
is remarkable for having two false windows
painted on one wall—one on each side a
doorway. Ann. Inst. 1832, pp. 285—9,
and Mon. Ined. Inst. I. tav. XLIII. Real
windows so situated are not uncommon in
Etruscan tombs, and occur most frequently
at Cervetri, Bieda, and Chiusi.

been questioned. I have no doubt of the former, not only because it is found on urns and tombs which are evident repre-sentations of houses, but on account of the high probability that these rows and streets of sepulchres were designed to imitate the buildings in the city opposite.

CONICAL TOMB, HEWN IN THE ROCK.

Among the sepulchral varieties of Bieda, two claim particular notice. One of these, which lies in the glen to the east of the town, is a cone of rock, hewn into steps, or a series of circular bases, tapering upwards. Of these, four only now remain, and the cone is truncated, but whether this were its original form, it is not easy to say. Like the conical tombs of Vulci and Tarquinii, it was probably surmounted by a sphinx, lion, pine-cone, or some other funereal emblem, or by a *cippus*, or statue. The rock around it is cut into a trench and rampart. Within the cone is the sepulchre, which is double-chambered, entered by a level passage—not lying beneath the surface as in the conical tombs of Tarquinii. There is a monument at Vulci very similar to this rock-hewn tumulus of Bieda.

The other tomb to which I have referred retains some traces of colour on its walls—the only instance of this among the multi-tudinous sepulchres of Bieda now open. It is also remarkable for being supported in its centre by a column, with base, capital, and abacus, of simple character. Whatever figures may have been painted on its walls, are now obliterated; but ribbons of various hues, and the Greek wave-ornament, can be distinguished through the soot from the shepherd's fires, which thickly coats the walls.

The tombs of Bieda present no great variety in their interiors. They are usually surrounded by benches of rock, about two feet and a half from the ground ; sometimes merely for the support of sarcophagi, but more frequently hollowed out for the reception of bodies. The fronts of these benches are adorned with pilasters, often in imitation of the legs of a banqueting-couch, which the bench itself is designed to resemble. The niches hollowed in the cliffs are usually for entire bodies, whence it may be inferred that the custom of burning the dead was not prevalent on this site. Double-chambered tombs are by no means rare, though I saw no instance of one with more than two chambers.

In one of our excursions to Bieda, we varied the route by passing through San Giovanni di Bieda, a wretched village two or three miles from the former place, in the midst of park-like scenery, but with no antiquities in its neighbourhood.[7]

Bieda, it has been said, was on the Via Clodia, or Claudia. This Way parted from the Cassian a few miles from Rome, ran by Ad Careias, or Galera, to Sabate on the Lacus Sabatinus, and through Forum Clodii, Blera, and Tuscania to Cosa, where it fell into the Aurelian.[8]

---

[7] Gell has stated that there are tombs at this spot with genuine Etruscan mouldings, but it is evident that he had never visited it, since he places it "on the road between Vetralla and Viterbo," whereas it is three miles on the other side of Vetralla.

[8] See p. 61.

CHAPTER XX.

PALO.—*ALSIUM*.

Necnon Argolico dilectum littus Haleso
Alsium.   SIL. ITALICUS.

The place of tombs,
Where lay the mighty bones of ancient men,
Old knights, and over them the sea-wind sang,
Shrill, chill, with flakes of foam.—TENNYSON.

FEW roads in Italy are now more frequented than the coast-line of railway between Rome and Pisa, and none in point of scenery are more uninteresting. Yet along this coast lie some of the principal cities of Etruria—cities of the most hoary antiquity, foremost of old in power and in wealth, in arts and in arms, as well as in the intimate association of their history with that of Rome, and still prominent in interest for the wonders they have yet to display in their local monuments. So far as intrinsic beauty is concerned, it would be difficult to find in Italy a tract less inviting, more bleak, dreary, and desolate, than that which lies between Civita Vecchia and Rome, and to the traveller on first making an acquaintance with that land of famed fertility and beauty, as many used to do, and some still do, at that port, nothing can be more disappointing. He who approaches the Eternal City for the first time from this side has his whole soul absorbed in recollections of her ancient glories, or in conceptions of her modern magnificence. He heeds not the objects on the road, as he skirts the desert shore, or the more desolate undulations of the Campagna, save when here and there a ruined bridge or crumbling tower serves to rivet his attention more fixedly on the past. A thousand togaed phantoms rise before his eyes; or the dome of St. Peter's swells in his perspective, and the treasured glories of the Vatican and the Capitol are revealed to his imagination. Yet when he has attained the desire of his eyes, and can look from the Imperial City to objects around her, he will find along this desert, arid shore, or among the wooded hills inland, sites where he may linger many a delightful hour in contemplation of "the wrecks of days departed."

Most of these sites are now easily reached by the train which leaves Rome three times a day. It was not so when I first knew this coast some thirty and odd years ago, when, if the diligence chanced to be full, it was often impossible to find any conveyance, not even a donkey as a *monture*, between one point and another. To such straits have I been put, that I have a lively recollection of entering Rome one fine morning on a fish-cart, after a night's journey from Palo, spread-eagled some fifteen feet above the road, on a pile of fish-baskets.

An hour's run from Rome by the railway brings you to Maccarese (twenty-one miles), on the river Arrone. At the mouth of the same river stands the Torre di Maccarese, supposed to mark the site of the Etruscan town of Fregenæ or Fregellæ,[1]— and its position on a low swampy shore, and in the vicinity of a noxious marsh or fen, called Stagno di Maccarese, answers to the picture of Silius Italicus—*obsessæ campo squalente Fregellæ.*[2] In very early times it may have been of importance; for Tarquinius Priscus invited Turianus, an artist of this place, to Rome, to make the *terra-cotta* statue of Jupiter, for his new temple on the Capitol.[3] We hear no more of it, however, till it was colonized by the Romans in 509 (B.C. 245);[4] and in 563 (B.C. 191), with the other maritime colonies of this coast, it was compelled to assist in fitting out a fleet against Antiochus the Great.[5] It was in existence at the commencement of the Empire,[6] but after that we lose sight of it; and now, so far as I

[1] Cluver, II. p. 499. Nibby, Dint. di Roma, II. p. 281. The Maritime Itinerary places it between Portus Augusti and Alsium, nine miles from each.

[2] Sil. Ital. VIII. 477.

[3] Pliny, who records this fact (XXXV. 45), calls the place Fregellæ; but that he refers to the town of Etruria, and not to Fregellæ of the Volsci, is manifest from the context, as well as from a comparison with Liv. I. 56; and is confirmed by the extended renown of the Etruscans in the fictile art. Moreover, Silius Italicus calls the Etruscan town Fregellæ, and Pliny (III. 9) the Latin town, Freginæ, so that the names seem to have been used indifferently. Yet Müller (Etrusk. IV. 3, 2) takes the town whence Turianus came for the Fregellæ of the Volsci, on the ground that the fictile art was early practised in that land, as is proved by the celebrated bas-reliefs found at Velletri; but, to reconcile this view with the rest of Pliny's statement, he supposes this Volscian to have studied art in the Etruscan school. All this seems to me unnecessary, and the simplest and most rational interpretation is to suppose that Pliny referred to the Fregenæ of Etruria.

[4] Vell. Pater. I. 14; cf. Epitome of Livy, XIX.

[5] Liv. XXXVI. 3.

[6] Pliny (III. 8) classes it among the maritime colonies of Etruria. Strabo (V. p. 225) also cites it as a small town on this coast, and calls it Fregenia.

can learn, there are no local remains visible to mark the Etruscan
character of the site.

The next station is Palidoro, twenty-six miles and a half from
Rome, marked by a church and two large farm-houses. At a
spot not far from this, called Selva la Rocca, the Duchess of
Sermoneta, in 1839 and 1840, excavated some tumuli, and found
vases of the most beautiful Greek style, some resembling those
of Sicily and Athens; besides pottery of more ancient character;
together with articles in gold, bronze, amber, smalt, glass, and
alabaster.[7]

A mile or two beyond, at a spot called Statua, are some ruins,
supposed to mark the site of Ad Turres, a station on the Via
Aurelia.[8]

Palo station is forty-nine kilomètres, or thirty miles from
Rome by railway, though some miles less by the old high road.

Palo is well known to travellers as the half-way house between
Rome and Civita Vecchia; but few bear in mind that the post-
house, the ruined fortress, and the few fishers' huts on the beach,
represent the Alsium of antiquity—one of the most venerable
towns of Italy, founded or occupied by the Pelasgi, ages before
the arrival of the Etruscans on these shores.[9]

It is strange that no record is preserved of Alsium during the
Etruscan period; but this may be owing to its dependence on
Cære, with whose history and fortunes its own were probably
identical. That it was occupied by the Etruscans we learn from
history, confirmed by recent researches. The earliest notice of
it by Roman writers is its receiving a colony in the year 507.[1]
At no time does it seem to have been of much importance; the
highest condition it attained, so far as we can learn, being that of

---

[7] Abeken, Bull. Inst. 1839, p. 84; 1840,
p. 133; Mittelitalien, p. 267; Micali,
Monum. Ined. p. 374.

[8] Mentioned in the Itinerary of Antoninus, as 22 miles from Rome. Here it
is that Cramer (Ancient Italy, I. p. 208)
places Alsium.

[9] Dion. Hal. I. p. 16. Silius Italicus
(VIII. 476) refers its origin to the Argive
Halesus, son of Agamemnon, from whom
he supposes it to have derived its name.
Its Pelasgic origin being admitted, it seems
just as likely to have derived its name from
ἅλς—the sea; or from ἄλσος—a grove, as
Gerh. el opin. Ann. Inst. 1831, p. 205,
in reference to the dense woods on the

coast. For both he and Welcker are of
opinion that the Pelasgic tongue, though
differing from the Greek, bore sufficient
analogy to it, to enable us to trace by that
means the origin of the names of certain
ancient localities.

[1] Vell. Paterc. I. 14. As a maritime
colony it was compelled to furnish its quota
of troops in the year 547 (B.C. 207),
when in the Second Punic War Italy was
threatened with a second invasion of Carthaginians under Hasdrubal. Liv. XXVII.
38. Pliny (III. 8) and Ptolemy (Goog.
p. 68, ed. Bert.) certify to its existence as
a colony in their days.

a small town.[2]   This may have been owing to its unhealthy
position, on a low swampy coast.   Yet it was much frequented
by the wealthy Romans;[3] and even the Emperor Antoninus chose
it as his retreat, and had an Imperial villa on this shore.[4]

> Havova un bel giardin sopra una riva,
> Che colli intorno e tutto 'l mare scopriva.

At the beginning of the fifth century Alsium, like the neighbouring Pyrgi, was no longer a town, but merely the site of a
large villa ;[5] we have no subsequent record of it, and it was probably destroyed by the Goths or Saracens, who devastated this
coast in the middle ages.

Not a vestige of the Pelasgic or Etruscan town is now visible ;
but there are extensive substructions of Roman times along the
beach.   The fort, also, which was built in the fifteenth century,
has some ancient materials in its walls.   About a mile to the
east are some very extensive ruins on the shore, apparently of
one of the Roman villas.

Alsium, though its site had been pretty clearly indicated by
the notices of the ancients,[6] had been well-nigh forgotten, when
some years since the enterprise of a lady revived interest in the
spot.

About a mile and a half inland from Palo, close to the deserted
post-house of Monteroni, are four or five large tumuli, standing
in the open plain.   They bear every appearance of being natural

[2] Rutil. I. 224. Strabo (V. p. 225) also
speaks of it as a mere πολίχνιον.   Yet the
fact of giving its name to a lake—now Lago
Martignano—full 20 miles distant, seems
to imply an extensive *ager*, and no small
importance.   For the Lacus Alsietinus, see
Frontinus, de Aquæduct. II. p. 48.   Cluver
(II. p. 524) errs in taking the Lago Stracciacappa to be the Lacus Alsietinus.

[3] Pompey had a villa here.   Cicero, pro
Miloue, XX.   M. Æmilius Porcina also
built one on so magnificent a scale, that he
was accused of it as a crime, and heavily
fined by the Roman people. Val. Max.
VIII. 1, *Damn*. 7.   And the mother-in-law
of the younger Pliny had also a villa at
Alsium, which had previously belonged to
Rufus Verginius, who took such delight in
it, that he called it "the nestling-place of
his old age."—*senectutis suæ nidulum*—
and was buried on the spot. Plin. Epist.
VI. 10 ; cf. IX. 19.   An inscription, found

at Ceri, mentions a villa at Alsium. Visconti, Mon. Ant. di Ceri, p. 12.

[4] Fronto, de Feriis Alsiensibus.   Gruter
(p. 271, 3) gives a dedicatory inscription
to Marcus Aurelius, by the Decuriones of
the Colony of Alsium, which was found at
Palo.   Cf. Cluver. II. p. 497.

[5] Rutil. I. 224—

> Nunc villæ grandes, oppida parva prius.

[6] Strabo (V. pp. 225, 226) places it on
this coast between Pyrgi and Fregenæ. And
so also the Maritime Itinerary marks it as
9 miles from the latter, and 12 from the
former town.   The Peutingerian Table is
in error in calling it 10 miles from Pyrgi,
for 12 is the true distance.   These discrepancies are of little importance ; the general
position of a place being thus indicated,
the precise site can be determined by extant
remains.

hillocks—huge masses of tufo rising above the surrounding level. Hence their ordinary appellation of "Colli Tufarini." Yet their isolation and similarity to the sepulchral mounds of Cervetri, induced the Duchess of Sermoneta, in whose land they lay, to probe their recesses. This was in 1838. One of the most regular in form, which was about forty feet high, was found to be girt by a low basement wall of tufo masonry, which formed a periphery of nearly eight hundred feet. This wall had two buttresses on the north, sundry drains on the south, and on the west a hole containing a small stone cylinder. Though the sepulchral character of the tumulus was thus clearly indicated, the entrance to the tomb was long sought in vain; at length, some forty or fifty feet up the slope, a passage was found cut in the rock, and leading to the tomb; and it was remarked that the mouth of the passage was pointed at by the cylinder in the basement-wall. The tomb closely resembled the Grotta Regulini-Galassi of Cervetri; for it was a long passage, walled with regular masonry, the courses converging till they formed a rude Gothic-like arch, which terminated in a similar square channel or groove; and the high antiquity indicated by its construction was likewise confirmed by the character of its furniture. No painted vases of Greek form or design; nothing that betrayed the influence of Hellenic art; all was here closely allied to the Egyptian.[7]

No other tomb was discovered in this mound, but a well or shaft in the floor, twenty feet deep, opened into a horizontal passage, about a hundred feet long; and here were three other shafts, probably sunk to other sepulchral chambers on a still lower level. This system of shafts and galleries reminds us of the Pyramids, and is in harmony with the Egyptian character of the contents of this tomb.

At the foot of this mound, sunk beneath the surface of the plain, was discovered a double-chambered sepulchre, of more ordinary Etruscan character, and its contents showed only that general resemblance to the Egyptian which bespeaks a high antiquity.[8]

---

[7] Rude pottery of black earth, with figures scratched thereon; flat vases of smalt, ornamented with lotus-flowers, purely Egyptian in character, and ostrich-eggs painted, as in the Isis-tomb of Vulci, beads of smalt and amber, and gold *laminæ* with archaic reliefs.

[8] They consisted of pottery, and *terra-cotta* figures in the Oriental Etruscan style, some with four wings, forming the feet of vases. The description of these tombs I have taken from Abeken, Bull. Inst. 1839, pp. 81—84; 1841, p. 39; and also from his *Mittelitalien*, pp. 242, 267, 272, 274.

These tombs, from their position, must have belonged to the necropolis of Alsium; and thus, while one bears out Dionysius' statement of the existence of an Etruscan population on this site, the other confirms his testimony as to its prior occupation by a more ancient race.

Were excavations continued here, other tombs would doubtless be discovered. But since the Duchess's death, little has been done on this coast.

It is scarcely worth while to visit the tumuli of Monteroni, for the chambers are now re-closed with earth; even the basement-wall is re-covered or destroyed, and not a trace remains to attest their sepulchral character.

In spite of its venerable antiquity, Palo is a most dreary place. Without extant remains of interest, or charms of scenery, it can offer no inducement to the traveller to halt one hour, save that he will here find the best accommodation in the neighbourhood of Cervetri; and should he propose to take more than a passing glance at that site, he may well admit the claims of Palo to be his head-quarters. The fare is not such as the place once afforded—no "fatted oysters, savoury apples, pastry, confectionery, and generous wines, in transparent faultless goblets," dainties fit to set before a king—*convivium regium*[9]—but, for a wayside hostelry, the post-house is not to be despised. Yet the place itself is desolate enough. Beyond a copse on either side

See Canina's Etruria Marittima I., p. 126 and tav. XL., for plans and sections of these tombs. Micali, who takes his notices from the papers of the late Duchess, gives a somewhat different description of these tombs. He says, above the basement-wall of the tumulus the tufo was cut into steps to the height of 18 feet, and then levelled; and on this was raised a mound of earth to the height of 27 feet more. In the lower or natural part of the mound was discovered a sepulchre of four chambers, one of them circular, all with rock-hewn benches, and with bronze nails in the walls. These, from his description of their contents, are the least ancient of the tombs mentioned in the text. The passage-tomb he represents as 45 feet long, sunk in the same levelled part of the mound, though lined with masonry, regularly squared and smoothed. Upon it opened, by a door of the usual Etruscan form, another narrow passage, similarly lined but half the length, with a rock-hewn bench,

and numerous bronze nails in the wall. Here were found some articles of gold, and jewellery, fragments of Egyptian vases, and odorous *paste*, and a stone in the form of an axe-head, supposed to be Egyptian. There were no Etruscan inscriptions in any of these tombs. The masonry of the passage he represents (Mon. Ined. tav. LVII.) as *opus quadratum* of tufo blocks, but *pseud-isodomon*, or in courses of unequal heights. These tombs were drained by many channels cut in the rock, and branching in all directions. Mon. Ined. pp. 378—390. It must be the less ancient of these tombs in which Mrs. Hamilton Gray, who visited them shortly after they were opened, saw a pair of panthers painted over the door of the outer chamber, and two *hippocampi*, with genii on their backs, on the walls of the inner. Sepulchres of Etruria, p. 123, third edition.

[9] Fronto, de Feriis Alsiensibus, epist. III.

of the village, there is nothing to relieve the bare monotony of the level waste.   It is hard to believe Alsium could ever have been " the voluptuous sea-side retreat " it is described in the time of the Antonines.[1] Now the traveller is ready to exclaim—

"Oh, the dreary, dreary moorland ! oh, the barren, barren shore !"

Yet the lover of sea-side nature may find interest here, as well as in the sparkling bay of Naples.   Though to me this is no *dilectum littus*, as it was to Halesus, yet memory recalls not without pleasure the days I have spent at Palo.   The calm delight of a sunny shore finds its reflex in the human breast.   The broad ocean softly heaving beneath my window, ever murmured its bright joy; mirroring " the vault of blue Italian day."   A few *feluccas*, their weary sails flapping in the breeze, lay off shore, lazily rocking with the swell, which broke languidly on the red ruins at my feet, or licked with foam the walls of the crumbling fortress.   Away to the right, was the distant point of Santa Marinella ; and to the left, the eye wandered along the level shore, to which the dunes of Holland were mountains, uncertain whether it were traversing sea or land, save when it rested here and there on a lonely tower on the coast ; or when it reached a building on the extreme horizon, so faint as now to seem but a summer-cloud, yet gleaming out whitely when the evening sun fell full on its flank.   This was the fort of Fiumicino, at the mouth of the Tiber, the port of modern Rome.   Such were the standing features of my prospect ; which was varied only by scenes of domestic life, at the doors of the huts opening seaward, or by herds of long-horned cattle, which came down to pick their evening meal from the straw scattered over the beach.   When the sun's last glories had faded from the sky, then began the life and stir of Palo.   The craft, which had lain in the offing all day, stood in after dark, and sent the produce of their nets to land.   Then what bustle, what shouting, on board and ashore ! Red-capped, bare-legged fellows with baskets—my chubby host of Palo bargaining for the haul—sky-blue *doganieri*, and cloaked quidnuncs, looking on—all common-place features enough, but assuming, from the glare of torches, a rich Rembrandtish effect,

---

[1] Fronto, loc. cit. Were it not that the author was writing to an Emperor, we might suspect him of irony ; but sovereigns, especially despots, are edged tools ; which

Pollio remembered when challenged to banter by Augustus.   Macrob. Saturn. II. 4.   Fronto, however, qualifies his praises of Alsium by mentioning the *raucis, cludes.*

to which the dark masses of the vessels, magnified by the gloom,
formed an appropriate background.

APPENDIX TO CHAPTER XX.

The ancient sites on this coast, between Rome and Centum Cellæ, are
thus given, with their distances, by the Itineraries :—

ANTONINE ITINERARY.
(*Via Aurelia.*)

Roma	
Lorium	M.P. XII.
Ad Turros	X.
Pyrgos	XII.
Castrum Novum	VIII.
Centum Cellas	V.

MARITIME ITINERARY.

Roma	
In Portum	M.P. XVIIII.
Fregonas	VIIII.
Alsium	VIIII.
Pyrgos	XII.
Castrum Novum	VIII.
Centum Cellas	VIII.

PEUTINGERIAN TABLE.
(*Via Aurelia.*)

Roma	
Lorio	M.P. XII.
Bobiana	—
Alsium	VI.
Pyrgos	X.
Punicum	—
Castro Novo	VIIII.
Centum Collis.	IIII.

ANOTHER MARITIME ITINERARY.

Portus Augusti	
Pyrgos	M.P. XXXVIII.
Panapionem	III.
Castrum Novum	VII.
Centum Cellas	V.

ETRUSCAN SARCOPHAGUS OF TERRA-COTTA, FROM CERVETRI.

CHAPTER XXI.

CERVETRI.—*AGYLLA* or *CÆRE.*

—saxo fundata vetusto
Urbis Agyllinæ sedes ; ubi Lydia quondam
Gens, bello præclara, jugis insedit Etruscis.—VIRGIL.

Buried he lay, where thousands before
For thousands of years were inhumed on the shore.
What of them is left to tell
Where they lie, and how they fell ?—BYRON.

FROM the railway-station at Palo the traveller will espy before him a small village with one prominent building sparkling in the sun, at the foot of the hills which rise to the north, dark with wood. This is Cervetri, the modern representative of the ancient city of Cære. Should he come by train with the intention of visiting that site, he will probably be disappointed in finding a conveyance. A *corriere* conveys to Cervetri the mails dropped by the morning train from Rome, but the *baroccino* seats only two, and a place is not always to be had. If the traveller then

do not care to have a walk of five miles over the downs, he
should write the day beforehand to Giovanni Passeggieri of
Cervetri, who will have a *vettura* in readiness at the Palo station.

The pedestrian or horseman on his way to Cervetri, will leave
the high road for a shorter path, just after crossing a streamlet,
known by the ominous name of La Sanguinara.[1] If the traveller
be in a vehicle, he must keep the high road as far as a second
rivulet, the Vaccina, or Cow-stream, where a country-track turns
to the right and crosses the downs to Cervetri. Insignificant as
this turbid brook may appear, let him pause a moment on the
bridge and bethink him that it has had the honour of being sung
by Virgil. It is the *Cæritis amnis* of the Æneid,[2] on whose
banks Tarcho and his Etruscans pitched their camps, and Æneas
received from his divine mother his god-wrought arms and the
prophetic shield eloquent of the future glories of Rome,—

> clypei non enarrabile textum.
> Illic res Italas, Romanorumque triumphos,
> Fecerat Ignipotens.

The eye wanders up the shrub-fringed stream, over bare
undulating downs, the *arva lata* of ancient song, to the hills
swelling into peaks and girt with a belt of olive and ilex. There
frowned the dark grove of Silvanus, of dread antiquity, and there, on
yonder red cliffs—the "ancient heights" of Virgil—sat the once
opulent and powerful city of Agylla, the Cære of the Etruscans,
now represented, in name and site alone, by the miserable village
of Cervetri. All this is hallowed ground—*religione patrum latè
sacer*—hallowed, not by the traditions of evanescent creeds, nor
even by the hoary antiquity of the site, so much as by the
homage the heart ever pays to the undying creations of the
fathers of song. The hillocks which rise here and there on the
wide downs, are so many sepulchres of princes and heroes of old,
coeval, it may be, with those on the plains of Troy; and if not,
like them, the standing records of traditional events, at least the
mysterious memorials of a prior age, which led the poet to select
this spot as a fit scene for his verse. The large natural mound
which rises close to the bridge may be the *celsus collis* whence

---

[1] Livy (XXII. 1,) relates that, in the
year 537, "the waters of Cære flowed
mingled with blood." Cf. Val. Max. I. 6,
5. The Aquæ Cæretes, here mentioned,
are generally supposed to be the same as
the Θερμά Καιρετανά of Strabo (V. p 220),
now called the Bagni del Sasso, four miles
west of Cervetri. May not the above tradition be preserved in the name of this
stream?

[2] Æn. VIII. 597. Pliny (N. H. III. 8)
calls it, "Cæretanus amnis."

Æneas gazed on the Etruscan camp.[3] No warlike sights or
sounds now disturb the rural quiet of the scene. Sword and
spear are exchanged for crook and ploughshare; and the only
sound likely to catch the ear is the lowing of cattle, the baying of
sheep-dogs, or the cry of the *pecorajo* as he marches at the head
of his flock, and calls them to follow him to their fold or to fresh
pastures.[4] Silvanus, "the god of fields and cattle," has still
dominion in the land.[5]

After two miles of the country-road the traveller passes the
chapel of Sta Maria de' Canueti, and presently ascends between
the walls of Cervetri and the heights of the ancient city.

Cervetri, the representative of Agylla, is a miserable village,
with 300 or 400 inhabitants, and is utterly void of interest. It
is surrounded by fortifications of the fourteenth and fifteenth
centuries, and stands just without the line of the ancient walls,
so that it is annexed to, rather than occupies, the site of the
original city. The village, and the land for some miles round it,
are the property of Prince Ruspoli, whose palace forms a conspicuous object in the scene. This noble seldom makes excavations himself, but allows them to be carried on by his friends,
who are of a more speculative or philarchaic turn of mind. It is
to the enterprise of the Marchese Campana, of General Galassi,
of the arch-priest Regulini, and subsequently of Signor Capranesi,
and of the brothers Boccanera, that we owe the numerous and
remarkable objects of Etruscan antiquity that have been brought
to light here of late years.

The *cicerone* of whose services and keys the visitor who would
see the tombs must avail himself, is Giovanni Passegieri, a
tobacconist, to be found in his shop in the little piazza. Most
travellers will find it sufficient to lionize the site in a day's
excursion from Palo, where there is a tolerable inn; but those
who would devote more than a hurried day to the antiquities of
Cære, and to avoid the transit to and from Palo, are willing to
put up with village accommodation, will find a clean bed and

---

[3] Æn. VIII. 604.

[4] This scene, of sheep following their
shepherd, attracted by his voice, often
meets the eye of the traveller in the East;
and beautiful allusion is made to it in Holy
Writ (St. John X., 3, *et seq.*). Oxen and
goats also in Corsica, and even swine in
Italy, of old, used to follow their herdsman at the sound of his trumpet. Polybius

(XII. pp. 654, 655, ed. Casaub.), who
records this fact, remarks that while the
swineherds of Greece walked behind, those
of Italy invariably preceded their herds.

[5] This region was famed for its cattle in
the olden time. Lycophron (Cass. 1241,
speaks of the valleys or glens of Agylla,
abounding in flocks.

refreshment in the house of the said Giovanni, although they must not expect the delicacies for which Cære was renowned of old.[6]

Remote as are the days of the Etruscans, this city boasts a far prior antiquity. It was originally called Agylla, and is classed by Dionysius among the primitive towns of Central Italy, which were either built by the united Pelasgi and Aborigines, or taken by them from the Siculi, the earliest possessors of the land, ages before the foundation of the Etruscan state.[7] That it was at least Pelasgic and of very remote antiquity there can be no doubt;[8] though we may not be willing to admit that that occupation of Italy can be referred with certainty to the third generation before the Trojan war.[9] Traditions of ages so long prior to the historic period must be too clouded by fable, or too distorted by the medium of their transmission, to be received as strictly authentic. In its early days Agylla seems to have maintained intercourse with Greece, which corroborates, if need be, the uniform tradition of its Pelasgic origin.[1]

It would appear that at its conquest by the Etruscans its name

[6] Martial relished the *perna* of Cære (XIII. 54), and compared her wines to those of Setia (XIII. 124). Colomella (de Re Rust. III. 3) testifies to the abundance of her grapes.

[7] Dion. Hal. I. p. 16; cf. III. p. 193.

[8] Dionysius is confirmed by Strabo (V. pp. 220, 226), Pliny (III. 8), Servius (ad Æn. VIII. 479; X. 183), and Solinus (Polyh. cap. VIII.), who all record the tradition that Agylla was founded by the Pelasgi. Servius states that they were led to select this site on account of a fountain; not being able to find water elsewhere in the neighbourhood. Strabo says these Pelasgi were from Thessaly (cf. Serv. ad Æn. VIII. 600). Virgil corroborates the tradition by referring the grove of Silvanus on this site to the Pelasgi —

Silvano fama est veteres sacrâsse Pelasgos.

Lycophron (Cass. 1355) calls Agylla, Ausonian. It is justly remarked by Lepsius (Ann. Inst., 1836, p. 202) that there are more witnesses to the Pelasgic origin of Cære, than of any other city of Etruria. Mommsen (Hist. Rome, I. c. 10) asserts that Agylla is not a Pelasgic name, as generally supposed, but a word of purely Phœnician origin, signifying "round city,"

for such a form the town must have presented when viewed from the coast.

[9] It is stated by Hellenicus of Lesbos, that the Siculi were expelled from Italy at that period; Philistos of Syracuse gives the date as 80 years before the Trojan War; while Thucydides refers the expulsion to a period much subsequent to the fall of Troy (ap. Dion. Hal. I. p. 18).

[1] That Agylla had a Greek origin cannot be deduced from the circumstance of its having dedicated treasure to the Delphian Apollo (Strabo, V. p. 220), and of its consulting that oracle (Herod. I. 167), for other people than the Greeks are recorded to have made similar dedications and consultations. Crœsus, king of Lydia, consulted the oracle of Delphi and other Greek oracles (Herod. I. 46; Paus. III. 10, 8; X. 8, 7), and Tarquinius Superbus sent his two sons with gifts to consult the Delphic oracle. Liv. I. 56. The language of the city, however, in very early times, if Strabo may be believed, was Greek: or if we refuse credence to the tradition he records, we may, at least, receive it as evidence of the general belief in the Greek origin of the city, which gave rise to the legend. Servius (ad Æn. VIII. 597) derives the name from a *heros eponymos*, Agella.

was changed into Cære, but the reason of this alteration we know not, unless we choose to attach credit to the old legend, which tells us that when the Lydian or Etruscan colonists were about to attack the city, they hailed it and inquired its name ; whereon, a soldier from the ramparts, not understanding their motives or language, replied with a salutation—χαῖρε—"hail!" which they receiving as a good omen, on the capture of the city applied to it as its name.[2] But this, like most of the etymologies of the ancients, savours strongly of, what Pliny terms, the *perversa subtilitas* of the grammarians.

In the time of Æneas, the city is represented by Virgil as under the sway of Mezentius, a cruel and impious tyrant, who was expelled by his subjects and fled to Turnus, king of the Rutuli ; while the liberated Agyllans joined the ranks of the Trojan prince.[3]

In very early times, Cære is said to have cultivated the arts ; for Pliny asserts, that in his day paintings were here extant, which had been executed before the foundation of Rome ; and he cites them as examples of the rapid progress this art had made, seeing that it appeared not to have been practised in the days of Troy.[4] Cære, even as early as the time of the first Tarquin, is represented as among the most flourishing and populous cities of Etruria ;[5] and she was undoubtedly one of the Twelve of the Confederation.[6] But what, above all, distinguished Cære was, that she alone, of all the cities of Etruria, abstained from piracy, from no inferiority of power or natural advantages, but solely from her sense of justice ; wherefore the Greeks greatly honoured her for her moral courage in resisting this temptation.[7]

---

[2] Strabo, loc. cit. Steph. Byzant. *v.* Agylla. Servius (ad Æn. VIII. 597) relates the same story, but on the authority of Hyginus (de Urbibus Italicis) refers this blunder to the Romans. Müller (Etrusk. einl. 2, 7, n. 40) thinks the original Etruscan name was "Cisra." Lepsius (die Tyrrhen. Pelasg. p. 28) regards Cære as the original name, which came a second time into use ; and thinks it was Umbrian, not Etruscan, in conformity with his theory of the Umbrian race and language being the foundation of the Etruscan. Canina (Cere Antica, p. 25), who is of the old or literal school of historic interpretation, thinks that "the change of name, and the mingling of the Agyllans with the Etruscan invaders can be established in the first ten years after the fall of Troy ;" while Niebuhr, on the other hand (I. p. 127, cf. p. 385), will not allow it to have been made even so early as the year of Rome 220 (B.C. 534).

[3] Virg. Æn. VII. 648 ; VIII. 481, *et seq.* ; cf. Liv. I. 2.

[4] Plin. N. H. XXXV. 6.

[5] Dion. Hal. III. p. 193.

[6] This may be learned from the passages of Dionysius and Strabo already cited, as well as from the prominent part the city took, in conjunction with Veii and Tarquinii, and the independent course she subsequently followed with regard to Rome. Livy (I. 2) also represents Cære as a powerful and wealthy city of Etruria.

[7] Strabo, V. p. 220. Mommsen (loc.

The first mention of this city in Roman history is, that it maintained a war with Tarquinius Priscus.[8] It also joined Veii and Tarquinii in the twenty years' war with his successor, Servius Tullius, and at the re-establishment of peace, in consequence of the prominent part it had taken, it was punished by the Roman monarch with the forfeiture of a portion of its territory.[9]

At the same period, or about the year of Rome 220 (534 B.C.), the Cærites joined their fleet with that of Carthage on an expedition against a colony of Phocæans, who had seized on Alalia in Corsica, and after a severe combat, all the prisoners taken by the allies were brought to Cære and there stoned to death. In consequence of this cold-blooded massacre, the city was punished with a plague; men, herds, and flocks—whatever animal passed near the spot where the bodies of the Phocæans lay, became afflicted with distortion, mutilation, or paralysis; whereon the Cærites sent to Delphi to consult the oracle how they might atone for their crime, and were ordered to perform solemn expiatory rites, and to institute games of gymnastic exercises and horse-racing in honour of the slain; which they continued to observe in the time of Herodotus.[1]

On the expulsion of Tarquinius Superbus from Rome, he and his two sons took refuge in Cære,[2] probably on account of his family connections there; but it is not recorded that this city took part in Porsenna's expedition to re-instate the exiled prince. Unlike Veii, Fidenæ, Falerii, and other cities in this part of Etruria, Cære, though but twenty-seven miles from Rome, seems to have been for ages on friendly terms with that city.[3] When, in the year 365, Rome was attacked by the Gauls, Cære opened her gates and gave refuge to the Flamen Quirinalis, and Vestal Virgins, and eventually restored them in safety to their home.[4]

cit.) thinks that Strabo in this passage did not refer to piracy, but meant that Cære protected and encouraged foreign commerce, by refraining from exactions, and that she thus became a sort of free-port, both for the Phœnicians and Greeks, to which fact she owed her great wealth and importance in early times.

[8] Dion. Hal. III. p. 193.

[9] Dion. Hal. IV. p. 251; cf. Liv. I. 42. Herod. I. 166, 167.

[2] Liv. I. 60. Dionysius (IV. pp. 276, 279) however, asserts that it was to Gabii he fled, where his son Sextus was King. Livy says it was Sextus alone who went to

Gabii.

[3] This fraternity and intimate connection were probably owing to the Pelasgic origin of Cære, and the consequent want of a complete sympathy with the Etruscans. Niebuhr (I. p. 386) was even inclined to the opinion that Rome was a mere colony of Cære—an opinion which he afterwards modified. Lepsius (Ann. Inst. 1836, p. 203) thinks that the Pelasgic population of Cære was preserved more or less pure to a late period.

[4] Liv. V. 40. Strabo, V. p. 220. Val. Max. I. i. 10. Cf. Plut. Camil.; Flor. I. 13. See also an inscription in the Vatican,

Nay, we are told that the Cærites attacked the retreating Gauls, laden with the spoil of Rome, routed them, and recovered all the booty they were bearing away. For these services the senate decreed that the Cærites should receive the *hospitium publicum*, or be admitted into the most intimate relations with the Roman people[5]—in fact, they received the full privileges of Roman citizens, save the suffrage.[6] The origin of our word ceremony— *cærimonia*—has been ascribed to this event.[7]

A year or two before the capture of Rome by the Gauls, Cære was engaged with another enemy, Dionysius of Syracuse, who, in 362, attacked Pyrgi, and spoiled its celebrated temple of Eileithyia. As this was the port of Cære, the inhabitants of the latter city rushed to the rescue, but, being probably unprepared for war, not expecting an attack, they were easily routed by the Sicilians.[8]

Cære, though closely allied to Rome, continued to maintain her independence; but it is probable that this was threatened, otherwise "the sympathy of blood" alone would hardly have induced her, in the year 401 (B.C. 353), to take up arms to assist Tarquinii against Rome, when she had for ages been intimately associated with the Republic. She must have received some provocation when she sent an army into the Roman territory, and laid it waste up to the mouth of the Tiber. Ere long, however, conscious of her unequal strength, she repented of this step, and besought pardon and peace, reminding the Romans of the services she had rendered in their distress. The senate referred her ambassadors to the people, who, moved by their touching appeal and the remembrance of past services, rather than by the excuse then urged, listened to their prayer and

---

given by Gruter, p. 492—7, and Muratori, p. 172, 4.

[5] Liv. V. 50. Strabo, loc. cit.

[6] This condition became proverbial, and what had originally been conferred as an honour was subsequently made significant of disgrace; for *tabulæ Cærites* and *cera Cæritis* came to imply the condition of Roman citizens, who had been deprived of the right of suffrage. Hor. I. ep. VI. 62. Aul. Gell. XVI. 13, 7. Strabo, loc. cit. Niebuhr (II. pp. 60, 67) is of opinion, from the classification of Festus (v. Municipium), that Cære was really degraded from the highest rank of citizenship, in consequence of her conduct in the year 401; and thus

he accounts for the proverbial reference to the Cæritan franchise as a disgraceful condition.

[7] Val. Max. loc. cit. Festus, v. Cærimonia. The etymologies of the ancients are rarely to be trusted; but Niebuhr (I. p. 386) thinks this derivation very plausible. The first syllable of the word may not have been originally Cæri, but Cœri (for Curi) monia—Coerare being an early form of Curare (A. Gell. IV. 2)—which, at least, is expressive of the meaning; the two diphthongs, it is well known, were sometimes interchangeable,

[8] Diod. Sic. XV. p. 337. Serv. ad Æn. X. 184.

granted them a truce for a hundred years.[9]   It is highly probable
that the Cærites paid the penalty of their error by the loss of
their independence, for we have no record of any further conquest
of them by the Romans; indeed, we next hear of Cære as a
Roman dependency, providing corn and other provisions for the
fleet of Scipio, in the year 549,[1] and otherwise assisting in the
Second Punic War.[2]

At the commencement of the Empire this "splendid and illustrious city" had sunk into utter insignificance, retaining mere
vestiges of its past greatness, being even surpassed in population
by the Thermæ Cæretanæ—the hot baths in the neighbourhood, which the Romans frequented for health's sake.[3]   It
revived, however, as appears from monuments and inscriptions
found on the spot, and became a *municipium*.[4]   Nor was it at
any period wholly blotted from the map, but continued to exist,
and with its ancient name, till, at the beginning of the thirteenth
century, part of its inhabitants removed to a site about three
miles off, on which they bestowed the same name, and the old
town was distinguished by the title of Vetus, or Cære Vetere,
which has been corrupted into its present appellation of Cervetri,
the new town still retaining the name of Ceri.   This has misled
antiquarians, who have sought the Etruscan city on the site
which seemed more clearly to bear its name,[5] but inscriptions and

---

[9] Liv. VII. 19, 20.

[1] Liv. XXVIII. 45.

[2] Sil. Ital. VIII. 474.

[3] Strabo, V. p. 220.   Now the Bagni
del Sasso, so called from a remarkable bare
crag on the summit of the neighbouring
mountain.   It lies about five miles west of
Cervetri, and is visible from the road between Palo and Sta Severa.   Mannert
(Geog. p. 379) places the Aquæ Cæretanæ
at Ceri ; Canina (Etr. Marit. I. p. 163) at
Caldane, five or six miles to the S. E.
of Cervetri.   Cluver (II. p. 493)confounds
them with the Aquæ Apollinares, on the
upper road from Rome to Tarquinii.   Westphal (Rom. Kamp. p. 160) makes a similar
mistake.   But Holstenius (Annot. ad Cluv.
p. 85) distinguishes between the two Aquæ,
placing one at Stigliano, the other at Bagni
del Sasso.   The true site of the Aquæ
Apollinares has been fixed by M. Desjardins
at Vicarello, on the Lago Bracciano.   Ann.
Inst. 1859, pp. 34—60.

[4] Festus v. Municipium.   Gruter, pp.

215, 1 ; 485, 5 ; cf. 235, 9.   Cluver, II.
p. 493.   Bull. Inst., 1840, pp. 5—8.—
Canina.   In excavations made in 1840 on
the site of the city, some beautiful marble
statues of Tiberius, Drusus, Germanicus,
and Agrippina were discovered, together
with a singular bas-relief bearing the names
and emblems of three Etruscan cities, Tarquinii, Vetulonia, and Vulci, which monuments are now among the chief ornaments
of the new Museum of the Lateran.   In
the season of 1845–6, the Augustine monks
of Cervetri discovered many more statues
and *torsi*, with altars, bas-reliefs, beautiful cornices, and other architectural fragments of a theatre, coloured tiles and
antefixæ, and numerous fragments of Latin
inscriptions, with one in Etruscan, "CU-
SIACH," which is unique in having the
letters cut in marble and inlaid on a darker
stone.

[5] A bull of Gregory IX., in 1236, distinguishes between these two towns, speci-
fying "plebes et ecclesias in Cere Nova,"

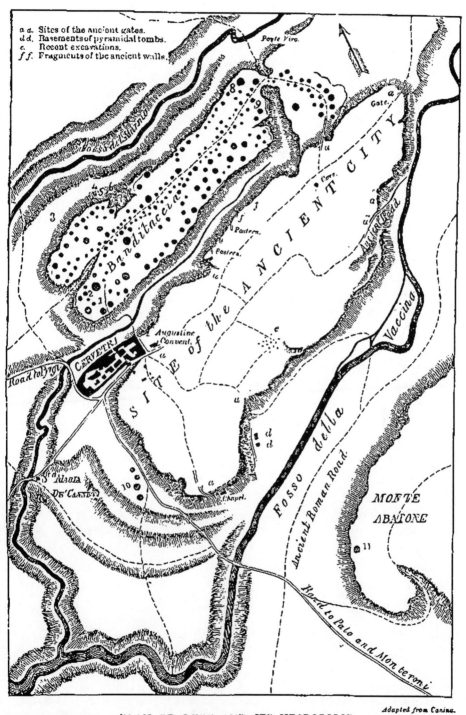

PLAN OF CÆRE AND ITS NECROPOLIS.

1. Tomb with pilasters.
2. Grotta della Sedia.
3. ,, delle Cinque Sedie.
4. ,, dell' Alcova.

5. Grotta dei Tarquinj.
6. ,, dei Sarcofagi.
7. ,, del Triclinio.
8. ,, dei Rilievi.

9. Grotta degli Scudi e Sedie.
10. ,, Regulini-Galassi.
11. ,, Campana.

other monuments found at Cervetri of late years, have established
its identity with Cære beyond a doubt.[6]

Of the ancient city but few vestiges are extant; yet the outline of its walls is clearly defined, not so much by fragments,
for there are few remaining, as by the character of the ground
which the city occupied. This is a height or table-land, rising
in steep cliffs above the plain of the coast, except on the northern
side where it is united by a neck to the high land adjoining.
Within the space thus marked off by nature, not a ruin of the
ancient city now rises above ground. Temples, towers, halls,
palaces, theatres—have all gone to dust; the very ruins of Cære
have perished, or are overheaped with soil; and the peasant
follows his plough, the husbandman dresses his vines, and the
shepherd tends his flock, unconscious that he is treading over
the streets and buildings of a city among the most renowned of
ancient times, and thirty times more extensive than the miserable
village which has retained its name.

Let not the traveller omit to visit the site of Cære under the
impression that there is nothing to be seen. If of antiquarian
tastes, he will have the satisfaction of determining the extent,
form, and position of the city,—he will perceive that it was four
or five miles in circuit, and therefore fully substantiated its
claim to be ranked among the first of Etruria,—that it was of
oblong form,—that it had eight gates, all distinctly traceable, some
approached by roads sunk in the rock and lined with tombs,
others retaining their flanking walls of masonry,—he will see in
the cliffs around the city, the mouths of sewers above, and more
frequently tombs of various forms below; and he will learn from
the few fragments that remain, that the walls of Cære were
composed of rectangular blocks of tufo, of similar size and arrangement to those in the walls of Veii and Tarquinii, and utterly
different from those of Pyrgi, which are supposed to have had a
common origin.[7]

and also, "in Cere Vetere et finibus ejus."
Nibby, Dintorni di Roma, I. p. 355.

[6] Bull. Inst. 1840, pp. 5—8; 1846,
p. 129. Canina in his Cere Antica, published in 1838, claims to have been the
first to indicate the true site of this
city. But Gruter (pp. 214; 652, 8) had
long before given some inscriptions referring to Cære, which were found at Cervetri.

[7] Canina (Etruria Marit. tav. 45) illustrates some fragments of the wall on the

north of the city. Foundations may, in
several parts, be traced along the brow of
the cliffs, and on the side opposite the Banditaccia, for a considerable extent. Many
of the ancient blocks have been removed of
late years to construct walls in the neighbourhood, and I was an indignant witness
of this destruction, on one of my visits to
the site. Nibby (I. p. 358) speaks of traces
of the more ancient or Pelasgic walls in
large irregularly squared blocks, along the

If he be an artist, or lover of the picturesque, taking no interest in the antiquities of the place, he will still find abundance of matter to delight his eye or employ his pencil; either on the site of the city itself, with its wide-sweeping prospect of plain and sea on the one hand, and of the dark many-peaked hills on the other, or in the ravines around, where he will meet with combinations of rock and wood, such as for form and colour are rarely surpassed. The cliffs of the city, here rising boldly at one spring from the slope, there broken away into many angular forms, with huge masses of rock scattered at their feet, are naturally of the liveliest red that tufo can assume, yet are brightened still further by encrusting lichens into the warmest orange or amber, or are gilt with the most brilliant yellow—thrown out more prominently by an occasional sombering of grey—while the dark ilex, or oak, feathers and crests the whole,

> "And overhead the wandering ivy and vine
> This way and that, in many a wild festoon,
> Run riot, garlanding the gnarled boughs
> With bunch and berry and flower."

The chief interest of Cære, however, lies in its tombs. These are found on all sides of the city, but particularly on the high ground to the north, now called La Banditaccia. Let not the traveller conceive vain fears from a name of so ominous a sound, and which his imagination may lead him to suppose was derived

cliffs on the east of the city, and still more distinct on the western side. I could perceive no such remains; all the fragments I observed being of an uniform character—rectangular tufo masonry, of smaller blocks than usual, and very similar in size and arrangement to the fragments of walling at Veii (p. 12), and Tarquinii (p. 427), and to the ancient fortifications on the height of S. Silvestro near the Tiber, which I take to mark the site of Fescennium (p. 122). It is nevertheless possible that these walls are of Pelasgic construction; for, as the only material on the spot is soft tufo, which has a rectangular cleavage, the Pelasgic founders of the city could not avoid using it except by fetching limestone, at a great expense of labour, from the mountains inland; and, using the tufo, they would naturally hew it into forms most easily worked and arranged, as they did in the Regulini-Galassi tomb, and other early sepulchres of Cære, whose contents authorise us to regard them as Pelasgic. The objection to assign such an origin to the remains of the city walls, lies not in the rectangularity of the blocks, but in their small size; seeing that all the ancient fortifications we are best warranted in ascribing to the Pelasgi, are composed of enormous masses. Though I acknowledge the influence of the local materials on the style of masonry, I do not think it amounts to a constructive necessity; and though I believe the Pelasgi may have employed one style of masonry at Cosa, another at Cortona, and a third at Agylla, I cannot admit that they exercised no preference, or that any other people with the same materials would have arrived at the very peculiar style which they seem always to have followed, where practicable, and which is generally called after their name. For further remarks on this subject, see chap. L.

from the number of bandits infesting the spot.[8] The name is
simply indicative of the proprietorship of the land, which once
belonging to the *comune*, or corporation of Cervetri, was *terra
bandita*—"set apart;" or "forbidden" to the public, and, as it
was uncultivated and broken ground, the termination descriptive of
its ugliness was added—*banditaccia*. It retains the name, though
it has passed into the hands of Prince Ruspoli. To reach it from
Cervetri, you cross the narrow glen to the north. Here in
the cliffs opposite is hollowed a range of sepulchres, all greatly
injured within and without.[9]

This Banditaccia is a singular place—a Brobdignag warren,
studded with mole-hills. It confirmed the impression I had received at Bieda and other sites, that the cemeteries of the Etruscans were often intentional representations of their cities. Here
were ranges of tombs hollowed in low cliffs, rarely more than
fifteen feet high, not piled one on another as at Bieda, but on the
same level, facing each other as in streets, and sometimes branching
off laterally into smaller lanes or alleys. In one part was a
spacious square or piazza, surrounded by tombs instead of houses.
None of these sepulchres, it is true, had architectural façades remaining, but the cliffs were hewn into smooth, upright faces, and
here and there were fragments of an ornamental cornice cut in the
rock. Within the tombs the analogy was preserved. Many had
a large central chamber, with others of smaller size opening upon
it, lighted by windows in the wall of rock, which served as the
partition. This central chamber represented the *atrium* of
Etruscan houses,[1] whence it was borrowed by the Romans; and
the chambers around it the *triclinia*, for each had a bench of rock
round three of its sides, on which the dead had been deposited,
reclining as at a banquet. The ceilings of all the chambers had
the usual beams and rafters hewn in the rock; and in one

---

[8] Mrs. Gray (Sep. Etruria, p. 367) may
be excused for having fallen into this error,
when the same had been stated by the
highest archæological authorities in Rome.
Cere Antica, p. 51. Bull. Inst. 1838, p. 171.
In truth, a spot so swarming with caverns,
might well suggest such an appellation.

[9] One of them has a small pilaster against
its inner wall, with capital and abacus
quite Doric, and shaft also of early Doric
proportions, though resting on a square
base.

[1] Described by Vitruvius (VI. 3), Varro
(L. L. V. 161), and Festus (v. Atrium).
The *atrium* in this case was not a true
cavædium, not being open to the sky; but
had it been, the purpose of concealment
would have been defeated. Indeed it was
sometimes deemed necessary to support the
ceiling by a massive pillar of rock. Yet
that the analogy was intended, and was
preserved as far as possible, is evident from
the windows around, which suppose the
light to have been received from the central
chamber.

instance there was a fan-like ornament in relief, and walls panelled, precisely as in a tomb at Vulci;[2] whence it may be inferred that such decorations were at one period fashionable in Etruscan houses.

Many of the tombs of the Banditaccia are surmounted by tumuli. Tumuli, indeed, are scarcely less numerous here than at Tarquinii. Some of them are still unexcavated, the entrance being below the surface; in others the doorway opens in the basement, which is often of rock, hewn into mouldings and cornice, and more rarely of masonry. The cone of earth which originally surmounted these tumuli is in most cases broken down, in some almost to the level of the soil. As at Tarquinii, there are no architectural façades in this necropolis; the decoration is chiefly internal. Nor could I perceive more than two instances of inscriptions on the exterior of tombs; and those were no longer legible.

Tombs of great interest have been opened on this spot at various periods, and not a few still remain open. The first you reach is a large tomb, lying deep below the surface of the hill, with two square pillars in the centre, and a row of long niches for bodies recessed in the walls; beside which the chamber is surrounded by a deep bench, separated into compartments for corpses, which were arranged, not in lines parallel with the niches, but at right angles, with their feet pointing to the centre of the tomb. There is nothing further remarkable in this sepulchre beyond an Etruscan word—CVETIIN—cut in the rock over one of the recesses, which, from its position in the corner, seems to be the commencement of an inscription never completed. This tomb, in size, form, and arrangements, is very like that of the Tarquins, represented in the wood-cut at page 242. It was discovered in 1845. It is marked 1 in the Plan.

GROTTA DELLA SEDIA.

Hard by, on the slope between Cervetri and the Banditaccia, is a sepulchre, on the plan of those of Bieda, with two small chambers, separated by a wall of rock, in which are cut a door and two little windows, all surrounded by the usual rod-moulding. But the marvel of the tomb is an arm-chair, cut from the living rock, standing by the side of one of the two sepulchral couches in the outer chamber, as though it were an easy-chair by the bed-side,

or a seat for the doctor visiting his patient! But why placed
in a tomb? Was it merely to carry out still further the analogy
to a house? Was it, as Visconti suggests, for the use of the
relatives who came yearly to hold solemn festivals at the tomb?[3]
Or was it for the shade of the deceased himself, as though he
were too restless to be satisfied with his banqueting-couch, but
must have his easy-chair also to repose him after his wanderings?
Or, as Micali opines, was it to intimate the blissful repose of the
new life on which his spirit had entered?[4] Was it not rather a
curule chair, the *insigne* of the rank or condition of the deceased,
showing him to have been a ruler or magnate in the land?[5] It
may have been for the support of a cinerary urn; for in the tombs
of Chiusi, *canopi*, or vases in the form of human busts, which
were probably the effigies of the deceased whose ashes they
contained, have often been found placed on earthenware seats of
this form. Such *canopi* have also been discovered at Cære. This
tomb was opened in 1845.[6]

Crossing the western end of the Banditaccia, we reach a tomb
opening in its northern slope, called the

GROTTA DELLE CINQUE SEDIE.

It has three chambers, one in the centre, which has its roof
carved into beam and rafters, and a smaller one on each side,
opening on the passage by which the tomb is approached. The
rock-cut doorway to each chamber is arched—an unusual feature.
In the little chamber to the left, are five small seats in a row,
hewn from the rock, but without decorations. They give its
name to the sepulchre. I found this tomb full of water in June,
1876. It faces W.N.W.

GROTTA DELL' ALCOVA.

A little beyond that just described, and lying beneath a tumulus,
is another sepulchre which I shall call the " Tomb of the Alcove,"

---

[3] Antichi Monumenti di Ceri, p. 31.

[4] Micali, Mon. Ined. p. 152.

[5] The form of this and similar rock-hewn
seats in other tombs of Cervetri is very like
that of the beautiful marble chair, with
bas-reliefs, in the Palazzo Corsini at Rome,
which is thought to be Etruscan, and a

genuine *sella curulis*. It will be borne in
mind that the curule chair was one of the
Etruscan *insignia* of authority; and
adopted by the Romans from the Etruscans.

[6] Canina gives a representation of this
tomb. Etruria Marit. I. tav. 65.

from a large recess in the further wall, almost like a chapel in a Cathedral.[7] There are in fact three of these recesses, like so many apsides, but the central one is the most spacious, and is obviously the post of honour, the last resting-place of the most illustrious dead here interred. In it is a massive sepulchral couch, with cushion and pillows at its head, ornamented legs in relief, and a low stool, or *hypopodium* in front—all hewn from the living rock. It may represent a *thalamus* or nuptial-couch, rather than the usual festive κλίνη or *lectus,* for it is double, and must have been occupied by some noble Etruscan and his wife, whose skulls still serve as a *memento mori* to the visitor, though a confused heap of dust on the couch is all that is left of their bodies and integuments.

The tomb bears a striking resemblance to a temple—in its spaciousness—in its division into aisles by the pillars and pilasters which support the rafter-carved roof—in the dark shrine at the upper end, raised on a flight of steps—and in the altar-like mass of the couch within. Nor are the many large *amphoræ* which strew the floor, unpriestly furniture ; though they hint at copious libations to a certain jolly god, poured forth on the occasion of the annual sepulchral festivals.

This tomb has other features of interest. The two fluted pillars which support the roof, and the pilasters against the inner wall, present specimens of capitals and mouldings of a peculiar character, and throw light on that little-understood subject—the architecture of the Etruscans. Cære, indeed, is particularly rich in this respect—more so than any other Etruscan site. Many of the tombs still open have singular or beautiful architectural features ; and others of the same character are now lost sight of, or reclosed with earth ; one in particular, from its spaciousness and the abundance of such decoration, had acquired the name of "Il Palazzo." Of the students of ancient architecture who yearly flock to Rome, none should omit to visit the tombs of Cervetri— and none would regret it. This tomb was discovered in 1845.[8]

— — — — — — — — —

At the back of this tomb is one by far the most interesting

[7] Canina calls this tomb "Sepolcro dei Pilastri," and gives a plan and sections of it. Etruria Maritt. I. tav. 67, p. 195. It faces N.N.W.

[8] The deep pit which forms the entrance to most of these tombs is generally lined with tufo masonry. The style is not uni-

form ; in this instance over the doorway it is *emplecton*, precisely resembling the walls of Sutri, Falleri, and Nepi, though of rather smaller dimensions. In every instance it is *opus quadratum*, or regular masonry, even in those tombs which are manifestly of the most ancient construction.

that has been found in this *necropolis*, since the discovery of the celebrated Grotta Regulini-Galassi.   It must be called

GROTTA DE' TARQUINJ,

or, the "Tomb of the Tarquins!"   Yes, reader—here for the first time in Etruria has a sepulchre of that celebrated family been discovered.   The name had been met with, a few times, on

TOMB OF THE TARQUINS, CERVETRI.

urns, and funeral furniture,[9] but never in any abundance.   Nor are we yet assured that it was a common name in Etruria. We only know that there must have been a numerous family of Tarquins settled at Cære.   But can this have been of the same race as the celebrated dynasty of Rome?   Nothing more

The frequent traces of the passages having been vaulted by the gradual convergence of the horizontal courses, establish their high antiquity, as being prior to the invention or at least the practice of the arch.

[9] On a spherical *cippus*, found at Chiusi, was inscribed "TARCNAL" (Passeri, Acheront. p. 66, ap. Gori, III.)—"TARCHNAS" on a cornelian *scarabæus*, found near Piscille (Vermiglioli, Iscriz. Perug. I. p. 81, tav. V. 2)—"TARCHI," on a column in the Museo Oddi at Perugia (id. I. p. 148) —"TARCHIS," on one of the urns in the Grotta de' Volunni at Perugia —"TAR-

CHISA," on an urn in the Museum of Florence (Lanzi, Saggio, II. p. 417).—"TARCHV," on a black cinerary pot from Chiusi, now in the same collection.   TARCH was no doubt the primitive form, with the inflexion of Tarch-*i-u*, or *un* ; from this the adjective was formed by the usual addition of *na* or *nas* — Tarchnas (Tarquinius),   Tarchnai (Tarquinia).   The termination *sa* or *isa* is indicative of connection by marriage, or Tarchisa may be equivalent to Tarquitia— an Etruscan family renowned for its skill in divination. See p. 7.

probable. We know that when the royal family was expelled, the king and two of his sons, Titus and Aruns, took refuge at Cære; Sextus, the elder—

> "the false Tarquin
> Who wrought the deed of shame,"—

retiring to Gabii, where he was soon after slain.[1] What more likely then than that the family here interred was descended in a direct line from the last of the Roman kings? Though Aruns, one of the princes, was slain soon after in single combat with the consul Brutus, at the Arsian Wood,[2] he may have left his family at Cære, and his father and brother still survived to perpetuate the name of Tarquin.[3] However it be, let the visitor to this sepulchre bear in mind the possibility, to say the least, that the skulls he handles, and the dust he gazes on, may be those of that proud race, whose tyranny cost them a crown—perhaps the Empire of the World.

The first chamber you enter is surrounded by benches of rock, and contains nothing of interest; but in the floor opens a long flight of steps, which lead down, not directly, but by a bend at right angles, to a lower chamber of much larger size.[4] It is called by the peasantry the " Tomb of the Inscriptions," and well does it merit the name; for it has not merely a single lengthy legend, as on the pillar of the Pompey-Tomb at Corneto, nor a name here and there, as in the Grotta delle Iscrizioni at the same place; but the tomb is vocal with epigraphs—every niche, every bench, every portion of the walls speaks Etruscan, and echoes the name of Tarquin.

This chamber is a square, or nearly so, of thirty-five feet, with two massive pillars in the centre, and a row of thirteen recesses

---

[1] Liv. I. 60. Dionysius says the king fled to Gabii, where Sextus was prince, and after staying there some time in the vain hope of inducing the Latins to take up his cause, he removed to the city of Etruria, whence his mother's family had come, i.e. Tarquinii (V. pp. 276, 279); but no mention is made of Cære.

[2] Liv. II. 6.

[3] Livy (II. 6, 9) says the elder Tarquin and his son Titus subsequently went to Tarquinii, Veii, and Clusium, to raise the cities of Etruria in their cause, and when the campaign of Porsenna had failed to reinstate them at Rome, they retired to Tusculum, to their relative Mamilius Octavius (Liv. II. 15). We hear no more of them at Cære, yet from their choosing that city as their *first* place of refuge in their exile, it is highly probable that they had relatives residing there, as well as at Gabii, Tarquinii, and Tusculum. The existence of this tomb at least establishes the Etruscan origin of the Tarquins, which Niebuhr has called in question (I. pp. 376, 511).

[4] The depth of the floor below the surface must be very considerable—hardly less than 50 feet. The upper chamber faces S.S.E. The tomb was discovered in 1845.

for corpses, in the walls; while below is a double tier of rock-
hewn benches, which also served as biers for the dead. The
walls, niches, benches, and pillars, are all stuccoed, and the
inscriptions are painted in red or black, or in some instances
merely marked with the finger on the damp stucco. Observe
these scratched epigraphs. They are remarkable for the wonderful freshness of the impression. The stucco or mortar has
hardened in prominent ridges precisely as it was displaced; and
you might suppose the inscription had been written but one day,
instead of much more than two thousand years. No finger, not
even the effacing one of Time, has touched it, since that of the
Etruscan, who so many centuries ago recorded the name of his
just departed friend.

Were I to insert all the inscriptions of this tomb, I should
heartily weary the reader.[5] Let one suffice to show the Etruscan
form of the name of Tarquin.

ᛘᚨᛚᚦ·ᛚᚨᛟᚤᚨᛚ·ᛚᚨᚤᚾᚨᛅᛏ·ᛄᛚᚨᛘ

which in Roman letters would be

AVLE · TARCHNAS · LARTHAL · CLAN

The name, either in Etruscan or Latin,[6] occurs no fewer than
thirty-five times! How much oftener it was repeated in parts
where the paint has run or faded, or the inscriptions have become
otherwise illegible, I cannot say, but should think that not less
than fifty epitaphs with this name must have been originally
inscribed in this tomb. One fact I noticed, which seems to
strengthen the probability that this family was of the royal race
—namely, that it appears to have kept itself in great measure
distinct by intermarriages, and to have mingled little with other
Etruscan families—at least when compared with similar tombs,

---

[5] I have given all the inscriptions that remain legible, whether Etruscan or Latin, in Bull. Inst. 1847, pp. 56—59. Compare Dr. Mommsen's version of some of them (p. 63) which differs from mine, though I cannot think in every instance so correct. For the plan, sections, inscriptions, &c., of this tomb see Canina, Etr. Maritt. I. tav. 62.

[5] The Latin inscriptions in this tomb do not necessarily indicate a very late date; if the family were of the royal blood of Rome, the occasional use of the Latin character may be explained, without referring these epigraphs to the period of Roman domination. Moreover, even though in Latin letters, the name sometimes retains its Etruscan form — "TARCNA" — which is quite novel, and a presumptive evidence of antiquity.

those of Perugia for instance, this sepulchre will be found to contain very few other family-names introduced in the epitaphs as matronymics.[7]

Most of the niches are double, or for two bodies. Some, beside inscriptions, have painted decorations—a wreath, for instance, on one side, and some *crotala*, or castanets, on the other, or a wreath, and a small pot or *alabastos*, represented as if suspended above the corpse. Between the niches are elegant pilasters, and in front are the legs of couches, and the usual long, paw-footed stools, all painted on the stucco, to make each mortuary bed resemble a festive couch. On one of the square pillars which support the beamed roof, is painted a large round shield. In the ceiling between the pillars is a shaft cut through the rock, from the plain above, still covered by the slabs with which it was closed when the last of "the great house of Tarquin" was laid in this tomb.[8]

Like most of the tombs of the Banditaccia, which are below the surface, this was half full of water, as it generally is in winter. At the expense of wet feet, I contrived to examine them all; but after heavy rains, a visit to Cære would, to many, prove fruitless. One tomb was completely reclosed with earth washed down from above, so that I was obliged to have it re-excavated for my especial inspection.

GROTTA DE' SARCOFAGI.

Close to the Tomb of the Tarquins is another sepulchre, sunk deep below the surface, and approached by a similar narrow passage lined with masonry. I designate it the "Tomb of the Sarcophagi," from its containing three of those large monuments, which are very rarely found at Cære, the dead being in general laid out on their rocky biers, without other covering than their robes or armour. The sarcophagi here are of marble. Two have the draped figure of a man on the lid, in an archaic style of art. The first reclines on his back, his right hand rest-

---

[7] In more than forty inscriptions, I could find only eleven names of other families; and of these, seven only were in Etruscan characters, and connected with the name of Tarchnas: the other four were in Latin, and quite distinct.

[8] See the woodcut at page 242. The shaft was either used as an entrance after

the doorway had been closed, by means of niches cut for the feet and hands; or may have served, by the removal of the covering slabs, to ventilate the sepulchre, in preparation for the annual *parentalia*. Such shafts are most common in the tombs of Falerii; but there they open generally in the antechamber, rarely in the tomb itself.

ing on his belly, and his left holding the torque, which encircles
his neck.   He has remarkably fine features, and wears mustachios
and beard, and a chaplet of leaves round his brow.   Four small
lions, of most quaint and primitive art, surround his couch, one
at each angle.   The other figure reclines on his left side, wears a
chaplet, and holds a *phiala* in his right hand, while his left rests
on his bosom.   His hair is arranged in the stiff crisp curls which
are seen in the earliest Etruscan bronzes ; his eyes are painted
black, his lips red ; the rest of the monument is uncoloured.   At
each shoulder is a small sphinx, and a little lion at each foot.
Another sarcophagus of similar character was found in this tomb,
even more interesting than those described, as it bore a number
of figures in relief and coloured, but it has been transferred to
the Gregorian Museum.

There is a peculiarly primitive air about these figures ; they are
unlike those generally carved on the lids of sarcophagi, which, in
truth, are seldom archaic in character.   They bear a strong resemblance to some archaic sarcophagi very recently found at
Tarquinii, and now in the Museum of Corneto.

The third sarcophagus is of temple-form, with a tiled roof, but
without sculptured decorations.

The marble of which these monuments are formed is pronounced
by Canina to come from the Circæan promontory, where, from a
town near the quarry, and from its transparency, it is known as
the alabaster of S. Felice.   The same marble was employed in
the archaic sarcophagi of Tarquinii and Vulci, and the Etruscans
made use of it, though not extensively, until they became
acquainted with the marble of Luna.

On the wall of this tomb is scratched an Etruscan inscription,
which in Roman letters would be v: APUCUS : AC. and on a slab
which served as a *cippus*, I read LARTHI AP. VCUIA, in Etruscan
characters.   Hence it appears probable that the sepulchre was
that of a family named Apucus (Apicius ?) [9]

The front of the couches is painted with sea-monsters, dolphins,
lions, and other animals, on a stuccoed surface.   There are traces
of painting also on the walls of the tomb, but nothing is now intelligible beyond a band of the usual wave-pattern on the inner
wall.

Immediately above the tomb last described, is one opened in

[9] For illustrations of these sarcophagi, see Canina, Etr. Maritt. I. tav. 60, 61, p. 192.

the spring of 1846, which has paintings on its walls. It is designated the

GROTTA DEL TRICLINIO.

The tumulus under which it lies is enclosed by a wall of loose stones, and the door of the tomb is surmounted by three courses of masonry. This tomb has but a single chamber, twenty-four feet by sixteen, surrounded by deep benches of rock, on which the dead were laid, and at the head of each compartment, when I first saw it, lay a skull, which startled the eye on entering the sepulchre. Just within the door are bas-reliefs—a wild-boar on one side, and a panther tearing its prey on the other. But the paintings?—It requires a close and careful examination to distinguish them, so much have they suffered from the damp; and if unaware of their existence, you might visit the tomb without perceiving them. The white stucco on which the scenes are painted has been changed by the damp to a hue dark as the native rock. In a few places only where it has remained dry has the painting retained its distinctness. On the left-hand wall you perceive the heads of a man and woman, who are reclining together at a banquet; and beautiful heads they are, with features of Greek symmetry, and more mastery and delicacy in the design than are commonly found in the sepulchral paintings of Etruria. He is garlanded with laurel and wears a short beard; and his flesh is of the usual deep red, the conventional colour of gods and heroes; but hers is of the white hue of the stucco, though her cheek is touched with red. He pledges her in a *phiala*, or bowl of wine, to which she replies by an approving look, turning her head towards him. Her face and expression are extremely pretty, and a variegated skull-cap, and a full rich tress at the side of her face add to her charms. She wears also a necklace and torque of gold. A round table, resting on three deer-legs, stands by them, with meat, fruits, eggs, and goblets; and a large round shield is suspended on the wall behind. You might fancy it a portrait of Pericles, who had just laid his armour by, and was pledging the fair Aspasia.

> A maraviglia egli gagliardo, ed ella
> Quanto si possa dir, leggiadra e bella.

From these heads we must judge of the rest in this tomb; for a similar scene is repeated again and again on the walls—eight other couples recline on the festive couch, each with a tripod-table by their side, and a shield suspended above.[1] But the women have lost the fairness of their sex, and, from the discoloration of the stucco, have become as dusky as negresses; while the men, from their brick-dust complexions, are much more distinct. The men are not half-draped, as in the earlier tombs of Corneto, but are all dressed in white tunics, the women in yellow. In the centre of the inner wall stand a couple of slaves, at a large table or sideboard, which has sundry vases and goblets on and beneath it, and a tall *candelabrum* at its side, the counterpart to which is seen also on the side-wall.[2] On a mixing-vase which stands on this table or sideboard is inscribed the word "IVNON" in Roman letters, which can hardly here allude to the "white-armed," "ox-eyed" goddess, but must rather refer to the Juno, or presiding spirit of some fair Etruscan,[3] probably of the principal lady interred in this tomb.

The face of the sepulchral couches is also painted—above, with the usual wave-pattern—below, with animals, of which a pair of winged *hippocampi*, in a very spirited style, and a dragon with green wings, are alone discernible.[4]

The colours in this tomb have been laid on in distemper, not *al fresco*. The freedom of the design, so far as it is discernible,

---

[1] A singular feature is, that instead of a separate *lectus* for each pair, the revellers here are depicted reclining on a continuous couch, which, as it occupies three walls of the tomb, may be supposed to represent a *triclinium*, such as the Romans used. The figures here lie under a red and white, or blue and white, striped coverlet, or *stragulum*. The small tables by the side of the *triclinium* are not the usual τράπεζαι (*i.e.* τετράπεζαι), or with four legs, as in most of the paintings of Tarquinii, but τρίποδες, or with only three feet.

[2] Banquets by lamp-light are rarely represented in Etruscan tombs; the revellers are generally depicted lying under the shade of the ivy or vine, or amid groves of myrtle. Even in the Grotta Querciola, at Corneto, though a *candelabrum* is introduced, the festivo couches are surrounded by trees. In the Tomba Golini, at Orvieto, however, *candelabra* are depicted with lights burning, but the paintings there evidently represent scenes in the Etruscan Hades. The *candelabra* in this tomb of Cære are worthy of particular notice, as they are depicted with

a number of little vases tied to the stem in clusters, and with fruit and flowers at the top. *Candelabra*, with vases so attached, have been discovered in Etruscan tombs at Vulci. Bull. Inst. 1832, p. 194. From this we learn a secondary use to which these elegant articles of furniture were applied.

[3] See the Appendix to this Chapter, Note II.

[4] In the floor of this tomb is an oblong pit, just such as opens in the ceilings of so many sepulchres at Civita Castellana, and as is shown in the roof of the tomb of the Tarquins, in the wood-cut, at page 242. Whether it be the shaft to a second sepulchral chamber beneath this, as analogy suggests, or is merely intended to drain the tomb, I cannot say, for I found it full of water. In the so-called "Tomb of Solon" at Gombet Li, in Phrygia, described by Steuart in his work on Lydia and Phrygia, a similar well or shaft is sunk in the middle of a sepulchral chamber. I have found the same also in Greek tombs in Sicily.

the Greek character of the features, and the full faces of some
of the males, are clear proofs of a late date—a date certainly
subsequent to the Roman conquest; and this is confirmed by the
presence of the Latin inscription.[5] This tomb faces the S.E.

A painted tomb at Cervetri has peculiar interest, for this is the
only site in Etruria where we have historical record of the existence of ancient paintings. Pliny speaks of some extant in his
day, which were vulgarly believed to have been executed prior to
the foundation of Rome.[6] Those in this tomb can scarcely lay
claim to a purely Etruscan antiquity. Another sepulchre, however, was discovered some forty years since, which contained
figures of men and animals in a very archaic style, bearing in
their singular parti-coloured character much resemblance to those
in the Grotta Campana at Veji. The tomb is still open, and
lies on the slope to the N. of Cervetri, and not far from the
"Tomb of the Seats and Shields," but it is not easy to find,
and is full of water in the winter.[7]

Traversing the long street of tombs and tumuli, at the N.E.
extremity of the Banditaccia, next to a large tumulus with a
circular, rock-hewn base, we reach the

GROTTA DEI RILIEVI,

or "Tomb of the Reliefs," so called from its peculiar decorations. It was discovered in 1850 by the late Marchese Campana,
and is entered by a long flight of steps sunk deep in the rock, the
passage being lined with *emplecton* masonry. The entrance to

---

[5] For notices of this tomb see Bull. Inst.,
1847, pp. 61, 97, and Canina, Etruria
Marit. vol. I. p. 194, tav. 63, 64. Canina
calls it the "Tomba delle Pitture," and
ascribes it to the end of the Republic.

[6] Plin. XXXV. 6.

[7] The paintings in this tomb are said by
Mr. Ainsley to be more archaic than any at
Tarquinii. A description of them has been
given by Kramer (Bull. Inst. 1834, pp. 97
—101), who represents them as of the
rudest character, painted on the bare porous
tufo, which has undergone no preparation,
not being even smoothed, to receive them.
The tomb was nearly elliptical, and had an
upper and lower band of figures; those in
the lower were almost effaced; but above,
there was a man with pointed beard, and

close vest, shooting an arrow at a stag—a
lion devouring a stag, while a second lion,
squatting by, looked on—a ram flying from
another lion—and fragments of other
animals, and of a second man with a bow.
There was much truth and expression in
the beasts, in spite of their unnatural
parti-colouring. The only hues used in
this tomb are black, white, and red. The
face and legs of the archer were painted
white—a singular fact, as that was the
conventional hue of women. The door-
moulding was striped diagonally, as in
Egyptian architecture, with red, white, and
black. Many of the above figures have
now disappeared, and unless some means
are taken to preserve them, the rest will
soon perish. Cf. Ann. Inst. 1835, p. 183.

the passage is guarded by two lions of tufo, of life-size. This tomb resembles that of the Tarquins in its plan, being surrounded by broad benches of rock, having a series of sepulchral recesses hollowed in its walls, and its roof supported by two similar pillars hewn from the living rock. But its interest is of a very different character. That of the former tomb lies in the historical associations connected with the family there interred, and in its numerous epitaphs recording the name of Tarquin. The interest of this sepulchre, which belonged to an Etruscan family unknown to fame, lies in its singular and abundant decorations, in the numerous representations of weapons and other implements, generally domestic, sometimes religious, both sculptured and painted on its walls, pillars, and pilasters. In this particular it stands alone among the extant sepulchres of Etruria.

It is of smaller size than the tomb of the Tarquins, being only about twenty-five feet in length, by twenty-one feet in width ; the height above the benches of rock on which the pillars rest being about seven feet. The roof, which is nearly flat, is carved into a broad beam and rafters. The benches which surround the chamber are not the usual narrow ledges projecting from the walls, but broad terraces of tufo, on which the dead were laid at right angles to the walls, the beds, of which there are thirty-two, being separated by narrow ridges left in the rock. Recessed in the wall above the benches are a number of horizontal niches, thirteen in all, each for a body, and each with a rock-hewn pillow, painted deep red. These niches are separated by fluted pilasters, and each pilaster bears a shield carved in relief, having Ionic-like capitals, with lotus flowers pendent from the volutes. Above the niches runs a frieze, decorated with a series of weapons, offensive and defensive, all carved in high relief and coloured. Here are casques, greaves, swords, shields, and double strings of large balls, apparently of stone, and probably the missiles used in slings.[8] Over the doorway, however, the weapons give place to two bulls' heads, bound with fillets, as if for sacrifice, and to a bronze *patera* suspended between them for the libation. To the left of the doorway also hangs a flat quadrangular dish representing metal, probably for carrying meat, as it closely resembles the

---

[8] M. Noël des Verges (Étrurie et les Étrusques, III. p. 2) takes them to be the *phaleræ*—metal plaques used to decorate the breasts of victorious heroes, or ornaments used for the heads of horses—which Florus (l. 5) tells us the Romans received from the Etruscans. He draws them in his plate as tassels, but to my eye they appeared to represent a number of balls of large size, strung on a pair of stout ropes, the lowest ball being much the largest.

TOMB OF THE RELIEFS CERVETRI.

butcher's trays used now-a-days in Italy. On each jamb of the
doorway hangs a large two-handled dish (*lepaste*), probably of
metal, and beneath it a circular trumpet or horn.[9] Over the
central niche in the inner wall, on the frieze are two shields
flanking a helmet of peculiar form, and a sword suspended in its
sheath. On the narrow cornice above this frieze are represented
swords, some naked, others sheathed, between red and yellow
skull-caps.

In many of the sepulchral niches were found suits of bronze
armour—cuirass, helm, and greaves—though the heroes who had
worn them had long crumbled to dust, but in the central niche,
which was evidently the post of honour, the skeleton of the
warrior who occupied it still lay, when the tomb was opened,
stretched in his metal shroud. The wall beneath him is carved
with legs so as to resemble a couch, and under it is represented
one of the mysterious divinities of the Etruscan Hades, Typhon
or Charun, bearing a rudder in his right hand and a snake in his
left, while the serpent-coils, in which his body terminates, seem
to float just above the *hypopodium* or low stool, the usual supple-
ment to the banqueting-couch. Behind the stool stands Cerberus,
his three heads painted of different colours, red, white, and black,
and his neck bristling with a collar of snakes. To the left of
this scene stands a square chest or closet, painted red and white,
with a keyhole. On the pilasters, which flank the central niche,
are represented two heads much defaced;[1] one evidently representing a bearded man; and beneath him hang a black *kylix*, and
a red *olpe*. The other head is almost obliterated; the face is
quite gone, but, from a chaplet, some strings of red beads, and
a circular fan suspended beneath it, we may infer that it represented a woman. A walking-stick, on the other hand, resting
against the couch, is hardly in character with this inference.
As this central niche contained two bodies, the busts on the
pilasters were in all probability the portraits of the warrior and
his wife.

On all the side pilasters which separate the niches are shields
in relief, painted yellow, as if to represent brass or gold—of that
circular Argolic form, which alone seems to have been used by

[9] The κέρας which we learn from
Athenæus (IV. 82) was invented by the
Etruscans.

[1] M. Noël des Vergers represents these
as hand-bags (Etrurie, III. pl. 2), but to
Sir Gardner Wilkinson, as well as to myself, they appeared clearly to represent
heads in relief. The curly beard of the
male head is most distinct. The other has
something tied round the throat in a knot,
as is often the case with female figures in
Etruscan reliefs.

the Etruscans, and which the Romans adopted, in preference to the square shield they had previously used.

The two pillars in the centre of the tomb are about twenty inches square, and have capitals akin to the Ionic, but with an *anthemion*, or honeysuckle ornament, dependent from each volute, which gives them a singular though far from inelegant appearance. Two faces of each pillar are represented as hung with a variety of instruments, sacred and domestic, which demand a detailed description. On the pillar to the left, and on the side facing the door, you see hanging on nails, close under the capital, a pair of those mysterious twisted rods, which are represented only in two other monuments of Etruria—the procession of souls and demons on the walls of the Typhon-tomb at Corneto, and that beneath the portico of the Temple-tomb at Norchia. Their use was evidently religious, and their presence in this tomb probably indicates the interment of some *augur* or *aruspex*, or it may be of some Lucumo of high rank in the Etruscan hierarchy. These rods are coloured white and yellow, as if to represent wood. By their side hangs a leathern strap in several coils, probably a sling; and such may also be the coil of rope suspended below it near the base of the same pillar. On the other side of the rods hang a large *olpe*, or pitcher, and a stout stick or club suspended by a rope; lower down an axe, and a long-bladed knife or sword, while at the foot of the pillar a spotted cat is sporting with a mouse.

On the same pillar, but on the side opposite the other pillar, are suspended high up a long straight *lituus*, or trumpet, a painted *kylix* or drinking bowl, and a bottle hanging by a string round its neck. Below hang a dagger in its sheath, a hand-bag of very modern appearance, with a small bottle and a plate hanging over it; and a nondescript piece of furniture, more like a double lamp-bracket than anything else. At the base of the pillar a goose is picking up corn.

On the other pillar we see suspended another pair of the twisted rods, and by their side a large disk or drum, hanging by a leathern strap. Below hang an axe, a wooden case or frame, holding a pair of knives, a bundle of seven long spits, strung and bound together, the counterpart of which, in bronze, may be seen in the Gregorian Museum, a mace, and a small pot like an inkstand; and at the base of the pillar is a large globe, apparently of metal, resting on a wooden stand, which, from the short heavy mallet suspended by its side, we take to represent an Etruscan gong.

On the inner face of the same pillar hangs a long broad tablet, with two handles, ruled as if to take an inscription. It is flanked by a *lituus*, similar to that on the opposite pillar, and by what seems to be a spoon or ladle. On it hangs a small red bag, fastened with a long pin. Beneath it are suspended a pair of pincers, a mace, and a mallet, and between them is represented a duck. At the foot of the pillar are a tortoise, and a dog, with a bell round his neck, seizing a lizard.

At the entrance to the tomb stand two marble *cippi*, shaped like the hat of a Calabrese peasant, one of which bears the Etruscan inscription—

> " MATUNAS LARISAL
>   AN. CNEVTHIKER CHUNTHE."

In three of the niches also the name "Matunas" occurs, whence we may infer that the sepulchre belonged to a family of that name.[2] The tomb faces S.S.W.

A little to the west of the Matunas tomb is another beneath a tumulus, which has a chamber on each side of the doorway, a spacious *atrium*, or central hall, with a flat roof supported by two decagonal pillars, with bastard Ionic capitals, and three inner chambers, with Etruscan doors, and small windows opening on the *atrium*. The roof is carved into beam and rafters, and the spaces between the latter are filled with diagonal patterns, almost like chevrons.

A short distance to the S. of the Tomb of the Reliefs, and beneath a large tumulus, lies a sepulchre, called, from its peculiar furniture,

GROTTA DELLE SEDIE E SCUDI,

or the "Tomb of the Seats and Shields." This tomb was discovered in 1834, but not having been preserved under lock and key, like most of those just described, it is now choked with rubbish, so as to be hardly accessible. Yet it is one of the most interesting sepulchres on the Banditaccia. It contains no less than six chambers, and from their arrangement and furniture, and from its manifest resemblance to an ancient house, we may regard it as a typical monument. The large

----

[2] For further notices of this curious tomb, see M. Noël des Vergers, Étrurie et les Étrusques, III. p. 1—3, pl. I.—III. Sir Gardner Wilkinson, on "An Etruscan tomb at Cervetri." Ann. Inst. 1854, p. 58.

chamber in the centre, marked *e* in the annexed plan, represents the *atrium*, the inner ones, marked *f, f, f*, the *triclinia* or *cubicula;* those outside the door marked *c, c*, the πυλώρια, or *cellulæ janitoris.*

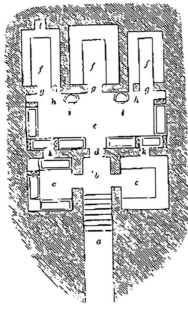

PLAN OF THE TOMB OF THE SEATS
AND SHIELDS.

The following is the explanation of the plan :—

a.	Rock-hewn steps leading down to the tomb.
b.	The vestibule.
c, c.	Chambers on each side of the entrance.
d.	Doorway to the tomb.
e.	Principal chamber, or *atrium.*
f, f, f.	Inner chambers, or *triclinia.*
g, g, g.	Entrances to the inner chambers.
h, h.	Windows to the same, cut in the rock.
i, i.	Arm-chairs and foot-stools, hewn from the rock.
l.	Niche recessed in the wall.
k, k.	Windows cut in the rock.

The sepulchral benches which surround each chamber are here indicated; sometimes with a raised, ornamental head-piece.

The shaded part of the plan represents the rock in which the tomb is hollowed.

But the most singular feature of this tomb is two arm-chairs, with footstools attached, hewn from the living rock, and a shield carved in low relief, suspended against the wall over each. On

TOMB OF THE SEATS AND SHIELDS.

looking round the principal chamber, you perceive no fewer than fourteen similar shields represented in relief, hanging around the walls. They are circular, like Argolic shields, about a mètre in diameter, and quite plain, without rim or boss. The above woodcut, which gives a section of the tomb, shows the chairs standing between the doors of the inner chambers, with the shields hanging above them.[3]

GROTTA DELLE LASTRE DIPINTE.

About one hundred paces from the "Tomb of the Reliefs," the Signori Boccanera in 1874 discovered a tomb of very small size, with a doorway only just large enough for a man to creep through, which, nevertheless, contained objects of rare interest. Lying, some on the rock-hewn benches, which flanked the tomb, some on the floor, were found five large tiles of terra-cotta, about 40 inches long, by 22 wide, painted with figures of very archaic character, and which bore traces of having been originally attached to the walls as decorations, just as the chambers in the royal palace at Nimroud were lined with marble slabs covered with reliefs. Two bore the figure of a sphinx, and appeared to have been placed one on each side the doorway. The other three formed a continuous series, and seemed to have occupied the inner wall.

The tomb is now closed, and has lost its interest. But the painted slabs are preserved in the Palazzo Ruspoli at Cervetri, where I saw them in June 1876, in the possession of the brothers Boccanera. As they were for sale, and the Italian government was then in treaty for the purchase, they will probably not long remain on the site of their discovery, but will pass into some native or foreign Museum.

Though these paintings are of high antiquity, the colours retain their freshness in a remarkable degree. They are limited to red, yellow, black, and white. The sphinxes alone are somewhat faded. They stand facing each other, each with one fore paw raised, their flesh white, eyes, eyebrows, and hair, black, the latter falling loosely on their shoulders and deep bosoms. Their open wings raised behind their backs, with their tips curling up like elephants' trunks, have the feathers coloured alternately red, white, and black.

The other three tiles bear three figures each, not more than half the height of the slab, which is ornamented above with a triple guilloche pattern in colours, and below the figures with a

---

[3] This tomb has been described and delineated in Bull. Inst. 1834, p. 99. Ann. Inst. 1835, p. 184. Mon. Ined. Inst. II. tav. XIX. Canina (Etr. Mar. I. p. 197, tav. 71) makes the mistake of placing this tomb on the Monte d'Oro, near Ceri. For further remarks on the shields, see the Appendix to this Chapter.

deep band composed of broad vertical stripes, red and white. Of
the nine figures, seven are females, two males, distinguished, as
in the painted tombs, by the flesh, which in the men is a deep
red, in the women, white. The interpretation of the scene they
represent is not clear. It is easier to say that it is not a banquet,
nor a dance, nor public game, nor any such scene of festivity as
was usually selected by the Etruscans to decorate their sepulchres
and coffins ; nor is it a scene of mourning. It might represent a
procession, were all the figures walking in the same direction.
The nature of the scene not being intelligible, I can only describe
the figures which compose it.

The women are draped to their feet in red, white, or yellow
chitones, and where the material represented is of very light
texture, this character is expressed by black wavy lines, as in
the woodcut at p. 262. Over the *chiton* they wear a mantle, red
or black, sometimes covering the head, in which case the lady is
depicted lifting it with one hand like a veil. Sometimes it hangs
on her shoulders, and her long black hair descends in a mass
below her waist. Their shoes with long sharp points, turned
back at the toes, as in the earliest painted tombs of Corneto, are
red and black, in alternate figures ; two wear buskins like the
men ; and one is bare-footed. Three of them carry vases of
different kinds in their hands, and two hold branches of pomegranates. The men, who stand together, conversing, have short
hair and pointed beards. One wears a black cap and mantle,
and holds a red bough. The other, whose head is covered with
a sharp pointed *petasus*, wears a black *pallium* over a white tunic,
and carries in one hand a chaplet, and in the other a long wand
tipped by the figure of a small bull. Both have buskins reaching
half way up the leg, where they are fastened by large buttons ;
as shown in the woodcut at p. 261. These male figures are thick-
limbed and clumsy, their muscular development exaggerated but
not detailed, and their knee-caps distinctly though conventionally
expressed.[4]

These paintings evidently belong to the infancy of Etruscan
art. The clumsiness and extreme rigidity of the figures, the

[4] An elaborate and able article on these
tile-paintings will be found in the Bull.
Inst. 1874, pp. 128–136, from the pen of
Signor E. Brizio. He puts an interpretation on the scene, which, in my opinion, it
will hardly bear. He views in it a love-
scene ; taking two of the figures, whose
female sex seems to be clearly indicated by
their white flesh, to be young men, and
infers, from their carrying branches of
pomegranates, that they are making love to
one of the women, who accepts their
advances, while she rejects the attentions of
the two bearded men.

very archaic though careful design, the utter want of expression,
the limited scale of colour, the incapacity of the artist to delineate
active movements, and even to express the folds of drapery,
though conscientiously indicating those details which were within
his power, all mark these paintings as among the most primitive
works of Etruscan pictorial art yet brought to light.

But these painted slabs are not unique. In 1856, the Marchese
Campana disinterred at Cervetri, six tiles of very similar character, which, on the breaking up of his collection at Rome, were
transferred to the Louvre. A few years afterwards, another
series of painted terra-cottas, said also to have been dug up at
Cervetri, appeared in the market at Rome. But these were
eventually pronounced to be fabrications, and the knowledge of
that fact naturally threw suspicion on those of the Campana
collection, and also on those from the Boccanèra *scavi*, when
their discovery was first made known. But these latter, while
they confirm the doubts as to the second batch, vindicate the
genuineness of the first; for the similarity between the two series
in style, design, colouring, ornamentation, and general treatment,
though not in subject, is so striking, that it is impossible to
doubt their equal antiquity, and difficult to believe they are not
by the same hand.

Not being able to procure copies of the quaint and curious tiles
now at Cervetri, I offer for the reader's inspection, faithful transcripts of those in the Louvre. These, like the Boccanèra
series, were the decorations of a single tomb.

The principal scene is composed of three tiles, each about four
feet long by two wide. In the centre is a lofty altar, built up
with blocks of various colours, disposed chequer-wise, and carved
into architectural forms, among which the torus and owl's beak
moulding repeatedly occur. Behind the altar rises a slender
column, supporting a large bowl, or it may be a capital of peculiar form, and doubtless indicating the temple, before which the
altar stands. By the altar, on which a fire is burning, stands
a man, beardless, and with short hair, and wearing nothing
but a close-fitting yellow vest, and black boots. He rests one
hand on the altar and raises the other to his face, as if he were
smelling the incense. Behind him, and on the next tile,
stand three figures, two of men, clad in like fashion, in tight
vests, in one case, red, in the other, white, and in similar boots;
both are bearded, have a chaplet over their brows, and wear their
hair long and loose upon their shoulders. Both are armed, one

with bow and arrows, the other with a spear. Between them
stands a woman, distinguished by her white flesh, with her hair
reaching to her waist, and draped to her heels in a white *chiton*,
over which she wears a yellow tunic reaching to her knees, and
over all a red mantle with ornamented border. Her shoes are
yellow. She carries, what, but for its red colour, would be pronounced a branch, or a chaplet of leaves. Each of these figures
has one hand raised, as if in adoration. The procession was
continued on another tile, but as it is imperfect, I omit a description of the figures upon it.[5]

The tile to the right presents a singular scene. The figures
already described are standing still or moving slowly towards
the altar, but those on this tile are rushing at full speed towards
it. The foremost is clad like the other men, and carries a bow
and arrows. He who follows also resembles the rest in his
costume, though he has no beard, but the parti-coloured wings
at his shoulders and heels, mark him as no creature of flesh
and blood, but as a genius or demon of the Etruscan mythology
—one of those spirits so frequently introduced on sepulchral
monuments into scenes of death and destruction. As he rushes
to the altar he bears in his arms the body of a woman, who from
her helpless attitude, and her arms swaddled beneath her mantle,
either represents a corpse, or is intended for a victim.

The sacrifice of Iphigenia, a favourite subject on Etruscan
urns of late date, is naturally suggested by this scene. But to
this interpretation it may be objected that the art is here so
purely Etruscan, so entirely free from all Hellenic influence,
that it would be an anomaly to regard it as the representation
of a Greek myth. "These figures," says Dr. Brunn,[6] "are
Etruscans of the purest blood, not ideal but real, so far as the
style of that remote epoch permitted them to be represented."
The man at the altar, again, has none of the attributes of a
priest, not even a beard, and is the least imposing figure of the
group.

On a fourth tile, belonging to the same series, although it does
not fit on to the others, two grey-headed men are sitting, face to
face, on folding-stools, each dressed in a long white tunic of
some light material, covered by a red mantle. One, who holds a

---

[5] The said tile in all probability originally
contained three figures, but it has been
reduced in width, apparently to fit it into
a narrow space, so that two figures only, of
opposite sexes, now remain, and that of the
woman is mutilated.

[6] Ann. Inst. 1859, p. 334.

PAINTINGS ON TILES, FROM AN ETRUSCAN TOMB, CERVETRI.

wand, appears to be talking on some serious subject to the other,
whose attitude, as he rests his chin on his right hand, is expressive of meditation, or of profound grief. The small female
winged figure in the air behind him, with one hand stretched

PAINTED TILE, FROM AN ETRUSCAN TOMB.

out towards him, evidently represents a soul, as we learn from
analogous scenes on other Etruscan monuments, and may justly
be taken for the soul of the woman who is borne away by the
winged demon, and who was probably the wife or daughter of the
sorrowful old man, and we may infer that it is for her loss that
his friend is endeavouring to console him.

The fifth tile does not belong to the same series, for it differs
from the rest in dimensions and decorations; yet it was found in

the same tomb, and was painted apparently by the same hand.
It represents a man in a white shirt, covered by a brown tunic,
sitting, wand in hand, on a *plicatilis*, or folding-stool, in front of
an altar or pedestal, not unlike that already described, on which

PAINTED TILE, FROM AN ETRUSCAN TOMB.

stands, with open arms, the image of a goddess, with *tutulus* and
ampyx on her head, and white talaric *chiton*, with a brown tunic
over it, open in front, and girdled round her waist. At the foot of
the altar a snake is seen approaching the leg of the sitting figure,
which has given rise to the suggestion that he may represent
Philoctetes in the island of Lemnos.[7] This view, however, is

7 Ann. Inst. 1857, pp. 251, 359. But   bow and arrows of Hercules, and not with
Philoctetes would be represented with the   a wand or sceptre.

difficult of acceptation, for the reasons already assigned, and he more probably is merely the priest of the unknown divinity, and the serpent, like the wand, is one of his attributes.[8]

A glance is enough to satisfy one as to the high antiquity of these paintings. It will be remarked that the figures show none of the anatomical development so ostentatiously exhibited in many of the early wall-paintings of Etruria. The artist has contented himself with marking out, which he has done with decision and purity, the bald outlines of his figures, merely expressing in some cases the rounding of the hip, and in a conventional manner the prominence of the knee-pan, and elbow, and indicating the nails. Nor in the drapery has he attempted to represent folds, save by thin wavy lines, where the material is either wool, or of a very thin texture. Yet in every part the desire to delineate nature with fidelity, so far as lay within the limits of his ability, is most apparent. His ability, however, did not enable him to design with correctness the human figure in motion. Everything indicates a very imperfect knowledge of his art. In point of antiquity, indeed, these painted tiles of Cervetri are pronounced by the most competent judges, to be second only to the very archaic wall-pictures of the Grotta Campana at Veii, and anterior to all the other tomb-paintings of Etruria.[9]

The colours are indelible, being burnt in with the tiles. The ground is white, and the flesh of the women, and the parts of the dresses and furniture which are of that hue, are left untouched. The other colours used are black, red, brown (a mixture of the two), and yellow. No blue, or green, is introduced, probably from the inability at that early age to produce pigments of those hues.

GROTTA REGULINI-GALASSI.

The sepulchre at Cervetri which has most renown, and possesses the greatest interest from its high antiquity, its peculiar structure, and the extraordinary nature and value of its contents, is that which has received the name of its discoverers,—the archpriest Regulini, and General Galassi. This is one of the very few

---

[8] For the part that serpents were made to play by the priesthood of Etruria, see p. 331. An interesting analysis of the scenes on these tiles is given by H. Brunn, Ann. Inst. 1859, pp. 325—353.

[9] Helbig thinks they are separated by a long space of time from the Veientine paintings. Ann. Inst. 1863, p. 341. Brunn admits an interval, but does not think it a wide one. Ann. Inst. 1866, p. 423.

virgin-tombs, found in Etruscan cemeteries. It was opened in
April 1836. It lies about three furlongs from Cervetri, to the
south-west of the ancient city, and not far from the walls. It is
said to have been inclosed in a tumulus, but the mound was so
large, and its top has been so broken by frequent excavations,
and levellings of the soil for agricultural purposes, that its
existence is now mere matter of history.

The sepulchre opens in a low bank in the middle of a field.
The peculiarity of its construction is evident at a glance. It is a
rude attempt at an
arch, formed by the
convergence of hori-
zontal strata, hewn to
a smooth surface, and
slightly curved, so as
to resemble a Gothic
arch. This is not,
however, carried up
to a point, but termi-
nates in a square
channel, covered by
large blocks of *nenfro*.
The doorway is the
index to the whole

MOUTH OF THE REGULINI-GALASSI TOMB.

tomb, which is a mere passage, about sixty feet long, constructed
on the same principle, and lined with masonry.[1] This passage
is divided into two parts or chambers, communicating by a doorway of the same Gothic form, with a truncated top.[2]

The similarity of the structure to the Cyclopean gallery at
Tiryns is striking; the masonry, it is true, is far less massive,

[1] The masonry is of rectangular blocks of
red tufo, containing large nodules; in the
outer chamber, small and irregular, the
courses, which are not always horizontal,
being from 12 to 15 inches deep; in the
inner it is of more massive dimensions.

[2] The outer chamber is 33 feet, the
inner 24½ feet long, and the thickness of
the partition-wall, 3 feet; making the entire length 60½ feet. The inner doorway
is 6½ feet high and 4½ wide at the bottom,
narrowing upward to 1 foot at the top.
Similar passage-tombs have been found
elsewhere in this necropolis, especially in
that part called Zunbra (Bull. Inst. 1840,

p. 132), as well as at Palo and Selva la
Rocca. Tombs of this passage-form are
generally of high antiquity. These bear
an evident relation to the Treasuries of
Mycenæ and Orchomenos, and to the
Nurhags or Nuraghe of Sardinia and the
Talajots of the Balearics, in as far as they
are roofed in on the same principle. And
they are probably of not inferior antiquity.
Like the Nuraghe they may with good
reason be regarded as the work of the
Tyrrhene-Pelasgi. The Druidical barrows
of our own country sometimes contain
passage-formed sepulchres like these of
Cervetri.

but the style is identical, showing a rude attempt at an arch, the true principle of which had yet to be discovered. It is generally admitted, not only that such a mode of construction must be prior to the discovery of the perfect arch, but that every extant specimen of it must have preceded the knowledge of the correct principle. It is a mode not peculiar to one race, or to one age, or the result of a particular class of materials, but is the expedient naturally adopted in the formation of arches, vaults, and domes, by those who are ignorant of the cuneiform principle; and it is therefore to be found in the earliest structures of Egypt, Greece, Italy, and other parts of the Old World, as well as in those of the semi-civilised races of the New.[3] The Cloaca Maxima, which is the earliest known instance of the perfect arch in Italy, dates from the days of the Tarquins; this tomb then must be considered as of a remoter period, coeval at least with the earliest days of Rome—prior, it may be, to the foundation of the City.[4]

The great antiquity of this tomb may be deduced also from its contents, which were of the most archaic, Egyptian-like cha-

---

[3] Stephens' Yucatan, I. p. 429, et seq. This traveller's description and illustrations show the remarkable analogy between these American pseudo-vaults and those of ancient Europe. The sides of the arch in certain of these vaults are hewn to a smooth curved surface, as in the Regulini tomb, and terminate not in a point, but in a square head, formed by the imposition of flat blocks; the peculiarity consists in the courses being often almost at right angles with the line of the arch, showing a near approach to the cuneiform principle.

[4] Canina (Cere Antica, p. 80) refers its construction to the Pelasgi, or earliest inhabitants of Agylla, and assigns to it and its contents an antiquity of not less than 3000 years, making it coeval with the Trojan war. He says it can be determined that precisely in the reign of Tarquinius Priscus, the change in the mode of constructing the arch was effected in Rome, for Tarquin introduced the style from Tarquinii. But though we were absolutely certain that Tarquin built the Cloaca Maxima, we have no authority for determining when the first true arch was erected in Rome. The principle may, for aught we know, have been known and

practised at an earlier period. At any rate, it is highly probable that it had been known in Etruria some time before the construction of the Cloaca Maxima, and if at Tarquinii whence Tarquin migrated, why not at Caere, a neighbouring city belonging to the same people? As regards this tomb all are agreed on its very high antiquity. Even Micali, who sees everything in a more modern light than most archaeologists, admits that the style of architecture shows it to be prior to the foundation of Rome (Mon. Ined. p. 359). Canina is of opinion that the tomb in its original state was surmounted by a small tumulus, but that after the arrival of the Lydians, another tumulus of much larger size was constructed about it, of which it formed a part; traces of such a second tumulus having been found in an encircling basement of masonry and several chambers hollowed in the rock below the original tomb,—and that the piling up of the earth around the latter was the means of preserving it intact from those who in ages past rifled the rest of the sepulchral mound. This has been pronounced by an able critic, to be "a sagacious analysis." Bull. Inst. 1838, p. 172.

racter.[5] Scarcely any pottery, and none painted, was found here; but numerous articles of bronze, silver, and gold, so abundant, so quaint, and so beautiful, that it is verily no easy task to describe them. I shall here do little more than specify the position which they occupied in the tomb.

In the outer chamber, at the further end, lay a bier of bronze, formed of narrow cross-bars, with an elevated place for the head. The corpse which had lain on it, had long since fallen to dust. By

TERRA-COTTA LARES, FROM THE REGULINI-GALASSI TOMB, CERVETRI.

its side stood a small four-wheeled car, or tray, of bronze, with a basin-like cavity in the centre, the whole bearing, in form and size, a strong resemblance to a dripping-pan; though ornamented in a way that would hardly become that homely instrument. On the other side of the bier lay some forty little earthenware figures; probably the Lares of the deceased, who certainly was no worshipper of beauty. At the head and foot of the bier stood a small iron altar on a tripod, which may have served to do homage to these household gods. At the foot of the bier also lay a bundle of darts, and a shield; and several more shields rested against the opposite wall. All were of bronze, large and round like the Greek ἀσπίς, and beautifully embossed, but apparently

[5] Lepsius, no mean authority on Egyptian matters, remarks the evident imitation of Egyptian forms (Ann. Inst. 1836, p. 187). The ordinary observer would not hesitate to pronounce the figures on some of the vessels to be purely Egyptian.

for ornament alone, as the metal was too thin to have been of
service in the field. Nearer the door stood a four-wheeled car,
which, from its size and form, seemed to have borne the bier to
the sepulchre. And just within the entrance stood, on iron
tripods, a couple of caldrons, with a number of curious handles
terminating in griffons' heads,[6] together with a singular vessel—a
pair of bell-shaped vases, united by a couple of spheres.[7] Besides
these articles of bronze, there was a series of vessels suspended
by bronze nails from each side of the recess in the roof.[8] The
caldrons, dripping-pan, and bell-vessel, are supposed to have
contained perfumes, or incense, for fumigating the sepulchre.

This tomb had evidently contained the body of a warrior; but
to whom had the inner chamber belonged? The intervening
doorway was closed with masonry to half its height, and in it
stood two more pots of bronze, and against each door-post hung
a vessel of pure silver. There were no urns in this chamber, but
the vault was hung with bronze vessels, and others were suspended on each side the entrance. Further in, stood two bronze
caldrons for perfumes, as in the outer chamber: and then, at the
end of the tomb, on no couch, bier, or sarcophagus, not even on
a rude bench of rock, but on the bare ground,[9] lay—a corpse?—
no, for it had ages since returned to dust, but a number of gold
ornaments, whose position showed most clearly that, when placed
in the tomb, they were upon a human body. The richness,
beauty, and abundance of these articles, all of pure gold, were
amazing—such a collection, it has been said, "would not be
found in the shop of a well-furnished goldsmith."[1] There were,
a head-dress of singular character—a large breastplate, beautifully embossed, such as was worn by Egyptian priests—a finely

[6] Similar to this must have been the
brass *krater* dedicated to Juno by Colœus,
the Samian, out of the profits of his successful voyage to Tartessus, about 630 B.C.,
for Herodotus describes it as having griffons'
heads set in a row around it; IV. 152.

[7] Much like that shown at page 275.

[8] The nails thus supporting crockery or
bronzes in Etruscan tombs, throw light on
the use of them in the so-called Treasury
of Atreus, at Mycenæ, where they have
long been supposed to have fastened the
plates of bronze with which it was imagined the walls were lined. It has been
suggested, however, that no nails ever
existed in that celebrated Thesaurus, but
that certain nodules in the blocks have

been mistaken for them. Bull. Inst.
1836, p. 58—Wolff. But admitting that
there were really nails, it is far more probable that they served to support pottery
or other sepulchral furniture, than a lining
of metal, seeing it is now generally believed that the so-called "Treasuries" of
Greece were no other than tombs.

[9] Canina (Cere Ant. p. 75) states that
the floor under the corpse, in both tombs,
was paved with stones embedded in *cement—
selci collegati in calce*—an unique feature,
and worthy of particular notice in connection with the very remote antiquity of
the tomb.

[1] Bull. Inst. 1836, p. 60.

twisted chain, and a necklace of very long joints—earrings of great length—a pair of massive bracelets of exquisite filagree-work,—no less than eighteen *fibulæ* or brooches, one of remark-able size and beauty—sundry rings, and fragments of gold fringes and *laminæ*, in such quantities, that there seemed to have been an entire garment of pure gold. It is said that the fragments of this metal crushed and bruised, were alone sufficient to fill more than one basket.[2] Against the inner wall lay two vessels of silver, with figures in relief.[3]

This abundance of ornament has led to the conclusion that the occupant of this inner chamber was a lady of rank—a view con-firmed by the inscriptions found in the tomb.[4] But may it not have been a priest with equal probability? The breastplate is far more like a sacerdotal than a feminine decoration; and the other ornaments, if worn by a man, would simply mark an oriental character,[5] and would be consistent enough with the strong Egyptian style observable in many of the contents of this sepulchre.[6]

[2] Bull. Inst. loc. cit. Though this de-scription is somewhat vague, it conveys the idea of the great abundance of this metal, which was found crushed beneath a mass of fallen masonry.

[3] A silver vessel of precisely similar character has since been found at Pales-trina. Ann. Inst. 1866, p. 203.

[4] Canina, Cere Antica, p. 76. Cavedoni, Bull. Inst. 1843, p. 46. The inscriptions were on several of the silver vessels, and consisted merely of the female name "LARTHIA," or "MI LARTHIA," in Etrus-can characters. This was conjectured to signify the proprietor of these vessels, who, it was concluded, was also the occupant of the tomb. Larthia is the feminine of Lar, Lars, or Larth, as it is variously written.

[5] The necklace appears too massive and clumsy for a woman's neck; and we have abundant proof in sarcophagi and painted tombs that such ornaments were worn also by men; *fibulæ* would be applicable to either sex; earrings were not inappropriate to Etruscan dignitaries, as we learn from the sarcophagus of the "Sacerdote" in the Museum of Corneto; and bracelets of gold, we are taught by the old legend of Tarpeia, to regard as the common ornaments of Sabine soldiers in very early times. And though Niebuhr (I. p. 226) has pronounced

these golden decorations of the Sabines to have had no existence, save in the imagina-tion of the poet who sang the lay, the discoveries made since his day, especially in Etruscan tombs, prove the abundance of gold ornaments in very early times, and also their warlike application; so that whatever improbability there be in the story, arises merely from its inconsistency with the simple, hardy manners of the Sabines. Yet even here, the analogy of the golden torques of the rude and warlike Gauls might be cited in support of the legend.

Micali (Mon. Ined. p. 60) thinks the breastplate and *fibulæ*, from their fragility, were evidently mere sepulchral decorations; and the bracelets show a funereal subject—a woman attacked by lions, and rescued by two winged genii—which he interprets as the soul freed from the power of evil spirits by the intervention of good. It may be re-marked that the form of this tomb is that prescribed by Plato (Leg. XII. p. 947, ed. Steph.) for Greek priests—"a grave under ground, a lengthened vault of choice stones, hard and imperishable, and having parallel couches of rock." The benches alone are here wanting.

[6] Micali (Mon. Ined. p. 62) is of opinion that this, and the Isis-tomb of Vulci, con-

On each side of the outer passage was a small circular, domed
chamber, hewn in the rock, one containing an urn with burnt
bones, and a number of *terra-cotta* idols ; the other, pottery, and
vessels of bronze. These chambers seem of later formation.
Canina indeed is of opinion that the inner chamber alone was the
original tomb ; that the outer, then serving as a mere passage,
was subsequently used as a burial place, and that, at a still later
period, the side-chambers were constructed.[7]

All this *roba*, so rich and rare, has been religiously preserved,
but he who would see it, must seek it, not on the spot where it
had lain for so many centuries, but at the Gregorian Museum at
Rome, of which it forms one of the chief glories. That revolving
cabinet of jewellery, whose treasures of exquisite workmanship
excite the enthusiastic admiration of all fair travellers, is occupied
almost wholly with the produce of this tomb. The depository
which has yielded this wealth, now contains nought but mud,
slime, and serpents—the *genii* of the spot. It has been gutted of
its long-hoarded treasure, and may now take its fate. Who is
there to give it a thought? None save the peasant, who will ere
long find its blocks handy for the construction of his hovel, or
the fence of his vineyard, as he has already found a quarry of
materials in neighbouring tumuli ; and the sepulchre, which may
have greeted the eyes of Æneas himself, will leave not a wreck
behind. Much of the masonry of the inner chamber has been
already removed, and the whole threatens a speedy fall. Surely
a specimen of a most ancient and rare style of architecture has
public claims for protection, as well as the works of the early
painters, or the figures of bronze, clay, or stone, which are preserved in museums as specimens of the infancy of their respective
arts. Were its position such as to render it difficult to preserve,
there would be some excuse for neglect, but when a wooden door
with lock and key would effect its salvation, it is astonishing that
it is suffered to fall into ruin.[8]

tain the earliest monuments of Etruscan
primitive art, as it existed before it had
been subjected to Hellenic influence. He
considers the silver vessels to show perfect
imitations of the Asiatic or Egyptian style
of ornamentation ; yet with all this, to
have the stamp of nationality so strongly
marked, as to distinguish them altogether
from purely Egyptian works. Dr. Brunn,
on the other hand, from the analogy of a
similar vase in the Louvre, regards all
these silver vases as importations from the
East, and probably from Cyprus, which
would explain their mixed Asiatic and
Egyptian character. Ann. Inst. 1866,
p. 413.

[7] Cere Ant. pp. 75, 78.

[8] The above was written in 1847. I
was grieved on a recent visit (June, 1876)
to find that nothing has yet been done to
save this curious monument from destruction. The outer chamber is choked

Another tomb, of precisely similar construction, was found near the one just described; but, having been rifled in past ages, it contained nothing but an inscription rudely scratched on the wall.[9]

At the same time with the Regulini-Galassi tomb, several others were opened in the neighbourhood; in one of which was

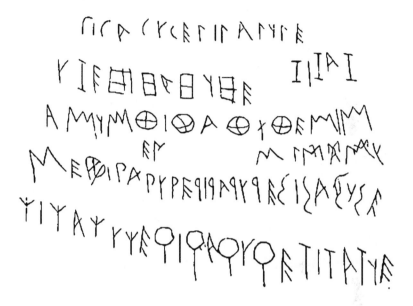

PELASGIC ALPHABET AND PRIMER.

found a relic of antiquity, insignificant enough in itself, but of high interest for the light it throws on the early languages of Italy. It is a little cruet-like vase, of plain black ware, a few inches high, and from its form has not unaptly been compared to an ink-bottle. What may have been its original application is

with débris, and in the inner the lower courses have been carried off, and the upper overhang in such a manner, that the whole structure appears on the point of collapsing.

For the foregoing description of the contents of this tomb and their arrangement, I am indebted to Canina, Cere Antica, parte terza; Braun, Bull. Inst. 1836, pp. 56—62; 1838, p. 173. Canina in his later work, Etruria Marittima, gives

a plan, and numerous illustrations of this tomb and its contents, tav. 50—59. Grifi, in his Monumenti di Cere Antica, endeavours to prove from the contents of this tomb the oriental, and especially Mithraic, character of the Etruscan worship.

[9] Bull. Inst. 1836, p. 62. The writer does not mention in what characters was this inscription, though he says it was not worth copying! I could not learn if the tomb is still open.

not easy to say; probably for perfumes, as it resembles the *alabastos* in form; or it may have served as an ink-stand, to hold the colouring-matter for inscriptions. Whatever its purpose, it has no obvious relation to a sepulchre, for round its base is an alphabet, in very ancient characters, shown in the bottom line of the subjoined fac-simile; and round the body of the pot the consonants are coupled with the vowels in turn, in that manner so captivating to budding intelligences. Thus we read—"Bi, Ba, Bu, Be—Gi, Ga, Gu, Ge—Zi, Za, Zu, Ze—Hi, Ha, Hu, He—Thi, Tha, Thu, The—Mi, Ma, Mu, Me—Ni, Na, Nu, Ne—Pi, Pa, Pu, Pe—Ki, Ka, Ku, Ke—Si, Sa, Su, Se—Chi, Cha, Chu, Che—Phi, Pha, Phu, Phe—Ti, Ta, Tu, Te." Now, it must be observed, that this inscription, though found in an Etruscan tomb, is not in that character, but in Greek, of very archaic style;[1] and there is every reason to believe it a relic of the earliest possessors of Cære, the Pelasgi, who are said to have introduced letters into Latium.[2] From the palæography, this is indubitably the most ancient monument extant which teaches us the early Greek alphabet, and its authentic arrangement.[3] This singular relic has now past from the hands of General Galassi, its original possessor, into the Gregorian Museum of the Vatican.

---

[1] The difference between this alphabet and the genuine Etruscan one, found on a vase at Bomarzo, is very apparent. See the fac-simile at p. 172. That has but twenty letters, this twenty-five, and both in their form and collocation there are wide differences. That has the Etruscan peculiarity of running from right to left. In Greek letters this alphabet would be thus expressed:—A, B, Γ, Δ, E, F (the digamma), Z, H (the ancient aspirate), Θ, I, K, Λ, M (this is the letter effaced), N, Ξ, O, Ọ (koppa), Π, P, Σ, T, Υ, X, Φ, Ψ. It will be remarked that the same force has not been assigned to certain of these letters where they occur in the primer, and the reader will be ready to dispute my accuracy. Let him break a lance then with Professor Lepsius, who is my authority, and who gives his views of this inscription in the Ann. Inst. 1836, pp. 186—203.

[2] Solinus, Polyhist. cap. VIII.

[3] The letters here are of the most archaic forms known, some of them strongly resembling the Phœnician; and the presence of the *vau* and the *koppa*, and the want of

the *eta* and *omega*, establish the high antiquity of the pot. There are some singular features to be remarked. The arrangement of the letters in the alphabet does not correspond with that in the primer, and in both it differs from that generally received. The vowels in the primer are placed in an order entirely novel, and which is at variance with that of the alphabet. There is a curious instance of *pentimento* or alteration in the fourth line. Some of the characters, moreover, have new and strange forms, and their force appears doubtful. I have given that assigned to them by Lepsius, who has eruditely discussed the palæography of this inscription. Notwithstanding its Greek or Pelasgic character, there are circumstances which seem to betray that it was scratched by an Etruscan hand. For evidences of this, I refer the curious reader to the said article by Lepsius, merely mentioning that this inscription bears a strong affinity to an alphabet and primer inscribed on the walls of an Etruscan tomb at Colle, near Volterra. (See Chapter XLII.)

Another small black pot, found by Gen. Galassi in the same excavations, has an inscription similarly scratched around it, and then filled in with red paint, which Professor Lepsius determines to be also in the Pelasgic, not the Etruscan, character and language. The letters are not separated into words, but run in a continuous line round the pot. Lepsius thus divides them—

> MI NI KETHU MA MI MATHU MARAM LISIAI THIPURENAI
> ETHE ERAI SIE EPANA MINETHU NASTAV HELEPHU,

and remarks that "he who is so inclined may easily read them as two hexameter lines, after the manner of the old Greek dedicatory inscriptions." Though he pronounces that in this inscription we possess one of the very rare relics of the Pelasgic tongue, he regards the date of it as uncertain, as he conceives that the population of Cære remained Pelasgic to a late period.[4]

The high ground to the east of Cære, on the opposite side of the Vaccina, is called Monte Abatone. This Canina[5] regards as the site of the sacred grove of Silvanus, described by Virgil,[6]

> Est ingens gelidum lucus prope Cæritis amnem,
> Religione patrum latè sacer : undique colles
> Inclusere cavi, et nigrâ nemus abiete cingunt,
> Silvano fama est veteres sacrâsse Pelasgos ;

and thinks that its name is derived from the fir-trees—*abietes* —which are said by that poet to have surrounded the grove.[7]

[4] See the above-cited article by Lepsius, where the inscription is given in its proper characters ; and his more recent remarks in his pamphlet, "Ueber die Tyrrheniscben Pelasgor in Etrurien," pp. 39—42, where he lucidly points out the peculiarities both in the language and characters which distinguish this inscription from the Etruscan, and mark it as Pelasgic. He states that Müller agreed with his opinion on this point, though it was disputed by Franz (Elementa Epigraphices Græcæ, p. 24), who admitted, however, that the language was not Etruscan.

[5] Canina, Cere Ant. p. 53. So also Abeken, Mittelitalien, p. 37. Gell (Topog. of Rome, I. p. 1) places the grove on the hills on the opposite side of the Vaccina.

[6] Virg. Æn. VIII. 597. Livy (XXI. 62) mentions an oracle at Cære.

[7] Cavaliere P. E. Visconti (Ant. Monum. Sepolc. di Ceri, p. 17) would derive it from ἄβατον—a spot sacred, not to be trodden— on the ground that this was the name applied by the Rhodians to the edifice they raised round the statue of Artemisia to conceal it from the public view. Vitruv. II. 8, 15. But Cav. Canina rejects this derivation, on account of the necropolis of Cære being on the opposite side, in the Banditaccia. When two Roman knights are breaking a lance together, who shall venture to step between them? Yet the probability seems in favour of the fir-trees ; unless the word is derived from some Abbey that in the middle ages stood on the spot. I would remark that the cemeteries of the Etruscans were not confined to any one side of their towns, though one spot might, for convenience sake, be more especially

None, however, are now visible. Ceres has usurped the greater part of the hill, and has driven Pan to its further extremity.

The interest of Monte Abatone is not its doubtful claim to the site of a sylvan shrine, but its positive possession of tombs of very singular character. About a mile to the east of the Regulini sepulchre, after crossing the Vaccina, you find a path leading up to the southernmost point of the Monte. Here, at the very edge of the cliff, facing the city, a tomb was opened in May, 1845, which might formerly be seen with all its furniture, just as it was found. The traveller was indebted for the pre-servation of this monument to the late Marchese Campana, its discoverer, a gentleman whose zealous exertions in the field of Etruscan research are too well known to require laudation from me. Since his death the tomb has been neglected, and is no longer under lock and key. The traveller, therefore, will hardly expect to find its actual condition answer to the description which follows.

Grotta Campana.

This tomb bears considerable similarity to that of the same appellation at Veii—not so much in itself as in its contents. It lies beneath a crumbled tumulus, girt with masonry.[8] There is but a single sepulchral chamber, but it is divided, by Doric-like pilasters, into three compartments. The first has a fan-like ornament in relief on its ceiling, just as exists in a tomb in the Banditaccia, and in another at Vulci,[9] and which being here found in connection with very archaic furniture, raises a pre-sumption in favour of its being a most ancient style of decoration. Just within the entrance, on one hand, is a large jar, resting on a stumpy column of tufo, which is curiously adorned with stripes and stars in relief, though not in the approved Transatlantic arrangement. In the opposite corner is a squared mass of rock, panelled like a piece of furniture, and supporting small black vessels. The second compartment of the tomb is occupied by

devoted to interment; in the case of Cære the city was completely surrounded by tombs.

[8] The entrance, as usual in the tombs of Cervetri, is lined with masonry. The doorway is cut in the rock in an arched form, and around it is a groove, into which fitted the ancient door, a slab of stone. For the plan, sections, &c., of this tomb, see

Canina, Etruria Marit. I. tav. 68.

[9] In one of the two side-chambers which open on the entrance-passage of this tomb, the walls also are panelled in relief with the very same pattern as decorates the said tomb of the Sun and Moon at Vulci. The two-fold coincidence in this sepulchre is remarkable. See p. 449.

two sepulchral couches, hewn from the rock, and containing nothing of their occupants beyond some dark dust, mixed with fragments of metal, surrounded by sundry articles of crockery, though their skulls are still left at the heads of their respective biers. Between these couches, on a square mass of rock, retaining traces of colour, rests an earthen pan, or brazier, for perfumes, with archaic figures in relief round the rim; and at the foot of each couch stands a huge jar, almost large enough to hold a man, which probably contained the ashes of the slaves or dependents of those whose bodies occupied the couches. In the inner compartment, against the wall, are two benches of rock; on the upper, stand several similar large jars, together with smaller vessels; and on the lower, is a curious, tall, bell-shaped pot, of black earthenware, similar in form to one of bronze found in the Grotta Regulini-Galassi. It was probably a *thymiaterion*, or incense-burner. It is shown in the annexed woodcut.

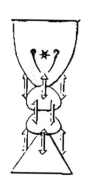

ETRUSCAN FUMIGATOR.

About a mile from the Grotta Campana, but still on the Monte Abatone, are two remarkable sepulchres, well worthy of a visit. They are not under lock and key, yet can scarcely be found without a guide. The spot is vulgarly called Il Monte d'Oro, from a tradition of gold having been found there. On the way to it, you may observe traces of a sepulchral road, flanked with many tumuli—some with architectural decorations. The tombs lie in a small copse, and are not easily accessible to ladies. To explore them, indeed, demands much of the sportsman's spirit in the ruder sex, for they are often half-full of water. The first is called the "Tomb of the Seat," and is distinguished from the other of that name, already described, by its position on Monte Abatone.

GROTTA DELLA SEDIA.

This tomb lies under a large tumulus, with a square basement of masonry, which makes it highly probable that the superincumbent mound was in this case of pyramidal form.[1]

---

[1] The basement is 63 feet by 56. Visconti makes it larger—108 by 91 Roman palms. At the back, or on the side opposed to the entrance, is a square projection or buttress in the masonry. The blocks are of tufo, and the courses recede

Half-way down the passage which leads to the sepulchre, you pass through a doorway of masonry, which marks the line of the tumulus-basement. The passage is lined with masonry, whose converging courses indicate the existence originally of a vault overhead. The tomb consists of two chambers, and has nothing extraordinary, except an arm-chair, with a footstool attached, hewn out of the living rock, as in the two tombs of the

C Dennis.

ROCK-CUT CHAIR AND FOOT-STOOL.

Banditaccia, already described. Here it is not by the side of a sepulchral couch, but against the wall of rock which separates the two chambers.[2]

This tomb had been rifled in ages past, but carelessly, for, when reopened in 1835, some gold leaf, and several *fibulæ* of the same metal were discovered in one of the chambers. Other furniture was found, indicative of a high antiquity.[3] A singular feature was the skeleton of a horse, lying by the bier of his

as they ascend, as in the walls of Servius Tullius at Rome. Similar square basements of masonry, generally *emplecton*, and probably the bases of pyramids, are not uncommon in this necropolis, especially in the glen of the Vaccina, beneath the cliffs of the city.

[2] Micali, in his last work, in which he seeks to establish oriental analogies in Etruscan monuments, expresses his opinion that these seats are Mithraic symbols—and so he also regards the celebrated marble chair of the Corsini Palace. Mon. Ined. p. 152.

[3] Here were fragments of embroidery in flowers of smalt of Egyptian workmanship —a piece of blue *pasta* inscribed with hieroglyphics—*alabasti* in the form of Egyptian females—and bits of amber and other oriental gums placed around the corpse. A morsel of one of these gums being put to the fire emitted so powerful an odour as to be insupportable, says Visconti, even in the spacious hall of the Ducal palace at Ceri. Ant. Mon. di Ceri, pp. 29—32. The vault at the entrance proves this tomb to be very ancient.

master, and suggesting that he had been slain at the funeral obsequies.[4]

GROTTA TORLONIA.

The sepulchre under the adjoining tumulus has received is name from the proprietor of the land, Prince Torlonia, who opened it in 1835. The basement is here of the usual circular form.[5] The entrance to this tomb is its most singular feature. At a considerable distance a level passage opens in the hill-side, and runs partly underground towards the tumulus, till it terminates in a vestibule, now open to the sky, and communicating with the ground above, by two flights of steps. The inner part of this vestibule is recessed in the rock, like the upper chambers of the tombs of Castel d'Asso; for there is a similar moulded door in the centre, and on either hand are benches of rock which, being too narrow for sarcophagi, suggest that this chamber was formed for the funeral rites—probably for the banquet, and generally for the convenience of the relatives of the deceased in their periodical visits to the tomb. This chamber is decorated with rock-hewn pilasters of Doric proportions, but with peculiar capitals, and bases somewhat allied to the Tuscan.

In the floor of this vestibule opens another flight of steps leading down to the sepulchre.[6] There is an antechamber at the entrance, which opens into a spacious hall, having three compartments, like chapels or stalls, on either hand, decorated with Tuscan pilasters, and a chamber also at the upper end, which, being the post of honour, was elevated, and approached by a flight of steps. Each chamber contained several sepulchral couches, altogether fifty-four in number. At the moment of opening the tomb, these were all laden with their dead, but in a little while, after the admission of the atmosphere, the bodies crumbled to dust and vanished, like Avvolta's Etruscan warrior

[4] For a detailed description of this tomb and its contents, and for illustrative plans and sections, see the work of Cav. P. E. Visconti, Antichi Monumenti Sepolcrali di Ceri. Canina (Etruria Marit. I. p. 197, tav. 70) dates this tomb from before the second century of Rome.

[5] This tumulus is about 75 feet in diameter. The masonry of the basement has this peculiarity, that at the distance of every 10 or 11 feet a pilaster projects so as to give the whole a resemblance to a vast cog-wheel lying on the ground. In the masonry, just above the entrance, is a pit shaft, as in the tombs of Civita Castellana.

[6] Visconti (Ant. Mon. di Ceri, p. 20) conjectures that this flight of steps was originally concealed, so that a person entering the passage or descending the steps from above, would take the vestibule with its moulded doorway for the real sepulchre.

at Corneto, leaving scarcely a vestige of their existence.[7] The external grandeur of this tomb augured a rich harvest to the excavator, but it had been already stript of its furniture—not a piece of pottery was to be seen—so completely had it been rifled by plunderers of old.[8]

In that part of the necropolis, called Zambra, which lies on the west of Cervetri, towards Pyrgi, some very ancient tombs were opened in 1842. In construction they were like the Grotta Regulini-Galassi, being long passages similarly walled and roofed in with masonry, and lying beneath large tumuli of earth, and their furniture betrayed a corresponding antiquity.[9]

It is worthy of remark that though sepulchres are found on every side of Cære, those towards the sea are generally the most ancient.[1] It may also be noticed that the tombs face all points of the compass.

I have already mentioned that in very early times, Cære was renowned for her cultivation of the pictorial art, and that in the

[7] Visconti, p. 21. A full description of this tomb, with illustrations, will be found in the said work of Visconti. Also in Canina (op. cit. I., p. 196, tav. 69), who refers the tomb to the second or third century of Rome.

[8] An external analogy to houses is not very obvious in these tumular sepulchres. They have been supposed to have the funeral pyre for their type (Ann. Inst. 1832, p. 275), but the usual analogy may, perhaps, be traced in the habitations of the ancient Phrygians, who, dwelling in bare plains, on account of the scarcity of wood, raised lofty mounds of earth, weaving stakes above them into a cone, heaping reeds and stubble around them, and hollowing them out for their habitation. Such dwellings were very cool in summer, and extremely warm in winter. Vitruv. II. 1, 5. Externally they must have resembled the shepherds' capanne, which now stud the Campagna of Rome. Indeed, if the tumular form of sepulture were not one of natural suggestion, and which has therefore been employed by almost every nation from China to Peru, it might be supposed that the Lydians, who used it extensively, had copied the subterranean huts of their neighbours the Phrygians, and introduced the fashion into Etruria. The conical pit-houses of the ancient Armenians might in the same way be regarded as the types of the tombs

of that form which abound in southern Etruria, and are found also south of the Tiber, as well as in Sicily; for the description given of them (Xenophon, Anab. IV. 5, 25; cf. Diodor. XIV. pp. 258–9) closely corresponds. The interiors of these subterranean huts of Armenia presented scenes very like those in an Italian *capanna*.

[9] The word Zambra seems of Saracenic origin, and recalls the old romances of Granada; but it was used in Italy in the middle ages for *camera*; and it seems probable that this spot derived its name from the sepulchral *chambers* here discovered. The word is also met with in several parts of Tuscany, but attached to streams and torrents (see Repetti, *sub voce*); so that it is difficult to trace a connection with the Moorish dance. For an account of the tombs, see Abeken, Bull. Inst. 1840, p. 133; Mittelitalien, pp. 236, 268, 272; Micali, Mon. Ined. p. 375, *et seq.* tav. LVI. Canina gives plans of four of these tombs, which he thinks belonged to the necropolis of Pyrgi (op. cit. I., p. 198, tav. 73).

[1] Abeken (Mittelital. p. 240) fancied there might be some reason for this westward position of the oldest tombs, as though it were chosen for its approximation to the sea, the peculiar element of the Tyrrheno race. He notices the analogy of the Nuraghe on the western shore of Sardinia.

first century of our era, paintings were extant on this site, which were believed to be prior to the foundation of Rome.[2] There can be little doubt that, although not expressly named, Cære was also one of the cities of Etruria, which at a very remote period excelled in the plastic arts.[3] Of her sculpture in marble we have instances in the "Grotta dei Sarcofagi," already described. Some choice specimens of terra-cotta statuary have fortunately come down to us to attest her skill in moulding clay.

What visitor to the Louvre has not been startled, on first entering the Musée Napoléon, at the sight of a loving pair, as large as life, reclining on a couch in the centre of the room? The life-like character of these figures, who appear engaged in animated conversation, their strange costumes, and still stranger cast of features—differing widely both from the Greek and from the Egyptian, yet decidedly oriental and akin to the Calmuck; the varied colouring of the group, which faithfully imitates nature throughout; the unusual material for statuary, which is soon recognized as burnt clay—cannot fail to call forth wonderment. What do they mean? Whence do they come? What people do they represent? To what age do they belong? are the questions to which they naturally give rise. This group is an early work of Etruscan plastic art from Cervetri, discovered by the Marchese Campana in 1850. The monument is a sarcophagus, in which were deposited the bodies of the pair whose effigies recline on the lid, or rather form the lid, as the urn is moulded into the couch on which they are reposing. The lady lies in front, and is draped to her feet in a yellow *chiton*, or chemise, with short sleeves, over which she wears a red mantle with a broad border of white. Her neck is encircled with a gorget; her ears are pierced for rings, which have been removed; her cap is the *tutulus*, the national head-dress in the early days of Etruria, from beneath which her hair descends in long tresses on her bosom and shoulders. Her husband, who lies behind her, wears merely a short tunic or shirt; his beard is trimmed to a point, his hair hangs loosely behind his head. The hands and feet of both are modelled to the life, though certain other parts of the figures betray a careless treatment. A strange incongruity in the group can hardly fail to strike the observer. With this Asiatic pomp of colour, with these features, not only un-European, but absolutely Tartar-like, and barbaric, the ornaments of the couch are purely Hellenic, identical with those which are found decorating Greek

---

[2] Plin. N. H. XXXV. 6.   [3] *Ib.* XXXV. 46.

vases of the best style and period, which fact limits the antiquity of the monument to the fifth century B.C. This incongruity is accounted for by Dr. Brunn, by supposing that in very early times the native art of Etruria was subjected in a powerful degree to Hellenic influences, which more or less overlaid or obscured the indigenous element, yet that the latter was never entirely subdued, but exerted a reaction from time to time, developing the native peculiarities' sometimes to such an extent, especially when the monument was of large size, that it produced the feeling of strangeness and novelty, which we lose however on further investigation, when we perceive that the elements are already familiar,—only developed in a manner novel and unexpected.[4]

Of yet more primitive character, and evincing more clearly the peculiarities of Etruscan indigenous art, with even less alloy of foreign elements, is a similar sarcophagus of terra-cotta, also found at Cervetri, and now in the British Museum. The woodcut at the head of this chapter is copied from a photograph published in "the Castellani Collection," by Mr. C. T. Newton, whose description of it I cannot do better than transcribe.

"This Etruscan sarcophagus consists of a coffin, richly decorated with reliefs all round, the four corners of which rest each on a pedestal ornamented with the bust of a Siren or Harpy. On the cover of the coffin are a male and female figure reclining on a mattress. The male figure is naked, and his meagre and emaciated condition seems caused by age and sickness, though perhaps much of the peculiarity of the type may be due to the want of skill in the artist in the representation of nude forms. The female figure wears a close-fitting *chiton*, which does not reach to the feet. Her hair falls in long tresses over her bosom, and is gathered into a thick queue behind. Round her neck is a necklace with pendants, resembling some very ancient ornaments in silver and amber found at Palestrina, and now in the Castellani collection of jewels. Her right hand is raised as if she held out something which the male figure advances his right

<hr>

[4] Ann. Inst. 1861, pp. 391–404. I mention Brunn's view of this singular monument, but cannot admit his explanation of the peculiar characteristics it displays to be satisfactory. He rejects all affinity to Pelasgic or Lydian art, and ascribes the peculiarities of physiognomy simply to the attempt of the Etruscan artist to represent a smile! The unmistakable resemblance, however, these figures bear to the Mongol type, cannot fail to be recognised by any one who has lived, as I have done for years, among Tartar races. For an illustration of this monument see Mon. Inst. vol. VI. tav. 59. See also an article by Dr. Emil Braun. Ann. Inst. 1850, p. 105.

hand to receive. His left elbow rests on two flat cushions, on which a painted Meander is still visible. The style of these figures is archaic, the treatment throughout very naturalistic, in which a curious striving after truth in anatomical details gives animation to the group, in spite of extreme ungainliness of form, and ungraceful composition. The groups seem to have been made in parts, fitted on after passing through the furnace. The relief on the front of the coffin represents a battle between two warriors, each attended by one male and two female figures. At either end of the scene is a winged figure; these probably represent the souls of the two warriors. On the opposite side of the coffin is represented a banquet, at which a male and female figure recline. At one end are two warriors, each of whom appears to be taking leave of two female relations. At the other end are two pairs of females, seated in chairs, in a mourning attitude. It is to be presumed that the four scenes thus represented on the sides of the coffin have relation to one another, and that the four subjects represented are, the leave-taking of two warriors before going to single combat; the death of one of them; the mourning for that death; and the funeral feast, or possibly the reception of the slain warrior in the realms of bliss. But the particular single combat represented has not yet been identified. It should be noticed that in the single combat a lion is represented fastening on the leg of the falling warrior.

"Above the battle-scene is an Etruscan inscription painted in two lines, one of which is along the edge of the mattress, the other immediately below. The letters are identical with the earliest forms of the Greek. The inscription is very similar to that on a gold fibula found at Chiusi, but its interpretation is not yet determined.

"In the Louvre is a terra-cotta sarcophagus found at Cervetri, and formerly in the Campana Collection, on which are two reclining figures, very similar in type and composition to these, but showing more sense of beauty, and more artistic skill in their design and execution.

"These two sarcophagi may be reckoned among the earliest known specimens of the fictile art of Etruria. There is no positive evidence as to their age, but they can hardly be later than B.C. 500."

To this description I will venture to add that the Tartar physiognomy is even more pronounced in this pair than in that on the Louvre sarcophagus; and there can be no doubt that this

is the earlier monument. The figures in relief below are closely
akin in style to those on the most archaic *cippi* of Chiusi. The
inscription, as Mr. Newton observes, is in very early Greek
characters, rather than Etruscan, yet, like the latter, it is written
from right to left.   Italian antiquaries generally doubt its
genuineness. It is certainly not easy to decipher.

The ancient pottery of Cære is in keeping with the archaic,
oriental character of the rest of the sepulchral furniture. The
large, fluted, or fantastically moulded cinerary jars, of red or
black ware, with figures of centaurs, sphinxes, and chimæras in
flat relief, resemble those of Veii; and so the rest of her early
unpainted pottery, which Lepsius takes to be Pelasgic rather
than Etruscan.[5]   The most ancient painted vases are also found
on this site, not only those of the so-called Phœnician style, but
others of a much rarer class and peculiarly Doric character,
resembling the ancient Corinthian pottery, as we know it
through the celebrated Dodwell vase, and others from Greece
and her colonies.[6] These very early vases are of course found
in the most ancient tombs, but in those of later date, imitations
of this early pottery not unfrequently occur. It is not difficult to
detect these pseudo-archaic vases, which are probably the work
of Etruscan hands.   One of the most striking examples of these
imitation vases is a *hydria*, with black figures representing the
myth of Hercules slaying Busiris and his attendant priests.[7]
Busiris was King of Egypt, and to propitiate the gods during a
protracted famine, was advised to sacrifice yearly a foreigner to

[5] To the Pelasgi, says Lepsius, must undoubtedly be referred the vases of black
earth of peculiar, sometimes bizarre, but
often elegant forms, adorned with fantastic
handles, figures, nobs, flutes, and zigzag
patterns — as well as the fine old gold
articles, of archaic and extremely careful
style, very thinly wrought, and sown with
minute gold grains, and studded with short
stumpy figures, with marked outlines and
Egyptian characteristics. Tyrrh. Pel. p. 44.

[6] Of this rare class of vases from Cære,
there are two in the Gregorian Museum.
One, an *olpe*, represents the combat of
Ajax (Aivas), and Hector, who is assisted
by Æneas. The palæography of the inscriptions, just like that of the Dodwell
vase, determines this also to be Doric;
especially the use of the Q instead of the
K; for the *koppa* is quite foreign to Attic
inscriptions. Mon. Ined. Inst. II. tav. 38;

Ann. Inst. 1836, pp. 306—310, Abeken.
The other vase, a *hydria*, represents a
boar-hunt, as on the Dodwell vase. Mus.
Gregor. II. tav. 17, 2. Another good
specimen of this class of Cæritan pottery
is at Berlin, and represents the combat
between Achilles and Memnon, with birds
flying over the horses' heads—a frequent
symbol on painted vases, which has been
interpreted as a type of swiftness, or as an
augury—and also with peculiar palæography. Mon. Ined. Inst. II. tav. 33;
Ann. Inst. 1836, pp. 310—311. The
figures on these vases are black and violet,
on a pale yellow ground; and the outlines
are scratched, as on other vases of the
most ancient style.

[7] Ann. Inst. 1863, pp. 210—232, Helbig; 1865, pp. 296-306. Bull. Inst.
1865, p. 140. Mon. Inst. VIII., tav.
16, 17.

HERCULES SLAYING BUSIRIS FROM AN ETRUSCAN VASE, CERVETRI.

Jupiter. Hercules, travelling through Egypt, was seized when asleep by the priests, who led him to the altar as a victim; but he burst his bonds, slew the king, his son, and the priests, as he is represented doing in the woodcut on the last page. The fair people represent the Egyptians, the dark, negroes. As usual in representations of this myth, there is much of the burlesque in the treatment; the manner in which the demi-god strangles half a dozen of his foes at the same moment is highly ludicrous.

Though the pottery of Cære is generally of a more archaic character than that of Vulci or Tarquinii, yet beautiful vases of the later, or Greek, styles are also found here.

Between Cære and Veii, and in the territory of the former city, lay a very ancient Etruscan town, called Artena, which was destroyed by the Roman kings. Speculations have been raised as to its site, but it will probably always remain a matter of conjecture.[8]

APPENDIX TO CHAPTER XXI.

NOTE I.—SHIELDS AS SEPULCHRAL DECORATIONS. See p. 257.

THE shields carved or painted in this and other tombs of Cære, probably mark them as the sepulchres of warriors, and are only a more permanent mode of indicating what is expressed by the suspension of the actual bucklers. This was a Greek as well as Etruscan custom. The ancient pyramid between Argos and Epidaurus, mentioned by Pausanias (II. 25. 7.) contained the shields of the slain there interred. The analogous use of them as external decorations of sepulchres by the people of Asia Minor and by the Etruscans, has already been pointed out. Vide p. 200. The shield was a favourite *anathema* with the ancients, who were wont, at the conclusion of a war, to suspend their own bucklers, or those of their vanquished foes, in the temples of their gods—a very early and oriental custom, for David dedicated to God the gold shields he had captured from the men of Zobah. 2 Sam. viii. 7, 11. Crœsus the Lydian offered a gold shield to Minerva Pronœa, to be seen at Delphi in the time of Herodotus (I. 92 ; cf. Paus. X.

---

[8] Livy (IV. 61) alone mentions this town, and he does so to distinguish it from the Artena of the Volsci, which is thought to have occupied the heights above Monte Fortino. He says the Etruscan Artena belonged to Cære, and not to Veii as some supposed. Nibby placed it at Castellaccio in the *tenuta* of Castel Campanile, where he found traces of an Etruscan town; but Gell thought it more likely to have stood at Boccea, or Buccea, near the Arrone, twelve miles from Rome, for "there is here a high and insulated point, which has all the appearance of a citadel, and which seems to have been occupied at a subsequent period by a patrician villa." (I. p. 195.) Canina places it at a spot six miles to the east of Cære, and about two to the north of Le Caldare, which he takes to be the Thermæ Cæretanæ. Etr. Mar. J. p. 164.

8, 7,), and sent another to Amphiaraus, which was preserved in the temple of Apollo at Thebes. Herod. I. 52, 92. After the battle of Marathon, the Athenians dedicated their shields to the Delphic Apollo, and fixed them to the entablature of his temple. Paus. X. 19, 4. And traces of shields in the same position may still be observed on the eastern front of the Parthenon— one under each triglyph, with the marks also of the bronze letters of the inscriptions which alternated with them. The Roman conquerors of Corinth suspended a number of gilt shields on the entablature of the temple of Jupiter Olympius ; and in the pediment of the same building was a golden shield, also a dedicatory gift (Paus. V. 10, 4, 5.) ; and so shields have been found carved in the pediments of the rock-hewn, temple-like tombs of Phrygia. Shields may sometimes have been symbols of protection received from the gods, and thus acknowledged ; but were often, like *anathemata* in general, mere emblems of the profession of those who dedicated them ; as was the case with the twenty-five shields of the armed runners in the Olympic *stadium*. Paus. V. 12. 8. Sometimes they seemed to have served merely decorative purposes, as when Solomon adorned his palace with five hundred gold targets (1 Kings, x. 16, 17) ; or as when, in Asia Minor, they were carved on city walls, and the *proscenia* of theatres. And they were a conventional decoration also with the Romans, who emblazoned them with the portraits of their ancestors, and suspended them in temples or in their own houses. Plin. XXXV. 3, 4. The use of shields, however, as fields for personal devices, is as old as the War of the Seven against Thebes, if we may believe Æschylus ; and for family emblems is also very ancient, for Virgil (Æn. VII. 657) introduces one of his early Italian heroes with a formidable escutcheon—

> Pulcher Aventinus, clypeoque insigne paternum,
> Centum angues, cinctamque gerit serpentibus Hydram.

The shields borne by the figures of Minerva on the Panathenaic vases are supposed by Canina to contain the devices of the Italian cities. Bull. Inst. 1843, p. 75. But this is open to question. We must look beyond the days of chivalry for the origin of armorial bearings, and for their emblazonment on shields. For an ingenious theory of the Egyptian origin of heraldry, see Mr. Wathen's interesting work on " Ancient Egypt," pp. 20 *et seq.*

NOTE II.—GENII AND JUNONES. See p. 248.

The spirits which were believed by the Romans to attend and protect human beings through life, were supposed to be of the same sex as their individual charge ; the males being called Genii, the females Junones. Tibul. IV. 6, 1 ; Seneca, epist. 110. Such spirits were supposed not only to have presided over, but to have been the cause of birth, which is in fact implied in the name—*Genius, a genendo* (Festus, v. Geniales ; Censorinus, de Die Natali, III.) ; and hence the nuptial couch was called *lectus genialis*, and was sacred to the Genius. Fest. s. v. ; Serv. ad Virg. Æn. VI. 603. Some maintained that every man at his birth, or rather at his conception, had two Genii allotted to him, to attend him through life—one inciting him to good deeds, the other to evil—and whose office it was also after death to attend him to the presence of the infernal judges, to confirm or refute his pleadings, according to their truth or falsehood : so that he might be raised to a better

state of existence, or degraded to a lower. Serv. ad Virg. Æn. VI. 743 ; cf.
III. 63 ; Euclid. Socrat. ap. Censorin. III. A similar doctrine of protecting
and attendant spirits was held by the Greeks, who called them demons—
δαίμονες—and believed them to be allotted to men at their birth, as guardians,
always present, and cognisant not only of deeds but of thoughts, and
commissioned also to accompany them to the other world. Also to act as
interpreters and messengers between the inhabitants of earth and heaven.
Plato, Phædo, pp. 107, 108, ed. Steph., and ap. Apuleium, de Deo Socrat.
p. 80, ed. 1493 ; cf. Hesiod. Opera et Dies, I. 121 et seq., 250 et seq. ; Pind.
Olymp. XIII.

Genii were distinguished from the Manes and Lares, inasmuch as these
were the deified spirits of the dead, while the Genii were the offspring of the
great gods (Fest. vv. Genium, Tages), and the givers of life itself, wherefore they were called Dii Genitales. This distinction, however, was not
always preserved, for the Genii were sometimes confounded with the Manes
and Lares, and supposed, after the death of their charge, to dwell in his
sepulchre. Serv. ad Æn. III. 63 ; Censorin. loc. cit. ; cf. Plin. II. 5.

A man was believed to be born under the influence of a favourable or
unlucky Genius (Pers. IV. 27—genio sinistro) ; and the Genius or Juno, as
the case might be, was also supposed to be pleased or offended with the
actions of the individual. Thus Quartilla, in Petronius (cap. 25), exclaims,
" Junonem meam iratam habeam, si unquam," &c. And if a man restrained
his passions and appetites, he was thought to " defraud his Genius," or if he
gave way to them, to " indulge his Genius." Persius, V. 151 ; Serv. ad Virg.
Georg. 1. 302 ; Terent. ap. eund.

As the Genius was a god he received divine honours, especially on the
birthday of the individual, when he was propitiated by libations, and offerings of flowers (Horat. Ep. II. 1, 144 ; Tibul. I. 7, 50 ; IV. 5, 9 ; Pers. II.
3,) ; and so also the Juno of a woman (Tibul. IV. 6) ; and it was customary
to anoint the head of the image, to adorn it with chaplets, and to burn
incense before it. Tibul. I. 7, 51 ; II. 2, 6 ; Ovid. Trist. V. 5, 11. Even
after death offerings were made to the Genius of the deceased, as Æneas
to that of his father (Ovid. Fast. II. 545), to whom he offered gifts—

Ille patris Genio sollemnia dona ferebat—

a custom which explains the inscription, " ιυνοΝ " (Junoni), on the vase
painted on the wall of this tomb at Cervetri.

Women were in the habit of swearing by their Juno (Tibul. III. 6, 48), as
men by their Genius ; and a lover would even swear by the Juno of his
mistress (Tibul. IV. 13, 15), exalting her above every other divinity. Juvenal
(II. 98), denouncing the effeminacy of the Romans, sets it in the strongest
light by saying that a servant swears by the Juno of his lord—

Et per Junonem domini jurante ministro.

Not only men and women, but places and things, had their Genii, according to the Roman creed (Festus, v. Genium ; Serv. ad Georg. I. 302 ; Æn.
V. 85, 95). Cities, as well as their component parts—streets, houses, baths,
fountains, &c.—had their individual Genii ; and so also with regions,
provinces, armies, nations—every portion, as well as the whole collectively,

had its presiding spirit. The Genius of the Roman People is often represented on coins, though Prudentius might well question his individual
character—

> Quanquam cur Genium Romæ mihi fingitis unum,
> Cum portis, domibus, thermis, stabulis, soleatis
> Assignare suos Genios ? perque omnia membra
> Urbis, perque locos, Geniorum millia multa
> Fingere, ne propriâ vacet angulus ullus ab umbrâ ?

These *genii loci* were supposed to take the visible form of a serpent (Virg.
Æn. V. 95 ; Serv. ad loc.) ; and so they are constantly represented on the
household shrines of Pompeii, eating meat or fruits from an altar.

The doctrine of Genii and Junones as held by the Romans, there is little
doubt, was received from the Etruscans with that of the Lares. We know
that the latter people worshipped Genii. A Genius Jovialis was one of
their four Penates (Arnob. adv. Nat. III. 40 ; cf. Serv. ad Æn. II. 325) ; and
Tages, their great lawgiver, was himself the son of a Genius (Fest. *v.*
Tages). And that the Etruscans held the doctrine of good and evil spirits
attending the soul into the other world, is demonstrated by their monuments ;
by none more clearly than by the paintings in the Grotta del Cardinale at
Corneto. This dualistic doctrine is thought by Gerhard (Gottheiten der
Etrusker, p. 57) not to be Hellenic ; Micali refers its origin to the East. It
is not so clear that the Etruscans held the distinction between Genii and
Junones ; for the sex of the ministering spirit is often not accordant with
that of the human being, who, whether man or woman, is generally attended
by a female spirit. Thus the majority of the demons represented on
Etruscan urns, sarcophagi, and mirrors, are females. Therefore it is not
strictly correct to term such she-demons, Junones. Passeri (Paralipom. in
Dempst., p. 93) employed the name "Geniæ." Nor is it always easy to
distinguish between the attendant spirits, good or bad, and the ministers of
Fate, who are introduced as determining or directing events, or the Furies,
who, as ministers of vengeance, are present at scenes of death, or assisting
in the work of destruction. All have the same general characteristics.
Wings at the shoulders—high buskins, often with long flaps, which are apt
to be mistaken for *talaria*—a short, high-girt tunic—a double strap crossing
the bosom, the upper ends passing over the shoulders, the under, behind the
back, and united between the paps in a circular stud or rosette. The
distinction must be drawn from the nature of the scene into which these
demons are introduced, from their attitude and expression, but chiefly from
the attribute in their hands, which, in the case of a Fury, or malignant Fate,
is a hammer, sword, snakes, shears, or a torch ; in the case of a decreeing
Fate, is a scroll, or a bottle or ink-horn, with a *stylus*, or in a few instances,
a hammer and a nail ; and in the case of a Genius or Juno may be a simple
wand, or nothing at all. The demons of vengeance, who are often attendants
on Charun, from their resemblance to the Furies of Greek mythology, are
thought by Gerhard to have a Hellenic origin. Gottheiten der Etrusker,
p. 17. Their Etruscan appellation is not yet ascertained, although the name
" NATHUM " is attached to a wingless male-demon with brutes' tusks, who,
armed with snakes, presides at the slaughter of Clytæmnestra, on a mirror
now in the Berlin Museum (Gerhard, op. cit. taf. VI.) ; and although the
demon who exults over Theseus and Pirithous in Hades, as depicted in a
painted tomb at Corneto (see p. 355), is designated " TUCHULCHA." Against

some of the she-demons of milder character, especially those which have the
attributes of Fates, the name "LASA" has been found attached on Etruscan
mirrors (Lanzi, Sagg. II. tav. VI. 6. ; Gerhard, Etrusk. Spiegel, taf. XXXVII.,
CLXXXI. Bull. Inst. 1846, p. 106), though a similar goddess is sometimes
designated "MEAN" (Etrusk. Spiegel, taf. LXXXII., CXLI., CXLII.). Lasa,
from its connection with other names in the instances cited, seems a generic
appellation. It must be equivalent to "Lara," the r and s being interchangeable letters ; wherefore we find "Lases" for Lares in the Carmen Arvale.
Lara or Larunda is considered by Müller (Etrusk. III., 4, 13) to be identical
with Mania, the Mother of the Manes and Lares. The origin of "Lasa" has
also been referred to the Aἶσα of the Greeks (Bull. Inst. loc. cit.) ; but the
. analogy seems to be one of office rather than of appellation, for the derivation from the Etruscan "Lar" is perfectly satisfactory. Gerhard (Gottheiten
der Etrusker, p. 16) on this ground translates Lasa as the "mistress," not
only of the Genii of men, but of the analogous Junones of women, yet
thinks a Lasa must never be mistaken for a Juno.

Though the female ministering spirits of the Etruscan mythology are not
in every respect analogous to the Roman Junones, it may be well, in default
of a specific name, to apply to them the same appellation. To the mild or
decreeing Fates, the name of "Lasa" may be confidently attached ; and
the malignant Fates, or demons of vengeance, whose Etruscan name has
not yet been clearly ascertained, from their resemblance to the Erinyes or
Eumenides of Grecian fable, may well be designated Furies. In many instances they seem to be closely allied to the Kῆρες of the Greek poets—the
she-demons of doom and violent death, who haunted battle-fields and scenes
of mortal strife ; but I do not remember an instance on an Etruscan monument, of a female demon being drawn with the fangs and claws of a wild
beast, as the "Ker," presiding at the mutual slaughter of the Theban Brothers,
was represented on the celebrated Chest of Cypselus. Pausan. V. 19, 6.
On the large sarcophagus of the Casuccini collection, now at Palermo, on
which the final parting of husband and wife is represented in relief, a demon
armed with shears and torch is seen issuing from the gate of Orcus, and over
her is inscribed the word "KULMU ;" but whether this name applies to her,
or to the gateway, is matter of dispute. Another demon by her side is
named "VANTH," but neither her attribute nor her character is clearly intelligible. The same name is also attached to a she-demon in the François
tomb of Vulci, in the scene where Achilles is sacrificing Trojan captives to
the shade of Patroclus; but here again it is doubtful if she be a good genius
introduced in antagonism to Charun, as M. Des Vergers opines (III. p. 20),
or an evil spirit urging the son of Peleus to his vengeance, as Dr. Brunn
(Ann. Inst. 1861, p. 358) prefers to regard her. The generic appellation of
the malignant demons of the Etruscan mythology has yet to be ascertained.

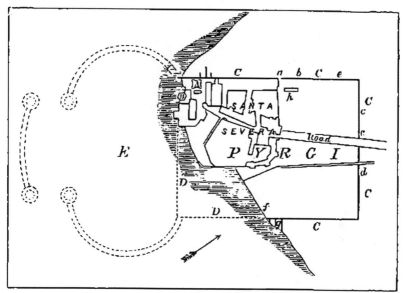

PLAN OF PYRGI.

Adapted from Canina.

A. The keep.	*a*. Site of an ancient gate.
B. Round tower.	*b*. Wall, here 16 feet thick.
C, C. Line of Pelasgic walls.	*c*. Wall, 12 feet thick.
D, D. Outline of ancient city seaward, accord-	*d*. Wall, 8½ feet thick.
ing to Canina's supposition.	*e*. Roman repairs of Pelasgic wall.
E. Ancient Harbour, according to Canina ;	*f*. Blocks on the beach.
but no traces of such moles and break-	*g*. Roman walls.
water are visible.	*h*. Fountain.

CHAPTER XXII.

SANTA SEVERA—*PYRGI*.

Pyrgi veteres.—VIRGIL.

Grandia consumpsit mœnia tempus edax.—RUTILIUS.

NINE miles beyond Palo is the fortress of Santa Severa, standing on the shore, about a furlong from the high-road. It is a square castle, with a square keep at one angle, and a lofty round tower, with machicolated battlements, rising near it. To the casual observer, it has nothing to distinguish it from other mediæval forts; but if examined closely, it will be seen that its walls on the side of Civita Vecchia are based on foundations of far earlier date, formed of massive, irregular, polygonal blocks, neatly fitted together without cement,[1]—precisely similar to the walls of Cora,

---

[1] Under the walls of the fortress, however, the blocks are imbedded in mortar.
The traveller must not be misled by this,
which is a modern addition, as at Orbetello.

Segni, Palestrina, Alatri, and other ancient towns in the Latin and Sabine Mountains—in short, a genuine specimen of what is called Pelasgic masonry. This wall may be traced by its foundations, often almost level with the soil, for a considerable distance from the sea, till it turns at right angles, running parallel with the shore, and, after a while, again turns towards the sea—enclosing a quadrangular space two or three times larger than the present fort, and sufficiently extensive for a small town.[2] This is the site of "the ancient Pyrgi."[3]

These, and the slight remains on the Puntone del Castrato, presently to be mentioned, are the only specimens of polygonal masonry in this part of Etruria, though such masonry is found on three other sites further north. The strict similarity to the walling of cities south and east of the Tiber, seems to imply a common origin, and that not Etruscan. Moreover, the position of this town in the plain, scarcely raised above the level of the sea, is so unlike purely Etruscan sites, which are always strong by nature as well as by art, and the materials of its walls—limestone, travertine, crag, sandstone, all aqueous formations—so distinguish them from the volcanic fortifications of the other ancient sites in the southern district of Etruria, that we are led to the conclusion that it was built by a different race, or in a different age. Now, though we have no express assertion in ancient writers that Pyrgi itself was of Pelasgic origin, we know that its temple of Eileithyia was built by that people, and that it was the port of Agylla or Cære,[4] which was founded or occupied by the same

One block is 9 ft. 6 in. long, 3 ft. 9 in. high, and 1 ft. 9 in. thick.

[2] Canina (Ann. Instit. 1840, pp. 39, 40) gives the dimensions as 850 by 650 Greek feet. Abeken calls it 750 by 600 ft. (Mittelitalien, p. 133), which nearly agrees with my measurement of 720 by 650 English ft.

[3] The Itinerary of Antoninus describes Pyrgi as 34 miles from Rome, which is the true distance, and 8 miles from Castrum Novum. The Maritime Itinerary makes it 30 miles from Portus, at the mouth of the Tiber, 12 from Alsium, and 8 from Castrum Novum. The Peutingerian Table calls it 10 miles from Alsium, which is correct, but 9 from Castrum Novum; see p. 226. These discrepancies in the distances are of little consequence, since Pyrgi occupies the relative position assigned to it between Alsium and Castrum Novum.

[4] Strabo, V. p. 226 ; Diod. Sic. XV. p. 337, ed. Rhod. Pyrgi can hardly have been founded originally as the port of Cære, for it was at least 8 miles from that city, which lay only 4 miles from the sea ; and there can be no reason why a site should not have been chosen for a port much nearer Cære, as there is nothing in this spot to recommend it in preference to any other part of the neighbouring coast, and the harbour it once possessed must have been entirely artificial. I think it much more probable that the earliest structure on this site was the celebrated temple, and that the castle sprung up subsequently to protect that wealthy shrine, and that the existence of a fortress here determined the people of Cære to adopt the spot for their port, instead of constructing another on a more convenient site—Alsium, for instance.

race, and we have Virgil's authority as to its high antiquity,[5] and its name in proof of its Greek origin. So that while history gives us the strongest presumptive evidence that Pyrgi was a Pelasgic town, its existing remains confirming that evidence, may be considered decisive of the fact.[6]

The small size of the town, scarcely more than half a mile in circuit, as determined by the remains of its walls, is another feature which distinguishes it from all the Etruscan sites already described. Yet in this particular it quite agrees with the description we have of Pyrgi, as " a castle "[7] and " a small town."[8] It must, nevertheless, have been a place of considerable importance as a port, naval station, and commercial emporium,[9] and it was renowned as the head-quarters of those hordes of pirates, who long made the Tyrrhenians as much dreaded throughout the seas of Italy and Greece,[1] as the corsairs of Barbary have been in later times.

Much of the importance of Pyrgi must have arisen from its temple of Eileithyia or Lucina, the goddess of childbirth,—a

Canina (Ann. Inst. 1840, p. 37) cites Dionysius, in support of his opinion that this temple was founded by the Pelasgi at least two generations before the Trojan War.

[5] Virgil (Æn. X. 184) calls it ancient even in the days of Æneas ; and though at liberty to indulge in the proverbial licence of a poet, he was too good an antiquary to commit a glaring anachronism.

[6] Canina (Ann. Inst. 1840, p. 40) thinks that as the site itself did not afford the Pelasgic builders of Pyrgi materials for the polygonal masonry, to which they were accustomed, they cut the blocks from the neighbouring mountains, now called Monti del Sasso, which yield a calcareous stone naturally assuming polygonal forms. Some antiquaries, with Micali (Mon. Ined. p. 373), and Bunbury (Class. Mus. V. pp. 147—186), will not admit that this polygonal masonry shows a Pelasgic origin, but ascribe it rather to a constructive necessity, arising out of the nature of the building materials at hand. My reasons for regarding the polygonal masonry of Italy, in type at least if not always in construction, as Pelasgic, will be given in Chapter L. It is evident that a *choice* was exercised in this instance, for the local rock is all volcanic, either soft tufo, or black lava, which lines

the shore between Pyrgi and Civita Vecchia ; but this may have been rejected as too hard, or it might not have given the desired cleavage. The variety of materials employed —all alike thrown into polygonal forms— proves that the adoption of that style in this instance was not accidental, but intentional. At Agylla, however, where the rock is a volcanic tufo, the Pelasgi seem, at least in their tombs, to have hewn it into rectangular blocks.

[7] Serv. ad Æn. X. 184.

[8] Rutil. I. 224. Strabo also (V. p. 225) classes it among the πολίχνια of the Etruscan coast.

[9] Pyrgi was also a fishing-town (Atheu. VI. c. 4). It seems to have suffered the usual evils of a seaport, that—"quædam corruptela ac demutatio morum"—as Cicero terms it (de Rep. II. 4) ; for Lucilius (ap. Serv. ad Æn. loc. cit.) mentions the "scorta Pyrgentia."

[1] Serv. loc. cit.—"Hoc castellum nobilissimum fuit eo tempore, quo Thusci piraticam exercuerunt ; nam illic metropolis fuit." The small size of Pyrgi, as Müller remarks (Etrusk. I. 4, 8) is no proof against its importance in ancient times, seeing that the once renowned ports of Greece astonish the modern traveller by their confined dimensions.

shrine² so richly endowed with gold and silver, and costly gifts, the *opima spolia* of Etruscan piracy, as to have tempted the cupidity of Dionysius of Syracuse, who, in the year of Rome 370 (B.C. 384), fitted out a fleet of sixty triremes, and attacked Pyrgi, ostensibly for the sake of repressing its piracies, but really to replenish his exhausted treasury. He surprised the place, which was very scantily garrisoned, spoiled the temple of not less than a thousand talents, and carried off booty to the amount of five hundred more, defeating the men of Cære, who came to its rescue, and laying waste their territory.³

This is all we know of Pyrgi in the days of Etruscan independence. Her history must in great measure be identical with that of Cære, on which she was so intimately dependent. We find her mentioned as a Roman colony in the year 563 (B.C. 191), when with Fregenæ, Castrum Novum, and the maritime colonies of Latium, she was compelled to add her quota to the fleet fitting out against Antiochus, king of Syria.⁴ It is evident that under the Roman domination she lost much of her former importance.⁵ We find nothing more than mere statements or hints of her existence,⁶ till in the fifth century after Christ she is said to have dwindled from the condition of a small town to that of a large

---

² Rite maturos aperire partus
  Lenis Ilithyia, tuere matres ;
  Sive tu Lucina probas vocari
            Seu Genitalis ! &c.
                Hor. Carm. Sæc. 13.
Aristotle (Œconomic. II. 20) and Polyænus also (V. cap. II. 21) call this goddess Leucothea. Niebuhr (II. pp. 478, 493, Engl. trans.) and Müller (Etrusk. III. 3, 4) call her Mater Matuta, who was identified by the Romans with the Leucothea of the Greeks. But Matuta is also allied with Eos or Aurora (Lucret. V. 655) ; and Gerhard (Gottheiten der Etrusker, pp. 9, 25) suggests an analogy between Eileithyia-Leucothea, and the Etruscan Aurora, who was called "*Thesan.*" Etrusk. Spiegel, I. taf. LXXVI. The natural relation of the goddess of the dawn with the goddess of births is easily understood ; that with a goddess of the sea, is not so evident. As Leucothea was deemed powerful in preserving from shipwreck, and was the patron-deity of sailors, it is an argument in her favour in this instance. Were this shrine sacred to her, it would seem to imply that the port was prior to the temple. On the

other hand, it may be said, that Eileithyia being but one form of Juno, the great goddess of Argos (Hesych. *s. v.* Εἰλειθυίαι), the Pelasgic colony may well have raised a temple to her honour—as did the Argive colony, called by Dionysius (I. cap. 21) Pelasgic, which settled at Falerii. She is sometimes called the daughter of Juno (Paus. I. 18, 5 ; Iliad. XI. 271). Homer, however, elsewhere (Iliad. XIX. 119) speaks of this goddess in the plural number. So also Hesychius. For a new view of the derivation of the name, *vid.* Ann. Inst. 1842, p. 95 (Henzen).

³ Diodorus Sic. XV. p. 337 ; Serv. ad Æn. X. 184. See also Aristot. Œcon. II. 20 ; Strab. V. p. 226 ; Polyæn. Strat. V. cap. II. 21 ; cf. Ælian. Var. Hist. I. 20.

⁴ Liv. XXXVI. 3.

⁵ Servius (loc. cit.) speaks of Pyrgi as "nobilissimum" in early times, and implies that she had lost her importance with her piracies.

⁶ Liv. XXV. 3 ; Cic. de Orat. II. 71 ; P. Mela, II. 4 ; Plin. III. 8 ; Ptol. p. 68, ed. Bert. ; Mart. XII. epig. 2 ; Strab. loc. cit. ; Serv. loc. cit.

villa.[7] We hear no more of her as Pyrgi, but find mention of her in A.D. 1068, as the Castle of Sta Severa.[8]

Of the celebrated temple there are no traces extant; nothing to determine even the site it occupied. Canina suggests that, from the period in which it was built, it may have been in the most ancient Doric style.[9] If so, it must have resembled the great temples of Pæstum, standing like them on the shore, and rearing its massive capitals and entablature high above the towers and battlements of the inclosing walls, at once a beacon to the mariner, and a stimulus to his devotion.

The foundations show the walls of Pyrgi to have been in parts of great thickness, implying, what might be expected from its exposed situation in the plain, that its fortifications were of unusual strength and loftiness.[1]

The port, as already said, must have been wholly artificial, which seems indeed to be expressed in the term applied to it by ancient writers.[2] Nothing remains to determine the shape of the harbour, but Canina thinks it was formed by two curved moles, each terminating in a tower, with a third mole in front of the opening between them, like the "island" at Civita Vecchia.

There are no tombs visible around Sta Severa, not even a tumulus on the plain, but at the foot of the heights which rise inland, sepulchres have been discovered. On one spot, called Pian Sultano, the Duchess of Sermoneta has excavated, and the tombs she found were of very simple character, similar to those of Palo and Selva la Rocca.[3]

---

[7] Rutilius (I. 224), speaking of Alsium and Pyrgi, says—

"Nunc villæ grandes, oppida parva prius."

[8] Nibby, Diotorni di Roma, III. p. 94.

[9] Annal. Inst. 1840, p. 42.

[1] The name of Pyrgi denotes the existence of "towers" in the ancient walls, yet there are no traces of any now visible. It is evident they did not project beyond the line of walls, as at Cosa and Falleri, though Canina, in his restored Plan of Pyrgi, has so represented them, for the outer face of the foundations is in parts clearly definable for a considerable distance; nor are there traces of towers within. Perhaps they rose only on the side towards the sea, where huge masses of ruin, the wrecks of the fortress and port, now lie on the shore, fretting the waves into everlasting foam. There are traces of Roman work on this side, of opus incertum and reticulatum. The ancient walls seem to have varied from 8 to 12 and 16 feet in thickness.

[2] Canina points out that Strabo and Dionysius both used the term ἐπίνειον, instead of λιμήν, in describing Pyrgi—the former term implying an artificial port, constructed with moles or breakwaters—the latter a natural harbour only. Ann. Inst. 1840, p. 43. This view is favoured by Hesychius when he says that ἐπίνειον is smaller than λιμήν.

[3] Micali, Mon. Ined. pp. 375, 385. The tombs which Abeken (Mittelitalien, pp. 239, 242, 267) describes as belonging to Pyrgi, or to a village dependent on her, are those at the Puntone del Castrato, treated of in the next chapter. The tombs at Zambra, mentioned at p. 278, are supposed by Canina to have belonged to the necropolis of Pyrgi.

CHAPTER XXIII.

SANTA MARINELLA.—*PUNICUM.*

I wandered through the wrecks of days departed,
Far by the desolated shore.
                                      SHELLEY.

FIVE miles beyond S. Severa is the station of Santa Marinella.
Here the railroad crosses the shoulder of a low headland, on
which stand a few buildings and a lonely date-palm. The promontory half embraces a tiny bay, with some ruins of a Roman
mole or breakwater. A few fishing-boats are drawn up on the
beach; the half-draped tawny fishermen are sitting beneath their
shade, mending their nets; and two or three similar craft, with
their latteen sails glistening like snow in the sunbeams, are
gliding with swan-like motion over the blue waters. The hamlet
is supposed to mark the site of Punicum, a station on the Via
Aurelia.[1] A few furlongs before reaching it, in a field by the
road-side, are many traces of Roman habitation, probably
marking the site of a villa. Here on the shore are a couple of
ancient bridges standing in picturesque ruin near the road, and
marking the course of the Via Aurelia along the coast. Excavations have been made in this neighbourhood by the Duchess of
Sermoneta, and many remains of Roman magnificence have been
brought to light.[2]

[1] Punicum is mentioned only by the
Peutingerian Table. Nibby (Dintorni di
Roma, II. p. 313) thinks it must have
taken its name from the pomegranates
(*malum punicum*) which flourished here,
or from some heraldic device of this
character; but it is more likely to have
arisen from some association of the place
with the Carthaginians. Mommsen (Röm.
Gesch. I. c. 10), indeed, is of opinion that
there was a Phœnician settlement or factory
on this spot, the only one on the shores of
the Italian peninsula. But were that the
case, it is strange that we find no mention
of such a settlement in Roman writers.

[2] In the winter of 1837, on the shores
of the little bay, were found remains of
baths and other buildings, with mosaic
pavements, together with a singular column,
and a beautiful statue of Meleager, now in
the Museum of Berlin. Mon. Ined. Inst.
III. tav. LVIII. For further notices, see
Bull. Inst. 1838, p. 1; 1839, p. 25; 1840,
p. 115; Ann. Inst. 1843, p. 237, *e seg.*

Were the traveller now to leave the train, and pursue the high-road towards Civita Vecchia for about a mile, and then cross the heath to the extremity of the range of wooded hills which here rise from the coast, he would find some remains of far prior antiquity to those at Santa Marinella, which prove the existence of a long-forgotten Etruscan town or fortress on this spot. Let him ask for the "Puntone del Castrato," or "Sito della Guardiola," and he may obtain a guide at the little *osteria* of Santa Marinella.

I know not what induced the Duchess of Sermoneta to commence excavations on this site. No traces of sepulchres are now visible. More than once have I wandered long over the heathy crag-strewn ground at the foot of these hills, vainly seeking vestiges of a necropolis. It is certain, however, that here have been discovered many tombs of a remarkable character, being rude chambers hollowed in the rock, lined with rough slabs, and roofed in either by a single large cover-stone, or by two slabs resting against each other, gable-wise—extremely similar, so far as I can learn from the description, to those still to be seen at Saturnia. There is some analogy also to the tombs of Magna Græcia, and yet more to the *cromlechs* of our own land, and other parts of Europe and of the East. The oriental character of the furniture they contained confirms their high antiquity.[3]

Abeken speaks of a huge tumulus rising in the midst of these tombs. This, however, I found to be nothing but the termination

---

[3] These tombs were found in 1840. The slabs which lined them were, some calcareous, some volcanic, partly hewn, partly rough, but always put together so as to present a tolerably even surface. A single massive slab often lined each of the three side-walls of the tomb, and a fourth, leaning against the front, closed the door-way. Sometimes the tombs had two chambers, the outer of which served as a vesti-bule. They contained benches, or sepul-chral couches, of rock. Abeken thinks that these gable-roofed tombs, from their resemblance to guard-houses, may have suggested to the peasantry the name of La Guardiola, conferred on this site. Over every tomb rose a tumulus, of which Abeken saw few or no traces; but he says that the most remarkable feature was a *cuniculus*, or passage, lined with slabs, surrounding one of these tombs; and he thinks it served to separate the sacred space of the sepulchre from the surrounding soil, or to prevent one tomb from inter-fering with another. It bears an analogy to the trench cut in the rock round the conical tomb at Bieda. See p. 217. Among the sepulchral furniture was found an *alabastos* with hieroglyphics. Abeken, Bull. Inst. 1840, p. 113, *et seq.* ; Ann. Inst. 1841, p. 31 ; Mittelitalien, pp. 239, 267. Micali (Mon. Ined. p. 356) considers tombs of this simple character the most ancient in style, though not always in con-struction, as they must have continued in use for ages, and probably never went out among the peasantry. He describes some as built up of many blocks, regularly cut and smoothed, but without cement (p. 386, tav. LV.).

of the range of hills which here sink to the coast; and what he took for a vast sepulchre inclosed by masonry, I perceived to be the *arx* of an ancient town, marked out by a quadrangle of foundations, almost level with the soil; and what he regarded as an outer circuit of walls to his tumulus, I discovered to be the fortifications of the town itself, extending a considerable way inland, along the brow of the hill, till their vestiges were lost among the crags with which the ground is strewn. Traces of several gates also I clearly observed; and in more than one spot remains of polygonal masonry.[4]

Here then stood the town in whose cemetery the Duchess of Sermoneta made excavations. What was its name? We have no mention by ancient authors of any town on this coast between Alsium and Centum Cellæ, whose site has not been determined. That this was of very ancient date, may be inferred from the silence of Roman writers, as well as from the character of the remains, which mark it as Etruscan. Now, on the coast immediately below it stands the Torre di Chiaruccia, the Castrum Novum of antiquity; a name which manifestly implies the existence of a more ancient fortress, a Castrum Vetus, in the neighbourhood; which, there can be little doubt, is the place whose remains occupy the Puntone del Castrato.[5] This may have fallen into decay before the domination of the Romans, or it may have been destroyed by them at the conquest, and when a colony was to be established, a fresh site was chosen on the coast

---

[4] I have given notices of this site in Bull. Inst. 1847, pp. 51, 93. On the summit of the mound or tumulus, says Abeken, is a quadrangular inclosure of wall, within which rises a second, still higher, at the very summit of the mound. The ground between the two inclosures is paved with marine breccia. Within the upper quadrangle a sepulchral chamber has been discovered about 14 feet below ground, originally lined with masonry, but now much ruined. The entrance is not distinguishable. The whole seems to have formed a cemetery, and perhaps the inclosing walls served to support different stories, rising above the sepulchral chamber; a plan adopted by the Romans in the Mausolea of Augustus and of Hadrian, and in the Septizonium of Severus. Abeken, Bull. Inst. 1840, pp. 113—5; and Mittel-italien, p. 242.

Abeken elsewhere (Ann. Inst. 1841,

p. 34) suggests that the inner and higher quadrangle of masonry may have marked the *area* of a temple, like that of the Capitol. If so, the presence of bones in the passage, is explained by the well-known connection between temples and tombs.

[5] This conjecture of mine is confirmed by the actual name of the site, as Dr. Braun suggests (Bull. Inst. 1847, p. 94—*Castrato* being, probably, a mere corruption of the ancient name. I am indebted to the Cav. Canina for the information that a mosaic discovered a few years since at Sta Marinella, bore the representation of a town on a height, which he suggests may have been this on the Puntone del Castrato. In the old fresco maps in the galleries of the Vatican, some ruins are indicated on this height, though no name is attached. This shows that the site was recognised as ancient at the close of the 16th century, when those maps were executed.

below, probably for convenience sake; or it may be, that the entire population of the old town was transferred to the new, for the same reasons that led to the foundation of the duplicate cities of Falerii and Volsinii.

About two miles beyond Santa Marinella stands, close to the shore, the solitary square tower of Chiaruccia, marking the site of Castrum Novum, mentioned above. All we know of it is that it was a station on the Via Aurelia and a colony on this coast,[6] and that, with other neighbouring colonies, it reluctantly furnished its quota to the fleet which was despatched in the year 563 (B.C. 191) against Antiochus the Great.[7] In the time of Rutilius it was in utter ruin—*absumptum fluctuque et tempore.*

Some miles nearer to Civita Vecchia, by the roadside, near a tower called Prima Torre, are two large barrows, which, from a slight excavation made some years since, are thought to give promise of valuable sepulchral furniture.

---

[6] Liv. XXXVI. 3; Plin. III. 8; Ptol. Geog. p. 68, ed. Bert.; Mela. II. 4.

[7] Liv. loc. cit. The Castrum Inui of Virgil (Æn. VI. 776), which was on the coast of Latium, seems to have been confounded by Servius (ad loc.) and by Rutilius (I. 232) with this Castrum Novum in Etruria—the former a place of great antiquity, the latter probably only of Roman times. But Müller (Etrusk. III. 3, 7) thinks from Rutilius' mention of an ancient figure of Inuus over a gate at Castrum on this coast, that the god may have been worshipped at both sites. Inuus was a pastoral deity, equivalent to Pan, or Faunus. Holstenius (Annot. ad Cluver. p. 35) and Mannert (Geog. p. 375) took Sta Marinella for Castrum Novum, though Cluver (II. p. 488) had previously indicated the ruins at Torre di Chiaruccia to be the site—an opinion which is now universally admitted to be correct.

CHAPTER XXIV.

CIVITA VECCHIA.—*CENTUM CELLÆ.*

Ad Centumcellas forti defleximus Austro ;
　　Tranquillâ puppes in statione sedent.
Molibus æquoreum concluditur amphitheatrum,
　　Angustosque aditus insula facta tegit ;
Attollit geminas turres, bifidoque meatu,
　　Faucibus arctatis pandit utrumque latus.
Nec posuisse satis laxo navalia portu,
　　Ne vaga vel tutas ventilet aura rates.
Interior medias sinus invitatus in ædes
　　Instabilem fixis aëra nescit aquis.—RUTILIUS.

WHOEVER has approached the Eternal City from the sea must admit the fidelity of the above picture. As Civita Vecchia was 1400 years since, so is it now. The artificial island, with its twin-towers at the mouth of the port ; the long moles stretching out to meet it ; the double passage, narrowed almost to a closing of the jaws ; the amphitheatre of water within, overhung by the houses of the town, and sheltered from every wind—will be at once recognised. It would seem to have remained in *statu quo* ever since it was built by Trajan. Yet the original town was almost utterly destroyed by the Saracens in the ninth century ; but when rebuilt, the disposition of the port was preserved, by raising the moles, quay, and fortress on the ancient foundations, which are still visible beneath them.[1]

It is possible, in ancient times, when the ruler of the world made it his chosen retreat, and adorned it with his own virtues and the simple graces of his court, that Centum Cellæ may have been, as the younger Pliny found it, " a right pleasant place"— *locus perjucundus.*[2] Now, it is a paradise to none but *facchini*

---

[1] There are other remains of the Roman town on the shore without the walls ; and the aqueduct which supplies the town with water is said to be erected, for the most part, on the ruins of that constructed by Trajan. On the shore, at this spot, was discovered that colossal arm in bronze now in the Gregorian Museum, which, though of the time of Trajan, is said to "surpass in beauty perhaps all ancient works in this metal with which we are acquainted."

[2] Plin. Epist. VI. 31.

and *doganieri*. What more wearisome than the dull, dirty town of Civita Vecchia? and what traveller, who in former times was condemned to wait here for steamer or diligence, did not pray for a speedy deliverance from this den of thieves, of whom Gasperoni, though most renowned, was not the most accomplished? *Tempora mutantur.* No one need now be delayed at Civita Vecchia, when there are four trains running daily to Rome, three to Orbetello, and one to Leghorn and Pisa.

It does not appear that this site was ever occupied by an Etruscan town. Yet relics of that antiquity are preserved here, some in the Town-hall, mostly from Corneto,[3] and some in the house of the Marchese Guglielmi, an extensive proprietor of land in the Roman Maremma,[4] besides a collection of vases, bronzes, and other portable articles in the shop of Signor Bucci, in the Piazza.

Three miles from Civita Vecchia, on the road to Corneto, at a spot called Cava della Scaglia, Etruscan tombs have been opened,[5] which seemed to have belonged to the neighbouring Algæ, though that place is known to us only as a Roman station, mentioned in the Maritime Itinerary. Its site is marked by Torre Nuova, on the sea shore, three miles from Civita.

Three miles to the east of Civita Vecchia, on the road to Allumiere, are the Bagni di Ferrata, the hot springs lauded by Rutilius under the name of Thermæ Tauri,[6] and mentioned by Pliny[7] as the "Aquenses cognomine Taurini," in his catalogue

---

[3] These consist of three sarcophagi of *nenfro* with recumbent figures on the lids, found in the Montarozzi; two-winged sphinxes and half a dozen female heads in stone, painted in imitation of life, and very archaic in character. Besides these, there are sundry Roman *cippi* and monumental tablets, among which will be found the names of Pompeius and Cæsennius—families of Tarquinii—Veturius, which answers to the Velthur in the Grotta degli Scudi (p. 337)—and several milestones, probably of the Via Aurelia.

[4] The collection in the house of the Marchese Guglielmi is composed of articles found in his own land. One of the most remarkable objects is an urn of *nenfro*, found near Montalto, in 1840. It is in the form of a little temple, supported on Ionic-like columns, with a moulded doorway at one end, and a male figure, in relief, holding a wand and *patera*, at the other—probably

representing the deceased, whose name is inscribed in Etruscan characters around him. In the opposite tympanum is a human head set in a flower; and the angles of the pediments rest on lions' heads. Micali, Mon. Ined. pp. 403—7, tav. LIX. Canina, Etr. Marit. tav. CIX. Bull. Inst. 1850, p. 124 ; 1869, p. 166.

[5] Excavations were made here in 1830 by Signor Bucci, but with no great success. His attention was drawn to the spot by a Figaro of Civita Vecchia, who, fifteen years previous, had found there a shoe of bronze, which he had esteemed of no value, till a foreigner, entering his shop, seized upon it and carried it off, leaving a napoleon in the palm of the astonished barber.

[6] Rutil. I. 249—

Nosse juvat Tauri dictas de nomine thermas,
Nec mora difficilis millibus ire tribus.

[7] Plin. III. 8.

of Roman Colonies in Etruria. They are still much resorted to by the citizens of Rome during the summer.

Twelve miles from Civita Vecchia in the same direction, near Allumiere, or the alum-works, is the town of Tolfa, perched high on the wooded slopes of the mountains which bear its name. In the wide valley beneath it, through which flows the Mignone, rise several of those cliff-girt plateaux of tufo, which in this land are at once recognised as the probable sites either of Etruscan habitation, or of Etruscan sepulture. The loftiest of these heights shows on one side remains of fortifications of tufo masonry, resembling that of the ancient walls of Cære, and a hollow way below the walls seems to mark the line of road which formerly led up to one of its gates. The site of an ancient town is manifest, and its Etruscan origin is proved by the cemetery in its neighbourhood, but the name it bore of old is utterly unknown.

The existence of Etruscan tombs on this site had long ago been noted,[8] but systematic excavations were first undertaken in the winter of 1865, by some inhabitants of Tolfa. Numerous sepulchres were opened—small, unadorned chambers hollowed in the tufo, generally beneath tumuli, which were sometimes of square form; one tomb only was discovered containing rock-hewn benches, and these were carved to resemble couches, and below them were two dogs and a stag in relief in an archaic style of art. Beautiful painted vases, some with black, others with red figures, were brought to light, together with two very fine mirrors, and other objects in bronze, and some gold jewelry. Among the tombs were found a number of wells, about a mètre in diameter, which were probably sepulchres, like those of Poggio Renzo at Chiusi, and of Marzabotta, near Bologna, but they do not seem to have been sufficiently explored to determine the fact.[9]

Corneto is now so easy of access by railway from Civita Vecchia, that the traveller who approaches the Eternal City by that port, should make a point of visiting the painted tombs of the Montarozzi, which will open to him clearer and more comprehensive views of the early civilization of Italy than he can derive on any other site, and which form an excellent introduction to the works of ancient art in Rome.

[8] Bull. Inst. 1831, p. 210.

[9] For an account of the excavations on this site, see Bull. Inst. 1866, pp. 225—231. Otto Benndorf.

SALTATRIX AND SUBULO, GROTTA DEL TRICLINIO.

CHAPTER XXV.

CORNETO.—*TARQUINII.*

THE CEMETERY.

What men or gods are these? What maidens loath?
What mad pursuit? What struggle to escape?
What pipes and timbrels? What wild ecstacy?—KEATS.

Dead men
Hang their mute thoughts on the mute walls around.—SHELLEY.

FROM Viterbo to Corneto there is an excellent road, and a
daily service by diligence. The thirty miles between them are
professedly accomplished in six hours; but "between the word
and the deed there is a long distance," as the proverb saith.
The country is most sparsely inhabited. In the twenty-one
miles of undulating downs of heath or corn which separate
Vetralla from Corneto, there is but one village, that of Monte
Romano, lying beneath the tufted hill of that name, which
forms a striking feature in the scenery of this district, and in
whose neighbourhood Etruscan antiquities have been discovered.

The most easy method of reaching Corneto from Rome is by
the Maremma railway, by which it is 101 kilometres, or 63 miles
distant. After leaving Civita Vecchia, the line follows the coast,
but at some distance, traversing wide downs of corn, and being
flanked inland by a long olive-clad ridge, on whose further
extremity sits enthroned the "Queen of the Maremma," crowned

with a tiara of many towers. The station is nearly three miles
from the town, but carriages always await the arrival of the
trains, and take a good hour to crawl up the wooded steep to the
gate.

By the carriage-road from Civita Vecchia the distance is about
the same, and the time consumed on the journey not much
greater. The country traversed is a desert of undulating heath,
overrun with lentiscus, myrtle, and dwarf cork-trees, the haunt
of the wild-boar and roe-buck. The road is a continuous
ascent till it reaches the crest of the long barren ridge, where
Corneto comes into view at the distance of several miles. The
strangely broken surface of the down at once arrests the eye.
To the right, separated from it by a deep vale, stretches a parallel
ridge, browed with white cliffs. That once bore the walls, the
temples, the palaces of ancient Tarquinii—this contained its
sepulchres. The one was the city of the living; the other the
city of the dead. Formerly, how different! now, but too similar
—rivals in desolation! It is a wild and dreary scene. Not a tree
on either height, or in the vale between—wide sweeps of bare
country on every hand—the dark, serrated range of the Tolfa
hills to the south—an aqueduct of many arches in the foreground; and the sunny blue of the Mediterranean, the only
cheerful feature in the landscape, gleaming on the horizon.

The road here branches to Vetralla on the one hand, and to
Corneto on the other. The latter track traverses the hill of the
Necropolis, the whole surface of which is rugged with tumuli, or
what have been such, but are now shapeless mounds of earth,
overgrown with lentiscus, myrtle, wild olive, broom, and rank
grass, and giving to the hill, even when seen from afar, a strange,
pimply appearance. Hence its appellation of "Montarozzi."

"Fanno i sepolcri tutto 'l loco varo."

Towards the sea the eye passes over lower grounds, in which
are olive-groves, a farm-house or two, and several tumuli of large
size. Lower still lies the flat, barren strip of coast—the region
of salt-works and deadly fevers. There, on the beach, stands a
hamlet, dignified with the title of Porto Clementino: a few small
craft are at anchor off shore, waiting for cargoes of corn and
salt.

It is a drive of nearly three miles over the Montarozzi to the
gate of Corneto. Here a glance brings the thoughts from the
most remote antiquity, down to the days of chivalry. Long lines

of yellow battlemented wall stretch along the crest and down the slope of the hill; and the style of masonry, the absence of bastions and ravelins, and of embrasures, show these fortifications to date from before the invention of artillery.

Though the chief city of the Papal Maremma, having a population of nearly five thousand souls, and lying on the high-road from Civita Vecchia to Leghorn, Corneto has no inn, where the traveller, *fessus viarum*, may repose and recruit in comfort. A picturesque Gothic building in the lower Piazza, styled from its original application and actual condition Il Palazzaccio—"the great ugly Palace" has long served as a hostelry; but he who expects the luxury suggested by its twisted mullions and graceful tracery, will meet with disappointment. He will find such comfort and cleanliness as may be looked for in an Italian country town, and much civility and attention from the hostess, Luigia Benedetti, and her daughters. A new hotel, better suited to the requirements of modern travellers, is about to be opened by the Municipality of Corneto.

Corneto possesses little interest, save to those who love to dwell with the past. The scenery around it, though wild, and occasionally grand, is not—for Italy at least—picturesque. Bare, hog-backed heights—the broad desert strip of shore—no wood but olive plantations, dull, grey, formal, and monotonous, less cheerful even than treeless tracts, and which are to scenery what a drab coat is to humanity—these are not promising materials for the portfolio. The city itself is the finest feature in the scene, and viewed from the north, on which side the ground sinks precipitously to the banks of the Marta, it is particularly bold and imposing. With this exception, the scenic delights of Corneto may almost be summed up in what none but the determined admirer of nature will appreciate—

"Watching the ocean and the sky together,
Under the roof of blue Italian weather."

With so little of the beautiful or picturesque around it, with dulness and dirt within its walls, the atmosphere in summer leaden and febrile, Corneto has no attractions beyond the relics of ancient days in its neighbourhood.

The antiquity of Corneto is questionable. The fond pride of its citizens has assigned to it an origin in the remotest ages, identifying it, on the strength of the first syllable—on the Macedon and Monmouth principle—with the Corythus of

Virgil;[1] a pretension too absurd to need refutation. If it had an existence in Etruscan times, it were less unreasonable to suppose, with Gell, that it occupies the site of Cortuosa, or Contenebra, towns in the territory of Tarquinii, which were captured and destroyed by the Romans, A.U.C. 366.[2] But it is most unlikely that either of these towns stood so close to the great city of Tarquinii; and as there are no traces whatever of ancient habitation, it is more probable that this site was not occupied in Etruscan times, or at most by an outpost or fort.

There are not a few relics of antiquity, however, in Corneto. In the Cathedral, beside some curious inscriptions of the middle ages, is a marble slab, forming a step in the aisle, and bearing an Etruscan epigraph, probably sepulchral.[3] In several private houses there are collections of Etruscan antiquities,—in the Palazzo Bruschi, a most numerous and valuable collection; and a Museum has recently been formed by the Municipality, which already contains some most interesting articles discovered on the spot. But a description of these collections we must leave to a subsequent chapter, and hasten to the painted tombs, which are the real lions of Corneto.

When I first visited Corneto, I had the advantage of the guidance of Signor Carlo Avvolta, the *gonfaloniere*, or chief magistrate of the town. He was a lively, intelligent, old gentleman, experienced in excavations, deeply interested in the antiquities of this his birthplace, ever ready to impart information, and displaying as much courtesy to strangers as cordiality to his friends. He might be consulted with profit also on the more rousing matters of Maremma sports. Though nearly eighty years of age, he was still a keen sportsman, and entered on the fatigues and perils of the chase with the ardour of a man of thirty. Wherever his activity might lead him during the day, in the evening he was sure to be found at the *caffè*, or at

[1] So sings a poet of the fifteenth century (Bull. Inst. 1839, p. 68).

Cardinal Garampi (ap. Tiraboschi, Litter. Ital. I. p. 50, ed. Milano, 1822) dates the origin of Corneto from the eighth or ninth century of our era, and says it was first called Corgnitum, perhaps from the abundance of cornels in the neighbourhood. Canina suggests that it may have received its name from the height it occupies, which terminates in a double projection, like the horns of an animal. Etr. Marit. II., p. 38.

Corneto was formerly much better populated than at present, for its walls are now half empty.

[2] Liv. VI. 4. Gell, Rome, I. p. 373. We have no clue whatever to the site of these towns. The position which has been assigned to them on the Marta, where it issues from the Lake of Bolsena, and again at and near Norchia, is matter of mere conjecture.

[3] In Roman letters it would be—LARTH. VELCHAS. TITUIRESU.

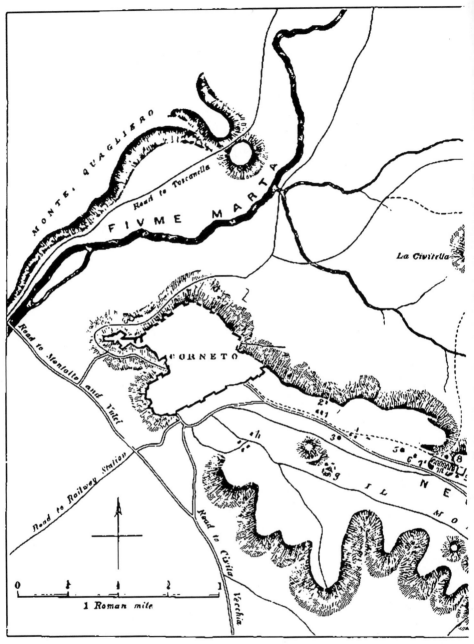

MAP OF TARQUINII AND 1

La Castellina

T A R Q V I N I I

Road to Viterbo

Adapted from WESTPHAL.

NECROPOLIS.

g. La Mercareccia.
h. Caves.
i. Sites of the ancient Gates.
k. Fragments of the ancient Walls.
l. Ara della Regina.
m. Aqueduct.
————— Carriage roads.
— ·· — Bridle paths.
········ Ancient roads.
Where this connects the portions of *m*, it marks
the subterranean course of the aqueduct.

the *spezieria*, where he would descant, with all the enthusiasm of his nature, on the last boar or roe-buck he had made to bite the dust, or on the paintings and furniture of Etruscan tombs.

It was owing to his antiquarian zeal, that the painted tombs on the Montarozzi, after remaining exposed to the wantonness of travellers and the ignorance of shepherds for years—in one case for more than a century—were fitted with doors by order of the government. The keys were intrusted to a citizen of Corneto. This man, Agápito Aldanesi, after exercising his vocation of *custode* for some thirty years, departed this life in 1873, bequeathing his keys and his mantle to his son-in-law, Antonio Frangioni, who now worthily does the subterranean honours of the spot.

The following is a list of the painted tombs in the Montarozzi now open, which I shall describe in the order in which they are generally visited :

		Discovered				Discovered
Grotta	Querciola	1831		Grotta	del Vecchio	1864
,,	de' Cacciatori	1873		,,	dei Vasi Dipinti	1864
,,	della Pulcella	1865		,,	del Moribondo	1872
,,	del Letto Funebre	1873		,,	delle Iscrizioni	1827
,,	del Triclinio, or G. Marzi	1830		,,	del Barone	1827
,,	del Morto	1832		,,	del Mare	1827
,,	del Tifone, or G. Pompei	1832		,,	Francesca	1833
,,	degli Scudi	1870		,,	delle Bighe	1827
,,	del Cardinale	1699		,,	del Pulcinella	1871 [4]
,,	dell' Orco, or di Polifemo,	1868				

This is a long programme; therefore, should the visitor want either the time or the inclination to accomplish it, I would recommend him to make the following selection. Grotta de' Cacciatori, G. Querciola, del Triclinio, del Morto, del Tifone, del Cardinale, dell' Orco. These are all within a mile of Corneto, and of easy access. But the earliest, and some of the most interesting tombs are beyond this point, and can only be reached on foot. The nearest are the Grotta del Vecchio, and G. dei Vasi Dipinti; but the most ancient of all the painted tombs is the Grotta delle Iscrizioni, which lies at the further end of the necropolis. Somewhat nearer to Corneto, but still in the heart of the Montarozzi, are the Grotta del Barone, and G. delle Bighe—typical tombs of their respective classes.

My descriptions of the paintings in these tombs may seem

[4] To these may be added three other nameless tombs, very recently discovered, but not at present accessible, being temporarily reclosed with earth (June, 1876).

tedious to the ordinary reader, but he who reads them on the spot will, I trust, accord them the merit of accuracy. The frequent visits I have made to Corneto, the long days I have spent from sunrise to sunset,

"Hid from the world in the low-delved tombs,"

the paintings in many of which I have copied and coloured on the spot, so as to familiarise myself with all their details, and the attention I have paid to the subject, warrant me in laying claim to greater accuracy than can be attained by the observation of a passing tourist.

About half a mile from Corneto, a deep pit to the right of the road marks the entrance to the

GROTTA QUERCIOLA,

a name derived from the owner of the ground in which the tomb lies.

A descent of about twenty steps, hewn in ancient times from the solid rock, leads to the entrance of the tomb, which is closed by a modern door. This opens into a spacious chamber. The first impression is one of disappointment. The chamber is in the form of an Etruscan tomb—but where are the paintings?—why close a sepulchre with naked walls? Presently, however, as the eye becomes accustomed to the gloom, figure after figure seems to step forth from the walls, and you perceive two rows of them, separated by a striped coloured ribbon—the upper row being nearly four feet, the lower little more than half that in height. In the pediment, left at each end of the chamber by the ceiling sloping down from the central beam, is a third row, not more than twelve inches high.

The next impression is one of surprise. Can this be the resting-place of the dead?—Can these scenes of feasting and merriment, this dancing, this piping, this sporting, appertain to a tomb? There on the inner wall, and occupying the principal row, is a banqueting scene—figures in richly-broidered garments recline on couches, feasting to the sound of the lyre and pipes; attendants stand around, some replenishing the goblets from a sideboard hard by; a train of dancers, male and female, beat time with lively steps to the notes of the instruments, on which some of them are also performing; while in the lower row are depicted field-sports, a boar-hunt being the most conspicuous.

But observe that fond and youthful pair on the central couch. The woman, of exquisite beauty, turns her back on the feast, and throws her arms passionately round the neck of her lover, who reclines behind her. The other guests quaff their wine without heeding them. The elegant forms of the couches and stools, the rich drapery, the embroidered coverlets, show this to be a scene of high life, and give some idea of Etruscan luxury.[5] Even the dancers are very richly attired, especially the women, in figured robes of bright colours, with embroidered borders of a different hue.[6] A simple mantle, either the *chlamys* or scarf, or the *himation* or blanket, suffices for the men; but the attendants at the sideboard have unornamented tunics. The dancing-girls are decorated with jewellery—earrings, necklaces, and bracelets —and have also a frontlet on their brows;[7] while the men wear chaplets of myrtle. A *tibicen*, or *subulo*, as the Etruscans called him, blowing the double-pipes,[8] and a *citharista* with his lyre, stand at one end of the banqueting-scene, and a *subulo* at the other; another performer of each description mingles in the dance.[9] All this feasting and merry-making is carried on in the

---

[5] Diodorus Siculus (V. p. 316, ed. Rhod.) and Posidonius (ap. Athen. IV., c. 38) tell us that the Etruscans were wont twice a day to have a sumptuous banquet prepared, and to recline under flowered coverlets, drinking out of silver vessels of various forms, and attended by a multitude of handsome slaves, magnificently apparelled. Each *lectus* or couch in this scene has beneath it the usual long stool—*hypopodium* or *subsellium*—and, though both are intended to have four legs, two only are represented. The dogs beneath the couches answer to the κύνες τραπεζῆες of Homer. Il. XXIII., 173; Odyss. XVII. 309.

[6] They wear the Ionic *chiton*, or long tunic, with short, loose sleeves; and over it a shawl, in some instances the *peplos*, in others the lighter *chlamys*.

[7] It is the *ampyx* or *sphendone*—the same frontlet as is generally given by ancient artists and poets to Juno, Diana, and the Muses.

[8] Varro, de Ling. Lat. VII. 35; Festus, v. Subulo. Both these writers cite Ennius as saying—

Subulo quondam marinas propter adstabat plagas—

a position in which a fife-player has never, I believe, been found on an ancient monument, though in a parable which Herodotus (I. 141) puts into the mouth of Cyrus, one is represented as playing—not preaching, like St. Anthony—to the fishes. Varro adds that the root of *subulo* must be sought in Etruria, not in Latium. Vossius went to the East for it, and fancied he had found it in the Arabic—*sunbul*—spica, calamus. Macrobius (Saturn. II. 1) represents this class of men as being proverbial for their indecent language—subulonis impudica et prætextata verba. The pipes used by the Etruscans at sacrifices were of ivory (Virg. Georg. II. 193), or of box-wood; those at public festivals, of lotus-wood, of asses' bones, or of silver. Plin. XVI., 66. Pliny says these double pipes were of Phrygian origin. VII., 57.

[9] The union of the pipes and lyre in ancient music, as exemplified in this and other Etruscan tombs, is frequently mentioned by classic writers. Horace (Epod. IX. 5) gives us to understand that a Doric

open air, as is shown by the trees behind the festive couch, and alternating with the dancers; yet the *candelabrum* indicates it to be by night.

The *biga*, or two-horse chariot, over the doorway, from its disproportionately small size, seems hardly to belong to the foregoing scene, and was, perhaps, introduced merely to fill an awkward space; though it may also have reference to the funeral games.

To hunt the wild boar of Etruria—*Tuscus aper*—was a favourite sport of the old Romans,[1] as it is still of their modern representatives. From this and other ancient monuments we learn that it was the delight of the Etruscans also. The bristly monster is here depicted brought to bay by the dogs. Men on foot and horseback are rushing eagerly to the attack; the former, while brandishing a spear in one hand, have an axe in the other to cut their way through the thickets, or to sever the boar's head from his carcass. Behind these figures are the nets into which it was the custom to drive the game, in order to bring it to bay. Such a scene is described by Virgil,[2] in his usual circumstantial and picturesque manner, and with more conciseness, but not less accuracy, by Horace;[3] and that such was the ordinary mode of hunting the boar and deer among the Greeks and Romans we have abundant evidence in ancient writers. In this lower band there seem to have been chariot-races also, though many figures have been obliterated from the wall.

In each pediment are two warriors, with short curved swords, leading their horses by the bridle;[4] and the angles are filled by panthers—animals frequently portrayed in Etruscan tombs, and generally over the doorway; whence it has been concluded that they were introduced as figurative guardians of the dead. But their presence in tombs may be explained by their being

---

song accompanied the lyre, and a "barbarian," *i.e.*, most probably a Lydian, the pipes—as he elsewhere (Od. IV. 15, 30) says—Lydis remixto carmine tibiis. Lydian was frequently used by the ancients as synonymous with Etruscan, on account of the generally received tradition, that Etruria had been colonised from Lydia, but the pipe was really of oriental origin. See Müller, Etrusk. IV. 1, 3, p. 203.

None of the *subulones* in this tomb wear the φορβειά, or *capistrum*—the bands fastened behind the head, to assist the action of blowing, by compression of the cheeks.

[1] Juven. Sat. I. 22; Stat. Silv. IV. 6, 10; Mart. VII. epig. 27; XII. ep. 14, 9. The boars of Umbria (Horat. Sat. II. 4, 40), and of Lucania (Sat. II. 3, 234; 8, 6) were also celebrated as a dish, but that of Etruria had more reputation, at least than the former, for Statius says—Tuscus aper generosior Umbro.

[2] Virg. Æn. X. 707—715.

[3] Horat. Epod. II. 31.

[4] Gerhard (Ann. Inst. 1831, p. 321) considers these warriors to represent the souls of the deceased, figured in a heroic and deified aspect.

sacred to Dionysus, who, according to the tradition which made him the son of Zeus and Persephone, the goddess of death, was himself an infernal deity.

This tomb was discovered in April, 1831. It is larger and loftier than any other sepulchre in this necropolis, whose walls are completely covered with paintings,[5] and in its original state must have been truly magnificent; but the colours have now almost faded from the walls, and it is to be feared that ere long they will vanish entirely. They have faded very much during the last few years, and the stucco has also fallen from the inner wall, so as almost to have destroyed the banqueting-scene.[6] This is the more to be regretted, on account of the peculiar beauty of the design here exhibited, which places this among the best of the painted tombs of Tarquinii. In fact the design is almost Hellenic, yet accompanied by features purely Etruscan; Gerhard regards this as the most instructive monument extant for the history of pictorial art in Etruria.[7] Yet though the influence of Greek art be manifest in this tomb, the subject is genuinely Etruscan. The most striking peculiarity is the presence of the two sexes on the same festive couch. It is evident that the fair one in this scene, from her amorous attitude, and from the absence of any other of her sex at the banquet, is as frail as fair —in short, that she is a *hetœra*.[8] But in others of these painted tombs women of most modest appearance are represented reclining with the men. And this is rarely found in Greek works of art—bas-reliefs, or even painted vases. For, with all their refinement, the Hellenes never attained to such an elevation of

---

[5] It is about 18 feet square, and about 10 feet high at the sides, and 12 to the central beam of the ceiling, which is without decoration. It looks S.

[6] This may be owing to the action of the atmosphere, for it is probable that the colours lose some of their freshness by exposure. On the other hand, nothing is more injurious than humidity, which conceals the true colours, and ultimately effaces them. To obviate its effects, iron gratings are now substituted for the wooden doors with which the tombs were formerly closed.

[7] Ann. Instit. 1831, pp. 313, 319, 357. A strong Greek character is seen not only in the general style of the design, but in the details of the drapery, the furniture, the crockery; yet the high-necked *krater* on the sideboard is very un-Hellenic in

form, nor have I ever seen its counterpart. The two *amphorœ* at its side are not much superior in form. The folded cushion under the elbow of each banqueter is the ὑπαγκώνιον of the Greeks, answering to the *cubital* or *pulvinar* of the Romans. The flowered bedding (ἀνθινὴ στρωμνή) of the figure in the corner, is one of the articles cited by Posidonius (ap. Athen. IV. c. 38) as a proof of the extravagant luxury of the Etruscans.

[8] Gerhard (Ann. Inst. 1831, p. 347) makes her an honest woman and the wife of her feast-fellow. Mrs. Gray (Sep. of Etruria, p. 193), with a praiseworthy tenderness for her sex, is blind to the amorous *abandon* of this fair Etruscan, and can see in her only "an afflicted mother consoled by her remaining son."

sentiment towards the fair sex, as to raise it to an equality with the male. In the feeling with which they regarded, and the suspicion with which they treated their women, they were half-orientals; the polished Athenians in this respect were even behind their ruder Dorian rivals. Their wives and daughters were never suffered to share the festive couch with their lords. *Hetæræ* alone were admitted to that equivocal honour. The superiority of the Romans in this point,[9] there is little doubt was owing to the example of the Etruscans, who as is abundantly proved from their monuments, as well as from history,[1] admitted their women to an equal place at the board. Such, however, was not the custom of the early Romans, for they reclined at table, while their women sat on chairs;[2] and so also they used to represent their deities in the *lectisternia*, or sacred feasts, for the statue of Jupiter was laid on a couch, while those of Juno and Minerva, his sister-wife and daughter, were placed in a sitting posture.[3]

One peculiarity of this tomb is, that there are no chaplets represented, either suspended from the walls, or in the hands of the dancers. The colours used in these paintings are red, yellow, blue, grey, black, and white. It is said that when the tomb was

---

[9] Quem Romanorum pudet uxorem ducere in convivium? . . . multo fit aliter in Græciâ—triumphantly exclaims Corn. Nepos (præfat.).

[1] Aristot. ap. Athen. I. c. 42. That the same custom prevailed among the Volsci seems proved by certain reliefs discovered at Vellotri. Theopompus (ap. eund. XII. c. 14), while he admits that the Etruscan women took their meals with the other sex, maligns them by saying, that it was with any one rather than with their own husbands. But the simple fact of the two sexes reclining together at meals, must have appeared so outrageous a breach of decorum to the Greeks, who always associated such a position with *hetæræ* alone, as to lead them naturally to regard the women as immodest; just as a Persian on hearing of distant lands, where all the women go unveiled, would set them down as dead to all shame and virtue. Before the discovery of these painted tombs, the union of the two sexes at the banquet had been remarked by Micali (Italia avanti il dominio de' Romani, II. p. 86, tav. 37) on certain Etruscan monuments; but Inghi-

rami (Mon. Etrus. I. p. 665) would not admit it—each considering his own view most flattering to his Etruscan forefathers. "How so licentious a custom," exclaims Inghirami, commenting on his opponent, "can be termed refinement, delicacy, and the elegant custom of a civilised people, as he declares the Etruscans to be, I leave to the judgment of any one who has the most superficial idea of decency." Yet in the same work (l. p. 408) he admits that both sexes are sculptured on Etruscan urns reclining together at banquets; but he interprets such scenes symbolically, fancying the men to represent heroes, the women, souls!

[2] Varro, ap. Isid. Orig. XX. 11.—Viri discumbere ceperunt, mulieres sedere, quia turpis visus est in muliere accubitus. Valer. Max. II. 1, 2.

[3] Valer. Max. loc. cit. Yet Livy (V. 13) and Dionysius (Excerp. Mai, XII. 7) describe Latona and Diana reclining with male divinities at the first *lectisternium* exhibited at Rome A. U. c. 355, just before the capture of Veii.

opened, an Etruscan inscription was legible near the principal
figures of the banquet; but it has completely disappeared, the
surface of the wall in this part having sadly suffered from time.[4]

GROTTA DE' CACCIATORI.

On the other side of the road, and rather nearer to Corneto,
on a spot called the "Calvario," is a group of tombs. The first,
called the "Tomb of the Sportsmen," was discovered in 1873.
You descend into it by a steep passage as into the last. It has
two chambers. The outer, about fifteen feet long, by ten wide,
is surrounded by trees, or rather by a series of olive saplings,
painted on the walls, from which are suspended fillets and chaplets, ribbons in festoons, mirrors, and in one instance a bird-cage.
Alternating with the trees are male figures, those on the left hand
almost obliterated; but on the opposite wall, you can distinguish
two, each with a cloth about his loins, engaged in a frantic dance;
one especially, who throws his head back and raises his knee to
the level of his chin, might be taken for one of the infuriated
marabouts sometimes seen in eastern lands. On the ground
behind him a *subulo*, similarly clad, but with a *tutulus* for a cap,
lies on his back playing his pipes, and kicks his legs in the air as
if beating time to his own music, or as if inspired with the fast
and furious mirth of the dancers. Dancing figures seem originally to have been carried all round the room, but are now almost
obliterated, by the falling away of the surface.

In the pediment over the door leading to the inner chamber is
the scene which gives its name to the sepulchre. Two horsemen,
one on a red, the other on a green steed, are represented
returning from the chase, preceded by a man on foot, who seems
to be pointing out the way through the thickets, and followed by
a slave carrying the game on a pole across his shoulder, and by a
peasant, with dogs, two of which are on the scent of a hare in the
right-hand corner.

The inner chamber, which is only ten feet square, displays yet
more remarkable scenes on its walls. Here the artist, not content

---

[4] For notices and opinions of this tomb,
consult Bull. Instit. 1831, p. 81-3 ; Ann.
Inst. 1831, p. 313, *et seq.* (Gerhard); 1831,
p. 325 (Ruspi); 1831, pp. 346—359 (Gerhard); 1834, p. 56 (Bunsen); 1863, pp.
348—351 (Helbig) ; 1866, p. 427 (Brunn) ;

1870, p. 63 (Helbig). For illustrations,
see Mon. Ined. Inst. I. tav. 38. Copies
of these paintings are preserved in the
Museo Gregoriano at Rome, and are engraved in the work of that name, tom. I.
tav. CIV.

with the representation of the human figure and domestic animals, as in the other painted tombs of Etruria, exhibits his skill in the delineation of landscape, for he gives us three sea-side subjects, unique in character, and full of interest. On the wall facing the door is depicted a boat with a high sharp stern, and a low bow, on which is painted an enormous eye, a fashion that has descended from Etruscan times to the fishermen of modern Italy. It is steered by a man with a broad oar; several other figures are sitting or standing in the boat, and one is leaning over the bow, with ropes in his hand, as if he had just made a cast of his line or net. A dolphin is sporting in the waves around the bows, water-fowl are pluming themselves on the rocks, and the air is full of birds of different colours and species, which a man, standing on a rock in the foreground, is attempting to knock over with a sling. On the left-hand wall is a somewhat similar scene. The boat in the centre is occupied by three naked men, watching a fourth who is plunging headforemost from a high rock into the waves. Behind him is another man, climbing the cliff like a monkey, apparently with the intention of following suit.[5] The scene on the right-hand wall is almost obliterated, but you can distinguish a third boat with a man standing in the bow, and endeavouring with a barbed trident to harpoon not the fish, but a pair of geese. Here again a man standing on the rocks in the foreground is slinging stones at the wild-fowl which fill the air around him.

On each side the door of this inner chamber is depicted a panther so frequently introduced into Etruscan sepulchres.

In the pediment opposite the door, a fond couple are reclining on a couch, laid on the ground; he naked from the waist upwards; she, robed in red, black, and green, with a red *tutulus* on her head, encircled with two blue chaplets. The difference of sex, as in all these painted tombs, is marked by the colour of the flesh; the man being depicted red, the woman white.[6] She is decorated

---

[5] Signor Brizio, in his description of this tomb, thinks this man has fallen into the sea, by the brow of the cliff giving way, and that the man behind him is trying to save him (Bull. Inst. 1873, p. 82); but from the nudity of the falling figure, and of the men in the boat, I am inclined to regard this as a bathing scene.

[6] A similar distinction in the colour of the sexes was observed by the Egyptians in their paintings. Vermilion seems to have been the conventional hue of male

rank and dignity also among more Eastern nations. "She saw men portrayed upon the wall, the images of the Chaldeans portrayed with vermilion. . . . all of them princes to look to, after the manner of the Babylonians of Chaldea, the land of their nativity." Ezek. xxiii. 14, 15. Just so are the Assyrian sculptures coloured, now in the British Museum. That it was also an ancient custom in Italy to represent gods and heroes of this red hue is evident from Pliny (XXXIII. 36), who states that the with large round earrings, snake-bracelets, and a necklace or band round her throat. He also wears a necklace with large pendants in the shape of dogs' heads. While he holds a goblet of wine in one hand, he throws the other arm lovingly round her neck, and his bare foot also over her loins, as she turns towards him to offer him a chaplet. Two slave-girls, each with long hair hanging down her back, and each holding a chaplet, sit at the foot of the couch; one turns her head round to watch the amorous pair; the other turns her back on the scene as if it had no interest for her. A youthful *subulo* plays his pipes by the side of the couch; and at its head stands a naked slave boy, holding up a small black cross, perhaps a *plectrum*, for a lyre hangs on the wall behind him. In the corner a large *krater* and three other vases rest on the ground, and a cup-bearer approaches them to replenish his pitcher with wine.

The figures in this tomb are rudely and carelessly drawn, yet are of an archaic style and with no lack of character. The outlines are strongly marked with black. A broad band composed of sixteen stripes of different colours surrounds the chamber beneath the roof, and from it depend garlands and chaplets of various hues. The ceiling is carved into a broad beam painted red; and the slopes on either hand are studded with flower-like spots, alternating with squares. This tomb faces the S.[7]

Very near the tomb just described, but on the verge of the height facing the long ridge on which Tarquinii once stood, is another tomb, called

GROTTA DELLA PULCELLA.

It was discovered in 1865, but reclosed, and opened again in November, 1873. It is entered by a horizontal passage, forty-five yards in length, sunk in the rock, and opening to the N.E.

---

statue of Jupiter was wont to be fresh painted with *minium* or vermilion on high festivals, and that Camillus, the conqueror of Veii, so bedaubed himself on his triumph. He adds that in his day the custom prevailed in Æthiopia, where all the great men painted themselves of this hue; and the images of the gods were similarly bedyed. The Romans doubtless derived the custom from the Etruscans, with whom, as these painted tombs and the recumbent figures on their sarcophagi testify, it was a conventional mode of expressing a state of glorification and beatitude. Tibullus (II. I. 55) says the husbandman of old was wont to dance before the gods—minio suffusus rubenti.

[7] A full description of these curious scenes, differing from mine in some particulars, is given by Signor E. Brizio, Bull. Inst. 1873, pp. 79-85, and 97-98.

You descend three steps, and find yourself in a small chamber, only ten feet square. In the wall opposite is a sepulchral recess, hollowed in the rock, just long and deep enough for a body, quadrangular below, but terminating above in a high-pitched pediment, from the apex of which a huge Gorgon's head, with winged brows, greets you with bristling teeth, and out-thrust tongue; but whatever effect it may have had in ancient times, it no longer preserves the tomb from intrusion. On the inner wall of the niche you can discern traces of two winged genii or demons, holding up a veil with which to cover the corpse. On one side-wall hangs a casket, on the other, two fillets. Externally the niche is decorated with a broad egg and tongue border, and with a wave pattern as a fringe, and is flanked at each end by a short Doric column, not carved but painted. On the wall on either hand are two musicians, one with the lyre, the other with the double-pipes, as if playing to the corpse which lay in the niche between them.

The side-walls of the tomb display banqueting-scenes, each wall having two couches, on which recline pairs of opposite sexes, distinguishable not merely by their costume, but by their complexion. The men are bare to the waist, and wear garlands of myrtle leaves round their brows. The women wear yellow transparent *chitones*,[8] or chemises, spotted with black, and red *pallia* with rich borders of other colours. All have frontlets of gold, and are decorated also with earrings, snake-bracelets, and necklaces of different patterns; one especially, a deep network of gold terminating in tassels, is worthy of attention from lady visitors. The *stragula*, or coverlets, are white or blue bordered with red, or red bordered with blue. The cushions of the couches are of chequers alternating with meander patterns, in broad vertical bands. Beneath the couches are low footstools as usual.

On the first couch on the left-hand wall the gentleman holds a lyre, and lifts his right hand as if to strike its chords. His companion holds up both her hands, either to beat time to his music, or to testify her enjoyment. Notice the unnatural length of her fingers, an archaicism in Etruscan art. Her hair is red,

---

[8] Yellow, or saffron-coloured gowns were much worn by *hetaræ* in Greece (Aristoph. Lysist. 44; Eccles. 879; Thesmoph. 253), and also by married women when they wished to allure their husbands (Aristoph. Lys. 219). Young girls also, when taking part in the festivals of Diana, wore dresses of the same hue (Lys. 645). Crocus, or saffron, in fact, seems to have been the colour most attractive to a Greek eye, and most in fashion for full dress in the time of Aristophanes.

but her eye deep black, of that almond form so much admired in Spain and the East. At the foot of the couch stands a naked boy with wine-jug and drinking-bowl, ready to minister to the wants of the revellers. The scene is continued on the wall flanking the door, where are traces of another slave, jug in hand, at a table or sideboard.

The youth on the next couch holds a *phiala* over his head, tilting it to show that he has quaffed its contents,[9] while his lady, who is fair, with blue eyes and auburn hair, stretches one hand towards him in approbation. At the foot of this couch stands a pretty little girl, from whom the tomb has received its modern appellation. She has black hair and eyes, charming features, and a graceful figure; her bosom is bare, but her yellow tunic descends to her heels without concealing her red boots. She holds a *kantharus* in one hand, and points with the other to her mistress, as if to call her attention to the goblet of wine.

On the first couch on the opposite wall the lady is offering fruit or an egg to her mate, and both have their hands uplifted, as if in exultation. On the adjoining couch the man is chucking his fair companion under the chin, but she does not resent the liberty, for though chiding him coquettishly with one hand, she rests the other on his body. His face shows a *pentimento*. A female slave standing at the foot of the couch, and stretching out both arms to her mistress, completes the scene. The trees behind the couches show these revels to take place in the open air. On each side of the door is depicted a sideboard with vases —the complement to the feast. The ceiling is painted with four longitudinal beams down the middle, and with rafters on either slope. The figures in this tomb, though somewhat archaic, are very carefully drawn, and cannot be later than the fifth century, B.C.[1]

A little beyond the last tomb, is another, discovered in 1873, which has received the name of

Grotta del Letto Funebre,

or " Tomb of the Funeral Bier," from the most prominent object

---

[9] This *phiala* is decorated with a leaf pattern, which throws light on certain curious disks in the inner chamber of the Grotta Campana, Veii, proving them to represent drinking-bowls. See p. 41.

[1] An excellent description and able criticism of the paintings in this tomb are given by Signor E. Brizio, Bull. Inst. 1873, pp. 93-101.

depicted on its walls. This is a couch of extraordinary size, which almost fills the wall facing the entrance. It is not the low bed, on which the dead or dying man is represented as stretched in two other tombs in this necropolis, but an elevated bier or catafalque, on which a body might lie in state. But there is no corpse here depicted; the couch is empty, although a pair of double cushions suggest that it was prepared for two bodies, which is further indicated by a conical crown or *tutulus*, bound with a garland of ivy or laurel leaves, resting on each cushion. Beneath the bier is the usual footstool.

At the head of the bier, two men half draped, wearing green garlands round their brows, and long torques of ivy leaves about their necks, are carousing at a banquet, attended by two naked slaves; while an *auletris*, with black hair, a yellow band round her head, and a *capistrum* tied over her mouth, stands at the other end of the bier, playing the double pipes,[2] the instruments themselves being obliterated from the wall.

On either side-wall is a banqueting scene, but the revellers, though of opposite sexes, are here kept distinct; on the right are two men, half draped; on the left, three women, decorated with chaplets and torques, wearing yellow gowns, and red mantles. The men are served by boys, but the ladies are waited on by a female slave, in yellow *chiton* and red *tutulus*, who, while bringing them a jug of wine and a goblet, is stopped on her way by a slave of the opposite sex, who admiringly chucks her under the chin. A youthful *subulo* stands at a cypress tree, playing his double pipes. A girl dances to his music, footing it in a quaint attitude, which finds its counterpart in the Grotta del Triclinio.[3] Next, a *Pyrrhichistes*, with helmet, shield, and spear, is suggestive of an armed race or dance. A *discobolus*, nearly nude, follows, about to hurl his quoit, and there are other figures which, from the exfoliation of the surface, are no longer intelligible, though one exhibits much energy and excellent design. The scene terminates with two steeds on the wall to the left of the entrance, ridden by naked youths.

The banquet is represented as under shelter, which is indicated by festoons of white curtains, bordered with red, supported on

[2] This is the only instance among the wall-paintings of Tarquinii of a flute-player being furnished with a *capistrum*, although they are so represented in several painted tombs at Chiusi, and not unfrequently on Etruscan sarcophagi and vases.

[3] Her costume also resembles that of the *crotolistria* in the G. Triclinio, differing only in having a circular disk or brooch, red and yellow, on her bosom.

each side-wall by a blue column, over which the curtains hang. Two similar columns support the tent over the bier. All the other figures are represented in the open air, as is shown by the trees, and by the double row of ivy leaves with berries, in the band over their heads, which is interrupted only by the curtains.

On the right-hand wall, next the festive couch, is a group of figures on foot. A half naked man is dancing with frantic *abandon* to the music of the double pipes, played by a boy at a cypress tree. Then there is a gigantic pugilist, who, with one arm raised over his head, is striking a violent blow, while, with the other held out in advance, he parries the attack of his adversary. But no foe is visible; and it may be that he is exulting in his victory over another naked man behind him, who holds something, perhaps a sponge, to his nose, as if he had already received a smasher, for which he is comforted by a male slave, who is waiting on the revellers. Next to the pugilist, a pair of horses are being harnessed to a *biga;* the first, a grey steed, is caressed by the lad, who stands at his head, while his groom attaches him to the pole; the other, a black horse, is awaiting his turn. Another *biga*, on the wall flanking the door, is ready for the contest. Behind the first *biga*, a row of trees, more like blue paddles on long red stems, probably marks the *spina* of the hippodrome. The horses are remarkably well drawn, and their points carefully displayed. The red horse in the second *biga* especially, is formed like a blood-horse of to-day, with fine head and neck, head well put on, straight crupper, and deep quarters, and carries both head and flag like an Arab. In the pediments are the usual pair of panthers, or cats, each watching a bird over its head. The band of figures is about twenty-six inches in height. Beneath it, encircling the tomb, is a large wave-pattern, painted black, with fish, alternately blue and red, plunging above it. The decorations of the ceiling, as well as of the walls, so closely resemble those of the adjoining Grotta del Triclinio, and some of the figures also bear so near a resemblance, that it is difficult to resist the impression that the tombs have been painted by the same hand. There is nothing in the style of art opposed to this view, although there is rather less archaicism in this than in the neighbouring tomb, yet not more than may be explained by the difference of style at distinct periods of the same artist's life. The design certainly betrays a freer hand; the attitudes are more easy and natural, so in parts is the drapery, but there is hardly the same careful and conscientious delineation of details.

The blue in this tomb is remarkably brilliant, while in the Triclinio it is the colour that has most faded. Certain of the figures show a strong approximation to the Greek, the *discobolus* for instance, and the draped figure next him, but most of the others are purely Etruscan in character.[4] The tomb faces S.S.W.

Close to the tomb just described is the

GROTTA DEL TRICLINIO,

called also from the owner of the ground, GROTTA MANZI, but it is better known by the former designation. It was discovered in 1830, by Manzi and Fossati.[5]

The first peep within this tomb is startling, especially if the sun's rays happen at the moment to enter the chamber, which they do in the course of the afternoon. Such a blaze of rich colour on the walls and roof, and such life in the figures that dance around! In truth, the excellent state of preservation—the wonderful brilliancy of the colours, almost as fresh after three or four and twenty centuries, as when first laid on—the richness of the costumes—the strangeness of the attitudes—the spirit, the vivacity, the joyousness of the whole scene—the decidedly Etruscan character of the design, distinct from the Greek and yet in certain points approximating to it—render this one of the most interesting tombs yet opened in Etruria.

The paintings in subject, character, and arrangement, are very similar to those in the Grotta Querciola, but there is only a single band of figures. Here are the same scenes of joy and festivity; the banquet at the upper end; the dances on the side-walls; and on each side of the door a man on horseback. The broad beam of the ceiling is painted with ivy leaves and berries; the slopes are chequered with black, red, blue, yellow, and white. Where the painting has suffered, it is not so much from the colours fading, as

---

[4] Signor Brizio, who has written an able criticism on these paintings, is of opinion that in this, among the painted tombs of Corneto, you may first recognise decided traces of Greek influence upon Etruscan art, there being some figures conceived and designed on principles quite opposed to Etruscan art, and which are decidedly Hellenic. Bull. Inst. 1873, p. 102.

[5] This tomb faces S. by W. Its dimensions are 15 ft. by 11; nearly 8 ft. in height

in the centre, and 6 ft. 3 in. at the sides. The height of the figures is about 3 ft. 6 in. The floor of the inner half of the tomb is raised in a *dais*, about 2 or 3 inches high, in one corner of which are four holes, marking the place of the sarcophagus, which was found in it. Few of the painted tombs on this site seem to have been family sepulchres, which predominate over those for individuals in most of the Etruscan cemeteries.

in the Querciola tomb, as from the stucco peeling from the wall, and from streams of a semi-transparent deposit from the rock itself, which has obliterated a considerable portion of the banquet; but there still remain, little impaired, two figures of opposite sexes, reclining on a couch, attended by a female servant with an *alabastos*, or pot of ointment, and a boy with a wine-jug, while a *subulo* stands in one corner playing the double-pipes. The

G. D.

CITHARISTA AND SALTATRIX, GROTTA DEL TRICLINIO.

man on the second couch is almost obliterated; and of the single male figure on the third couch, hardly a fragment is now to be traced. The sex of the figures is distinguishable by the colour; that of the men is a deep red; that of the women, being left unpainted, is of the ground-colour of the wall—a rich creamy white. This distinction holds in all the tombs; and is also made on the painted vases of the Second or Archaic Greek style, where the female flesh is always painted white. In front of each couch is an elegant *trapeza* or four-legged table, bearing dishes full of refreshments; and beneath are a cock, a partridge, and a cat. Depending from the ceiling above the banquet are chaplets of different colours.[6]

---

[6] An erudite explanation of the paintings of this tomb is given by Professor Gerhard, Ann. Instit. 1831, p. 337—346. In illustration of the analogy between the banquets of the Greeks and Etruscans, he quotes Amphis (ap. Athen. XIV. c. 49), who describes a banquet as composed of "cheese-cakes, sweet wine, eggs, sesame-cakes, ointment, a chaplet, and a female flute-player"—

Ἄμητες, οἶνος ἡδύς, ᾠά, σησαμαῖ,
Μύρον, στέφανος, αὐλητρίς.

The flute-player is not here of the fair sex,

Each couch, it will be observed, is covered with a cloth, on which the cushions are laid; and each figure lies under a separate coverlet, differing in this respect from the recorded custom of the Etruscans.[7]

Much more animated is the action of the dancers in this tomb than in the Querciola. There are five of them on each wall,

males and females alternating, separated by trees, with birds amid the foliage. Their steps are regulated by the lyre and pipes played by two of the men, and by the castanets rattled by one of the women.[8] All enter heartily into the spirit of the dance; but here, as now-a-days, woman asserts her right to excel, and the nymphs step out more merrily than their partners; especially one, who with head thrown back and hands raised, betrays true Terpsichorean *abandon*, and might pass for some *Gaditana puella*—some "lovely girl of Cadiz" of the

c. v.

ETRUSCAN DANCING-GIRL.

nor is this so general on Etruscan as on Greek monuments, though instances occur in the painted tombs of this same necropolis, of women blowing the *tibiæ pares*. Gerhard (loc. cit. p. 340) declares that all the figures in this tomb wear garlands of myrtle, and so they are represented in the copies in the Vatican and British Museums (cf. Ann. Inst. 1831, p. 327), but no signs of such garlands have I been able to perceive. Perhaps, being blue, they have faded from the wall, like the leaves of the trees in this tomb. In the above woodcuts the figures are represented without chaplets, as they now appear on the walls.

[7] Aristotle (ap. Athen. I. c. 42) records that the Etruscans reclined at their banquets under the same *himatia* with their wives. The *iμάτιον* in this sense is the same as the *στρῶμα*, and is equivalent to the *pallium*, *stragula*, or *straguium* of the Romans. The undercovering of the couch was probably designated *περίστρωμα*.

[8] Castanets—*crotala*—were used at the dances of the Greeks and Romans, by whom they have been transmitted to the southern

people of modern Europe. Thus the "Copa Syrisca," attributed to Virgil, was—

"Crispum sub crotalo docta movere latus."

So the senatorial youths of Rome in early times were wont to dance—*crotala gestantes*—Macrob. Saturn. II. 10. The castanets of the ancients were of various materials—wood, shell, brass, or sometimes of split reed. Suidas, v. *κρόταλον*. Eustath. ad Iliad. XI. 160. Those of the Etruscans seem never to have varied from the straight form shown in this tomb; though on the vases, which, however, represent Greek rather than Etruscan life, they have sometimes the extremities crooked. On the bronzes they are of the same form as in this tomb (Ann. Inst. 1836, p. 64; Mon. Ined. Inst. II. tav. XXIX.); and in the Tomb of the Tarquins, at Cervetri, they are also like these, and are painted on the wall as if suspended over the head of a corpse. *Crotalon* was used by the Greeks as a term of reproach, equivalent to our "rattle," or "chatterbox." Eurip. Cycl. 104; Aristoph. Nub. 260, 448.

olden time. The attitudes, as in many archaic Greek and Etruscan designs, are sometimes unnatural and unattainable, which arises from the inability of the artist to foreshorten—the limbs and features being represented in profile, even when the body is in full.[9] The form of the hands, too, is remarkable—fingers of such undainty length are seen only in the most archaic painted tombs of Etruria, though general on black-figured vases of the Archaic style, and also in the early bronze figures of Etruscan deities. Most of the dresses of both sexes are transparent, representing some light material, which shows the forms beneath; but in a display of this sort these ancient Taglionis and Ceritos cannot rival those of modern days. The richness of the borders of the garments, and the strange stiffness and regularity of the folds, are quite Etruscan. So also is the physiognomy of the figures. Yet there is something Jewish in the female profiles. Mark this, ye seekers of the Ten Tribes! The cheeks show that a high colour was as much admired in Italy in former days as at present; and probably the Etruscan fair ones, like the Greek and Roman, heightened their charms with rouge.

It is worthy of remark that all the women in this tomb, even the slave who is waiting on the banqueters, are decently robed. So it is in the other tombs; and this tends to belie the charge brought against the Etruscans by the Greeks, that the men were waited on by naked handmaids.[1] No such representation has been found on any Etruscan painting or relief yet discovered; on the contrary, the women are draped with more than Greek modesty.[2] Only in one tomb in this necropolis, that of the Scrofa Nera, is a woman depicted with bosom bare. The Etruscans may not have been better than their neighbours in such matters, but any reproach of this sort comes from the Greeks with a very bad grace.

It is evident that this tomb is of earlier date than the Querciola. That shows the dominance, this the partial influence

---

[9] An awkward instance of this may be observed in the female attendant behind the couch, whose body is in full, but head and feet in profile, and turned in opposite directions. The left foot of the dancing girl in the woodcut on p. 320 is the only instance of foreshortening in this tomb.

[1] Timæus ap. Athen. XII. c. 14; IV. c. 38.

[2] To the nudity of the Spartan women I

need not refer; the Thessalian women are described by Persæus dancing at banquets naked, or with a very scanty covering (ap. Athen. XIII. c. 86). The maidens of Chios wrestled naked with the youths in the gymnasium, which Athenæus (XIII. 20) pronounces to be "a beautiful sight." And at the marriage feast of Caranus the Macedonian, women tumblers performed naked before the guests. Athen. IV. 3.

only of Greek art. Gerhard considers that "with all the delicacy of the ornaments, and all the archaic Greek character of the design, there is still an awkwardness about the former, and a rudeness in the latter, which mark these paintings as imitations of the Greek, spoilt in the execution."[3] The woodcuts, which are faithful transcripts of copies carefully made from the originals with the *camera lucida*, speak for themselves on this point.

Every one, on entering these tombs, must be struck with the inappropriateness of such scenes to a sepulchre; but happily for us we regard them from the high vantage-ground of Christianity, and our view is not bounded by a paradise of mere sensual gratification. If we cast ourselves back into antiquity and attempt to realise the sentiments and creed of a Greek, Etruscan, or Roman, we shall perceive how well such scenes as this represent, or at least typify, the state of bliss on which a departed spirit was supposed to have entered. They believed in the materiality of the soul; and their Elysium was but a glorification of the present state of existence; the same pursuits, amusements, and pleasures they had relished in this life they expected in the next, but divested of their sting, and enhanced by increased capacities of enjoyment. To celebrate the great event, to us so solemn, by feasting and joviality, was not with them unbecoming. They knew not how to conceive or represent a glorified existence otherwise than by scenes of the highest sensual enjoyment.[4]

The funeral feast is still kept up by the most civilised pagans of our own day, the Chinese, and even by certain people of Christendom,—by such as on account of their isolated position, or of national prejudices, have adhered most closely to the customs and usages of antiquity. The wakes of the Celtic races

---

[3] Ann. Inst. 1831, p. 319.

[4] The funeral feast in honour of the dead was called by the Greeks νεκρόδειπνον, or περίδειπνον, the latter term being applied, it may be, from the feast being held "round about" the sepulchre, though some would derive it from the position of the guests, or make it equivalent to a *circumpotatio*. The Romans held a similar feast, and called it *silicernium* (Festus, *sub voce*) the etymology of which word is uncertain; though Servius (ad Æn. V. 92) suggests a very probable one—*silicernium* quasi *silicenium*, super silicem positæ (cœnæ)—because the meal was spread upon the rocks. If the upper and open chamber in the tombs of Castel d'Asso and Norchia were for the funeral feasts, it well illustrates this etymology. That the ancients did hold these feasts in the open air, and among the tombs, is pretty evident. At Pompeii a *triclinium* for such purposes stands in the midst of the sepulchres. Lucian (de Luctu. p. 813, ed. 1615) tells us that the feast was held to comfort the relatives of the deceased, and induce them to take food.

of our own land have in all probability an identity of origin—in feeling at least—with the funeral feasts of the Greeks, Etruscans, and Romans.

Dances, among the ancients, had often a direct religious meaning and application, and were introduced at sacrifices together with songs in honour of the Gods.[5] Music, to our ideas, is hardly consistent with a scene of mourning, yet it might be solemn and dolorous. That such was intended to be its character in this case, the accompanying figures forbid us to suppose; it must have been lively and animated, in harmony with the action of the dancers. But on other Etruscan monuments it seems to have been of a different character. Not a few bas-reliefs represent the *præficæ*, or hired mourners, wailing over a corpse, beating their breasts and tearing their hair, while a *subulo* chimes in with his double-pipes.

It may be questioned whether such scenes are emblematical of the bliss of the departed, or representations of the actual feasts held in their honour;[6] in either case there can be no doubt that they are truthful delineations of Etruscan costumes and manners. I am inclined to a descriptive interpretation, admitting at the same time the symbolical character of certain objects, some of which were probably introduced on that account at the actual feasts. It seems to me, however, quite unnecessary to regard all the pictorial furniture of these tombs as symbolical, as some have done. In this case, for instance, the trees which alternate with the dancers, are most probably introduced merely to indicate that the festivities were held in the open air;[7] and the animals seem only ornamental accessories, or whims of the

---

[5] Plato, de Leg. VII. 799. Tibul. II. 1, 56. Quintil. 1. 11. Of this character were the Corybantian, or armed dances of Phrygia in honour of Cybele; the Hyporchema and Geranos in honour of Apollo (see Müller, Dor. II. 8, 14); and the Salian dances of the Etruscans and Romans in honour of Mars. The Dionysiac, though also religious, were peculiar in their mimetic character—in representing the deeds of the god. Servius (ad Virg. Eclog. V. 73) gives us the philosophy of sacred dancing among the ancients:—"hæc ratio est, quod nullam majores nostri partem corporis esse voluerunt, quæ non sentiret religionem: nam cantus ad animum, saltatio ad mobilitatem pertinet corporis." The bodily expression of some sentiment was the essence of all the dancing of the Greeks, and what poetry effected by words, dancing told by movements. Becker, Charicles, sc. VI.

[6] Micali (Mon. Ined. p. 364) views them as symbolical. Gerhard (Ann. Inst. 1831, p. 321) thinks the dances symbolize the welcome given to the deceased in the abodes of the blessed; and is of opinion that these festive scenes represent the bliss of souls in the other world. (Ann. Inst. 1831, p. 346, 350).

[7] The trees are either olives, known by their small black berries, or myrtles, or the lotus, or ivy, now represented only by large black berries, the shrubs to which they were attached having almost entirely faded from the walls.

artist. The known relation of the panther to Bacchus is suggestive of a funeral signification of the two over the doorway, and
the same may be said of the ivy which surrounds the room in a
broad band above the heads of the figures; but why seek a
symbolic interpretation in the cat and domestic fowls gleaning
the crumbs of the feast, or in the cats and birds among the
trees, or in the hare and fox at their feet? The men on horseback seem introduced by a sort of pictorial *synecdoche*—a portion
being put for the whole—to indicate the races which usually
formed part of the funeral entertainments.[8]

Did not the archaic character of the paintings in this and
similar tombs of Tarquinii, forbid us to assign to them so
recent a date, the frequent occurrence of Bacchic emblems might
lead to the supposition that these festive scenes represent the
Dionysia, which were imported from Greece into Etruria about
two hundred years before Christ, and thence introduced into
Rome.[9]

The colours in this tomb are black, deep red, or maroon,
light red, blue, and yellow. In few of the painted tombs in
this necropolis do we meet with green. All the colours, except
the blue which in the leaves of the trees has much faded, retain
their original brilliancy; and it must be remembered that three
or four-and-twenty centuries have elapsed since they were laid on,
and that they are on the bare rock, the natural creamy hue of
which forms the ground to the whole. Damp does not seem here
to have affected them as in some other tombs.[1]

I have said that the colours were laid on the bare rock. The
surface of this, however, has undergone some preparation.
The rock is a calcareous stone, of tertiary formation, full of
minute marine substances. It is soft, even plastic when damp,
but acquires a considerable degree of hardness on exposure to

[8] Gerhard, as already mentioned, p. 308,
regards such mounted figures to be emblems
of the souls of the defunct. The birds are
thought by M. Lajard (Ann. Inst. 1833, p.
90–98) to be emblematical of gods, such being
the usual mode of expressing divinity on the
ancient monuments of the East. He finds
a sacred or funeral symbol in each of the
animals in this tomb, and says that ribbons
tied to trees, as in this scene, have a religious meaning in Persia. M. Lajard
perceives still further oriental analogies in
this tomb, especially in the dancing women,

whom he declares to be similar, in their
attitudes and costume, to the *bayadères* of
modern Persia.

[9] Liv. XXXIX. 8. 9.

[1] Ruspi (Ann. Inst. 1831, p. 326) maintains that the damp has been a preservative
of the colours. He remarks, that when the
sun enters this tomb, and dries the surface
of the wall, the figures in that part appear
more natural and beautiful than the rest,
because they then lose their extreme depth
of colour, and acquire just the tint the
ancient artist intended.

the atmosphere. Where the surface of the wall has crumbled away, it is evident that it is composed of a stucco, scarcely differing in texture and colour from the rock itself. It seems to be made of the finer particles of the rock, sifted and plastered over the coarser surface, and subsequently dried and indurated, perhaps by artificial heat. The colours were laid on *al fresco.*[2] These remarks apply to all the painted tombs of this necropolis, except those of the Typhon, the Cardinal, and the Orcus, which are stuccoed with a different material.

CAMERA DEL MORTO.

About a hundred yards beyond the Grotta del Triclinio is another painted tomb called "The Dead Man's Chamber," discovered in 1832.

Most of the tombs hitherto described contain festive scenes; but here is a painting of another character. On one of the side-walls, the body of a hoary-bearded man in red drapery is seen stretched on an elegant couch, and a young woman standing on the stool by his bedside, leans over him, apparently in the act of drawing his hood over his eyes.[3] A man stands at the bottom of the couch, and seems with one hand to be pulling the clothes over the old man's feet, while he raises the other to his head, according to the conventional yet natural mode of expressing grief among the Etruscans. Behind him stands another man, who with more violent gestures appears to be manifesting his

---

[2] So thinks Ruspi; and Mr. Ainsley, who has paid great attention to these paintings, is of the same opinion. "From the circumstance," he says, "of the colour brushing off on the slightest contact, it might be concluded that the paintings are in distemper, but the proof is by no means complete, for a stain is left inward, and the whole substance of the stucco is so decayed as to rub off with great facility; the outline also is frequently traceable, scratched in the stucco, which would have been unnecessary in distemper." Otto Donner declares himself unable to find any paintings in these tombs executed in distemper, and pronounces all that he examined to be in fresco. Bull. Inst. 1869, p. 205.

For details and criticisms of the paintings in this tomb see Bull. Inst. 1830, p. 231; Ann. Inst. 1831, p. 324 (Ruspi); 1831, p. 327; 1831, pp. 337–346, 359–

361 (Gerhard); Bull. Inst. 1831, p. 5; Ann. Inst. 1863, pp. 347–352 (Helbig); 1866, pp. 426–7 (Brunn); 1870, pp. 58–63 (Helbig). The criticisms of the last two writers are particularly valuable. For illustrations, see Mon. Ined. Inst. I. tav. XXXII. Mns. Gregor. I. tav. CII. Good copies of these paintings are in the British Museum, but the colouring is too hard and crude, and in parts incorrect, particularly in the absence of the distinction between the sexes. Mrs. Gray also has given a plate of these paintings (Sepulchres of Etruria, p. 188), but inaccurate and characterless in outline, and of imaginary colouring throughout.

[3] This is the figure which Mrs. Gray (Sepul. of Etruria, p. 69) likens to a Capuchin monk, from the cowled tunic in which he is dressed. But *cucullus non facit monachum.* It is as much like the *bornous* of Barbary.

sorrow in a similar manner,[4]—if he be not dancing—a supposition which his attitude and the analogy of other figures in this tomb, seem to favour. A third man, who stands at the head of the couch, has also his hand to his head. The precise attitudes and meaning of these figures it is impossible now to determine, owing to the dilapidated state of these paintings, but two of them at least appear to be giving manifestations of deep sorrow.

Turn to the other walls of the tomb, and the scene changes from grave to gay in an instant! Here all is tipsy dance and jollity! These naked men, crowned with chaplets, and dancing with Bacchanalian frenzy, seem unconscious of, or indifferent to, the mournful scene adjoining. On the inner wall, one fellow is playing the fife,[5] though not moderating his saltatory action a whit on that account; the other is brandishing a *kylix* or flat bowl, which he appears to have just emptied, but a large *krater* of wine stands at his feet, whence he may replenish it at pleasure. Of the two figures on the adjoining wall, one is in the act of quaffing from a similar bowl; the other is whirling a chaplet in his hand; and all four, though torn into fragments and almost destroyed by time, display in their *disjecta membra* such feats of capriole agility, that the seeker for Celtic analogies might declare them to be dancing an Irish jig or a Highland reel. Similar chaplets are represented hanging from the wall around the chamber, even over the death-bed, and some are seen suspended from the olive-trees which alternate with the dancers, and from the handles of the *krater*.

The fourth wall of this tomb has no paintings beyond the usual pair of panthers in the pediment. In the corresponding position on the opposite wall are two parti-coloured lions and two blue pigeons, probably introduced as mere ornaments; or, if symbolical, perhaps representing the ministers of death about to seize the soul.

You are struck with the archaic character of the paintings in this tomb, compared with those in the Querciola and Triclinio.

---

[4] He has been described as placing a chaplet on his head (Bull. Inst. 1832, p. 213); and so he is represented in the restored copies in the Gregorian and British Museums. The other two male figures in this scene may be striking their brows to betoken grief.

[5] The *tibia* is here introduced in one of the three occasions on which it was frequently used, according to Ovid (Fast. VI.

657) by the early inhabitants of Italy :—

Cantabat fanis, cantabat tibia ludis ;
Cantabat moestis tibia funeribus.

We have already seen it represented at games and scenes of festivity. Here it is an accompaniment to the mourning of survivors over the corpse. Instances of its employment at such scenes are not unfrequent on Etruscan bas-reliefs.

This character is most strongly marked in the physiognomy, in the eyes, which are always full though the face be in profile, in the shape of the heads, in the cut of the beards, and in the contour of the bodies of the dancers. You may observe this archaic character particularly in the figure of the woman, in her stiff, ungainly form, and may remark that her dress differs from that of the females in the two said tombs, principally in her hair hanging down in long braids, and in her long and sharp-toed boots. Her name, written in Etruscan characters over her head, is "THANAUEIL,"[6] and its similarity to that above the old man "THANARSEIA," together with the duties she is performing, seems to mark her as a relative, probably his daughter. The two men at the foot of the couch are now anonymous, but the third has the inscription "ENEL" above him, which formed, however, but a portion of his name.

This is one of the earliest tombs yet discovered at Tarquinii, second in point of antiquity to the "Tomb of the Inscriptions" alone. The art is purely Etruscan, without any traces of Hellenic influence.

It is also one of the smallest of the painted sepulchres of Tarquinii; indeed, it is rare to meet with tombs of such confined dimensions.[7] The colours, in as far as they are preserved, retain all their original depth, but the surface of the wall is greatly dilapidated. The flesh of the males is a very deep red, save that of the corpse, which is paler, perhaps intentionally so represented. That of the woman, as usual, is left uncoloured. The average height of the figures is about two feet and a half.[8]

GROTTA DEL TIFONE.

About sixty paces farther on, in a pit of more than ordinary depth, is the entrance to the "Cave of the Typhon" or, as it is

---

[6] The Etruscan letters are very small, and have almost faded from the wall. A very slight alteration—the insertion of one stroke and the omission of another—would make her name "Thanachvil," which by metastasis might be "Thanchavil," the known Etruscan form of Tanaquil—a name which is not of unfrequent occurrence on monuments of this antiquity.

[7] It is only 8 ft. square, 5 ft. high at the sides, and somewhat more than 6 ft. in the centre. The beam of the ceiling is painted red, and is represented as resting on a large double modillion or bracket of the same colour, in the pediment. The tomb faces S.W.

[8] A plate of the scenes in this tomb will be found in Mon. Ined. Inst. II. tav. 2; also in Mus. Gregor. I. tav. XCIX. Copies, of the size of the originals, exist in the Gregorian Museum at Rome, and in the British Museum. For criticisms, see Ann. Inst. 1863, pp. 342-3 (Helbig); 1856, p. 423 (Brunn); 1870, pp. 47, 48 (Helbig).

otherwise called, the "Tomb of the Pompeys,"—Grotta de' Pompej—discovered in 1832. Before the door are vestiges of a small antechamber, with a shaft to descend from the ground above, as in the tombs of Civita Castellana and Falleri.

The door is opened—and, oh! the gloom of this dark-walled cavern!—the blackness, the solemn silence, the sepulchral damp, chill and awe the senses and oppress the spirits. It is a very Tartarus after the gay, Elysian air of the tombs you have just quitted.

Cernis, custodia qualis
Vestibulo sedeat? facies quæ limina servet?

No Fury, no Cerberus, no panther even, nor lion, mounts guard at the door of this Orcus, but the stone figure of a grand, though rude old Lucumo, decked with fillet and torque, reclines just within the entrance—the first object that meets your eye when the door is opened.

Descend these half-dozen steps to the floor, light your tapers, and look around. This tomb differs in many respects from those you have already seen. It is of considerable size;[9] its flat roof is supported in the centre by a massive square pillar; and a triple tier of benches, all hewn from the living rock, surrounds the chamber. In fact it more nearly resembles the sepulchres of Cære than those of Tarquinii. Its size, and the many sarcophagi which lie scattered and broken about the tomb, prove that this was a family vault, the last resting-place, it may be, not merely of a single family, but of a *gens*, or, I may say, a clan of ancient Tarquinii.

The walls of this tomb are not covered with paintings, but simply adorned with a double band—the upper, of dolphins sporting above the waves; the lower, of sun-like flowers—except on one wall where a small space is occupied by a funeral procession of singular interest. The square pillar in the centre is also painted. On three of its sides is a divinity of Etruscan mythology; that at the back a female, terminating in foliage instead of legs, the other two, males, conventionally called Typhon—whence the tomb receives its vulgar appellation.[1]

---

[9] The area, or the arena, so to speak, of this tomb, is 26 ft. by 15½; but if to this be added the depth of the benches, the dimensions will be 41½ ft. long, by 31 wide. The height is 11 ft., and the floor cannot be less than 30 ft. below the surface of the ground. The pillar is nearly 5 ft. square. The roof is flat, stuccoed, and painted with broad red beams intersecting each other at right angles. The tomb faces the E.

[1] The Etruscan name of this mythical

They have human bodies of life size, winged and terminating in

TYPHON, PAINTED ON THE PILLAR.

being is not yet known to us. But he bears an analogy to the Typhon of the Egyptians and Greeks, and is significant of the principle of Destruction ; just as the Typhon of Egypt was the evil and destructive power, in opposition to Osiris, the good and productive. With the Egyptians he was, in particular, the personification of whirlwinds and storms,—and so Hesiod (Theog. 307) describes him—δεινόν θ᾽ ὑβριστήν τ᾽ ἄνεμον; cf. Pliny, II. 49, 50. In the Greek mythology Typhon was one of the giants who made war on the gods, and were smitten by Jove's thunder, and cast beneath Ætna and other volcanoes, where their belchings caused eruptions, and their writhings occasioned earthquakes. Pindar, Pyth. I. 29, et seq. Æschyl. Prom. 351—372. Ovid. Met. V. 346, et seq. ; cf. Virg. Æn. III., 578. Under this same snake-tailed form were the giants described by the ancients. Apollod. I. 6, 2. Ovid. Trist. IV. 7, 17. Pausan. VIII. 29. Serv. ad Æn. loc. cit. Macrobius (Saturn. I. 20) gives us the symbolic meaning of these

limbs, and says that Æsculapius and Salus were also thus imaged. The Giants are also frequently represented of this form, on ancient monuments. It is obvious that these Giants are symbols of volcanic powers. Their contests with the Gods took place in the Phlegræan Fields, or in other volcanic regions. Pindar, Nem. J. 100 ; Strab. V. p. 245, VI. p. 281 ; Pausan. loc. cit. The very name of Typhon indicates this meaning —being derived from τῦφος, "smoke," metaphorically, "conceit, arrogance." The origin of the myth is manifest in the volcanoes, the smoking sons of Earth, who dared to brave Heaven, and hurl rocks and fire against the gods. That the Etruscans should have had such a being in their demonology is not surprising, when the volcanic character of their country is remembered. In this tomb, he is represented under a solemn, imposing aspect, not with that exaggeration of the horrible that amounts to the grotesque and to caricature, which we see in the Grotta Dipinta at Bomarzo.

serpents instead of legs. The female figure is tame and stiff,
but the other two are most spirited and grand. Such as these
it is with which Tasso peoples hell—

> Oh come strane, oh come orribil forme !
> Quant' è negli occhi lor terrore e morte ! . . . .
> E 'n fronte umana han chiome d' angui attorte ;
> E lor s'aggira dietro immensa coda !—

> Oh what unearthly, oh what fearful shapes !
>   Terror and Death are flashing from their eyes !
> Their human heads are haired with writhing snakes,
>   And their vast tails coil back in loathsome guise !

Both of these figures are fine; one remarkably so. The attitude of the body—the outspread wings—the dark massy coils of
the serpent-limbs—the wild twisting of the serpent-locks—the
countenance uplifted with an expression of unutterable woe,
as he supports the cornice with his hands[2]—make this figure
imposing, mysterious, sublime. In conception, the artist was the
Michael Angelo of Etruria.[3]

On the front of the pillar is an Etruscan inscription of nine
lines, scratched on the stucco, now much injured, but the name
of "Pumpus" is distinctly visible in the first line.[4]

In front of the pillar and attached to it, is a large squared
mass of rock, which has been conjectured to be an altar, on which
offerings were made to the Manes. Its front and sides were
painted with figures in procession; but these have now almost
utterly perished.[5] A few years more, and no trace will be left of

---

[2] The Greeks introduced Typhons or
Giants into their architecture as Atlantes,
as is proved by statues found beneath the
Theseum at Athens. Similar monsters
were used by the Romans in architectural
decoration as Telamones. At Pompeii, in
the "Casa della Camera Nera," are many
of them painted, supporting the cornice
with both hands, as in this Etruscan tomb.

[3] The woodcut on p. 329, which is taken
from a slight sketch by the author, serves
to show the nature of the Typhon, but fails
to give the vigorous design, the Satanic
sublimity of the original painting. The
expression of the countenance is altogether
incorrect. Down to the knees the figure
is flesh-coloured. The serpent tails, as also
the wings, are painted grey.

[4] This inscription is given by Kellermann
(Bull. Inst. 1833, tav. suppl. n. 4). On
the cornice of the pillar is a band of wild
beasts' heads painted, and below the Typhons is a Doric frieze with patera-like
flowers in the metope.

[5] This procession, as it existed when the
tomb was opened, is represented in Mon.
Ined. Inst. II. tav. V. The face of one
figure, and the lower part of another in
tunic and sandals, are alone now distinguishable; but these fragments suffice to
show this scene to have been inferior in
style and more archaic in character than
the other paintings in this tomb. The
altar, or whatever it be, is 5 feet high,
7 feet wide, and 3 feet deep.

the paintings in this tomb, which will be known only from prints and descriptions as things that have passed away.

The procession painted on the wall of this tomb has given rise to as much speculation as any other local relic of Etruscan antiquity. Its resemblance to the relief on the temple-tombs of Norchia is visible at a glance.[6] In both are *genii* or demons leading souls into the unseen world; but that of Norchia is so much injured as scarcely to be intelligible without the aid of this painting, which is a key to its interpretation. Here are no shields, helmets, or weapons suspended—it may be because this was of the inglorious days of Etruria, when she had sunk to the tame condition of a Roman province; but here are six figures bearing those singular twisted rods, the symbols of the Etruscan Hades, which are sufficient to identify the character of this painting with that of the Norchian relief. Here are no winged *genii*, but the attributes of certain of these figures mark them to be demons. There are three of them in prominent positions—at the head, in the rear, and in the centre of the procession. They are of different colours; that in front is of fair complexion, and seems to represent a female; that in the rear seems to be of the male sex, from his deep red flesh; while he in the centre is of negro hue and features, and is recognised as the Etruscan " Charun." All are distinguished by the hammer borne aloft, a frequent emblem of supernatural power,[7] and also by serpents bound round their heads, like the Furies of Greek mythology.[8]—

> Serpentelli e ceraste avean per crine
> Onde le fiere tempie eran avvinte.— DANTE.

[6] See Chapter XVIII. pp. 200, 201. This procession is 9 feet in length, and the figures are as large as life, covering the entire wall from the upper bench to the ceiling. In this respect also they correspond with those in the Norchian procession.

[7] The hammer savours much of the East, thinks Inghirami (Mon. Etrus. I. p. 254), who cites Pococke as saying that the Turks believe in two black demons, who dwell in the sepulchre with the dead, judge him, and punish him with hammers if found guilty. Dr. Braun (Ann. Inst. 1837, 2, p. 274) calls it the solemn symbol of the Cabiri, in whose mysterious worship the Etruscan Charun had his seat and origin.

The hammer with which Charun is generally armed, is rather an attribute than an instrument. Demons with hammers, however, who seem to have much analogy

with Charun, are sometimes represented in the act of tormenting souls, as in the Grotta Cardinale, and the now lost Grotta Tartaglia, in this same necropolis, or of striking them down, as on the Admetus and Alcestis Vase, the frontispiece to Vol. II. of this work.

[8] Æschylus, Choeph. 1049. Pausanias (I. 28, 6) says Æschylus was the first so to describe the Furies, for in their temple at Athens they were not so represented, nor indeed with any features of the horrible. In the Orphic Hymns (LXVIII. 19. LXIX. 10), they are described with serpent-locks—ὀφιοπλόκαμοι. So also Ovid, Met. X. 349—atro crinitas angue Sorores—and Catullus, LXIV. 193. Virgil also (Æn. VI. 280) so describes—

> Discordia demens
> Vipereum crinem vittis innexa cruentis.

Euripides (Iphig. Taur. 287) seems to mean

Among the Egyptians also the snake-bound brow was emblematical of sovereignty, whether of gods or men. The import of the snake in the mythological system of the Etruscans seems to have been very similar; it was an emblem of divine or supernatural power, of mystery, perhaps of eternity, certainly of sacredness, and it had evidently a funereal meaning.[9] On many Etruscan monuments it is seen wound round the arm of Charun, as in the case also of the leading demon in this painted procession, who might well pass for Tisiphone, one of the Furies.[1] The same figure bears in her other hand a flaming torch, another attribute of the Furies, who are often represented brandishing a snake in one hand, and a torch in the other.[2] She may therefore be regarded as one of the "daughters of gloomy Night," though she has been designated "the wife of Charun;" while the red-faced demon in the rear has been called the son of the said dignitaries, but what authority there is for supposing "the pilot of the livid lake" to have been a family-man, I know not. It is clear that the black, hideous, bearded, brute-eared demon in the middle of the procession, who towers above all the rest, is no other than the conveyer of souls—*terribili squalore Charon*[3]—

Che intorno agli occhi avea di fiamme ruote.

the same thing — ἐχίδναις ἐστομωμένη. Horace (Od. II. 13. 35) and Virgil (Georg. IV. 482) describe the snakes as being woven in with the hair of the Furies; and the latter speaks of them as being blue—the colour generally given to those in Etruscan tombs.

[9] See Chap. XV., page 169.

[1] Virgil, Æn. VI. 571—

Tisiphone . . . torvosque sinistrâ
Intentans angues.

[2] So they are represented on monuments, Etruscan or Roman, when persecuting Orestes—as in the celebrated sarcophagus of the Lozzano tomb, now in the Lateran Museum; and on many Etruscan urns and sarcophagi.

There are two events in Etruscan history which throw light on this singular painting. The first occurred in the year 328, when the citizens of Fidenæ, finding themselves unequal to the Romans in the field, rushed out from their gates, like Furies, armed with torches, and bearing particoloured chaplets like serpents, in order to strike terror into their foes. But the Roman dictator, seeing his men give way under this novel attack, taunted them with being overcome, like bees, by mere smoke, rallied them to the charge, beat back the Fidenates with great slaughter, and captured their city. Liv. IV. 33; Flor. I. 12; Frontin. Strat. II. 4, 17. The second time was in the year 398, when the priests of Tarquinii and Falerii resorted to the same mode of attack, advancing like Furies in the van of their army, armed with flaming torches and brandishing serpents in their hands, and struck a temporary panic into the Romans by the unwonted sight. Liv. VII. 17; Frontin. loc. cit. It is interesting to find such a confirmation of history in this very necropolis of Tarquinii. The seekers of analogies between the Celts and Etruscans might find somewhat in Tacitus (Ann. XIV. 30), who relates that the women of Mona ran about like Furies armed with torches among the ranks of the Britons who were drawn up on the shore to oppose the landing of the Romans.

[3] Virg. Æn. VI. 299, et seq.; cf. Seneca, Herc. Fur. III. 764, et seq.

The second figure in the procession is a *cornicen*, or blower on the horn,[4] and probably represents an attendant on the infernal deities. One of the other figures bears a *lituus*, or augur's crooked staff in his hand,[5] and the rest, with the exception of two or three in the centre, have the singular twisted rods, which are seen in the Norchian bas-relief, and are evidently of funereal import. Whether all these, or only those who do not bear the rods, are souls, is difficult to determine, but there can be no doubt that the two principal figures of the group—the man on whose shoulder old Charun has set his fearful paw,[6] and the woman behind, under the charge of the young demon—are intended to represent the spirits of the defunct. Each of these has a designatory inscription in Etruscan characters attached—the man, indeed, has two of these titles, but the lower one is now almost destroyed. That above his head is very distinct, and runs thus :—

In Roman letters it would be— LARIS. PUMPUS. ARNTHAL. CLAN. CECHASE.[7] The first two words, or his *prænomen* and *nomen*, are repeated in the lower inscription. There was a third inscription behind the red demon, of which only the last two words are now legible.

---

[4] So it is described by Orioli (Ann. Inst. 1834, p. 160), but it might as well represent a *tibicen* playing on the curved *tibia* of Etruria (Virg. Æn. XI. 737), though that is said to have been used at festive scenes. Compare Tibullus (II. 1, 86), who calls the crooked pipe Phrygian. The *tuba* or *cornu*, however, being used at funerals (Virg. Æn. XI. 192. Ovid. Amor. II. Eleg. 6, 6. Petron. Satyr. LXXVIII. A. Gell. XX. 2), may well have a place in such a procession as this.

[5] The lituus was used by the augurs in their divinations to mark out the heavens into "regions," (Cic. de Divin. I. 17. Liv. I. 18. Plut. Romul. A. Gell. V. 8. Macrob. Sat. VI. 8.) of which the Etruscans had sixteen, the Romans only four. Cic. de Divin. II. 18. There was also a sort of trumpet called by the same name, probably because it was similarly crooked (Festus v. Lituus. Cic. de Divin. I. 17. A. Gell. loc. cit.): but it was a question whether the trumpet was called from the staff, or the staff from the trumpet. A player on

this trumpet was called "*liticen*," as a *tuba* "*tubicen*," a *cornu* "*cornicen*." A. Gell. XX. 2 ; Varro, de Ling. Lat. V. ; Festus, loc. cit. Müller (Etrusk. IV. 1. 5,) suggests that the word *lituus* probably meant *crooked* in Etruscan.

[6] Ambrosch (de Charonte Etrusco, cited by Dr. Braun, Ann. Inst. 1837, 2, p. 263) regards this paw as belonging to a lion's skin hanging from Charun's shoulders ; but it seems to me to be the brachial termination of the demon.

[7] In other words it means—Lars Pompeius, son of Aruns . . . . The last word does not seem to be a proper name, but is more like a verb. Whoever gives a careful attention to Etruscan sepulchral inscriptions, can hardly fail to arrive at the conclusion that the word "Clan" signifies *natus* or *filius*. Orioli (Ann. Inst. 1834, pp. 169, 171) regards it as one of the very few Etruscan words which have survived the lapse of ages. "I know not if it have any relation to the *clan* of Scotland and Sir W. Scott—I should think not ; but I find it

It is evident that these two figures are portraits of the persons interred in this sepulchre. But why represent the souls of the departed in the clutches of demons ?—such a sight could have been little grateful to the feelings of survivors, on their annual visits to the grave. Mrs. Gray's lively imagination conceives a romantic tale of woe, and sees in this pair an Etruscan Paolo and Francesca.

> O lasso !
> Quanti dolci pensier, quanto desio,
> Menò costoro al doloroso passo !

But it is not necessary to suppose this a scene of retributive justice. The Charun of the Etruscans is represented of this fearful character, rather as the messenger of the grim King of Terrors than as a persecutor and tormentor of guilty spirits. Charun is in general but the guide, the infernal Mercury of the Etruscans; whose office it is to conduct disembodied souls into the unseen world; and such seems to be the duty he and his fellow-demons are performing in this fresco.[8]

It is obvious at a glance that the paintings in this tomb are of much later date and of more advanced art than those in the sepulchres already described. There is nothing archaic about them. Here are grouping, perspective, foreshortening, full faces, chiaroscuro—never attained or even attempted in the earlier paintings; here are correctness and ease of design, modelling of form instead of mere outline, a natural and harmonious tone of colour in place of conventionalities and startling contrasts, drapery no longer in stiff, formal plaits, but hanging in broad easy folds. In a word, these frescoes are so like those of Pompeii, that they might be pronounced Greek, were it not for their national peculiarities.[9] There is no doubt that they belong to the period of

---

still existing among the Tuscans in the word *Chiana*, corrupted from the Latin *Clanis*, *Glanis*, or *Clanius*, which is evidently the Etruscan *clan* with a Latin termination." He proceeds to show that *Chiana*, in the language of modern Tuscany, means a canal, or water-course, whence the emissary of the lake of Perugia has received this name, as also the celebrated Val di Chiana ; wherefore he infers that the primary meaning of *clan* was *derivation*, whether applied to children, to water, or to anything else.

[8] Urlichs (Bull. Inst. 1839, p. 47) conceives this procession to represent the triumphal ingress of the dead into the infernal regions, and draws a parallel between it and the triumphal processions of the Romans, as represented on their monuments. Dr. Helbig also sees in the figures in this procession a strong analogy to the reliefs on Roman triumphal arches. Ann. Inst. 1870, p. 71.

[9] The figures on the pilaster, both as regards idea and invention, are perfectly Greek, says Dr. Brunn, while those in the procession on the wall are entirely Etruscan ; the grouping may be due to Greek influence, but in the character of the heads and figures the true Etruscan realism is displayed. Ann. Inst. 1866, p. 437.

Roman domination in Etruria. Read the inscription on one of the rock-hewn benches, and you have proof that the tomb was used by the conquerors :—

AVRELIA· L· F· OPTVMA· FEMINA
VIXSIT· AN· XLV

On one of the sarcophagi you find another Latin epigraph with the name of L. PERCENNA or TERCENNA[1]—an Etruscan name in Roman letters. But with these exceptions everything is Etruscan—the form and character of the sepulchre, the sarcophagi, the dolphin-band, the procession, the Typhon figures, and the inscriptions on wall, pillar, and sarcophagi—are all purely Etruscan. From the recurrence of the name of "Pumpus" twice on the wall, attached to the principal figure in the procession, and again in the inscription on the pillar, it is highly probable that this was the sepulchre of a family of that name, from which the Roman *gens* of Pompeius was descended ;[2] if so, there may have been no mixture of Etruscan and Roman bodies in this tomb; as appears to be the case, for those with Latin epitaphs may have been Etruscans by birth, education, customs, religion—in everything but language; their native tongue, though not perhaps extinct, being in their time no longer a polite language, but confined to the lower orders, like the Erse and Gaelic with us.

Milton is said to have drawn the scenery of the "Paradise Lost" from that of Tuscany. With more perhaps of truth may it be said that Ariosto often introduced the peculiarities of Cisapennine scenery into his great epic. This has often been brought to my mind in my wanderings through Etruria. What is the grotto where Orlando found the fair Isabella,[3] or the cave of the sage Merlin,[4] but one of these ancient sepulchres, which the poet has drawn from nature ? There is the mouth of the tomb in the face of the hill, choked with bushes and brambles—the passage of many steps hewn out of the rock, and leading straight down to the door of the sepulchre—the spacious gloomy chamber within, retaining the marks of the chisel on its walls and ceiling, and

---

[1] This inscription is also given by Kellermann (loc. cit.).

[2] The name of "Pumpu," "Pumpus," or "Pumpuni" (Pompeius or Pomponius) is frequently found among the sepulchral inscriptions of Chiusi, Cortona, and Perugia. At the last-named site a sepulchre of the "Pumpu" family was discovered in 1792 containing many urns inscribed with this name.

[3] Orlando Furioso, XII. 88, 90.

[4] Orlando Furioso, II. 70, 71 ; III. 6, 7, 15.

resembling a temple or church supported by columns with architectural adornments, having even a sort of altar in the midst, as
in this Grotta Pompej, and with sculptures or paintings on the
walls around, only revealed by the light of the torch.   The poet
may have indulged slightly in his professional licence, but who
can doubt, on seeing the tombs of Etruria, especially those of
Tarquinii and Cære, whence the portraiture was drawn?   One
could wish the poetical description borne out in every point—that
there was still some *genius loci*, some wise Merlin—

> Che le passate e le future cose
> A chi gli dimandò, sempre rispose—

to unravel the mysteries of antiquity here interred.[6]

Grotta degli Scudi.

About 400 yards beyond the Grotta de' Pompej, through a
hollow spanned by the arches of a mediæval aqueduct, runs a
road, leading from the ancient city across the Montarozzi towards the sea, and probably of Etruscan formation.   Here in a
bank to the left, opens the Grotta degli Scudi, or "Tomb of the
Shields," which was discovered in December, 1870.   It contains
a large central chamber, and three others of smaller size opening
upon it, each with a door and two windows cut through the intervening wall of rock.   This sepulchral arrangement in imitation
of a house, is not uncommon at Cervetri, but unique, so far as I
am aware, at Corneto.   These doors are of the usual Etruscan
form, but the lintel and jambs are painted with black stripes
to represent the rod mouldings which usually surround them.
Across one jamb of the doorway which faces the entrance is an
Etruscan inscription.   On the opposite jamb is depicted a
naked boy, carrying a wine-jug.   Turning to the window on the
right hand of this door, you perceive, painted on the wall above
it, a small sarcophagus, behind which sits in mournful attitude, a
naked and winged genius, whose red flesh shows him to represent
a good demon, apparently engaged in reading an inscription on
the lid, which is inverted, so that he can read it, while to the
spectator in the tomb it is upside down.   A second inscription on

[6] For further details and opinions of this
tomb, see Ann. Inst. 1834, p. 52 (Bunsen);
pp. 153—181 (Orioli); 1837, 2, p. 268
(Braun); Bull. Inst. 1832, p. 214 (Avvolta);

1839, pp. 46—48 (Urlichs).   A plan of the
tomb, with illustrations, will be found in
Mon. Ined. Inst. II. tav. 3, 4, 5.

the body of the sarcophagus is upright, though hardly distinct enough to be legible.

On the wall to the right of this window, on a festive couch adorned with the usual meanders and chequers, is a pair of figures, but the man alone is recumbent; his fair companion sits on the couch at his feet. He is depicted with a full face, his head crowned with laurel, and his body naked to the waist, below which it is covered with a white *himation*. She is drawn in profile, and a charming profile it is, of the Greek type; the bloom of youth is shown in her lips and cheeks; her golden hair would hang loosely about her neck, were it not partly confined by a fillet. She wears a necklace, snake-bracelets, and earrings resembling a small bunch of grapes. Her white drapery is in harmony with her youth and beauty. The repast seems to have just begun, for she holds out her hand to receive an egg offered to her by her partner. Bread, grapes, and other fruit lie on the table in front. A female slave, robed in white, holds an elegant fan behind her mistress. The wall behind these figures bears inscriptions, some in large, others in small characters, but for the most part illegible.

On the adjoining wall is depicted a similar scene, but the man reclines with his right hand on his companion's shoulder, holding a *phiala* in the other. He regards her fondly, but she casts her large black eyes into space, and clasps her hands before her, as if in deep thought. The accessories are very similar to those in the last scene, but in the corner behind the lady stand two musicians half draped in white, one playing the lyre, the other the double-pipes. The couple on this couch have their names attached; he was a Velthur; she of the Aprthnai family.

To the right of the door in this wall is a pretty figure of a naked boy, much injured. Beyond the adjoining window the figures of a man and two women are traceable, he with white *pallium* over his shoulder, but of the first woman little beyond her head with yellow fillet-bound hair is now visible. The second stands in the corner, draped in white, with bare arm raised to her bosom, looking towards a male figure on the wall at right angles; but this figure has lost all distinctive character. Next is seen a helmeted head, followed by a trumpeter blowing a curved horn or *lituus*, jointed, as if of brass, and by another blowing a long straight horn.

We have now been half round the tomb, and have returned to the entrance door. On the wall to the left of this door, are

vestiges of three figures, now almost obliterated, two males and
two females; one of the former blows a *lituus*. By the side of
the first window on the left of the chamber is a long Etruscan
inscription, of two lines, running vertically up the wall, but
hardly legible. Nothing more is distinguishable on this wall, till
you reach the further window, where there is an inscription on
the right jamb. In the corner beyond, you perceive a pair, of
opposite sexes. The man is sitting on a wooden chair, holding
a long black staff; while the woman either sits or stands by his
side, and points with her right hand to his mouth. He has black
hair and beard, and is half draped in a white *pallium* bordered
with black, which offers a strong contrast with his deep red flesh;
his feet, shod with sandals, rest on a stool. She has black eyes
and brown hair, and wears, over a yellow chemise, a similar
pallium to that worn by her companion. An inscription, no
longer legible, was attached to each.[6]

On the wall adjoining at right angles stand two male figures,
also in white robes bordered with black. Above the window by
their side is depicted a youthful Genius, or male-demon, with
open wings, sitting in an easy attitude, and resting his hammer
on the ground, as if to show he had finished his task.

The figures in this tomb are about 45 inches high. All, or
nearly all, have inscriptions over their heads, now for the most
part illegible. A wave pattern in black runs round the chamber
beneath the figures. This chamber is about 20 feet square.
The roof is not painted, but carved into beam and rafters. The
art displayed is of the latter days of Etruria. Nothing is here
archaic. Here we have chiaroscuro, foreshortening, and three-
quarter faces; and a freedom of style which marks the decadence
rather than the progress of art towards perfection. There is so
striking a resemblance in these paintings to some of those in the
neighbouring Grotta dell' Orco, that I do not hesitate to pronounce them to be of the same school, if not by the same hand.

The chambers to the right and left of the central one have no
decorations, but that opposite the entrance is surrounded with
shields, depicted as suspended against the walls, six on each side,
and four on the inner wall. They are merely outlined in black,
with a rim painted yellow; the diameter of the whole being about
thirty-five inches. Most of them bear sepulchral inscriptions,
in some within the shield itself, in others crossing the disk,

[6] There is considerable similarity between
this pair of figures and that of Pluto and
Proserpine in the Tomba Golini, near
Orvieto.

and continued on the wall beyond. The name of "Velchas" is repeated so frequently in the inscriptions in this tomb, as to leave little doubt that the sepulchre belonged to a family of that name.[7]

This tomb faces the S.E.

Further down the hollow in which the tomb just described lies, a long passage in the right bank leads to the

GROTTA DEL CARDINALE,

the "Tomb of the Cardinal," the earliest discovered of the painted tombs of Tarquinii, found as long since as 1699, re-opened in 1738, again in 1760, and finally in 1780, by a certain Cardinal Garampi, bishop of Corneto, from whom it derives its vulgar appellation. A more appropriate name would be Grotta del passagio delle Anime—"Tomb of the passage of Souls;" or Grotta Vesi, from an Etruscan inscription on the wall.[8] It is the largest single-chambered tomb in this, or perhaps in any other Etruscan necropolis, being no less than 54 feet square, with a flat ceiling, so low that a tall man can scarcely stand upright, coffered in concentric squares and oblongs, and supported on four pillars, six or seven feet square, hewn out of the rock in which the chamber is hollowed. On first entrance, when the feeble light of the tapers just reveals the forms of these massive pillars, one behind the other in dim perspective, you might fancy yourself in one of the rock-hewn temples of Egypt or India. In truth, in its general aspect this tomb bears no small resemblance to a temple; yet the paintings on the walls determine its sepulchral character. These paintings are on the right hand only of the tomb,[9] on the walls and pillars, in a frieze of small figures scarcely a foot in height, and are now almost obliterated by the smoke of the fires, which the shepherds of generations past were wont to make in the tomb, before it was taken

---

[7] The Grotta dell' Orco belonged to the same family. I am not aware that the paintings in this tomb have been described, or illustrated.

[8] This inscription is of two lines painted in black letters on the wall to the left of the doorway, and is now much injured; but the name of VELUS VESI is still distinct. I have given it in Etruscan characters, as it now exists, in Bull. Inst. 1845, p. 138. Vesi seems to be the family or gentilitial name of the owners of the tomb—a name which is found not unfrequently among Etruscan inscriptions, generally in its derivatives—Vesial, and Vesialisa.

[9] One third of the tomb is in an unfinished state. In the central portion, the ceiling is coffered as in the tombs of Chiusi, and the Pantheon at Rome; in the remaining part it is cut into rafters highly decorated with patterns in colour.

under the protection of the government. So sadly, indeed, have these paintings suffered through neglect and wantonness, that a stranger unaware of their existence might go round the tomb without perceiving them. Where they can be made out, they are seen to be drawn with much spirit and masterly ease, especially those on the pillars, and mark a later epoch than belongs to any other sepulchre in this necropolis, save that of the Typhon. From the style of art and the character of the decorations in this tomb, it is highly probable that it dates from the times of Roman domination, as late, it may be, as the sixth century of the City.[1] The subjects of the paintings, nevertheless, are for the most part unquestionably Etruscan, representing the passage of souls into the unseen world, and their condition therein; and opening to us a clearer and more comprehensive view of Etruscan religious belief, than is to be gathered from any other monument extant.

Representations of these paintings, as they existed many years since, are given by Micali and Inghirami, but the fullest delineations of them have been published of late years from the drawings of Mr. Byres, an English artist resident in Rome in the middle of the last century, who, on the re-opening of this tomb, proceeded to Corneto to make drawings of the contents.[2] Signor Carlo Avvolta assured me that Byres was sent by the British government, and was accompanied by several other artists, among whom was the celebrated Piranesi. Avvolta declared that he had a distinct remembrance of the party, because, there being no inn at Corneto, they were entertained by his father, one of the principal inhabitants. The visit of these strangers, their foreign tongue, and the rich presents they made his mother on their departure, made a deep impression on his boyish memory; and the old gentleman used to produce from the recesses of some quaint cabinet, a number of portraits of the party, which they made of each other, and left as a memorial of their visit.

The illustrations of Byres are valuable records of the original state of this and other tombs at Corneto, which are now almost

[1] Gerhard does not think that the paintings betray the decadence of art (Ann. Inst. 1831, p. 319). Brunn, on the other hand, is of opinion that the national element is here seen in decay and decomposition, no longer having a distinct character and style, but mixed with and contending feebly against the Hellenic element. Ann. Inst. 1866, pp. 437-8.

[2] The drawings made by Byres were engraved, but never reached publication during his lifetime, and after lying *perdus* in Italy for sixty or seventy years, they were brought to light and published in London—"Hypogæi, or the sepulchral caverns of Tarquinia, by the late James Byres, Esq., of Tonley, Aberdeenshire. Edited by Frank Howard. London, Colnaghi, Cadell, Pickering, 1842."

destroyed, or reclosed and forgotten. Many of the figures in this tomb which are given by Byres, are now entirely obliterated, and of others nothing but a faint glimmering is now discernible through the thick smoky coating of the walls; while a few still remain sufficiently preserved to approve the general accuracy of his drawings.[3] Much as these paintings have suffered from smoke, they have been further defaced by the wantonness of visitors. Micali says, "they have been pilfered piece-meal by trans-Alpine travellers, who boast of their intelligence." Such an assertion is in accordance with the rampant nationality of that writer, but of such pilferings I could perceive few signs, and of the names scratched on the wall, which have done the most injury, I saw none but Italian. Though Englishmen have an extended reputation for this sort of barbarism, they by no means monopolise it. "I am afraid this great lubber, the world, will prove a cockney" in other portions than Britain. Throughout Spain, Portugal, Italy, and the Levant, I have always found the same propensity to record individual insignificance prevalent—to fulfil, what some one calls, "tous les petits devoirs d'un voyageur;" and on any remarkable site or building, especially in the neighbourhood of large cities, have always remarked the great majority of names inscribed to be those of natives.

The figures painted in this tomb may be divided into two classes or worlds—the living and the dead; which in some instances, however, are scarcely distinguishable. In the latter must be included another class, not less numerous, for the tomb teems

> "With all the grisly legions that troop
> Under the sooty flag of Acheron."

[3] There is, however, a tame mannerism about his drawings, which, after having carefully compared them with the originals, I am compelled to refer to the artist alone. Indeed, from the superior spirit and energy of the original figures, and from the inaccuracy of some of Byres' details, I am of opinion that the engravings were made from slight sketches, in the course of reworking which, much of the character and spirit of the originals was lost. Agincourt's evidence is to the same effect—"J'en ai vérifié l'exactitude sur les lieux mêmes; elle est entière quant aux sujets, mais le style du dessin m'a paru amélioré, et n'avoir pas le caractère de celui qui était propre aux Etrusques." Hist. de l'Art, III. p. 9. It must be confessed, however, that Byres' task cannot have been much easier than it would be at present; for in his time these figures seem not to have been in much better condition than they are now. Winckelmann speaks of them as very indistinct. Cardinal Garampi, in 1786, said certain of the colours only were preserved, and the figures were in general dark shadows, with the attitudes and outlines distinguishable. And even in 1760, Pacciaudi said they had almost vanished, and were to be made out only by putting the light quite close; the red alone being very apparent. Some are now only to be traced by the scratched outline, while others which were merely coloured have entirely faded from the wall.

To the living belong the combats on the frieze of the pillars, where the figures are represented almost or entirely naked, and armed with sword and shield. In attitude and action they are in general spirited and expressive. One of these scenes is remarkably fine and spirited, approximating more closely to the Greek than any other in the tomb.[4] Here indeed, as in the Typhon tomb, the art displayed on the pillars is almost purely Greek, while that on the walls is unmistakably Etruscan.

The mythological scenes are yet more curious and interesting. They represent numerous souls, in the form of men, robed in white, conducted into the other world by genii of opposite characters, the good being depicted red or flesh-colour, the evil black, like the Furies of Grecian fable ;[5] both alike in human form, but with wings, red or white, at their shoulders.[6] Sometimes a good and evil spirit seem contending for the possession of a soul,—as where this is pursued by the malignant demon, and hurried away by the better genius ; sometimes they are acting in unison—as where they are harnessed to a car, and are driven by an old man, who may possibly represent the Minos or Rhadamanthus of the

[4] It has been copied by Micali (Ant. Pop. Ital. tav. LXVI.), and from him by Mrs. Gray (Sepulchres of Etruria, p. 203). According to Sir W. Gell (Rome, I. p. 376), "many of these figures are positively the same as those represented in the Phigaleian marbles, and particularly the group in which one warrior prevents another from killing his wounded foe." I confess myself unable to perceive any close resemblance between the groups, though it exists between particular figures.

[5] Æschylus (Eumen. 52) describes the Furies as "black and utterly horrible"— (cf. Orph. Hym. 69, 6.—κιανόχρωτοι. Eurip. Orest. 321.—μελαγχρῶτες), and so they were always represented on the Greek stage. Æschylus also describes them as clad in sable robes. (Eumen. 375.— μελανείμονες, cf. 352. Choeph. 1049— φαιοχίτωνες). Inghirami (Mon. Etr. I. p. 277, et seq.) opposed the idea that the demons in this tomb were genii, good and bad ; and pronounced them all to be Furies. But though many have the attributes of the Eumenides, even as they are represented on Etruscan monuments, the distinctive, nay antagonistic, character is clearly set forth.

[6] Byres has drawn these figures with wings at their ankles, sometimes fastened to the leg, and sometimes like those at their shoulders, growing from the flesh—the talaria of Mercury and Perseus being represented in both ways on ancient monuments. Nothing of this sort could I perceive ; it was manifest to me that these were not talaria, but simple buskins with peaked flaps, such as are commonly depicted on Greek vases, and on Etruscan urns and sarcophagi, as the distinguishing attributes of genii or demons, as well as on the legs of Lares in the frescoes of Pompeii. This fact is most clearly marked, for where the flesh is black, as in the case of the evil spirits, the flaps and all the leg below them are red ; and where the flesh is red, the buskins are black. Talaria, however, would not be unapt attributes of the evil demons, for the Furies are described by Æschylus (Eumen. 74, 131, 147, 231, 246) as chasing guilty souls as hunters chase their prey, and are represented by other ancient writers as being winged (Eurip. Orest. 317. Iphig. Taur. 287. Orph. Hymn. 68. 5. Virg. Æn. XII. 848) ; and so they are often represented on Greek and Etruscan vases, running rapidly with wings both at their shoulders and ankles. Æschylus (Eumen. 51,250) however describes them as wingless.

Etruscans. In another instance a similar pair of antagonist spirits are dragging a car, on which sits a soul shrouded in a veil.[7] We may conclude they are attending the soul to judgment, for such was their office, according to the belief of the ancients, in order that when their charge was arraigned before the infernal judge, they might confirm or contradict his pleadings, according to their truth or falsehood.[8] When the good demons have anything in their hands, it is simply a rod or wand, but the malignant ones have generally a heavy hammer or mallet, as an emblem of their destructive character; and in some instances, probably after condemnation has been pronounced, they are represented with these instruments uplifted, threatening wretched souls who are imploring mercy on their knees. In a somewhat similar scene, a soul is in the power of two of these demons, when a good genius interposes and arrests one of the evil ones by the wing. In another scene the soul is represented as seizing the wing of the good genius, who is moving away from him.[9] The same dark demons are in more than one instance mounting guard at a gateway, doubtless the gate of Orcus—*atri janua Ditis*—which stands open day and night. One of these figures is very striking, sitting at the gateway, resting on his mallet, his hair standing on an end, and his finger raised as if to indicate the entrance to some approaching souls. Were this figure a female, it would answer in every respect, even to the colour of its raiment, to the Fury Tisiphone, whom Virgil places as guardian to the gate of Hell.[1]

Some of these scenes are now but faintly traceable, while others are still distinct. But there is one of very remarkable character delineated by Byres, which is not now to be verified. It represents two children, Cupid and Psyche, the latter with butterfly-

---

[7] Ann. Inst. 1837, 2, p. 261.

[8] Plato ap. Apuleium, de Deo Socratis, p. 80. ed. Venet. 1493.

[9] Byres has represented almost all these demons, both good and bad, as females. But two or three of the former only can now be distinguished as of that sex; a few are clearly males; but the majority preserve no sexual distinction. Yet it is not improbable that Byres is correct in this particular, judging from the analogy of the sepulchral urns, on which the winged demons, especially those who are mere messengers of Death, are commonly represented of the fair sex, but those with hammer or mallet, as allied to Charun, are generally males, though Byres here represents them as females. So in the copies made by Cattol, by order of Millin (Inghir. Mon. Etrus. I. p. 273, VI. tav. E. 3), and so Agincourt also represents them (Histoire de l'Art, IV. pl. 10, and Ingh. I. p. 275, IV. tav. 27); but Micali makes them almost all males.

[1] Virg. Æn. VI. 555—

Tisiphoneque sedens, pallâ succincta cruentâ
Vestibulum exsomnis servat noctesque
diesque.

A female demon, in a similar position and attitude, is represented on an Etruscan urn in the Campo Santo of Pisa.

wings, embracing each other; with a good genius on one side and an evil one on the other. They appear to have the same symbolical meaning as the Cupid and Psyche of the Greeks, for the evil genius is drawing Cupid, *i.e.*, the bodily appetites and passions, towards the things of this world, represented by a tree and a labourer hurrying along with a huge stone on his head, as if to intimate that man is born to trouble, and his lot below is all vexation of spirit; while on the other hand Psyche, or the more exalted part of human nature, draws him back, and her persuasions are seconded by the good genius, who, be it remarked, does not seize the soul, like the antagonist principle, but tries, with outstretched arms and gentle looks, to win it to herself. Behind her is a gate, through which a soul is calmly passing, as if to contrast the tranquil bliss of a future existence with the labour, unrest, and turmoil of this.[2]

I have spoken of souls on cars; others are seated on horseback; one is led by a good genius; another genius is leading a horse to a soul for him to mount, which reminds one of the old ballad—

> " Ho, ho ! the dead can ride apace—
> Dost fear to ride with me ?"

These favoured spirits may represent the great and wealthy of this world, or may merely indicate more clearly the journey into another state of existence, which is frequently symbolised by a horse on the Etruscan monuments of Chiusi and Volterra. The majority of souls are on foot—some full of horror, eager to escape; others imploring mercy from their malignant tormentors; but many are calm, resigned, melancholy beings, gliding along with rods in their hands. There is abundant room here for the imagination. Here it will perceive the warrior, arrested in his

---

[2] Though I have heard the truth of this scene, as represented by Byres, called in question, I see no reason to doubt it. It is certain that the figures on the wall, so far as it is possible to make them out, correspond with those in his plate, though almost all distinctive character has vanished. The stone-bearer and the tree are the most distinct portions; the two genii are far from clear; and it is only possible to perceive that something like two children has existed in the centre of the scene. The soul in the gateway appears to me to be leaning indolently against the wall. Moreover, as I have compared the whole series of Byres' plates with the original paintings, so far as it was practicable, and have found them to correspond in subject and general character, though not always in minute detail, I am willing to accord him credit for accuracy, in the subject at least of this scene. The apparent confirmation of his correctness afforded by Lanzi (II. p. 252) who mentions a representation of Psyche with butterfly-wings in the paintings of this tomb (cf. Inghirami, Mon. Etrus. IV. p. 112), is open to suspicion, as Lanzi had evidently seen his drawings, and may have written his description from them, not from the originals.

career of glory; here the augur, for whose sacred functions Death has no respect;[3] there the bride, giving her hand, not to an earthly husband but to a ghostly visitor; the village maiden with her water-pot on her head; the labourer with his spade or pitchfork on his shoulder, hurried away by one who knows no distinction of ranks;[4] and the infant in its mother's arms, fetched by a pale messenger, ere it had known aught of the joys or sorrows of the life it was called on to resign.[5]

GROTTA DELL' ORCO.

On the height above the Grotta del Cardinale is the enclosure of the new Campo Santo. Beneath the wall of this cemetery, on the side facing the S.W., is the entrance to the "Grotta dell' Orco," more vulgarly called "Grotta di Polifemo." This tomb was discovered in 1868, by an officer of the French army, then quartered in the Roman State, who, in his patriotic zeal to secure for the Louvre the remarkable frescoes on its walls, destroyed, it is said, some of the paintings, and defaced others. The tomb is so irregular in form that it is difficult to say into how many chambers it was originally divided, for the roof has fallen in parts, so as to have destroyed the partition-walls, and is now propped up by piers of masonry. It is clear that the paintings on its walls are not all by the same hand, or even of the same epoch, and, to judge from them, there seem to have been three distinct sepulchres, now thrown into one by the fall of the partition-walls. The paintings nearest the entrance being the earliest, we will commence with the wall to the right of the door, and take our readers round the tomb to the left.

We first notice traces of an elegant floral decoration, running round the wall into a deep recess. On the projection beyond

---

[3] This figure is represented leaning on a *lituus.* Byres draws him with wings, but could perceive no traces of them. He has a snake on the ground by his side. None of the genii in this tomb have these reptiles bound round their brows, as in the Grotta Pompej; but Byres gives drawings of two monstrous serpents, designed with great boldness, each bestridden by a boy, who is lashing it with a cord. They are no longer visible.

[4] These figures are represented by Micali (Ant. Pop. Ital. tav. LXV.) as bearing agricultural implements, which, as he gives

them, are very like those used in this part of Italy at the present day; but in Byres' plates no such instruments are given, nor could I perceive them in the paintings.

[5] This tomb has been described by Pacciaudi, in Caylus, Antiq. Egypt. Etrus. IV. p. 110; Piranesi, Maniere d' adornar gli edifizi, p. 22; Winckelmann, Storia delle Arti. I. lib. III. cap. 2, § 23, 24; Garampi, ap. Tirabos. Litter. Ital. I. p. 50; Micali, Italia avanti il dominio de' Romani, — all quoted at length by Inghirami, Mon. Etrus. IV. Ragion. VI. The tomb faces N.W.

this recess are a pair of figures on a couch, which is richly ornamented with chequers and meander-patterns. The greater portion
of this scene has disappeared. Of the man, little is left beyond
his head, crowned with laurel, and his right hand holding a twig.

THE WIFE OF ARNTH VELCHAS, GROTTA DELL' ORCO, CORNETO.

His partner has one of the most beautiful heads depicted in the
tombs of Etruria. She has deep hazel eyes, rich auburn hair,
and a profile of the ideal Greek type. She wears a double necklace, a chaplet of laurel leaves, and a yellow chemise, with a brown
battlemented border.[6] Of her name, inscribed above her, three

[6] The Frenchman had evidently the intention of detaching this head from the
wall, but fortunately could not put it into
execution. See her portrait above. The
artist, from whose drawing this woodcut is
copied, has mistaken a curl for the ear,
and represented this feature too low in the
head. It is in its proper place in the
original, as I can attest.

letters only are left; his was "Arnth Velchas." Her figure is
thrown out by a background of black rugged masses, somewhat

ARNTH VELCHAS AND HIS WIFE IN ELYSIUM, GROTTA DELL' ORCO, CORNETO.

resembling clouds, and clouds they seem intended to represent,
for these figures, as may be inferred from the proximity of the
demon on the adjoining wall, represent the souls of those who

were here interred, in a state of beatitude, rather than the said persons in the enjoyment of the pleasures of their earthly existence. In short, there is little doubt that we are here introduced to the Etruscan Hades or Orcus.[7]

The wall at right angles is occupied by a hideous dusky demon, with an eagle's bill for a nose, open mouth, black beard and eyebrow, brute's ears, and hair bristling with red, snake-like locks. His flesh is not black, but a livid blue.[8] He has open wings, grey above, and blue, black, and red on the pinions. His dress is a white tunic with a red girdle, and a yellow spotted band crossed over his bosom. He holds aloft a stout red pole, whether terminating as a hammer or a torch is not now discernible. A huge crested and bearded snake springs from his right shoulder, and his only leg now visible is buskined with the coils of yellow serpents, which depend from it like *talaria*. A sort of halo surmounts his head. No inscription now remains to determine his appellation, but there can be little doubt that he represents the Etruscan Charun.

The wall again recedes, and we come to a second banqueting-couch, which has suffered even more than the former. The man's head is only in part preserved, though the yellow *pallium*, thrown over his shoulder, is still distinct. The upper portion of the woman's figure is quite effaced, but the white drapery covering her lower limbs is drawn with much freedom and correctness. The fragment of a boy's face, who appears to have been standing in front of the couch, may be traced, as well as the head and shoulders of a slave girl in white with gold torque and *bulla*, occupying a similar position, but her features are obliterated. From the fragments which remain of this scene, we perceive that it was drawn with much boldness and freedom, and belonged to the best period of Etruscan art. The figures of the pair on the couch are thrown out from the wall by black clouds, as in the scene just

---

[7] Similar clouds have been found in only one other painted tomb in Etruria, the Tomba Golini at Orvieto, which, like this of Corneto, represents souls in Elysium in the presence of Hades and Persephone. But, as in that tomb, they are introduced only where the white drapery might otherwise be confounded with the white stucco ground, Count Conestabile was led to regard them as a mere artistic device. Pitture Murali, p. 110. Here, however, similar clouds surround the entire figures, whatever may

be their colouring, which has led Dr. Helbig to the conclusion that they were intended to represent the Ἀΐδης ζόφον ἠερόεντα of Homer (Iliad XV. 191), the cloudy gloom of the realms of Hades. Ann. Inst. 1870, p. 20.

[8] The infernal demon Eurynomos, as represented by Polygnotus on the Lesche at Delphi, was of a colour between black and blue, like that of the flies which settle upon meat. Pausan. X. 28, 7. The Etruscans generally depicted Charun of this livid hue.

described.   Over the lady is an Etruscan inscription of five lines,
only in part legible ; and over the man's head is a long epigraph
in smaller characters in a single line, a continuation of that on
the side wall of the recess.   When the tomb was first opened
there was a shield, it is said, resting on the couch in front of the
man, which shield bore an inscription, but no traces of either
shield or inscription are now visible.

These two festive scenes belong to the earliest portion of the
sepulchre.

The tomb has been so much injured—how far by the patriotism
of its discoverer, it is now difficult to say—that large portions of
its walls present nothing but blank rugged surfaces of rock ; but
of the paintings still remaining, those already described alone
have a personal character, or bear reference to the individuals
here interred.   The rest present us with scenes from the Etruscan Hades, with a mixture of Hellenic myths, and with one from
the heroic cycle of the Greeks.

This latter scene, which gives its popular name to the sepulchre,
we find in a large recess more to the left.   Here Ulysses, whose
name in Etruscan, " UTHUSTE," is inscribed in large characters
on the wall, is depicted in the act of blinding Polyphemus.   The
hero's head has quite disappeared, and his figure, which occupied
the side-wall of the recess, is almost obliterated, but his hands
guiding the enormous brand well sharpened to a point, as described by Homer, are still visible.   The figure of the Cyclops,
designated " CUCLU " in the Etruscan inscription, fills the inner
wall of the recess.   `He is a vast, misshapen monster, with head
disproportionately large, his enormous eye almost filling his forehead, mouth bristling with teeth, and fringed with long white
moustache and beard, shaggy black locks hanging about his
shoulders like snakes, but not concealing his monstrous ear.   He
is just springing from his bed of rushes as the hissing brand
enters his solitary orbit ; one leg is stretched convulsively across
the recess, his right arm falls powerless over the brand.   His
flesh is a deep red, and his figure is broadly outlined with black.
He is as hideous a giant as ever imagination conceived, or Jack
of nursery renown encountered, and answers well to his description given by Virgil in the well-known line—

Monstrum horrendum, informe, ingens, cui lumen ademptum.[9]

[9] Æn. III. 658. Polyphemus as here
depicted certainly does not answer to the
flattering portrait he draws of himself.
Theoc. Idyl. VI. 34, et seq.

A square door in the middle of this wall marks the entrance to his cave. On the side-wall to the right is represented his flock.

This scene from the Odyssey is so incongruous with the others in this tomb, which have all reference to the unseen world of the Etruscans, that we may regard it as forming the decoration of a separate sepulchre, or as an interpolation of a subsequent age, a view confirmed by the style of art ; the free yet careless design, the coarse execution, and the chiaroscuro indicating the decadence of Etruscan art.

A little further on we come to a projecting portion of the wall, where is represented a majestic figure with an animal's skin over his head, which at first suggests Hercules, but his concomitants and the inscription on the wall before him, "AITA" (Hades), mark him as the Pluto of the Etruscan mythology. He sits on a throne, the upper part of his body bare, the lower covered with brown drapery. His flesh is deep red, his beard black, and there is a grand and gloomy air about him well becoming the King of the Shades. With his left hand he holds aloft a snake; with his right he appears to be giving orders to the triple-headed warrior who stands before him. At his feet, and behind his throne, clouds are rolling ; some dusky, resembling those depicted in the scenes nearer the door, others grey, of more etherial and unmistakable character. At his right hand stands his wife, the fair Persephone, "PHERSIPNEI," as it is here inscribed ; her face of the Minerva type, so far as the features can be distinguished, her head bound with green snakes, and her form wrapped in white drapery, with a deep vandyked fringe, like a tippet over her shoulders. The skin Pluto wears on his head is that of a dog or wolf, the "Ἄϊδος κυνέη, which Hesiod describes as spreading "the terrible gloom of night" around him.[1] Over their heads an arch or dome is marked, to indicate "the resounding mansions of the mighty Hades, and of dread Persephone."[2] Before this august pair stands a figure, with three heads, yet with but one body, which, armed with cuirass, spear, and shield, stands erect before the throne, as if to receive the commands of the god. The inscription by his side is "KELUX," but there can be no doubt that the figure is intended to represent Geryon—forma tricorporis umbræ.[3]

---

[1] Hesiod. Scut. Herc. 227.

[2] Hesiod. Theog. 767. It will be observed that the names attached to these deities are not Etruscan, though written in that character, but are native corruptions of the Greek.

[3] The name may have been written "KENUX," but a portion of the middle letter becoming obliterated, it now reads as "KELUX." The poets placed this monster in Tartarus, with the Gorgons, the Harpies, and the giant Tityus, (Hor.

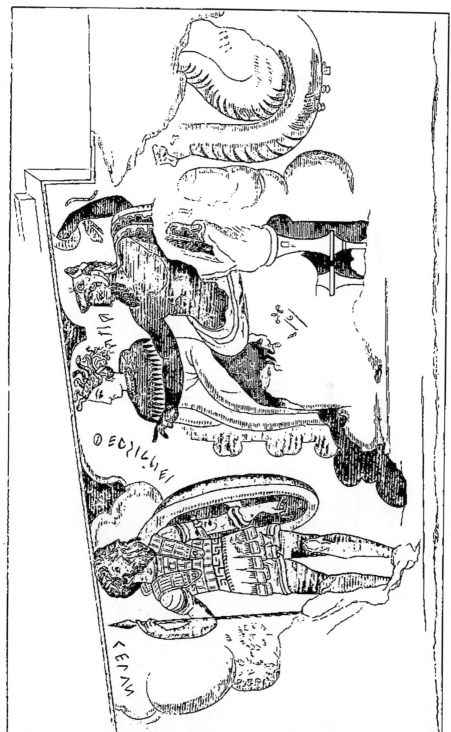

PLUTO, PROSERPINE, AND GERYON, IN HADES, GROTTA DELL' ORCO, CORNETO.

His triple heads are extremely handsome, as if to bear out the description of Hesiod[4]—

Βροτῶν κάλλιστον ἀπάντων
Γηρυονέα.

Behind him a large wing marks a demon, whose white arm shows her sex, but the rest of the figure is obliterated.

On the wall, at right angles to the last, are vestiges of a procession of figures. The first, of which but a fragment remains, is designated "Eivas," which Dr. Wolfgang Helbig, who has written an elaborate and learned article on this tomb—to which I am partly indebted for my description—takes to mean Ajax Telamonius.[5] He is preceded by a venerable man with white hair and beard, and head covered with a black mantle. His attitude, as well as the expression of his countenance, is expressive of deep dejection. Further examination shows him to be blind, and the inscription above him, "Hinthial Teriasals," proves him to be "the Shade of Tiresias."[6] Next him is a personage of very different character, a bold majestic figure, designated "Memrun," which can be no other than the handsome son of Aurora, "the divine Memnon."[7] His long hair hangs in golden tresses over his shoulders, though his beard is black. He is half-draped in white robes, and a broad band of the same hue encircles his waist, passes over one shoulder, and is wound round his left arm. He appears to be holding a staff in his right hand. The wing of a demon, at the head of the procession, shows there were four figures on this wall; but that was not all, for a leafless tree, which rises between Memnon and Tiresias, is full of Lilliputian human figures, climbing among the branches, and probably representing the souls which populate the regions of the dead. The tree, with its tiny inhabitants, strongly reminded me of the bamboo-clumps I have often seen in South America, swarming with marmosets or sackiwinkies.

Next follow fragments of figures, but none intelligible, save a demon with open wings, till we reach the front wall of the tomb. Here, in a recess, are two figures carved in the rock in high relief, one on each side. That to the right is naked, save a *chlamys* over

---

Od. II. 14, 8; Virg. Æn. VI., 289), and he had a further connection with Pluto, as both possessed oxen in the island of Erytheia in the extreme west, or at the gates of Night.

[4] Hesiod, Theog. 981.

[5] Annal. Inst. 1870, pp. 16–42; 64–70.

[6] A mirror with the shade of Tiresias—Hiuthial Terasias—supported by "Aitas" and "Turms," Hades and Hermes, is illustrated in the Mon. Instit. II. tav. 29.

[7] Odyss. IX. 522.

his shoulder.   His right hand is raised, but his head and all the
rest of his figure are gone.   Of the figure on the opposite wall
the legs alone are left, with a large snake rising from the ground
between them.

On the wall, at right angles to this, we have a scene differing
from any yet described.   So far, we have seen souls represented
in a state of beatitude, in the enjoyment of the pleasures which
most highly gratify the senses on earth.   We have seen the dread
King and Queen of the Shades in their own dominions; we have
seen the souls of heroes and prophets in solemn procession
headed by a demon, whether of good or evil character we cannot
determine, as her attributes are wanting, but we have seen nothing
to prove that they were not in Elysium.   Here, however, we behold a hideous and evidently malignant demon, more hideous
even than that first described, threatening, or triumphing over, if
not actually tormenting two beings who have fallen into his power.
The more prominent of these is denominated "THESE" or Theseus,
and the other, who has no inscription, doubtless represents
Pirithous, the audacious Lapith, who, with the assistance of his
friend, attempted to carry off Persephone from Hades.[4]   If this
view be correct, these paintings represent those heroes in the life,
and not as disembodied spirits.   The demon, who bears the novel
name of "TUCHULCHA," has asses' ears, two hissing snakes bound
round his brows and mingling with his shaggy locks, an enormous
eagle's beak, which serves at once for nose and mouth, and from
which, being wide open, he seems to be uttering horrible roars.
He appears to be seizing Pirithous by the neck with one hand,
while with the other he brandishes a huge black and blue
serpent over the head of Theseus.   His open wings also are
painted along the upper edge with a snake-like border, and the
very feathers seem to have caught the hue of a serpent's skin.
Of Pirithous little remains beyond his head, but the figure of
Theseus is truly beautiful.   His face and attitude are expressive
of utter resignation, and as he sits, half-draped in white, with
one hand on his knee and the other dropping at his side, his
whole figure might serve for that of Our Saviour, when buffeted
or scourged by the servants of Pilate.[5]   Immediately behind

[4] There can be no doubt that the opinion
of Dr. Helbig (Ann. Inst. 1870, p. 37) as
to the name of the second figure is correct.
It was a favourite subject of Greek artists
to represent these two friends in Hades.
Polygnotus depicted them, on the Lesche

at Delphi, as sitting in Hades, Theseus
holding the swords of both, while Pirithous
looked at the weapons with indignation that
they had proved of no service in their
nefarious enterprise.   Paus. X. 29, 9.

[5] The woodcut on p. 355, while it gives

Theseus springs an enormous serpent crested and bearded, which, with head erect, appears to be attacking a figure on the adjoining wall, who seems to be endeavouring to escape from it; but as this figure has grey flesh, and as he carries a pole over his right shoulder, he may represent a demon, followed by the snake as his instrument.[6]

On the adjoining wall, at right angles, we see a *kylikeion*, or sideboard, with five large jars; the two outer ones resting on kneeling figures, evidently representing metal. In front of it stand two tall *amphoræ*, and a *lebes* or mixing-basin. Here stands a naked slave boy, with a wine-jug and a drinking-bowl in his hands. He wears an armlet of gold, with two *bullæ* depending from it. By his side, but turning from him, is a youthful winged figure, wearing a similar armlet, whom we at once recognise as a good Genius, not only by the human colour of his flesh, but by his mild and benevolent expression. If such a figure were found on the walls of a Christian catacomb, instead of an Etruscan tomb, it would at once be declared, were it not for its nudity, to represent an angel. This genius carries in one hand a large *alabastos*. The group seems to have been accessory to other figures, which originally covered the long blank wall, up to the entrance of the tomb. What these figures were must ever remain matter of conjecture, unless they have been removed to Paris; but from the analogy of other tombs, we may surmise that the scenes here obliterated were of a joyous, festive character, such as would display the bliss of souls in Elysium. There were probably more couples reclining at the banquet, as the sideboard and wine-bearer strongly suggest; there may have been illustrations of the games, which the ancients believed to have formed a part of the delights of Elysium, but at least we may conjecture that the figures of dancers and musicians decorated the long tracts of wall, now blank, up to the banqueting-couch first described.

The resemblance between the paintings in this sepulchre (excluding the Polyphemus scene) and those in the Tomba Golini at Orvieto is striking. In both tombs the same subject is depicted, though it is treated in a different manner. Here

---

the general features of the scene with accuracy, fails altogether in rendering the expression of the head of Theseus, and thus makes the observations in the text appear inappropriate.

[6] This figure is too much mutilated to be intelligible. Dr. Helbig takes it to represent Charun, armed with the hammer, his usual attribute.

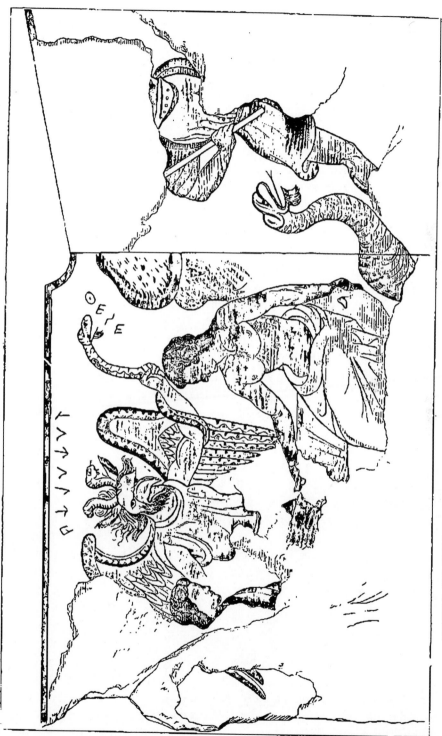

THESEUS AND PIRITHOUS IN HADES, WITH THE DEMON TUCHULCHA, GROTTA DELL' ORCO, CORNETO.

characters from the Greek mythology are introduced into the Etruscan Hades; there, the scenes are purely and entirely native. Though the art displayed in both instances is apparently coeval, or nearly so, the predominance of the Hellenic element is manifest in this Grotta dell' Orco.   Dr. Helbig pronounces these paintings to be the first yet brought to light at Corneto which represent with purity the tradition of the free Greek style, with its tendency to the beau-ideal.   But, as he truly remarks, the artists of Tarquinii seem almost always to have caught the spirit of Hellenic art, and to have been more deeply imbued with it than those of other Etruscan sites,[7]—a fact in accordance with the old tradition of Eucheir and Eugrammos.

Emerging from this tomb, you continue your walk over the Montarozzi, which here assumes that peculiar rugged character whence it derives its name.   Tumuli, or the remains of them, are scattered on every hand in hundreds—here and there cut into by spade or mattock, but generally overgrown with myrtle, broom, and lentiscus; tombs yawn around you at every step, once the resting-places of the princes and merchants of Tarquinii, now the dwelling of the fox, the bat, and the lizard, the shelter of the shepherd from the storm, or of the homicide from his pursuers; the very pathway resounds beneath your tread, and is full of chinks, which let daylight into the subterranean abodes of the dead.   Here you are stopt by piles of large hewn stones, dug out by the peasantry from the substructions of the tumuli, to be applied to the construction of hovels or cattle-sheds; there you cross a road hewn in the rock, with tombs in its cliffs to attest its antiquity.

At the distance of nearly two miles from Corneto, you find, at the verge of the steep facing the site of the ancient city, two other painted tombs, approached by level passages cut in the rock. One of them is called

Grotta del Vecchio.

These two tombs, which were discovered in 1864, bear a close resemblance in form, size, decoration, and style of art.   They lie close together.   That we shall first describe receives its designation from an old greybeard depicted on a festive couch on the wall facing the door.   The chamber is very small, not more than ten fect square. A glance suffices to prove that this is one of the earliest painted tombs of Corneto : for here, as in the Grotta delle Iscrizioni, everything betrays the primitive Etruscan style, before it had been modified and improved by the influence of Hellenic art. The old gentleman and his fair partner have a purely Oriental physiognomy, and so closely resemble that quaint Etruscan pair in terra-cotta, who, for some year or two, have excited the wonder and amusement of cockneys at the British Museum, that, if that strange sarcophagus had been discovered at Tarquinii instead of at Cære we might well conclude it had been found in this sepulchre. The old man, unlike most of the male figures in these tombs, wears a white shirt, his hoary head is bound with a red chaplet, and he holds a large *phiala* in one hand, while with the other he is about to caress the young girl who shares his couch. She, nothing loth, turns gaily towards him, and, with a "*grata protervitas*," which he seems fully to appreciate, offers him a striped chaplet, which she holds daintily between her finger and thumb, her other arm resting the while on his body. She is as youthful as he is venerable, and might be his daughter or grand-daughter, but more probably is the May to this December. She has no ornaments beyond a necklet or band round her throat, unless a large rosette which covers her ear is intended to represent an earring. She wears a high yellow *tutulus*, bound with two red chaplets crossing each other, a yellow spotted *chiton*, and a red *himation* over her shoulder. The drapery of the couch is red bordered with blue. On the wall behind hang chaplets ; and beneath the table, by the side of the couch, stand a couple of red-legged partridges. Vestiges of a male figure, probably a *subulo*, or a cupbearer, standing at the foot of the couch, are also discernible.

The wall to the right seems to have exhibited a similar scene of revelry, but the surface has been so defaced by a coating of saltpetre percolating through the rock, that little can now be made out. You can trace, however, a banqueting-couch, with red, blue, and yellow drapery, on which reclines a woman in yellow *chiton*. Her head is not visible, but from the position of her body she seems to be lying in the arms of her partner, and to be raising one arm, which shows a snake-bracelet, as if to resist him as he stretches out his right arm to embrace her. The rest of his figure is obliterated. At the foot of the couch stands a woman in a white *chiton*, with long brown hair and disk-earrings, who raises her arm as if addressing the pair on the couch.

Behind her a male figure draped in red may be traced by fragments.   On the opposite wall all is equally confused and indistinct, but a couch may be made out, though its occupants have
disappeared, and a female figure in yellow *chiton* is standing with
her back to it.

In the pediment over the banquet-scene, a broad yellow
modillion supports the roof-beam, which is decorated with disks
and ivy-leaves.   This modillion is flanked on either side by a
white spotted deer attacked by a particoloured lion; both bearing
a strong resemblance to the fantastic animals in the Grotta
Campana at Veii, the earliest painted tomb yet discovered in
Etruria.   This tomb faces E.S.E.[8]

Grotta dei Vasi Dipinti.

The inner wall of this tomb, as of the last, shows a banqueting-
couch, on which repose a similar couple.   The man, bare to the
waist, and with a chaplet round his head, holds an enormous
kylix in one hand, whose white hue is suggestive of silver, while
with the other he chucks under the chin the pretty young girl
who shares his couch.   But though she turns her face towards
him, she seems indifferent to his caresses, and with hand upraised
appears even to repel his advances.   Observe the strange way in
which she bends the fingers of this hand.   She has black hair,
hazel eyes, and regular features, and is decorated with a
sphendone round her brows, large circular earrings, and a necklace of gold.   In her other hand she holds a chaplet studded
with black beads.   She wears a red *tutulus* on her head, the
flaps of which reach to her waist, and a yellow short-sleeved

---

[8] Dr. Wolfgang Helbig, who gives a detailed
description of this tomb (Ann. Inst. 1870,
pp. 14, 45, 49, 72), pronounces the artist
to be a mere bungler as compared with him
of the "Tomb of the Painted Vases," very
inferior both as regards conception and
execution, and points out that the figures
are drily outlined, without any expression
of anatomical details.   Admitting the artistic inferiority, I would ascribe it to the
greater antiquity of this tomb, which to me
seems second in that point to none in this
necropolis, unless it be that of "The Inscriptions."   Dr. Helbig, however, after a
careful comparison of the archaisms in
each tomb, has arrived at a different opinion,
and regards them as contemporaneous, ascribing the shortcomings of the paintings
in this tomb to the incapacity of the artist,
rather than to the infantile condition of art
at the period they were executed (pp. 49–
51).   I find it more easy to agree with this
critic when he pronounces the design in
this tomb to be wanting in sentiment—that
the young girl here depicted has none of the
graceful coyness displayed by her follow in
the "Tomb of the Vases," but conducts herself with a joyous *abandon*; while the old
roué of Tarquinii, as he terms him, displays,
in the presence of his young mate, an un-
bridled delight which is truly comical.   For
an illustration see Mon. Ined. IX. tav. 14.

BANQUET SCENE, TOMB OF THE PAINTED VASES, CORNETO.

chemise spotted with black. Of the lower part of her body little remains visible. The couch is draped with red, bordered with white, and in front of it, beneath the usual footstool, lies a dog, looking up as if jealous of the attentions his master lavishes on the fair young girl. Sundry chaplets and neck-laces depend from the wall behind, together with a casket suspended by a cord.

In the corner to the left a young maiden, clad and decorated much like the lady on the couch, is seated on a low chair, covered with a leopard's skin. A naked boy sits on her lap, and testifies his fondness by throwing one arm round her neck. He holds a white duck in the other hand. The youth of these figures dispels all idea of sensual love, and suggests a scene of fraternal affection.

At the head of the couch a naked boy stands with a pair of metal *simpula,* or ladles, and a *colum,* or wine-strainer, ready to minister to the wants of his master, for close behind him on the right-hand wall stands a *kylikeion,* or sideboard, on which are arranged the vases of the banquet. See the opposite woodcut, which represents the scene adjoining that on p. 359. The large *krater* in the centre is yellow, to mark it as of plain clay. But the figured *amphorœ* which flank it are coloured precisely like real vases, with black figures on a reddish ground, and the scenes they represent—a dance of satyrs, and a man between two horses—are the counterparts of those on many vases of this archaic character. Two *kylikes,* also painted, lie inverted beneath the table. Then succeeds a dance of both sexes, carried round the rest of the tomb; trees, hung with chaplets or fillets, alternating with the dancers. The men, distinguished as usual by their red flesh, wear chaplets round their heads, and are naked, save that a deep red *chlamys* is tied round the waist, the ends of which curl up grotesquely, as if agitated by the lively movements of the dance. One of them, shown in the opposite woodcut, holds a *kylix* as large as a washhand basin, which from its white hue, and the nails which stud it, seems to represent silver; the others have nothing in their hands, but toss them about in a wild manner. There were two female dancers; of one a few fragments only are left, but from these you learn that her attitude showed much animation, and even *abandon.* The other *saltatrix* is in better preservation; her feet are gone, but her arms are swaying in the dance as she rattles the long castanets to her partner. There are vestiges of a *subulo* with his double-pipes on one side

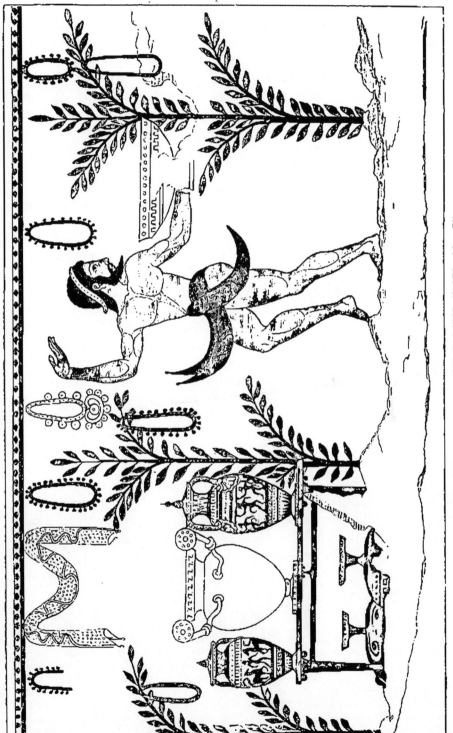

DANCING FIGURE, TOMB OF THE PAINTED VASES, CORNETO.

of the door, and on the other a fragmentary figure holds what appears to represent a tambourine.[9]

The paintings in this tomb show the archaic style of Etruscan art, tempered in some measure by Greek influences. These are betrayed in the strongly marked anatomical details, in the character of certain of the figures which show an analogy to those of the archaic Greek vases, and in the profiles which in some instances depart from the early Etruscan type and approximate rather to the Greek. The vases on the sideboard alone suffice to mark a period when the fictile art of the Greeks was familiar to the Etruscans, and aid us in determining the antiquity of the tomb.

We recognise in these paintings great carefulness and correctness in the design, and a truthful delineation both of the human form and of the accessories introduced. The outlines are clear and decided, yet delicately drawn; the details conscientiously expressed; and everything betrays a hand striving after a faithful rendering of nature, and working fully up to the power it possessed. In these respects the scenes in this tomb stand preeminent among the archaic wall-paintings of Corneto, showing a manifest improvement on the misshapen, ungainly figures of the " Iscrizioni," and on the rigid forms and blurred outlines of the " Barone."[1]

Grotta del Moribondo.

A further walk of three-quarters of a mile along the brow of the Montarozzi leads you to another painted tomb, facing the ancient city. It is called the " Tomb of the Dying Man," and was discovered in 1872. Like the last two described it is very small, hardly eight feet square. It faces N.N.W.

On entering, your eye is caught by the figure of a red horse,

---

[9] In the pediment over the banquet are two *hippocampi*, particoloured, red and white, followed by red eels. The ceiling is yellow, studded with clusters of red spots. The tomb faces S. E.

[1] "In the paintings in this tomb," says Dr. Helbig, "we recognise the hand of a true artist, distinguished by a feeling for the beautiful, and by the endeavour to ennoble his subjects. These paintings display, within the limits of the archaic style, a great advance towards perfection in the individual characters. In the countenance of the man on the couch we recognise delight mingled with an elevated dignity; in the attitude of the woman an elegance somewhat refined; in the figures of the young boy and girl, a sentiment so natural that it sheds over the entire group an air of innocence." For his description and critical analysis of this tomb, see Ann. Inst. 1870, pp. 8–14, 45–50, 72; cf. Mon. Ined. Inst. IX. tav. 15–13c.

with blue mane and tail, on the wall opposite. A naked youth runs behind him, holding the reins in one hand, and in the other a crook, with a sort of noose depending from it. With this exception the paintings in this tomb are very similar to those in the Grotta del Morto.

On the wall to the right the body of a man wrapped in red drapery, with a hood over his head, is stretched on a couch, behind which stands a woman, watching him anxiously. Her face is obliterated, but you can distinguish her brown hair, a red necklet, a rosette earring, her white *chiton* striped with red, and her sharp-toed blue boots. At the foot of the couch a male figure, in a grey *chlamys*, stretches one hand out towards the dying man, and raises the other over his head—the counterpart of the mourner in the other tomb. A girl in long grey *chiton*, and of a graceful though archaic figure, stands behind him, on the adjoining wall, and extends both arms towards the dying man. Blue and red chaplets are suspended above the couch. The rest of the paintings in this tomb have been destroyed by a deep fissure in the rock, extending quite across the chamber, and obliterating the figures on the left-hand wall; but enough remains to show that there were two male dancers very similar to those in the Grotta del Morto, represented in those quaint conventional attitudes introduced in archaic Etruscan monuments, to express violent motion.

In the pediment over the central scene are two blue leopards, one on each side of the usual modillion. The roof-beam is carved in relief and decorated with red disks. The blue in this tomb, wherever it occurs, is of wonderful brilliancy.

The rigid and angular forms, the exaggerated muscular development, and the stiffness of the drapery, all indicate an archaic period of art; yet it is an archaicism that betrays the influence of a freer development of art. The subject is almost identical with that of the Grotta del Morto, yet the treatment shows a great improvement on that scene. The dying man is designed with much more truth and feeling; the other figures are not inferior; but the naked groom holding the horse, which probably symbolises the passage of the soul to another world, is far better delineated, and with much more anatomical correctness, than any figure in the other tomb.[2]

These paintings cannot be of later date than those in the

---

[2] For an able criticism on the paintings in this tomb, see an article by Sig. E. Brizio, in Bull. Inst. 1873, pp. 196–200.

Grotta dei Vasi Dipinti, and must be at least coeval with the
earliest Greek vases, having black figures on a yellow ground.

GROTTA DELLE ISCRIZIONI.

Several hundred yards beyond this tomb, in the face of the
same cliff, is another, of yet higher antiquity, called, from the
number of Etruscan inscriptions on its walls, the " Tomb of the
Inscriptions ; " known also as the " Grotta delle Camere Finte,"
from the false doors painted, one in the centre of each wall, as
if to indicate entrances to inner chambers.[3]

The figures here depicted have several peculiarities.   They are
almost or entirely naked ; the colour of the flesh is not the usual
brick-red, but a paler tint, more true to nature ; and there is a
marked approximation to the oriental, or rather, I should say, the
figures are quite un-Hellenic in character, and betray the pure and
primitive style of Etruscan art.

The subjects are games and dances.   To begin with the wall
immediately to the left of the entrance.   Here two naked men
seem to be playing at dice, on a small table which stands between
them.   The dice are not depicted, but the attitudes of the men
indicate their occupation.   If it be so, it shows that the Etruscans
at their funerals had games of chance as well as of strength and
skill ; and explains the frequent discovery of dice in Etruscan
tombs among the relics of the funeral feast.[4]

The next two figures on the side-wall are also naked, and are
boxing with the *cestus* over an upright stick, crossed like a T,
which limits their advances ; these figures are much injured by a

---

[3] This tomb is 15 ft. 6 in. long, by 12 ft.
3 in. wide ; 6 ft. 6 in. high at the sides,
and 6 ft. 9 in. from the ground to the central beam of the ceiling. It was discovered
in 1827. The door was closed by a large
rectangular slab of stone, divided into small
square compartments, containing figures of
wild beasts or monsters, which Micali (Ant.
Pop. Ital. tom. III. p. 105, tav. LXVII. 7)
conceives to be emblems of the infernal
spirits to whom the guardianship of the
tomb was entrusted ; set there to terrify
those who would violate its sanctity. The
slab still lies within the tomb, which faces
N. E.

[4] The invention of dice is ascribed to
the Lydians, during the eighteen years'
famine, which drove a portion of them

from their native land to colonise Etruria.
Herod. I. 94.   That the Etruscans played
with dice we have historical evidence in
Livy (IV. 17), who records a tradition of
Lars Tolumnius, King of Veii. Not a few
Greek vases have been found in Etruria
and Campania, which represent Achilles
and Ajax playing at this game—the most
beautiful of them is in the Gregorian Museum.   Of the celebrated pair of dice
found by Campanari at Toscanella, marked
with words instead of pips which some
suppose to be the first six Etruscan numerals, and on which a theory of the origin
of the nation and language has been
founded, we shall have occasion to speak
elsewhere.

deep fissure in the rock. They are boxing to the music of a *subulo*, or piper,[5] in blue tunic and red boots. Next is a pair of athletes wrestling, and in spirited attitudes—one having lifted the other from the earth, and thrown him completely on his shoulder. The victor has a cloth round his loins; the other is quite naked. Each of these figures had his name in Etruscan characters above his head, but the inscriptions are now mere fragments, many of the letters having faded, or peeled from the wall.

The false door in this wall separates these combatants from an equestrian procession, which fills the space up to the false door in the centre of the inner wall. There are four mounted figures, preceded by another on foot, all perfectly naked. From the exultation of the first horseman, who throws his arms into the air, and from the anxiety of his followers to urge on their steeds, it is clear that the scene represents a race, which has just been won; the victor alone having his name recorded. The man on foot in front is probably an umpire. The steeds would hardly pass muster at Newmarket or Ascot, though they show no lack of spirit. Yet there can be little doubt that the favourite points with the turf-lovers of Etruria are here set forth;[6] resulting in a conventional form of singular uncouthness, which has not its counterpart in any other tomb of this necropolis, though bearing considerable affinity to the steeds in the Grotta Campana at Veii. These horses are alternately red and black, the manes and hoofs of the former being blue, of the latter, red or white; and all alike have long white tails.

The eight figures between the next two false doors—i.e., three on the inner, and five on the side-wall—form a Bacchic dance, as is apparent from the goblets and vases in their hands, and from the tipsy excitation of their gestures. The leading figure appears at first a female, from its form and necklace; though the flatness of the bosom, and the sameness in complexion with the men who follow, favour the ruder sex. The same may be said of the third figure, whose name seems to mark it as a male.[7] A more decided masculine character is seen in the anonymous *subulo* between

---

[5] This scene confirms the statement of Eratosthenes and Alcimus (ap. Athen. IV., 39; XII. c. 14), that the Etruscans boxed to the sound of the *tibia*; the latter adds that they also scourged, and kneaded bread to the same music.

[6] The Etruscans, be it remembered, were renowned for their race-horses. Liv. I. 35. Their passion for the turf must have led them to cultivate the breed.

[7] In the description given in the Musco Gregoriano, tom. I., they are called women, and for such Micali also took the first (III. p. 103).

these two. Each of the three has a chaplet round his brow, but
the first has a high white cap, or *tutulus*, in addition, which is
also worn by the two grey-beards who follow on the side-wall.
The first of these also wears a necklace, his arms are hung with
red chaplets, and he is brandishing a *phiala*, the contents of
which he has either just quaffed, or poured forth as a libation.
The second also holds a *kylix*, and is dancing with more energy
than his fellow. He is followed by a younger man with black
beard and red necklace, also carried away by Bacchanalian furor.
The three with the *tutulus* may be priests, yet that head-dress in
the painted tombs is sometimes given to males who have no
distinctive mark of the sacerdotal character.[8] Four of these
figures have a cloth wrapped round the loins, two are entirely
naked, save that their legs are cased in long peaked boots, such
as are worn by the women in the tombs of the Morto and Moribondo, and such as came again into fashion in Italy during the
middle ages. The procession is brought up by two slaves, who
are differently attired from the rest, without chaplets or necklaces, or even boots, but who wear a close-fitting jacket, or
spencer; both carry wine-jugs, and one bears a large *krater* on his
shoulder. The jugs and drinking-bowls are precisely similar to
those which modern excavations are bringing to light in abundance; the *krater* is somewhat peculiar in form. Why the fifer
alone in this procession is nameless is not easy to say, for even
the dog under the foot of the leading figure has its appellation
inscribed.

On the other side of the painted door on this wall is a bearded
figure in red *pallium*, and with a pair of chaplets round his head,
who from his attitude appears to represent some one in authority,
commanding the slave in the corner, who bears several branches
of trees in each hand, to follow the Bacchic dance. He appears
to have just arisen from a couch, where the slave has probably
been fanning him with the boughs.

The scene on the right of the entrance is difficult of explana-

---

[8] The *tutulus* is described by Varro (de
Ling. Lat. VII. 44) as a sort of *meta* or
cone, worn on the heads of priests. Festus
tells us it was the head-dress of the Flam-
inicæ, who wore their hair piled up above
their head, and bound round with a purple
fillet; and also a woollen cap of the same
form as the Flamines and Pontifices used.
Varro adds that matrons who wore their
hair twisted round the top of their heads,
applied to it the same appellation. The
tutulus appears to have been worn by
Etruscan women and girls of all classes in
very early times; as we find it continually
represented in the most archaic wall-
paintings, and it seems to disappear as
Etruscan art became subject to that of
Greece.

tion. It represents an old man, naked, holding in one hand a
forked rod ; and standing before a low stool, on which a boy, also
naked, is about to lay a blue fish. It is possible that the stool is
a sort of altar, and that the boy is making an offering to the other
figure, which may represent a divinity. I have heard it designated "The God of Chastity ; " and there are features which
favour this conjecture. It might be explained could we interpret
a long inscription in Etruscan characters over the head of this
figure.[9]

Around the tomb beneath the ceiling runs a broad band
of thirteen stripes or ribbons of different hues, from which
depend many chaplets, red or blue, over the heads of the
figures.

Over the door is the usual pair of panthers, and in each angle
of the pediment is a recumbent satyr, phallic, with brute-ears,
and human legs terminating in goats' hoofs—figures that seem
taken from the Greek mythology. A goose stands at the feet of
each. In the opposite pediment are a pair of lions *dos-à-dos*, of
deer, and of panthers—all parti-coloured, and curious examples
of Etruscan conventionalities in pictorial art.

The paintings in this tomb are of a more quaint and archaic
character than those in any other sepulchre in this necropolis ; and
they bear a closer affinity than any other Etruscan paintings yet
discovered, both in design and colouring, to the remarkable scenes
in the Grotta Campana at Veii—unquestionably the most ancient
specimens of pictorial art extant in Italy or in Europe. The
resemblance in the form of the horses has already been mentioned ;
it may be seen also in the parti-coloured animals, especially the
stags, in the inner pediment. The peculiarities in the human
figures are the exaggerated development of the thighs and buttocks,
the meagre waists, the round shoulders, the disproportioned
limbs, and attenuated extremities. In the general contour of the
bodies, and the elongated form of the eyes, there is some similarity
to the black figured vases of the Archaic Greek style. Yet it
cannot be said that these paintings betray a Greek influence.
The points of resemblance are rather such as they have in
common with other ancient works, executed in a like infantile
condition of art. The art they exhibit, in fact, is more nearly
allied to the Egyptian than to the Greek, yet differs essentially

[9] In our present *ignorance* of the Etruscan language, all attempts at translating
this or other inscriptions, except proper
names or oft-recurring formulæ, must be
mere guess-work.

from both. It may more correctly be characterized as the primitive style of Etruscan art.[1]

Moore to the west, or towards the centre of the Montarozzi, is the

Grotta del Barone,

or "Grotta del Ministro," as it is otherwise called, because it was discovered by Baron Stackelberg, and Chevalier Kestner, the late Hanoverian minister at Rome.[2] It is remarkable for the brilliancy of its colours, and for the simplicity of its subjects, which are contained in a single frieze of figures, about thirty inches high, bounded above and below by a broad band of variegated stripes. On the inner wall are a man and boy, both wearing a *pallium* over the left shoulder; the latter playing the double-pipes; the former, with blue hair, or it may be a cap, and black beard, has his arm round the boy's neck, and is offering a *kylix* to a dignified female figure, who with both arms raised seems to reject the gift. She is draped to her heels in a long white *chiton*, bordered with brown, and wears pointed bright blue boots, and a lofty cap or *tutulus*, from which depends a red mantle, not shrouding but displaying her form. She is adorned with necklace and earrings, and with a broad *ampyx* or frontlet of gold, which seems to mark her as a goddess, or at least as a priestess.[3] On each side of this

[1] Gerhard (Ann. Inst. 1831, p. 319) thinks this tomb displays archaic Greek art, partaking of the Etruscan manner, and with a rudeness in the countenances and drapery rather Tyrrhene than Greek. Yet Brunn (Ann. Inst. 1866, p. 423) and Helbig (Ann. Inst. 1863, p. 343) can perceive but very slight traces of Greek influence in these paintings. For other notices see Ann. Inst. 1829, p. 106, *et seq.*; Gell's Rome, I. p. 282, *et seq.*; Micali, Ant. Pop. Ital. III. p. 102, tav. LXVII. 5, 6. Copies of the paintings exist in the British Museum, and also in the Vatican, and have been engraved in the Museo Gregoriano, I. tav. CIII. The illustrations given by Mrs. Hamilton Gray (Sepulchres of Etruria, pp. 179, 183) are caricatures, such as ladies only dare indulge in.

[2] This tomb is 15 feet by 13, and of the usual height, from 6 to 8 feet. It was opened in 1827.

[3] By some she has been supposed to represent Ceres, or Cybele, or Proserpine; by others a priestess, as well from her broad *ampyx*, or frontlet, as from her high cap, or *tutulus*. The latter, however, cannot have been a distinctive mark of sacredness or divinity, since it was the head-dress of Etruscan women generally in very early days, as is abundantly proved by the most archaic painted tombs of Corneto. Nor does the frontlet afford a decided test of the condition of this figure, for though in Greek works of art it was introduced as an attribute of Juno, Venus, and other fair divinities, it was worn also by women, as by Andromache (Iliad XXII, 469), and in these very tombs of Corneto we see it decorating the brows of the *hetæra* in the Grotta Querciola, and of a dancing-girl in the Grotta Francesca. We learn from Aristophanes (Lysist. 1316) that it was the custom of Greek women to bind their hair

group is a man on horseback, and both riders appear from their whips with barbed handles to be preparing to contend in a race for the chaplets or crowns which hang above them.

On the right-hand wall the scene seems to denote a foregone conclusion. The race has apparently terminated, and the competitors, standing by the goal which is indicated by a fillet suspended from the wall, are respectively claiming the prize—each holding up a chaplet to attest his victory. The point in dispute seems to be referred, on the opposite wall, to the decision of the woman or priestess already described, who here stands between the rival horsemen; but to which she awards the prize is not evident, unless her turning her face to one, and her back on the other, decide the question; though, as the artist was obviously unable to depict a figure otherwise than in profile, this was an unavoidable position.

The inner pediment contains a pair of particoloured seahorses and some dolphins, on a ground of grey—a thin solution of black. In the opposite pediment is the usual pair of panthers.

The freshness of the colours in this tomb is remarkable. The blue of the man's hair or cap, of the long-toed boots, and of the borders of the garments, seems actually to have a bloom upon it; whereas in certain other tombs, this is the colour which has most faded. The red is also very strong and bright; that of the horses and of the men's flesh is exactly the same tint. Brown occurs in the *pallia* of the racers and in the border of the woman's *chiton*. The trees which fill up the spaces on the walls, are more correctly delineated than usual, and their leaves are either red, or a faint green—a colour rarely seen in the tombs of Tarquinii.[4] Of the oft-recurring conventionalities and contrasts in colour, which give Etruscan paintings so peculiar a character, this tomb presents excellent specimens—one man having blue, the rest white or yellow hair;[5] and some of the horses having blue hoofs, and all white manes and tails, though their bodies are black or red.

These figures are of very archaic design. Those of the women especially have all the rigidity of very early art, or, as Kestner

---

with the *ampyx* in preparation for the dance.

[4] A decided green is rarely seen in early Etruscan paintings. Perhaps they refrained from using it, because their yellow was thick and heavy, and would not make a brilliant green—brightness and striking contrasts of colour being the great aim of their artists,

often to the neglect of nature and correctness.

[5] The hair was probably coloured yellow, which has turned to a dirty white or grey. So also the ornaments of the female figures, which were doubtless coloured to represent gold.

expresses it, much of the grandiose spirit of the Egyptian and archaic Greek; [6] while the man and boy on the inner wall are stepping out with the ease of more advanced art. But the figures of the racers are very inferior, showing great stiffness and clumsiness, though their horses are drawn with considerable correctness and spirit, and with more compact forms than those in the Grotta delle Iscrizioni. These differences in style have led to the opinion that these figures are not the work of a single artist, or of the same period, and that they have been repainted after the lapse of centuries, and the outlines altered in the process.[7] But all the figures in this tomb are unquestionably referable to the infancy of Etruscan art. There is certainly a great want of distinctness in the outlines, but this appears to me to be owing to the imperfection of the materials used. I see no traces of retouching or repainting, and think that the brown mistiness which envelops the figures may be owing to some preparation used as a ground for the pigments, which ground has changed colour in the course of ages.[8]

Grotta del Mare.

Close to the tomb last described is a small, double-chambered one, called "Tomb of the Sea," probably from the character of its paintings, which are confined to the pediment of the outer chamber, and represent four seahorses—two on each side of a large ornament, which bears some resemblance to a scallop-shell.

Seahorses and other marine animals and emblems are of such frequent occurrence in Etruscan tombs, as well as on sarcophagi and funeral urns, as not to be without a meaning. As already stated, they probably have reference to the passage of the soul to

---

[6] Ann. Inst. 1829, p. 112. Gerhard thinks they are imitations of the Greek, executed by Etruscan artists. Ann. Inst. 1831, p. 319. But later critics see few traces of Greek influence in these paintings. Both Brunn and Helbig pronounce them to be only somewhat subsequent to those in the tombs of the "Iscrizioni" and "Morto." Both regard the composition as more harmonious, and Brunn perceives in the calm attitudes of the figures the influence of sculpture. Ann. Inst. 1866, p. 424 (Brunn); 1870, p. 47 (Helbig). nckelmann (Storia delle Arti, lib. III.

c. 2, § 24), speaks of similar female figures of Egyptian rigidity, placed motionless among a group of dancing-women, in certain painted tombs of Tarquinii open in his day; and he took them for divinities.

[7] Ann. Inst. 1829, p. 113—Kestner.

[8] For further notices of this tomb see Micali, Ant. Pop. Ital. III. p. 102, who also gives an illustration of a portion of its paintings (tav. LXVII.). The best copies are preserved in the Museo Gregoriano, and have been published in the work of that name. I. tav. C.

another state of existence, according to the general belief of the ancients that the disembodied spirit had to cross a lake or river on its way to its future abode. By some they have been regarded as symbols of demons or infernal monsters. It seems not improbable that in some cases they may be emblems of the maritime power of Etruria, who long ruled the waves, and gave her name in ancient times to that portion of the Mediterranean which separates Italy from Spain.

GROTTA FRANCESCA.

The tomb of this name, which is also called the " Grotta Giustiniani," from a young lady who was present at its opening, is not far from the group just described.[9] The walls are sadly dilapidated, so that the greater part of the figures which once adorned the tomb are effaced. Here, as in the Grotta Barone, no feasting is depicted, but only the dances and sports which attended the funerals of the Etruscans. On the inner wall, the principal figures are two women, playing, one the double-pipes, the other the castanets; the latter wears the *ampyx* or frontlet, and from her dress and attitude, as she rests one hand on her hip, while she brandishes the castanets with the other, might pass as the prototype of the modern *maja* of Andalucia. Her companion the *tibicina*, has yet more of a modern air; pipes and bare head excepted, she is just such a dame as a few years ago you might have met any day in Regent Street. Nothing is new under the sun—shawls, pelerines, and flowered gowns with deep flounces and ribbon borders, seem to have been as well known in Etruria twenty-two or three centuries ago, as they are to us.[1]

I cannot say as much of the dress of the two men on this wall, which would scarcely be deemed becoming now-a-days. He on foot, with the crook in his hand, has nothing but a blue *chlamys*

---

[9] This tomb was discovered in 1833 by Chevalier Kestner. It is 14 feet by 12, and of the usual height. It faces S.S.W. The beam of the ceiling is only marked out, not relieved; and the rafters are represented by broad stripes of red paint. In the left-hand corner is a rock-hewn bench for a sarcophagus, or for the corpse.

[1] Both these women wear necklaces and bracelets. She with the castanets has blue eyes and red hair. Her *chiton*, or gown, which reaches only half down her leg, is yellow, covered with red spots, and terminates in a deep flounce of the same colour, but studded with much smaller spots. She wears a red jacket, with white shoulder straps, the jacket being fastened round her waist by a white belt, perhaps representing silver. Her companion also wears a yellow spotted *chiton*, with a red mantle, bordered with white, over her shoulders—in form just like a modern pelerine.

or shawl over his shoulders; he driving the *biga* in the opposite corner wears simply a short white tunic or shirt, so short that it scarcely serves its purpose; each from the middle downwards is bare, or, as Hood would say,—

> " Thence, further down, the native red prevails
> Of his own naked fleecy hosiery."

The horses in the chariot are one red, the other blue, and their tails are curiously knotted or clubbed, as they are often represented on the painted vases. In the pediment are two blue panthers, one on each side of the usual bracket.

Turn to the right-hand wall. What spirit, what life, what nature, in this dancing-girl! Her gown of gauze or muslin floats around her in airy folds; the broad blue ribbon which binds her " bonny brown hair," and the red scarf hanging from one shoulder across her bosom, stream behind her with the rapidity of her movements; while she droops her face and raises her arm to give expression to her steps. Her other arm is a-kimbo, so that you might declare she was dancing the *salterella*. For spirit, ease, and grace she has no rival among the *ballerine* of Tarquinii. Her dress is peculiar—I remember nothing like it on painted wall or vase. It is as modern as that of her neighbours. It is hard to believe she has been dancing in this tomb for many centuries. She has now unfortunately but a short time to live; she will soon take her last step—from the wall. Her partner in the dance is almost obliterated, though enough remains to mark his attitude as easy and graceful. Next to him are some fragments of another woman; but everything else on this wall is effaced.

The opposite wall is also much dilapidated, but several figures are traceable. A man and woman standing in the corner, in long, broad-bordered robes, do not seem to be dancing. Hard by are two men half draped, apparently encountering a wild boar, or some animal no longer visible, for one of them holds a spear as if in the act of piercing it; behind them stand two bay horses, from which they may have dismounted.

The figures in this tomb, though rudely executed, show much more freedom and are of later date than those in most of the tombs of the Græco-Etruscan class in this necropolis. They appear decidedly later even than those in the Grotta Querciola.[2]

---

[2] For particulars of this tomb see Bull. Inst. 1833, p. 74, *et seq.* Ann. Inst. 1834, p. 190, *et seq.* Bull. Inst. 1875, p. 204.

GROTTA DELLE BIGHE.

Not far from the Grotta Francesca is the "Tomb of the Chariots," or "GROTTA STACKELBERG," as it has been styled from the gentleman who first copied and described its paintings.

Though the scenes in this tomb are in many parts greatly injured, a glance suffices to show that in its original state it must have been more richly decorated than any other painted sepulchre in this necropolis. Walls and ceiling must have blazed with colour. Like the Querciola tomb, this has a double frieze of figures; but here the arrangement is reversed, and the smaller frieze is above the larger. As in that tomb, the end-wall is here occupied by a banquet, and the side-walls by dances, of very similar character.[3]

This banquet differs from those in the tombs already described, in the absence of the fair sex; so that it is rather a *symposium* than an ordinary feast. The absence of edibles on the tables confirms this view. The guests, however, though all males, recline in pairs, on three couches; and are attended by two naked slaves and by a *subulo* playing his pipes. Beneath the couches are several blue ducks.

The dancers are of both sexes, distinguished by their colour; the women draped with tunic and *chlamys*, and wearing the *tutulus* on their heads; the men with merely a slight scarf round their loins. All, as well as the banqueters, are crowned with myrtle. In action and character they are very similar to those in the Grotta del Triclinio, yet inferior in spirit. One girl, however, playing the pipes is full of life, a true

> meretrix tibicina cujus
> Ad strepitum salias terræ gravis.

The dance was continued on three sides of the tomb, but is now scarcely distinguishable on more than one, the paintings having been greatly injured by the damp.

The ground of this frieze has the peculiarity of being a deep red; whereas in the upper and smaller frieze it is left of the colour of the rock, a creamy white. This small band is more

---

[3] This tomb was discovered in 1827. It is about 15 ft. square, 6 ft. high at the sides, and 8 ft. 6 in. from the floor to the central beam of the ceiling. This beam is painted with ivy-leaves, and circles, not unlike compass-dials; the slopes on either hand are chequered with various colours, as in the Grotta del Triclinio. The lower frieze of figures is 3 ft. in height, the upper only 18 inches.

remarkable than the other. It contains a multitude of figures scarcely more than a foot in height, and not fewer originally than one hundred in number, though not so many are now remaining. They represent the public, probably the funeral, games of the Etruscans.[4] On one wall are several *bigæ*, or two-horse chariots —whence the appellation of the tomb—not in the act of racing, but apparently preparing for the contest. The horses are red, blue, or white—a variety of colour introduced for the sake of contrast. On the other walls are figures on horseback—others boxing with the *cestus*—wrestling—hurling the *discus*—leaping with poles—while some, with helmets, spears, and shields, seem preparing for the Pyrrhic dance or for gladiatorial combats. All these were the games of the Greeks also, save the last, which were unknown to that people, but had their origin in Etruria, and were borrowed thence by the Romans.[5] Among these figures are two serpent-charmers, each with a reptile round one arm, and a rod in the other hand;[6] and this presents a fresh link between Etruria and the East, besides affording a confirmation of the fact, made known by other monuments and by history, that the control of serpents was an art cultivated in Etruria—probably as a means by which the priesthood impressed a sense of its superiority on the minds of the vulgar.

Most of these figures are naked; a few only have red or blue

[4] If such scenes as these, which occur frequently in the painted tombs of Etruria, especially in those of Chiusi, be more than representations of the solemn games held at funerals, it is probable that they not merely typify the state on which the souls of the blessed had entered, but portray the actual pursuits in which they were supposed to be engaged. Virgil gives authority for this suggestion, when he describes the delights of the Elysian fields as similar to those the blessed had enjoyed on earth—

Pars in gramineis exercent membra palæstris
Contendunt ludo, et fulvâ luctantur arenâ,
Pars pedibus plaudunt choreas, et carmina, dicunt.—Æn. VI. 642.

And again,

quæ gratia currûm,
Armorumque fuit vivis, quæ cura nitentes
Pascere equos, cadem sequitur tellure repostos.—Æn. VI. 653.

[6] See page 71. The figures with spears in this scene may be intended to represent

the ἀκόντιον, or contest of hurling the dart, which was one of the five games of the Greek *pentathlon* : the other four—leaping, running, casting the quoit, and wrestling—being also here represented. The *pentathlon* was introduced at the public games of Greece, in the 18th Olympiad (708 B.C.) ; boxing and horse and chariot-racing were subsequent novelties. Müller (Etrusk. IV. 1, 8, 9,) considers that the Etruscans were imitators of the Greeks in their public games, with the exception of gladiatorial combats, which were peculiarly their own.

[5] This seems to have escaped the observation of every one who has written on the tomb—at least I can find no statement to this effect. The figures are not so represented in any copies of these paintings that I have seen—not even in those on the same scale, in the Vatican and the British Museum, where what they hold in their hands rather resembles the so-called *acrostolion*, or scroll of victory, often depicted on vases. But to me it seems clearly to have been intended for a serpent.

tunics. In the same frieze at the corners of the walls are stands, or platforms, on which spectators of both sexes, richly clad, are seated, looking on at the sports; while beneath them the lower orders, mostly naked, are seen reclining on the ground.   There is nothing here to give us a high idea of the morality or decency of the Etruscan *plebs*.[7]

In the pediment above the banquet is a large wide-mouthed *krater*, supported by two small naked figures, each with a jug and dipping-ladle; and each angle of the pediment is occupied by a sitting figure, half-draped, garlanded for the banquet, pledging his opposite neighbour with true convivial earnestness. In the pediment over the doorway is the usual pair of panthers, and also a pair of geese; which, like the former, may be regarded as guardians of the tomb.   Remember

> " Those consecrated geese in orders,
>   That to the Capitol were warders;
>   And being then upon patrol,
>   With noise alone beat off the Gaul."

The correctness, freedom, and spirit of these paintings mark them as of a good school of Etruscan art, and of a later date than those in most of the painted tombs of Tarquinii, always excepting the Orcus, the Typhon, and the Cardinal. The relative position, however, that they occupy among the other wall-paintings of Etruria on this site, has been disputed. Professor Gerhard pronounces them to be of the purest archaic Greek style, and of earlier date than those of the Triclinio and Querciola, which display a free and perfect manner, whereas these partake of the primitive manner of Greek art.[8] Dr. Brunn also places them next the Grotta Barone in point of antiquity, and regards them as decidedly earlier than the Triclinio and Querciola, suggesting that the fineness and delicacy of execution for which they are remarkable makes them appear less archaic than they really are.[9] Dr. Helbig, on the contrary, considers them as of a more

---

[7] When Tarquinius Priscus built the Circus Maximus at Rome, be had seats constructed for the Patres and Equites, raised 12 feet from the ground. Liv. I. 35; cf. Dionys. III. 68. But the seats here depicted are too low for a man to stand upright beneath them. The outlines of the figures in this frieze have been scratched in before the colours were laid on, so that where the colour has entirely faded, the figure may yet be clearly distinguished. Here is an analogy to the vases of the earlier styles, with this difference, that the outlines on the vases are scratched *after* the paint has been laid on, for the sake of force and detail.

[8] Ann. Inst. 1831, p. 319.

[9] Ann. Inst. 1866, p. 425.

advanced period of art, and less archaic in character than the
paintings in the Triclinio, though earlier than those in the Querciola.[1]   To me it appears that the figures in the lower frieze are
much more archaic than those in the upper, which show more
freedom and spirit, as well as more Greek feeling, but whether
they are of later date, or by a different hand, I do not pretend to
determine.[2]

At the farther end of the Montarozzi, just above the spot where
the high road to Viterbo forks to Civita Vecchia, is another
painted tomb, the

GROTTA DEL PULCINELLA,

called also "Tomba Baietti" from its discoverer, who opened
it in 1871. It faces S.S.W. It is of very small dimensions,
hardly ten feet square. On the wall opposite the entrance one
figure only is depicted, that of a naked man, dancing, with
one hand to his head, amid red trees with blue leaves. Several
red chaplets are suspended from the wall, and in the centre
hangs a heptachord lyre to which a *plectron* is attached by a
string.[3]

On the wall to the right five figures are still extant—first a
male almost obliterated; then another man with a boy before
him, whose shoulder he seems to be striking with a long lance or
pole, while the boy appears to be claiming protection from a
third man on horseback, who is holding a branch over his own
head, as though it were a whip. His horse is painted pale blue
or green, with red mane, tail, and hoofs. Of the last figure on
this wall the lower limbs only are preserved.[4]

Turning to the opposite wall, you see a man dancing with

---

[1] Ann. Inst. 1863, p. 352 ; cf. 1870,
p. 64. Bunsen (Ann. Inst. 1834, p. 57)
gives the preference to this tomb over
the Querciola, as exhibiting the beauty of
the Greek ideal in the countenances, movements, and attitudes.

[2] Helbig (op. cit. pp. 57—63) considers
the evident archaicism in the lower hand
to be conventional, but does not attempt to
explain the absence of this feature in the
upper frieze. Illustrations of the paintings
in this tomb are given in the Museo Gregor.
tav. 101, and in Micali, Ant. Pop. Ital. tav.
68. Copies are also preserved in the British

and the Gregorian Museums.

[3] Brizio takes this man for a *cithar-
ædus*, about to take his lyre from the wall.
Bull. Inst. 1873, p. 75.

[4] Brizio (loc. cit.) takes the man with
the long pole to be the gymnasiarch,
teaching two pupils how to leap, and cites
similar scenes in the François and Casuccini
tombs at Chiusi ; but it is not easy to
accept this interpretation, seeing that two
of the figures on this wall are now almost
obliterated. The man on horseback, as he
suggests, probably represents the horse-
races held in honour of the deceased.

energetic action in front of another armed and mounted on a white horse, whose mane, tail, and hoofs are coloured blue, and whose neck he appears to be caressing. The warrior wears a white helmet with a blue crest, a cuirass or jerkin, painted deep red, as if to indicate leather, and greaves coloured blue to represent steel. He carries also a circular shield, deep red, with a white border—probably indicating leather with a metal rim. The next figure is bearded, and wears on his head a *tutulus*, or rather a foolscap, striped white and red, and tipped with a tassel; his jacket is short, close-fitting, and chequered black, red, and white, and over it hangs something like a tippet with a long fringe. From this fantastical costume, not unlike that of the Pulcinella of the Italian stage, the tomb has taken its name.[5] This and the warrior are the only figures that are clad; all the rest in this tomb are naked. Trees as usual intervene between the figures, and chaplets hang from their branches and from the walls above.

These figures are painted on a stucco surface, and rudely and carelessly drawn. They have been sadly injured, but enough remains to show them to be very quaint and curious, and of an early period of art, though not in the most archaic style.

In the pediment, on each side of the bracket, is a yellow lion, with open mouth, red tongue, and blue mane.[6]

———

Among this group of painted tombs was one which, so far as I can learn, I was the first to describe, and I took on myself the privilege of naming it, from its most remarkable feature, GROTTA DELLA SCROFA NERA. As it is no longer open, and has never been under lock and key, I shall transfer my account of it to the Appendix to this Chapter, in case it should at some future day be brought again to light.

GROTTA DEL CITAREDO.

A tomb with paintings of a remarkable character was discovered in this necropolis in 1862, which, from a prominent figure on its walls, received the appellation of " Tomb of the Lyrist." The

---

[5] Brizio takes this figure to represent a *histrio*, or mimer. He is the only figure in the tomb who wears a beard. In the tombs of Chiusi where dwarfs are introduced, they have large beards, and are dressed somewhat like this Pulcinella.

[6] For a description of this tomb, see Bull. Inst. 1873, pp. 73-79. E. Brizio, in this article, refers the paintings to the first period of Etruscan art, but considers them later than those in G. Iscrizioni, G. Morto, and G. Barone.

paintings it contained were of so much beauty and interest as to
merit a description, although they are now things of the past; for
the tomb has been reclosed, whether ever again to admit the
light of day is quite uncertain.

The figures on its walls were all those of dancers, with the
exception of a pair of naked pugilists flanking the entrance.   On
the wall to the right were five men, alternating with   shrubs

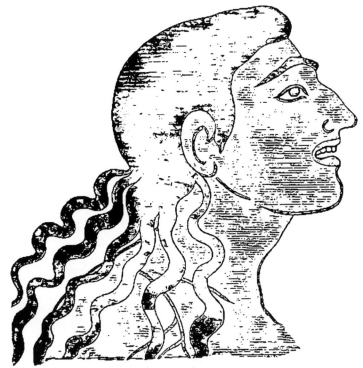

HEAD OF THE CITHARŒDUS, GROTTA DEL CARDEDO, CORNETO.

hung with fillets and chaplets.   He in the centre was quite nude,
and his fellows had but a light *chlamys* on their shoulders, which
did not conceal their nakedness, and all wore their hair hanging
in long thin curls down their backs.   Two were wreathed with
laurel, one with oak-leaves.   One played the double-pipes, and
another flourished a huge *kylix* over his head, just as an Irishman
in his tipsy jollity might brandish the empty punch-bowl.

On the opposite wall the dance was kept up by four women in
talaric *chitones* of gauze or muslin, which covered but did not
conceal their limbs.   Each wore a light scarf over her shoulders,
and her hair in loose dishevelled masses, which floated on the
wind with the movements of the dance; one of them rattled the

castanets, and another blew the double-pipes.   In the midst of
these nymphs danced a young man, with no covering beyond a
chlamys on his shoulders, his hair in long loose locks, and his
mouth open, indicating that he was accompanying with his voice
the notes he was eliciting from his lyre.   The woodcut shows
the head of this remarkable figure.   The dance was continued
on the inner wall of the tomb, where, on each side of two large

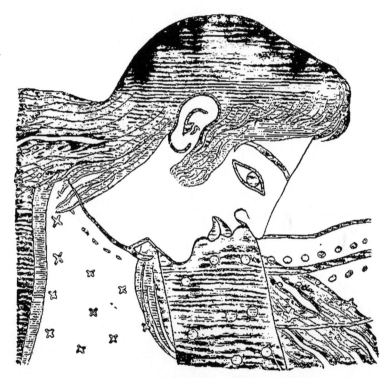

HEAD OF A SALTATRIX, GROTTA DEL CITAREDO, CORNETO.

windows painted on the wall, was another female dancer, in
every respect similar to those just described.   Beyond the usual
snake bracelets, these women wore no ornaments, not even the
customary chaplets or fillets round their heads, but their lips and
cheeks were coloured with vermilion.

   The separation of the sexes in this tomb—the men with a single
exception dancing on one side, the women on the other—is unique
among the numerous similar scenes of merriment in Etruscan
wall-paintings.   The head-dresses also of both—the loose hair
of the women, and the long thin tresses of the men—have no
counterpart in any other painted tomb of Etruria.   Still less in

any other monument of equal antiquity in this land do we find an attempt to express individual character and elevation of feeling, such as are here successfully portrayed in the countenance of the *citharœdus.*

In point of antiquity, the art-critics are agreed in placing this tomb at the head of the second class of Etruscan painted tombs, and pronounce the figures to display a decided advance on those of the most archaic class, both in design and colouring. They consider them to be composed of a strange mixture of Greek and Etruscan elements—the attitudes, the movements, and the design being Etruscan, while the countenances of the *citharœdus* and of some of the other figures manifest the pure beauty of the Greek ideal.[7]

To arrange these painted tombs in the order of their antiquity is no easy task; still more difficult, if not impossible, is it to assign to each its precise date. We must limit our endeavours in this direction to a general classification of these tombs. They may be divided into three classes :—

    1st. The Archaic, or purely Etruscan.
    2nd. The Græco-Etruscan.
    3rd. The Romano-Etruscan.

All critics agree in assigning the first place in point of antiquity to the Grotta delle Iscrizioni and the Grotta del Morto. Then follow the Grotta del Barone, the Grotta del Vecchio, Grotta dei Vasi Dipinti. In the same class I would place the Grotta del Moribondo and Grotta del Pulcinella, ascribing to them a somewhat later date than to the foregoing.

The second class comprehends the Grotta del Citaredo (now reclosed), the Grotta del Triclinio, Grotta delle Bighe, Grotta Querciola, Grotta della Pulcella, Grotta del Letto Funebre, Grotta dei Cacciatori, Grotta Francesca, and Grotta della Scrofa Nera (now reclosed).

In the third class are Grotta dell' Orco, Grotta degli Scudi, Grotta Bruschi (now reclosed), Grotta del Cardinale, and Grotta del Tifone.[8]

---

[7] Ann. Inst. 1863, p. 344 et seq.; Bull. Inst. 1863, p. 107, et seq. (Helbig.); Ann. Inst. 1866, p. 425 (Brunn). For illustrations see Mon. Ined. Inst. VI. tav. 79.— tav. d'agg. M.

[8] For able criticisms on the character and antiquity of these painted tombs, see the articles in the Annals of the Institute, 1863, pp. 336–360 (Helbig) ; 1866, pp. 422–442 (Brunn) ; 1870, pp. 5–74 (Helbig). These distinguished critics agree in the main points of the classification, and

To the precise date of these paintings we have no direct clue. Those of the earliest class we can only compare with the archaic productions of Hellenic art, which extend back to an undefined antiquity, and come down almost to the full development of that art in the fifth century B.C. Though we cannot fix the precise limits of the second class, we are not wholly without data for our guidance. We can assert that they must be later than Polygnotus, who flourished about the middle of that century, because he was the first, Pliny informs us, to draw women with transparent garments, to represent figures with open mouths, displaying the teeth, and to give expression and character to the countenance;[9] and we know that they must be prior to the sixth century of Rome, to which period we must assign the paintings of the third class. In this direction we have a landmark in the celebrated *cista* of the Kircherian Museum, which dates from the end of the fifth century of Rome, and which, though found at Palestrina, displays an art almost purely Greek, and yet so closely allied to Etruscan art on bronze works of the same description, as not to be distinguished from it.[1]

differ principally as to the position to be assigned to the Grotta delle Bighe ; Brunn ranking it with the Grotta del Citarœdo, Holbig placing it after the G. Triclinio and before the G. Querciola.

[9] Plin. N. H. XXXV., 25.

[1] Ann. Inst., 1863, p. 357. Some have taken the beard as a test of the antiquity of early Italian monuments, on the ground that prior to the year of Rome 454 there were no barbers in Italy ; for in that year, says Varro (de Re Rust. II. cap. 11), "barbers first came from Sicily, and that there were none in earlier times is indicated by the statues of the ancients, which for the most part have large beards." Compare Chrysippus (ap. Athen. XIII. 18), who says the practice of shaving originated in the time of Alexander, and Pliny (N. H. VII. 59), who adds that Scipio Africanus was the first Roman who shaved daily. But this test, as applied to Etruscan monuments, is not to be relied on. Not because the Etruscans are known to have used depilatories of pitch instead of razors, and to have had houses for the removal of the hair, as the Greeks had barbers' shops (Athen. XII. 14 ; Ælian. de Nat. Anim. XIII. 27). But because in some of the earliest monuments of Etruria, such as the paintings in the Grotta

Campana at Veii, and the archaic *cippi* of Chiusi, no beards are introduced ; while on others of late date, even of Roman times, like the Grotta Dipinta at Corvetri, figures are represented with beards, and these not mythological personages, like some who are bearded in the Orcus and Typhon-tombs in this necropolis of Tarquinii. Moreover, it is highly probable that the figures in Etruscan scenes of festivity were often represented beardless, to indicate the eternal youth they were supposed to enjoy in Elysium. So that the fact of a monument having all its male figures beardless, does not necessarily stamp it as subsequent to 300 B.C. Notwithstanding the weighty authority of Dr. Brunn in its favour (Ann. Inst. 1860, p. 488), I cannot but regard this test of the beard as a very unsafe guide to the relative antiquity of Etruscan monuments, whether of painting or of sculpture, in comparison with that afforded by the style of art.

In our inquiry into the antiquity of Greek monuments, we have certain grand landmarks for our guidance ; and though it may well be that art in Etruria was less rapid in its development than in Greece, yet, as we cannot doubt that in very early times it was subjected to Hellenic influences,

It will be observed that the tombs of the third class differ from all the rest in making a direct reference to Etruscan mythology. The figures in the earlier sepulchres represent creatures of this world in the most joyous moments of life—feasting, dancing, hunting, sporting—though there are valid reasons for regarding such scenes as descriptive of funeral rites and customs. But the later tombs disclose another state of existence ; with few exceptions, the scenes are no longer of this world—the principal actors are divinities or demons—the figures are disembodied spirits. Why are such representations not found in the earlier tombs ? It can hardly be accidental. The demonology of the Etruscans must have existed from the remotest period of their history, yet it is not set forth on their earlier monuments. On the most ancient pottery, whether relieved, scratched, or painted, we rarely find more than detached figures of divinities—as frequently perhaps symbolised as portrayed. So also in the earlier works in metal and stone—the religious creed is rather hinted at, and obscurely, than clearly expressed. It is only on urns, sarcophagi, mirrors, and other monuments of later date, that we see *genii* or other divinities taking part in human affairs.

The only solution I can suggest is, that in the earlier ages of Etruria the system of religion was thoroughly oriental—like her art, it savoured of Egypt—the people were so enthralled by the hierarchy, that they may not have dared to represent, perhaps scarcely to contemplate, the mysteries of their creed ; but that after their intercourse with Greece, their religion, as well as their arts, gradually lost that orientalism which had characterised it ; the distinctions of esoteric and exoteric were in great measure broken down, and the people dared to look within the veil, hitherto lifted by none but the augur and aruspex.

In contemplating these painted walls, the question naturally arises—Are they fair specimens of Etruscan art ?—are we justified in judging from them of the state of pictorial art among this ancient people, any more than we should be in drawing conclusions of modern Italian art from the painted decorations of chambers, from sign-posts, or from stage-scenery ? Can we suppose that any but inferior or provincial artists would con-

whether we regard the recorded settlement of Demaratus at Tarquinii about 657 B.C. as history or fable, and that it continued to feel those influences in a greater or less degree throughout the subsequent course of its existence, we are justified in applying to its productions the same tests as we should apply to works of Greek art, making such allowances for a somewhat slower development, as we should make in the case of works of art from Greek colonies in other parts of Italy.

descend to apply their pencil to the walls of a tomb, only for their work and their reputation to be buried from the world? Micali thought all these wall-paintings were the work of provincial artists;[2] but I cannot agree with him. With regard to this individual site, it is the cemetery of Tarquinii, the ecclesiastical if not the political metropolis of Etruria, the source of her religious doctrines and rites, the fount of the Etruscan Discipline; the city which long maintained an extensive intercourse with Greece, and whither Eucheir and Engrammos of Corinth resorted— whether actual beings or symbols of the arts implied in their names, it matters not. Here, if anywhere in Etruria, art must have flourished. Nothing can here be termed provincial. Moreover, to take a more general view, there was a sacredness attaching to tombs among the nations of antiquity, to which we are strangers, and which must be realised by us before we can judge correctly on this matter. The Pyramids attest to all time the honour paid by the Egyptians to their dead. The Greeks, besides their recorded opinions, have left palpable memorials of the importance they attached to well-furnished and decorated sepulchres: to such a pitch, indeed, were they inclined to carry their extravagance, that their legislators were at times obliged to curb it by sumptuary laws for the dead. The Romans raised still prouder *mausolea*—such enormous piles as serve their descendants for fortresses and amphitheatres. Why then should not the wealthy princes of Tarquinii have engaged the most celebrated artists of their day, to decorate their family sepulchres? They furnished them with treasures of gold and jewellery, and with the choicest specimens of fictile and toreutic art—why should they have been content with inferior performances on the walls? I see no reason to doubt that these paintings are the works of the Giottos, the Signorellis, the Raphaels, the Caraccis, of Etruria.[3] Analogy confirms this view; for Nicias, the Athenian, an artist of such eminence as to be extolled by Praxiteles,[4] did not disdain to decorate the walls of sepulchres with his pencil.[5]

[2] Micali, Ant. Pop. Ital. II. p. 246.

[3] Gerhard (Bull. Inst. 1834, p. 12) is of opinion, from the strong Greek character of certain of these paintings, that they are the work of Greeks resident in Etruria, influenced by the native taste; and Bunsen (Ann. Inst. 1834, pp. 57, 74) thinks they are by Greeks, or by native artists who had studied in Greece, or in her colonies in Italy.

[4] Plin. XXXV. 40.

[5] Pausan. VII. 22, 6. See page 38 of this work. We are not told that Polygnotus, the celebrated wall-painter of Greece, of whose works at Delphi Pausanias gives a detailed account (X. 25—31), ever exercised his brush in the adornment of tombs. From the paintings in certain of these tombs, however, we may form some idea of the character and style of his works.

I have described all the painted tombs now to be seen in the necropolis of Tarquinii. Many others have been discovered in past ages; but some have been immediately ruined by the admission of the light and atmosphere; others have fallen more gradually to decay; some have been wantonly destroyed; and a few have been re-closed, lost sight of, and forgotten. Some, again, of late years have been purposely closed by the excavators immediately after their discovery, as a future means of obtaining money. It is no uncommon thing for a stranger on making the tour of the Montarozzi to be accosted by some labouring man, who engages to open for him a painted tomb, "which nobody else has seen," for a douceur of from 20 to 50 francs. In this way the disappearance of the Scrofa Nera and other painted tombs in this necropolis may be accounted for. Records of not a few lost tombs are in existence. Among the earliest found was one opened in 1699, close to the walls of Corneto, in the *tenuta* Tartaglia, whence it has received its name. It was illustrative of the religious creed of the Etruscans, representing souls in the charge of winged genii. Three of these souls, in the form of naked men, were suspended by their hands from the roof of the chamber, as appears in the copy that has been preserved; and the demons stood by, one with a mallet, some with torches, and some with singular nondescript instruments, with which they seemed about to torture their victims. To a Protestant the scene was suggestive of the horrors of the Inquisition; to a Roman Catholic of the pains of purgatory.[6]

Another early account of the now lost tombs of Tarquinii was written about the year 1756, by an Augustin monk of Corneto, Padre Giannicola Forlivesi, who, at a time when Etruria was little regarded in Europe, interested himself in her antiquities, and wrote a minute account of the painted tombs of this necropolis.[7] This work, which has never been printed, was some years

[6] Passeri (Paralipom. ad Dempst., p. 139) regarded it as a scene in the Etruscan purgatory. Notices and illustrations of these curious paintings will be found in Buonarroti, p. 42, ad Dempst. II. tab. LXXXVIII.; Gori, Mus. Etrus. III. p. 91.

[7] He described several tombs no longer to be found. One was decorated with a painting of Cybele, with turreted crown, and a spear in her hand, seated on a car drawn by four lions, and preceded by twelve musicians, with fifes, cymbals, and tambours — probably the Corybantes or Galli, who danced at her festivals; for they used such instruments, though the former at least always danced armed like the Curetes of Crete.—Strab. X. p. 468, et seq. Cf. Horace, Od. I. xvi. 7. In another tomb was depicted Ceres, drawn by a pair of serpents. In a third was represented a galley, with oars and sails, with a king seated on the deck between two women, while Tritons were sporting in the waves, and blowing shell-trumpets. In a

since in the hands of Avvolta of Corneto; but he lost it by lending
it, and whether it was still in existence he could not tell.   The
marrow of it, however, has been extracted by Gori, who acknowledges his obligations to the Augustin;[8] and Avvolta also has
given to the world a sketch of its contents.[9]

In the work of Byres, already mentioned, plates are given of
several other painted tombs, once existing in this necropolis, but
no longer to be seen ; and the peculiar characteristics of Etruscan
art are better preserved in these than in his illustrations of the
Grotta Cardinale.[1]

Other painted tombs, no longer visible, have been known in
our own time.   There was one thirty or forty years ago near the
Grotta del Morto, which had a pillar in the centre, niches around
the tomb, and large figures painted on the walls, with Etruscan
inscriptions attached.   The surface had so much decayed that
the paintings were almost destroyed, but the figure of a woman in
magnificent apparel, with a very remarkable head-dress, was then
visible.[2]   The tomb is now lost sight of.

Another painted tomb was opened, near the Grotta Querciola,
in 1844.   It contained but four figures, rudely executed—two of
human beings, two of demons.   The former were taking a last
farewell of each other ; a grim Charun, mallet in hand, was
seizing one of them to lead him away, while a similar demon
stood at the gate of Orcus, resting on his hammer, which was
encircled by a serpent—a representation quite unique.   The
meaning of the scene seems to be this.   One soul is borne by the
messenger of Death to the other world ; the other has yet to live
awhile, as is gracefully indicated by the repose of his attendant
spirit.   This tomb was left open but a short time, during which
a record of it was fortunately preserved by Dr. Henzen,[3] and
then it was re-closed; *per le vigne*—"for the sake of the vineyards."

Several other painted tombs, opened of late years, and now

---

fourth was a procession of nine "priests,"
with lotus-flowers, birds, or vases in their
hands.   But the most remarkable scene
described by the Padre was a man crowned
with laurel, seated on an elephant, and
attended by a number of spearmen on foot.
This probably represented the Indian
Bacchus.

[5] Gori, Mus. Etrus. III. p. 90 ; cf. Maffei, Osservaz. Litter. V. p. 312.

[9] Bull. Inst. 1831, p. 91.

[1] For an account of these tombs, see the
Appendix, Note III.

[2] Bull. Inst. 1832, p. 214.

[3] Bull. Inst. 1844, p. 97.   This appears
to be the same tomb described by Dr.
Brunn, Ann. Inst. 1866, p. 438, tav.
d'A. W., but neither in the article nor in
the illustration is a serpent introduced.
The tomb was first opened in 1832, and it
is possible that after the lapse of 34 years,
the serpent may have been obliterated.

reclosed, have been described by Signor E. Brizio, in the Bulletins of the Archæological Institute of Rome.[4]

It is worthy of remark, that all the painted tombs now open are beneath the level surface; not one has a superincumbent tumulus, though such monuments abound on this site. More than six hundred, it is said, are to be counted on the Montarozzi

alone; and they may be considered to have been originally much more numerous. They seem to have been all circular, surrounded at the base with masonry, on which the earth was piled up into a cone, and surmounted probably by a lion or sphinx in stone, or by a *cippus*, inscribed with the name of the family buried beneath. After the lapse of so many ages, not one retains its original form, the cones of earth having crumbled down into shapeless mounds, though several have remains of masonry at their base. One is nearly perfect in this respect. It is walled round with travertine blocks, about two feet in length, neatly fitted together, but without cement; forming an architectural decoration which, from its similarity to the mouldings of Norchia and Castel d'Asso, attests its Etruscan origin. It rises to the height of five or six feet,

MOULDING OF THE MAUSOLEO.

and on it rests a shapeless mound, overgrown with broom and lentiscus.[5] The entrance is by a steep passage, leading down to a doorway beneath the belt of masonry. The sepulchral chamber is not in this case remarkable; but beneath a neighbouring tumulus is one of very peculiar character. The rock is hollowed into the shape of a Gothic vault, but the converging sides, instead of meeting in a point, are suddenly carried up perpendicularly, and terminated by a horizontal course of masonry. The form is very primitive, for it is precisely that of the Regulini tomb at Cervetri, one of the most ancient sepulchres of Etruria, and also bears much resemblance to the Cyclopean gallery of Tiryns in Argolis.[6]

[4] See Note IV. in the Appendix to this Chapter.

[5] This tomb is called "Il Mansoleo." Other tumuli, much akin to this, but with some variety in the masonry, were in existence a few years since, but have been destroyed by the peasantry, who, it is to be feared, will soon pull this also to pieces, for the sake of the hewn blocks around it. One had a cone cut into steps, like the tomb at

Bieda, shown in the woodcut at p. 217.

[6] A tomb has been found in this necropolis, vaulted over with a conical cupola, formed by the gradual convergence of horizontal courses of masonry, exactly as in the Treasury of Atreus at Mycenæ. It was about 18 feet in diameter. Gell, Rome, II. p. 106; Mon. Ined. Inst. I. tav. XL. b. 4. It has either been reclosed, or its site is forgotten. I have sought it long in vain.

These tumuli are probably the most ancient description of tomb in Etruria. Such, indeed, was the form of sepulchres among the primitive nations of the world. It varied in different lands. The Egyptians, Assyrians, and Hindoos assumed the pyramid ; while in Asia Minor, and by the early races of Europe —Greeks,[7] Italians, Scythians, Celts, Scandinavians, and Germans—the cone was preferred. The ancient tribes of America

IL MAUSOLEO, ON THE MONTAROZZI.

also adopted the same mode of sepulture ; and the vast pyramids rising from the plains of Mexico and Yucatan,[8] rivalling those of Egypt in dimensions, and the conical mounds of Peru, seem to

[7] Pyramids, however, are found in Greece, though of much inferior size to those of Egypt. Pausanias (II. 25, 7) speaks of one existing in his day on the road from Argos to Epidaurus ; and there are several still extant, the best preserved of which is near Argos. It is 49 feet by 39 at the base, and built of polygonal masonry, inclining to the horizontal and rectangular. A plate and description of it are given by Colonel Mure, in his very interesting Tour in Greece (II., p. 195, et seq.), who ascribes it to the same primitive school of architects that built the Treasury of Atreus.

[8] The two pyramids of the Sun and Moon in the plain of Teotihuacan, are particularly remarkable for their size ; and one of them has shafts and galleries within it, like those which have been discovered in the Pyramids of Egypt. A further analogy with the cemeteries of the old world is displayed in the multitude of smaller pyramids, all sepulchres, ranged in avenues or streets around these colossal monuments. The counterpart of this Micoatl, or "Path of the Dead," may be seen in the Montarozzi of Tarquinii, but still more strikingly in the Banditaccia of Cervetri. See Prescott's Hernan Cortes, II. p. 354-7, and Stephens' Yucatan for a description of these Transatlantic monuments.

attest a relation between the people of the Old and New World. Tumuli were in use among the Lydians, the traditional colonisers of Etruria, and the tombs of the Lydian Kings described by Herodotus and Strabo, which still in hundreds stud the bare ridges between Sardis and the Gygean Lake are—*magna componere parvis*—just like the mounds of the Montarozzi. The Turks call the spot Bin Tépé, or the Thousand Hills. The largest of these tumuli was the sepulchre of Alyattes, the father of Crœsus, and as described by Herodotus it was very like the "Mausoleo" of the Montarozzi; "having a basement composed of huge stones, the rest of the monument being a mound of earth."[9] The description given by Dionysius of the necropolis of Orvinium, a city of the Aborigines, a most ancient people of Italy, long prior to the foundation of the Etruscan state, answers so strikingly to the Montarozzi, that we might imagine he was writing of Tarquinii. His words are—"The foundations of its walls are visible, and certain tombs of manifest antiquity, and inclosures of cemeteries lengthened out in lofty mounds."[1]

It was within one of these tumuli of the Montarozzi that Avvolta, in 1823, discovered "the celebrated virgin tomb which gave rise to all the excavations subsequently made in the neighbourhood of Corneto." The discovery was owing to accident. He was digging into the tumulus for stones to mend a road, when he perceived a large slab of *nenfro*, part of the ceiling of the tomb. Making a hole beneath it, he looked in, and there (to give his own words)—"I beheld a warrior stretched on a couch of rock, and in a few minutes I saw him vanish, as it were, under my eyes; for, as the atmosphere entered the sepulchre, the armour, thoroughly oxydised, crumbled away into most minute particles; so that in a short time scarcely a vestige of what I had seen was left on the couch.[2] . . . Such was my astonishment,

---

[9] Herod. I. 93. The tomb of Alyattes is extremely large—a mere mound of earth, or rather of artificial concrete—and has no masonry now visible around its base; but this may be concealed by the sinking of the earth from above. The other tumuli of the Bin Tépé are of various sizes, though all save two much inferior to that of Alyattes, none of them now showing basements of masonry. They are all composed of artificial concrete, more difficult to penetrate than rock. I speak from experience, having spent a winter in exploring them. Huge sepulchral mounds abound all along the coast of Asia Minor, from the Troad southwards. Many are still to be seen in the Morea, which the Greeks of old ascribed to the Phrygians, who were traditionally believed to have come to Greece with Pelops. Heraclides, ap. Athen. XIV. 21.

[1] Dion. Hal. I. p. 12, ed. Sylb.

[2] The same singular effect of the atmosphere is narrated of the Grotta Torlonia at Cervetri. — Visconti, Antichi Monumenti Sepolcrali di Ceri, p. 21.

that it were impossible to express the effect upon my mind produced by this sight; but I can safely assert that it was the happiest moment of my life." [3]

The contents of this tomb, so far as they can be judged of from Avvolta's description, indicate a high antiquity; and the golden crown and rich bronzes show it to have belonged to some person of consequence. This tomb had evidently never been opened since the days of the Etruscans, and such sepulchres being exceedingly rare, are of immense importance to the archæologist. We visit Museums, and see the produce of cemeteries in objects rich and rare, but as to their arrangement as sepulchral furniture we gather not an idea. Or even should we be present at the opening of a tomb, if it has been rifled in past ages, as is the case with the vast majority, we can have no confidence in the genuineness of the arrangement; we cannot regard it with the same interest as if we were convinced every object occupied its original position. Or, should we be so fortunate as to hit upon a virgin-tomb, it is not unlikely that it is full of earth—that the roof has fallen in, deranged the original collocation, and destroyed the furniture; and happy shall we be if we can save anything uninjured from the wreck.

The necropolis of Tarquinii was of vast extent. Avvolta assured me that it covered sixteen square miles. Others tell us it stretched eight miles in length and six in breadth [4]—an extent hardly to be credited. It covers not only the whole of the Montarozzi, which is so thickly sown with tombs, that almost every step you take is on hollow ground, but it extends far down the slope towards the sea, and comprehends also Monte Quagliero, on the opposite bank of the Marta, and to the north of the ancient city, as well as the Poggio della Vipera higher up the same stream. It is highly probable that the heights around the city in every other direction would be found to contain tombs, for the Etruscans did not confine their cemeteries to one spot, but availed themselves of any advantages afforded by the disposition of the ground or the nature of the soil, and sometimes quite encircled the city of the living with a " city of the dead."

The necropolis on the slope of Monte Quagliero was discovered only in 1829. A sepulchral road, sunk in the tufo, crossed the

[3] For further particulars of this tomb, see Ann. Inst. 1829, pp. 95—98; and for the plan and sections of the tomb, showing the arrangement of its contents, see Ann. Inst. 1829, tav. d'agg. B.

[4] Pacciandi, quoted by Lanzi, II. p. 465 cf. Inghir. Mon. Etr. IV. p. 111.

hill, and contained sepulchres in both its walls.   Other tombs were sunk beneath the surface, for there were no tumuli on this spot.[5]

Excavations were carried on in this necropolis pretty briskly some thirty or forty years ago, but the attention of the tomb-burglars has since been absorbed by the more lucrative operations at Vulci and Chiusi.   For, though tombs are so abundant that almost every step you take in the neighbourhood of Corneto is over a sepulchre, yet the cemetery has been so well rifled in bygone ages, that it is rare to find anything to repay the expense of exploration.   Certain excavators on this site are of opinion that this rifling took place in the time of Julius Cæsar, when the painted vases were much prized, and were sought for eagerly in the tombs of Campania and Corinth.[6]   The reason assigned for this opinion is, that the more ancient tombs have been plundered, while those of later date have generally been spared.   This, however, may be accounted for by the superior wealth treasured in the older sepulchres; for these same gentlemen inform us that the poorer tombs of equal antiquity are often intact—a fact which is to be wondered at, seeing there is no external distinction now visible, whatever there may have been of old.   Nor is there any local separation—nothing like classification in the arrangement—but sepulchres of all ranks and of various dates are jumbled together in glorious confusion.   It seems as though, after the necropolis had been fairly filled, the subsequent generations of Tarquinians thrust in their dead in every available spot of unoccupied ground; and so it continued to a late period, for there are tombs of Romans, as well as of Etruscans, and some apparently even of the early Christians.   From the number of painted vases yielded by this necropolis, I should conclude that the rifling was of much later date than Julius Cæsar; more probably of the time of Theodoric (A.D. 489—526), when grave-spoiling was general throughout Italy.   For that monarch thought, with the Wife of Bath—

"It is but waste to bury preciously,"

and sanctioned the search for gold and silver, yet commanded everything else to be spared.[7]

Taking all classes of tombs into account, those which are virgin or intact are said to be not one per cent.; but those which, like Avvolta's tomb, contain articles of value, are in much smaller proportion.

[5] Bull. Inst. 1829, p. 8; Ann. Instit. 1830, p. 38—Westphal.

[6] Suet. Jul. 81; Strab. VIII. p. 381.
[7] Cassiodor. Variar. IV. 34.

On the slope of the Montarozzi, towards the sea, there are some tumuli of great size, which promise well to the excavator. In this neighbourhood is a remarkable tomb, which, though now in a very dilapidated state, should not fail to be visited by the traveller. Let him leave Corneto by the Civita Vecchia gate, and, instead of pursuing the road to that port, let him take a lane a little above it, which will lead him through olive-woods, till, at the distance of a mile or more from the city, he will enter a grass-grown area, inclosed by low cliffs, which are hollowed into caverns, some of vast extent. Among them is the tomb in question. The spot is called

LA MERCARECCIA,

and the tomb is known by that name, or is called Grotta degli Stucchi. Its outer wall has fallen, so that the tomb is quite exposed. The walls of the first chamber have been covered with reliefs, now scarcely traceable, save in a frieze beneath the ceiling, where animals—apparently wild beasts—are represented in combat, or devouring their prey—a frequent subject on Etruscan vases and bronzes of archaic character.[8] Among them is the figure of a boy distinctly traceable, who seems to be struggling with a huge beast like a hyæna. Another animal on the same wall appears to be a winged sphinx. The walls below the frieze bear traces of figures almost as large as life—men and horses—now almost obliterated, nothing remaining distinct. It would be surprising were it otherwise, for the rock is a friable tufo, and the tomb, for the last sixty or eighty years at least, has been used as a cow-shed or sheep-fold. The walls have been hollowed into niches for the lamps of the herdsmen, holes made in the reliefs for their pegs, and the whole tomb is blackened with the smoke of their fires. Were it not for this, traces of colour would doubtless be discernible on the reliefs, as on those of Norchia.[9]

It is lamentable to see this, almost the sole instance known, of an Etruscan tomb with internal sculptural decorations, in such a state of ruin. Had any care been taken to preserve it, were it a mere door or fence to keep out mischievous intruders, the sculptures would in all probability be still as fresh as the reliefs

---

[8] This subject is very common on early Greek works of art, the Doric vases to wit —and is also found on Lycian and Asiatic Greek monuments. See Fellows' Lycia, pp. 174, 176, 197; and the reliefs from Xanthus, in the British Museum; also the reliefs from Assos in Mysia, in the Louvre.

[9] A century ago, according to Gori, the cornice or frieze was red, and the beams of the roof red and blue.

on the sarcophagi and ash-chests. How long it has been subject to neglect on the one hand, and wantonness on the other, is not known. There is no record of its discovery.[1] A century ago, according to Byres, the sculptures were at least intelligible; but even then the outer wall had fallen, and the tomb was open to all intruders.[2] From the spirit and freedom evident in the remains yet visible, as well as from Byres' plates, which betray too much mannerism, we may learn that these reliefs belong to a late period of Etruscan art—a period apparently agreeing with that of the best sarcophagi and ash-chests.

The ceiling of this tomb is hewn into the form of a trapezium, with beams on each of its sides, sloping off from the centre, which is occupied by a square aperture, tapering up like a funnel through the rock for twenty feet, till it opens in a round hole in the surface of the plain above. In the sides of this chimney or shaft are the usual niches for the feet and hands. This can hardly have been the sole entrance, though tombs so constructed have been found—some in this very necropolis, illustrated by Byres, and described by Winckelmann, and others in the plain of Ferento already mentioned. A similar tomb has been discovered on the Aventine Hill, the necropolis of early Rome.[3] Yet it seems strange that a sepulchre so elegantly decorated as this, should be so carefully concealed—that there should be so much "art to conceal the art." It is worthy of remark that in its roof this tomb, which is unique in this respect, represents that sort of *cavædium*, which Vitruvius terms *displuviatum*,[4] or that descrip-

<hr />

[1] The earliest mention of it is by Maffei (Osserv. Letter. V. p. 311), who published in 1739. Gori in 1743 gave a description and illustrations (Mus. Etr. III. p. 90, class II. tab. 7, 8).

It is not improbable that this is the tomb referred to by Pope Innocent VIII. at the end of the fifteenth century, in a letter which he wrote to the citizens of Corneto, about a certain "sepulcrum marmoreum" just then discovered. This cannot have reference to a marble sepulchre, such as flanked Roman roads, for it was evidently subterranean; it must mean a tomb with reliefs, which are vulgarly designated "*marmi*" by the Italians, just as we speak of the "Elgin marbles." The tomb must have been highly adorned in itself, and rich in furniture; for the Holy Father sent "a beloved son" to Corneto expressly to see it, charging the authorities to show

him the sepulchre "in our name," and to compel those who had abstracted the contents to restore them forthwith. The civic powers, it appears, were themselves the culprits, for they replied that nothing had been found but some gold, which they had expended on repairing the fortifications. Bull. Inst. 1839, p. 69. Or this tomb may be the monument which is described in a poem of even earlier date, and which so astonished the natives with its magnificence as to be taken for the palace of Corythus. The benches around, the carved ceiling, with its chimney, and the sculptures on the walls here described, all tally with the description given in the poem.

[2] Byres, Hypogæi, part I. plates 5—8.

[3] Bartoli, Sepolcri Antichi, tav. L. It was discovered in 1692.

[4] Vitruv. VI. 3. No specimen of such a *cavædium* is, I believe, extant, but a

tion of court, the roof of which slopes from within, so as to carry
the rain outwards, instead of conveying it into the *impluvium* or
tank in the centre of the *atrium*. It may be, however, that this
opening represents—what it more strictly resembles—a chimney ;
for we know it was the practice of the Greeks of old to have a
vent for the smoke in the centre of their apartments.[5]

A steep passage cut in the floor of the tomb leads down to an
inner chamber, the roof of which is level with the floor of the
first. Byres represents a procession painted on its inner wall—
a number of souls, one of whom seems of princely or magisterial
dignity, conducted by winged genii ; but hardly a trace of
colour now remains, and no forms are distinguishable.[6] It is a
fair inference, however, that a tomb so richly decorated with
sculpture and painting was not of the *commune vulgus*, but
the last resting-place of some Lucumo, or prince of Etruria.[7]

In the cliffs which surround the Mercareccia are the mouths of
several caverns, which seem to have been tombs, subsequently
enlarged into "antres vast." But between this and Corneto are
others of much larger size. One day I joined a party on an exploring expedition to them. We went provided with torches, for
without them it were dangerous, as well as useless, to penetrate
these　　　" Grots and caverns, shagged with horrid shades."

The mouths of the caves are generally low and shapeless, affording no index to the extent and character of the interiors, which
stretch far into the bowels of the earth, sometimes in galleries or
passages, sometimes in spacious halls, whose lofty ceilings are
sustained by enormous pillars hewn out of the rock, presenting a
rude analogy to the subterranean temples of Egypt and Hindostan.
Their artificial character is manifest ; but whether they are

painting of it may be seen on the walls of
the Casa de' Capitelli Dipinti, and also of
the Casa de' Dioscuri, at Pompeii.

[5] Orph. Hymn. LXXXIII. 2; cf. Herod.
VIII. 137 ; though Becker (Charicles, Exc.
I. Sc. III.) cannot understand the καπνοδόχη
here as a regular chimney.

[6] As regards the relation of the inner to
the outer chamber, this tomb is not unique.
The tapestried sepulchre, represented by
Byres, and now lost sight of, was constructed on the same plan, as is also the
singular "Tomb of the Tarquins" at Cære.

[7] This tomb was described and drawn by
the Padre Forlivesi, to whom Gori (Mus.
Et. III. p. 90) owns himself indebted for

the materials he published. According to
his account, the beams of the outer chamber
were painted red and blue—"a very
pleasant effect." The cornice also was
painted, as well as some of the reliefs. The
inner wall of the second chamber was
painted almost as Byres represents it,
though each figure had its name in Etruscan letters ; but the other walls also had
figures of men alternating with trees, as in
many of the tombs of Corneto. The men
were all naked, save a light *chlamys* or
scarf, and some had birds in their hands,
one a lyre, and one was watering a tree
from a vase. These seem to have disappeared before Byres' time.

natural caverns, subsequently fashioned by man, or are wholly artificial, it is difficult to say. There is not enough regularity to evince plan, nor anything to indicate a definite object in the construction, so that I am inclined to agree with the popular belief, which regards them as quarries, opened for the building of Corneto. Nevertheless, when we remember what burrowers were the ancient Etruscans, the extent, number, and variety of their subterranean works, we cannot despise the opinion, held by some, that these caverns are of very early date, and associated with Etruscan times and rites.[8]

APPENDIX TO CHAPTER XXV.

Note I.—Chaplets in Etruscan Tombs.

The frequent occurrence of chaplets depicted on the walls of these tombs cannot fail to arouse inquiry as to their signification. If these sepulchral paintings be nothing more than representations of actual feasts, the presence of chaplets is sufficiently explained by the well-known custom of the ancients of wearing crowns and garlands at banquets and other festive occasions. By both Greeks and Romans they were assumed after the meal and before the drinking-bout which followed; wherefore to wear a garland was equivalent to being in cups (Plaut. Amphit. act III. sc. 4. 16). By the Greeks they were generally composed of myrtle-twigs, as in the Grotta Querciola and other tombs of Tarquinii, or of ivy, both of which were deemed an antidote to the effects of wine (Plato, Sympos. 37. Plutarch. Sympos. III. q. 1, 2. Athen. XV. 17, 18); or of poplar (Theocrit. Idyl. II. 121);—sometimes bound with ribbons, and with flowers, roses or violets, interwoven. Hence Athens derived her epithet of "violet-crowned," (ἰοστέφανοι Ἀθῆναι—Aristoph. Equit. 1323; Acharn. 638). The Greeks made them likewise of wool, for crowns of victory (Pind. Isth. V. 79). The Romans also made chaplets of the same simple materials—Nature's best ornaments—sometimes fastening flowers to strips of bast (nexæ philyrâ coronæ—Hor. Od. I. 38, 2. Ovid. Fast. V. 335—337); and likewise of wool bound round with ribbons, which was the most ancient material (Festus v. Lemnisci). That the Etruscans also wore woollen chaplets is shown by the sarcophagi and urns which bear the effigy of the deceased reclining on the festive-couch, for such seems to be the texture represented, and that flowers were bound into them by ribbons—lemnisci—is proved by many of the same monuments, especially those of terra-cotta. Of similar materials seem to be the chaplets depicted in these tombs, which often show a ribbon twisted round them, the red or white spots in them probably representing flowers, or it may be gems. Of the same description are the longer garlands worn by the Etruscan sepulchral statues on the breast,

---

[8] Urlichs (Boll. Instit. 1839, p. 67) considers these caverns to be the quarries mentioned by Vitruvius and Pliny, under the name of Lapidicinæ Anitianæ. See Chapter XIV. p. 161. But those quarries are expressly stated to be near the lake of Volsinii.

equivalent to the ὑποθυμιάδες of the Greeks (Plut. Symp. III. loc. cit. ; Athen. XV. 16, 22), and the breast-garlands of the Romans (Ovid. Fast. II. 739 ; Tibul. I. 7, 52 ; Hor. Sat. II. 3, 256). It may be observed that in the earlier tombs, garlands of leaves are never represented, but always chaplets of wool. On Greek vases the heads of banqueters of both sexes are sometimes represented bound with fillets—ταινίαι, vittæ—the long ends of which hang down behind (Mon. Ined. Inst. III. tav. XII.), but in Etruscan scenes the males are never so represented. The Etruscans on triumphal or other solemn occasions wore chaplets of pure gold in the form of leaves, sometimes set with gems, and terminating in ribbons of the same metal (Plin. XXI. 4, XXXIII. 4 ; Appian. de Reb. Punic. LXVI. ; Tertul. de Coronâ Milit. XIII.), nearly such as are found in their tombs. But the Romans in the height of their luxury used golden chaplets at their entertainments, as well as on occasions of great pomp or solemnity. On a few of the latest Etruscan monuments these ornaments are gilt, but in the generality, which belong to earlier times and more simple manners, the chaplets represent wool or other primitive materials.

With woollen wreaths, also, the ancients adorned their wine-vessels, especially those for mixing—krateres, kelebæ—(Theoc. Idyl. II. 2), and, perhaps, also crowned them with flowers (Virg. Æn. I. 724 ; Serv. ad locum ; III. 525 ; VII. 147) ; though some think these and similar passages in Homer mean only " filling to the brim." In reference to this custom we are said metaphorically to—

> " Wreathe the bowl
> With flowers of soul."

An analogy to this may be observed in the Camera del Morto of Tarquinii, where the krater-like vase between the dancers is decorated with chaplets.

But the chaplets in these tombs may be more than festive—they may have a sacred and funereal import. If so, they have an analogy to the infulæ of the Romans, which were used at solemn rites and festivals, suspended on the statues of gods, on altars, in temples or at their doors, on the victims to be sacrificed, or were worn by priests about their brows—or were used as symbols of supplication. For authorities, see Smith's Dictionary of Antiquities, v. Infula, Vitta ; to which may be added Varro, de Ling. Lat. VII. 24, and Frontin. Strat. I. 12, 5, who are the only ancient writers that mention infulæ in connection with sepulchres. But the tæniæ, which were analogous, are mentioned in such a connexion by Cæcilius (ap. Festum, s. voce), who speaks of " a tomb full of them, as usual." Pliny (XXI. 8) says that " crowns were used in honour of the gods, of the Lares public and private, of sepulchres, and of the Manes " (cf. Ovid. Fast. II. 537 ; Trist. III. 3, 82 ; Tibul. II. 4, 48) ; they were also offered to the Lares (Plaut. Aulul. prol. 25, and II. 7, 15 ; Tibul. I. 10, 22 ; Juven. IX. 138), whose images were even decorated with them (Tibul. II. 1, 60 ; Fest. v. Donaticæ). The Greeks crowned the funeral urns of their friends (Plut. Demetr. ad fin.). Philopœmen's urn was so covered with chaplets as scarcely to be visible (Plut. Philop. ad fin.) ; Hannibal crowned the urn of Marcellus (Plut. Marc. ad fin.) ; and on ancient vases, funeral stelæ are often represented hung with chaplets or bound with fillets (Stackelberg, Graeber der Hellenen, taf. XLV. XLVI. ; Millingen, Vases Grecs, collect. Coghill, pl. XXVI. ; Ingbir. Mon. Etr. VI. tav. L. 5). Even the dead themselves were sometimes crowned

(Eurip. Troad. 1143; Aristoph. Eccles. 538; Lysist. 602—4; Cicero pro Flac. 31; Tertul. de Coron. X.; Clem. Alex. Pædag. II. p. 181), especially when they had acquired in their lifetime a crown as a distinction (Cicero de Leg. II. 24; Plin. XXI. 5). Clemens of Alexandria explains this custom of crowning the dead, by the crown being a symbol of freedom and delivery from every annoyance. Claudian (Rapt. Proserp. II. 326, et seq.) represents the Manes themselves feasting at a banquet, and decorated with crowns.

As there is abundant evidence that crowns and chaplets were used by the ancients as sepulchral furniture, it is highly probable that those depicted in these tombs, though primarily festive, had at the same time a sacred import —which is strongly intimated in the Grotta del Iscrizioni, where they are worn and carried by priests and musicians in a Bacchic procession. The only hues of which such chaplets seem to have been made, are white, purple or red, and blue, in which case they were sacred to the Manes, and very rarely black.

For the use of festive chaplets among the Greeks, see the Fifteenth Book of Athenæus' Deipnosophistæ, which is devoted to this subject; and for the use of chaplets by the Romans, see Plin. Nat. Hist. XXI. 1—10.

An erudite article on the tæniæ represented on ancient vases, and their various applications and significations, will be found in the Ann. Inst. 1832, p. 380, et seq., from the pen of Professor Welcker. See also Becker's Gallus. Sc. X. excurs. 2.

NOTE II.—GROTTA DELLA SCROFA NERA (see p. 377),

(see p. 377)

or "Tomb of the Black Sow." This tomb had no passage cleared down to its doorway; but among the half destroyed tumuli of the Montarozzi was a pit, six or eight feet deep, overgrown by lentiscus; and at the bottom was a hole, barely large enough for a man to squeeze himself through. Having wormed my way through this aperture, I found myself in a dark, damp chamber, half-choked with the débris of the walls and ceiling.[1] Yet the walls had not wholly fallen in, for when my eyes were accustomed to the gloom, I perceived them to be painted, and the taper's light disclosed on the inner wall a banquet in the open air, for the ivy which forms a cornice round the chamber is depicted springing from the ground in one corner. The painting is so much injured that some of the figures are almost obliterated. I made out, however, three separate lecti on this wall, each with a pair of figures; one only of whom, on the central couch, is a woman, distinguished by her white flesh; the rest are males. From the absence of other women, and of the tables, the usual concomitants of the banquet, this seems to be rather a symposium or drinking-bout, than a regular deipnon. This view is corroborated by another feature: in front of the couches, besides the usual male attendant, bare from the waist upwards, stands a woman playing the lyre, her lower limbs wrapped in blue richly bordered robes, but her shoulders and bosom bare. Her foot rests on a low tripod stool. This is the only instance I remember of a semi-nude female introduced into the mural paintings of Etruria. Beneath the couch stand some domestic fowl; and one of the

[1] This tomb is 14 ft. 6 in. long, by 11 ft. 6 in. wide. It has the broad beam of the ceiling painted with red circles, and the rafters indicated with red paint. The figures on the walls are about 3 ft. 6 in. high.

pigeons presents an instance of that curious foreshortening of animals, which is not uncommon on black-figured vases, but is rarely to be seen in the painted tombs of Etruria. Of the eight figures in this scene only two retain their heads; but these enable us to judge of the character and expression of the painting in its original state. The drapery of the couches is particularly worthy of notice, being marked with stripes of different colours crossing each other, as in the Highland plaid; and those learned in tartanology may possibly pronounce which of the Macs has the strongest claim to an Etruscan origin.

The banquet was continued on the wall to the left, but there it is now almost obliterated. It was continued also on the wall to the right, by another couch with two male figures, each raising aloft a *kylix* he has just emptied; and both, as well as the other revellers whom Time has not beheaded, having their brows bound with blue wreaths of myrtle. They are attended by two servants, one of whom is bringing a fresh supply of wine. The scene seems to have terminated on this wall in a hunt, probably of the wild boar, in all ages the favourite sport of the inhabitants of the Etruscan Maremma. No such beast is visible in the present dilapidated state of the wall, but there is a man in a grove of trees hurling his long lance, and having his *chlamys* wound round his left arm for a shield, as the Highlander uses his plaid, and the Spaniard his *manta*.

The same sport is represented in the pediment above the banquet, where an enormous sow, not such as met the eyes of Æneas on the wooded shore, with thirty little ones as white as herself, but black as night, with crimson dogs and mane, is attacked in front by a huntsman with knotted lance, and from behind by several dogs, which another huntsman is setting upon her.[2]

In this tomb there is nothing Egyptian or archaic in the countenances, or the forms, as in the neighbouring Grotta del Barone. The features here are Greek, though with much of an Etruscan character. The eyes are in profile, and not in full, as in the earlier tombs. There is an absence of rigidity, a freedom, and correctness of design, which show an advanced state of the art, and which cannot belong to a very remote age. This is particularly visible in the limbs of the man attacking the sow, which display, not merely in outline, but in the modelling of the muscles, no small acquaintance with anatomical design. This tomb, then, must be classed among those of more recent date, such as the Bighe and the Querciola—yet considerably earlier than the Cardinal and the Typhon. It belongs to the latter part of the second period, when Etruscan art had not wholly lost its archaicism and distinctive features, but was acquiring a more full development under Hellenic influence.

The site of this tomb is not known even to the *custode*, and I fear it will now be vain to seek it among the countless mounds and pitfalls which chequer the surface of the Montarozzi. I know not why it was not furnished with a door at the time of its discovery. It can hardly be on account of the somewhat obscene character of one of the figures, or the same cause should render two other of these painted sepulchres unfit for eyes polite.[3]

---

[2] This may perhaps represent Theseus and the Sow of Crommyon, a not unfrequent subject on the painted vases, where the hero, however, is sometimes armed with neither sword nor shield, but with a conical mass of stone, which he is hurling at the brute. The same subject was represented on one of the sarcophagi in the Grotta Dipinta, Bomarzo, and a cone of metal, 8 lbs. in weight, was found within the tomb.

[3] Round this tomb, as round many others

Note III.—Lost Tombs delineated by Byres.   See p. 385.

One of the painted tombs illustrated by Byres (part I., plates 2, 3, 4) was unique in character.   It was somewhat on the plan of the Grotta Tifone, surrounded by a double tier of rock-benches, having a massive square pillar in the centre, and divided by a partition-wall of rock, into two chambers. The dimensions of the entire tomb were not less than 59 feet by 53 ft. 6 in., which surpass even those of the Grotta Cardinale ; so that this was the largest sepulchre yet discovered in this necropolis.   The interior chamber was surrounded by a double border of vine-leaves above, and of the wave-pattern below.   In one pediment was painted a rabbit between two triple-headed serpents ; and on the wall below was a long inscription in four lines of Etruscan characters, scarcely legible in Byres' plate, which, fortunately, is not the only record of it in existence.[4]   The pillar, like that in the Grotta Tifone, had a colossal figure, ten feet high, painted on at least two of its sides.   One was a young man, naked, save a cloth about his loins, holding a bough.   His full face, foreshortened limbs, and correctly drawn figure, prove a late date—certainly not earlier than the days of Roman domination in Etruria.   The other figure was that of a winged genius in the act of running.   He was bearded, and draped with a short tunic worn over a longer one reaching to his feet ; his brow was bound with snakes, a pair of the same reptiles formed his girdle, and he brandished a third with one hand, and held a rod in the other.

Another tomb represented by Byres (part IV., plates 1, 2, 3) displayed two figures of opposite sexes, one on each side a moulded doorway containing a niche, and each holding a pair of snakes, which the man controls with a wand, the woman with an olive branch.   The walls of this tomb were painted with an imitation of tapestry, fastened up by nails, hanging in folds, and terminating below in a vine-leaf border.

A third painted tomb given by Byres (part IV., plates 4—8) was adorned with banqueting-scenes.   On each side-wall were two couches, each bearing a pair, of opposite sexes.   One of the fair ones wore a Phrygian cap, and turning round to her mate, seemed to be pressing him to drink ; another was quaffing wine from a *rhyton*, and her companion from a *phiale* ; the third was chatting about a fillet, which her fellow was about to bind on her ; and in the fourth scene, the man had a lute, and the woman held up to his

---

in Etruscan cemeteries, may be observed nails, much rusted, on which articles of pottery or bronze were suspended against the walls. Lanzi (II. p. 267) and Inghirami (IV. p. 112) thought they originally supported *aulæa*. But though the Etruscans probably decorated their apartments with such hangings, their funeral feasts are generally represented as—

Cœnæ sine aulæis—

perhaps because they were held in the open air. In one tomb only, the Grotta del Letto Funebre, are curtains painted on the wall over the funeral banquet.

[4] This is clearly the same tomb described by Maffei (Osserv. Letter. V. p. 310 and Gori (Mus. Etrus. III. p. 89, who gives an inscription of four lines (class II. tab. VII. 3), and vouches for its correctness, as it was carefully copied a few days after the tomb was opened. Gori says it is in the Montarozzi, four miles from Corneto. He gives a second inscription of two lines on the opposite wall. (Cf. Inghir. Mon. Etrus. IV. tav. 19.) The first begins with the name of "Ramtha Matuluei"—the second with "Larth. Ceisiuis." A lady of this family, Cæsennia, is mentioned by Cicero (pro Cæciná, IV.) as being of Tarquinii and the wife of his client Cæcina. The name of "Ceises" also occurs on a tomb at Castel d' Asso (see page 186), which is worthy of notice, as Cæsenuia had an estate at Castellum Axia.

view a drawing of a boar-hunt, which she had just unrolled. This was a remarkable scene—quite unique. At one end of each conch was a slave—a boy by the man, a girl by the woman—bringing wine-jugs or chaplets; and on the inner wall were other slaves at a sideboard, or tending a candelabrum, burning among the trees. In spite of the mannerism of the artist, there was a more archaic character about the paintings in this tomb, than in any other he has illustrated.

Inghirami (Mon. Etrus. IV. tav. 29, 30, 31) gives some interesting coloured friezes and architectural decorations from certain lost tombs of Tarquinii, which attest their origin by Etruscan inscriptions.

Note IV.—Painted Tombs, opened of late, and reclosed. See p. 386.

Of the Grotta Bruschi, already mentioned, a description will be given in the next chapter, when I treat of the Museo Bruschi, where fragments of its paintings are preserved.

Other painted tombs, discovered many years since, but immediately filled with earth, have been re-opened within the last three or four years by Signori Rosa and Brizio, on behalf of the Government, and the latter gentleman has preserved records of the subjects depicted on their walls, from which I have gathered the following brief notices. The tombs were in so ruinous a condition, that they were re-closed almost immediately.

I.—A tomb of very small size, and simple decorations, at the extremity of the Montarozzi, about three and a half miles from Corneto. On each side of the door was depicted a pugilist in the attitude of boxing, and in the pediment above, a pair of panthers. In the opposite pediment were two lions devouring stags. Of the other figures three only remained distinguishable. Two were dancers, the man girt round the loins with a red *chlamys*; the woman, wearing a light vest, with a red *chlamys* also about her hips, and adorned with disk-earrings and snake-bracelets; she was dancing with lively steps to the rattle of her own castanets, and to the music of a lyre, played by a *citharœdus* on the adjoining wall. The style was archaic, very similar to that of the Grotta del Vecchio and Grotta de' Vasi Dipinti, and the paintings evidently belonged to the same early period of Etruscan art. Bull. Inst. 1873, pp. 194-6.

II.—A tomb about thirty paces from the Grotta del Moribondo, having a false door on its inner wall, painted to resemble bronze. Here three figures only were extant. On each side of the said door was a *citharœdus* crowned with laurel, playing a heptachord lyre, and dressed in tunic, mantle, and sharp-toed boots. The mantles had a tricolour border, red, white, and green. A man naked, save a *chlamys* about his loins, was dancing to their music. These figures were all stunted, their limbs thick and clumsy, very unlike the slender and graceful forms usually depicted on the walls of Etruscan tombs. The art here had not much of an archaic character, and bore considerable resemblance in some respects to that in the Grotta del Citaredo. Bull. Inst. 1873, pp. 200-4.

III.—Another tomb in the slope opposite Tarquinii, about two miles from Corneto. The colours had here faded to a great extent, so that the figures, which represented the usual games and dances, were but dimly visible. The best preserved was that of a *saltatrix*, described as truly beautiful, her long black hair falling on her shoulders, and her attitude full of spirit and animation. Then there were dancers of the male sex; one flourishing a goblet;

another with a buckler on his arm ; a third naked, dancing the Pyrrhic dance, with helmet, spear, and shield ; two pugilists contending ; and two musicians with the double-pipes. These paintings showed a stage of development in which art, freeing itself from archaic trammels, was assuming a broad and grandiose style, as in the Grotta Querciola, and Grotta Francesca. Bull. Inst. 1874, pp. 99–102.

IV.—Near the last was another tomb, which from the inscriptions on its walls, seems to have belonged to the family of " Eizenes." Here a soul was depicted between two demons, each bearing a hammer in one hand, and a snake in the other, with which he was threatening his victim. The design was coarse, vulgar, and conventional ; showing the hand of an artisan, rather than that of an artist. Bull. Inst. 1874, pp. 102–4.

Other painted tombs, referred to at p. 305, are of even more recent discovery. They have neither been described, nor illustrated, and as I found them in June, 1876, temporarily re-closed, I am indebted for the following brief notices to the intelligent observation of Antonio Frangioni, the cicerone. These tombs all lie close to the road, and in the near neighbourhood of the Grotta Triclinio. One, which was opened on 13th November, 1874, displays a banquet, or rather *symposium*, for on each side-wall four men are reclining in pairs, under green coverlets, the couches being separated by red columns —a novel feature. On the wall facing the entrance stands a large wine-jar, in the midst of a group of dancers of both sexes, one of whom plays the lyre, another the double-pipes. In the pediment above them are two large lionesses, from which Antonio designates the tomb. From his description I gather that the art here displayed is of archaic character and date.

Very near the last is a tomb, opened 5th April, 1875, which, from the description Antonio gives, must be well worthy of preservation. It contains some eighteen or twenty figures, arranged almost precisely as in the neighbouring Grotta del Triclinio, and as the style of art, so far I can learn, and the decorations of the tomb are also similar, there is a great probability that the paintings are by the same hand. On the wall facing the doorway are three pairs, of opposite sexes, reclining at a banquet, waited on by two naked boys. In the pediment above this scene are two panthers painted to the life. On each side-wall are five dancers, male and female alternating, separated by trees. One of them holds a cup and a wine-jug, and another plays the double-pipes. All the figures are said to be of beautiful design, and, with the exception of three dancers, in excellent preservation. Copies have already been made for the Archæological Institute of Rome.

Another tomb, adjoining that of the Triclinio, was opened 7th April, 1875. On the inner wall a pair of figures are reclining on a banqueting-couch, the woman wearing a *tutulus*, and both betraying a close analogy to the pair in the Grotta del Vecchio. On one side-wall a single figure only, that of a *subulo*, is extant ; but the wall opposite shows three men dancing, one with a lyre, and all bearing a strong resemblance to the group of bacchanals in the Grotta delle Iscrizioni. From Antonio's description I gather that the art here is quite archaic, and that this tomb is to be classed among the earliest in the necropolis of Tarquinii.

It is to be hoped that these three tombs will soon be fitted with doors, and placed under Antonio's protection.

BRONZE DISK, WITH THE HEAD OF THE HORNED BACCHUS.

CHAPTER XXVI.

CORNETO-TARQUINIA.—THE MUSEUMS.

"Remnants of things that have passed away."—BYRON.

BY royal decree of 10 September, 1872, the town of Corneto assumed the above as her legal appellation.

The Municipality for 50 years past has permitted private speculators to excavate in the Montarozzi. The art-treasures thus brought to light were dispersed to all parts of Italy and Europe, while the spot that yielded them had nothing to show. Corneto has at length the good fortune to possess an enlightened and patriotic chief in its present Sindaco, Signor Luigi Dasti, who, determining to secure for his native town whatever monuments of value and interest may illustrate its ancient history, has not only put a stop to all private enterprise in the Montarozzi, but has instituted systematic excavations on behalf of the Municipality, and has moreover devoted a suite of rooms in the Town-hall for the exhibition of the articles that may be disinterred.

The "Museo Etrusco Municipale," is quite in its infancy. It was commenced only in 1874, yet has already no mean show of antiquities, and with the measures now taken to secure its enrich-

ment, it has a fair prospect of possessing, in a few years, one of
the most interesting collections of Etruscan relics to be seen in
Italy.

On the ground floor of the "Palazzo Governativo," are some
choice sarcophagi, the first fruits of the excavations of 1876.   In
one tomb, at the further extremity of the Montarozzi, were found
no less than fifteen of these coffins, three of them of marble, a
rare material in Etruscan monuments.

Foremost in interest is the sarcophagus of the "Sacerdote,"
or priest, remarkable both as regards its character, and its admirable state of preservation.   On the lid reclines on his back a
man of middle age, his right hand raised as if in the act of
blessing, his left holding a small covered incense-pot, coloured
yellow, to resemble gold.   His flesh is painted red, his eyes
and hair retain traces of colour; his beard is crisp with curls,
and he wears large rings in his ears.   His long *chiton* reaches to
his toes, showing his bare feet, shod with stout sandals.   His
skeleton was found within the sarcophagus, and his skull is
preserved in a glass case hard by, together with two spear-heads,
much rusted.   From an inscription on the lid, behind his head,
we learn his name to have been "Laris Partiun"—(Partiunus or
Partunus).

The sarcophagus has no architectural decoration, but each of
its sides is adorned with paintings, now dimly visible through
a semi-transparent film with which the marble is encrusted.
These paintings, so far as they can be discerned, display a
strong resemblance to those on the celebrated Amazon sarcophagus in the Etruscan Museum at Florence; indeed, as that
monument was also found on the Montarozzi, they may well be
by the same hand.   The subjects on three of the sides are the
same—the combat of the Greeks with the Amazons—though the
treatment is different.   Here both parties are contending on foot,
so there is necessarily less of that variety and striking contrast
which characterize the other monument, where the Amazons are
depicted fighting either from chariots, or on horseback.   Yet
these scenes seem full of incident and spirit, so far as we can
judge from the lower limbs only of the figures, not a single head
being visible.   At each small end of the sarcophagus an Amazon
is represented on horseback, charging her foe, and these figures
being more distinct give some idea of the character and beauty of
the other scenes.   On the second long side, the paintings are
almost obliterated, but from the fragments discernible we learn

that the figures here were of both sexes, apparently moving in procession.

Another fine marble sarcophagus found in the same tomb has been designated the "MAGNATE," from the effigy of an elderly man who reposes on the monument which contains his remains. The inscription attached, which shows his name to have been "Velthur Partunus," states him to have reached the age of 82, though the sculptor has represented him some 20 years younger. He holds a bossed *phiala* in his right hand, as he reposes, as usual, half draped, on his left side. On the lid at the back of his head a female bust is painted to the life, whether representing a woman or a divinity is not easy to determine. On each side of her, at the angles of the bed on which the old gentleman is reposing, crouches a little lion with a yellow mane extending along his back in a double row of curls, quite to his tail. In corresponding places at the foot of the couch, is a head of the horned Bacchus between two winged sphinxes.

Each side of the sarcophagus is adorned with a band of small figures in relief, and coloured on a dark grey ground, representing combats—on one side of Greeks and Amazons, on the other of Centaurs and Lapiths. The art is of the Decadence and poor, yet the scenes are evidently copies of superior designs, the composition and motive being generally good, and many of the figures displaying much spirit in spite of stumpy forms and unskilful execution. The colouring is bright and harmonious, the various hues being thrown out by the grey ground so as to produce an effective whole, although the surface is somewhat waxy in appearance.

The scene which depicts the Centaurs and Lapiths, comprises also two Furies brandishing torches and snakes, against two armed youths, who probably represent Theseus and his Lapith friend Pirithous.

A third sarcophagus of white veined marble, without inscription or decoration of any kind, bears on its lid the effigy of a most corpulent gentleman, a true *obesus Etruscus*, who reclines in the attitude of one satiated with his debauch, one hand supporting his head, the other resting on his belly.[1]

In another room on the ground floor are two sarcophagi of *nenfro*, recently discovered, with reliefs of an unusual character. On the lid of the first, the effigy of the deceased lies flat on his

---

[1] For a description of these sarcophagi, see Bull. Inst. 1876, pp. 70—75, written by the Sindaco, Signor Luigi Dasti.

back, *patera* in hand. On each side of the sarcophagus, a lion and lioness are devouring a stag; at each end are two winged sphinxes *vis-à-vis*; at each angle a Lasa or Fury draped to the feet but with bosom bare, stands with wings upraised, brandishing a snake in either hand. The other sarcophagus, instead of the effigy of the deceased, bears that of Cerberus, very rudely carved on its lid, and at each angle a little lion devouring his prey. The relief on the sarcophagus itself is no less curious, representing combats of men with wild beasts. At one end a man kneeling on a rock seizes a hippogriff by the throat, and is about to stab it with his sword; at the opposite end, a naked man armed with a lance combats a lioness or leopard. In the middle two men armed with shields alone are contending with a wolf; one of them has fallen to the earth and covers himself with his shield, while the beast leaps over him. A Lasa, or it may be a woman, lifts a stone to hurl at the wolf. This subject is repeated on the other side, but in a ruder style of art. Its meaning I am at a loss to understand. The contests of the amphitheatre are naturally suggested, but the presence of the female figure is opposed to such an interpretation.

In the court-yard are several other sarcophagi of *nenfro*, most of them plain, but with epitaphs in Etruscan,—some of the same family, " Partunus : " one with the novel name of " Spantus."

In the first room upstairs are several heads of *nenfro*, of life-size—probably portraits—dug up in forming the New Cemetery on the Montarozzi; portions of figures in the same stone from the Grotta dell' Orco; a lion rudely sculptured; a slab with very archaic reliefs; and another, which represents a man falling on his sword, probably Ajax Telamonius.

In another chamber is a large *nenfro* sarcophagus, on whose lid reclines an old man half-draped, who from a *phiala* is giving drink to a doe, which lies in his lap. This is a singular scene,—though not quite unique. The reliefs on one side of the sarcophagus show the favourite subject of the Greeks contending with the Amazons; on the other side is also a battle-scene, but represented with so little spirit, that the combatants seem rather to be practising the use of arms, than fighting in earnest. The art is of the Decadence, and the monument is evidently of the latter days of Etruria.

Another room is hung with illustrations of many of the painted tombs of the Montarozzi.

On a central table in the third room upstairs stands a *kylix* of rare beauty and interest, brought to light in 1874. It is of large size, more than 21 inches in diameter. The figures are yellow on a black ground, yet the design is that of the black figured vases—severely archaic. Round the bowl all the gods of Olympus, distinguished by their names as well as by their attributes, are depicted in appropriate positions and relations. The names of "Oltos" and "Euxitheos" commemorate the artist and potter.[2] These, like all the other inscriptions on the bowl, are in Greek, but on its foot is an Etruscan inscription of 38 letters in one line, without the usual stops between the words, scratched in by some Etruscan who once possessed the vase. In Roman letters it would run thus—ITUNTURTKEVENELATELINASTINASKLINTIARAS.[3]

There are many other painted vases, chiefly of a late period; also a few articles of *bucchero*, like the black ware of Chiusi, rarely found at Corneto, and only in tunnel or passage-like tombs, which are the earliest on this site. Among the painted vases, the following are the most noteworthy :—

Two large *œnochoœ*, in the most archaic style, each with three bands of animals or chimæras, on a pale yellow ground.

Two *amphoræ*, with black figures, showing, one a Bacchic, the other a Pyrrhic, dance. These are Etruscan imitations of Greek vases.

Kylix, with yellow figures, of beautiful yet somewhat archaic design, displaying a race of fifteen naked youths on horseback. The ease and grace with which these boys sit their steeds, and the variety of action and sentiment they display, render this cup quite charming.

Kylix. Of the same character as the last, in the best style of severe art. In the disk within the bowl a warrior, holding a nymph by the wrist, endeavours to lead her away; that his persuasion is not without effect is expressed by the mingled coyness and coquetry of her attitude and countenance. On the outside of the cup are depicted Theseus and Ariadne. The "beautiful-tressed" nymph, with one arm over her head, is sleeping on a rock beneath the shade of a vine; over her hovers Eros, bearing a fillet or ribbon in his hands. The faithless Theseus is stooping in the foreground to pick up his sandal, and carries a short stick to

[2] A *kylix* found at Vulci bears the same names, as those of its painter and potter. Bull. Inst. 1875, p. 171.

[3] This vase, which is styled by Dr. Helbig the *chef-d'œuvre* of Euxitheos and Oltos, is fully described by him in Bull. Inst. 1875, pp. 171—3. The version he gives of the Etruscan inscription is not so correct as that given above, as I have proved by a comparison with the original.

mark his preparation for a journey. Behind him stands Hermes, with his usual attributes, pointing outwards, as if to hasten his departure. Another scene, on the same vase, represents Cassandra seeking refuge at an altar from the pursuit of Ajax, while Hecuba sits under a Doric column of the temple.[4]

Amphora; with black figures. Hercules and Apollo contending for the tripod. Minerva and Venus behind them.

Amphora. Black figures. Achilles and Hector fighting over the body of Patroclus.

Kylix. Small, with the head of a Satyr painted on it in yellow and white pigments.

Among the relics of Etruscan antiquity in other materials, notice,—

In bronze—a disk, about a foot in diameter, with the head in relief of the horned Bacchus, or the river-god Achelous, in almost perfect condition,[5] represented in the woodcut at the head of this chapter—a pretty female head in the same metal—a few mirrors, the best, gilt, representing the Judgment of Paris.

A tiny flask of variegated glass, flat, with rings at the shoulders; very delicate and pretty.

The building in which this collection is exhibited was formerly the " Ergastolo," or prison and house of correction for priests—the only institution of the kind in the Papal State. It is a spacious building, containing about seventy cells, a few under ground, but the greater part spacious and airy enough, where the peccant ecclesiastics, barring penances and want of liberty, must have been at least as comfortable as in a convent.

Museo Bruschi.

Count Bruschi, a landed proprietor of Corneto, has a large collection of Etruscan antiquities found at various periods in his land, which he courteously allows to be exhibited to strangers. These treasures have not been subjected to any systematic arrangement, but are scattered throughout his palace, so as to make it no easy matter to give such a description of them as will serve for a guide. There are, however, two small cabinets devoted to these antiquities, where some of the choicest articles are deposited. The first contains several vases in the earliest Greek style, and

---

[4] This beautiful *kylix* is described by Helbig, (Bull. Inst. 1875, pp. 174—6) but he attaches no names to the figures.

[5] The eyes are supplied by some material in imitation of life. These bronzes are too small and thin ever to have served as shields, and were probably suspended as ornaments on the wall of the tomb.

of unusually large size—*amphoræ, olpæ,* or *œnochoæ*—with bands
of figures of animals and chimæras on a very pale ground. Here
are also a few fine specimens of the black *bucchero,* or genuine
Etruscan ware, found, though rarely, in this necropolis, with
archaic figures in relief. In striking contrast with these are
some vases of the latest Greek style, showing the debased art of
the Decadence; but the greater part of the pottery in this cabinet
is of the Second, or Archaic Greek, style, with black figures on a
yellow ground. I will briefly point out some of the most remarkable of these vases, premising that, where not specified to the
contrary, all those described are of the Second style.

Two *amphoræ,* with Hercules overcoming the Nemean lion, in
the presence of Pallas and Hermes.

Amphora. A spirited combat between a warrior in a *quadriga,*
and two on foot.

Amphora. Hercules overcoming the triple-headed Geryon.

Amphora. Spirited contest between the Greeks and Trojans
over the body of Patroclus. One of the combatants has an octopus
painted on his shield, as his device.

Amphora. Hercules with the Centaur Nessus.

Amphora. Apollo playing the lyre to two nymphs; Mercury
and Neptune standing by.

Pelike. Birth of Minerva.

Amphora. A spirited race of *quadrigæ.*

Amphora. Ariadne seated on a goat, and holding a *kylix.*

Amphora. Quadriga foreshortened, as in the well-known
metope from Selinus. The inscriptions are unintelligible, which
makes it probable that this vase was an Etruscan imitation of the
Greek.

Amphora. Peleus seizing Thetis round the waist.

Kylix. In the Third style—the same subject; the goddess
having her name attached.

Pelike. A horse's head only, on each side of the vase.

These vases are mixed with others of different styles and
epochs, with articles in terra-cotta, bronze, ivory, glass, and
alabaster. Among the bronzes are two disks, with heads of the
horned Bacchus, like that in the Corneto Museum; and among
the terra-cottas there are pomegranates, figs, quinces, and other
fruits—very fair imitations.

In various rooms, on the higher floors of the palace, I noted,
two *œnochoæ* in the earliest style—two archaic heads of terra-
cotta,—an *amphora,* in the Second style, showing Hercules con-

tending with three Titans, Cerberus, with two heads only, lying on his back between the combatants,—a small *kylix* in the Third style, with a pretty bath-scene, in which a number of youths are using the strigil;[6] a large *skyphos*, adorned with the figures of six guinea-fowls, an unique subject for a Greek vase!—a small bronze pot, with beautiful figures in relief.

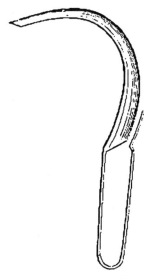

ETRUSCAN STRIGIL.

In the gallery, above the principal saloon, is a sarcophagus of terra-cotta, with a female figure on its lid. A cup in the form of a negro's head. Eggs and chicken-bones, the relics of some Etruscan funeral feast. Two very early pots, one of black, the other of yellow ware, with ornaments scratched upon them. The former has an inscription round the neck, in very archaic (Pelasgic?) characters.

The best vases are kept in a cabinet upstairs, and very choice and beautiful vases these are, mostly of the Second style, and not a few intact, perfect and fresh as when they were deposited in the tombs 500 years before Christ. The following are all of the Second style, with black figures on a yellow ground.

Amphora. Europa seated on the bull, and holding his horn.

Amphora. Minerva and Hercules in a *quadriga* vanquishing the Giants. There is another *amphora* with the same subject, treated with more spirit; on the reverse, Hercules at an altar is playing the lyre to Minerva, who stands opposite, armed.

Amphora. Hercules overcoming Hippolyta. The Queen of the Amazons is in Greek armour, but wears tight drawers, decorated with the meander pattern.

---

[6] The *strigil* was a metal scraper used after bathing to remove the perspiration from the skin; as a groom would remove the foam from a horse's coat with a bit of iron hoop. The curved part of the instrument is hollow like a boat; either to hold oil to soften the effect on the skin, which was far from pleasant if the *strigil* was too often or violently used, as Augustus experienced (Sueton. Aug. 80); or to allow the grease scraped from the body to run off as by a gutter. See the Scholiast on Juvenal III., 262. It was generally of bronze, sometimes of iron (*curvo destringere ferro,* Mart. XIV., ep. 51), and, very rarely, of silver. The metal is always very thin; and it is rare to find strigils in a perfect state. They are occasionally found bearing Etruscan inscriptions. Roman strigils were of different forms, but those of the Etruscans were invariably shaped like that in the above woodcut.

Amphora. Theseus slaying the Minotaur.

Amphora. Bacchus sitting, *kantharus* in hand, in a galley, whose prow is in the form of a pig's snout, the eye being prominently marked. The crew is composed of Satyrs of very small size, one of them steering. Two Mænads are also on board, one of whom sits in the stern playing the lyre. The reverse shows a similar subject; but here Bacchus is represented in pursuit of a Satyr in the bow of the ship, whom a Mænad endeavours to stop. Behind Bacchus a Satyr is playing the lyre, and another, with arm raised, is beating one of the crew. In the stern sits another nymph or Mænad, and below deck are other women with tiny Satyrs, sitting at the oars. This is a very curious subject, and, so far as I know, unique.

Amphora. A spirited scene of a warrior in a *biga*, overthrowing his foes. Instead of the letters which should compose the names, there are mere spots, which seem to mark this vase as an Etruscan imitation of a Greek original.

Amphora. Bacchus, *kantharus* in hand, between two loving couples, each composed of a Satyr and a Mænad.

Amphora. Three Mænads appear to have been dancing with castanets, when a Satyr rushes in, and carries off one of them on his shoulder.

Amphora of small size. Peleus seizing Thetis, whose attendant nymphs rush away in alarm. A scene exquisitely elaborated.

Amphora. A Panathenaic vase; Athene Promachos between two Doric columns, surmounted as usual by cocks. No inscription. On the reverse, a contest of pugilists.

Amphora. Bacchus seated on a *plicatilis*, or folding-stool, between two harpies.

Olpe in the form of a negro's head. A Bacchic scene round the neck.

Amphora. A very early and beautiful vase, but with a subject not easy of explanation. A woman, or goddess richly veiled and draped sits on a handsome chair, beneath which are a small sphinx and a dog. A mirror, suspended from the wall, shows the scene to be within doors, and in the *gynækonitis*. Before her stand Mercury and Minerva; behind her a naked man, wearing a chaplet, and another man draped, holding a spear and a fish. The vase was broken of old, but mended with many metal rivets. This is one of the best vases in the collection.[7]

---

[7] Bull. Inst. 1869, p. 170.

The following are in the Third style :—

Krater. A beautiful vase, showing "Pelias" on his way to be chopped up and boiled. The old man, walking feebly with a stick, is dragged along by one of his daughters, who seizes him by the wrist with one hand, and carries a sword in the other, with which she is about to put into execution the advice of the treacherous Medea. On the reverse is another of his daughters. There is much character and truth in the figures and countenances.

Kylix. Within the bowl, Hercules is attacking the Centaur Nessus, as he carries off Deïanira. On the outside is represented the combat between the Centaurs and Lapithæ, in the fine style of Greek art.

Kylix. Another, precisely similar, found in the same tomb.

Kelebe. Apollo sitting on a rock, bough in hand, while a Muse offers him a lyre.

Kylix. Three Satyrs, one of whom has seized a Mænad, and is carrying her away on his shoulder, while she strikes at him with a *thyrsus.*

Stamnos. Hercules and the Centaur Pholus at a large vase, into which the demi-god dips a wine-jug.

Kylix. In the disk, within the bowl, an *ephebus* is admiring a suit of armour on the ground before him. On the outside are two combats, full of spirit and truth to nature.

Kylix. Within the bowl a Discobolus with a quoit. On the outside two combats, of equal merit with the last.

Kantharus. Bacchic revels.

Lekythus, with a single figure outlined in black, on a white ground. Vases of this class are so rarely found in Etruria, that we may pronounce this an importation from Athens, or from Sicily.

Phiala. Two bowls of this form, called *omphalike,* from the boss or navel in the centre, of black ware, each with reliefs of four *quadrigæ.*

There are many small terra-cotta heads and masks around the walls. In a case are a few beautiful vases of variegated glass, called Babylonian, but found in Etruscan tombs. Of jewellery there is a choice collection, comprising, besides *scarabei,* specimens of almost every stage in the development of Etruscan gold-work; but the most remarkable objects are three necklaces of gold, one composed of little bottles, like *vinaigrettes ;* another of small *bullæ,* and a third of tiny *fibulæ.* A case of bronzes contains some choice works in this material, especially strigils, and mirrors bearing mythological subjects, with some female heads; *candelabra;* elegant bronze handles to caldrons, or to wooden furniture, which has long since perished; and several

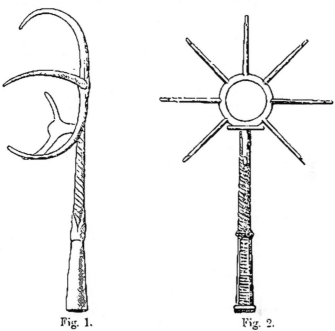

Fig. 1.   Fig. 2.

KREAGRÆ, OR FLESH-HOOKS.

kreagræ, or flesh-hooks, with six or eight long curved prongs, like grappling-irons, which have greatly puzzled modern sages.[8]

[8] These hooks were at first supposed to be instruments of torture, with which the early Christians had their flesh torn from their bodies. But being frequently found in tombs purely Etruscan, that notion was repudiated; and it remains a question whether they were mere kitchen-utensils, or implements used in sacrifices, either for taking up or turning over the burnt flesh, as such instruments were employed by the Jews (I. Sam. ii. 13)—for offering the entrails to the divinity—or for putting out the fire by pieces of fat at the end of the prongs—or were employed at the funeral pyre for separating from the embers the ashes of the deceased. Bull. Inst. 1840, p. 59. There is no doubt that they are the *kreagræ*—ἀπὸ τοῦ τὰ κρέα ἀγρεύειν—referred to by Aristophanes (Equit. 772), and described by the Scholiast (ad locum) as culinary instruments; though also mentioned by the great comedian (Eccles. 1002,

Vesp. 1155), as serving more general purposes of grappling or holding fast. It has been supposed, from the small ring to which the lower prong is often attached,—not clearly shown in the above woodcut, fig. 2,—that they may have served as torch-holders, especially as the handle proves them to have been generally attached to a pole of wood. But many are without this ring, and have a claw instead, as shown in fig. 1: besides, it would be difficult to account for the prongs at all on this supposition. From the prongs being sometimes blunted, it is argued that they were for mere show, and served no practical purpose. Yet in almost all those I have seen so blunted, it has been clear that this was not their original form, but that the prongs had been broken off. These *kreagræ* were called by the Romans *harpagones;* and it must have been a similar instrument on a larger scale which was used for grappling

Grotta Bruschi.

Other most interesting relics of Etruscan antiquity are preserved in this chamber. These are portions of a painted tomb, discovered in 1864, on the Montarozzi, not far from the Grotta Cardinale. When the tomb was opened, the paintings were in a ruined condition; a great part of the figures had disappeared, and what remained threatened, from the softness of the rock, soon to fall from the walls. After careful drawings had been made, the Count had the best preserved portions of the paintings detached from the walls and conveyed to his palace. From the drawings, which have been published by the Archæological Institute of Rome, we learn the character of these paintings and their style of art.[9] The chamber was surrounded by a band of figures, beneath which ran a large Greek fret, with dolphins plunging above the waves. There were no banqueters at their revels, no funeral games, no scenes of joy and merriment. Long solemn processions of figures, robed in white, surrounded the tomb. On one wall was a large male figure on horseback, probably representing the soul of the Etruscan here interred, attended by other figures on foot, all in white tunics, the foremost among them blowing a long straight trumpet. In front of this procession stood a woman, in long white or yellow *chiton*, with a dark mantle round her waist, a garland on her head, and a pomegranate in her hand. Before her a slave girl, also draped in white, held up a mirror to her mistress. This pair of figures also has been rescued from the tomb, and is preserved in this collection. On another wall, was another long procession of men, in white togas, or rather two processions meeting. Those marching from the left, bore, some, circular horns, others, straight horns of the *lituus* form, and preceded a figure of larger size, and more richly clad, whose epitaph was inscribed on the wall behind him. The *cortége* was brought up by a black demon, with open wings, who appeared to be driving the rest before him. A similar series of figures came from the right, all in white togas, and with inscriptions over their heads, in great part obliterated. They were headed by a small boy, and followed by a red demon in a dark tunic, with snakes coiled round his legs for *talaria*, and a long

ships, and was sometimes termed an "iron hand "—*ferrea manus*—(Liv. XXVI. 39; cf. XXX. 10. Flor. II. 2. Frontin. Strat. II. 3, 23. Lucan. III. 635. Dion Cass. XLIX. 3; L. 32, 34,) and figuratively "a

wolf." Hesych. v. λύκος. They are said to have been an invention of Pericles. Plin. VII. 57, ad fin.

[9] Mon. Ined. Vol. VIII. tav. 36.

inscription by his side.　He led a soul on horseback, draped in white, and indicated by a long epitaph.　This figure and his attendant demon have been cut from the walls, and are preserved in the Palazzo Bruschi.

On another wall was a similar procession, headed by figures bearing *fasces* and curved trumpets, and in the centre walked two figures, male and female, of much larger size than the rest.　All the figures described, which retained their heads, were represented in profile; but in one corner stood a pretty female figure, in white drapery, whose face was drawn in full; while in the opposite corner sat a hideous Charun, half-draped, and buskined, with monstrous nose and gaping mouth, and an enormous hammer on his shoulder, apparently content to see his realms so well peopled with souls from the upper world.

The art in these paintings betrayed a late date, quite as late as that of the Grotta Tifone.　The processions, in fact, in the two tombs, bore a close resemblance in many respects.　There was nothing archaic here; everything bespoke an advanced period of art, but there was a want of dignity in the conception, and a carelessness in the execution, that, in the opinion of a most competent critic, stamp the art in these paintings as "altogether municipal."[1]

The Bruschi gardens, outside the city on the road to Civita Vecchia, are worthy of a visit, even from the antiquary.　The parterres are adorned with altars, sarcophagi, fragments of columns, and other relics of Etruscan and Roman antiquity; and in the lower garden are some stone lions, of amusing quaintness.

The brothers Marzi, of Corneto, have a collection of vases and bronzes, the fruit of their own excavations; but it has not a permanent character, being increased by fresh discoveries, or diminished by sales.

In 1869 these gentlemen had the good fortune to disinter a singular and most interesting sarcophagus, eleven feet long, not lying in a tomb, but sunk beneath the surface.　It contained the skeleton of a warrior, which fell to dust on exposure to the atmosphere, cased in his armour, with his weapons by his side, and the various implements of his daily life around him, all of most archaic character, yet in excellent preservation.　There was his shoulder-strap (*gyalon*) of elastic bronze, retaining its lining of cloth; his breastplate of the same metal, covered with a

---

[1] H. Brunn, Ann. Inst. 1866, pp. 439—442.

sheet of gold decorated with bands of ducks and other figures in relief; his circular shield, lined with leather, and stamped with archaic ornaments in concentric circles. No helmet, no greaves, no sword, but his dagger and his knife were there, with handles encased in ivory and amber; the head and the but-end of his lance, and the heads of his double battle-axe. All these weapons, as well as most of the other articles, were of bronze; no trace of iron or steel being found in the coffin. Among the objects of personal use or ornament were, a razor of the crescent form usual in very early times, a travelling-flask, two horse-bits, sundry *fibulæ* of gold, silver, or bronze, rings of bronze, and an Egyptian *scarabæus*, set in silver.

Around the corpse were numerous articles of domestic use— two large vases, made of bronze plates fastened together with nails, in the earliest style of metal-work; many cups, pots, and plates of bronze; two bowls of quince-wood, studded with nails; and several bowls and a plate of silver. There were no Greek vases here; only a few articles of pottery of very archaic and oriental character, resembling the earliest ware of Rhodes and Cyprus. The most remarkable piece was a little *guttus* terminating in a pig's head, and adorned with ducks and geometrical patterns, which, like the decorations on the breastplate, are said to bear an affinity to the ornamentation of Nineveh and Babylon. The contents of this sarcophagus mark it as unquestionably one of the earliest sepulchral monuments yet discovered in this, or any other necropolis of Etruria.

The articles in this "Warrior's Tomb" were purchased in 1873 by Mr. George Bunsen, by whom they have been transferred to the Museum at Berlin.[2]

— — — — —   — —   —

Painted pottery is far less abundant on this site than at Vulci. It is of various descriptions and degrees of merit; from the coarse, staring, figured ware of Volterra, to the florid forms and decorations of Apulia and Lucania, and the chaste and elegant Attic designs of Vulci—which, in fact, is its general character. And this is singular, for we might expect that the Corinthian artists who settled here with Demaratus, the father of Tarquinius Priscus, would have introduced a Doric style of

---

[2] For a detailed description of the contents of this tomb, see Bull. Inst. 1869, pp. 257–260; and Ann. Inst. 1874, pp. 249 —260; both articles by Dr. Helbig. For illustrations see Mon. Inst. X. tavv. x–x⁴.

pottery; whereas there is here little or nothing that reminds us of Corinth or Sicyon; but much of the Attic character so prevalent at Vulci.[3] The best ware of Tarquinii is in no degree inferior, either in form, material, varnish, or design, to that of Vulci; and, if there be a difference, it is that it is generally less archaic in character.

Besides vases, many fine sarcophagi of *nenfro* and of marble have been found here—"ash-chests" rarely; for the Tarquinians were accustomed to *bury*, rather than *burn*, their dead. Bronzes are not very abundant on this site; yet I have seen some of great beauty, with reliefs of mythological subjects. In one tomb were found eleven bronze disks, about sixteen inches in diameter—seven of them with a lion's head, and the rest with a face of the horned Bacchus, or river-god Achelous, in high relief, in the centre, but none so perfect as that in the Municipal Museum.

The most beautiful work in bronze, however, that this necropolis is known to have produced, was a group of Venus and Cupid, found in 1855 by Signor Giosafat Bazzichelli of Viterbo. The laughter-loving goddess was sitting in a majestic attitude, while her son stood by her side in the act of drawing his bow. Unfortunately the group was but a fragment; the heads were gone, and the limbs of both were injured, yet even in its mutilated state Dr. Brunn describes it as " resplendent with the most sublime Greek beauty." He does not hesitate to compare it with the celebrated bronzes of Siris, now in the British Museum, and assigns it to the same period, that of Alexander. He characterises the style as less severe and chaste, more broad, soft, and delicate, yet notices the majesty, which, in spite of the pervading elegance, triumphs in the conception of the Venus; and pronounces the group worthy to be named by the side of those renowned works of Hellenic art.[4]

At the same time and by the same hand were discovered, in a virgin tomb, which also contained some beautiful jewellery, four remarkable reliefs in ivory, which had formed the decorations of a wooden box or casket. These reliefs, which retained traces of colour and gilding, represented a banquet—a *biga* at full gallop

[3] Niebuhr (I. p. 133) is mistaken in asserting that there is a striking similarity between the vases of Corinth and Tarquinii. Occasional resemblances may occur, but they are by no means characteristic. Gerhard (Ann. Inst. 1831, p. 213) remarks that there is little like the infancy of

Greek art in the vases of Tarquinii, and thinks the companions of Demaratus were workers in metal, for which branch of art the Dorians were renowned.

[4] Ann. Inst. 1860, pp. 489—493. Mon. Inst. VI. tav. 47. 6.

drawn by winged horses—a huntsman, winged, transfixing a stag —a marine demon, reclining on a couch, and holding a fish in each hand.   They are said to bear much analogy to the reliefs of the temple of Assos, to be executed in the style of the purest and most refined archaicism, and to belong to an epoch in which Etruscan art still remained perfectly unaffected by Greek influences.[5]

I must not omit to mention that some of the best imitations of Greek vases I have ever seen are made by Signor Scappini, of Corneto, under the auspices of Monsignor Sensi.

---

[5] Ann. Inst. 1860, pp. 478--488, Brunn.   Mon. Inst. VI. tav. 46.

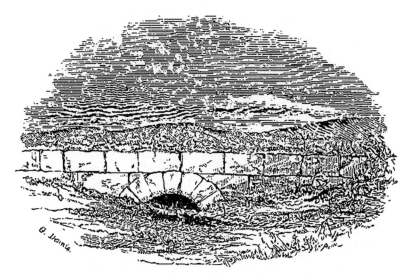

HALF-BURIED GATEWAY IN THE WALLS OF TARQUINII.

CHAPTER XXVII.

TARQUINII—THE CITY.

Giaco l'alta Cartago ; appena i segni
Dello alte sue ruine il lido serba.
Muojono le città, muojono i regni ;
Copre i fasti e le pompe arena ed erba.—TASSO.

That castle was the strength of all that state,
Untill that state by strength was pulled downe ;
And that same citie, so now ruinate,
Had bene the keye of all that kingdomes crowne.—SPENSER.

AFTER beholding the wonders of the Montarozzi, the attention
is naturally directed to the city from which these tombs were
peopled. "If such were its sepulchres," we may exclaim with
Lanzi, "what must have been its palaces!" Its antiquity,
power, and magnificence are naturally inferred,—what was its
history ?

The origin of Tarquinii is wrapt in the mists of fable. The
story told by the ancients, is this :—Soon after the Trojan War,
Tyrrhenus, son of Atys, king of Lydia, being compelled by
famine to quit his native land, brought a colony to this part of
Italy, and built the Twelve Cities of Etruria, appointing to that
work his relative Tarchon, from whom the city of Tarquinii, one

of the Twelve, received its name.[1] From this tradition there is one dissentient voice, that of Justin, who says that Tarquinii was built by the Thessali and Spinambri,[2] or, in other words, by the Pelasgi.[3] This Tarchon was a man of such wonderful wisdom, which he had displayed even from his childhood, that he was traditionally said to have been born with a hoary head.[4] He it is who is introduced by Virgil as leading his forces to the assistance of Æneas, against Turnus and Mezentius.[5]

Here, in the neighbourhood of Tarquinii, and about the period in question, it came to pass, said the Etruscan tradition recorded in the sacred books of the nation, that as a certain peasant was ploughing the land, and chanced to make a furrow deeper than usual, up sprang a wondrous being, a boy in appearance, but a patriarch in wisdom, Tages by name, the son of a Genius, and grandson of Jove.[6] The peasant, amazed at this apparition, uttered a loud cry; a crowd gathered round; and, "in a short time," says Cicero, who relates the story, "all Etruria was

---

[1] Strab. V. p. 219 ; Herod. I. 94; Vell. Paterc. I. 1. Strabo calls the city Ταρκυνία, Stephanus Ταρχώνιον; Dionysius (III. p. 184) Ταρκυνίοι. So also Strabo, elsewhere (p. 220). From the Tomb of the Tarquins we may conclude that its Etruscan name was Tarchna. Whether Tarchon was the son or brother of Tyrrhenus ancient writers are not agreed (Serv. ad Æn. X. 198 ; Cato, ap. Serv. ad Æn. X. 179; Lycoph. 1246 ; but Müller (einl. 2, 8 ; IV. 4, 2) regards them as identical—as respectively the Etruscan and Greek names of the same individual. Müller's theory is this :—A Tyrrhene is a man of Tyrrha, the Lydian Torrha ; the vowel was pronounced short, and therefore obscurely ; the Etruscans aspirated strongly ; what was more natural, then, than that a Tyrrhene should be called by them Tarchun ? That the Tyrrheni were Pelasgi from Tyrrha in the interior of Lydia, says Grote (History of Greece, III. p. 239), "is a point on which we have not sufficient evidence to advance beyond conjecture ;" and the evidence on which Müller built "seems unusually slender."

[2] Justin. XX. 1.

[3] Niebuhr, I. pp. 36, 116. Müller (Etrusk. einl. 2, 7) also regards Tarquinii as of Pelasgic origin, but thinks that this Pelasgic colony came from the Lydian coast, thus reconciling the two traditions. He

fixes the date of this emigration about the year 290 before the foundation of Rome, or 1044 B.C., which he considers the commencement of the Etruscan Era (einl. 2, 2). Gerhard (Ann. Inst. 1831, p. 203) also thinks Tarquinii was Pelasgic.

[4] Strab. loc. cit.

[5] Æneid. VIII. 506 ; X. 153. Joannes Lydus (de Ostent. III.) speaks of two Tarchons—one, the founder of the Etruscan state ; the other, the ally of Æneas—and distinguishes them as the elder and the younger.

[6] Festus, v. Tages. The Etruscans, however, regarded Tages as the son of Hercules and Minerva, as we learn from an Etruscan mirror, confirmed by other monuments.—Ann. Inst. 1841, p. 94—Braun. An argument confirmatory of the Pelasgic origin of Tarquinii may be drawn from this very name. Tagus was the title of the chieftain of the confederate cities of Thessaly (Xenoph. Hist. Græc. VI. 1 ; Pollux, I. c. 10), whence Tarquinii, according to Justin, derived her origin ; and the word Thessali was used as a synonym with Pelasgi (Strab. V. p. 220), the latter people having one of their principal seats in that land. Grote (Hist. Greece, II. p. 373) shows that the title Tagus was once applied by a Roman consul to the chief magistrate of the several cities of Thessaly.

assembled on the spot." The mysterious boy then made known to them the practice of divination by the inspection of entrails and the flight of birds; they treasured up all he had said or sung, and committed it to writing; and these records formed the code of the sacred Discipline of the Etruscans, which regulated their entire polity, civil and religious, and was by them transmitted to the Romans.[7] Though all this is evidently fable,[8] yet through the mists of tradition we catch a glimpse of substantial forms; we can perceive the high antiquity of the city of Tarquinii, dating from the very foundation of the Etruscan state—its importance, in the derivation of its name from the mythical hero of the land, the founder of the Twelve Cities; and as the spot selected for the divine revelation of the national system of polity. That it was one of the Twelve, none can doubt. Nay, it can urge claims to metropolitan supremacy; and, if not the political head, it must at least be regarded as the ecclesiastical metropolis of the land, the city peculiarly honoured by the gods, the spot where the religious system and the peculiar civilisation of the Etruscans took their rise.[9]

[7] Cic. de Divin. II. 23, 39; Ovid. Metam. XV. 553—9; Censorin. de die Nat. IV.; Serv. ad Æn. VIII. 398; Lucan. I. 636; Amm. Marcell. XXI. 1, 10; Arnob. II. 69; Isid. Orig. VIII. 9; Mart. Capella de Nupt. II. p. 27; VI. p. 134; Joan. Lydus de Ostentis, II. III. Müller credits the version of the last named writer, that the husbandman who ploughed up the oracular child was no other than Tarchon himself (Etrusk. III. 2, 3). Elsewhere (III. 2, n. 14) he says, in reference to Tarchon's hoary head, "It is very clear that Tarchon and Tages were personages of the same legend, who might be easily confounded." Cluver (II. p. 519) seems to regard them as identical.

[8] Cicero (de Div. II. 23) so regarded it, and laughed to scorn any who should credit it. Müller considers these traditions of Tarchon and Tages as local and genuinely Etruscan (Etrusk. einl. 2, 1, and 8; IV. 4, 2). Cluver (Ital. Ant. II. p. 520) suggests that the legend of Tages was a mere version of the creation of Adam, who first taught his children and children's children the practice, not of divination, but of all divine worship and sacred rites, which he had received from God himself.

[9] It is nowhere expressly stated that Tarquinii was the chief city of the Confederation, yet it is implied in the fact of its being the spot where the civil and religious polity of the Etruscans had their origin, and of its *eponymus* Tarchon being the traditional founder of the Twelve Cities. The metropolis, in the primary sense of the term, it undoubtedly was. Müller remarks (Etrusk. einl. 2, 1, 2), that "the Etruscans themselves regarded Tarquinii as the metropolis of their Twelve Cities." And again (einl. 2, 16)—"Tarquinii is that particular spot of Etruria, to which are attached all traces of a permanent unity and a close connection of the Etruscan cities under one head." Cluver (II. p. 520) also thinks the metropolitan supremacy of Tarquinii is clearly implied. If this be so, it must, *a fortiori*, have been one of the Twelve, and no proof of this is requisite. Yet I may add that Dionysius (III. p. 184) calls it "a great and flourishing city" in the time of Demaratus, which is confirmed by Cicero, Repub. II. 19. Its eminence is also strongly implied by its conduct in the war with Servius Tullius (Dion. Hal. IV. p. 231), and again in the war of 398, when Tarquinii and Falerii took the lead of all the Etruscan states (Liv. VII. 17).

Of the early history of Tarquinii we are utterly ignorant ; as we find no mention of it from the time of Tarchon till the close of the first century of Rome, when Demaratus, a wealthy merchant of Corinth, being compelled to fly from his native city on the usurpation of Cypselus and the expulsion of the Bacchiads, migrated to Etruria, with which he had long been in the habit of commercial intercourse, and settled at Tarquinii. He married a lady of that city, and begat two sons.[1] He brought with him a large band of fellow-refugees, among them two potters or workers in clay, Eucheir and Eugrammos—names indicative of their skill—and a painter named Cleophantos. Whether these were real existences, or mere symbols of their respective arts, the tradition obviously meant that Demaratus introduced the civilization of Greece and her refinement in the arts into the land of his adoption.[2] He was well received by the Tarquinienses,—one account, indeed, represents him as attaining to the supreme power in that city, in consequence of his great wealth.[3]

Lucumo or Lucius, the eldest son of Demaratus, and heir of his vast possessions, married an Etruscan lady of noble birth ; but though thus allied to their aristocracy, and himself a native of Tarquinii, he was looked down on by the Etruscans on account of his foreign origin. Unable to brook this wound to his pride, he quitted the city of his birth, and seeking a fairer field for his ambition, migrated to Rome, where his talents and wealth eventually raised him to the throne, which he filled as Tarquinius Priscus.[4] With his history after he quitted his native city, we

[1] Liv. I. 34 ; Dion. Hal. III. p. 184 ; Strab. V. p. 219 ; Cic. Tusc. Quæst. V. 37; de Repub. II. 19 ; Macrob. Saturn. I. 6. Dionysius says he had made his immense fortune by trading with Etruria alone.

[2] Plin. N. H. XXXV. 5, 43. He says that these two *fictores* first introduced the plastic art into Italy. Tacitus (Ann. XI. 14) says Demaratus taught the Etruscans alphabetical writing ; and according to Cicero (de Repub. II. 19) and Dionysius (loc. cit.), he instructed his sons in all the arts of Greece, for which Rome was indebted to Tarquin, who—Græcum ingenium Italicis artibus miscuisset—says Florus, I. 5.

[3] Strab. VIII. p. 378.

[4] Liv. I. 34 ; Dion. Hal. III. p. 185 ; Polyb. VI. 2, ap. Suid. v. Λεύκιος. All this pretty legend of Demaratus falls to the ground at a touch of the critical wand of Niebuhr, who shows (I. p. 372, *et seq.*) that the chronological basis on which it rests is utterly unsound. He does not positively deny the existence of such a man as Demaratus, but totally rejects his relationship with Tarquinius Priscus, whom he regards not as an Etruscan at all, but as a Latin—which he deduces from his *cognomen*, Priscus. The two potters he looks on, not as real personages, but as symbols of moulding or painting on clay. Yet these names were not always mere abstractions ; for I have seen that of "Eucheir" inscribed as the potter on a Greek vase, and there is a *kylix* in the British Museum, with the inscription ΕΥΧΕΡΟΣ ΕΠΟΙΕΣΕΝ. Müller (einl. 2, 16, n. 32) agrees with Niebuhr in considering the two legends of Demaratus and L. Tarquinius as originally in no way connected. He regards (einl. 5, 4) the legend of Demaratus as purely Corinthian,

have nothing more to do than to mention that, if chroniclers may be credited, he had his revenge on his fellow countrymen, by the conquest of the entire Etruscan Confederation, which sent him twelve *fasces*, and the other *insignia* of empire in acknowledgment of its submission to his authority.[5] It may be, however, that the legend of Tarquin's migration to Rome and his attainment of the kingly power are merely significant of the conquest of that city by an Etruscan prince, who introduced the institutions of his country, and made Rome the capital of a powerful state in connection with the national Confederation.[6] In this case we may regard the legend of Tarquin's conquest of the Twelve Cities as significant either of the metropolitan power of Tarquinii over the rest of Etruria,[7] or as an invention of the annalists to account for the introduction of the Etruscan *insignia* of authority into Rome.[8]

When Servius Tullius ascended the throne, the Etruscans, who had been subdued by his predecessor, says Dionysius, revolted; and Tarquinii, with Veii and Cære, took a prominent part in the war, which lasted twenty years, and ended in the entire subjugation of the Confederation.[9]

not Italian, and as showing, whether true or false, the early commerce of Tarquinii with Corinth.

[5] Dion. Hal. III. p. 195; Flor. I. 5. See Niebuhr's objections to this tradition of Tarquin's conquest of Etruria, I. p. 379. Müller (einl. 2, 16) also regards this legend of Tarquin's conquest as "impossible;" for Etruria was then at the zenith of her power. Mannert (Geog. p. 333) also points out the impossibility of this conquest, as being opposed to all the occurrences of the later history of Etruria. The silence of Polybius, Cicero, and Livy, proves—thinks Niebuhr—that they did not credit it.

[6] Niebuhr (I. p. 384) is of opinion that the legend of the Tarquinius Priscus "clearly implies a belief that there was a time when Rome received Toscan institutions from a prince of Etruria, and was the great and splendid capital of a powerful Etruscan state." Müller (einl. 2, 16) is much of the same opinion. Arnold (Hist. of Rome, I. p. 56) also considers the Etruscan dynasty of Rome to show the dominion of Etruria over the Latins, and the expulsion of the Tarquins to signify the decline of the city of Tarquinii, and the liberation of Rome from the Etruscan yoke.

[7] Müller (einl. 2, 16) so interprets this tradition of Tarquin's conquest of all Etruria. "If you will," says he, "you may view the two Tarquins as regents of Tarquinii in Rome; but this seems in both cases open to doubt." He would rather consider Priscus and Superbus as names descriptive of an earlier and later tyranny; and the two kings so specified as being in fact "nameless in history." Niebuhr (I. p. 383) suspects a connexion between the Roman legend of Tarquin, being the supreme ruler of all Etruria, and the Etruscan one of Tarchon, who conquered that land and founded the Twelve Cities.

[8] Strabo (V. p. 220) ascribes the introduction of the Etruscan *insignia* into Rome to Tarquin himself, who brought them from Tarquinii; Livy (I. 8) to Romulus. The statement of Strabo that "Tarquin adorned Etruria"—which from the context would seem to refer more particularly to his native city, Tarquinii—"by means of resources derived from Rome," seems opposed to the tradition of his subjugation of that land, and more consistent with his conquest of Rome as an Etruscan prince.

[9] Dion. Hal. IV. pp. 214, 231. To this

After Tarquinii Superbus had been expelled from Rome, he sought assistance from the Tarquinienses and Veientes on the plea of consanguinity. It seemed good to the people of Tarquinii that their race should reign at Rome, and in conjunction with Veii they sent an army to reinstate Tarquin. In the battle which ensued, the Veientes, who had been often beaten by the Romans, turned and fled; but the Tarquinienses, "a new enemy, not only maintained their ground, but even repulsed the Romans." This was the battle of the Arsian Wood, in which Junius Brutus, the First Consul, and Aruns Tarquinius fell by each other's hands; and the Etruscans had to learn from divine lips that they were beaten.[1]

We hear nothing further of Tarquinii for more than a century, till in the year of Rome 357 (397 B.C.), she took up arms to assist Veii, then closely besieged by the Romans, but was severely punished for her interference.[2]

The next mention we find of her is in the year 366 (388 B.C.), when the Romans invaded her territory, and destroyed the towns of Cortuosa and Contenebra.[3]

In the year 395 (359 B.C.) her citizens retaliated by ravaging the Roman territory, routed their army, and put to death in the Forum of Tarquinii three hundred and seven of the captives, as a sacrifice to their gods—the disgrace of the Romans being increased by the ignominy of the punishment.[4] In 397 the Tarquinienses were joined by the Falisci,[5] and in the following year occurred that singular scene, already referred to, when the Etruscan priests, with flaming torches and serpents in their hands, led the van of their force against the Romans, who, terrified at this charge of Furies, at first gave way; but being laughed out of their fears by their leaders, rallied, and put the foe to the rout. Hereupon the allied cities gathered all the force of the Confederation, and marched to the Salinæ, at the mouth of the Tiber, where, being suddenly attacked by the

conquest of Etruria by S. Tullius, the same objections will apply that are urged against that by his predecessor. Niebuhr (I. p. 367) rejects it as fictitious.

[1] Liv. II. 6, 7 ; Dion. Hal. V. pp. 279, 286, et seq. Livy, in representing Tarquinii on this occasion at war with Rome for the first time, is quite opposed to Dionysius; but seems to corroborate the opinion above mentioned of the early Etruscan conquest of Rome, and to show that the Tarquinienses

regarded the expulsion of the Tarquins as a rebellion against their authority in particular. The expedition of Porsena seems, however, rather to indicate that it was regarded as a rebellion against the entire Confederation.

[2] Liv. V. 16.
[3] Liv. VI. 4.
[4] Liv. VII. 12, 15.
[5] Liv. VII. 16.

Romans, eight thousand of them were captured, and the rest slain or driven out of the Roman territory.[6] But Tarquinii was not yet subdued; she continued the war manfully, and in the year 400 (354 B.C.) sustained another signal defeat, in which a vast number of her soldiers were taken prisoners, who were all slain in cold blood, save three hundred and fifty-eight of noble birth, who were sent to Rome, and there in the Forum were scourged to death, or perished by the axes of the lictors. Thus bitterly did the Romans avenge the sacrifice of their countrymen in the forum of Tarquinii. Not yet, however, was the spirit of the Tarquinienses subdued; they still maintained the war, aided by the Cærites and Falisci. But their allies of Cære proved faithless, and made a separate peace with Rome, and the other two cities continued a fruitless struggle, till in the year 403 (351 B.C.), when the Romans had laid waste their lands with fire and sword, "doing battle," as Livy says, "with fields rather than with men," they besought and obtained a truce for forty years.[7]

At the expiration of that period they, in conjunction with the rest of the Confederate cities, save Arretium, again took up arms, and besieged Sutrium, then in alliance with Rome, which made vain efforts to raise the siege; till in the following year, 444 (310 B.C.), Fabius routed the Etruscans with a shower of stones in the neighbourhood of that town; and followed up his victory by crossing the Ciminian Mount.[8] Tarquinii, though not expressly mentioned, doubtless took part in the great struggle and defeat at the Vadimonian Lake in 445; for in the next year she was compelled to furnish corn for the Roman army, and to petition for another truce of forty years.[9]

Though we find no further mention of Tarquinii in Etruscan times, there is little doubt that she took part in the final great struggle for independence, and joined her confederates in the second fruitless stand made at the Vadimonian Lake in the year 471 (283 B.C.).[1] At what precise period she fell under Roman domination we know not; but it must have been at the close of the

---

[6] Liv. VII. 17; Frontin. Strat. II. 4, 17; Diod. Sic. XVI. p. 432. The latter writer says nothing memorable was effected—only the *ager Faliscus* was devastated. Yet Rutilus the dictator had his triumph—Fasti Capitolini, anno 397.

[7] Liv. VII. 19—22.

[8] Liv. IX. 32, 33, 35, 36; cf. Diod. Sic. XX. p. 773, ed. Rhod.; Flor. I. 17; Fasti Capitolini, anno 444.

[9] Liv. IX. 39, 41; Diod. Sic. XX. p. 781. Niebuhr (III. p. 276) regards Tarquinii as the only bitter enemy that Rome possessed among the Etruscans, after the fall of Veii.

[1] Of this final war we have but scattered notices. A connected and detailed account was doubtless given in the lost second decade of Livy.

fifth century of Rome. In the Second Punic War she furnished Scipio's fleet with sail-cloth.[2] The city was subsequently a colony and a *municipium*;[3] and inscriptions found on the spot prove it to have been flourishing in the time of Trajan and the Antonines. It is supposed to have been desolated by the Goths and Lombards in the sixth, and by the Saracens in the ninth century of our era, at which time its inhabitants removed to the opposite hill, and founded Corneto ; but it was not finally deserted till the year 1307, when its last remains were destroyed by the Cornetans.[4]

The site of the ancient city is still called Turchina,[5] or Piano di Civita. From the Montarozzi nothing is to be seen of it but the high, bare table-land on which it stood, girt about with white cliffs. This table-land lies inland from the Montarozzi, and parallel to it, and rises five or six hundred feet above the sea. It is nearly two miles from Corneto, across the deep intervening valley ; and as there is no road or even track, the excursion must be made on foot or horseback—the latter being advisable for ladies, as the slope is steep and rugged. The highest part of the city is to the west, opposite Corneto. Here and in many other parts around the brow of the cliffs are a few massive rectangular blocks, the foundations of the ancient walls, but other trace of a city, above ground, there is none—a long, bare platform, overrun with weeds or corn-stubble, meets the eye, with not a sign of life, on its melancholy surface, or at most a few cattle grazing, and a lonely herdsman seated on some prostrate block, or stretched beneath a lowly bush. Yet that this has been the site of a city will not be doubted by him who regards the soil on which he treads ; which is composed of brick-bats, earthenware, hewn stone, and marble—ineffaceable traces of ancient habitation. A practised eye might even perceive in these fragments records of the city's history—that it was originally Etruscan is proved by the pottery, which resembles that on purely Etruscan sites ; while the intermixture of marble tells of the domination of the Romans, and the frequent fragments of

² Liv. XXVIII. 45.

² Plin. III. 8 ; Frontin. de Col. ; Cicero, pro Cæcinâ, cap. IV. ; Ptolem. Geog. p. 72, ed. Bert.

⁴ Garampi, ap. Tirabos. Letter. Ital. I. p. 50.

⁵ This is very nearly the Etruscan appellation, which, as we learn from the

Tomb of the Tarquins at Cære, must have been TARCHNA. The name of "Turchina" is also given by the Cornetani to a height halfway between the ancient city and Monte Romano, whence water is still brought to Corneto by the aqueduct. It is marked by this name also on Canina's map. Etr. Marit. tav. 74.

verd-antique, and other rare and valuable stones, determine it to have been a place of wealth and consequence under the Empire.[6]

The lover of nature will turn from these dim traces of antiquity to the bright scene around him. He looks across the deep, bare, lonesome valley to the opposite height of the Montarozzi, whose long, rugged mass bounds the view to the south and west, terminating abruptly in yellow cliffs, which are crowned by the many towers of Corneto. The lofty bare height to the north-west is Monte Quagliero, part of the ancient necropolis; the trees in the intervening hollow mark the course of the Marta; and stretching away over a tract of level shore, the eye reaches the broad blue of the Mediterranean, and travels on to the graceful headland of Monte Argentaro, to the Giglio and Giannuti, its islet satellites, and if the weather be clear, to the peaks of Elba, dim and grey on the blue horizon. From this quarter round again to the south stretches the wide sweep of the Etruscan plain, broken and undulating—no longer here richly wooded as in days of yore,[7] but for the most part naked and barren; with the dark crests of the Canino mountains on the north; the giant mass of Santa Fiora, a wedge of snow, towering behind; Monte Fiascone rising like a long wave in the north-east; the loftier double-peaked Ciminian at its side; and bounding the view to the south, the long, serrated, and forested range of the Tolfa, sinking to the sea at Civita Vecchia.

On the way from this point eastward to a lofty part of the ridge several remains are passed—here mere substructions, there fragments of walling—here a well, there a vault opening in the slope. Still more numerous are such vestiges on the summit of this height, which seems to have been the Arx of Tarquinii. Here are nothing but substructions, yet the outline of several buildings may be traced,[8]—possibly temples of the three great divinities, Jupiter, Juno, and Minerva, which were usual in Etruscan cities,[9] and which analogy teaches us to look for on the Acropolis, or most elevated position. This spot is known by the

---

[6] It is said that scarabei and beautiful cameos are often brought to light by the plough. Ann. Inst. 1829, p. 93.

[7] Stat. Sylv. V. 2, 1 ; Varro, de Re Rust. III. 12. The latter writer speaks of a park here, stocked with wild animals, not only deer, roebuck, and hares, but also wild sheep.

[8] On the side facing the Montarozzi, the blocks are arranged in terraces down the slope, possibly the steps by which the superincumbent buildings were approached, but more probably so placed for the sake of a firmer foundation.

[9] Serv. ad Æn. I. 426.

name of Ara della Regina, or "The Queen's Altar." It is three miles and more from Corneto as the crow flies, and double that distance by the high road.

At a little distance behind these substructions, a semi-circular line of blocks is to be traced, which appears to mark the outline of the citadel. On the east of it are traces of a gate; and on the opposite side, in the slope facing the Montarozzi, is a half-buried arch, which must be an ancient gateway, now encumbered with *débris*. It is shown in the woodcut at the head of this chapter.[1]

From the Arx the hill is seen to turn to the north-east, showing the form of the city to have been that of an obtuse angle. The arm most remote from Corneto is bounded at the distance of nearly a mile by a high sugar-loaf mound, and the intervening slopes are thinly strewn with blocks of the ancient walls—one stone rarely standing upon another. The conical, or rather wedge-shaped, height, called La Castellina, appears to have been without the limits of the city, from which it is separated by a hollow.[2] Were it excluded, the city must still have been about five miles in circuit.

The line of walls may be traced in many detached portions by substructions. The blocks, though sometimes volcanic, are generally cut from the calcareous cliffs of the city, in dimensions and arrangement resembling the remnants of masonry at Veii and Cære, and with equal claims to be considered Etruscan. In fact, where the outline of a city is almost determined by nature, the original line of wall at the verge of the cliff may well have been preserved in all ages, and how often soever the upper portions may have been renewed, it is highly improbable that the foundations would have been disturbed. There seem to have been

---

[1] The arch is only 6 ft. 6 in. in span, and about 3 ft. thick, inwards; so that it must have been a mere postern. The depth of the voussoirs is 21 inches, and of the courses in the surrounding masonry, 17 or 18 inches.

Canina gives an illustration of this archway (Etruria Marit. tav. 77), yet speaks of it as on the north side of Tarquinii, and as opening in the substructions of a causeway, which crossed the valley in this direction to the heights of Santo Spirito, and also served as an aqueduct to convey water thence to the ancient city (II., pp. 35, 57). He was either misinformed as to the posi-

tion of the arch, or if speaking from personal observation, he must have referred to another similar monument, for the archway mentioned in the text, and illustrated from a sketch by my own hand, is on the south of the city, and was undoubtedly a gate in the city-walls.

[2] Westphal (Ann. Inst. 1830, p. 37) took this height for the acropolis. Its slope, indeed, bears fragments of ancient walling, but whether these belonged to a fortification, or mark, as Canina supposes, the precinct of a temple which crowned the summit, now occupied by mediæval remains, I could not determine.

many gates. The sites of some are very discernible—especially in that part nearest Corneto.

The principal remains within the walls are evidently Roman. Just under the Arx to the west are traces of Baths, excavated in 1829. Little is now to be seen, but when opened there were painted walls, broken statues and columns, Latin inscriptions, beautiful mosaics, and other remains which told of

> " What time the Romaine Empire bore the raine
> Of all the world and florisht most in might."

Traces of other buildings have been discovered—a *nymphæum*, temples, reservoirs—in fact, every excavation brings some ruin to light, for the entire surface of the hill is a thick stratum of *débris;* but as such researches, however valuable to science, are seldom lucrative to the speculator, we cannot expect many excavations to be made.[8]

In the winter of 1875–6, however, a company of thirteen gentlemen of Corneto, with the Sindaco at their head, influenced by the love of antiquarian research, rather than by the hope of gain, commenced excavations on the site of the ancient city. They continued their labours for three months, and though they did not find much of value to reward their enterprise, they had the satisfaction to disclose a large portion of the southern walls of the Arx, extending for at least sixty metres. These walls are of regular masonry in six or seven courses, each course being about eighteen inches in height. The blocks, which are of the local stone, are all arranged with their ends outwards, and often immediately over each other in a hap-hazard manner, as in very primitive masonry. In front of the wall ran an ancient road about ten feet wide, with a pavement of squared slabs laid diagonally. This is now covered up, as are also sundry wells or pits beneath the wall, the contents of which I could not learn from my guide, one of the excavators. Within the walls, were opened several subterranean structures, in which were found fragments of marble, terra-cottas, and articles in bronze and gold, as well as coins. One of these chambers contained a great number of

---

[8] For notices of the excavations on the site of Tarquinii, see Bull. Inst. 1829, p. 197; 1830, pp. 72, 238; 1831, p. 4; 1835, p. 27.

Micali (Ant. Pop. Ital. II. p. 222) mentions a large *cloaca*, similar in construction to the Cloaca Maxima, at the foot of the hill of Tarquinii. I have sought it in vain; nor is it mentioned by any one but himself. He can hardly mean the half-buried arch, of which a woodcut is given at the head of this chapter.

terra-cotta heads. Multitudes of large iron nails, probably used for fastening timber, which has long ago perished, lay in heaps on the ground, together with many fragments of glass, and of red Aretine pottery, with adornments in relief.

A remarkable relic on the site of the city is a tomb, or what is precisely similar to those found in abundance on Etruscan sites —a chamber hollowed in the rock below the surface, of the ordinary size, with walls slightly converging as usual, and ceiling carved into beam and rafters. As it is in the very heart of the city, it naturally suggests a doubt if it were really a tomb, and not rather a cellar or underground apartment. But in the records of these excavations I find it mentioned as a tomb, and as containing, when opened, fragments of beautiful, painted vases, mingled with burnt bones.[4] It must then be regarded as an exception to the rule of Etruscan burial—as the tomb of some illustrious individual, who was honoured with sepulture within the city-walls.[5]

Such are the extant remains of the city which formerly occupied this site—a city among the most ancient, and once, it may be, the chief in all Italy—the metropolis of the Etruscan Confederation—which was in the zenith of her power and splendour when Rome was but a group of straw-built huts on the Palatine—which gave a dynasty to the Seven Hills, and exchanged with the cities of Greece, even in that early age, the products of her skill and labour. Who can behold unmoved her present desolation? Where stood temple and tower, palace and forum, where shone the glories of art and the lavishments of wealth and luxury, nature now displays, as in mockery,

---

[4] Bull. Inst. 1830, p. 72. Instances of similar intramural sepulture I have observed on the site of the ancient Cære. I am assured by Signor Luigi Dasti, the Sindaco of Corneto, that in the excavations made on the site of this ancient city in the spring of 1876, several subterranean tombs were brought to light. I visited the spot in May, to assure myself of the fact, but found that all these structures had been reclosed with earth.

[5] This was the custom with the Romans. Cic. de Leg. II. 23 ; Plut. Publicola, ad finem. And in Greece, though in early times the dead were buried in their own houses (Plato, Minos, II. p. 315, ed. Steph.), and though in Sparta and some of her

colonies it was usual to inter within the city (Plut. Lycurg. ; Polyb. VIII. p. 533, ed. Casaub.; Paus. I. 43, 3), yet in the historic period it was the general custom to bury without the walls, as at Athens (Cic. ad Div. IV. 12), except when peculiar honour was to be shown to the dead ; as when Themistocles was interred in the forum of Magnesia (Plut. Themist. ad fin.), and Timoleon in that of Syracuse (Plut. Timol. ad fin.). Polybius (loc. cit.) tells us that at Tarentum the citizens always buried their dead within the walls, in fancied obedience to an ancient oracle, which had declared that the city would be happy and prosperous in proportion to the number of its inhabitants.

her summer tribute of golden corn—*seges ubi Troja fuit.* Or where the rock-strewn soil refuses to yield, all is a naked waste—

> " The mighty columns are but sand,
> And lazy snakes trail o'er the level ruins."

The sage or artist from Athens or Corinth—the Egyptian priest or magician—the Phœnician merchant—the Samnite ally —the subject Umbrian—the rude Gaul or stern Roman marvelling at the magnificence—the stately augur—the haughty Lucumo —the fierce corsair—the crowd of luxurious citizens, the rank, the wealth, the beauty of Tarquinii—where are they? Your voice passes over the lonely waste, and meets not the wall of temple, mart, or palace, to echo the cry, " Where are they? " The city is no more—one stone of it is scarcely left upon another. And its inhabitants? They lie in the depths of yonder hill. Not one abode of the living is left, but sepulchres in thousands. There lie the remains of Tarquinii and of her citizens, their treasures of gold and silver, of bronze and pottery, of painting and sculpture, all they prized in life, lie not here, but there—buried with them. Strange that while their place of abode on earth is mute, their sepulchres should utter such eloquent truths !

ANCIENT CLOACA ON THE MARTA.

CHAPTER XXVIII.

GRAVISCÆ.

Inde Graviscarum fastigia rara videmus
Quas premit æstivæ sæpe paludis odor.
Sed memorosa viret densis vicinia lucis,
Pineaque extremis fluctuat umbra fretis. —RUTILIUS.

As Tarquinii carried on an extensive commerce with foreign countries, yet was situated some miles from the sea, she must have had a port. This is nowhere expressly named by the ancients, yet as the only town on this coast below Tarquinii was Graviscæ,[1] said by Livy to have belonged to that city,[2] it is highly probable that Graviscæ was its port.

Of Graviscæ a few scattered notices only have come down to us. We have no record of its foundation, yet we learn that it was of high antiquity.[3] It was probably a colony of Tarquinii,

---

[1] Called also Gravisca, and Graviscium. Plin. III. 8 ; Strab. V. p. 225 ; Mela, II. 4 ; Ptolem. p. 68, ed. Bert.

[2] Liv. XL. 29.

[3] Virgil (Æn. X. 184) mentions it among the Etruscan cities of the time of Æneas. Sil. Italicus (VIII. 475) characterises it as veteres Graviscæ.

There are certain coins—with the legend ΓΡΑ, and the head of Jupiter, two eagles on a thunderbolt, and two dots as the sign of a *sextans*,—which have been attributed to Graviscæ. Lanzi, Sagg. II. pp. 26, 68. But numismatists now refer them to Acragas in Sicily.

established solely for purposes of commerce; and it must have followed the fortunes of its mother-city. Yet it fell into the hands of the Romans at an earlier period, for it was taken from Tarquinii. In the year 573 (181 B.C.) it became a Roman colony,[4] and it appears to have been in existence as late as Trajan,[5] but in the time of Rutilius it was in utter ruin, and scarcely a vestige of it was visible.[6] If this were the case nearly 1500 years since, what can we expect to find now? Its general position on the coast below Tarquinii is pretty clearly indicated by the geographers and Itineraries,[7] but its precise site has not been satisfactorily determined,—most antiquaries placing it at or near the Porto San Clementino, between the mouths of the Marta and Mignone;[8] some at the mouth of the latter stream;[9] Westphal alone pointing out a site on the right bank of the Marta.[1] I have visited all three spots, and am of opinion that the last is the true site of Graviscæ, or at least of the port of Tarquinii.

S. Clementino, or Le Saline, as it is called from the neighbouring salt-works, is a small port, four or five miles below Corneto. Though called a port, it is scarcely a village—a large Dogana, a puny fort, and a few hovels inhabited by the labourers in the salt-works, being its sole ingredients. A little commerce, however, is carried on, for it exports salt to Fiumicino for the capital, and corn in some quantities to France and England, as in ancient times to Rome.[2] This is in the cool season. In the summer months the place is well nigh deserted. Not a soul enters this fatal region, save under imperious necessity. The *doganiere* turns his face to the waveless, slimy expanse, which

---

[4] Liv. loc. cit.; cf. Fabrotti, X. p. 748. Frontinus (de Coloniis) speaks of a later colonisation of Graviscæ by Augustus, and says that Tiberius marked out its *ager* by huge stones.

[5] This is learned from an inscription found at Tarquinii, which refers to Graviscæ. Ann. Inst. 1832, p. 152.

[6] Rutil. Itin. I. 281.

[7] Strabo (loc. cit.) describes it as 300 *stadia* (37½ miles) from Cosa, and somewhat less than 130 (22½ miles) from Pyrgi. The Maritime Itinerary of Antoninus gives the distance from Pyrgi as 27 miles. The Peutingerian Table is defective in the distances on this side of Graviscæ, but states that from Cosa to be 21 miles, which is much too small. Ptolemy indicates it as

lying between Cosa and Castrum Novum. Precision in distances is not to be looked for from the ancient geographers, on account of their imperfect means of information, nor from the Itineraries, because of the great facility for the commission of errors in the transcribing of figures. We must be content with an approximation to truth.

[8] Cluver, II. p. 434. Cramer, Ancient Italy, I. p. 197. Micali, Ant. Pop. Ital. I. p. 146. Abeken, Mittelitalien, p. 36.

[9] Canina, Boll. Inst. 1847, p. 92. This view is based on the Itineraries.

[1] Ann. Inst. 1830, pp. 28, 30.

[2] Liv. IX. 41. I cannot learn that coral is found on this coast as in ancient times. —Plin. XXXII. 11.

mocks his woe with its dazzling joy, and sighs in vain for a breath of pure air to refresh his fevered brow;—the lonely sentinel drags his sickening form around the pyramids of salt which stud the shore, using his musket for a staff, or he looks out from his hovel of reeds on the brink of a salt-pit, to the bare trembling swamp around, and curses the fate which has consigned him to this lingering death. It is a dreary spot, where danger is not masked in beauty, but comes in its native deformity. Such has ever been the character of this coast. Virgil describes it as most unhealthy—and the very name of Graviscæ, according to Cato, is significant of its heavy pestilent atmosphere.[3] The curse on Moab and Ammon is here realised—"Salt-pits and a perpetual desolation."

These salt-works produce annually eight pyramids, each containing nearly a million of pounds. It is strange that none of this salt is consumed at Corneto, which receives her supply from France—the heavy duties on the native product, still, as in the days of Porsena,[4] a government monopoly, making it more expensive than that imported.

At San Clementino are traces of ancient habitation—two vaults and a sewer of Roman date, and fragments of pottery mingled with the soil. The space thus strewn is very circumscribed; nothing above ground is of Etruscan character, and no remains of an ancient port are visible. Yet traces of Etruscan burial have been found in the neighbourhood which favour the view, though they do not warrant the conclusion, that this is the site of Graviscæ.[5]

Three miles along the shore to the south, stands the lonely Tower of Bertaldo, at the mouth of the Mignone.[6] It is more commonly called Sant Agostino, from a legend of that saint. The holy man, as he once strayed along this shore, was pondering on the mysteries of the Trinity, and doubts, suggested by the evil powers whose attacks he deplores in his "Confessions," were arising in his mind, when on reaching this spot, he beheld a

---

[3] Virg. Æn. X. 184 ; Serv. in loc.; Rutil. I. 282. Cato, ap. Serv. loc. cit.

[4] Liv. II. 9.

[5] Westphal is in error in denying the existence of ancient remains on this site. Ann. Inst. 1830, p. 28. Painted vases have been found here, not in tombs, but in sarcophagi of stone or earthenware, buried at a very little depth below the surface, and in a circumscribed spot of ground. In one were found all the bones of a horse, and (as if the owner had left to his steed the post of honour) by its side lay a human skeleton of gigantic size. Ann. Inst. 1829, p. 95— Avvolta.

[6] Anciently the Minio, mentioned by Virgil, Æn. X. 183 ; Serv. in loc. ; Mela, II. 4 ; Rutil. I. 279. Cluver (II. p. 483) regards the Rapinium of the Maritime Itinerary as a corruption of Minio.

child busied in filling with water a small hole in the sand. St. Augustine asked what he was about. "Trying to put the sea into this hole," replied the *criatura*. "Impossible!" cried the saint, laughing at the boy's simplicity. "More easy this," said the other, who now stood confessed an angel, "than for thee to comprehend those sublime mysteries thou art vainly seeking to penetrate." This cannot have been the site of Graviscæ, which, as we learn both from Rutilius and the Itineraries, stood considerably to the north of the Minio. It probably marks the site of Rapinium, a station on the Via Aurelia, half-way between Centum Cellæ and Graviscæ.

To reach the site on the right bank of the Marta, it is necessary on leaving Corneto to take the road to Leghorn, as far as the Marta, two miles distant; then, crossing the bridge, turn at once to the left, and after a couple of miles in a country-road, you will reach some Roman ruins by the way-side. A few furlongs beyond is an eminence, some thirty or forty feet high, on and around which are scattered sundry large blocks of tufo, and fragments of travertine columns. This I take to be the site of Graviscæ. That more than a temple or villa occupied it is clear, from the extent of the broken pottery, and from several circumstances presently to be mentioned. True, it is almost two miles from the sea, yet scarcely a furlong from the Marta, which here swells into a respectable stream, and bears palpable evidence of having been of much more importance in ancient times than at present, and of having been in direct connexion with this eminence.

To discover these traces of antiquity, you must follow the course of the stream from the point where you first meet with the Roman ruins; and at the distance of two or three furlongs you will come upon some large blocks rising from the soil. Further examination will show them to be the crest of an arch. Look over the bank—you will perceive the vault beneath you; and if you clamber down, you will find it to be one of the finest specimens of an ancient arch in all Etruria. My astonishment on making this discovery was great. A friend who had previously visited this site, had remarked the blocks rising from the soil, but had not perceived the grand relic of antiquity at his feet. Grand it is, for the vault is not inferior to the Cloaca Maxima in span, or about fourteen feet, while the masonry is on a much larger scale.[6]

[7] The *roussoirs* are from five to six feet in depth; those of the Cloaca Maxima are scarcely two feet and a half; but there is a triple row of them.

The arch opens in a long embankment of regular masonry, which, rising some twenty feet above the stream, extends in fragments a considerable distance towards the sea. The masonry of both arch and embankment is of tufo, uncemented, and is of manifest antiquity. The vault must be the mouth of a sewer or stream, as is clearly shown by the mound of earth which chokes it. Were it not for this, and the trees which have taken root in it, the arch could not be examined from this bank; and to the boughs of the said trees I acknowledge my indebtedness for the sketch which is copied in the woodcut at the head of this Chapter.

Remounting the bank, I descried a double line of substructions stretching away in connection with the arch, in a direct line towards the height of the town. I traced it across the plain, till the modern road, which skirts the base of that eminence, obliterated its vestiges. It was obviously the ancient road or causeway from the stream to the town. Scarce a block of the pavement remained, but the skeleton—the double line of kerb-stones— was most palpable. This causeway explained the long embankment to have been a quay, and a port was at once confessed.[7] I could not doubt that this was a quay, for the opposite bank was very low, and entirely without masonry. The whole seemed the counterpart of the Pulchrum Littus and the Cloaca Maxima; the embankment being of the same height, the vault of the same dimensions, and the object being doubtless similar—to drain the low grounds on this bank,[8] to permit vessels to lie alongside, and to serve as a barrier against occasional floods—the Marta being the natural and only emissary of the Lake of Bolsena. This must have been one reason, added to the all-cogent one of superior salubrity, which led the founders of the town to select a site, not on the sea-shore, or on the banks of the stream, but on the first convenient eminence, though it were two miles inland. This quay, sewer, and causeway, prove to a certainty that this

---

[8] The river would not serve as a port now-a-days, but must have been quite deep and broad enough for the galleys of the ancients. The causeway may possibly have formed part of the ancient Via Aurelia, but the absence of all traces of a bridge across the Marta at this point seems opposed to that view.

[9] The arch may have been a bridge over a small stream, which fell into the Marta, but no traces of a channel could I perceive in the plain. The proprietor of the ground, Signor Falzacappa, of Corneto, is of opinion that the arch, called by the peasantry Il Pontone, is a bridge originally crossing the Marta itself, which has since changed its course. But the comparatively narrow span of the arch, the absence of all vestiges of a former channel, and the long embankment, forbid me to entertain this view.

site, whatever may have been its name in ancient times, was the port of Tarquinii.[9]

West of the town is a rising ground, in which are some caves, and here, it is said, tombs have been found. Sepulchres richly decorated and furnished, are not likely, however, to be discovered here; for this town can have been little more than a place of business to the parent city—a landing-place for goods—where the merchant princes of Tarquinii had their warehouses and offices.[1] No one would have dwelt in the pestilent atmosphere of this swampy coast, who could have afforded a residence on the comparatively salubrious heights of Tarquinii. The fever-fraught climate of the summer months is the only feature which the site retains of its ancient character. Nothing can be more dreary and desolate than the scene around. The sun calls forth no beauty; the showers no verdure or luxuriance. Of the dense pine-groves which overshadowed the waves of old,[2] not a tree remains—the vineyards which still earlier gave Graviscæ renown,[3] have now no existence,—a patch of corn here and there in the plain, and the grey olive-woods on the distant slopes of the Montarozzi, are the only signs of cultivation within view.

[1] I stated my opinion that this was the site of Graviscæ in Bull. Inst. 1847, p. 92. To this, Canina, who placed that town near the mouth of the Mignone, which site, he says, agrees with the distance of rather less than 180 *stadia*, laid down by Strabo as that between Pyrgi and Graviscæ, objected, and pronounced the remains discovered by me to belong to a station on the Via Aurelia, indicated in the Maritime Itinerary under the name of Maltanum, which, he thinks, from the agreement of the other Itineraries, stood precisely at the mouth of the Marta. Now the Itineraries, to which Canina appears to have yielded implicit credence, are often in error, or widely at variance—as a comparison of them in this very instance will attest. The principal objection to this being the site of Graviscæ is the position to the south of the Marta assigned to that town by the Itineraries. (See Westphal's observations on this subject. Ann. Inst. 1830, p. 32.) On other points I may appeal to them in support of my view that this is the site of Graviscæ. For if, with Canina, I cite the Maritime Itinerary in evidence, I find Graviscæ placed 12 miles from Centumcellæ, but the Mignone, where Canina places Graviscæ, is only 7 or 8 miles distant; the Saline, where others have placed it, is but 10, whereas my site is just 12½ miles from that port. And while Strabo's distance of 180 *stadia* from Pyrgi is better answered in the Saline than in either of the other sites; the Maritime Itinerary in stating it at 27 miles, favours the site on the right bank of the Marta. This shows how little dependence is to be placed upon the Itineraries for precise information.

[2] It was probably, like Alsium and Pyrgi, a mere—oppidum parvum (Rutil. I. 224); for Strabo (V. p. 223) and Pliny (III. 8) assert that there was but one Etruscan *city* on this coast—Populonia.

[3] Rutil. Itin. I. 283.

[4] Plin. N. H. XIV. 8, 6.

APPENDIX TO CHAPTER XXVIII.

VIA AURELIA.

(Continued from page 226.)

ANTONINE ITINERARY.			PEUTINGERIAN TABLE.	
Pyrgi			Pyrgi	
Castro Novo	M. P. VIII.		Punicum	—
Centum Cellis	V.		Castro Novo	M.P. VIIII.
Martha	X.		Centum Cellas	IIII.
Forum Aurelii	XIIII.		Mindo fl.	—
Cossam	XXV.		Gravisca	—
			Co	—
ANTONINE MARITIME ITINERARY.			Tabellaria	V.
Pyrgi			Marta	II.
Panapionem	M.P. III.		Foro Aurelii	III.
Castrum Novum	VII.		Armenita fluv.	IIII.
Centum Cellas	V.		Ad Nonas	III.
Algas	III.		Succosa	II.
Rapinium	III.		Cosam	II.
Graviscas	VI.			
Maltannin	III.			
Quintianam	III.			
Regas	VI.			
Arming fluv.	III.			
Portum Herculis	XXV.			

Some of the distances given after Centum Cellæ are very incorrect, and show that the Table in this part is not to be trusted.

For a continuation of the Via Aurelia from Cosa to Luna, see Chapter XLV.

ETRUSCAN KRATER.

CHAPTER XXIX.

VULCI.

Ruine di cittadi e di castella
Stavan con gran tresor quivi sozzopra.—ARIOSTO.

What sacred trophy marks the hallowed ground? . . .
The rifled urn, the violated mound.—BYRON.

VULCI is a city whose very name, fifty years since, was scarcely known, but "which now, for the enormous treasures of antiquity it has yielded, is exalted above every other city of the ancient world, not excepting even, in certain respects, Herculaneum or Pompeii."[1] Little is to be seen, it must be confessed, on its site; yet a visit to it will hardly disappoint the traveller. It lies about eighteen miles north-west of Corneto. The road, for the first eleven or twelve, or as far as Montalto, is the coast-railway from Rome to Pisa, and follows the line of the ancient Via Aurelia; traversing a country bare and undulating, and of little beauty. Let the visitor descend at the station of Montalto, about half a

---

[1] Dr. Braun, Ann. Inst. 1842, p. 39.

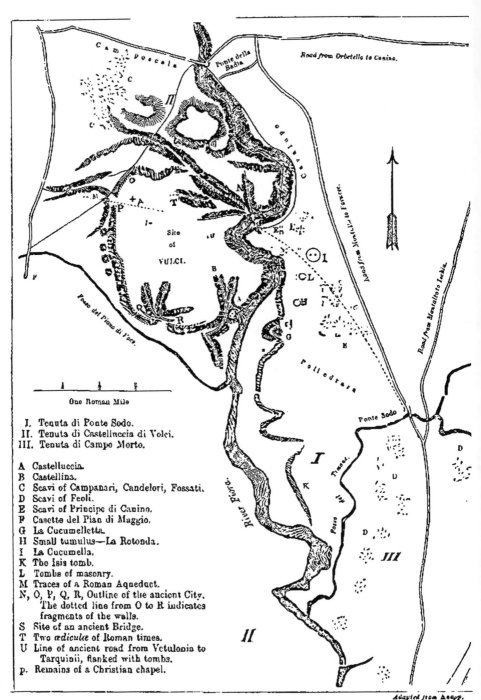

I. Tenuta di Ponte Sodo.
II. Tenuta di Castelluccia di Volci.
III. Tenuta di Campo Morto.

A Castelluccia.
B Castellina.
C Scavi of Campanari, Candelori, Fossati.
D Scavi of Feoli.
E Scavi of Principe di Canino.
F Casette del Pian di Muggio.
G La Cucumelletta.
H Small tumulus—La Rotonda.
I La Cucumella.
K The Isis tomb.
L Tombs of masonry.
M Traces of a Roman Aqueduct.
N, O, P, Q, R, Outline of the ancient City.
    The dotted line from O to R indicates
    fragments of the walls.
S Site of an ancient Bridge.
T Two ædiculæ of Roman times.
U Line of ancient road from Vetulonia to
    Tarquinii, flanked with tombs.
p. Remains of a Christian chapel.

One Roman Mile

PLAN OF VULCI AND ITS NECROPOLIS.

Adapted from Ahaep.

mile from the town.   This is a small, dull place, with no attraction beyond a tolerably comfortable inn.   It is supposed to be the site of the Forum Aurelii, a station on the Via Aurelia.[2]   At the mouth of the Fiora, on which it stands, are a few Roman remains.   On the shore, about three miles to the south-east, stood Regæ, the site of a very ancient Pelasgic settlement, Regisvilla, whose king Maleos, or Malæotes, the legendary inventor of the trumpet, abandoned his throne, and migrated to Athens.[3]   The site is now called, from its prominent rocks, Le Murelle.[4]

Vulci lies near the Ponte della Badia, seven or eight miles inland from Montalto, and is accessible in a *carretino*, or light vehicle.[5]   All this district is a desert—a desert of corn, it is true, but almost uninhabited, so deadly is the summer-scourge of *malaria*.   One house alone is passed on the road to the Ponte della Badia, and that is a little mill, on the Timone, which is here spanned by a natural bridge, called, like that of Veii, Ponte Sodo.   Beneath it is a cavern, grotesquely fretted with stalactites.

On passing the Ponte Sodo we entered on a vast treeless moor, without a sign of life, save a conical *capanna* of rushes here and there rising from its surface, and a dark castle, standing in lonely pomp in the midst, nearly three miles before us.   All this moor, from the other side of the Ponte Sodo, up to the castle and far beyond it, was the necropolis of Vulci ; but no signs of sepulture were visible, except one lofty tumulus—the Cucumella—half-way between us and the castle.   As we proceeded, however, we observed numerous pits, marking the spots where tombs had been recently opened, and partly reclosed with earth.

We alighted at the castle-gate.   It is a fortress of the middle ages, and in most other lands would be a piece of antiquity. Here it is a modern work, with little interest beyond its pic-

---

[2] Cluver. II. p. 485 ; Mannert, however (Goog. p. 370), places Forum Aurelii at Castellaccio, near the mouth of the Arrone, half-way between the Fiora and the Marta; a site more in accordance with the Peutingerian Table.   The Fiora is the Armenita of the Table, and the Arnino of the Maritime Itinerary.   Some singular Etruscan monuments have been found in the neighbourhood of Montalto.—Micali, Mon. Ined. p. 195, tav. XXXIV. ; p. 403, tav. LIX.

[3] Strab. V. p. 225 ; Lactant. ad Stat. Theb. IV. 224.   Müller (Etrusk. einl. 2, 6) thinks he derived this name from the headland of Malea in Laconia.   Regisvilla

is probably a Roman corruption of the more ancient name of Regæ, which afterwards came again into use.   Welcker (cited by Gerhard, Ann. Inst. 1831, p. 205) derives it from ῥηγαί, clefts, a name indicative of its situation.

[4] Holsten. Annot. ad Cluver. p. 34 ; Westphal, Ann. Inst. 1830, p. 30.

[5] There are two roads from Montalto to Vulci, both practicable for light vehicles. The shorter runs on the right bank of the Fiora, but that on the left bank is preferable.   This it is which is described in the text.   It is marked in the Map.

turesque character. When I first knew it, it was a Papal custom-house; and a few *doganieri* mounted guard here over the neigh-bouring frontier, and took toll on the cattle and goods which crossed it. The castle stands on the verge of a deep ravine which is here spanned by a narrow bridge, fenced in with parapets so tall as to block all view. Not till I had crossed it had I any idea of its character; and then, from the slope below, it burst on me like a fresh creation. It is verily a magnificent structure, bestriding the rocky abyss like a colossus, with the Fiora fretting and foaming at a vast depth beneath.[6] But what means this extraordinary curtain of stalactites which overhangs the bridge on this side, depending in huge jagged masses from the parapet, and looking as though a vast cataract had rolled over the top of the bridge, and been petrified in its fall, ere it could reach the ground? One might almost fancy the bridge had been hewn out of the solid rock, and that the workmen had abandoned it before its completion,—like Michael Angelo's statues with unfinished extremities. How else came this rugged appendage fixed against the very top of so lofty a structure? The only solution is—it is the result of an aqueduct in the parapet. I observed the rocks around fretted in the same manner, and then comprehended that the water flowing from the table-land of the necropolis, charged with tartaric matter, in its passage through the aqueduct had oozed out of its channel, and by the precipitation of the earthy matter it held in solution, had formed this petrified drapery to the bridge. The stalactites stand out six or seven feet from the wall, and depend to a depth of fifteen or twenty feet. Independently of their remarkable conformation, their colouring—a clear creamy white—combines, with the grey or reddish masonry, to add to the effect of the bridge. The solemn castle, high on the cliff by its side, rearing its dark-red tower against the sky— the slopes clothed with the ilex and shrubs—the huge masses of rock in the hollow—the stream struggling and boiling through the narrow cleft—the steep frowning cliffs seen through the arch —are so many accessories in keeping with the principal object,

---

[6] The height of the arch above the stream is said to be 96 French feet, and its span 62 feet. The width of the bridge is only 10 feet, and its entire length 243 feet. Ann. Inst. 1832, p. 261. There is a second arch, only 15 feet in span, formed merely to lighten and strengthen the long wall of masonry on the right bank. It has a draped figure in relief on its key-stone. There is a third arch, still smaller, close under the castle, not perforating the structure, but merely recessed in it. Being on the southern side of the bridge, it is not shown in the annexed woodcut. A view of the bridge from that side is given in Mon. Ined. Inst. I. tav. 41.

PONTE DELLA BADIA, VULCI.

Drawn by G. Dennis.

forming with it as striking and picturesque a scene as I remember in Etruria.

What is the date of the bridge, and by whom was it constructed? Signor Vincenzo Campanari, who first made it known to the world, took for granted that it was of Etruscan architecture;[7] but M. Lenoir, who exercised a more critical eye, entertained doubts of this. The truth is, that the bridge is of different periods. It has three projecting piers of red tufo, much weather-worn, which are obviously of earlier construction than the neat and harder *nenfro* masonry which encases them. Both the tufo and *nenfro* portions are in the same *emplecton* style, like the walls of Sutri, Nepi, and Falleri; and the latter portion is, in part, rusticated. This style, having been adopted by the Romans, affords no decided clue to the constructors of the bridge. The return-facing of the arch, however, is of travertine, and may with certainty be referred to that people, as it possesses features in common with bridges of undoubted Roman origin—the Ponte d'Augusto at Narni, and the celebrated Pont du Gard. The aqueduct, also, I take to be Roman, simply because it passes over arches of that construction; for the skill of the Etruscans in hydraulics is so well attested, as to make it highly probable that to them were the Romans indebted for that description of structure.[8] The tufo buttresses are very probably Etruscan, for they are evidently the piers of the original bridge; and may have been united, as Lenoir suggests, by a horizontal frame of wood-work, a plan often adopted by the Romans—in the Sublician bridge, to wit—which subsequently gave place to the *nenfro* masonry of the time of the Republic, and to the arches. This seems a plausible hypothesis; and, in default of a better, I am willing to adopt it. The *nenfro* and travertine portions are, in any case, of Roman times, whatever be the antiquity of the tufo piers.[9]

The enormous masses of stalactite which drape the bridge seem to indicate a high antiquity for the whole structure; and, doubtless, they must have been the formation of centuries: yet

---

[7] Ann. Inst. 1829, p. 195.

[8] Canina takes the aqueduct to be of Imperial times, and probably of the time of Claudius, in whose reign the greatest arched works of the Romans were constructed, and to have been made to convey water to the Thermae in the city, which are unquestionably of Roman origin. To the same period he also refers the bridge, but does not notice the difference in the anti-quity of the projecting piers. Etruria Marit. II., pp. 87, 92, 101.

[9] These piers are merely encased, not connected with the rest of the structure. Lenoir points out an analogy, as regards these tufo piers, between this bridge and the Ponte Nonno, on the Via Praenestina, near the site of Gabii, which is known to be of high antiquity. Ann. Inst. 1832, p. 261.

we need not refer them to too remote a period; for, in a parallel
case at Tivoli, a vault in the face of a cliff, lined with Roman
reticulated work, has had its mouth blocked by an immense sheet
of this fantastic formation, many tons in weight.

About a mile below the bridge, on the right bank of the Fiora,
stood the ancient city of Vulci. It occupied a platform of no
great elevation, and, except on the river side, not defended by inaccessible cliffs; yet it is the only height in the wide plain at all
adapted to the site of a city. Its surface is now sown with corn;
and, besides the usual traces of ancient habitation in broken
pottery, there are ruins of extensive baths, and the wreck of a
small temple, with *cella* and niches still standing, and the statues
of its divinities and the columns which adorned it lying in
shattered fragments around.[1] All these are Roman, and of
Imperial times. Of the Etruscan city there are no traces, beyond
portions of the walls, of tufo blocks, on the brow of the cliffs to
the south and west. The sites of five gates can be recognised.

The city was of no great size—not larger than Fæsulæ or
Rusellæ, or about two miles in circuit.[2] Yet, at the period of its
greatest prosperity, it must have been extremely populous; for
its sepulchres disclose this fact. Its vast wealth, which is learned
from the same source, must have been obtained by foreign commerce; yet the position of the city, seven or eight miles from the
sea, and on no navigable stream, is such as could have been
chosen only by agriculturists.

It is a remarkable fact, and one which proves how limited is
our acquaintance with antiquity, that though this city, from its
population, wealth, and magnificence, must at some period have
been among the first in Etruria, we have absolutely no account
of its history in Livy, Dionysius, or any other ancient writer—
nothing beyond a bare record of its existence in the catalogues
of geographers.[3] The history of Vulci is chronicled in its

---

[1] From the variety in these fragments,
in size, style, and material, it would seem
that several public buildings had occupied
this site—all of the Empire. For notices
of the remains on the site of the city, see
Bull. Inst. 1835, p. 177; 1836, p. 36; and
1835, p. 122; where an account is given
of an ancient furnace, containing fragments
of pottery—suggesting a native manufactory
of vases.

[2] Micali, Ant. Pop. Ital. I. p. 147.
Some have thought it once spread over the
adjacent heights. The Prince of Canino

imagined it to have occupied both banks of
the river, and that its two parts, thus
divided, were connected by bridges.
Museum Etrusque, p. 10.

[3] Pliny (III. 8) mentions its inhabitants
as—Volcentini, cognomine Etrusci,—and
states that Cosa was in their territory—
Cossa Volcientium. Ptolomy (p. 72, ed.
Bert.) calls it Οὐόλκοι, and Stephanus says
—Ὄλκιον, a city of Etruria; according to
Polybius, VI., the name of its people was
Ὀλκιῆται and Ὀλκιεῖς. The name has
been supposed of Greek origin, yet its

sepulchres. Were it not for these, and the marvellous secrets they disclose, Vulci might have remained to the end of time in obscurity—its site unheeded, its very existence forgotten.[4]

The only event in the annals of Vulci, which has come down to us, is recorded in the Fasti Consulares, preserved in the Capitol. It is the defeat of its citizens, in concert with the Volsinienses, by T. Coruncanius, the Roman Consul in the year 474 (B.C. 280).[5] This date proves the power and importance of Vulci, that, after the disastrous defeats the Etruscans had experienced at the Vadimonian Lake, in the years 444 and 471, where the strength of the nation was completely broken, Vulci could still make head against Rome; and its conjunction with Volsinii, which at that time must have been one of the mightiest cities in Etruria, is a further evidence of its importance.[6] It is even probable that at this late period of the national independence, after Veii, Falerii, and other cities south of the Ciminian, had been conquered, Vulci took rank among the Twelve.[7] That it was

genuine Etruscan character is evident at a glance. Its initial syllable places it in the same category with Volaterræ, Volsinii, Voltumnæ Fanum, Felsina, Falerii, and the names of numerous Etruscan families—some of which bear a close analogy, as Velcia, Velscia, Phelces or Phelcia, Velchas, Velchnas, Velczna, Velzina. The M. Fulcinius of Tarquinii, whom Cicero (pro Cæcinâ, IV.) speaks of as owner of an estate near Castellum Axia, seems to have derived his name from Vulci.

[4] Gerhard (Ann. Inst. 1831, p. 101) is inclined to date the foundation of Vulci after the battle of Cuma, or about the year of Rome 278; but, I think, without adequate reason. His arguments are, the silence of ancient writers, the close vicinity of Tarquinii and Regisvilla, the former of which he imagines began to decline in power about that period, leaving Vulci to rise into importance. But if Cosa, as some suppose from Pliny's mention of it, were a colony of Vulci, the latter must have existed in very early times.

The similarity between the names of Volci or Vulci, and Volsci or Vulsci (sic Cato, ap. Priscian. V. 12; VI. 8), is very apparent. But what real connection existed is not so easy to determine. We know that the land of the Volsci, as well as all Campania, was at one period subject to the Etruscans (Cato, ap. Serv. ad Æn.

XI. 567; ad Georg. II. 533; Strab. V. p. 242; Polyb. II. 17, 1); and thence Micali (Ant. Pop. Ital. I. p. 149) infers that a colony of Volsci may have settled at Vulci during that domination. Niebuhr (I. p. 120, cf. p. 70) thinks, from the mention by Livy (XXVII. 15), of a people bearing almost the same name, the Volcentes, in connection with the Lucani and Hirpini, that there is substantial ground for conjecturing that the Vulcientes were not Etruscans, but an earlier people, who had kept their ground against those invaders; or, in other words, that the Etruscans, by their conquest, separated two portions of the same primitive Italian race —just as the Gaels of Scotland were widely severed from their Celtic brethren of Gaul by the Roman and Teutonic conquests of Britain. If Niebuhr (I. p. 72) be correct in supposing a close affinity between the names and races of the Falisci and Volsci, the same may also have existed between the Falisci and Vulcientes.

[5] The Fasti, which follow the Catonian æra, have it 473. See Gruter, p. 296.

[6] Müller, Etrusk. einl. 2, 17; II. 1, 2.

[7] This view, which is favoured by the immense treasures of its necropolis, is almost established by a monument discovered a few years since at Cervetri, and now preserved in the Lateran Museum. It is a bas-relief, which seems to have formed one

not at its conquest destroyed, as has been supposed,[8] is proved
by the Roman remains—baths, statues, inscriptions, coins—
which have been here brought to light. Pliny and Ptolemy
prove its existence under the Empire; and coins of Constantine,
Valentinian, and Gratian, show it to have stood at least as late
as the fourth century after Christ.[9]

The name of the ancient city has been preserved traditionally;
and this site has been known, from time immemorial, as the
Pian di Voce.[1] Yet the Prince of Canino, Lucien Bonaparte,
who owned the greater part of the necropolis, fancied this to be
the site of the long-lost Vetulonia, on whose ruins rose the city
of Vulci.[2] The Prince, however, had but shallow ground for his
conjecture, and stood almost alone in this view; the general and
better supported opinion being, that Vetulonia occupied some site
on this coast more to the north.

The city of Vulci stood on lower ground than its necropolis;
not so much therefore is to be seen from its site, as from the
opposite cliffs, from which spot the stern grandeur of the scene
is most imposing. The wide, wide moor, a dreary, melancholy
waste, stretches around you, no human being seen on its expanse;
the dark, lonely castle rises in the midst, with the majestic bridge
spanning the abyss at its side; the Fiora frets in its rocky bed
far beneath your feet, and its murmurs conveyed to your ear by
the tall cliffs you stand on, are the sole disturbers of the solemn
stillness. Deep is the dreariness of that moor. Not the Landes
of Gascony, not the treeless plains of the Castilles, not the shores
of the Gygæan Lake, surpass it in lifeless desolation. The sun

side of a marble throne. On it are three
separate figures, each with the name of a
people of Etruria attached—VETULONENSES
—. . . CENTANI—and TARQUINIENSES. The
middle word can have been no other than
Vulcentani; there is just room for the
three initial letters in the space where the
inscription is defaced. It seems highly
probable that the names of the Twelve
people of Etruria, and their several devices,
were recorded on this monument. Bull.
Inst. 1840, p. 92 (Canina); Ann. Inst.
1842, pp. 37—40 (Braun), and tav. d' Agg.
C. Even Annio of Viterbo made a happy
guess at this eminence of Vulci, and in
his Comments on his Catonis Origines,
called "Volcen" one of the Twelve.

[8] Bull. Inst. 1831, p. 163—Gerhard.
[9] Bull. Inst. 1835, pp. 121, 177; cf.

Gruter, pp. 301, 447, 1. Tombs purely
Roman have also been discovered, and
some even with Christian inscriptions.

[1] Micali (Ant. Pop. Ital. I. p. 147)
claims the merit of having first pointed out
this as the site of Vulci, yet Holstenius
(Annot. ad Cluver. p. 40) more than a century before, had mentioned this as the
Piano di Volci—the site of the ancient city.
All doubt of its identity has now been removed by the discovery of Latin inscriptions
on the spot. Bull. Inst. 1835, pp. 11, 121.

[2] Ann. Inst. 1829, pp. 188—192; Mus.
Etr. pp. 13, 163. His opinion was based
principally on an inscription in a vase
found in this necropolis—VIΘΛONOXEI,
written against a figure in a Bacchic scene.
See Bull. Inst. 1829, p. 140; 1830, p.
187; Ann. Inst. 1831, p. 186.

gilds but brightens it not.　The dark mountains, which bound it
on the north and east, are less gloomy in aspect, and afford a
pleasing repose to the eye wearied with wandering over its
surface.

> "All is still as night!
> All desolate!—Groves, temples, palaces—
> Swept from the sight; and nothing visible
> Amid the sulphurous vapours that exhale,
> As from a land accurst, save here and there
> An empty tomb, a fragment like the limb
> Of some dismembered giant."

Can it be that here stood one of the wealthiest and most luxurious cities of ancient Italy—the chosen residence of the princes
of Etruria?　Behold the sole relics of its magnificence in the
stones scattered over yonder field on one side, and in the yawning
graves of the vast cemetery on the other, a surer index than the
crumbled city presents to the civilisation once flourishing on this
site, but long since extinct—the one desolated, the other rifled—
both shorn of their glory.　The scene is replete with matter for
melancholy reflection, deepened by the sense that the demon of
malaria has here set up his throne, and rendered this once
densely-peopled spot " a land accurst."

The remains of two bridges, it is said, may be traced, connecting
the city with the necropolis; but none could I perceive, though
it is highly probable that there was some more direct communication than the distant Ponte della Badia.　Were it so, it may have
been at a spot called·Il Pelago, where the stream widens into a
small lake or pool, and its banks lose their precipitous character.[3]
It is a spot which has claims on the artist as well as the antiquary.　The range of lofty cliffs, fretted with stalactites, feathered
with hanging wood, and washed by the torrent, presents, in conjunction with the distant castle, the broken ground of the city,
and the wild mountains, rare morsels of form and colour for the
portfolio.

In the cliffs near the Ponte is a natural cavern, scarcely worth
the difficulty of the descent to it.

Fifty years ago the existence of this vast cemetery was utterly
unknown.　In the early part of 1828 some oxen were ploughing
near the castle, when the ground suddenly gave way beneath

---

[3] The Prince of Canino asserts the existence of two bridges in ruins (Ann. Inst.
1829, p. 192); Westphal (Ann. Inst. 1830,
p. 40) speaks of the remains of one only,
more than a mile below the Ponte della
Badia, which agrees with the position of
Il Pelago.　It is marked S in the Plan.

them, and disclosed an Etruscan tomb with two broken vases.
This led to further research, which was at first carried on unknown to the Prince of Canino, but at the close of the year he
took the excavations into his own hands, and in the course of
four months he brought to light more than two thousand objects
of Etruscan antiquity, and all from a plot of ground of three or
four acres.[4]   Other excavators soon came into the field; every
one who had land in the neighbourhood tilled it for this novel
harvest, and all with abundant success; the Feoli, Candelori,
Campanari, Fossati,—all enriched themselves and the Museums
of Europe with treasures from this sepulchral mine.   Since that
time the Prince or his widow has annually excavated on this site,
and never in vain; and the glories of ancient ceramographic art,
which he thus brought to light, and diffused throughout Europe,
have made the name of Lucien Bonaparte as well known, and
will, perhaps, win for him as lasting a renown as his conduct on
the 19th Brumaire, or the part he played in the councils of his
Imperial brother.

The necropolis embraced both banks of the Fiora.   In the
tract between the city and the Ponte della Badia, on the right
bank, known as the *tenuta* Camposcala, excavations were commenced by the Campanari in 1828; and thence came most of the
vases in the Vatican and the British Museum.   Of the multitude
of tombs here opened, few remain unclosed; but of these one,
discovered in 1830, and called Grotta del Sole e della Luna—
" Tomb of the Sun and Moon," particularly deserves attention,
It has eight chambers; the walls of some are curiously adorned
with panels, and the ceilings with mouldings in regular patterns,
all carved from the rock, in relief, in evident imitation of wood-
work.   One of these ceilings has a singular fan-pattern,[5] the
counterpart to which is found in two tombs at Cervetri; whence
we may conclude it was no uncommon decoration of Etruscan
houses.   In this same *tenuta*, under the walls of the city, was
found in 1833, a painted tomb of remarkable character, the first
discovered on this site.   It is now utterly destroyed, but a record
of it has been preserved, and copies of its paintings now in the
British Museum rescue it from oblivion.[6]

---

[4] Museum Etrusque, p. 12.

[5] This pattern is given in Mon. Ined.
Inst. I. tav. XLI., together with the plan
and sections of this tomb.   The moulding
round one of the doors, besides being of the
usual Etruscan form, is painted with red
and black ribands, diagonally, so often seen
in Egyptian door-mouldings.

[6] For a description of it see the Appendix
to this chapter.

In April 1857, another painted tomb of still greater interest and importance, was discovered in this necropolis, by Signor Alessandro François, from whom it takes its name. On the banks of the Fiora, on the verge of the cliffs opposite the ancient city, and at the height of 100 feet above the stream, François found a passage cut in the rock, which he followed out until it led him to a magnificent tomb of eight chambers, hewn in the travertine. Two of these only were painted; the central chamber, and the inner room beyond it, which however had only floral decorations; but the principal chamber, which was 23 feet by 20, was surrounded with scenes of striking interest. On the left half of the walls was represented the sacrifice of Trojan captives to the shade of Patroclus, Achilles himself and Ajax being the butchers. M. Noël des Vergers, under whose auspices François was excavating, calls this scene an Etruscan translation of Homer's description of the sacrifice, and not a faithful translation either, since personages of the Etruscan spirit-world are here mixed up with those of the Greek mythology.[7] Charun with his hammer and a winged Lasa are present at the slaughter; and the shade of Patroclus himself, as he appeared to his friend in a dream, stands watching the sacrifice offered to his manes. Other scenes of slaughter were there: Ajax about to murder Cassandra; and the Theban Brothers dying by each other's hands. The other half of the chamber exhibited scenes no less sanguinary, though illustrative not of Greek, but of Etruscan traditions. Here was Mastarna, better known by his Roman name of Servius Tullius, cutting the bonds of his friend Cæles Vibenna; here was Tanaquil, the wife of the first Tarquin; and "Cneius Tarquinius of Rome" meeting his death from the hands of an Etruscan; and here were other scenes of blood, in which unarmed men were falling beneath the sword—victors and victims all designated by Etruscan appellations. I merely mention in this place the discovery of this wonderful tomb, as nothing is now to be seen on the spot. Prince Alessandro Torlonia, to whom the ground belongs, had these frescoes detached from the walls, and removed to Rome, where after lying in his palace for many years, they have very recently been transferred to the Collegio Romano. They will be further described when we treat of the Museo Kircheriano, where they are now exhibited.

It is on the left bank of the Fiora that most of the excavations

7 Étrurie et les Étrusques, III. p. 18. For illustrations of these paintings see the said work, planches XXI.—XXX.

have been, and are, annually made. Here, about a mile from the castle, towards the Cucumella, we came upon a gang of excavators, in the employ of the Princess of Canino; most of the necropolis on this bank of the Fiora being her property. And a pretty property it is, rendering an excellent return to its possessor; for while her neighbours are contenting themselves with well-stocked granaries, or overflowing wine-presses, the Princess to her earlier is adding a latter harvest—the one of metaphorical, the other of literal gold, or of articles convertible into that metal. Yet, in gathering in the latter harvest, the other is not forgotten, for, to lose no surface that can be sown with grain, the graves, when rifled, are re-filled with earth. On this account, excavations are carried forward only in winter.

At the mouth of the pit in which they were at work, sat the *capo*, or overseer—his gun by his side, as an *in terrorem* hint to his men to keep their hands from picking and stealing. We found them on the point of opening a tomb. The roof, as is frequently the case in this light, friable tufo, had fallen in, and the tomb was filled with earth, out of which the articles it contained had to be dug in detail. This is generally a process requiring great care and tenderness, little of which, however, was here used, for it was seen by the first objects brought to light that nothing of value was to be expected—*hoc miseræ plebi stabat sepulcrum*. Coarse pottery of unfigured, unvarnished ware, and a variety of small vases in black clay, were its only produce; and as they drew them forth, the labourers crushed them beneath their feet as things "cheaper than seaweed." In vain we pleaded to save some from destruction; they were *roba di sciocchezza*— "foolish stuff"—the *capo* was inexorable; his orders were to destroy immediately whatever was of no pecuniary value, and he could not allow us to carry away one of these relics which he so despised. It is lamentable that excavations should be carried on in such a spirit; with the sole view of gain, and with no regard to the advancement of science. Such is too frequently the case. Yet they are occasionally conducted by men whose views are not bounded by money-bags, but who are actuated by a genuine love and zeal for science. The man to whom the Princess had intrusted the superintendence of her *scavi* was "a lewd fellow of the baser sort," without education or antiquarian knowledge, though experienced, it may be, in determining the localities of tombs, and the pecuniary value of their contents. Excavations were differently conducted during Lucien's lifetime, for he per-

sonally superintended them.[8]   Since the period of which I write
matters have much improved.   The present government of Italy
watches more carefully over antiquarian researches, and appoints
experienced men to superintend the progress of *scavi* in the
various districts of Etruria, who note the character of the
sepulchres, the nature and arrangement of their contents, and
report all discoveries of importance, to the Commission of Antiquities at Rome.   The additional light thus thrown on antiquarian science is most valuable.   As it was, facts, often, it may
be, of great importance, were unnoticed and unrecorded.   We
saw, in the Museums of Europe, from Paris to St. Petersburg,
the produce of these Vulcian tombs, we admired the surpassing
elegance of the vases and the beauty of their designs, and
marvelled at the extinct civilization they indicate; but they
afforded us no conception of the places in which they had been
preserved for so many centuries, or of their relations thereto.
Besides the official record, notices of the discovery of remarkable
tombs or objects are given periodically in the publications of the
Archæological Institute of Rome, and of other antiquarian
societies of Italy.

In watching the excavations at Vulci I learned that the contents of adjoining tombs often differed widely in antiquity, style,
and value—that sepulchres of various ranks, and different periods,
lay mixed indiscriminately, and that the same tomb even sometimes contained objects of several ages, as though it had been the
vault of one family through many generations.

The external difference between the cemeteries of Tarquinii
and Vulci is striking enough.   There you have a hill studded
with sepulchral mounds, and distinguishable afar off by its rugged
outline; here is a vast uniform level, with scarcely an inequality
on its surface—one lofty barrow alone rising from it, to mark,
like the tumulus on the plain of Marathon, or the lion-crested
mound on that of Waterloo, that this is a field of the dead.   The
tombs of Vulci are sunk beneath the level surface.   They are
not in general of large size, and are usually of oblong form,
surrounded with benches of rock, on which the dead were laid,
generally without any inclosure or covering beyond their armour

---

[8] Gochard (Bull. Inst. 1831, p. 88) complains of the incivility and vandalism of
most of the excavators at Vulci, making a
particular exception in favour of the Prince.
Bunsen (Ann. Inst. 1834, p. 85) pronounces
the same condemnation.   The mercenary
character and barbarism of Italian excavators are notorious, and prompt one to cry—
Desino scrutari quod tegit ossa solum !

or habiliments. Yet some sarcophagi of great beauty and interest have been found here. The abundance of bones, and the rarity of cinerary urns or vases, show that interment was more in fashion than cremation. The doorways to the tombs are of the usual Egyptian form, and, though sunk deep beneath the soil, are often adorned with the square lintelled moulding so common at Bieda. Some thirty years ago, it was calculated that more than six thousand tombs had already been opened in this necropolis;[9] which number had increased in 1856 to more than 15,000.[1]

La Cucumella.[2]

This singular tumulus, which, standing in the midst of the bare plain, is visible at the distance of many a mile, is a vast cone of earth, like Polydore's tomb—*ingens aggeritur tumulo tellus*—above two hundred feet in diameter, and still forty or fifty in height, though much lowered from its original altitude by time and the spade of the excavator. It was encircled at its base by a wall of masonry, which was traceable by fragments in 1830, though not a block is now left. The mound was opened by the Prince of Canino, in 1829. Above this wall were found sundry small sepulchral chambers, as in the tumuli of Cervetri and Chiusi; but all are now re-closed. They were probably tombs of the dependents and slaves of the great personage or family for whom the mausoleum was erected.[3]

In the heart of the mound were unearthed two towers, one square, the other conical, both between thirty and forty feet in height, of horizontal, uncemented masonry, but extremely rude and irregular, and so loosely put together as to threaten a speedy

---

[9] Micali, Mon. Ined. p. 361.

[1] Noël des Vergers, Etrurie, III. p. 16.

[2] Cucumella—probably *a cacumine*—is a term commonly applied in Central Italy to a mound, hillock, or barrow. This Vulcian *tumulus* is called the Cucumella, *par excellence*, as there is no other on this site to rival it. There may be some affinity in the word to the Etruscan, for we find the proper name of "Laris Cucuina," on a tile in the Pasquini collection at Chiusi. Mus. Chius. II. p. 124.

[3] Micali (M. m. Ined. p. 361) regards the tumulus as a mark of distinction and dignity. It may be in this case, but can

hardly be so at Tarquinii and Caere, where tumuli are so abundant. Knapp (Ann. Inst. 1832, p. 280) accounts for the general adoption of the tumulus on certain sites, by the inferior hardness and compactness of the rock in which the tombs were excavated. But this notion is quite upset by an extended view of Etruscan cemeteries. For in the friable arenaceous earth of Chiusi and its neighbourhood, artificial tumuli are never found, whereas at Cervetri, where the tufo is as hard as on any other site, they are most numerous. The reason of this peculiarity certainly does not lie in a constructive necessity.

fall.[4] The conical tower appears to have been hollow; but neither this, nor the other, has any visible entrance; and it seems probable that they served no more practical purpose than to support the figures with which the monument was crowned.[5]

At the foot of these towers is now a shapeless hollow; but here were found two small chambers, constructed of massive regular masonry, and with doorways of primitive style, arched over by the gradual convergence of the horizontal courses. They were approached by a long passage, leading directly into the heart of the tumulus; and here on the ground lay fragments of bronze and gold plates, very thin, and adorned with ivy and myrtle leaves. Two stone sphinxes stood guardians at the entrance of the passage, and sundry other quaint effigies of lions and griffons were also found within this tumulus.[6] No other furniture was brought to light; whence it was evident that the tumulus had been rifled in by-gone ages. The masonry of the towers, the primitive doorways, and the character of the few articles found, tend to prove this tomb to be of very ancient date—much prior to the generality of sepulchres in this necropolis.[7]

Signor François, the great explorer of Etruscan cemeteries, persuaded that the real sepulchre, over which the tumulus had been raised, was still concealed, made excavations in 1856 for its discovery, in connection with M. Noël des Vergers. He ran a trench completely round the base of the mound, but without success. He fell a victim the year following, to the deadly atmosphere of the site, and "the Cucumella still rears its head like the mysterious sphinx of these dangerous solitudes."[8]

This tumulus bears a striking analogy to that at Sardis, known to be the sepulchre of Alyattes, king of Lydia, and father of Crœsus, which had a basement of huge stones, surmounted by a mound of earth. Five *termini*—ούροι—stood on the summit,

---

[4] Gerhard (Bull. Inst. 1829, p. 51) accounts for the rudeness of this masonry by supposing it to have been faced, probably with metal, as marble was not used in architecture by the Etruscans. This supposition is quite unnecessary, for the towers were not intended to be seen, being buried in the earth.

[5] According to Micali (Ant. Pop. Ital. p. 148) several sphinxes were found on the summit of the towers, and it may be presumed that they were for the external decoration of the tumulus.

[6] Ann. Instit. 1832, p. 273.

[7] For an account of the opening of this tumulus, see Bull. Inst. 1829, p. 50, *et seq.* (Gerhard) ; and Micali, op. cit. III. p. 94. For a plate of the monument, see Mon. Inod. Inst. I., tav. 41, 2, and Micali, op. cit. tav. 62, who represents the square tower with a door.

[8] Noël des Vergers, Étrurie, III. p. 15. Illustrations of some of the fruits of M. des Vergers' excavations at Vulci, are given in his beautiful work.

says Herodotus, and on them were carved inscriptions, recording
the construction of the monument, and that it was raised principally by the hands of young women. The tumulus was six
stadia and two *plethra* (3,842 ft. 8 in.) in circumference, and
thirteen *plethra* (1,314 ft. 1 in.) in diameter.[9] As the Lydians
are traditionally the colonisers of Etruria, when we find similar
monuments in this land, we may regard them as strengthening
the probability of the tradition, and may assign them an early
date in style, if not always in actual construction. The tumulus
of Alyattes was six or seven times as large as the Cucumella, yet
the affinity is not the less striking. But there are scores of
sepulchral mounds on the Bin Tépé at Sardis, whose dimensions
agree with those of the Cucumella. It is in character and
arrangement alone, not in size, that the mound of Alyattes is to
be regarded as a type of Lydian tombs, for Herodotus specifies
this as among the marvels of the land on account of its size—
ἔργον πολλὸν μέγιστον—inferior only in magnitude to the works of
the Egyptians and Babylonians. The five *termini* on the Lydian
monument are not clearly and definitely described; but the
inscriptions on them show an analogy to the *stelæ* of the Greeks
and Etruscans; and as they could not, consistently with the
rest of the monument, have been on a small scale, the probability
is that they were either cones surmounting towers, or the termi-
nations of such towers, rising above the body of the mound.[1] It
is a remarkable fact, that the tomb of Porsena, at Clusium, the
only Etruscan sepulchre of which we have record, bore a close
affinity to the only Lydian sepulchre described by the ancients—
the square merely taking place of the circle; for it is said to
have had "five pyramids" rising from a square base of masonry,
"one at each angle, and one in the centre."[2] And the curious
monument at Albano, vulgarly called the tomb of the Horatii and
Curiatii, has a square basement of masonry, surmounted by four
cones, and a cylindrical tower in the midst.[3] Five, indeed, seems

[9] Herod. I. 93.

[1] When writing the above, I was not
aware that anything remained on the tumulus of Alyattes to verify the statement of
Herodotus; but having since passed a
winter on the Bin Tépé, encamped beneath
the shadow of this gigantic mound, I can
testify that on its summit still lies a shapeless fragment of one of the *termini* which
decorated its crest; but I failed to perceive
in it any resemblance to a *phallus*, such as

Von Prokesch and Von Olfers who cites him
(Lyd. Königsgräber bei Sardes) appear to
have recognised. It is about 9 feet in
diameter, and bears not a vestige of an inscription, not answering in this respect to
the description given by Herodotus.

[2] Varro, ap. Plin. XXXVI. 19, 4.

[3] It is supposed by some to be the sepulchre of Pompey the Great, erected hereabouts by his wife Cornelia—Plut. Pompeius, ad finem. To this opinion Canina is

to have been the established number of cones, pyramids, or columnar *cippi*, on tombs of this description; whence it has been suggested that three other towers are probably buried in the unexcavated part of the Cucumella.[4]

Southward from this is a much smaller mound, called "La Cucumelletta," because it is a miniature of the other. It was opened by the Prince in 1832, and was found to contain five chambers.

Still nearer the Cucumella is a low tumulus, called "La Rotonda," about thirty feet in diameter, and walled round with a single course of travertine blocks. The cone of earth which surmounted it is now levelled to the top of the masonry. There is a trench and rampart around it, as in the conical rock-hewn tomb of Bieda. The chamber is now choked with earth; but in it were found vases of great beauty.[5]

Another tumulus, on the right bank of the Fiora, near the site of the ancient city, was opened by Campanari, in 1835. In the middle of the chamber, stretched on the ground, lay the skeleton of a warrior, with helm on his head, ring on his finger, and a confused mass of broken and rusted weapons at his feet. Against the wall of the tomb, depending from a nail, which, from rust, could hardly support it, hung a large bronze shield, lined with wood. An elegant bronze vase and a tripod were also there, but no pottery. In an adjoining chamber, however, where articles of jewellery, strewed on the ground, indicated a female occupant, there were some beautiful painted vases.[6]

These warrior-tombs are not uncommon, scattered indiscrimi-

---

inclined—Ann. Inst. 1837, 2, p. 57. Others regard it as the tomb of Aruns, son of Porsena, who fell at Aricia, contending with the Greeks of Cuma in the year 250 of Rome (Liv. II. 14; Dionys. V. 36; VII. 5). Piranesi first started this opinion, and is supported in it by Nibby, Gell, and the Duc de Luynes, Ann. Inst. 1829, p. 309. But there is no valid reason for regarding this tomb as of very early date, or of Etruscan construction. The basement was faced with *emplecton* masonry, now destroyed by the recent repairs, but above this, where the original structure is disclosed, it is seen to be of *opus incertum*, in strata alternating with courses of masonry. This stamps it as Roman; no instance of such a construction having been found in genuine Etruscan monuments. The mouldings also, as Canina

observes, mark the latter days of the Republic. It must be a Roman tomb—in imitation of those in use in the early days of Italy—whether of Pompey, or of some other wealthy Roman, is a matter of mere conjecture. The *gens Pompeia*, however, had an Etruscan origin, as we learn from the Grotta del Tifone at Corneto; and the great Pompey is known to have possessed a villa near Alba. Plut. Pomp. loc. cit.

[4] Ann. Inst. 1832, p. 273—Lenoir. I much doubt this. There may be one or two more, but from the position of the disclosed towers in the mound, there can hardly have been five.

[5] Ann. Inst. 1832, p. 277. Mon. Ined. Inst. I., tav. 41, 3.

[6] Bull. Inst. 1835, p. 203, *et seq.*

nately among those of men of peace. In some are found arms of various descriptions, the iron generally much oxydised, the helmets frequently bearing marks of the battle-fray, in "good old blows" of sword or lance, and sometimes encircled with chaplets of ivy, myrtle, or oak-leaves, in pure gold, of the most delicate and exquisite workmanship; as if to show that the departed had fallen in the moment of victory, or, it may be, to typify the state of triumphant bliss into which his spirit had entered. Not always are there remains of the corpse itself. When the soil is unusually dry, bones may be found not entirely decayed; but it more often happens that on the rocky bier lie the helmet, breastplate, greaves, signet-ring, weapons—or, if it be a female, the necklace, ear-rings, bracelets, and other ornaments, each in its relative place; but the body they once encased or adorned, has left not a vestige behind. In some of the warrior-tombs of this necropolis, as also on other sites, the bones of a horse and dog have been found by the side of those of the man;[7] whence we may infer that the Etruscan believed in a future state of existence for the brute creation,

> "And thought, admitted to that equal sky
> His faithful dog would bear him company;"

a doctrine held by the civilised nations of antiquity, as well as by "the poor Indian;" for Virgil pictures the souls in Elysium as practising equitation; and Homer mentions the sacrifice of horses and household dogs at the pyre of Patroclus.[8]

Among the tombs, in that part of the necropolis to the south, called the Campo Morto, are scattered here and there sundry square areas paved with large flags, and surrounded by walls of regular masonry. It seems probable that they were *ustrinæ*, or spots appropriated to the burning of the dead, which, though not a common custom with the Etruscan inhabitants of Vulci, may have prevailed among their Roman successors.[9]

---

[7] Bull. Instit. loc. cit.

[8] Virg. Æn. VI. 655. Hom. Il. XXIII. 171—4. Lucian (de Luctu, p. 810, ed. Bourd.) says that horses and concubines were sometimes slain at the funeral pile, and clothes were cast on it, or buried with the defunct, as though he would use such things in the other world as he had been wont to enjoy in this.

[9] The *ustrina* or *ustrinum* differed from the *bustum* or τύμβος, in being the place

where the corpse was burnt alone, whereas in the *bustum* it was also buried. Festus, v. Bustum. The best specimen of an *ustrina* extant is that large quadrangle on the Via Appia about four or five miles from Rome, which Gell took to be the Campus Sacer Horatiorum, mentioned by Martial (III. epig. 47. 3). A detailed description of it is given by Fabretti (Inscrip. Ant. III. p. 230).

GROTTA D'ISIDE.

One of the most remarkable tombs discovered in Etruria was opened in 1839, in a part of this necropolis called Polledrara, to the west of the Ponte Sodo. In interest and importance it rivalled the Regulini-Galassi tomb at Cervetri; for, besides objects of native art, of very high antiquity, anterior to all Hellenic influence, it contained articles purely and unequivocally Egyptian, attesting the very early intercourse between Etruria and Egypt. This tomb had nothing remarkable in its con-

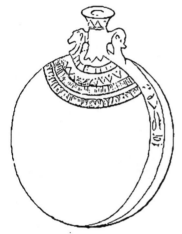

EGYPTIAN FLASK.

OSTRICH-EGG, PAINTED.

struction; it was hollowed below the surface, like the other tombs of Vulci, and had an antechamber and three inner chambers. From the character of its contents, it received the name of the "Tomb of Isis;" but it was really the sepulchre of two Etruscan ladies of rank, whose effigies are still in existence, though nearly three thousand years may have elapsed since their decease.

The tomb is now reclosed, but its contents have been fortunately kept together. They were once in the possession of the Prince of Canino, son of Lucien Bonaparte, but have now passed into the British Museum. All have a strong Egyptian or oriental character; but with the exception of those evidently imported from the banks of the Nile, they are Etruscan imitations of Egyptian art, with the native stamp more or less strongly marked. The genuine Egyptian articles consist of six ostrich-eggs,[1] one

Imitations of ostrich eggs, in terra cotta, have been found in the tombs of Vulci (Micali, Mon. Ined. p. 57), which seems to indicate that they were of funereal

painted with winged camels shown in the woodcut; four carved
with figures in very low relief—griffons and other chimæras, or

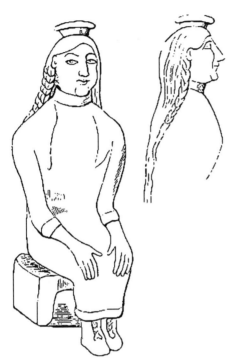

UNGUENT-POT IN THE FORM OF A WOMAN.

wild beasts fighting or devouring their prey; and the
sixth with a warrior in his
biga, attended by another
chariot, and four horsemen,
carved in the same manner
on the shell. The eggs have
holes in them, as if for suspension, and bring to mind
the great rock's egg of the
Arabian Nights; or, rather,
recall the fact of ostrich-
eggs being suspended in
mosques at the present day.
Genuinely Egyptian also are
five vases of greenish enamel,
flat-sided like powder-flasks,
and with hieroglyphics round
the edge.[2] But three *alabasti*,
terminating above in female
busts, with hands on the
bosoms, are mere imitations
of Egyptian articles; so also
are two unguent-pots, in the shape of small sitting figures of
women, about six inches high, one of them shown in the above

application, and that the demand was
greater than the supply. Yet the eggs of
smaller birds, imitated in that material,
have also been found in this necropolis.
Ann. Inst. 1843, p. 351. We know that
the eggs of the ostrich were sometimes used
as vases by the ancients. Plin. X. 1. Hens'
eggs are often found in tombs, not only in
Etruria, but in Greece and her colonies,
and are sometimes inclosed in vases. They
are not always fragile, for many museums
in Italy contain specimens of this singular
sepulchral furniture. Whether mere relics
of the funeral feast, or intentionally left in
the tomb with the wine, honey, milk, &c.,
as food for the Manes, or for some purely
symbolical purpose, it is not easy to determine. The signification of fertility, ordinarily attached to eggs, can hardly apply

to a sepulchre. The egg was more probably,
in this case, an emblem of resurrection.
It was used by both Greeks and Romans
in lustrations. (Lucian. Diog. et Poll. p.
114, ed. Bourd.; Juven. Sat. VI. 518;
Ovid. Ars Amat. II. 329). By the latter
people it was sometimes supposed to possess
strange efficacy; for Livia Augusta, when
pregnant with the Emperor Tiberius, in
order that her child might prove a male,
hatched an egg in her own bosom. Plin.
X. 76.

   [2] See the woodcut on p. 457. The hieroglyphics have been deciphered, and "contain invocations to the gods to grant a
happy New Year to the owner of the vase."
Vases of precisely similar character, found
in Egyptian tombs, are also to be seen in
the British Museum.

woodcut; and a vase with many colours, which is unique in Etruscan pottery—the ground being dark-grey, and the figures black, red, blue, yellow, and white. So Egyptian-like are the chariots, and the procession of females painted on this vase, that the general observer would at once take it for an importation; yet the learned have pronounced it Egyptian only in character, and native in execution, though of most archaic style and early date,[3] the myth which represents Theseus and the Minotaur being purely Hellenic.

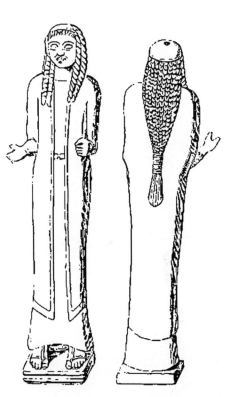

The effigies of the two ladies differ in material, as well as in taste. One is a full-length figure of stone, two feet nine inches high, clad in a long *chiton*, reaching to her feet, and over it a shorter tunic open in front and clasped at the waist, sandals on her feet, but no ornaments beyond those with which nature honoured her head—two long tresses being left on each side of her face to fall to her bosom, just such as are cherished now-a-days by misses in their teens; and her "back-hair" being plaited into a number of

STATUE OF AN ETRUSCAN LADY.

tails, clubbed together at the end. What magic power may have lain in her eyes, we know not, as they have been taken from their sockets, probably being of some precious material. Nor can we compliment her on her form, which is stiff and masculine, though such may have passed for elegant among the daughters of Ham, to whom she bears a striking resemblance. The above woodcut gives a front and back view of this fair Etruscan.[4]

[3] Micali, Mon. Ined. p. 30, tav. IV. 1.
[4] This figure, though Egyptian in character, is admitted to be a work of Etruscan art, and among the earliest examples extant.

If we cannot say of this

> " Sweet *Tyrrhene* maid, a very shower
> Of beauty was her earthly dower,"

no more can we declare her companion to be—

> " A lovely lady, garmented with light
> From her own beauty."

She had her bust taken in bronze, and being of vainer mood than her fellow, and less modest withal, had it represented bare, taking

care to put on her best necklace—and a gorgeous one it must have been, though stiffening her neck like a warrior's gorget—and to have her hair carefully arranged and curled when she sat to the artist. And she seems to have worn a broad gold frontlet, for such an ornament, embossed with figures, was found in the tomb. Then she affected modesty, and with a gilt bird on her hand, thought to make herself more engaging. Yet posterity, whom she intended to enchant, will hardly accord this Etruscan Lesbia credit for great charms; and will be apt to exclaim with Juvenal, denouncing bedizened dowagers—

Intolerabilius nihil est quam femina dives.

The pedestal is in keeping with the bust, being richly adorned with figures of lions, sphinxes, and chariots. The antiquity of this bust is proved, not only by its style, but by its workmanship; not being cast, but formed of thin plates of bronze, hammered into shape, and finished with the chisel—the earliest mode of Etruscan toreutics.[5]

BRONZE BUST OF AN
ETRUSCAN LADY.

---

[5] The earliest works of the Greeks in bronze must have been so formed, for we know that the most ancient statue in bronze —that of Jupiter on the Acropolis of Sparta —was wrought in separate pieces, nailed together (Pausan. III. 17, 6). This hammered work — *sphyrelaton* — can hardly have been later than the beginning of the sixth century B. C., because Pausanias (VIII. 14, 8 ; X. 38. 6 ; cf. Plin. XXXV.

43) tells us that the art of casting statues in bronze — χώνευμα — was invented by Rhœcus of Samos, who built the great temple of Hera in that island (Herod. III. 60), and who is believed to have flourished before 600 B. C. On the revival of the arts in the middle ages, says Micali (Mon. Ined. p. 52), the earliest statues in bronze, as that of Boniface VIII. in Bologna, erected in 1301, were formed of plates.

In the same tomb were found two oblong bronze cars, on four wheels, and with a horse's fore-quarters springing from each angle. They must have been for fumigation, and may have been dragged about the tomb to dispel the effluvium, on the occasion of the funeral feast, or the annual *parentalia*, and were probably equivalent to the *focolari*, so common in the tombs of Chiusi. There were also found sundry quaint vessels in bronze, with some tripods and a lamp—all of mere funereal use, being too thin and fragile to have served domestic purposes—a spoon of

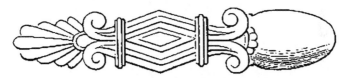

IVORY SPOON FOUND IN THE ISIS-TOMB.

ivory, and some plates and vessels of alabaster, which were probably used at the funeral feast, and left as usual in the tomb together with an abundance of the green *paste*, of which the Egyptians made necklaces and bracelets to adorn their mummies.[6]

On the painted pottery, found at Vulci, it were needless to expatiate. Every Museum in Europe proclaims its beauty, and, through it, the name of Vulci, little noised in classic times, and well nigh forgotten for two thousand years, has become immortal, and acquired a wider renown than it ever possessed during the period of the city's existence. Vulci has none of the tall black ware with figures in relief, so abundant at Chiusi and its neighbourhood; but of painted vases there is every variety—from the earliest, quaintest efforts, through every grade of excellence, to the highest triumphs of Hellenic ceramographic art. Of the early, so-called Doric, pottery, little is found at Vulci; nor of the Perfect style, which is predominant at Nola, is there so great an abundance here; the great mass of Vulcian vases being of the Attic style—of that severe and archaic design, which is always connected with black figures on a yellow ground.[7] The best

[6] For an account of the articles in this tomb, see Bull. Inst. 1839, pp. 71—73 —Urlichs; Micali, Mon. Ined. pp. 37—71, tav. IV.—VIII.; Ann. Inst. 1843, p. 350, Bull. Inst. 1844, p. 105.—Braun.

[7] A comparison of the pottery found at Vulci and Tarquinii is greatly in favour of the former. The subjoined table shows the comparative per centage of each description of vases.

vases of Vulci, in the chaste simplicity of their style, closely
resemble those of Nola and Sicily; yet there are characteristic
shades of difference in form and design, which can be detected
by a practised eye. On this site, more than on any other in
Etruria, have been found those singular vases painted with eyes,
so common also in Sicily, the meaning of which continues to
perplex antiquaries. Specimens of them are given in the annexed
woodcut, and in that at the head of the following chapter—the

KYLIX, OR DRINKING-BOWL, FROM VULCI.

former, a *kylix*, or drinking bowl, in the possession of the
Marquis of Northampton; the latter, a scene copied from an
amphora in the British Museum.

I cannot here enter into further details of the vases of Vulci;
for a description of them would be almost identical with that of
the painted pottery of Etruria. It would not be too much to assert
that nine-tenths of the painted vases, that have been brought
to light in Etruria, are from this site. The extraordinary
multitude of these vases, bearing Greek subjects, of Greek design,
and with Greek inscriptions—the names of the potter and painter

	Tar- quinii.	Vulci.
Painted vases, with figures, (i.e., the two best classes)	4	45
Painted vases, with animals, (i.e., the Egyptian style)	16	10
Painted vases, with mere ornaments . . .	20	5
Plain, uncoloured ware . .	10	2
Black ware, with reliefs. .	1	4
Ditto, varnished . .	5	—
Ditto, unvarnished .	44	34
	100	100

The average produce of excavations on this
site is said to be thirty times greater than

at Tarquinii. At Vulci virgin-tombs are to
the rest as 1 to 90. In eight months of
excavation, Fossati found but three intact,
containing painted vases, though more than
twenty intact with ordinary black ware.
Ann. Inst. 1829, p. 128.

Gerhard considered the painted vases of
Vulci to belong to a period not earlier than
the 74th Olympiad (484 B.C.), nor later
than the 124th (284 B.C.), or between the
third and fifth centuries of Rome—an
opinion founded on the forms of the vases,
the subjects represented, and on palæo-
graphic evidences. Bull. Inst. 1831, p.
167. But the Doric vases are certainly
earlier than he supposed.

being also recorded as Greeks—has suggested the idea that Vulci must have been a Greek colony,[8] or that a portion of its inhabitants were of that nation, living in a state of isopolity with the Etruscans.[9]   But these views are opposed by the fact that nothing found on this site, except the painted vases, is Greek; the tombs and all their other contents are unequivocally Etruscan.   On this site it is that the very few vases, bearing Etruscan inscriptions and subjects, have been found.   The *krater* at the head of this chapter, which bears the strange scene that forms the frontispiece to the second volume, is a notable specimen of this class of vases.[1]

Although thousands on thousands of painted vases have been redeemed from oblivion, this cemetery still yields a richer harvest than any other in Etruria.   No site has been so well worked by the excavator—none has so well repaid him; yet it seems far from exhausted.   Nor is it rich in vases alone.   Bronzes of various descriptions, mirrors with beautiful designs, vessels, tripods, *candelabra*, weapons—are proportionately abundant, and maintain the same relative excellence to the pottery.   That exquisite *cista*, or casket, with a relief of a combat between Greeks and Amazons, now in the Gregorian Museum, and which yields not in beauty to any of those rare relics of ancient taste and genius, which the necropolis of Præneste has produced, was found at Vulci.   No site yields more superb and delicate articles in gold and jewellery—as the Cabinets of the Vatican, and of the brothers Castellani at Rome can testify; none more numerous relics in ivory and bone, or more beautiful specimens of variegated glass.[2]

To this we may add that no cemetery in Etruria has yielded more beautiful examples of statuary in terra-cotta than that of Vulci, though such works of art are of rare occurrence in

---

[8] Gerhard, Ann. Inst. 1831, pp. 106, 107. He subsequently (Bull. Inst. 1832, pp. 76, 78) rejected this hypothesis in favour of that of an isopolity of Greeks and Etruscans.   Welcker (cited in Ann. Inst. 1834, pp. 43, 285) thinks this colony was one of potters, living as a separate body for ages, preserving their peculiarities of religion and rites.

[9] Ann. Inst. 1834, p. 45.

[1] The fullest account of the vases of Vulci will be found in Gerhard's "Rapporto Vulcente," Ann. Inst. 1831.   See

also some admirable papers, by Bunsen, Ann. Inst. 1834, pp. 40—86.   Opinions of Müller, Boeckh, Panofka, and Gerhard, on various points connected with this subject, will also be found in Bull. Inst. 1832, pp. 65—101.   But every work on ancient vases, that has appeared during the last fifty years, treats more or less of the pottery of Vulci.

[2] For notices of the beautiful works in bronze and jewellery found on this site, see the Annali and Bulletini of the Archæological Institute of Rome —*passim.*

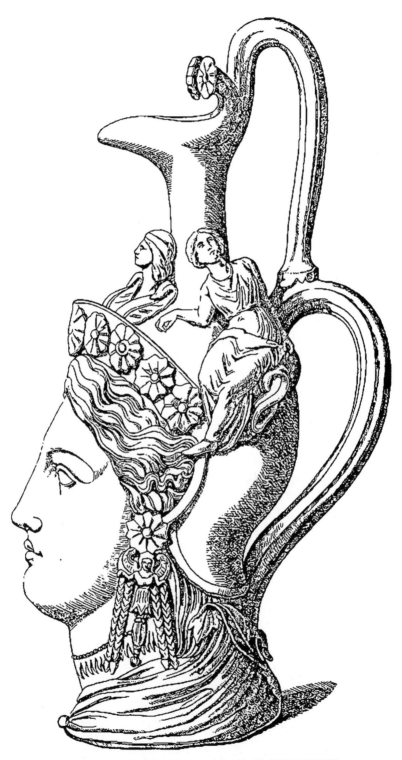

WINE-JUG, FROM VULCI, WITH THE HEAD OF PALLAS-ATHENE.

Etruscan tombs, save in the shape of portrait-busts, modelled from the life.

Among the choice and bizarre objects in this material, and a hybrid between sculpture and pottery, is a beautiful *œnochoë*, or wine-jug, from the tombs of Vulci, now in the British Museum. The body is in the shape of a female head, probably representing Pallas Athene, highly decorated, and wearing a helmet, the crest of which forms the spout of the vase. The pot has a double handle, the lower one for pouring, the upper for carrying. " The helmet," says Mr. Newton, " is ornamented on each side with a seated female figure in relief, and in front with a female head issuing from leaves ; over the forehead is a row of rosettes ; the earrings are in the form of winged female figures, surmounted by rosettes ; the necklace is formed of pendants ; the whole has been coloured, and the earrings gilt. The design of this vase is bold and original, the modelling excellent, and much taste is shewn in the application of the ornaments. It is further interesting from the correspondence in form of the jewels with those found in Etruscan tombs of the Macedonian period." Such graceful freaks as this are rare in Etruscan pottery, though not unfrequent in that of Magna Græcia, from which this is distinguished by its air of superior solidity. An illustration of this fantastic jug is given in the woodcut opposite, though no engraving, it has been truly said, can convey the polychromic charm which belongs to the original.[3]

APPENDIX TO CHAPTER XXIX.

NOTE.—THE CAMPANARI PAINTED TOMB AT VULCI. See p. 448.

THIS tomb, when opened, was in a very dilapidated condition ; much of the surface of the wall had fallen, and the external air speedily affected the remainder. Campanari, who discovered the tomb, made an attempt to detach the fast perishing painting from the damp, crumbling walls ; but, at the very commencement of the process, the stucco, rotted by the humidity of twenty centuries, gave way, and the painting fell in pieces at his feet. He had previously, however, had a copy made of it, which is now in the British Museum, and engravings of the same have been published in Mon. Ined. Instit. II. tav. 53, 54. Descriptions are also given in Bull. Inst. 1833, pp. 77 —80—Kestner ; Ann. Inst. 1838, pp. 249—252—Sec. Campanari. From these sources I obtain the following description.

[3] Ann. Inst. 1852, pp. 357—360 (Braun). Mon. Inst. V. tav. 48.

On the outer wall of the tomb, on one side of the door, stood the figure of Charun, or, as the inscription attached styles him, "CHARU," with hideous visage, leaning on his mallet. Within, on the opposite wall, sat, on an elegant curule chair or throne, a king arrayed in Tyrian purple, with crown on his head, and long sceptre in his hand, tipt by a lotus-flower. Before him stood his queen, in long *chiton*, mantle, and veil. This pair, in all probability, represented the king and queen of the Shades, Hades and Persephone, or, as the Etruscans called them, "Aite" and "Phersipnei." Behind the throne stood three draped male figures, whose venerable aspect seemed to mark them as the judges of the dead—Minos, Æacus, and Rhadamanthus. On either hand was a procession of figures, of both sexes, going towards the throne, supposed to be souls proceeding to judgment; though there was nothing in dress, appearance, or attributes, to mark them as of the lower world. The group on each side the throne was very similar; in fact it has been considered the same family—in one case going to judgment, in the other entering the abodes of the blessed. The figures were as large as life, except Charun, who was but half the size.

The style of art was more advanced than in any of the tombs of Tarquinii, not even excepting those of the Cardinal and Typhon. The paintings were quite Roman in character, and could hardly be earlier than the frescoes of Pompeii, which they resembled in freedom of design, truth and nature of the attitudes, and mastery over those difficulties which in every land attend the early stages of art. Yet the Charun who stood sentinel over this tomb was in a very different and more archaic style. He may have been painted at the first formation of this sepulchre, and the other figures added in the days of Roman domination, or the archaicism of his figure may be a conventionality of a later age. Another feature of late date was a massive column of *peperino*, supporting the ceiling, with a remarkable capital of the composite order, having heads, male and female, between the volutes. Campanari removed this to Toscanella, where it is still to be seen in his garden. See the woodcut at page 481.

This sepulchre seems to represent the lower world,—Charun mounts guard at the entrance, the King of Hades sits on his throne within; but the absence of Furies, as well as of Genii and Junones, essentially distinguishes this from the infernal scenes in the Pompey and Cardinal tombs of Tarquinii, as well as from those, to which in other respects it bears more affinity, in the Grotta dell' Orco in the same necropolis, and in the Tomba Golini at Orvieto.

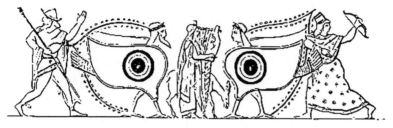

CHAPTER XXX.

CANINO AND MUSIGNANO.

Magni stat nominis umbra.—Lucan.

Quicquid sub terrâ est in apricum proferet œtas.—Horat.

THREE or four days may be pleasantly spent at Vulci, in exploring the neighbourhood and watching the progress of the excavations; returning every evening to Montalto, to secure the two greatest by-road luxuries in Italy—a decent dinner and a flealess bed. Let no one conceive that he may pernoctate at the Ponte della Badia with impunity. My fellow-traveller, on a previous visit to Vulci, had been induced to take up his quarters for the night in the guard-room of the castle, where the soldiers did their best to accommodate him; but he was presently attacked in his camp by legions of sharp-shooters, sure of aim and swift of foot—who compelled him, sighing for the skin of Achilles, to beat a precipitate retreat and take up a position in the court-yard of the castle—*sub Jove frigido*—for the rest of the night. As the nearest resting-places are Montalto and Canino, both seven or eight miles distant, and as in the latter village the traveller will find only a *hospitium miserabile*, with but slight diminution of the said annoyances, his better plan is to drive back nightly to Montalto, and comparative comfort.

Let the traveller also provide himself at the inn with such cold viands as he may, for the sustenance of his inner man during these day-long excursions. Not a mouthful will he otherwise procure for love or money; and a keen appetite, be it remembered, is the perquisite of hunters of antiquities and the picturesque, in common with their brethren in quest of ignobler game. With what relish, when the hour of twelve arrived, were we wont to throw our portfolios aside, and reclining in Etruscan fashion on our elbows, fall to our humble banquet of hard-boiled eggs, cold chicken, or cutlets, basking all the while "in the blue noon divine!" and we would pledge one another in draughts from the Fiora, with as much gusto as ever Etruscan prince or Lucumo emptied his *patera* of choice Graviscan or Cæritan, or as luxurious Roman quaffed

> " His wines of Setia, Cales, and Falerne,
> Chios or Crete."

Among the *videnda* of this neighbourhood, Musignano, the villa of the late Prince of Canino, and afterwards the residence of his widow, claimed a visit. Our road thither from Vulci lay across the plain, a treeless expanse of pasture or corn-land, till we approached the hills at whose foot lay the villa, embosomed in dense groves. These hills, called Monti di Canino, rise nearly 1500 feet above the sea, an isolated limestone mass in the midst of the volcanic plain—an inferior and tamer Soracte. As it was late in the day we passed the villa, and continued to Canino two or three miles further. This village, which gives its name to the principality, is of considerable size, the abode chiefly of those employed in the iron-foundries in the neighbourhood. It is built on the verge of a ravine, bearing in its cliffs traces of tombs, which mark the site of an Etruscan town, whose name has long been forgotten. The only accommodation for the traveller is a miserable " Locanda," the resort of carriers and iron-smelters, where, in the midst of a thousand discomforts, we were fain to pass the night.[1] In the morning we drove back to Musignano.

The villa is a very plain building, with no pretensions to external magnificence. It was originally an abbey, giving its name—La Badia—to the famous bridge, and it retains a gloomy monastic air. Were it in England, it might pass for a mad-house. The ponderous gateway was flanked by Etruscan lions and griffons in stone, and in the quadrangle within were several similar objects of antiquity—relics from the Cucumella. Signore Valentini, the son-in-law of the Princess, received us courteously, and showed

---

[1] By leaving Montalto early in the day, the traveller will have ample time to visit Musignano, and return the same night, or to push on to Toscanella—the next site of Etruscan interest. In the latter case, let him, on alighting at Musignano, send his vehicle on to Canino to bait the horses, and he can follow on foot at his leisure. It is a pleasant walk through the grounds.

us what vases and other relics her cabinet at that time contained. Few of the treasures of this unrivalled mine of Etruscan wealth were retained on the spot. The finest vases, as soon as discovered, were bought by the Pope for the Gregorian Museum, or found their way into foreign museums; and the richest and rarest articles of gold and jewelry met with ready purchasers in the Cavaliere Campana, and a few other kindred collectors of antique treasures.

The few vases in the Princess's cabinet were such as could not find a ready sale on account of their imperfect state. Most of this pottery had been found in fragments, and had been cemented together by an artist in the pay of the Princess. Articles thus restored are not materially lessened in value, if the paintings themselves be not injured; and even when these are imperfect, if the part deficient be not so large as to destroy the whole beauty and meaning of the subject; or if it be such as may be easily restored by a skilful pencil, the vase will not be greatly depreciated. Articles in a very imperfect state will sometimes fetch enormous prices. So skilful are some of these restorers, that they will make imperfect vases pass for perfect, so as almost to deceive the best judges.

Several of these vases had the mysterious eyes painted on them, which are so often found on the pottery of Vulci; and a curious specimen of which is given in the woodcut at the head of this chapter, copied from an amphora in the British Museum.[2]

The bronze articles in the cabinet, though not numerous, were in excellent preservation, and some of great beauty; indeed the bronzes of Vulci are inferior to none in elegance of form, and in the design and execution of their adornments.

But the most interesting feature of this mansion was its gallery of family portraits. There was Lucien himself at full length, the original of the well-known prints—his lady—and their handsome children, in family groups. There was the great Corsican in various periods of his career—the venerable Madame Letizia,

---

[2] This scene is remarkable, inasmuch as the eyes are made to represent the winged bodies of monsters, conventionally called Sirens, though here of both sexes. Such Sirens are commonly supposed to be emblems of souls; but Micali (Ant. Pop. Ital. III. p. 129) considers them in this instance to represent Bacchus and Libera, or the great infernal deities. Between them stands Apollo playing the lyre, with the hind at his feet; and behind them are Diana with her bow, and Mercury with his *petasus, caduceus* and *talaria*. On the other side of the amphora, the pair of human-headed, eye-bodied birds is repeated, but between them is the favourite subject of Peleus and Thetis (see Micali, op. cit. tav. LXXXIV.). For further remarks on the eyed vases, see the Appendix, Note I.

whose remains lie at Corneto—her brother, the Cardinal—the beautiful Pauline—and all, or nearly all, the members of this renowned family. In 1854 the villa passed into the hands of Prince Torlonia, and it has now lost its attractions.

The grounds attached to the villa are laid out in the English style; and the park-like scenery tempts the traveller to linger. Here, among the scattered sarcophagi, whose recumbent figures accord with the repose of the scenery, was one which arrested our attention. It bore a female figure, as large as life, rudely but boldly executed, not reclining as usual on her elbow, but stretched on her back, like the effigies on mediæval monuments. The bas-relief below displayed one of those scenes of domestic bereavement, so frequently and touchingly represented on the Etruscan urns of Volterra and Chiusi. Two winged genii, ministers of death, whose office was betokened by the snakes twisted round their arms, have seized upon a young girl—the same probably whose effigy reclines on the lid—and are about to lead her away, when a majestic figure, her father it must be, interposes, and with outstretched hands seems imploring them to release her; while her mother, with younger children in her arms and at her side, looks on in motionless woe. On one side of this group, but in a separate compartment, stood a winged Charun, resting on his oar, as if awaiting the arrival of the soul: and at the other side stood a similar figure with hammer uplifted, ready to strike the fatal blow.[3]

Two large sarcophagi of *nenfro* with male figures on the lids, and Etruscan inscriptions showing them to have belonged to the family of "Tute," are from the excavations made by Prince Torlonia. The relief on one displays the deceased in magisterial attire, standing in a *biga*, preceded by two lictors with *fasces*, and followed by two *apparitores* or servants, one bearing a large writing-tablet. The procession is moving to the music of two trumpeters. The subject, as well as the style of art, betrays the period of Roman domination.[4]

Two other sarcophagi of singular interest were also formerly at Musignano, and may still perhaps be seen at the Villa. They are described in the Appendix to this Chapter.

---

[3] Micali has described and illustrated this sarcophagus. Mon. Ined. p. 303, tav. XLVIII. 1. See also Ann. Inst. 1843, p. 365.—Braun. I have reason to believe that it has been removed from Musignano.

[4] Bull. Inst. 1869, p. 172.

APPENDIX TO CHAPTER XXX.

NOTE I.—EYES ON THE PAINTED VASES. See p. 469.

THE meaning of these eyes on the painted vases has not been satisfactorily determined. They are generally termed "mystic," and they are at least mysterious. They are found not only on vases of undoubted Greek origin, as on those of Nola, Sicily, and Adria, but are also often scratched on the black relieved ware of Chiusi and Sarteano, which has every evidence of a purely Etruscan character. It has been thought that they have a Bacchic import—an opinion which finds support in the figures or subjects with which they are often connected; such as vine or ivy branches—bunches of grapes—the god of wine himself standing, goblet in hand, between the eyes, or his head alone in that position—Satyrs and Mænads dancing—Silenus on his ass—Gorgons' heads, which are symbols of the infernal Bacchus—or subjects bearing reference to some one or other of the attributes or to the varied character of this great divinity of the ancients. They have been found also in the form of panthers' heads. The Bacchic nature of the scene in the woodcut at page 467, and the relation of Hermes, Apollo, and Artemis to Dionysus, are set forth by Micali (Ant. Pop. Ital., III. p. 129). But the subject is sometimes such as cannot easily be interpreted as Bacchic—warriors, represented singly or in combat, on horseback or in chariots—the deeds of Hercules, or other Greek myths—chimæras—Pegasi—athletes exercising—Furies, or other winged deities, as shown in the woodcut at p. 462.

There is some plausibility in the opinion that these eyes were charms against the evil eye, in which the ancients believed as strongly as the modern southrons of Europe.

> Nescio quis teneros oculus mihi fascinat agnos.—Virg. Buc. III. 103.

We know that the Gorgonion was supposed to have the power of averting evil (Lucian. Philopatris, p. 1120, ed. Bourdel.), and these eyes may be those of Gorgons, for they are evidently intended to represent a face, the other features even being sometimes introduced. Micali opines that the eyed vases were δῶρα ὀπτήρια—presents made by the bridegroom on seeing his bride unveiled (Mon. Ined. p. 268).

The introduction of eyes in such cases may perhaps be more satisfactorily accounted for by the resemblance and relation of vases to boats. The presence of eyes on the bows of ancient vessels, perhaps originating in the fancied analogy with fish, or to intimate the vigilance necessary to the pilot, is well known. The names of several sorts of goblets—such as σκύφος, σκάφη, κάνθαρος, κύμβη, κύπελλον, καρχήσιον, ἄκατος, ἀκάτιον—are common to them with boats; and it is on vases of this description that eyes are most frequently painted. This analogy between boats and cups is greatly confirmed by the fables of Hercules crossing the sea to Spain in a goblet (Apollod. II. p. 100, ed. 1599; Athen. XI. 38, 39; Macrob. Saturn. V. 21)—the prototype of St. Raymund.

Note II.—Singular Sarcophagi. See p. 470.

THESE two sarcophagi were found at Vulci, in the winter of 1845-46, and thence transported to Musignano. They are about seven feet in length. One is of a material unusual in this part of Etruria—a semi-transparent marble, often mistaken for alabaster, which Canina pronounces to come from the Circæan promontory. It bears on its lid not a single figure as usual, but a wedded pair, clasped in each other's arms—

gremio jacuit nova nupta mariti—

lying half-draped in that loving posture, described in the Canticles—"His left hand is under my head, and his right hand doth embrace me." Satisfactory, doubtless, to their Manes was this petrification of their conjugal fondness, but posterity could have taken it for granted—*ciò s' intende bene*. This unusual attitude seems to hint at some tragical event that cut down both at one stroke. The relief below represents, as if for contrast, a combat between Greeks and Amazons; and at the ends of the monument are lions and griffons devouring cattle.

The other sarcophagus is of *peperino*, and bears a similar pair on its lid. Its relief is in a superior style of art. It evidently represents a nuptial scene, for in the centre stands a female figure, embracing a youth. Other figures stand on either side. Behind the bride is a youthful slave who holds a large umbrella over her head; then another woman bearing a *hydria* on her head, and a *prochous* in her hand; a third with a large fan (ῥιπίς—*flabellum*), exactly like the Indian fans of the present day; and a fourth with lyre and *plectrum*. Behind the youth stands a man with a folding-stool (ὀκλαδίας—*plicatilis*); another with a *lituus* or augur's wand; a third with a large circular curved trumpet; and a female flute-player with double-pipes and a chaplet, or it may be a *capistrum*, in her hand. At one end of the monument a fond couple are sitting in a *biga* under a large umbrella, and in the act of embracing, which suggests, even more strongly than the recumbent figures on the lid, that the deceased pair were cut off at once; for the chariot indicates the passage to the other world, while the fatal event is also symbolised by a winged Fate or Fury with snakes round her arms, who accompanies the *biga*. At the other end a man of magisterial dignity is in the act of mounting a biga, accompanied by his *apparitor* with wand and *lituus*. At each end of the lid are three female heads, set in flowers.

These monuments are described in Bull. Inst. 1846, p. 86; critically examined by Dr. Braun, Ann. Inst. 1865, pp. 244-252; and illustrated in Mon. Ined. Inst. VIII. tav. 18-20.

THE SARCOPHAGUS OF THE NIOBIDS.

CHAPTER XXXI.

TOSCANELLA.—*TUSCANIA.*

Vedemo Toscanela tanto anticha
Quanto alcun altra de questo paese.
FACCIO DEGLI UBERTI.

ABOUT nine or ten miles to the east of Canino lies Toscanella, an Etruscan site of considerable interest, which may be reached in a carriage, either from Viterbo, Corneto, or Canino. This part of the great plain is diversified by oak-woods, which afford a pleasing contrast to the naked sweeps nearer the sea and the Ciminian Mount. Toscanella, with its many lofty towers, is the most conspicuous object in the thinly-peopled plain, and may be descried from a great distance. Yet it stands on no eminence, but on the very level of the plain, nearly surrounded by profound ravines. It is a mean, dirty town; and its interest lies in its picturesque situation, its Etruscan remains, and its churches, which are choice specimens of the Lombard style. Here and there in the streets is a rich fragment of mediæval architecture. The walls of the town are of the same period; no traces of the ancient fortifications remain, except on the adjoining height of San Pietro.

In such a by-road town as this, it were folly to expect a good inn. On my first visit to Toscanella, I procured tolerable accom-

modation in the house of a butcher, and afterwards in a little inn
kept by Filippo Pandolfini, who served me with a clean bed and a
decent meal. At that time Toscanella had interest as the
residence of the brothers Campanari, whose names are known
throughout Europe, wherever a love of Etruscan antiquities has
penetrated. The two brothers whom I knew are no more, but I
recall with respect and gratitude the many pleasurable and profitable hours I have spent in their society, and I take this opportunity of saying a word in tribute to their memory.

Carlo Campanari, the eldest, was well known in England by
his collection of Etruscan antiquities which he exhibited in London some forty years since, and great part of which was eventually
purchased by the British Museum. For many years he was the
active director of excavations, which he commenced in conjunction with his father, Signor Vicenzo, also an ardent labourer in
Etruscan fields, and greatly has the world benefited by his
patient and persevering labours, and by the light they have thrown
on the history, customs, and the inner life of the Etruscans. To
him am I indebted for much courtesy and kindness, and for his
readiness at all times to impart the results of his long experience.
Secondiano Campanari did not take so active a part in excavations as his elder brother, but devoted his attention to a critical
examination of Etruscan monuments; and many valuable papers
has he published, principally in the records of the Archæological
Institute. Domenico, the youngest brother, at the period referred to resided in London, where he acted as the agent for the
Institute in England, as well as for the sale of the articles transmitted by his brothers. Thus, in this fraternal triumvirate, the
old adage was verified :

> Tre fratelli —
> Tre castelli.

Besides their society, which rendered Toscanella at that period
a place of much interest to the antiquary, these gentlemen had
many things rich and rare, the produce of their *scavi*, to offer to
the traveller's notice. Their house was a museum of Etruscan
antiquities. In the vestibule were stone sarcophagi with figures
reclining on the lids ; and sundry bas-reliefs in *terra-cotta* were
embedded in the walls. Their garden was a most singular place.
You seemed transported to some scene of Arabian romance, where
the people were all turned to stone, or lay spell-bound, awaiting
the touch of a magician's wand to restore them to life and activity.
All round the garden, under the close-embowering shade of

trellised vines, beneath the drooping boughs of the weeping willow, the rosy bloom of the oleander, or the golden fruit of the orange and citron, lay Lucumones of aristocratic dignity—portly matrons, bedecked with jewels—stout youths, and graceful maidens—reclining on the lids of their coffins, or rather on their festive couches—meeting with fixed stare the astonishment of the stranger, yet with a distinct individuality of feature and expression, and so life-like withal, that, "like Pygmalion's statue waking," each seemed to be on the point of warming into existence. Lions, sphinxes, and chimæras dire, in stone, stood among them, as guardians of the place; and many a figure of quaint character and petrified life, looked down on you from the vine-shaded terraces, high above the walls of the garden.

In the garden wall was a doorway of Etruscan form and moulding, surmounted by a cornice bearing the formula "ECASU-THINESL" in Etruscan characters—all taken from a real tomb. The door opened into what seemed an Etruscan sepulchre, but was really a cavern formed in imitation of the said tomb, and filled with the identical sarcophagi and other articles found therein, and arranged pretty nearly as they were discovered. It was a spacious vaulted chamber, and contained ten sarcophagi— a family group—each individual reclining in effigy on his own coffin. It was a banqueting hall of the dead; for there they lay in festive attitude and attire, yet in silence and gloom, each with a goblet in his hand, from which he seemed to be pledging his fellows. This solemn carousal, this mockery of mirth, reminded me of that wild blood-curdling song of Procter's—

> "King Death was a rare old fellow—
> He sat where no sun could shine;
> And he lifted his hand so yellow,
> And poured out his coal-black wine!
> Hurrah! hurrah!
> Hurrah for the coal-black wine!"

In truth, he must have been of stern or stolid stuff whose fancy was not stirred at the sight of this frozen banquet.

The figures on Etruscan sarcophagi and urns are, with very few exceptions, represented as at a banquet—generally with *patera* in hand, but the women have sometimes an egg, or piece of fruit instead, as on the walls of the painted tombs; sometimes tablets; or a fan of leaf-like form, like our own Indian fans; or it may be a mirror, which with their rich attire and decorations betrays the ruling passion strong in death. In a few instances I have seen a bird in the fair one's hand—*passer, deliciæ puellæ*—and more rarely a drinking-cup, which, when we call to mind the character the Greeks have given them, we might expect to find of more frequent occurrence.[1] The men are generally only half-draped, and have torques about their necks.—

Flexilis obtorti per collum it circulus auri—

or wear the long breast-garlands worked round with wool, which were worn by Greeks and Romans.[2] The ladies have sometimes torques, sometimes necklaces, long ear-rings of singular form, and bracelets, and both sexes have often many rings on their fingers —*censu opimo digitos onerando*—a custom which Rome it is said, derived from Etruria.[3] The Etruscans, indeed, seem to have had an oriental passion for jewelry—a passion which was shared by the Romans,[4] and has been transmitted to their modern represen-

---

[1] Theopompus (ap. Athen. XII. 14) describes the fair Etruscans as "terrible women to drink, pledging any man who happens to be present," and he adds, as if to qualify his censure, "and they have very beautiful faces."

[2] Called ὑποθυμιάδες. Athen. XV. 16.

[3] Florus (I. 5). Livy (I. 11), and Dionysius (II. p. 105) ascribe the use of rings in very early times to the Sabines. Pliny, however, asserts that the custom of wearing rings was derived from the Greeks. He adds, that none of the statues of the early kings, save those of Numa and S. Tullius, were represented with them, not even those of the Tarquins (XXXIII. 4, 6), at which he greatly marvels. It is probable that the custom was introduced into either Greece or Etruria from the East. We learn from these sepulchral statues that rings were usually worn by the Etruscans, as by the Greeks and Romans, on the fourth finger of the left hand (A. Gell. X. 10; Macrob. Saturn. VII. 13; Isidor. Orig. XIX. 32); the reason of which is said to be, that the Egyptians had discovered by dissection, that a certain nerve—Isidore says a vein—led from that finger to the heart; and that digit was singled out for distinction accordingly. Ateius Capito (ap. Macrob. loc. cit.) gives a more plausible reason.

[4] In early times the Romans emulated Spartan severity, and wore iron rings for signets. It was long ere the senators circled their fingers with gold. Iron was emphatically the metal of the stern Romans of old, and it was a sense of the degeneracy induced by luxury that made Pliny (loc. cit.) exclaim :—"His was the greatest crime in life, who first arrayed his fingers in gold." Even Marius in his triumph over Jugurtha though an Etruscan crown of gold was held over his head from behind, wore a ring of mere iron ; and a similar ring, as Pliny remarks, was probably on the hand of the conqueror, and of the slave who held the crown. At first it was disgraceful for a man to wear more than one ring, and women wore none, except what a virgin received from her betrothed, and she might wear two gold ones. (Isid. Orig. loc. cit.) But, in after times, with the excess of luxury, the Romans used not only to wear a ring on every finger (Mart. V. epig. 6, 5), but many on each joint (Mart. V. epig. 11); and to cover their hands with them, so that Quintilian (XI. 3) was obliged to caution would-be orators on this subject. Martial (XI. epig. 59) speaks of a man who wore six on every finger ! and recommends another, who had one of a monstrous size, to wear it on his leg instead of his hand (XI. epig. 37). To such extravagant effeminacy was this habit carried, that even slaves, like Crispinus, had a different set of rings for summer and for winter, those for the latter season being too heavy for hot

tatives, as a Sunday's walk on the Corso will abundantly testify. These figures all rest on their left elbow, supported by cushions, and the sarcophagi beneath them are often hewn to imitate couches. Thus, as in the painted tombs, they are represented in the height of social enjoyment, to symbolise the bliss on which their spirits had entered;[5] or, it may be, to describe their actual pursuits in another world; and these effigies may image forth not the men but their *manes*, at the revels in which they were believed to indulge.

> Pallida lætatur regio, gentesque sepultæ
> Luxuriant, epulisque vacant genialibus umbræ.
> Grata coronati peragunt convivia Manes.[6]

These figures are of *nenfro*, coarsely executed, yet bold and full of character, and are manifestly portraits. The flesh of the men was originally painted a deep red—the hue of beatification—their drapery purple, blue, yellow, or white, and their ornaments yellow to represent gold; even the differences of complexion were marked, some having eyes of cerulean hue, and others, like Horace's Lycus,

> --nigris oculis nigroque
> Crine decori.

This varied colouring was completely preserved at the time of their discovery, but was exchanged, in those which lay in the garden, for an uniform weather-staining of green.[7]

The principal figure in the tomb was the patriarch of his race, whose name was set forth as " VIPINANAS VELTHUR VELTHURUS AVILS LXV." which would be Latinised by " Vibenna Voltur Volturius (Veturius?), vixit annos LXV."[8] Then there was a matron, some twenty years younger, probably his wife, with features worthy of a Cornelia; and various juniors of the family, among them a foppish youth of twenty, with twisted torque about his neck,

weather. Juven. Sat. I. 28 :—

> Ventilet æstivum digitis sudantibus
> aurum,
> Nec sufferre queat majoris pondera
> gemmæ.

Well might Juvenal add—

> Difficile est satiram non scribere.

[5] This was probably the conventional mode of expressing apotheosis. Thus, Horace (Od. III. 3, 11) represents Augustus, though living, as a demigod, reclining with Pollux and Hercules :—

> Quos inter Augustus recumbens
> Purpureo bibit ore nectar.

[6] Claudian. Rapt. Proserp. III. 326.
[7] Bull. Inst. 1839, p. 24. One figure is said to have been painted black, and to have had negro's features.
[8] This repetition of the name with an addition is not unique. It is found also on an urn at Perugia—"Ls Varna Varnas Ateinl." Vermigl. Sepolcro de' Volunni, p. 52. So occasionally in Roman names—L. Sextius Sextinus — Quintus Quinctius Cincinnatus.

his hair bound with a fillet, and the effects of early indulgence visible in his bloated frame; his sister, a pretty girl of fourteen, and another sweet damsel with Grecian features. Verily, if these be faithful portraits, Italian beauty has not improved in the last three or four-and-twenty centuries; and the Etruscan fair possessed other charms than those exerted by Tanaquil and Begoë.[9]

The walls of the tomb were hung with vases, jugs, goblets, of bronze as well as earthenware, while tall amphorae, and full-bellied jars of unglazed clay, with a rabble rout of pots and pans, and sundry bronze *candelabra*, strigils, flesh-hooks—lay about in glorious confusion.

In the centre of the chamber was a lidless sarcophagus, with a relief of a human sacrifice—a subject rarely met with on Etruscan monuments, except as illustrating the myth of Iphigenia.

I was surprised to hear that the greater part of these sarcophagi came from a single tomb. It was opened in 1839, in a spot called Il Calcarello, and contained no less than twenty-seven of these large coffins; those of the women forming a circle in the centre, and those of their lords arranged in a larger circuit around. The ceiling of the tomb had fallen in, though supported by three columns, which were not able to uphold the weight of a superincumbent pavement of large rectangular blocks. On this pavement lay a flat circular stone, like a solid wheel or thin millstone, with an Etruscan inscription round its edge, showing it to be the *cippus*, or tomb-stone to the sepulchre.[1]

One of these *nenfro* sarcophagi was among the finest I have

---

[9] The beauty of the Etruscan women is attested by Theopompus (ap. Athen. XII. c. 14). Begoë was an Etruscan nymph, who wrote on the Ars Fulguritarum, or art of divination from things struck by lightning, and her books were preserved at Rome, in the Temple of Apollo (Serv. ad Æn. VI. 72). Lactantius (ad Stat. Theb. IV. 516) speaks of an Etruscan nymph, who performed such feats as would have made Sullivan the Whisperer stare with astonishment. She whispered the dread name of God into the ear of a bull, and he fell dead at her feet. This nymph Müller (Etrusk. III. 4, 2) thinks was no other than Begoë. Gerhard (Gottheiten der Etrusker, p. 44) suggests the same. Tanaquil's powers of divination are well known. Liv. I. 34; Arnob. adv. Nat. V. 18; Claudian. Laus Serenæ, 16. Her magic

zone, with its amulet properties, is mentioned by Festus, v. Prædia.

[1] See the woodcut at p. 481. This disk-like *cippus*, which Canina takes for an Etrusco-Doric capital, calls to mind the stone laid on the tumulus of Phocus in Ægina, with which Peleus, according to the legend, using it as a *discus*, struck Phocus and slew him. Pausan. II. 29, 9.

The inscription on this *cippus* is Eca. Svthi. Larthial, Tar . . . . s. Sacniv. The fourth word, which is the gentilitial name, was most probably "Tarchnas," or Tarquinius, for there is just space sufficient for the missing letters. This seems to indicate the existence of a branch of the Tarquin family at Tuscania, as well as at Cære, where their tomb has been discovered. Kellermann, however, reads the name "Tarsalus." Bull. Inst. 1833, p. 61.

seen executed in this coarse material.[2] On the lid lay a man of middle age, a true *obesus Etruscus*—*turgidus epulis*, reclining, half-draped, on the festive couch. His face, as usual with these sepulchral effigies, had so much individuality of character, that none could doubt its being a portrait. A striking face it was, too,—with commanding brow, large aquiline nose, mouth speaking intelligence and decision, though somewhat sensual withal, and an air of dignity about the whole countenance, marking him as an aristocrat—one of the Patres Conscripti of Tuscania. No inscription set forth his name, pedigree, or age.

His sarcophagus bore a bas-relief of the slaughter of the Niobids. At each end sat one of the avenging deities, speeding the fatal arrows. In the centre of the group stood a bearded man, in tunic and buskins, perhaps Tantalus the father, but more probably Amphion the husband of Niobe; and at his side stood the fond mother herself, "all tears," vainly seeking to shelter her children with her garments,—

> Totâ veste tegens, Unam, minimamque relinquo !
> De multis minimam posco, clamavit, et unam !

She was not represented, according to the received version—

> Tra sette e sette suoi figliuoli spenti,

for their number was here but six, three of each sex, which is at variance with all the Greek and Latin authors who have recorded the myth;[3] indeed, it is rarely that the Etruscan monumental versions of well-known traditions agree in every particular with those recorded by classic writers. At one end of the sarcophagus was a Centaur contending with two Lapithæ, and at the other,

---

[2] An illustration of it is given in the woodcut at the head of this Chapter ; but the bas-relief is in a much better style of art than is there exhibited. The monument is about 7 feet in length.

[3] Lasus (ap. Ælian. V. H. XII. c. 36), Apollodorus (III. 5, 6), Ovid (Met. VI. 182), and Hyginus (Fab. IX. XI.), give her seven children of each sex. The same is implied by Euripides (Phœn. 162). Homer (Il. XXIV. 604) says they were twelve in number—

> Ἐξ μὲν θυγατέρες, ἒξ δ' υἱέες ἡβώοντες.

Eustathius (ad locum) and Propertius (II.

eleg. 20, 7) follow his version. Sappho (ap. A. Gell. XX. 7) increases them to eighteen ; Hesiod (ap. Apollod. loc. cit.) to twenty, in which he is followed by Pindar and Mimnermus, (ap. Ælian. loc. cit.), and Bacchylides (A. Gell. loc. cit.). Alcman (ap. Ælian. loc. cit.) reduces the number to half. Herodotus (ap. Apollod. loc. cit.) alone makes the number less than is represented on this sarcophagus—two sons and three daughters. This discrepancy is cited by A. Gellius as an instance of the strange and ridiculous diversity in Greek poetic fables. He adds, that some say there were only three children in all.

Achilles was dragging the corpse of Hector round the walls of Troy; but instead of the body being attached to the chariot by the heels, as Homer represents it, it was here fastened by the neck—a further instance of discrepancy between Greek and Etruscan traditions.[4] The style of art marked this sarcophagus as of no early date. It was probably of the time of Roman domination, perhaps even as late as the Empire.[5]

There is good reason for believing that the sarcophagi were not in general made expressly for the individual whose remains they inclose, as the lids must have been. From the symbolical or mythological character of the subjects in the bas-reliefs, which rarely bear any apparent reference to the individual interred, and from the frequent recurrence of the same scenes, it seems probable that the sarcophagi were manufactured wholesale by the Etruscan undertakers, and when selected by the friends of the deceased, they were fitted with effigied lids to order; or the recumbent figures were rudely struck out, and finished into likenesses of the departed. This will account for the not unfrequent incongruity between the two parts, which are sometimes even of a different stone. The likeness may have been taken after death, or from those small *terra-cotta* heads so often found in the tombs, and which were probably moulded from the life. Sarcophagi and urns of *terra-cotta* are frequently found at Toscanella, but are generally very inferior in style of art to those of stone, displaying much uncouthness and exaggerated attenuation—caricatures of the human form; yet some have been found of great beauty, as that of the wounded youth, commonly called Adonis, in the Gregorian Museum. These earthenware coffins are often found with those of *nenfro*, whence it would appear that the difference was a matter of choice or expense rather than of antiquity.[6] The former were used principally by women. It is clear that interment was much more general at Tuscania than cremation; yet large jars containing the ashes of the dead are often found in the same tomb with sarcophagi.

---

[4] On an Etruscan *amphora*, once in Campanari's possession, was a still more singular version of Achilles' triumph. His chariot dragging the corpse was driven by his *auriga* round the tomb of Patroclus; while he, though completely armed, and though the steeds were at full gallop, was giving proof of his "swift-footed" powers, by *running* at its side, looking back on the mangled corpse of his foe. Bull. Inst.

1841, p. 134—Braun.

[5] From coins of Augustus and other Roman remains found in the tomb, this sarcophagus has been considered as late as that Emperor. Bull. Inst. 1839, p. 40.—Abeken. See also 1839, p. 25—Jahn.

[6] Pliny (XXXV. 46) remarks that many people preferred being interred in coffins of earthenware—fictilibus soliis.

In this garden was a singular capital of a composite column, taken from the painted tomb of Vulci.[7] It was of *peperino*, and between each pair of volutes was a head, male and female alternately. From the Phrygian cap of the men, the relic received the name of "the column of Paris and Helen." Such capitals cannot be of very early date. There was a finish and freedom about this which would not allow us to claim for it an origin prior to the Roman conquest of Etruria. The other fragments shown in the annexed woodcut, are the disk-like *cippus* found above the tomb in the Calcarello, and a portion of the masonry which encircled a tumulus, interesting as a specimen of Etruscan moulding.

ETRUSCAN CAPITAL, CIPPUS, AND MOULDING.

Signor Lorenzo Valerj, the *speziale* or apothecary of Toscanella, has a collection of Etruscan antiquities for sale. As a man of experience and research, his acquaintance would be valuable to the visitor curious in Etruscan matters.

Several Etruscan sarcophagi of interest are to be seen at the Spedale, near the Viterbo Gate.

Of the origin and history of Tuscania we have no record. The only mention of it in ancient writers is found in Pliny, who classes it among the inland colonies in Etruria;[8] and in the Peutingerian

---

[7] See p. 466. The column on which the capital rests in the above cut does not belong to it. Several capitals of similar character have been found in various parts of Italy—one at Salerno, another at Cora, third, without volutes, is in the Museum

of Berlin (Bull. Inst. 1830, p. 136 ; Mon. Ined. Inst. II. tav. 20), a fourth has been discovered by Mr. Ainsley, at Sovana (see p. 512); and fragments of others have been found at Rome and Pompeii.

[8] Plin. III. 8.

Table, which shows it to have been on the Via Clodia, between Blera and Saturnia.[9] It is from its tombs alone that we know it to have existed in Etruscan times; yet it must have been a place of inferior importance, and was probably dependent on Tarquinii.

Of the original town there is no vestige beyond some substructions of the walls of *emplecton* masonry, and some sewers, cut in the cliffs beneath the height of San Pietro. Here, too, are traces of the Roman colony, in fragments of reticulated walling; and remains of a circus were discovered, some years since, in the ravine beneath.[1] The ancient town must have been larger than the modern, for it comprehended the height of San Pietro, which is without the modern walls, and which, being rather more elevated than the rest of the town, and at the extremity of the tongue of land, was evidently the Arx of Tuscania. That it was continued as a fortress during the middle ages, is proved by the tall, square towers of that period, which encircle, like a diadem, the brow of the hill. Eight are still standing, more or less impaired. They are double, like certain of the Round Towers of Ireland—a tall, slender tower being encased, with little or no intervening space, in an outer shell of masonry. Lest some should be led away by this analogy to cherish the idea that they are of very ancient construction, or, by a bold leap, should arrive at the conclusion that the Etruscans and Irish had a common origin, I must repeat that the masonry of these towers stamps them as indubitably of the middle ages.[2]

The richest jewel on this tiaraed height is the church of San Pietro, one of the most interesting ecclesiastical structures of Central Italy. The style is Italian Gothic. Though this church cannot compete in grandeur or richness with the celebrated Duomi in the same style, at Pisa, Siena, and Orvieto; yet, in the small and snug way, it is a gem, and will repay the lover of art for an express visit to Toscanella. Its charms lie chiefly in its façade, which, though rich in the general effect, is most grotesque in detail. Beasts, birds, and reptiles move in stone

---

[9] See pp. 61, 490. Vestiges of this road are to be seen in the glen beneath S. Pietro towards the Marta.

[1] Bull. Inst. 1839, p. 23.

[2] They have, however, been taken for Etruscan, and supposed to have been built over Etruscan graves, and to "have formed the centre of some immense sepulchral mound, similar to the Cucumella at Vulci."—Sepulchres of Etruria, p. 326. Nothing, however, is more improbable. This height, from its relative position, its local character, and the ancient walling and sewers, wa obviously a portion of the Etruscan town—most probably the citadel.

about the marigold window, the round-arched doorways, and the arcaded galleries—here stepping forth from the masonry, there chasing one another up and down the façade. Scarcely a square foot but displays some grotesquery in high or low relief, some grinning head, some uncouth form, some fantastic chimæra. The whole façade is teeming with life. This is not in harmony with the repose of architecture, still less with the solemnity and dignity of ecclesiastical edifices. Perhaps it was to qualify this profane character that a sprinkling is introduced of angels, saints, men, and devils. But what can we say of trifacial heads—grim caricatures of the Trinity—more than once seen on this façade? —or of artisans and tradesmen at their respective avocations, all in caricature? Yet such in a band of reliefs surround the porch of San Pietro.

The aisles of the church are divided by two rows of massive columns of Roman antiquity, probably from some temple which stood on this height. Beneath the choir is a crypt, supported by twenty-eight slender columns of no uniformity.

Of the same style as S. Pietro, inferior in richness of decoration, yet still more grotesque, is the church of Santa Maria, in the hollow at the back of San Pietro.

The necropolis lay in the broad, deep ravines round Toscanella, and on the opposite heights. There are many tombs in the cliffs, not with architectural façades, as at Castel d'Asso or Norchia, but with simple doorways, and interiors presenting little variety —unadorned chambers surrounded by rock-hewn benches. The most remarkable tomb on this site is in the cliffs below the Madonna dell' Olivo, about half a mile from the town. Here, a long sewer-like passage leads into a spacious chamber of irregular form, with two massive columns supporting its ceiling, and a rude pilaster on the wall behind. But the peculiarity of the tomb lies in a *cuniculus* or passage cut in the rock, just large enough for a man to creep through on all-fours, which, entering the wall on one side, after a long gyration, and sundry branchings now blocked with earth, opens in the opposite wall of the tomb. Formerly, this was the only instance known of anything like a subterranean labyrinth in an Etruscan sepulchre, but it is now quite eclipsed by that in the singular Poggio di Gajella of Chiusi. Be it remembered that the only Etruscan tomb described by the ancients, that of Porsena, at Clusium, is said to have contained a labyrinth.[3] Let the traveller inquire for the Grotta della

[3] Plin. Nat. Hist. XXXVI. 19, 4.

Regina, and let him provide himself, at Toscanella, with tapers and matches, or his excursion will be in vain.[4]

In the cliffs round the town are several instances of *columbaria*. They are large chambers in the rock, filled from floor to ceiling with small niches, like pigeon-holes, capable of holding an urn or pot, but differing from the niches in Roman *columbaria*, in the absence of the *olla*-hole. One of these tombs, in the cliff above the Viterbo road, is remarkable for its size, and its division into three chambers, with a massive pillar of rock supporting its roof. It is shown in the opposite woodcut, with Toscanella in the distance. The nearer height with the towers is the hill of S. Pietro. As the Romans seem to have taken the idea of their *columbaria* from the Etruscans, it is difficult, in the absence of all sepulchral furniture, to pronounce on the origin of these and similar tombs; yet I think it probable that these niched sepulchres were—in type at least—Etruscan.[5]

Most of the tombs of Toscanella, however, are sunk beneath the surface of the ground, as at Vulci. Campanari's excavations were principally in the table-land on the west of the town. Here it was that the tomb with the Niobe sarcophagus and twenty-six others, was discovered.

On my first visit to Toscanella, Signor Carlo Campanari was excavating in the *tenuta* of the Marchese Persiani. Here, in a shallow pit, he found a chest of stone, in size and form like a large dog-kennel, yet an evident imitation of a house or temple; for it had a door moulded at one end, and a gable roof, with beams beneath the eaves. It lay so little below the surface, that it was surprising it had not been brought to light by the plough. The form of this urn is not uncommon. What was most remarkable was, that it did not contain the ashes of the dead; for they lay on the ground hard by, covered by a tazza. It was merely a monumental stone.

After witnessing at Vulci the ruthless destruction of every article which bore no pecuniary value, it was pleasing to observe the different spirit in which the excavations at Toscanella were

[4] The tomb receives its name from the figure of a female found painted on the wall, when it was opened ages since, but now utterly obliterated. A plan and plate of this tomb are given by Micali, Ant. l'op. Ital. tav. LXIII., and by Canina, Etr. Marit. tav. XC.

[5] Abeken, while holding the same opinion, regards these Toscanella *columbaria* as Roman, about the fourth century of the City. Mittelitalien, p. 258. Similar *columbaria* have been discovered beneath the surface at Toscanella, but without inscriptions to determine their antiquity—nothing beyond small cinerary pots.

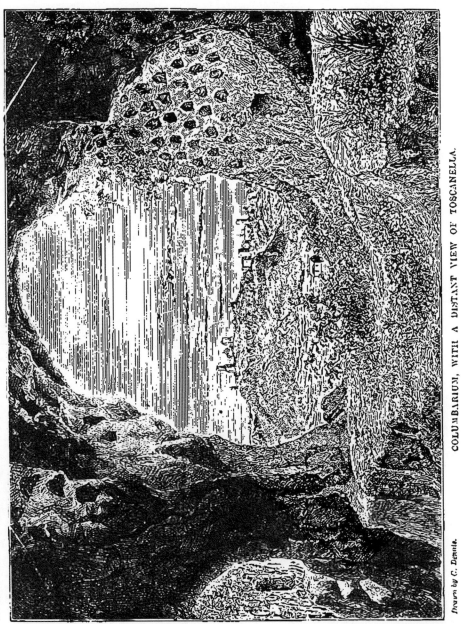

Drawn by C. Denile.

COLUMBARIUM, WITH A DISTANT VIEW OF TOSCANELLA.

conducted.   Here, every article, every fragment, was carefully
laid aside by the workmen, to be submitted to Campanari's
inspection.

The Etruscan pottery found at Toscanella is of very inferior
quality.   The beautiful painted vases, unearthed in thousands at
Vulci, are never found in this necropolis.   Yet the distance is
but fourteen or fifteen miles.   Are we to suppose that the Tus-
canienses could not afford to purchase such valuable furniture ?
That Tuscania was not poverty-stricken, is clear from the rich
bronzes, gold ornaments, and jewellery, found in its subterranean
chambers.   We must rather regard such differences in sepulchral
matters as the result of fashion, prejudice, or caprice.

Many years since, Signor Campanari, wishing to carry on his
excavations on a larger scale, set about forming a society or company for the purpose, when the Papal Government, suspicious of
all associations whatsoever, stepped forward and at once opposed
and furthered his design by offering itself as his coadjutor.   In
Italy then, as in Spain—

> Allá van leyes
> Do quieren reyes—

"Laws go as sovereigns please."   So he accepted the offer,—
and on these terms.   Expenses and returns to be shared equally;
but Campanari to receive a stated annual sum for his personal
superintendence and direction.   In the partition of the spoil one
party was to make the division, the other the selection; and as
Campanari knew the value of such articles better than most men,
the Government left the division to him, and reserved to itself
the choice.   Thus he laboured for some time in the Tenuta di
Camposcala at Vulci; and the result was—the Gregorian Museum.
The Government used to exchange with him the least valuable
articles which had fallen to its share for others of greater beauty
and rarity; for its aim was to form a perfect museum, which,
while comprehending specimens of the various objects found in
Etruscan tombs, should contain articles of first-rate excellence as
works of art, or of superior interest as illustrative of the manners,
customs, and creed of the ancient inhabitants of Italy.

The man of antiquarian tastes might spend a week or so of
winter pleasantly enough at Toscanella, watching the progress of
the excavations, exploring the sepulchres and the picturesque
ravines, examining or sketching San Pietro and Sta. Maria, and
the singular relics in Campanari's garden; and such quiet pur-

suits might be diversified by excursions to places in the neighbourhood, or by an occasional boar-hunt, in company with the squirearchy of Toscanella.

A ride of fifteen or sixteen miles will take him to Montefiascone, by a road too rugged for carriages, yet abounding in beautiful scenery—of which the wild open plain, with its belt of mountains, robed in purple or snow, groves of picturesque cork-trees, a mediæval castle in ruins, and the lovely lake of Bolsena, with its fairy islets, are the principal features. Viterbo is somewhat nearer, and the road is carriageable, though very inferior in beauty;[6] Vetralla is about eighteen miles distant, but the road is a mere bridle-path. Castel d'Asso, Norchia, and Bieda, are also within an easy distance, but not of easy access, owing to the numerous, perplexing ravines which intersect the plain; and a guide is indispensable. To Vulci it is fourteen or fifteen miles; and to Corneto about seventeen—both carriage-roads. So that within a morning's ride or drive lie all the most interesting sites of the great Etruscan plain.

---

[6] At a spot, called Cippolara, about half-way between Toscanella and Viterbo, are many tombs; and here Buonarroti, in 1694 (p. 99, ap. Dempst. de Etr. Reg. II.), found urns and *cippi* with inscriptions. See Santi Bartoli, Sepolcri Antichi, tav. XCVII. This site lies to the north of the road. Musarna lies off the road a mile or two to the south; see Chapter XVII.

CHAPTER XXXII.

ISCHIA, FARNESE, AND CASTRO.

Urbes constituit ætas, hora dissolvit. —SENECA.

A thousand years scarce serve to form a state,
An hour may lay it in the dust.—BYRON.

NORTH of Toscanella lies a group of Etruscan sites. The road, which is scarcely carriageable, passes through the villages of Arlena, Tessenano, and Celere, none of which betray an antiquity higher than Roman times, and at the distance of twelve or fourteen miles reaches Ischia, whose position on a tongue of land between profound ravines, full of tombs, marks it as of Etruscan origin. There is nothing of interest, however; the tombs are utterly defaced by their application to the uses of the inhabitants. The ancient name of the place is unknown. It was a small town, probably dependent on Tarquinii or Vulci. Its Etruscan character is not generally recognised; yet Campanari made excavations here some years since.

Four or five miles north of Arlena, and about the same distance from Ischia, lies Piansano, among the hills to the west of the Lake of Bolsena. On a height to the south of the village, excavations made a few years since by Count Cini disclosed the remains of an Etruscan town, or, at least, of a fortress, the periphery of whose walls can be traced, and the site of a gate recognised. Tombs also were found in the cliffs below. On an opposite hill were discovered the remains of an ancient building constructed of squared blocks of *nenfro*, and traversed by a canal.[1]

As Ischia is on the way to Pitigliano and Sovana, it may be well to state that accommodation is to be had at the house of Sabetta Farolfi—tolerable enough considering the intense squalor of the town ;

—quis enim non vicus abundat
Tristibus obscœnis ?—

[1] Bull. Inst. 1869, p. 174.

for here you meet with clean sheets, foul tables and tongues, unbounded civility and scanty comfort, wretched meals and good society. The house is patronised by the aristocracy of Ischia, and is the evening resort of the archpriest, the *medico*, the *speziale*, and other conscript fathers of the town, who showed their politeness by urging me, though *impransus* and way-worn, to a rubber of whist.

Two or three miles west of Ischia lies Farnese, a village in a similar, though less imposing, situation, and bearing the same evidences of Etruscan antiquity. As general on ancient sites where population has never ceased to exist, the sepulchres in the cliffs here have had their original character destroyed by their conversion to cattle-stalls and hogsties. Campanari has made slight excavations in the plain around Farnese. The village is more decent in appearance than Ischia, yet its *osteria* loses in comparison even with that of La Farolfi. The Chigi palace here was occupied, at the time of my visit, by Maréchal Bourmont, the hero of Algiers. Exiled from his country for the part he played in "the three great days of July," he fixed his residence at Farnese, exchanging the stirring life of the camp, and the brilliant saloons of the Tuileries, for the seclusion, monotony, and death-like tranquillity of this Italian village.

The antiquity of Farnese has long been acknowledged. Mannert and Cramer take it to be Maternum, a station on the Via Clodia;[2] Cluver holds the same opinion, but inclines to think it identical with Sudertum, a town mentioned only incidentally by ancient writers, without any hint as to its locality.[3] This is mere conjecture, for no remains which throw light on the subject have been discovered on the spot.

Two or three miles west of Farnese lies Castro, another Etruscan site. The path to it runs through a ravine, and at one point passes over a hill, whose entire slope from base to summit is strewn with huge masses of lava,—

---

[2] Mannert, Geog pp. 384, 388. Cramer, Ancient Italy, I. p. 245. Maternum is thus marked in the Peutingerian Table:—

Foro Clodii	
Blera	XVI.
Marta	VIIII.
Tuscana	—
Materno	XII.
Saturnia	XVIII.
Succosa	VIII.

[3] Liv. XXVI. 23. Pliny III. 8; Ptol. Georg. p. 72, ed. Bert. Cluver. Ital. Ant. II. p. 517. Holstenius (Annot. ad Cluver. p. 41) thinks Madernum the same as the Sudernum mentioned by Ptolemy, and says the site is now called "Madernò," on the left bank of the Fiora, a few miles below Castro, and has many remains. I regret that I have not been able to verify this statement.

"Crags, knolls, and mounds confusedly hurl'd,
   The fragments of an earlier world."

Castro lies in a wilderness—it is a city of desolation. You mount from the ravine to the plain, and see before you a dense wood, covering a narrow ridge between steep precipices. You enter the wood, not to thread your way over smooth turf or fallen leaves, but to scramble over heaps of ruins, broken columns, capitals, and rich cornices, mingled with coarser *débris ;* through all which vegetation has forced its way, and is striving in turn to conceal the wrecks of art which had displaced it. A truer picture of the place can hardly be given than that Byron has drawn of the Palatine.

All this devastation is but of modern date. Little more than two hundred years since, Castro was a flourishing city; the capital of a Duchy, which comprised the greater part of the Etruscan plain, and which gave a title to the king of Naples; but in 1647, Pope Innocent X. rased it to the ground, because the bishop of the see had been murdered—it was supposed by the Duke Farnese, lord of Castro—and the bishopric was transferred to Acquapendente.

Castro, as usual, stands on a tongue of land between two glens. Descend into them, and here, if a lover of nature, you will be charmed with the bold forms and rich colouring of the ilex-hung cliffs—with the varied covering of the slopes—with the pictur-esque windings of the sheep-tracks, the only signs of life in these wilds—with the meanderings of the rivulet, which "singeth its quiet tune," now to the darkling canopy of foliage, now to the bright blue sky. Or if a lover of antiquity, you will find interest in tombs hollowed in the rock—some of several chambers, some full of pigeon-holes, as at Toscanella, others mere niches, or long shelf-like recesses, one over the other, as in the necropolis of Falerii—in fragments of rock-cut cornices—in the ruins of two bridges—and in vestiges of an ancient road.

High in the cliff, opposite the extremity of the town, a hundred feet or more above the stream, is a circular hole, inaccessible from below, which seems to be a window to a tomb sunk in the plain above ; or it may be the mouth of a sewer.

The *columbaria* are generally in the cliffs immediately beneath the city-walls. Of the ancient fortifications I perceived no fragments, but considerable remains of mediæval date are extant on the south side, in small cemented masonry cut from the yellow tufo cliffs on which they stand. In these walls are sundry apertures like tall arched doorways, which, from their position, can only be the mouths of sewers. More ancient drains also are not wanting, of the usual upright form, cut in the cliff itself, and determining the antiquity of the town.

I left Castro with something like disappointment. Not that it is not worthy of a visit; but my expectations had been too highly raised, and I looked for more numerous and curious relics of Etruscan antiquity. Yet the only verbal reports of it that had reached my ears were from the peasantry of the neighbouring villages, since I had never met with any antiquary, native or foreign, who had visited the spot; and as to written descriptions, the most recent I know is more than two hundred years old, from the pen of Cluver, which is but a translation of that by Leandro Alberti, who wrote nearly a century earlier. "Castro," says the latter, "is so encompassed about with rocks and caverns, that it seemeth to them that behold it, rather a dark den of wild beasts, than the abode of domesticated man."[4] To this Cluver adds, that similar caverns and marvellous fissures are to be seen at Farnese.[5] Now the truth is that there are comparatively few rock-sepulchres around Castro—not half so many as around Norchia, Bieda, Toscanella, Pitigliano, Sovana, and other Etruscan towns, similarly situated; and such as are found here are rude, and roughly hewn, and in no way remarkable. Yet the description is so far true, that Castro is a most gloomy site—one of the gloomiest I remember in Etruria. It is not its desolation alone,—Capena, Norchia, Férento, Tarquinii, Vulci, and other sites, are also uninhabited and deserted. It is not its overgrowth of wood,—Rusellæ and Cosa are similarly covered. It is its general aspect. Nowhere is the wood more dark and dense— nowhere are the cliffs blacker and more frowning—nowhere are the ravines more solemn and apparently endless, more impressively lonesome and silent—nowhere is there a more utter absence of habitation within ken—on no site does the Past becloud the spirit with a deeper awe.

To the Etruscan name of this town we have no clue. Its present appellation seems to indicate its importance as a fortress in Roman times. Cluver regards it as the site of the ancient Statonia, but gives no satisfactory reasons for his opinion;[6] and

---

[4] Descrittione d'Italia, p. 53, ed. 1551. It must be remembered that in Alberti's and even in Cluver's time, Castro was inhabited.

[5] Cluver, Ital. Ant. II. p. 518.

[6] Cluver, II. p. 517. His opinion rests principally on the vicinity of Castro to the Lago Mezzano, which he says is without

until we have some more definite evidence, we must be content to remain in the dark as to the ancient name of Castro.[7]

If not on this site, where shall we place the ancient Statonia? It is a question not to be answered easily. Pliny indicates a site not far from the sea,[8] though not actually on the coast.[9] From his and other notices of it in connection with Tarquinii, it seems highly probable that it stood close to, if not actually within the territory of that city, as Vitruvius appears to intimate.[1] There is every reason to believe that Statonia stood somewhere in this northern district of the Etruscan plain, but to which of the ancient sites in this quarter, of undetermined name, to assign it, we have yet no means of deciding.

Four or five miles north-east of Ischia lies Valentano, on a hill of black ashes, part of the lip of the great crater-lake of Bolsena. It is larger than Ischia or Farnese, but can offer no better accommodation to the traveller. From a terrace outside the walls a magnificent view of the lake is to be had, but I saw it in lowering

---

doubt the Lacus Statoniensis of antiquity. Supposing him to be correct in this particular, Castro is not so near that lake as Ischia, Farnese, Pitigliano, Sorano, and Grotte San Lorenzo, all Etruscan sites, any one of which has on this score a stronger claim to be considered the representative of Statonia. Then he says that ancient inscriptions have been discovered at Castro, which prove its antiquity; but he does not tell us that any one of these bears reference to Statonia. An additional reason urged by him is that here, as well as at Farnese, are quarries of white rock, which he identifies with the *lapidicinæ* of silex, of which Vitruvius (II. 7) and Pliny (XXXVI. 49) speak as existing in the territory of Statonia. This stone, as already mentioned (Chap. XIV. p. 161), was proof against the action of fire and frost, peculiarly adapted to moulds for metal-casting, and of such hardness and durability as to render it invaluable for statues and architectural adornments. Now it is true that there are cliffs of a whitish rock to the east of Castro; but they prove nothing as to the identity of that town with Statonia; first, because the rock is not described by Vitruvius as white, but like the Alban stone, or *peperino*, that is a greenish grey, though Pliny seems to have blundered in copying from Vitruvius, *albi* for *Albani;* and next, because the rocks at Castro are of a soft,

volcanic character, with none of the properties of the *silex*—a term usually applied by the Romans to the lava or basalt of their paved roads (Liv. XLI. 27. Tibul. I. 7, 60), and occasionally to hard limestone, as in the well-known inscription on the walls of Ferentinum. It would not seem that the—viridis silex nusquam copiosus, et ubi invenitur lapis non saxum—mentioned by Pliny in the same chapter with these quarries, was also in the neighbourhood of Statonia. The said quarries, again, are not said to have been at the town of Statonia, but merely in its *ager*, just as those round the Volsinian lake were in the *ager* of Tarquinii.

[7] Mannert (Geog. p. 383) places Statonia either at Castro or at Farnese; Cramer (I. p. 223) and Abeken (Mittelitalien, p. 34), following Cluver, recognise it in Castro.

[8] Plin. XIV. 8, 5. He records the renown of its wine.

[9] Plin. III. 8; cf. Strab. V. p. 226.

[1] Vitruv. II. 7; Plin. XXXVI. 49; Varro, de Re Rust. III. 12. The last-named writer says there were immense preserves of hares, stags, and wild sheep, in the *ager* of Statonia. Cluver thinks that Statonia could not have stood in the direct line between Tarquinii and the lake of Volsinii, because the *ager Tarquiniensis* extended up to that lake.

weather, when the clouds lay like a grey pall on its waters, and only when they occasionally broke could I catch a glimpse of its broad, leaden surface, with its two islets of fabulous renown, and the headland of Capo di Monte appearing like a third. I could perceive no traces of ancient habitation on this site, Etruscan or Roman, nor could I learn that such exist. The walls are wholly mediæval, and of tombs, there are none; in truth, the volcanic ashes and scoriæ of which the hill is composed would render it impracticable to construct tombs here in the usual manner of the Etruscans.[2]

Canina would claim Valentano as the site of the Fanum Voltumnæ, the celebrated shrine at which the princes of Etruria were wont to meet in council on the affairs of the nation. Not that he cites the authority of ancient writers, or monumental evidence, in support of this collocation, but taking it for granted that the Fanum must have stood in the territory of Vulci, and yet near the Volsinian Lake, he selects Valentano as the most likely spot to answer these requirements.[3] Any site we may assign to the Fanum must be conjectural. But a strong objection to Valentano lies in the absence of all traces of ancient habitation on this height.

From Valentano there is a track, a mere bridle-path, to Pitigliano, about twelve miles distant to the north-west. About midway it passes the Lake of Mezzano, a small piece of water embosomed among wooded hills, which is pronounced by Cluver to be the Lacus Statoniensis.[4] That lake, however, is said by Pliny and Seneca to have contained an island, which this of Mezzano does not, so that we must either reject Cluver's conclusion, or suppose that the island has since disappeared. As there

---

[2] This town is supposed by Cluver (II. p. 516) to be the representative of Verentum, a place of which no express mention is made, but which he conjectures to have existed, from the persuasion of a corruption in the text of Pliny. But I cannot see that he has adequate ground for this opinion. He thinks that in Pliny's catalogue of Roman colonies in Etruria (III. 8), the "Veientani" of the ordinary version should be "Verentani," as some readings have it, both because it comes next in the list to Vesentini —Vesentum being the island Bisentino, in the lake of Bolsena—and because Veii had ceased to exist before Pliny's time. But I must venture to differ entirely from Cluver : Pliny's list is clearly alphabetical, and has

no reference to topographical relations ; and Veii, a century before Pliny's day, had been recolonised by the Romans, and was then existing as a *municipium*. The balance is also greatly in favour of "Veientani," inasmuch as Pliny in his catalogue would surely not omit all mention of that colony, which was the nearest of all, almost within sight of the Seven Hills, and whose past history was so intimately interwoven with that of Rome. If this be the correct reading, there is no proof of the existence of such a town as Verentum.

[3] Etruria Marittima II., p. 131.

[4] Cluver, II. p. 517. Mannert (Geog. p. 388) and Cramer (I. p. 223) agree with him.

is no other lake in central Etruria which can answer to the Statonian, we must take the alternative, and consider the island to have floated, as it is described,[5] and to have become eventually attached to the shores of the lake. Such seems to have been the case with the Vadimonian lake, which is now almost choked by the encroachment of its banks on the water ; and a similar process is going forward in the Lacus Cutiliæ, in Sabina, and in the sulphureous lakes below Tivoli ; where masses of vegetable matter, floating on the water, assume the appearance of islands, and having had their cruise awhile, become entangled at length by some prominent rock or tree on the shore, attach themselves permanently to it, and settle down into respectable portions of *terra firma*.[6]

[5] Plin. II. 96 ; Seneca, Nat. Quæst. III. 25. There are only four other lakes in Etruria which contain, or are said to have contained, islands—the Volsinian, the Vadimonian, the Thrasymene, and the Lacus Aprilis or Prelius. The first two are mentioned by Pliny, and the second by Seneca, in addition to the Lake of Statonia, so that it cannot be confounded with them.

The Thrasymene is too much inland, seeing that Statonia was not far from the coast. And of the Lacus Aprilis, now Lago Castiglione, may be said, what will apply with equal force to the Thrasymene, that it is much too remote from Tarquinii ; for Statonia, as already shown, was either close to or within the *ager* of that city.

[6] See Chapter XI. p. 144.

CHAPTER XXXIII.

PITIGLIANO AND SORANO.

Nihil privatim, nihil publice stabile est ; tam hominum, quam urbium, fata volvuntur.
SENECA.

Ay, now am I in Arden : when I was at home I was in a better place ; but travellers must be content.
AS YOU LIKE IT.

PITIGLIANO, an Etruscan site, and the principal town in this part of Tuscany, lies about twelve miles to the N.W. of Valentano. With a competent guide it may be reached also from Castro or Farnese, twelve miles distant. When I first knew this road it was on the border between the Roman and Tuscan States, and had a bad reputation as the resort of outlaws from both States. But these are Will-o'-the-Wisp perils, ever distant when approached. The appearance of the country, however, is not suggestive of security,—dense, gloomy woods alternating with open moors, and not a house by the wayside, save one farm on a green spot, half-way to Pitigliano.

This town stands on the northern limits of the great Etruscan plain, which is here bounded by a range of mountains, among which the snowy peak of Monte Amiata towers supreme in the north, and the nearer heights sink gradually in the east to the long-drawn ridge which girdles the Lake of Bolsena. In the west, a line of mist marks the course of the deep-sunk Fiora, and leads the eye southwards across the plain to the bare crests of the Monti di Canino, which rise like an island from a sea of foliage, with the blue Mediterranean gleaming beyond on one hand, and the grey mass of the Ciminian bounding the horizon on the other.

At a little distance, Pitigliano seems to stand on the unbroken level of the plain, but as usual occupies a tongue of land, flanked by ravines ; so that when you seem just at its gates, a deep chasm yawns at your feet, which must be traversed to its lowest depths ere you can reach the town. When you have surmounted the long steep, and passed the line of fortifications, which, as at Nepi, cross the root of the tongue—nature on every other side affording sufficient protection — seek incontinently Il Bimbo. This "Baby" is no painted effigy of sucking humanity, rocked by the breezes—nor even a living specimen of that "best philosopher, mighty prophet, seer blest," whom Wordsworth apostrophises—but is represented by the mature and portly person of a respectable townsman, Giuseppe Bertocci.

Pitigliano is a place of considerable importance, with some 3000 inhabitants, of whom more than a tithe are Jews, led to congregate here, as at Gibraltar, by the annoyances and persecutions they were formerly subjected to in the neighbouring State. In spite of the wealth thus created, Pitigliano is a mean and dirty town, without any interest inside its gates. A glance beyond them will convince you that it is an Etruscan site; though being never visited by antiquaries, it has not been recognised as such.[1] Its ancient name, even under the Romans, is quite unknown;[2] and its very existence is unrecorded before the eleventh century, when it is mentioned in a Papal bull as Pitilianum.

There is a fragment of the ancient walls on the northern side of the town; and if you leave it by the Porta di Sotto, you have, immediately on your right, a fine fragment of *emplecton* masonry of tufo, eight courses high—precisely similar to the walls of Sutri, Nepi, Falleri, and Bieda. As you descend the steep road you have tombs on every hand—from the brow of the town-crested height, down to the banks of the stream, and again up the opposite side of the ravine—slope, cliff, and ledge are honey-combed with sepulchres. Here too are portions of the ancient road, sunk in the tufo, with water-channel at its side, and niches in its walls. The tombs here, beyond the *columbaria*, which are unusually numerous, are not now worthy of particular notice.

[1] Even Repetti, who in his admirable "Dizionario della Toscana," gives a detailed account of the place, is at a loss to determine its origin; but he relies on literary, not on monumental evidence.

[2] Bertius in his edition of Ptolemy (Geog. p. 72) marks it as the site of Ἥβα—a colony mentioned by that geographer as in the neighbourhood of Saturnia and Suana. But may it not be Caletra, which must have been in this district? Saturnia is said by Livy (XXXIX. 55) to have been —in agro Caletrano; and Pitigliano is but ten miles from Saturnia, as the crow flies, and is by nature the most important Etruscan site in this vicinity. Cluver (II. p. 515) suggests Monte Pò, near Scansano, as the site of Eba. Cramer (I. p. 222) follows him. Canina (Etr. Marit. II., p. 95) suggests Capalbio, thirteen miles to the west of Vulci. Neither offers anything as to the site of Caletra. Or may not Pitigliano be Statonia ?—it is but a few miles from the Lago Mezzano, and its wine is celebrated in this district of Italy. It is singular that it is the only recognised Etruscan site, whose modern name possesses all the elements of the ancient and long-lost Vetulonia—P. t. l. n. = V. t. l. n.—but this analogy can be but accidental, as the position of Pitigliano is much too remote from the sea to answer to the site of that early and maritime city of Etruria.

Whatever may have been their decorations within or without, some two thousand years of profanation have well nigh effaced their original character, and left them as problems to be solved only by the antiquary. Thus it always happens where population has most flourished and longest endured. It is at the long-deserted sites of Castel d'Asso and Norchia that the sepulchres are best preserved. Man is ever the worst foe to the works of man.

The table-lands around Pitigliano are full of tombs, especially on the west, where for miles the plain is undermined with them. No excavations have been made; but accident, from time to time, brings sepulchres to light.[3]

Though there is little to interest the antiquary at Pitigliano, there is food enough for the artist. Few towns in volcanic Etruria are more imposingly situated, and in the midst of finer scenery. The spot that produced and inspired a Zuccherelli should have some claims to beauty. Its ravines, though darkly, damply profound[4]—grand as are their tall impending cliffs—gloomy and solemn as are their silent recesses—are at all seasons highly picturesque, at some even truly beautiful. In what rich and harmonious colouring were they decked when I beheld them! The many-tinted rocks had their blended warmth cooled and shadowed by the drapery of foliage—the tender green of the budding vegetation, the darker verdure of the ilex and ivy, the pale blue of the aloe; while, like silver bands on a mantle of green velvet, the streamlets flowed through the wooded hollows, here spanned by a rustic mill, there by a ruined bridge. One of these rivulets leaps at one bound from the plain to the depths of the ravine. Omit not to visit this "Cascatella;" it is worthy of a place in your sketch-book, and cascades do not often adorn the plains of Etruria. Though little more than a brook, the stream makes the most of itself in its plunge, and roars, raves, and foams in decent imitation of its betters, which make more noise in the world. At some distance, however, you perceive not this assumption, but have a waving sheet of foam, murmuring on a dark wall of rock.

On this height, called the Poggio Strozzoni, once stood the villa of the Counts Orsini, for more than three centuries the feudal lords of Pitigliano; but not one stone of their mansion now

---

[3] At Ponte di S. Pietro on the Fiora, between Pitigliano and Manciano, Campanari has made slight but promising excavations. On the heights on the opposite side of the river I observed unequivocal traces of an Etruscan town, with rock-hewn sepulchres and niches around it.

[4] Repetti says they are 180 *braccia*, or nearly 350 feet, deep.

remains on another. Vestiges of former magnificence, however, mark the spot, in two colossal recumbent figures hewn from the living rock. The popular voice calls them "Orlano (Orlando) and his wife,"—the Roland of chivalry and of song—he whose brand "was worth a hundred of Death's scythes,"—he who

> "With many a Paladin and Peer,
> In Roncesvalles died—"

These, however, are not chivalresque but allegorical figures, of *cinquecento* times. "Orlano" has not Durindana but a *cornucopia* by his side, and spills nothing but fruit and flowers. There are bas-reliefs of the same date on the rocks hard by. Tradition thus accounts for the ruin of the villa :—

The last Count kept a mistress at Sorano, yet was extremely jealous of his wife. She, fond and faithful, viewed his visits to the neighbouring town with great suspicion. On his return one day, finding her from home, he went to Pitigliano to seek her, and met her on the bridge which crosses the stream, just above the cascade. "What have they been doing at Pitigliano to-day?" asked he. "Much the same as at Sorano, I suppose," was the innocent reply. A guilty conscience and his jealous disposition caused him to misinterpret this answer, and regarding it as a confession, he seized her in his wrath, and hurled her into the torrent. He fled, and was never heard of more ; and his villa fell into utter ruin. So says tradition—history may tell another tale.[6]

Pitigliano, like Toscanella, is an excellent *point d'appui*, whence to make excursions to the neighbouring sites of interest—Saturnia, Sovana, Sorano, Castro, to wit;[6] and is fortunate in having a decent *hospitium*. "The Baby" belies his name, for he is a stout fellow, equally removed from first and second childhood ; and his wife, Lisa, is one of the most lively, obliging landladies that ever welcomed traveller, or ruled the frying-pan—

> Che donna fu di più gaia sembianza?

Their house is no inn—such a convenience exists not at Pitigliano ; it is a *casa particolare*, where you may be entertained for a consideration, moderate enough.

The traveller will not fare so well at Sorano, another Etruscan site, four or five miles to the north-east of Pitigliano. Inn, of course, there is none—for who visits this secluded spot ?—but

[5] For a sketch of this quarrelsome, tyrannical family, and their doings in this part of Italy, see Repetti, *v.* Pitigliano.

[6] Pitigliano is 2½ miles from Sovana, 5 from Sorano, 12 from Castro, 10 from Manciano, 16 from Saturnia by the high road, 30 from Orbetello, 35 from Grosseto, 18 from Acquapendente.

there is its usual substitute, where shelter may be had for the night. Ask for the house of La Farfanti, *detta* La Livornesa. Here, one large smoke-dried room serves for kitchen and *salle à manger;* and on the upper floor a single chamber, crowded with beds, accommodates the family and guests. I turned from the door to seek more comfort elsewhere, but in vain; the rain was descending in torrents, and I was fain to return, stipulating for the sole possession of one of the beds—a fantastic demand, which excited great ridicule at my expense, and was not granted without much hesitation. But with a proverb I carried my point—*Le ortiche non fan buona salsa, e due piedi non istan bene in una scarpa*—"Nettles don't make good sauce, nor can two feet stand well in one shoe." Here accordingly I passed the night, in company with eight men and two women—the former being knights of the spade and plough, who, reeking from their labours, shuffled off their habiliments, and kept up a tuneful chorus of such *tibiæ pares* as nature had furnished them with, till daylight recalled them to the field. Travelling, like "misery, acquaints a man with strange bed-fellows."

Let me however do La Farfanti justice, as I did the supper she provided, which would have done credit to the *cuisine* of the first hotel of Livorno, her native town, and went far to atone for other discomforts. "God never strikes with both hands," says the Spanish proverb. Rarely indeed does the by-way traveller in Italy meet with such

> Mundæ sub lare pauperum
> Cœnæ,

as fell to my lot at Sorano.

Sorano stands on a tongue of land at the extreme verge of the Etruscan plain. Cross the deep ravines around it, and you are at once among the mountains. On this side you have volcanic formation—on that, aqueous deposit. Its elevation preserves Sorano from the pestiferous atmosphere, which has depopulated the neighbouring Sovana. The town is small, mean, and filthy, with streets steep, narrow, and tortuous. In the centre rises a precipitous mass of rock, whose summit commands one of the most romantic scenes in this part of Italy,—the town clustering round the base of the height—the grand old feudal castle, with its hoary battlements, crowning the cliffs behind—the fearful precipices and profound chasms at your feet—and the ranges of mountains in front, rising in grades of altitude and majesty, to the sublime icy crest of Monte Amiata.

The picturesque beauties of Sorano are not less when seen from below; especially from the road leading to Castel Ottieri, whence the view of the town and castle-crowned cliffs can hardly be rivalled in Italy—that land of rock, ruin, and ravine.

Of antiquities, Sorano has little or nothing to show. There are some traces of an ancient road sunk in the rock beneath the town, which has been supplanted by a modern corkscrew gallery. There are vestiges also of a Roman road in the hollow, in blocks of lava, which lie in the stream. Tombs are not abundant, and with the exception of *columbaria*, which are unusually numerous, often at inaccessible elevations in the cliffs, they are of little interest, beyond serving to establish the Etruscan antiquity of the site. Most of the tombs are so defaced as to be hardly distinguishable from natural caverns. In the ravine to the west is a narrow ridge of rock, perforated, as at Norchia, so as to assume the appearance of a bridge; whence its vulgar name of Il Pontone.

In the neighbourhood of Sorano, in the direction of Sovana, was found a few years since one of the most beautiful mirrors of bronze that ever issued from an Etruscan tomb. The figures it bears are in flat relief, exquisitely chiselled, and represent the Judgment of Paris—a subject of common occurrence, but here treated in a peculiar manner. This mirror is now in the possession of the Marchese Strozzi of Florence, and will be further mentioned when we describe the monuments of Etruscan art in that city.[7]

What may have been the ancient name of Sorano, we have no means of determining. Cramer conjectures it may have been Sudertum;[8] but Cluver, with equal probability, places that town at Farnese.[9]

The attractions of Pitigliano and Sorano to the traveller lie in their scenery alone. At no other ancient sites in the volcanic district of Etruria are the cliffs so lofty, the ravines so profound, the scenery so diversified, romantic, and imposing; and it may be safely affirmed that among Etruscan sites in general, though few have so little antiquarian interest, none have greater claims on the artist and lover of the picturesque.[1]

---

[7] See Vol. II. p. 106.

[8] Cramer, Ancient Italy, I. p. 223.

[9] Cluver, Ital. Ant. II. p. 517.

[1] About two miles or more from Sorano to the east, is a deserted and ruined town called Vitozzo. I saw it only from the opposite side of a wide ravine, and can say nothing as to its antiquity; except that the abundant ruins on the site seem to mark it as chiefly of mediæval times. The peasants tell you it is extremely ancient, but they know no more of comparative antiquity than of comparative anatomy.

BRONZE BUST, FROM THE ISIS-TOMB, VULCI.

ADDENDA TO VOL. I.

Page 130, *to note* 6.—Lanciani places the Fanum Feroniæ on the hill of Sant Antimo, near Nazzano, where in 1868 the remains of a noble temple of the Ionic order were discovered, of circular form, 20 mètres in diameter. Bull. Inst. 1870, p. 30.

Page 154, *to note* 9.—In the Bazzichelli Collection was the celebrated vase of Euthymides, son of Polios. Ann. Inst. 1870, pp. 267—271. Klügmann, tavv. d'agg. 0, v.

Page 185.—In the castle and fosse of Castel d'Asso, many missiles of terra cotta in the form of acorns have been found—larger than those of lead, and of extremely hard clay. Bull. Inst. 1873, p. 109.

Page 264, *to note* 8.—But on a *stamnos*, illustrated in Mon. Inst. vi. tav. 8, on which Philoctetes is represented as bitten by the serpent, and rolling on the ground in agony, a goddess of very similar character, and with her hands in the same position, is introduced, standing on a pedestal, with fire on the ground before her. An inscription designates her as " Chryse."

Page 266, *to note* 4.—Professor Helbig takes the Regulini-Galassi tomb to be contemporary with the sepulchre at Palestrina, which has recently yielded even more wonderful but similar treasures in the precious metals and bronze, and he would refer both tombs to about the middle of the seventh century, B.C. He pronounces the silver bowls found in both tombs to be not Egyptian, but Phœnician imitations, and thinks they must have been imported into Italy by the Carthaginians about 650 B.C. See his article on Phœnician art, Ann. Inst. 1876, pp. 197—257.

Page 358, *last line.*—The flaps or lappets of her *tutulus* are probably the κρήδεμνα of Homer, Odys. I. 334 ; vi. 100 ; xvi. 416.

Page 366, *to note* 8.—The *tutulus* seems to have been also a Phœnician head-dress. See Layard's Nineveh, II. pp. 386, 389, where women wearing the *tutulus* are represented seated in Tyrian boats.

ERRATA IN VOL. I.

Page lviii, note 9, *for* "Samothraci," *read* "Samothrace."
„ lxxiii,   „   1, *for* "φιλοτέχνοι," *read* "φιλότεχνοι."
„ cxxvii, line 7, *for* "his discovery," *read* "this discovery."
„ cxxviii,   „   15, *for* "discovered," *read* "made known."
„   „   last line, *for* "discovered by Mr. Pullan," *read* "discovered by Count Bassi, and described by Mr. Pullan."
„ 11, note 6, last line, *for* "p. 79," *read* "p. 80."
„ 21,   „   7, *for* "πελάτοι," *read* "πελάται."
„ 32, line 9 from the bottom, *dele* "late."
„ 42,   „   1, *for* "bronze mirrors," *read* "bronzes."
„ 55,   „   22, *for* "with the tall *campanile*," *read* "and tall *campanile*."
„ 60,   „   13, *for* "coins," *read* "money."
„ 60,   „   15, *for* "money," *read* "coinage."
„ 83, note 3, line 14, *for* "The discovery since their day," *read* "The recent discovery."
„ 103, line 10, *for* "jet," *read* "jut."
„ 112, note 11, line 4, *for* "its size, much superior," *read* "its size, in which it was much superior."
„ 130, line 10. *for* "being struck," *read* "having been struck."
„ 135, note 7, line 3, *for* "95," *read* "65."
„ 172,   „   6,   „   17, *for* "also," *read* "however."
„ 200,   „   2,   „   10, *for* "εὐκύκλοι," *read* "εὔκυκλοι."
„ 208, line 5 from the bottom, *for* "were wont to recline," *read* "were reclining."
„ 249,   „   23, *for* "the late Marchese Campana," *read* "the Marchese Campana."
„ 250,   „   11 from the bottom, *transpose, and place* "and each pilaster bears a shield carved in relief," *at the end of the sentence.*
„ 274,   „   11, *dele* "late."
„   „   14, *for* "Since his death," *read* "Of late years."
„ 277,   „   4, *for* "is name," *read* "its name."
„ 304,   „   11, *for* "the Cathedral," *read* "Santa Maria in Castello."
„ 323,   „   7, *add* "Cf. Aristoph. Rane, 154—157."
„ 324,   „   8, *add* "For birds in Elysium, see Tibul. I. 3, 59."
„ 338,   „   1, *for* "three figures," *read* "four figures."
„ 352,   „   6, *after* "So far," *insert* "excepting the scene from the Odyssey."
„ 368,   „   2 from the bottom, *for* "which seems to mark," *read* "which has been supposed to mark."
„ 375, last line, *for* "makes," *read* "make."
„ 388, line 5, *for* "Gygean," *read* "Gygæan."
„ 396, last line, *for* "fowl," *read* "fowls."
„ 398, note 3, last line but 2, *after* "In one tomb only," *insert* "now open."
„ 405, line 7, *for* "Euxitheos," *read* "Euthsitheos."
„ 405, note 3, *for the concluding sentence,* "The version he gives," &c., *read* "and by Heydemann, Ann. Inst. 1875, pp. 254—267. See Mon. Inst. 1875, tav. 23, 24."
„ 406, line 13, *for* "representing," *read* "erroneously supposed to represent."
„ 408,   „   6, *after* "six guinea-fowls," *insert* "probably representing the sisters of Meleager."
„ 422, note 4, *dele* "12."
„ 459,   „   3, *add* "Helbig takes them for Phœnician or Carthaginian imitations. Ann. Inst. 1876, p. 241."
„ 461,   „   6, *add* "Ann. Inst. 1866, p. 409.—Brunn."
„ 463, line 21, *for* "yields not," *read* "scarcely yields."
„ 472,   „   20, *for* "Agdria," *read* "cista."
„ 489, note 1, *add* "It is supposed to be an Etruscan fountain and lavatory. Ann. Inst. 1870, pp. 227—231, tav. d'agg. K."

END OF VOL. I.

BRADBURY, AGNEW, & CO., PRINTERS, WHITEFRIARS.

1552296R1

Printed in Great Britain by
Amazon.co.uk, Ltd.,
Marston Gate.